Bible Secrets Series
Volume I

The Deep Things of God

A PRIMER ON THE SECRETS
OF HEAVEN AND EARTH

M.M. TAUSON

THE DEEP THNGS OF GOD:
A Primer on the Secrets of Heaven and Earth

Copyright © 2011 by Maximiano Maximo Tuason, Jr.

First printing: January 2012

ISBN 978-971-95293-0-9

Unless otherwise specified, Scripture quotations are from the Authorized King James Version (KJV) of the Bible.

Bayith Ha-Shem Publications: A ministry of
The Minister of Bayith Ha'Shem Messianic Ministries, Inc.
P.O. Box 3272, Makati City, 1200 Philippines
email:bayithashem@yahoo.com

To the Father,

For my Brethren

What some readers say about this book:

This "book is excellent! Highly recommended to our readers. It contains a wealth of knowledge in various areas: History, theology, science, Scripture. (The author's) insights are amazing... I kid you not. This book is phenomenal!" – Richard Chaimberlin, Litt. D.; editor-publisher, *Petah Tikvah* ("Door of Hope"), Rochester, New York, USA.

"Wow, what a book! ...It is a very interesting book, in many areas. I am reading it, a little everyday, along with my devotions... I would like to purchase 2 more copies... to share with brother Bill... and another friend." - Brian Allen, minister, The Indian Sabbath Trail, McEwen, Tennessee, USA.

This is "such an earth-shaking book. Turned my beliefs profoundly. I talk about it... in my radio program much... I discovered the Bible is truly fascinating, which you really brought out. From a former doubter, I was suddenly converted." - Manny Topacio, radio program host, "Somewhere in Time," DWBR 104.3 FM, Philippines.

"I thank you profusely with deep gratitude for this opportunity to learn of the really important matters. I truly believe you were led by the Holy Spirit... I would like to purchase 10 books... God bless you immensely... I would request some time to talk about your WORK. I have so many questions. God bless you." - Carlos A. Pedrosa, former president, Philippine National Bank, Manila, Philippines.

"What you wrote is excellent! This could have only been inspired by the One True God..." - Ferdy Corcuera, Bible student/researcher, Quezon City, Philippines.

Contents

Preface

"My people are destroyed for lack of knowledge..." (Hos 4:6a).

The primary purpose of this book is to address the concern of the prophet Hosea in the Biblical quotation above. Most people do not know the message the Scriptures have for them, because they do not read the Bible. This volume aims to arouse in them the desire to know more. Some do not believe in the Bible, because its contents sound like folk tales to them. This book can help prove the veracity of many of those narratives. Others entertain doubts about the truth of the Word of God, because the Bible seems to contradict itself in some places. This work can help harmonize a number of those misconceptions.

I thus hope to contribute in my own, albeit limited way towards the fulfillment of the prophecy in Daniel 12:4 – *"But thou, O Daniel, shut up the words, and seal the book, even to the time of the end: many shall run to and fro, and knowledge shall be increased."*

The "secrets" in this compendium consist mostly of little-known and hardly understood scriptural insights and scientific discoveries that relate to God and the Bible, the universe and our planet, mankind and Israel. Many of these concepts have been gleaned from prophetic symbols and encryptions uncovered in varying degrees of concealment in Scripture, as well as novel ideas and facts verified in the fields of both theoretical and experimental physics.

I must tell the reader that I am neither a scientist nor an authority on the Bible. As they say, "One who teaches the Bible is never a scholar, he is always a student." Aside from introducing a few original and innovative insights and suggestions, my main role in this book is that of a compiler and annotator.

As this work is intended for general readership, other items are no esoteric "secrets" at all but, rather, bits of general knowledge to provide a more comprehensive background to each topic. Some basic Biblical concepts have also been included for clarity. Hence, this book has something for everybody: from the unbeliever to the skeptic to the believer, from the beginner to the master.

This is admittedly an ambitious work – an effort to explain the nature of God, the origins of the universe, and the mysteries in the Scriptures. Yet, I had not planned to produce a book of this magnitude. The pieces of Biblical insights, scientific discoveries, and a plethora of related facts and concepts accumulated over the years and eventually jelled into an integral whole that asked to materialize in print.

When I began work on this book in July 2009, I originally intended to publish a little book that was mainly about the Sacred Names, now making up Chapters 10 to 12. As you can see, the book grew with the addition of numerous other topics, and what I had expected to finish in three or four months took all of twenty-nine months.

Much of the contents has been derived from the tracts, booklets, newsletters, newspaper and magazine articles, and Bible Study modules that I wrote and distributed among participants of the Sabbath School sessions and the Bible Study-by-mail program that I conducted, as well as to a number of friends, colleagues, and acquaintances.

I started writing tracts in late 1992 with my obsolescent PC-386. The computer became infected with a virus, and the files I had been working on were destroyed. Only three files were left: a short one, another of medium length, and a rather lengthy third one. Inexplicably, all three files were cut short and ended at the same Biblical quotation: *"And they that be wise shall shine as the brightness of the firmament; and they that turn many to righteousness as the stars for ever and ever"* (Dan 12:3). At the computer repair shop, I related the incident to the owner-technician, who happened to be an evangelical Christian well versed on the Bible. All he could say was, it probably was not a coincidence.

I grew up a lukewarm Roman Catholic knowing the Creator as "God," "Diyos" in Filipino, from the Spanish term "Dios." I became aware of the name "Jehovah," but for some reason I never heard anybody, not even the priests in church, invoke it. Most people I knew regarded the Jehovah's Witnesses as a curiosity. In hindsight, that time seems to have been a period of uncertainty regarding the Name of God. I got wind that God had another personal Name from a classmate in college who told me that the Name of God consisted of the five vowels of the English alphabet: "Iaoue."

In 1977, I was edified on the importance of the Sacred Names, together with the *Torah* ("law") and other Messianic doctrines, by international organizations promoting "Yahweh" as the name of the Father and "Yahshua" as that of His Son. In 1994, I looked into a group claiming the pronunciation of the Tetragrammaton or Four-Lettered Name of God was "Yaohu" and His Son's Name, "Yaohushua." I later found out that although the congregation said prayers in Hebrew, sang Hebrew worship songs, and had a Filipino founder based in Jerusalem, they were actually Sunday-keeping evangelical Christians.

I learned what I now regard as the true pronunciation of the Name of God in mid-1996 from a foreign ministry. The minister recounted vacillating between two forms of the Name when an angel confirmed to him the correct one in a dream. Going over copies of his research materials, I saw that his exegesis was simple, but impeccable. I was fully convinced it was the true sound of the Tetragrammaton. I wholly embraced his discovery and made it an integral part of my writings.

As I focused on the Sacred Names, I was soon led to the discovery of the pre-Mosaic Three-Lettered Name of God, together with the original Name of the Son, which has been set aside in the Sacred Name movement in favor of an erroneous form. I determined to teach the Sacred Names to all and sundry. I started a ministry, which I named *Bayith Ha'Shem*, Aramaic/Hebrew for "House of the Name."

In September 1997, I finished the booklet *Found: The Lost Names of the Father and the Son*. The night I completed the work, a dark entity attacked me in my sleep. It pressed down upon me, rendering me immobile under its oppressive presence. I tried wriggling my toes and fingers, to no avail. I felt I would die of *bangungot*, the vernacular term for a nightmare that causes sleep paralysis and culminates in cardiac arrest. Finally, I was able to gasp the saving Name of the Son. The entity faded away and left me.

The booklet received the concurrence of the foreign minister, who began using in his own tracts the other sacred Names I had found and authenticated. He requested me to write a second booklet detailing the discovery and etymological basis of the pronunciation of the Four-Lettered Name or Tetragrammaton.

From the Bible, I felt the urge to transfer to an upland location. *"Go up to the mountain, and bring wood, and build the house; and I will take pleasure in it, and I will be glorified, saith the LORD"* (Hag 1:8).

I moved in early 1998 to a highland community that spiritual seekers frequently went to. I saw that the town's name, read the Hebrew way, spelled out an archaic Name of God and the word "grape." I found a relatively big house, which had been empty since the seven elderly occupants died one after another. Neighbors said the place was haunted. The surviving brother, who lived nearby, was understandably willing to let it at an unusually low monthly rental. Inspecting the place, I felt the presence of unearthly entities. I exorcised the spirits with the Son's Name. (They left the house, but not the premises. My children would later tell of hearing my voice calling from the outside or seeing me coming home, when in reality I was still in the city. The voice and apparition seemed those of *doppelgangers*, ghostly impersonators.)

Sometime in March 1999, I finished the second booklet I entitled *Tetragrammaton: Restored in the Last Days*. That night, I was once again attacked by the shadowy entity. However, I was better prepared mentally and spiritually that time and managed to immediately utter the Name of the Son. The evil presence vanished at once, and has since never returned.

I had a sign made for Bayith Ha'Shem that I could post by the front door. In the morning of the day I was to put up the sign, my body began to ache from the loins upward. I felt some of my internal organs swelling, as though imperfections in my person were being set right. I broke into a cold sweat. When the ache and discomfort became so unbearable that I could hardly walk or even stand, I went back to bed. After several hours of deep sleep, I woke up fully refreshed, feeling like a new man.

At that time I had been a "born-again" Christian for seven years (although I had been loosely observing the seventh-day Sabbath on my own since the early 1980s.) Uninvited and unknown, I boldly went to a pastors' weekly meeting in the city and offered to reveal to them the Sacred Names. They refused to hear me, but instead quoted Matthew 16:17 to me: *"And Jesus answered and said unto him, Blessed art thou, Simon Barjona: for flesh and blood hath not revealed it unto thee, but my Father which is in heaven."* They expected no less than the Heavenly Father Himself to reveal the sacred Names to them!

A year later, I again had the impetus to relocate. *"And the hand of the LORD was there upon me; and he said unto me, Arise, go forth into the plain, and I will there talk with thee"* (Ezek 3:22). I moved to a populous lakeside community in May 1999. I later realized that the name of the town, read from right to left, spelled out "father" and "messenger" in Hebrew. Training to become a pastor, I enrolled in a local school of ministry and, later, in a nine-month course at the International School of Theology -- Asia, where I earned a certificate in Christian leadership. I also enrolled for a Master's degree at the Trinity Bible College and Seminary -- Philippine Extension. I became a member of the town's pastors' association, one of the most active in the province. I spiritually grew enormously. Indeed, God "talked" with me there.

I have glimpsed a few instances of the Sacred Names manifesting in my life. I was born on the 10th of May, whose *gematria* is 10-5 – the numerical value of the short form or Two-Lettered Name of God. I reached the age of independence on 10 May 1965 – 10-5-65 -- the same numbers of the Tetragrammaton or Four-Lettered Name. In 2010, when I opened a bank account for the ministry, the account number issued to Bayith Ha-Shem startled me. It was 10565!

In my Bible study, greatly aided by books and periodicals by Messianic and watchmen authors and ministries, complemented by many secular references, and in my final choice of materials for inclusion in this book,

I had always viewed things with the eyes of a child, call it naivete or gullible curiosity. After all, did not Christ say, *"Verily I say unto you, Except ye be converted, and become as little children, ye shall not enter into the kingdom of heaven"* (Matt 18:3)? I hope you will read this book in much the same way.

Biblical quotations here are from the Authorized King James Version (KJV), unless otherwise indicated. I have also made use of passages from a few apocryphal, pseudepigraphical, and kabbalistic works to provide more details to several brief Biblical accounts, as long as they harmoniously complement and do not contradict the generally accepted canonical texts. The books of the Apocrypha and Pseudepigrapha are comparable to extra-Biblical writings, such as those of the 1st century Jewish historian Flavius Josephus, which shed light on sketchy Biblical information. The Kabbalah, for its part, reflects the thinking of Jewish mystics. These works, after all, though non-canonical, had been written for the most part by men who believed in and loved God.

The chronology used in this book is primarily that of Archbishop James Ussher of Armagh, Ireland, produced in 1650-1654 and first printed in the margins of Bibles in 1701 (Old Testament Chronology, *The Treasury of Biblical Information*, Holman Bible Publishers, 1952).

It is my avid prayer that this volume will serve its purpose as an eye-opening aid to the layman eager to learn and the seeker in search of a deeper knowledge and better understanding of the Creator, the world we live in, and our earthly existence.

Finally, it is not my aim to convince the reader to believe any of the ideas presented in this work. The reader must decide for him- or herself. Should any of the deep things of God seem unusually obscure, the Bible advises us to pray for guidance: *"If any of you lack wisdom, let him ask of God, that giveth to all men liberally, and upbraideth not; and it shall be given him"* (James 1:5).

Amen!

M.M. TAUSON

1

Mysteries
of Our Maker

*Can you search out the deep things of God?
Can you find out the limits of the Almighty?"*

-- Job 11:7, NKJV.

Knowing God and the secrets of His being must have seemed impossible, even unthinkable, to men in ancient times. Thus suggested Zophar the Naamathite in the quote above to his suffering friend, Job, the central character in the oldest book of the Bible with the same name.

Have you, like many men in ages past and present, ever wondered what God is? Or, short of that, merely tried to guess at the reasons behind His actions? The apostle Paul sighed, *"O the depth of the riches both of the wisdom and knowledge of God! how unsearchable are his judgments, and his ways past finding out! (Rom 11:33).* Yet, he knew only too well that we are not completely in the dark.

Blissfully, much of what can be known about God we can find in the Scriptures. Yes, the Bible. All we have to do is prayerfully look. As Christ assures us, *"Ask, and it shall be given you; seek, and ye shall find; knock, and it shall be opened unto you (Matt 7:7).* Our quest for enlightenment will not be unaided. Sincere and earnest seekers will have the Spirit of God Himself as guide and revealer of His mysteries. *"But God hath revealed them unto us by his Spirit: for the Spirit searcheth all things, yea, the deep things of God* (1 Cor 2:10). Truly, *"He revealeth the deep and secret things..."* (Dan 2:22).

So, for the time being, let us take off the shoes from our mental feet, for the ground that we are treading is holy.

What are you?

However, even before trying to discern God's divine essence, it will perhaps be wise for us to first know a little more about you. After all, we are what we believe in. And this is probably one of the best times to ascertain where you actually stand. Two people talking about "God" may not be thinking of the same entity. Let us go back to basics then. All the people in the world may be divided into several distinct theological groups based on their belief, or unbelief, in God, a god, or gods.

Godless persons.

If you are not sure whether there is truly a God or not, then you are an *agnostic*. The term comes from the Greek *a* ("without") and *gnosis* ("knowledge") – that is, absence of knowledge about God. It is no wonder then that agnostics are unwilling to accept or reject the idea of a God. To play it safe, they simply say that the existence of an invisible power or supreme being can neither be proved nor disproved.

On the other hand, if you firmly believe that there is no God, you are an *atheist*. The Greek root-words *a* ("without") and *theos* ("god") together form the word. Atheists reject the existence of God or any god at all. They do not subscribe to the idea that a divine, supernatural entity exerts an influence on our lives.

There are two kinds of atheist, though. One, the *secular atheist* (from Latin *saeculum,* "world") is a worldly individual not affiliated with any religion. The other is the *religious atheist*, which sounds oxymoronic or self-contradictory. This second person practices a religion which has no God. A well-known example is Buddhism, named after its founder, the Buddha (Sanskrit for "enlightened"). Another is Confucianism, more of a philosophy than a religion, popularized by the Chinese sage Confucius (Latinized *Kongfuzi,* "Great Master Kong"). A lesser known group of religious atheists is India's Jainism, whose founder was called the *Jina* ("spiritual conqueror").

So! If you are an agnostic or an atheist, should you stop reading at this point? To the contrary, you probably need this book more than all the others. With all due respect to the reader, the Bible says it is foolish to deny the existence of God. *"The fool hath said in his heart, There is no God"* (Ps 53:1).

Godly people.

You are a *theist* if you believe in God or gods. Some writers say there was probably no period in history when men did not worship a god or gods. Fearfully aware of their mortal weakness, men made it a practice to appeal to unseen powers for help and protection. Theists thus believe in an invisible, supernatural Spirit or spirits who affect the lives of all men and creatures, as well as events and forces in nature. There are many kinds of theist.

One God. You are a *monotheist* (Greek prefix *mono*, "one," in combination with *theos*) if you believe in only one God. Most of the world's major religions are monotheistic. The best known are:

Christianity, established in the 1ˢᵗ century A.D. by Christ, a title transliterated from the Greek word *Christos* ("anointed"), which came from the Hebrew *Mashiach* ("anointed"), transliterated into English as Messiah. A believer in Christ, the Son of God, is a Christian. A Christian who obeys both the Old Testament commandments of Israel's God and the New Testament teachings of the Messiah is called a Messianic.

Islam, founded in 610 A.D., means "submission" in Arabic. An Islamic follower used to be called a Mohammedan, after the founding prophet Mohammed or Muhammad ("the praised one"). Nowadays, an adherent is known as a *Muslim* ("one who submits").

Judaism, rooted in a covenant between God and Abraham about 4,000 years ago, gave rise to Christianity and other religions. The name came from Judah (*Yahudah*, "praise God"), the fourth son of Abraham's grandson Jacob, who had been renamed Israel. Judah is the source of the words "Jew" and "Judea," land of the kingdom of Judah. Jews and Christians worship the same God under one name.

Zoroastrianism, today a much smaller group, has been named after its founder Zoroaster, Greek form of the Persian name Zarathustra ("he of the golden light"), who tradition says lived between the late 600s and mid-500s B.C..

Sikhism, whose partisans are called Sikhs ("disciples" in Hindi and Urdu), was established by Guru Nanak in the 1500s. With elements of both Hinduism and Islam, Sikhism teaches that there is one God, an invisible, all-present Creator.

Deism (from the Latin *Deus*, "God"), a religious philosophy that became popular in the 1700s during the "Age of Reason," holds that reason is the only guide to truth. Although God created the universe, He has left it on its own under the laws of nature. The U.S. Declaration of Independence and Preamble to the Constitution contain *deist* phrases like "in God we trust" and "we are endowed by the Creator with certain inalienable rights."[1]

God in everything. In contrast to other monotheists who worship a personal God, you are a *pantheist* (Greek *pan,* "all," prefixed to *theos*), if you think that the one God is in all things and all places in nature.

Your creed is slightly different should you be a *panentheist* (*pan-ent/*"within"*-theos*), who believes that the world is only a part of God's being. For example, the *Kabbalist*, a practitioner of the Jewish mystical system *Kabbalah* ("received tradition"), views the universe as merely a contracted aspect of the infinite God.

The more, the godlier?

You are a *polytheist* if you believe in many gods (Greek *poly* means "many"). The Greek and Roman mythologies in classical times had numerous gods and goddesses to whom the citizens paid homage. This form of religion, though, has several sub-categories.

You are a *henotheist* (Greek *hen-/heis,* "one," plus *theos*) if you pray to one God, but acknowledge the existence of other gods. Thus, adherents of Hinduism (from Hindu, "inhabitant of the Indus Valley") adulate a supreme world spirit, consisting of a trinity, but also serve some 33 million other gods![2] Practitioners of voodoo (African for "god," "spirit," or "sacred object") and Santería, ("way of the saints," from Spanish *santos,* "saints"), both admixtures of African, Roman Catholic, and Native American religions, revere one supreme being, in addition to many spirits or "saints." Tribal religions in Africa and the Pacific islands have similar beliefs.

You are an *anthropolatrist* (Greek *anthropos,* "human," plus *latreia,* "worship") if you venerate men as gods. Ancient Egyptians paid homage to their pharaohs as living gods. Some Roman emperors, starting with August Caesar, demanded worship. Before World War II, the state religion of Japan, Shinto ("the way of the gods"), deified the emperor as the descendant of the sun-goddess. The Japanese also revered ancestors as divinities. In Taoism ("the way" in Chinese), Taoists pray to dead heroes they have elevated to the status of gods.

You are a *theriomorphist* (Greek *therion,* "wild beast" and *morphe,* "form") if your gods have animal forms. The animals themselves are not worshipped, but their powers represented in the deities. The ancient Egyptians worshipped gods and goddesses with human bodies, but with the heads of wild animals, birds, reptiles, even insects.

You are an *animist* (Latin *anima,* "soul") if you believe that every thing in nature has a spirit. The Chinese, Japanese, Africans, and Native Americans, among others, worship many spirits thought to be in various aspects of nature and man, such as the sky, heavenly bodies, rain, thunder and lightning, mountains and hills, the sea, rivers, trees, rocks, hunting skills, agricultural and human fertility, and many others.

God is dead?

Or are you a spiritual member of the group of liberal theologians who, in the mid-1900s, espoused the philosophical idea that "God is dead"? They claimed that the traditional image of God as a father figure with supernatural powers was no longer consistent with the scientific view of the modern world.

That concludes our little soul-searching. Do you now know, if you have not been so sure before, what you are? Can we now proceed in our quest for a more intimate knowledge of God as He is portrayed in the Judeo-Christian Scriptures that we call the Bible?

What is God?

Is God real? Did He create man, or did man, fearfully conscious of his weakness and mortality, create God in his mind? If God is real, what is He like? Author Paul Johnson (*A Quest for God*, 1996) wrote: "The existence or non-existence of God is the most important question we humans are ever asked to answer."[3]

Before the creation.

The 13th century *Sefer HaZohar* ("Book of Splendor") describes God before the creation of the universe: "Before He gave any shape to the world, before He produced any form, He was alone, without form and without resemblance to anything else. Who then can comprehend how He was before the Creation? Hence it is forbidden to lend Him any form or similitude, or even to call Him by His sacred name, or to indicate Him by a single letter or a single point..."[4] God was all there was -- neither inside nor outside anything – having no spatial dimension whatsoever or frame of reference conceivable by the human mind.

Proof of His existence.

Today, the Scriptures tell us that the proof of God's existence is apparent in the created universe: *"For the invisible things of him from the creation of the world are clearly seen, being understood by the things that are made, even his eternal power and Godhead; so that they are without excuse"* (Rom 1:20).

Indeed, the breathtaking beauty of nature on earth and the awe-inspiring majesty of the heavens point to the hand of a Creator. But these are oftentimes subjective thoughts engendered by surges of human emotions.

Wernher von Braun, the German rocket scientist who became the father of the U.S. space program, wrote: "My experiences with science led me to God... Prove the existence of God? Must we really light a candle to see the sun?"[5] In today's world, we have been conditioned to demand rational and objective explanations for nearly everything. Surprisingly enough, modern science supplies many of the answers we seek – beginning with a number of the traditionally acknowledged characteristics of God taught by the Scriptures.

God, the Eternal

The Bible repeatedly avers that God has no beginning and will have no end. For instance, Moses exulted: *"Before the mountains were brought forth, or ever thou hadst formed the earth and the world, even from everlasting to everlasting, thou art God"* (Ps 90:2). John calls God *"him which is, and which was, and which is to come..."* (Rev 1:4b).

Jewish mystics refer to God as the *Ein Sof* ("Infinite Nothingness"), literally, "Without End," eternal, infinite. Without a past and a future, God is pure consciousness in timeless eternity. Yet, "Without End," according to some, implies a beginning, so it would perhaps be more appropriate to call God the *Ein Techila* – "Without Beginning." (But does that not imply an end?) Others insist that no name would be appropriate for the Creator, because the letters and sounds of names came only after the Creation.[6]

Beginning of time?

The very first words of the Scriptures relate that time had a starting point. *"In the beginning..."* (Gen 1:1a).

The apostle Paul repeated the idea no less than three times nearly 2,000 years ago: *"No, we speak of God's secret wisdom, a wisdom that has been hidden and that God destined for our glory before time began"* (1 Cor 2:7-8, NIV). *"Paul, a servant of God and an apostle of Jesus Christ for the faith of God's elect and the knowledge of the truth that leads to godliness -- a faith and knowledge resting on the hope of eternal life, which God, who does not lie, promised before the beginning of time"* (Titus 1:1-2, NIV). And... *"This grace was given us in Christ Jesus before the beginning of time"* (2 Tim 1:9-10, NIV).

If time had a beginning, "when" and how did it begin?

When time began.

Time must have begun with the Creation. *"In the beginning God created the heaven..."* (Gen 1:1a).

What is "heaven"? The word, in the ordinary sense, is synonymous with "sky" -- the expanse above the surface of the earth where the birds fly, where the clouds drift by and, farther out, where the sun, moon, and stars shine. In short, "heaven" is the space above, surrounding, and beyond our planet Earth in all directions. Space, science teaches, is a vacuum ("emptiness").

So, God created "heaven" or empty space to put His creation in. As the Jewish mystics tell it, the *Ein Sof* caused a part of His "Infinite Nothingness" to contract in order to make room for the emergence of the physical universe. Thus, empty "space" appeared. The "contraction" or "constriction" is called *Tzimtzum,* a term first used in his teachings by the Kabbalist master Isaac Luria (1534-72).[7] Critics, however, argue that "contraction" is an inaccurate and misleading term as it implies previously existing dimensions. The *Ein Sof* has no spatial dimension of any sort.

In any case, time came into existence when God created space ("heaven"). How? We measure space (or any object occupying space) by means of the three physical dimensions of length, width, and height. We measure a fourth, more subtle dimension – time -- through the movement of an object in space. The 12th century Jewish philosopher Maimonides noted: "Time is an accident consequent upon motion and is necessarily attached to it. Neither of them exists without the other. Motion does not exist except in time, and time cannot be conceived by the intellect except together with motion."[8] For example, a ball thrown from point A may take two seconds to reach point B. Without the dimensions of space as a frame of reference, there can be no movement and, therefore, no time.

As the *Encarta Encyclopedia* points out: "In Einstein's general theory of relativity, which was introduced in 1916, the very existence of time depends on the presence of space."[9] The editors speculate that "the big bang theory (of the birth of the universe) does not explain what existed before the big bang. It may be that time itself began at the big bang, so that it makes no sense to discuss what happened 'before' the big bang."[10]

Time will end.

Physicist Paul Davies, of the University of Adelaide, Australia, wrote: "Modern scientific cosmology is the most ambitious enterprise of all to emerge from Einstein's work. When scientists began to explore the implications of Einstein's time for the universe as a whole, they made one of the most important discoveries in the history of human thought: that time, and hence all of physical reality, must have had a definite origin in the past. If time is flexible and mutable, as Einstein demonstrated, then it is possible for time to come into existence – and also to pass away again; there can be a beginning and an end to time."[11]

Truly, the Scriptures also tell us that time will ultimately come to an end: *"But as for you, Daniel, conceal these words and seal up the book until the end of time..."* (Dan 12:4, NASU).

"Space-time" inseparable.

Space and time are so inseparably tied together that scientists refer to the continuum of space and time as simply one entity: "space-time."

The Jews had a 16th century saying: *"HaMakom V'HaZman Echad Hu."* ("Space and time, they are one.")[12] Writer Fred Alan Wolf, commenting on Albert Einstein's special theory of relativity, observes that "space and time are linked together and are interchangeable. The connection between space and time, however, is not apparent unless you are dealing with vast distances, very short times, or things moving very near to the speed of light."[13]

God outside space-time.

If God created space and time, then He obviously pre-existed and must be outside space-time. As the whole cannot be contained in any of its parts, infinite God cannot be confined in the finite universe He merely created. King Solomon asks: *"But will God indeed dwell on the earth? behold, the heaven and heaven of heavens cannot contain thee; how much less this house that I have builded?"* (1 Kings 8:27).

Moreover, everything in the universe functions according to the laws of physics. Would God subject Himself to the physical laws He Himself had established? If He did, He would no longer be infinite.

Space and time had a beginning, and their Creator existed before time began. He is therefore before, above, and beyond time, which has no effects on Him. Thus, God is timeless. Science confirms Scripture: God is eternal -- with no beginning and no end.

God, the Cosmic Intelligence

Did the universe, including man, come about simply by accident as most scientists would have us believe? Davies, a known atheist, notes: "A long list of additional 'lucky accidents' and 'coincidences' has been compiled... impressive evidence that life as we know it depends very sensitively on the form of the laws of physics, and on some seemingly fortuitous accidents in the actual values that nature has chosen for various particle masses, force strengths, and so on..."[14]

Scientists are awed and at the same time baffled by the incredible "natural" order and amazing "accidental" precision of forces in the cosmos. The balance and harmony of the laws of physics are so perfect, it is difficult to believe they all happened by chance.

Four fundamental forces.

Scientist have identified the four fundamental forces at work in the universe.

1. The strong nuclear force, which bonds the quarks that make up the protons and neutrons in an atom, and holds those protons and neutrons together to form the atomic nucleus in matter.

2. The electromagnetic force that keeps electrons orbiting around the atomic nucleus, and fastens together the molecules that make up all living organisms, as well as the planets and the stars.

3. Gravitation, the attraction between all forms of matter produced by their masses (amounts of matter), keeping objects and organisms on the ground, and regulating the motions of planets, stars, galaxies.

4. The weak nuclear force that causes radioactive decay in atoms and generates nuclear reactions that enable the Sun and the stars to produce light and heat.

Consider. All matter is mostly space. Quantum particles such as protons, neutrons, and electrons that form atoms are separated by vast distances. For instance, the nucleus of a hydrogen atom is about 10^{-13} cm, while the radius of its electron's orbit is some 10^{-8} cm. If the nucleus were as big as a pinhead, the electron would be a football field away![15] If any of the four fundamental forces fails to function, or is altered even one small fraction, all atomic components would fly apart and disintegrate. All matter would cease to exist, and all energy would disappear without a trace.

Something must have brought these forces into play. Or, should we say, Someone? Says Nehemiah, *"You alone are the LORD; You have made heaven, The heaven of heavens, with all their host, The earth and everything on it, The seas and all that is in them, And You preserve them all"* (Neh 9:6, NKJV).

The "laws of heaven."

The laws of physics do not seem to have evolved. They appear to have been present from the very beginning as matter formed almost instantly. Prof. Keith Ward of King's College, London University, wrote: "The universe began to expand in a very precisely ordered manner, in accordance with a set of basic mathematical constants and laws which govern its subsequent development into a universe of the sort we see today. There already existed a very complex array of quantum laws describing possible interactions of elementary particles, and the universe, according to one main theory, originated by the operation of fluctuations in a quantum field in accordance with those laws."[16]

The ancients knew that the universe has laws governing its existence and operation. Job asks quizzically: *"Do you know the laws of the heavens? Can you set up [God's] dominion over the earth?"* (Job 38:33, NIV). If the universe has laws, there must have been a "lawgiver." Albert Einstein said, "Everyone who is seriously involved in the pursuit of science becomes convinced that a spirit is manifest in the laws of the Universe – a spirit vastly superior to that of man."[17]

Jeremiah suggests who had set up the physical laws of the universe: *"This is what the LORD says: `If I have not established my covenant with day and night and the fixed laws of heaven and earth,...`"* (Jer 33:25, NIV).

An "intelligent designer."

Wernher von Braun, who was also the first director of the U.S. National Aeronautics and Space Administration (NASA), remarked: "One cannot be exposed to the law and order of the universe without concluding that there must be purpose and design behind it all. In the world around us, we can behold the obvious manifestation of an ordered, structured plan or design..."[18] He concluded: "The better we understand the intricacies of the universe... the more (we) marvel at the inherent design upon which it is based... the admission of a design... ultimately raises the question of a Designer..."[19]

British astrophysicist Sir Fred Hoyle marveled: "A common sense interpretation of the facts suggests that a super-intellect has monkeyed with the physics, as well as with the chemistry and biology, and that there are no blind forces worth speaking about in nature. The numbers one calculates from the facts seem to me so overwhelming as to put this conclusion almost beyond question."[20]

"Roger Penrose, professor of mathematics at Oxford University, has among his areas of expertise the study of the universe after its creation. He was awarded the Wolf Prize for his analytic description of the Big Bang, which forms the basis of all Big Bang models. Penrose finds the laws of nature tuned for life. This balance of nature's laws is so perfect and so unlikely to have occurred by chance that he avers an intelligent 'Creator' must have chosen them."[21]

Solomon said God introduced wisdom, or intelligence, before the Creation. *"I, wisdom, dwell together with prudence; I possess knowledge and discretion... The LORD brought me forth as the first of his works, before his deeds of old; I was appointed from eternity, from the beginning, before the world began"* (Prov 8:12, 22-23, NIV). God had, even before His very first creative act, set into motion the physical laws that would govern all creation.

The psalmist intones: *"O LORD, how manifold are thy works! in wisdom hast thou made them all..."* (Ps 104:24; also 136:5; Prov 3:19;8:12,22-23; Jer 10:12, 51:15).

God, the Immanent

Solar and galactic systems are held together by the gravitational force of the mass (matter) and energy they contain. The matter primarily comprises hydrogen and helium, while the energy consists mainly of electromagnetic radiation in many forms.[22]

Missing mass?

The Big Bang Theory of the birth of the universe assumes the presence of enough mass in the rapidly expanding universe for matter to come together and form stars and galaxies. However, estimates of the universe's actual mass consistently fall far short of the minimum amount necessary to hold the stars and galaxies together.

"In 1933 the late Fritz Zwicky pointed out that the galaxies of the Coma cluster are moving too fast: there is not enough visible mass in the galaxies to bind the cluster together by gravity. Subsequent observations verified this 'missing' mass in other clusters."[23]

Considering the observed velocities and apparent masses of the galaxies in the clusters, they should have broken up a long, long time ago. Something unseen is keeping them together. On a smaller scale, in the 1970s spiral galaxies were found spinning just as fast at the outer edges as they do at the center. It is a mystery how they have been doing this for countless eons without flying apart.

"Dark matter."

Author Walt Brown writes that "in almost every case the velocities of the individual galaxies are high enough to allow them to escape from the cluster. In effect, the clusters are 'boiling.' This statement is certainly true if we assume that the only gravitational force present is that exerted by visible matter, but it is true even if we assume that every galaxy in the cluster, like the Milky Way, is surrounded by a halo of dark matter that contains 90 percent of the mass of the galaxy."[24]

The missing mass, which does not emit, reflect, or absorb light or any kind of radiation, is called "dark matter," because no one can see or even detect it. Paul spoke about this to the Hebrews: *"By faith we understand that the universe was formed at God's command, so that what is seen was not made out of what was visible*" (Heb 11:3, NIV). The visible universe has been created from invisible things.

The *World Book* points out that the combined mass of all the stars, planets, and cosmic dust and gases accounts for only about 4% of the energy needed to hold the universe together. Of the remaining 96% that astronomers cannot detect, dark matter accounts for approximately 23%.[25] Would the scientists have believed Paul if he had spoken to them? "*He is before all things, and in him all things hold together*" (Col 1:17-18, NIV).

"Dark energy."

Big Bang theorists assume that the expansion of the universe should be slowing, in the same way that a ball thrown upward into the air must slow as it moves away from the earth's gravity. Cosmologists have taken measurements of this cosmic deceleration for decades. Their findings, rechecked many times, always show the same perplexing result: The universe's expansion is not decelerating, but is instead accelerating![26,27]

To preserve the viability of the Big Bang theory, an explanation had to be found. There must be an unknown energy actively counteracting gravity and causing stars and galaxies to accelerate away from each other. That unknown, undetectable energy must be, what else -- dark energy. It is said to represent the last 73% missing in the equation.[28]

The Spirit of God?

God, 2,600 years ago, said through the prophet Jeremiah: "*Can any hide himself in secret places that I shall not see him? saith the LORD. Do not I fill heaven and earth? saith the LORD*" (Jer 23:24). God said He fills the entire universe. But is not the *Ein Sof* or "Infinite Nothingness" outside the universe?

"*God is a spirit*" (John 4:24), and as many of us know "*the Spirit of God moved upon the face of the waters*" (Gen 1:2b) in the emerging universe. It appears that, although the *Ein Sof* remains outside of creation, His Spirit, which is energy, entered the physical world. Paradoxically, God is both apart from and a part of the universe!

Are the unseen and undetectable "dark matter" and "dark energy," as well as all observable matter and energy in the cosmos, God? Paul hints at the answer. "*While we look not at the things which are seen, but at the things which are not seen: for the things which are seen are temporal; but the things which are not seen are eternal*" (2 Cor 4:18). The unseen, eternal God is immanent in the universe.

God, the Immutable

The most striking characteristic of nature, from Aristotle's point of view, was "change."[29] Intellectuals who are of a like mind in our modern age have even coined a clever maxim: "Change is the only constant."

It is an established principle in physics that all things change. The second law of thermodynamics, entropy, states that spontaneous change in isolated systems proceeds from a state of order to one of disorder. In simple terms, all things break down, deteriorate, or decay through time. The general rule in the universe is change. Everything changes.

The only exception to that rule is God.

Outside time.

God declared through the prophet Malachi that He is immutable – He does not change. *"For I am the LORD, I change not..."* (Mal 3:6). David repeats that truth in a psalm: *"They shall perish, but thou shalt endure: yea, all of them shall wax old like a garment; as a vesture shalt thou change them, and they shall be changed: But thou art the same, and thy years shall have no end"* (Ps 102:26-27). God has passed on this immutability to His Son, who has the same nature. *"Jesus Christ the same yesterday, and to day, and for ever"* (Heb 13:8).

There are at least two reasons, both backed by modern scientific principles, why God does not change.

First, as we have already seen, God, as the *Ein Sof* or "Infinite Nothingness" is outside space-time. Changes take place only in time. Since God is not subject to the passage of time, He is timeless. And, being timeless, He cannot change. God is immutable.

God is light.

The clue to the second reason is in James's reiteration of God's unchanging nature. *"Every good and perfect gift is from above, coming down from the Father of the heavenly lights, who does not change like shifting shadows"* (James 1:17-18, NIV). An additional element, though, appears in the passage: *"Father of the heavenly lights."* As such, God must also be light, which is precisely what John says: *"This then is the message which we have heard of him, and declare unto you, that God is light, and in him is no darkness at all"* (John 1:5).

What is light? It is pure radiant energy -- a form of electromagnetic radiation consisting of photons, the fastest moving things in the universe. Having no mass, photons travel through space at some 186,000 miles per second (about 300,000 km/sec.) without any loss of energy. Nothing travels faster than light, whose velocity is the cosmic speed limit. At the speed of light, time stops. Light therefore, is also timeless and cannot change. Naturally no less is its Creator, God, who is light as well. Yes, God is truly immutable.

God, the Omnipresent

The Holy Scriptures tell us that God is in all places at the same time. Quite unexpectedly, recent discoveries in a relatively new field of science seem to provide evidence that God is truly present everywhere all at once. We refer to the young branch of physics called quantum mechanics (QM).

Quantum mechanics.

Quantum mechanics, or quantum physics, which developed in the 1920s, is the study of the smallest parts that make up matter and energy – such as protons, neutrons, electrons, positrons, quarks, photons, neutrinos, and a host of other minuscule entities. As a theoretical science, QM provides precise mathematical rules that describe how the universe works on the smallest scales. It has proven so successful in predicting results that entire industries have been built on QM -- microelectronics, computers, lasers. Nonetheless, QM is still oftentimes referred to as "weird science."

Many phenomena uncovered and predicted by quantum mechanics are so mind-boggling they leave physicists flabbergasted. Danish physicist Niels Bohr, winner of the 1922 Nobel Prize, said: "Anyone who isn't shocked by quantum physics has not understood it."[30]

As his fellow Nobel Laureate Richard Feynman wrote, "it is often stated that of all the theories proposed in this century, the silliest is quantum theory. Some say that the only thing that quantum theory has going for it, in fact, is that it is unquestionably correct."[31]

Cosmologist Andreas Albrecht of the University of California at Davis claims QM is "the fundamental language that Nature speaks. Nature doesn't answer questions for certain; it answers questions by giving probabilities... There's a possibility that almost anything happens... It comes out of the mathematics. It's forced down our throats."[32]

"Nonlocality."

Quantum physicists have observed that subatomic particles perform magical or, more appropriately, sci-fi-like acts. Fred Alan Wolf wrote in *Space-Time and Beyond*: "Particles don't behave as we might expect them to. For example, they vanish and reappear in unexpected places in violation of energy conservation rules." Particles make quantum jumps

-- that is, they go from one place to another without traveling across the space between the two locations![33] How are they able to do that?

In the 1940s American-born British physicist David Bohm, a friend and protégé of Einstein, observed in his work in plasma (gases of high density electrons and positive ions) that, on the subatomic level, location ceases to exist! Any point in space is equal to all other points in space. They are conjoined, no matter how distantly separated they may appear to be. In other words, any one quantum particle is present everywhere in the universe. Physicists have since accepted the phenomenon and call it "nonlocality." Paul Davis of the University of Newcastle upon Tyne has concluded that "the nonlocal aspects of quantum systems is therefore a general property of nature."[34]

According to the *Encarta Encyclopedia*: "The strong correlations observed in these experiments suggest to many that we inhabit a nonlocal reality, meaning that what happens here and now could depend upon something far away in space, time, or both."[35] Nonlocality demonstrates how God can be present in all points of the universe at the same time.

David wondered: *"Whither shall I go from thy spirit? or whither shall I flee from thy presence? If I ascend up into heaven, thou art there: if I make my bed in hell, behold, thou art there. If I take the wings of the morning, and dwell in the uttermost parts of the sea; Even there shall thy hand lead me, and thy right hand shall hold me"* (Ps 139:7-10).

Quantum mechanics proves God is omnipresent.

God, the Omniscient

Solomon asserts that God is all-knowing. *"The eyes of the LORD are in every place, beholding the evil and the good"* (Prov 15:3). No one person or thing, good or bad, escapes from His sight. *"Can any hide himself in secret places that I shall not see him? saith the LORD"* (Jer 23:24a).

Because He is the Creator of heaven and earth, including space and time, God knows their every nook and corner, as well as everything that has happened and will happen. *"Remember the former things of old: for I am God, and there is none else; I am God, and there is none like me, Declaring the end from the beginning, and from ancient times the things that are not yet done..."* (Isa 46:9-10a; also Acts 15:18).

God does not only see all our actions and hear all our words, He also knows our innermost thoughts and feelings. *"O LORD, thou hast searched me, and known me. Thou knowest my downsitting and mine uprising, thou understandest my thought afar off"* (Ps 139:1-2). He even knows what we are going to say even before it is formed on our lips.

"Before a word is on my tongue you know it completely, O LORD" (Ps 139:4, NIV). Thus, Christ told His followers: *"Do not be like them, for your Father knows what you need before you ask him"* (Matt 6:8, NIV).

Interconnectedness.

In traditional physics, the principle of separability states that connected objects once separated can no longer affect one another. Logical enough. Yet, quantum mechanics violates this principle and instead reveals a "quantum connectedness." An object can still affect another, even when there is no longer any physical contact between them.[36] How is that possible?

Fred Alan Wolf says that some subatomic processes result in the creation of pairs of matter and antimatter particles. The twins have identical or closely related properties, except that these are reversed. For example, a negatively charged electron's antimatter partner called positron has the same mass, but has an opposite positive charge (hence its name) and spins in the opposite direction.[37] QM predicts that attempts to measure complementary characteristics on the pair – even when traveling in opposite directions – would always fail. This had led Niels Bohr to speculate: If subatomic particles do not exist individually until they are observed, they probably do not exist as separate, independent entities. They must be parts of an indivisible whole that remains so even after their appearance.[38]

In the earlier mentioned work of David Bohm with plasma, particles would stop behaving individually and start behaving like parts of an interconnected system. It was as though each particle knew what the trillions of other particles in the universe were doing.

In 1964 John Stewart Bell, a theoretical physicist at CERN (the European center for nuclear research in Geneva), developed a mathematical approach, now called the *Bell Inequality*, on how connectedness could be tested. As the level of technological precision needed was not yet available at the time, the experiment was conducted only in 1982 at the Institute of Theoretical and Applied Optics in Paris. Nevertheless, just as QM had predicted, two photons, although spatially separated, appeared in contact with each other and nonlocally connected! It showed that, on the subatomic level, all things in the universe are interconnected -- nothing is separate from any of all the others.[39]

That finding provides us with more understanding about how God knows everything happening anywhere, anytime. *"And there is no creature hidden from His sight, but all things are naked and open to the eyes of Him to whom we must give account"* (Heb 4:13, NKJV). God is truly omniscient – all-seeing and all-knowing.

God, the Omnipotent

God's powers are truly awesome to His creatures. *"And I heard as it were the voice of a great multitude, and as the voice of many waters, and as the voice of mighty thunderings, saying, Alleluia: for the Lord God omnipotent reigneth"* (Rev 19:6). God is all-powerful. *"Is any thing too hard for the LORD?"* (Gen 18:14). The answer is obvious. *"Ah Lord GOD! behold, thou hast made the heaven and the earth by thy great power and stretched out arm, and there is nothing too hard for thee"* (Jer 32:17).

Manifested in "miracles."

God often manifests His power to men in miracles – extraordinary, supernatural phenomena that seem improbable or even impossible to the human mind. In Scripture, they are called "signs and wonders." Men's unbelief is one reason why God performs miracles. *"'Unless you people see miraculous signs and wonders,' Jesus told him, 'you will never believe'"* (John 4:48, NIV).

Some of the most spectacular miracles recorded in the Bible are those God did before and after the Israelites' Exodus from Egypt, as well as some which interfered with the natural movement of the sun.

The 10 plagues of Egypt. God inflicted ten successive ordeals on Egypt when Pharaoh obstinately refused to let the Israelites go: (1) The waters of the Nile River turned into blood (Ex 7:14-25). (2) Frogs covered the land of Egypt (Ex 8:1-14). (3) Lice formed from the dust and infested both men and animals (Ex 8:16-19). (4) Flies swarmed into all the houses of the Egyptians (Ex 8:20-31). (5) A plague killed all the livestock in Egypt, except those of the Israelites (Ex 9:1-7). (6) A pandemic of boils afflicted all the Egyptians and their animals (Ex 9:8-11). (7) Hail and fire rained down over all Egypt (except Goshen, where the Israelites lived), killing all men and animals out in the field (Ex 9:13-26). (8) Locusts covered the whole of Egypt and devoured all green vegetation and fruits on trees (Ex 10:3-6,12-19). (9) Darkness blanketed Egypt for three days, but the Israelites had light in their dwellings (Ex 10:22-23). (10) All the firstborn of the Egyptians and their animals died (Ex 11:1-7,12:12-13,29-31).

Miracles in the wilderness. (1) The parting of the Red Sea by an east wind that blew all night, enabling the Israelites to walk across to safety from their Egyptian pursuers (Ex 14). (2) The provision of quail in the evening of the day the LORD promised to give them bread and meat

(Ex 16:6-13), and when they longed for Egyptian food the LORD sent them a whole month's supply of quail (Num 11:4-32). (3) The daily supply of *manna* ("bread from heaven") that appeared on the ground daily for forty years (Ex 16). (4) Water from the rock in Horeb that Moses struck with his staff (Ex 17:1-6).

Miracles with the sun. (1) The sun stood still when Joshua asked the LORD to stop the sun until they would have defeated the Amorites (Josh 10:12-14). (2) The shadow moved back ten degrees on the sundial, the sign King Hezekiah had asked for to confirm that the LORD had truly healed him and added fifteen years to his life (2 Kings 20:8-11). (3) Darkness at noon over the whole land as Christ hung dying on the cross, from 12:00 noon until 3:00 in the afternoon (Luke 23:44-45).

Some miracles explained?

Unbelievers in ancient times tried to dismiss God's miracles as the works of magic or evil spirits.[40] In our modern day scholars offer reasons, scientific or otherwise, to explain many Biblical miracles.

The ten plagues. The Nile's turning into blood is said to be a natural effect of its annual flooding, with the water first turning green, then yellow, then ochre red starting around the 25th of June due to the proliferation of algae and other microorganisms, similar to "Red Tide" today. Frogs subsequently multiply in September. An infestation by flies and outbreak of animal plague supposedly often follow in December. So do a purported epidemic of boils, hailstones, a locust invasion, and darkness caused by fine sand blown by the southwest wind from the desert, filling the atmosphere.[41] Hence, Egypt's magicians were able to imitate the first two miracles of turning water into "blood" and causing frogs to appear (Ex 7:22; 8:7).

In contrast, the feats of Moses were undeniably miraculous in the suddenness of the change in the river and the over-abundance of the frogs. Trying to mimic the third miracle, the magicians were unable to turn dust into lice (or gnats), (Ex 8:18). It is doubtful if they even attempted to copy Moses's acts of bringing on swarms of flies, the animal plague, and the boil epidemic, from which they themselves terribly suffered (Ex 9:11), but not the Israelites. The hailstorm and locust invasion could not have been normal recurrences as they were said to be the worst ever in Egypt (Ex 9:24; 10:14). Lastly, the death of all the firstborn of both men and animals in Egypt, except those of Israel, has no parallel in human history. Can these be called anything other than miracles of God?

The Red Sea divided. The "Red Sea" that the LORD parted to let the Israelites escape from the Egyptians is in the Hebrew original *Yam*

Suf, which means "Reed Sea" or "Sea of Reeds." It was at the northern end of the Red Sea, where no reeds grow. Centuries after the Exodus, canal-building by pharaohs trying to link the Nile delta and the Red Sea drained the Reed Sea, leaving only marshes called Bitter Lakes. In 280 B.C., Jewish scholars translating the Hebrew Scriptures into the Greek Septuagint rendered "Reed Sea," which no longer existed, as *Erythra Thalassa* ("Red Sea"). In 300 A.D. Jerome had the name *Mare Rubrum* ("Red Sea") in his Latin Bible, the *Vulgate.* Martin Luther correctly translated *Yam Suf* as *Schilfmeer* ("Reed Sea") in his German version of the Old Testament in 1534.

In short, the sea the LORD parted *"with a strong east wind all that night"* (Ex 14:21) and the Israelites crossed on foot was not the Red Sea, which has an average depth of 1,765 feet, but the shallow Sea of Reeds. Does that make the event a non-miracle? Absolutely not. Just the same, the shallow Reed Sea posed an impassable barrier to the Israelites.

In a computer-aided study, calculations by Nathan Paldor and Doron Nof of the American Meteorological Society showed that a wind blowing at 40-45 miles per hour for 10 hours would reduce the level of a shallow body of water by 10 feet.[42] "Such heaping up of the waters by the wind is well known and sometimes amounts to 7 or 8 ft. in Lake Erie (Wright, Scientific Confirmations of the Old Testament, 106)."[43] That would have been enough to let the Israelites cross the sea and later drown the Egyptians and their horses weighed down by war implements. The miracle was, how did that east wind happen to blow with just the needed strength, at the right place, in the right direction, all night?

The provision of quail. The quail that fell on the Israelite camp were birds residing in or passing through Egypt and the Holy Land on their migrations northward in March and southward in September.[44] With strong wing muscles, quail can fly rapidly for a short time. When migrating, they spread their wings for the wind to carry them along.[45] The southeast wind blew the quail over the Red Sea,[46] across the mouth of the Gulf of Aqaba and Suez, and on to the Sinai peninsula. On their way north, they passed over narrow portions of the sea, but arrived so exhausted they could easily be caught by hand.[47]

It was not a miracle if Moses knew about the annual migration and encamped in the birds' path. What was truly miraculous was the number of the birds. God gave around two million Israelites enough quail to eat for a month! Can you imagine how many birds that was? The quails fell *"by the camp, as it were a day's journey on this side, and as it were a day's journey on the other side, round about the camp, and as it were two cubits high upon the face of the earth. And the people stood up all that day, and all that night, and all the next day, and they gathered the quails: he that gathered least gathered ten homers: and they spread them all abroad for themselves round about the camp"* (Num 11:31b-32).

A *"day's journey"* is about 20-22 miles, so the quail extended some 40-44 miles on the two sides of the camp combined, piled *"two cubits"* (3 feet) or about waist-high on the ground![48] No wonder the people went sleepless for 36 hours gathering them. A *homer* ("heap") is about 8 bushels or one donkey-load. The birds were so many *"they spread them all abroad,"* that is, they dried them in the sun.[49]

Some commentators, theologians even, cannot believe they were quail. "It is uncertain what sort of animals they were... The learned bishop Patrick inclines to agree with some modern writers, who think they were locusts, a delicious sort of food well known in those parts, the rather because they were brought with a wind, lay in heaps, and were dried in the sun for use."[50] Now, if the quail were not a miracle, what is?

The daily *manna*. The *World Book* says: "Some historians say manna was a gluey sugar from the tamarisk shrub."[51] The *Encyclopaedia Britannica* adds: "An edible, white honeylike substance known as manna forms drops on the stem of a tamarisk tree, *Tamarix mannifera*. A scale insect either punctures the stem, triggering the exudation, or secretes the manna itself."[52] *Fausset's Bible Dictionary* provides more details, saying manna is "the sweet juice of the *tarfa*, a kind of tamarisk. It exudes in May for about six weeks from the trunk and branches in hot weather, and forms small round white grains. It retains its consistency in cool weather, but melts with heat. It is gathered from the twigs or from the fallen leaves. The Arabs, after boiling and straining, use it as honey with bread. The color is a greyish-yellow, the taste sweet and aromatic. Ehrenberg says it is produced by an insect's puncture. It abounds in rainy seasons, some years it ceases. About 600 or 700 pounds is the present produce of a year. The region wady Gharandel (Elim) and Sinai, the wady Sheich, and some other parts of the peninsula, are the places where it is found. The name is still its Arabic designation, and is read on the Egyptian monuments (mennu, mennu hut 'white manna')."[53]

The *Encarta Encyclopedia* advances another theory: "Some experts believe that the manna of the Bible was the lichen *Lecanora esculenta*, or a related species. Arabs still gather this lichen and mix it with meal to produce bread. When dry, it can be torn from the soil and transported by the wind, producing a 'rain' of food."[54] The *Encyclopaedia Britannica* concurs: "Manna is the common name for certain lichens of the genus *Lecanora* native to Turkey, especially *L. esculenta*. In the Middle East lichen bread and manna jelly are made from *Lecanora*."[55]

The manna God gave the Israelites, though, differs on several points: (1) It was found on the ground after the morning dew had evaporated, not under trees. (2) The quantity gathered in one day far exceeded the present yearly production. (3) It appeared six days a week, all year round, not just occasionally or for several weeks. (4) None was found on the seventh-day Sabbath. (5) It appeared for 40 years while Israel wandered in the wilderness, but disappeared the day after the Israelites first ate of the produce in the Promised Land (Josh 5:10-12). Now, decide whether manna was a miracle from God or not.

Tests for our faith?

Some miracles, like the ones we have just discussed have elements that leave the door open for speculation. Why would the LORD, who is all-knowing, choose circumstances that would allow room for doubt? Perhaps, God's miracles are tests for our faith as well. By allowing alternative possibilities, He allows us to exercise our free will – to believe or not to believe. It is said: No miracle is needed for those who believe, but no miracle is sufficient for those who will not believe.

Yet, some miracles are truly inexplicable -- the darkness at noon at the Crucifixion, for instance. A solar eclipse was impossible, because it was the day of Passover, which always falls at the time of the full moon, when the Earth is between the sun and the moon. *"But Jesus beheld them, and said unto them, With men this is impossible; but with God all things are possible"* (Matt 19:26; also Luke 1:37). God is omnipotent.

God's image and traits

Abraham spoke with God (Gen 12, etc.). Jacob, his grandson, met God "face-to-face. *"And Jacob called the name of the place Peniel: for I have seen God face to face, and my life is preserved"* (Gen 32:30). So did Moses. *"And the LORD spake unto Moses face to face, as a man speaketh unto his friend."* (Ex 33:11a).

Anthropomorphic.

The Scriptures frequently portray God as anthropomorphic -- having the physical figure, facial features, and appendages (sometimes used figuratively) of a human being.

He has a head with hair (*"the hair of his head like the pure wool"* -- Dan 7:9b); eyes and ears (*"Now mine eyes shall be open, and mine ears attent unto the prayer that is made in this place"* -- 2 Chron 7:15; 1 Pet 3:12); a nose with nostrils (*"These are a smoke in my nose, a fire that burneth all the day"* -- Isa 65:5b; Ex 15:8); a mouth with lips (*"he shall smite the earth with the rod of his mouth, and with the breath of his lips shall he slay the wicked"* -- Isa 11:4b).

God has a torso with shoulders (*"the LORD shall cover him all the day long, and he shall dwell between his shoulders"* -- Deut 33:12b); a back (*"And I will take away mine hand, and thou shalt see my back parts: but my face shall not be seen"* -- Ex 33:23); a behind to sit upon (*"I beheld till the thrones were cast down, and the Ancient of days did sit"* -- Dan 7:9a).

He has arms (*"with a stretched out arm, and with fury poured out, will I rule over you"* -- Ezek 20:33b); hands (*"I will put thee in a clift of the rock, and will cover thee with my hand while I pass by"* -- Ex 33:22b); fingers (*"two tables of testimony, tables of stone, written with the finger of God"* -- Ex 31:18b); legs to walk with (*"And they heard the voice of the LORD God walking in the garden in the cool of the day"* -- Gen 3:8); feet (*"the place of my throne, and the place of the soles of my feet, where I will dwell in the midst of the children of Israel for ever"* -- Ezek 43:7a).

God in human form seems to feel discomfort under the heat of the sun and get hungry as well. *"And he took butter, and milk, and the calf which he had dressed, and set it before them (Elohim); and he stood by them under the tree, and they did eat (Gen 18:8).*

Human emotions.

The LORD likewise displays the wide spectrum of human emotions. He can have positive feelings, like satisfaction (*"And God saw every thing that he had made, and, behold, it was very good"* -- Gen 1:31); love (*"the LORD thy God turned the curse into a blessing unto thee, because the LORD thy God loved thee"* -- Deut 23:5b); amusement (*"I also will laugh at your calamity"* -- Prov 1:26a); pity (*"Like as a father pitieth his children, so the LORD pitieth them that fear him"* -- Ps 103:13); mercy (*"The LORD is gracious, and full of compassion; slow to anger, and of great mercy"* -- Ps 145:8).

On the other hand, God can also be filled with negative emotions, such as sadness and disappointment (*"And it repented the LORD that he had made man on the earth, and it grieved him at his heart"* -- Gen 6:6); anger (*"And my wrath shall wax hot, and I will kill you with the sword; and your wives shall be widows, and your children fatherless"* -- Ex 22:24); hatred (*"I hate, I despise your feast days, and I will not smell in your solemn assemblies"* -- Amos 5:21); spite (*"I will mock when your fear cometh"* -- Prov 1:26b).

The LORD can also feel regret and change His mind (*"And the LORD said, I will destroy man whom I have created from the face of the earth; both man, and beast, and the creeping thing, and the fowls of the air; for it repenteth me that I have made them"* -- Gen 6:7).

Based on these verses, it seems as though God is no different from any ordinary man!

The LORD's proxy

Despite the preceding descriptions of God, the Bible tells us that nobody has seen or heard God at any time at all! To begin with, God, being spirit, is invisible: *"Who is the image of the invisible God..."* (Col 1:15a). Moses reminded the Israelites: *"And the LORD spake unto you out of the midst of the fire: ye heard the voice of the words, but saw no similitude; only ye heard a voice"* (Deut 4:12).

Christ says it could not have been God Himself: *"And the Father himself, which hath sent me, hath borne witness of me. Ye have neither heard his voice at any time, nor seen his shape"* (John 5:37). The apostle John teaches the same truth. *"No man hath seen God at any time; the only begotten Son, which is in the bosom of the Father, he hath declared him"* (John 1:18). Paul confirms it: *"...God, the blessed and only Ruler, the King of kings and Lord of lords, who alone is immortal and who lives in unapproachable light, whom no one has seen or can see"* (1 Tim 6:15b-16, NIV). Who, then, did Abraham, Jacob, and Moses speak with "face-to-face"?

Aggelos, the messenger.

Let us go over one passage wherein Abraham met God in person. *"And the LORD appeared unto him in the plains of Mamre: and he sat in the tent door in the heat of the day; And he lift up his eyes and looked, and, lo, three men stood by him: and when he saw them, he ran to meet them from the tent door, and bowed himself toward the ground. And said, My Lord, if now I have found favour in thy sight, pass not away, I pray thee, from thy servant"* (Gen 18:1-3).

God appeared to Abraham as three men. The word in the original Hebrew Scriptures most frequently translated "God" is *elohim*, meaning "gods" (singular, *el* or *eloah*, "god"). Some Bible teachers interpret *elohim* as the three persons of the "Trinity." But, usually, when the term *Elohim* is used to refer to God, it is said to be used as a plural of magnitude and majesty. When used in reference to angels, *elohim* truly means the plural form – more than one.

Now, consider the meeting between God and Moses. *"And the angel of the LORD appeared unto him in a flame of fire out of the midst of a bush: and he looked, and, behold, the bush burned with fire, and the bush was not consumed. And Moses said, I will now turn aside, and see this great sight, why the bush is not burnt. And when the LORD saw that he turned aside to see, God called unto him out of the midst of the bush, and said, Moses, Moses. And he said, Here am I"* (Ex 3:2-4). Note that, first, the "angel of the Lord" appeared to Moses from the middle of a burning bush. Then, we read it was the LORD Himself. Next, it was God who called to Moses from the bush. The terms "angel of the Lord," "the LORD," and "God" are used interchangeably. We get the impression that all three are one and the same!

An "angel of the LORD" also appeared to Manoah, Samson's father-to-be. *"But the angel of the LORD did no more appear to Manoah and to his wife. Then Manoah knew that he was an angel of the LORD. And Manoah said unto his wife, We shall surely die, because we have seen God"* (Judg 13:21-22). The connection between the "angel of the LORD" and "God" is borne out clearly. Manoah knew that it was the "angel of the Lord," and yet he referred to the angel as "God" Himself!

The God whom Abraham, Jacob, Moses, Manoah, and even Adam and Eve conversed with was not the *Ein Sof* or "Infinite Nothngness," but the "angel of the LORD" – His alter-ego, proxy, representative, or emissary. (The English word "angel" comes from the Greek *aggelos*, which means "messenger.") The angel is also called "the LORD" by God's authority. *"Behold, I send an Angel before thee, to keep thee in the way, and to bring thee into the place which I have prepared. Beware of him, and obey his voice, provoke him not; for he will not pardon your transgressions: for my name is in him"* (Ex 23:20-21). Similarly, as a country's president today is addressed as "Excellency," his or her ambassadors are also called "Excellency."

When God destroyed Sodom and Gomorrah, there were two entities called "the LORD." *"Then the LORD rained upon Sodom and upon Gomorrah brimstone and fire from the LORD out of heaven"* (Gen 19:24). One called "the LORD" in the sky near the earth rained on the two cities fire and brimstone coming from another one also called "the LORD" higher up in heaven!

Author David Allen Deal (*The Mystic Symbol*) wrote: "The lesser YHWH (angel of the LORD), also called 'Metatron' in the Book of Enoch, is also well-attested to among the Jewish rabbinical sources. He is called the 'lesser YHWH,' and the use of the term acknowledges the existence of a greater YHWH, the Father, who is above all."[56]

The God with whom Abraham, Jacob, Moses, Manoah, even Adam and Eve, and the other blessed Biblical men had dealings and spoke "face-to-face" was the angel of the LORD.

The "Manufacturer's Mark"

Lest there be any confusion whose handiwork the created universe is, God left His mark imprinted upon His creation to let His creatures know that He is the Creator. The unmistakable trace of His hand is in virtually everything He has made and brought forth. His "manufacturer's mark" consists of just one character – the number "7."

Reputed to be the number of spiritual completeness and divine perfection, 7 is also the "indestructible" number – it is the only number that cannot be divided exactly except by itself, its fractions and multiples, and 1 (always leaving a seemingly infinite remainder). Apparently God's favorite number, 7, is all around us.

In the earth and nature.

The Earth has 7 distinct motions: (1) Rotation around its axis. (2) Revolution around the sun. (3) Wobble in its axis. (4) Slow vertical rotation of the magnetic core. (5) Movement with the Sun's 260-million-year circuit in space. (6) Up and down oscillation in its orbit around the Milky Way. (7) Acceleration with the galaxy toward the periphery of the universe.[57]

The globe has 7 continents (Europe, Asia, Africa, North America, South America, Australia, Antarctica). There are 7 distinct colors in the rainbow (violet, indigo, blue, green, yellow, orange, red). There are 7 whole tones in the musical scale (do, re, mi, fa, sol, la, ti).

In man and living things.

The human head has 7 orifices (2 eyes, 2 ear holes, 2 nostrils, 1 mouth). A man's face has 7 bones (2 nasal, 2 lacrimal/tearduct, 1 maxillary/upper jaw, 1 mandibular/lower jaw, 1 vomer/nostril partition). There are also 7 bones in the neck and 7 bones in the ankle.

A person's pulse slows down every 7 days throughout life. All the cells in the human body (except brain cells) are completely replaced every 7 years. A child attains the "age of understanding" at 7 years, when he or she can start learning. The 21st year (7x3) is regarded as the age of maturity in young men and women. Man's average life span is placed at 70 years (7x10) by both science and Scripture (Ps 90:10). The gestation periods for man and most animals are in multiples of 7, as shown here. Many fruit trees take 7 years to attain full production.

Gestation Periods

Entity	Days	Weeks	Multiples
Man	280	40	(7x40)
Sheep	147	21	(7x21)
Lion	98	14	(7x14)
Dog	63	9	(7x9)
Cat	56	8	(7x8)
Duck	28	4	(7x4)
Chicken	21	3	(7x3)

In the Scriptures.

In the Old Testament alone, "7" appears 287 times (7x41), "seventh" occurs 98 times (14x7), "seven-fold" is used 7 times, and "70" is seen 56 times (7x8) -- for a total of 448 (7x64) instances.[58]

Hidden heptadic structure. Dr. Ivan Panin of Russia, in the course of 40 years and 40,000 pages of mathematical compilations, discovered that the entire Bible (in both the original Hebrew and Greek) is totally interconnected with endless systems of 7s. Names, words, letters are all linked to one another by special arrangements of 7s. He accomplished his work by hand, before the advent of computers. Jewish and Christian scholars have verified his findings with the use of modern computer programs.[59]

The very first verse in the Bible in Hebrew has a hidden heptadic structure, an interwoven pattern of 7s, recurring many times, as shown below (Hebrew is read from right to left):

Hebrew characters						No.	Transliteration	English
ת	י	שׁ	א	ר	בּ	6	Bere'shiyt	In the beginning
			א	ר	בּ	3	bara'	created
מ	י	ה	ל	א		5	'Elohim	God
			ת	א		2	'et	the
מ	י	מ	שׁ	ה		5	hashamayim	heaven
		ת	א	ו		3	wa'et	and the
	ץ	ר	א	ה		4	ha'arets	earth
						28	7 words	

The sentence has 7 Hebrew words with 28 letters (7x4). The first three words have 14 letters (7x2), and the last four words have 14 letters (7x2). The fourth and fifth words together have 7 letters. The sixth and seventh words combined have 7 letters. The three key nouns (God, heaven, earth) have 14 letters (7x2). The four remaining words have 14 letters (7x2).[60] These groupings of 7s are repeated throughout Scripture in countless instances, in both the Old and New Testament original texts.

Let us go over some of the Biblical verses where 7 and its multiples are plainly seen.

The patriarchs. God told Noah to take 7 pairs of clean animals into the Ark (Gen. 7:2). Noah and his family went into the ark 7 days before the rains began (Gen 7:4-10). As the waters began to subside, the

Ark rested on the mountains of Ararat in the 7th month of the Flood (Gen 8:4), whereupon Noah sent out a dove every 7 days until it brought back an olive leaf as a sign that the waters had dried up (Gen 8:6-12). The olive tree is the symbol of *Zayin* ("Z"), the 7th letter of the Hebrew alphabet, which is also used to write the number "7."

God bestowed upon Abraham 7 blessings. *"And (1) I will make of thee a great nation, and (2) I will bless thee, and (3) make thy name great; and (4) thou shalt be a blessing: And (5) I will bless them that bless thee, and (6) curse him that curseth thee: and (7) in thee shall all families of the earth be blessed"* (Gen 12:2-3).

Jacob served 7 years for his first wife Leah, and 7 years for Rachel, his first love (Gen 29). There were 7 years of plenty and 7 years of famine in Egypt, when Joseph became Pharaoh's vicegerent (Gen 41).

The nation of Israel. God made 7 promises to Israel. *"Wherefore say unto the children of Israel, I am the LORD, and (1) I will bring you out from under the burdens of the Egyptians, and (2) I will rid you out of their bondage, and (3) I will redeem you with a stretched out arm, and with great judgments: And (4) I will take you to me for a people, and (5) I will be to you a God: and ye shall know that I am the LORD your God, which bringeth you out from under the burdens of the Egyptians. And (6) I will bring you in unto the land, concerning the which I did swear to give it to Abraham, to Isaac, and to Jacob; and (7) I will give it you for an heritage: I am the LORD"* (Ex 6:6-8).

The Tabernacle ("Tent of Meeting") in the wilderness (and later the Temple in Jerusalem) had 7 pieces of furniture: (1) brazen altar and (2) laver in the court (Ex 40:29-30); (3) table of showbread (Ex 39:36; 40:22-23), (4) golden lampstand (Ex 40:24-25), and (5) altar of incense (Ex 40:26-27; 9:2) in the Holy Place; and (6) Ark of the Covenant and (7) Mercy Seat with the cherubim (Ex 31:7) in the Holy of Holies. Aaron and his sons were consecrated for the priesthood in an elaborate 7-day purification ceremony (Ex 29:30,35,37).

God had 7 priests with 7 trumpets march around Jericho with the Israelite army for 7 days (7 times on the 7th day) and then make a long blast with their trumpets – the signal for the people to shout and cause the walls of the city to fall down (Jos. 6:1-20). It took the Israelites 7 years to conquer 7 nations in Canaan: the Hittites, Hivites, Amorites, Jebusites, Perizzites, Girgashites, and Canaanites (Jos 11:16-12:24). It then took them another 7 years to divide the land among the twelve tribes of Israel (Jos 13-22).

King Solomon built the Temple over 7 years (1 Kings 6:37-38). The Israelites kept a feast that lasted for 7 days in dedicating the Temple to the LORD (2 Chron7:4-8).

The Jews were held captive in Babylon for 70 years (Jer 25:11-12,29:10; Dan 9:1-2; 2 Chron 36:17-21). Thus, the land of Judea lay desolate for 70 years as foretold by Jeremiah (2 Chron. 36:20-21). The angel Gabriel told Daniel that 70 "weeks" (490 years) had been decreed for Israel to restore their relationship with God (Dan. 9:24).

Sabbaths and holy days. The Creation Week lasted 7 days. At the end of His creative work, the Creator blessed and rested on the 7th day. For that reason, our modern week has 7 days, ending on the 7th day Sabbath of rest.

God ordained 7 holy days for Israel: (1) Passover (Lev 23:5); (2) Feast of Unleavened Bread (Lev 23:6-8); (3) Feast of Firstfruits (Lev 23:10-14); (4) Feast of Weeks, or Pentecost (Lev 23:15-22); (5) Feast of Trumpets (Lev 23:24-25); (6) Day of Atonement (Lev 23:27-32); (7) Feast of Tabernacles (Lev 23:34-43). Each year, Israel observes 70 holidays.

70 Annual Holidays in Israel

Holiday	Days
Weekly Sabbath	52
Passover, Feast of Unleavened Bread, and Feast of Firstfruits	7
Feast of Weeks or Pentecost	1
Feast of Trumpets	1
Day of Atonement	1
Feast of Tabernacles	7
Last Great Day	1
Total:	70

The ministry of Christ. The prayer Christ taught His disciples has 7 parts: *"After this manner therefore pray ye: (1) Our Father which art in heaven, Hallowed be thy name. (2) Thy kingdom come. (3) Thy will be done in earth, as it is in heaven. (4) Give us this day our daily bread. (5) And forgive us our debts, as we forgive our debtors. (6) And lead us not into temptation, but (7) deliver us from evil"* (Matt 6:9-13).

Christ fed four thousand men, plus all the women and children with them, with 7 loaves of bread (Matt 15:32-38; Mark 8:1-9). He cast 7 demons out of Mary Magdalene (Mark 16:9; Luke 8:2). Christ said a man must forgive a brother 70 times 7 (Matt. 18:21-22). In contrast, the LORD told Israel: *"And after all this, if you do not obey Me, then I will punish you seven times more for your sins"* (Lev 26:18-19, NKJV).

Christ uttered 7 last words on the cross: (1) *"Father, forgive them; for they know not what they do"* (Luke 23:34b); (2) *"Verily I say unto thee, To day shalt thou be with me in paradise"* (Luke 23:43b); (3) *"Woman, behold thy son!" Then saith he to the disciple, "Behold thy mother!"* (John 19:26b-27a); (4) *"Eloi, Eloi, lama sabachthani?" which is, being interpreted, "My God, my God, why hast thou forsaken me?"* (Mark 15:34b; Matt 27:46b); (5) *"I thirst"* (John 19:28b); (6) *"It is* finished" (John 19:30b); (7) "Father, into thy hands I commend my spirit" (Luke 23:46b).

On His Second Coming, Christ will descend on the Mount of Olives (Zech 14:4). Today we regard as the emblem of peace the branch of the olive tree, symbol of *Zayin* ("Z"), the 7th letter in the Hebrew alphabet. Christ will usher in the 7th millennium, the thousand years of peace, and reign as King of kings and Lord of lords (Rev 17:14; 19:16; 20:4,6).

The Church and end-times. The Holy Spirit endows Christians with many gifts. Paul lists down 7 in Romans 12:6-8. *"We have different gifts, according to the grace given us. (1) If a man's gift is prophesying, let him use it in proportion to his faith. (2) If it is serving, let him serve; (3) if it is teaching, let him teach; (4) if it is encouraging, let him encourage; (5) if it is contributing to the needs of others, let him give generously; (6) if it is leadership, let him govern diligently; (7) if it is showing mercy, let him do it cheerfully"* ("Rom 12:6-8, NIV).

The end-time prophecies in the book of Revelation truly overflows with 7's: 7 churches (1:4, etc.); 7 spirits of God (1:4, 3:1, etc.); 7 golden candlesticks (1:12, etc.); 7 stars (1:16, etc.); 7 lamps (4:5); 7 seals (5:1,5); 7 eyes (5:6, etc.); 7 angels (8:2, etc.); 7 trumpets (8:2,6); 7 thunders (10:3,4); 7,000 men killed (11:13); beast with 7 heads and 7 crowns (12:3); 7 plagues (15:1, etc.); 7 vials or bowls (17:1; 21:9); 7 mountains or hills (17:9); 7 kings (17:10); etc.

How can we doubt who the real Creator of the universe and Author of the Scriptures is?

Gestation and holy days

Author and TV host Zola Levitt, writing a book for new parents with the help of a gynecologist, saw an amazing correspondence between the Jewish holy days and human gestation -- from conception to birth.

On the 14th day of each monthly cycle, a woman's ovary releases a mature egg into the uterus, a process called ovulation. Jews observe the first holy day, Passover, on the 14th day of the first month of the year with, among other traditional food items on the table, a roasted egg.

The woman's egg cell must be fertilized by a sperm cell within the next 24 hours for pregnancy to take place. The Feast of Unleavened Bread begins 24 hours after Passover.

Within 2-6 days, the fertilized egg or embryo attaches itself to the womb and starts growing. The Feast of Firstfruits, which is always kept on a Sunday, may fall 2-6 days after Passover.

Around the 50th day, the embryo begins to take shape as a human being. Jews celebrate the Feast of Weeks, or Pentecost, 50 days from the Feast of Firstfruits.

Starting in the 7th month, the baby is able to hear sounds outside the womb. On the first day of the 7th month, the Feast of Trumpets, rabbis sound their *shofars*, or trumpets of ram's horn, for the Jews to hear the signal beginning the civil new year in autumn. (Jews observe two new year days – the other being the religious new year in the spring.)

On the 10th day of the 7th month, the hemoglobin in the blood of the fetus begins to change from that of the mother to its own. The Day of Atonement, when the blood of a sacrificial animal was taken into the Temple's Holy of Holies for the sins of the people, is kept on this day.

On the 15th day of the 7th month, the lungs become fully developed, which will enable the baby to breathe if born prematurely. The Feast of Tabernacles begins on this day, exalting the Shekinah glory or Spirit of God. The Hebrew word for spirit is *ruach*, which also means "breath."

Birth, when the baby first sees the light of day, normally takes place 9 months and 10 days after fertilization of the egg. *Hanukkah*, the Feast of Lights, a holy day added only in the 2nd century B.C., is celebrated 9 months and 10 days after Passover – for 8 days. Male Jewish infants, as commanded by God, are circumcised on the 8th day after birth.[61]

This incredible parallelism strongly suggests that the LORD who ordained the Jewish holidays and the Creator who engineered the process of human gestation must be the same God who knows all things. David sang around 3,000 years ago: *"For You formed my inward parts; You covered me in my mother's womb. I will praise You, for I am fearfully and wonderfully made; Marvelous are Your works, And that my soul knows very well. My frame was not hidden from You, When I was made in secret, And skillfully wrought in the lowest parts of the earth. Your eyes saw my substance, being yet unformed. And in Your book they all were written, The days fashioned for me, When as yet there were none of them"* (Ps 139:13-16, NKJV).

2

Secrets
in Scriptures

he secret things belong unto the LORD our God: but those things which are revealed belong unto us and to our children for ever, that we may do all the words of this law"

-- Deuteronomy 29:29.

Are there really secrets in the Bible? Incredibly, beneath its plain surface text, numberless mysteries await discovery. Isaac Newton, the first modern scientist who discovered gravity and the mechanics of the solar system, believed there were secrets in the Bible. Past middle age, he studied Hebrew and spent the rest of his life trying to uncover those mysteries. He seemed quite sure the Bible, like the cosmos, was a "cryptogram set by the Almighty" and strove to "read the riddle of the Godhead, the riddle of past and future events divinely fore-ordained."[1]

Newton tried out many mathematical models but, despite his genius, did not succeed to his death in 1727. Found among his papers were about a million words, not about mathematics or astronomy, but mostly about esoteric theology. It seems that, in his last years, Newton regarded Bible secrets as more important than his Theory of the Universe.

Dare you follow Newton's footsteps? But, if Scripture to you is by and large unknown territory, let us first get familiar with the Bible.

In general, what people call Scriptures are the unified collection of manuscripts that forms the basic teachings of any one particular religion. Most of the major religions of the world have their own holy scriptures:

Islam has the *Koran*, Hinduism the *Vedas*, Buddhism the *Tipitaka*, Confucianism the *Analects*, Zoroastrianism the *Avesta*, Shinto the *Nihon shoki* and *Kojiki*. However, the Scripture we are concerned with in this book is that of the Judeo-Christian faith -- also known as the Bible.

What is the Bible?

The English word "Bible" came from an ancient Phoenician port city named Byblos. The Greeks imported *papyrus*, an Egyptian water plant used for making paper, from that city and thus called it *byblos*. Consequently, the Greeks called a book *biblio* and a small book *biblion*. Later, *Biblia*, meaning "little books," was the term used in Latin, since the Scriptures are not just a book, but actually a small library of 66 little books (70, if we count Psalms as actually having 5 books).

The Bible was written over a period of 1,600 years (*circa* 1500 B.C.-100 A.D.), in 13 countries on 3 continents, by 40 to 44 authors of various backgrounds: shepherds, prophets, warriors, judges, kings, poets, musicians, scribes, fishermen, an orchard dresser, a tax collector, a physician, a tent-maker. The contents come in a variety of forms: history, homily, biography, allegory, dramaturgy, prophecy, poetry, proverbs, parables, penal code, personal letters, and more. Besides religious verses with spiritual and moral lessons, the Bible contains topics touching on practically all aspects of life: art, science, medicine, sociology, agriculture, government, finance, etc., with lessons that remain sound to this day.

Despite having many authors writing centuries apart over one-and-a-half millennia of ever-changing mores and attitudes, the Bible exhibits an amazing unity and sameness of purpose. From the first book to the last, the Judeo-Christian Scriptures present consistent themes of faith, justice, and love – portraying an unchanging Creator-Father intent on saving His erring creatures from self-inflicted destruction.

Biblical origins

Where did the writers get the ideas and stories recorded in the Bible? Did these come from myths, legends, and folktales, or were they actual historical events?

One writer and speaker.

In the second book of the Bible, Exodus, we read that God Himself wrote part of the Scriptures. *"And he gave unto Moses, when he had made an end of communing with him upon mount Sinai, two tables of testimony, tables of stone, written with the finger of God"* (Ex 31:18).

According to Jewish tradition, Moses wrote the other parts during the forty days and nights that he spent with God on Mount Sinai. He copied the black letters of fire he saw against a background of white flame.[2] Later, God would dictate His other instructions to Moses over the Ark of the Covenant, God's symbolic throne on earth: *"And there I will meet with thee, and I will commune with thee from above the mercy seat, from between the two cherubims which are upon the ark of the testimony, of all things which I will give thee in commandment unto the children of Israel"* (Ex 25:22). Moses wrote the rest of the first five books of the Bible, called *Torah* ("law") in Hebrew, during the forty years the Israelites wandered in the wilderness after the Exodus from Egypt.

Angels, prophets, Christ.

After the time of Moses, God sent his messengers, the angels, to convey His messages to men: *"While I was speaking and praying, confessing my sin and the sin of my people Israel and making my request to the LORD my God for his holy hill -- while I was still in prayer, Gabriel, the man I had seen in the earlier vision, came to me in swift flight about the time of the evening sacrifice. He instructed me and said to me, 'Daniel, I have now come to give you insight and understanding'"* (Dan 9:20-22, NIV; also Rev 1:1; 22:6).

At other times, God spoke through His prophets, who gave voice to His holy words: *"As he spake by the mouth of his holy prophets, which have been since the world began"* (Luke 1:70).

When God's Only Begotten Son came to earth as a man, it was He who conveyed God's messages to men. *"God, who at various times and in various ways spoke in time past to the fathers by the prophets, has in these last days spoken to us by His Son"* (Heb 1:1-2, NKJV).

Inspired by the Holy Spirit.

After Christ ascended to heaven, it was the Holy Spirit who moved godly men to speak on behalf of God -- *"for prophecy never came by the will of man, but holy men of God spoke as they were moved by the Holy Spirit"* (2 Peter 1:21, NKJV).

For this reason, Scripture is said to have been inspired by God: *"All Scripture is given by inspiration of God, and is profitable for doctrine, for reproof, for correction, for instruction in righteousness"* (2 Tim 3:16-17, NKJV). The phrase *"given by inspiration of God"* comes from the Greek word *theopneustos*, which means God (*theo*) breathed (*pneustos*), indicating God was actively behind the writing of the Greek Scriptures or New Testament.

Thus, since the Biblical messages have been written by God Himself, spoken by Him through His angels, prophets, and Only Begotten Son, as well as inspired by His own Holy Spirit in godly men, believers have all the reasons to call the Bible the "Word of God."

Canonical books

The Bible is made up exclusively of canonical books, i.e., belonging to the canon or official list of books authorized as Holy Scriptures by the Church. Both the Latin *canon* and English cannon (artillery gun) come from the same Greek word, *kanon*, in turn derived from the Hebrew *qaneh*, "cane" or "reed," a tube-like water plant used as a measuring stick or standard in olden times. Hence, "canonical" books are only those that measure up to the "canon" or standards of the Church.

The early Church writers Clement and Origen were the first ones to use the word *canon* in referring to the Hebrew Scriptures in the 2nd and 3rd centuries, respectively. The canonical books are made up of two sets:

Hebrew Scriptures.

Jews call the Hebrew Scriptures the *TaNaKh*, an acronym for *Torah* ("the law"), *Nevi'im* ("prophets"), and *Ketuvim* ("writings").

The *Torah* (*Pentateuch* in Greek, meaning "five rolls") consists of Genesis (origin or creation), Exodus (emigration or mass departure), Leviticus (of Levites or priests), Numbers (counting the Israelites), and Deuteronomy ("second law" or "repetition" of the first list). With annotations, the *Torah* is called *Chumash*.

The *Nevi'im* comprises the written works of four "major" prophets with relatively long manuscripts and twelve "minor" prophets with brief accounts. (There are twelve "oral" prophets with no written records, but are also referred to in the *Tanakh*.)

The *Ketuvim* is made up of historical narratives, as well as scripts of wisdom and poetry, such as the Psalms, Proverbs, Song of Songs.

The *Tanakh* was faithfully copied and recopied over the centuries by Levitical scribes, who had been originally charged with the safeguarding of the holy writings since Mosaic times. Their descendants, the Jewish scribes, similarly exercise great care in their work, painstakingly counting the exact number of letters and lines. Any slight variation from the original renders a copy unfit for use.

In the Middle Ages, from the 6th to the 10th century A.D., scribes who became known as the Masoretes, compiled the *Masorah*, a collection of notes on the textual traditions of the *Tanakh*. The Old Testament (OT) text of the modern Bible is based on Masoretic texts dating from the A.D. 900s, which are considered authentic Hebrew manuscripts.

Greek Scriptures.

The Greek texts of the new covenant or New Testament (NT) tell the story of Christ and the growth of early Christianity.

The first section of the NT comprises the Gospels: the four books of Matthew, Mark, Luke, and John. "Gospel" comes from the Old English word *godspel*, which means "good message or story." In Greek the term is *euaggelion* ("good news"), which gave rise to the English words "evangel," "evangelist," etc. Next are the lone historical book of Acts, the 21 epistles or letters of the apostles (13-14 or about half of which had been written by Paul, the book of Hebrews being doubtful), and the solitary book of prophecy in the NT, Revelation.

A collection of Christian writings first began to be referred to as "New Testament" (*Novum Testamentum* or *Instrumentum*) in the late 2nd century by the theologian Tertullian (160?-220?) and was placed on equal footing with the "Old Testament.[3]

Unfortunately, the Greek texts of the NT did not all pass down to us in their original form.

Gnostic influence. In the ancient Greek and Egyptian cultures, centuries before and after Christ, mystics known as Gnostics (seekers of "knowledge") proliferated. They congregated in Alexandria, Egypt, where they established a school of Gnosticism, as evidenced by their recently discovered Nag Hammadi Library.[4] Some of the best known Gnostics were the early Church "fathers" Clement of Alexandria (150?-215?), Origen (185?-254?), and Theodoret (393?-458/466?).[5,6]

Many scribes embraced Gnostic teachings and became practitioners of "textual criticism" (scriptural editing). Whenever a Gnostic scribe came across a passage he did not agree with, he either edited it or removed it entirely. On the other hand, faithful members of the underground Church diligently copied and preserved the original apostolic writings word-for-word. This resulted in two schools of Christianity: the Gnostic, in Alexandria, and the Orthodox, centered around Antioch in Asia Minor (present-day Turkey).[7]

Author William Grady (*The Christian's Guide to the King James Bible*, 1993) wrote: "The ancient city of Alexandria, located in the Nile Delta, has had a reputation for its heretics. Philip Schaff, well-known church historian and chairman of the American Standard Version (1901) committee recognized that Alexandria was the source of 'a peculiar theology' set forth in the writings of Clement and Origen who developed 'a regenerated Christian form of the Alexandrian Jewish religious philosophy of Philo'."[8] Worse, "Origen and St. Gregory (540?-604) held that the gospels were not to be taken in their literal sense."[9]

Four textual sources. The changes introduced into the original Greek texts have resulted in four different sources for the NT:

1. *Codex Vaticanus.* In A.D. 313 the Roman emperor Constantine, after legalizing Christianity, asked Eusebius, the Bishop of Rome, to make fifty copies of the Greek apostolic writings. Unfortunately, Eusebius picked the Gnostic texts as his references. One of those codices became the *Vaticanus*.[10] (A *codex* is a book with pages as distinguished from a scroll.)

2. *Codex Alexandrinus.* Believed to have been written in Alexandria sometime in the 5th century, it is the second major, but similarly Gnostic-influenced set of Greek manuscripts, as one can tell from its name.[11]

3. *Textus Receptus* ("Received Text") or Majority Text. Towards the end of the 3rd century, Lucian of Antioch made a compilation of over 4,000 Greek manuscripts and fragments[12] of the original, unedited Orthodox texts. This formed the basis of the Eastern Church's Byzantine text, following the transfer of the Empire's capital from Rome to Byzantium in A.D. 330. In the 6th-14th centuries, most copies of the apostolic writings came from the Byzantine text. In 1525, the Greek scholar Erasmus, using five to six Byzantine copies from the 10th-13th centuries, published the first printed collection of the NT Greek texts. It became the *Textus Receptus*.[13]

4. *Codex Sinaiticus.* Regarded as the oldest extant manuscripts, this collection of Alexandrian Greek texts dates from the early 300s, but was discovered only in 1844 – salvaged from a trash pile in St. Catherine's monastery in the Sinai, Egypt.[14]

Some Bible scholars prefer the codices *Vaticanus, Alexandrinus,* and *Sinaiticus* over the *Textus Receptus* because they are older, but it should be noted that these Gnostic manuscripts differ considerably from one another as well as from the more authentic *Textus Receptus.*

Non-canonical books

Many books, considered non-canonical, have not been included in the Bible. Most of these writings fall under the following categories:

The *Apocrypha.*

Martin Luther was the first to use the Greek word *Apocrypha*,[15] meaning "hidden" or "secret," in the 16th century. The term was originally deemed complimentary as it seemingly referred to works too exalted or esoteric for laymen. In time, though, "apocryphal" acquired the meaning "non-canonical" or without the imprimatur (approval) of the Church and, hence, to be regarded as forbidden, even heretical. There are both OT and NT apocrypha.

The early Church leaders, however, quoted from the Apocrypha. The Roman and Byzantine churches regarded the books as Scripture. The scholar Jerome (347–419/420) called the Apocrypha "ecclesiastical books" that were good for spiritual edification, but not authoritative. Augustine (354–430), a renowned Church theologian, disagreed; and the Apocrypha became part of Jerome's Latin Vulgate ("common") version of the Bible. Later translations excluded the Apocrypha.

The Roman Catholic and Protestant Bibles were the same until the Reformation that Luther, John Calvin, and others led early in the 16th century. They questioned some practices of the Roman Church, such as indulgences and prayers for the dead, which were unscriptural (Heb 9:27; Deut 18:11). The OT *Apocrypha,* however, contained prayers for the dead (2 Mac 12:42). In 1546, the Council of Trent officially included the OT *Apocrypha* in the Catholic Bible.

Books belonging to the OT Apocrypha are: 1 Esdras, 2 Esdras, Tobit, Judith, Additions to the Book of Esther, Wisdom of Solomon, Ecclesiasticus (or Wisdom of Jesus the Son of Sirach), Baruch and the Epistle of Jeremiah, Prayer of Azariah and the Song of the Three Holy Children, Susanna, Bel and the Dragon, Prayer of Manasseh, 1 Maccabees, 2 Maccabees, 3 Maccabees, 4 Maccabees, Psalm 151.

The *Pseudepigrapha.*

Writings ascribed to other authors, typically well-known Biblical personages who were not the actual writers, are called *pseudepigrapha,* which means "falsely inscribed." The better known *pseudepigraphal* books are the Book of Enoch, Letter of Aristeas, Martyrdom of Isaiah, Apocalypse of Abraham, Testimony of Abraham, Sibylline Oracles, Testament of the Twelve Patriarchs, Book of Jubilees.

A few others are also quite interesting: Joseph and Asenath, Lives of the Prophets, Life of Adam and Eve, 5 Maccabees, 3 Baruch, Psalms of Joshua, Psalms of Solomon, Testament of Job, Paralipomena of Jeremiah the Prophet, Secrets of Enoch, Assumption of Moses.

A number of "missing" gospels have come to public attention in recent times. These are the Gospel of Thomas, Gospel of Philip, Gospel of Mary, Gospel of Barnabas, Gospel of Judas.

The Dead Sea Scrolls.

In 1947 Bedouin shepherds unwittingly discovered the most ancient Biblical manuscripts in the caves of Wadi Qumran near the western side of the Dead Sea. Called the "Dead Sea Scrolls," more than 800 texts and fragments so far found have been dated from as early as 200-150

B.C. Actually, discoveries in the area had been reported as early as the A.D. 100s through the Middle Ages.

All Old Testament books, except Esther, are represented in the Dead Sea Scrolls. However, the manuscripts appear to have been written by Essenes, a Jewish sect of ascetics, whose beliefs are known to have been heavily influenced by Greek Gnostics.

Biblical divisions

The Bible is essentially made up of two sets of books – one written before the birth of Christ, and the other, some years after His crucifixion and ascension to heaven. The subdivision of the text into smaller sections came centuries later.

Testaments.

The two main parts of the Bible -- the Old Testament and the New Testament -- are separated in time by the Inter-Testamental Period or "400 silent years" (circa 400-5 B.C.), with no canonically accepted writings between the last book of the OT (Malachi) and first book of the NT (Matthew).

The OT is about 99% Hebrew and 1% Aramaic (e.g., Ezra 4:8-6:18; 7:12-26; Jer 10:11; Dan 2:4-7:28).[16] The ancient Hebrew text did not have spaces between words, a form of script called *scripta continua*. The spaces were simply inferred. Spaces between words seem to have been introduced in the 5th century B.C., on the return of the Jews from Babylon to Judea during the time of the prophet Ezra.[17]

The NT was mainly written in *koine* (common) Greek (except the book of Matthew, which was probably penned in Hebrew)[18] from around 45 A.D. until no later than 100 A.D.

Books.

The Bible has 66 books in all. The Old Testament has 39 books, which contain 78% of all the text of the Bible.

The New Testament has 27 books, or 22% of the text, including many quotations, paraphrases, and allusions to OT scriptures.[19]

Chapters.

As early as the 3rd century, the Jews divided portions of the *Torah* into large sections called *Parashahs*, and the *Nevi'im* into sections called *HaphTarahs,* for convenience during readings in synagogues. Shorter sections called *Pesuqim* closely resemble modern Bible verses.

The numerical sequence of chapters in Christian Bibles came much later in the Latin translations. The present-day arrangement of chapters first appeared in the 13th century. Some scholars attribute the system to Cardinal Hugo de St. Caro (d. 1248), while others give the credit to Archbishop Stephen Langton of Canterbury (d. 1227).[20]

Verses.

Biblical passages were first marked in the 16th century, with verses appearing in Robert Stephens' edition of the Greek New Testament in 1551. His son Henry Stephens recounted how his father thought of the concept on horseback while traveling from Paris to Lyons.[21]

Shortly thereafter, the first Bible with the text divided into chapters and verses was published in 1560 – the Geneva Bible.

Parallel structures

Whether by divine or human design, the OT and the NT display analogous textual structures, divisible into four parts each: covenant, history, teachings, and prophecy.

The OT *Torah* and the NT Gospels are both covenants, in which the terms and conditions of the agreement or contract between God and man are spelled out. The books Joshua, Judges, Ruth, 1 and 2 Samuel, 1 and 2 Kings, 1 and 2 Chronicles, Esther, Nehemiah, and Ezra in the OT, and Acts in the NT constitute history. The OT books of Job, Psalms, Proverbs, Ecclesiastes, and Song of Songs, as well as the NT epistles of Romans, 1 and 2 Corinthians, Galatians, Ephesians, Philippians, Colossians, and 1 and 2 Thessalonians, 1 and 2 Timothy, Titus, Philemon, Hebrews, James, 1 and 2 Peter, 1, 2 and 3 John, and Jude, all present teachings. The books of prophecy are those of Isaiah, Jeremiah, Lamentations, Ezekiel, Daniel, Hosea, Joel, Amos, Obadiah, Jonah, Micah, Nahum, Habakkuk, Zephaniah, Haggai, Zechariah, and Malachi in the OT, as is Revelation in the NT. (Chart in the Appendix.)

Disparate views.

The Jews do not use the New Testament since they do not recognize Christ as the Messiah. On the other hand, evangelical Christians rely primarily on the NT for religious doctrine, using the OT only for spiritual and moral guidance, and considering the seventh-day Sabbath, feast days, and many other commandments of God as only for the Jews.

Messianic Jews, together with Gentile members of the Messianic movement, keep both the OT and NT teachings of the Bible.

Sola Scriptura.

Many Bible teachers hold that all religious doctrines must be based solely on the Scriptures. This is known in Latin as *Sola Scriptura*.

The prophet Isaiah declared: *"To the law and to the testimony: if they speak not according to this word, it is because there is no light in them"* (Isa 8:20). Accordingly, the "law" refers to the *Tanakh*, which embodies the Old Testament laws and teachings; while "testimony" points to the New Testament, which testifies to the truth and fulfillment of the Old. Thus, any teaching that is not based on both the OT and the NT has no "light" or truth in it.

Interesting statistics.

The King James Version (KJV) of the Bible, first published in England in 1611, has the following interesting statistics:

King James Version (KJV) Statistics[22]

Letters:	3,586,489 letters
Words:	773,692 words
Verses:	31,093 verses
Chapters:	1,189 chapters
Shortest verse:	John 11:35
Longest verse:	Esther 8:9
Middle verse:	Psalm 118:8
Shortest chapter:	Psalm 117
Longest chapter:	Psalm 119

The shortest verse in the KJV reads: *"Jesus wept"* (John 11:35). The exact middle verse of the Bible says: *"It is better to trust in the LORD than to put confidence in man"* (Ps 118:8). This seems to be the core message of the Bible – located in the very heart of the Scriptures. We must depend on God, never on unreliable man.

Because the KJV has 1,189 chapters, besides the one that contains Psalm 118:8 there are 1,188 other chapters. The numbers are repeated! But the oddity does not end there. Psalm 118 is preceded by Psalm 117, the shortest chapter in the Bible, and followed by Psalm 119, the longest chapter. The central verse lies "guarded" by the briefest and lengthiest chapters on both sides -- a puzzle that has long intrigued Bible scholars.

Bible translations

Numerous translations of the Holy Scriptures – as the OT alone, the NT only, the Bible as a whole, or just parts of the OT or NT -- have been made from as early as the 3rd century B.C. to our present day. Listed below are some of the major translations:

Septuagint, c. 280 B.C. Ptolemy II had the Torah translated into Greek for the Jews in Alexandria, Egypt. 72 translators, 6 from each of the 12 tribes of Israel, are said to have finished the work in 72 days.[23] The volume was named the *Septuagint* ("Seventy" or "LXX") after the number of translators – 70 being an approximation of 72.[24] From 250 to 150 B.C. "the remainder of the OT was translated, as well as some apocryphal and non-canonical books."[25]

Writer Larry Spargimino warns: "The manuscripts of the Greek Old Testament (Septuagint), however, are interspersed with apocryphal writings, never acknowledged by the rabbis, or by Christ or His apostles, as 'scripture'."[26] Thus, "nearly all (translators) acknowledge the general corruptness of the LXX..."[27] Moreover, some researchers question the existence of the Septuagint before Christ. "Moorman gives two examples of writers who argue that there is no pre-Christian era Septuagint... Paul Kahle... (Peter) Ruckman... point(s) out that no one has produced a Greek copy of the Septuagint dating from before A.D. 300. Instead of Jesus and the apostles quoting from the Septuagint, the Septuagint quotes from them."[28]

Aquila's translation, c. 140 A.D. Aquila, a 2nd century scholar, completed an extremely literal translation of the Old Testament in Greek. This replaced the Septuagint among Greek-speaking Jews. A Jewish convert to Christianity, Aquila returned to Judaism when censured for practicing astrology. Origen used Aquila's work in the 3rd century; Jerome, in the 4th-5th centuries.[29]

Onkelos Targum, c. 150. Translations of the Hebrew Scriptures into Aramaic or Chaldaic (Western Aramaic) for the benefit of Jews who had lost their knowledge of Hebrew in foreign lands are called *targums*. The *Onkelos Targum*, a literal translation in Aramaic, has become the official *targum* for the Torah. Legend ascribes the work to Onkelos, a Roman convert to Judaism who is said to have been the nephew of Titus, destroyer of Jerusalem in A.D. 70.[30]

Peshittah, 2nd c. The spread of Christianity into Syria made it necessary for the New Testament to be translated into Syriac, sometimes called "Christian Aramaic."[31] The principal Syriac translation, *Peshittah*, means "common" or "simple."

Vulgate, 383-405. The scholar Jerome, commissioned in 382 by Pope Damasus to do an official Latin version of the Bible, unfortunately made use of the *Codex Vaticanus*, which had been based on the corrupt Alexandrian texts.[32] He finished the Gospels in 383, followed by the rest of the NT. Translating the OT, he first used the Septuagint, but later shifted to the Masoretic texts, completing the Latin Bible called *Vulgate* ("common" or "popular") in 405.[33]

Wycliffe's NT, 1384. John Wycliffe, a Catholic priest later dubbed "the Morning Star of the Reformation," produced 150 handwritten copies of the first major English translation of the NT.[34] He had, however, based his work on Jerome's compromised Latin Vulgate.[35]

Gutenberg Bible, 1455. Following the development and use of the movable type by Johannes Gutenberg and his associates in the mid-1400s, the Gutenberg Bible was the first complete book (3 volumes) to be printed. Also called the "42-line Bible" because most of the pages had 42 lines, only 150 copies of this Latin Bible were printed.

Erasmus's Greek NT, 1516. Desiderius Erasmus, a Dutch priest and scholar, produced his Greek edition of the NT. It made available for the first time the original Greek text, which was naturally more accurate than the Latin Vulgate and became much preferred by reformers.[36]

Tyndale's NT, 1525. William Tyndale, using Erasmus's work, published the first printed NT in English. Portions of the OT appeared in 1530 and 1531. His translation was so precise and his language so magnificent later translators would adopt much of his phraseology. Ironically, the Roman Church burned Tyndale at the stake in 1536.[37] And within a year a Bible, 2/3 of it Tyndale's, was allowed in Britain.

Coverdale Bible, 1535. Miles Coverdale had the first complete English translation of the Bible and the Apocrypha printed in Germany. He used Tyndale's translation, portions of Luther's German Bible, and some Latin translations, apparently from Jerome's Vulgate.[38,39]

The Great Bible, 1539. Coverdale, commissioned in 1538 by England's vicar-general Thomas Cromwell to supervise the work on an official version of the Bible, published a pulpit Bible. It was called the "Great Bible" for its sheer size – the largest printed up to that time.

Geneva Bible, 1557-1560. Translated by English Protestants in exile in Geneva, based on Erasmus's work and texts preserved by the early Church, the Geneva Bible became the first authorized version of the Anglican Church, Puritans, and Pilgrims. It was regarded as simply a translation for laymen, though.[40]

Bishops' Bible, 1568. A revision by Anglican scholars and bishops to replace the Great Bible and Geneva Bible, the Bishops' Bible served as the second authorized version of the Anglican Church

The Jesuit Bible, 1582. This work was published in 1582 by Jesuits in the Anti-Reformation Movement to counter the Coverdale and Geneva Bibles used by Protestants to refute certain Catholic doctrines.

Rheims-Douay Bible, 1582/1610. Catholic refugees from England in France translated this first English Catholic Bible from Latin. The NT came out in Rheims in 1582, while the OT was finished in Douay in 1610.[41] Carefully translated and footnoted to support Catholic doctrines, it was the only officially approved Catholic Bible for over 350 years until 1966, when the Jerusalem Bible was published.[42]

King James Version, 1611. Commissioned by King James I of England in 1604 to make a third authorized version, the Anglican Church, using Erasmus's uncorrupted Greek text and about 90% of Tyndale's inspired phraseology, produced the Authorized or King James Version (KJV).[43] In honor of the royal sponsor, NT characters named "Jacob" were renamed "James" in the KJV.

Several minor revisions were made on the KJV -- in 1613, 1629, 1638, 1653, 1762, and 1769 -- e.g., to update words like *sith* and *fet*.[44] The KJV remained the only Protestant English translation for 270 years.

Westcott-Hort edition, 1881. In 1853, a Revision Committee commissioned Anglican churchmen Brooke Foss Westcott and Fenton J.A. Hort to produce "an acceptable alternative to the archaic language and grammar" of the KJV. The two were occultists who had helped found the Ghost Society, a club that dabbled in necromancy and spirit channeling.[45] Westcott and Hort preferred Gnostic texts that had edited many passages that underscore "the deity of Christ, His atonement, His resurrection, and other key doctrines."[46]

William Grady notes that the "corrupt manuscript tradition embodied in codices *Vaticanus* and *Sinaiticus*, the principal sources for the notorious Westcott-Hort Text, are Alexandrian texts... Alexandrian teachers, such as Origen, Clement, and Philo, were some of the most grievous corrupters of biblical Christianity."[47] Author Floyd Jones adds: "Moreover, it must be seen that the testimony of these two corrupted manuscripts are almost solely responsible for the errors being foisted upon the Holy Scriptures in both testaments by modern critics."[48]

As seen by author Chuck Missler, in the four gospels alone, there are more than 3,000 contradictions between the Westcott-Hort version and the *Textus Receptus* that they rejected. Their so-called critical edition differs from the traditional Greek text in no less than 8,413 instances![49]

Regrettably, the Westcott-Hort texts served as the basis for the 1881 English Revised Bible. In addition, most new Bible translations since then, except for the New King James Version (1979-1982), have been based on the corrupt texts of the Westcott-Hort edition.[50]

Types of translation

Today, there are over 60 popular versions of the Bible to choose from. Which one is right for you? It will be helpful to know that Bible translations are classified into three broad categories, as follows:

"Word-for-word."

The most faithful and accurate English translations from the original Hebrew and Greek texts are word-for-word or verbatim versions, such as the KJV, NKJV, and New American Standard Bible (NASB, 1970). Authors Norman Geisler and William Nix calculate that, compared with the texts of the Dead Sea Scrolls, the KJV is "98.33% pure."[51]

The latest version of the KJV is the 21st Century King James Bible, featuring modern English and punctuation, with the text in paragraph form, instead of verses.

"Meaning-to-meaning."

Valued as secondary references for their contemporary wording, "meaning-to-meaning" renditions include the New International Version (NIV, 1973-79), Revised English Bible, Good News Bible (1976), New Living Translation, Jerusalem Bible (1966). In the late 1980s, the NIV began outselling the KJV, which nonetheless remained a top favorite.

"Paraphrased."

With their interpretive translations, paraphrased versions are useful in making the Scriptures more understandable, but should not be used as basis for doctrines. Translators use figures of speech that conform to their own religious beliefs. The Living Bible (1971) and The Message are two examples of a paraphrased translation.

Most read book

In the early 17th century, the Bible became the most read book in the world. The widespread use of the movable type expedited the printing of more and more copies. In the 1990s, around 630 million Bibles were being distributed yearly by the American Bible Society and the British and Foreign Bible Society.[52] The American Bible Society stated at the end of 1997 that the Bible had been translated in full in 363 languages; the NT in 405 languages; and portions of it, usually one or more gospels, in 2,197 languages.[53] By the year 2000, more than 6 billion copies of the Holy Scriptures had been printed.

Scriptural Secrets

Now, for the secrets that Jewish sages and mystics have endeavored to pry from the Scriptures for ages. By the 12th century, rabbis believed the sacred texts could be interpreted on several levels of meaning.

Levels of meaning.

1. *Peshat*, the literal or plain meaning. The literal meaning may be lost in translation if some significant words are omitted. For instance, in the opening line of the Bible (Gen 1:1), *"In the beginning God created the heaven and the earth"* (*Bᵃre'shiyt bara' 'Elohim 'et hashamayim wᵃ'et*

ha'arets.), the translators left out the word *et* (which indicates that the verb action is on the object, not the subject).

2. *Remez*, the esoteric or allegorical hint of something deeper. In the same example, the word *et*, spelled with the first and last letters of the Hebrew alphabet (*aleph* and *tav*) alludes to the eternal nature of God. Hence, *"'Elohim 'et"* means God is *"Alpha and Omega, the beginning and the end, the first and the last"* (Rev 22:13b, etc.).

3. *Derash*, the homiletical or practical application. Each letter of the Hebrew alphabet has a meaning. The *aleph* in *et* stands for "bull," known for its power, while the *tav* symbolizes a "sign, mark, or cross." Combined, they can mean "power of the cross or mark of God."

4. *Sod*, the mystical or hidden meaning. The first letter of the first word, *"B^{a}re'shiyt,"* is *bet*, represented by a "house." A married man builds a house for his wife. So, when God created heaven and earth, He was building a house for His "bride."

The first three methods are closely similar to those used in Christian hermeneutics. The rabbis used the acronym *PaRDeS* ("Paradise") as a mnemonic device for remembering the four levels.[54] There are even more methods in the mystical Jewish Kabbalah. Practitioners hold that there are "seventy gates" of wisdom, that is, 70 different means of interpreting the text of the Torah.[55]

God keeps secrets.

Paul says that God, even before He created the universe, reserved secrets for us. *"No, we speak of God's secret wisdom, a wisdom that has been hidden and that God destined for our glory before time began"* (1 Cor 2:7, NIV; cf. Eph 3:9). The LORD often spoke through the prophets, but owing to the people's disobedience He sometimes blinded them to His messages. *"For the LORD has poured out on you The spirit of deep sleep, And has closed your eyes, namely, the prophets; And He has covered your heads, namely, the seers"* (Isa 29:10, NKJV).

God had revealed to Daniel many of His secrets. Oddly, at the outset of the 6th century B.C., the angel Gabriel told Daniel to hide the secrets already given him. *"But thou, O Daniel, shut up the words, and seal the book, even to the time of the end... And he said, Go thy way, Daniel: for the words are closed up and sealed till the time of the end"* (Dan 12:4a,9; cf. Isa 29: 10-14)). The secrets were to be revealed again only at the "time of the end."

Meantime, seeking to know some of God's secrets is not forbidden, but, rather, an honorable endeavor: *"It is the glory of God to conceal a thing: but the honour of kings is to search out a matter"* (Prov 25:2). Surprisingly, to gain spiritual insight, all we have to do is ask: *"If any of you lack wisdom, let him ask of God, that giveth to all men liberally, and upbraideth not; and it shall be given him"* (James 1:5; Luke 11:9).

Secrets will be known.

Christ said all secrets would eventually be uncovered. *"For there is nothing covered, that shall not be revealed; neither hid, that shall not be known"* (Luke 12:2). However, God's secrets cannot be discerned through men's insight or intelligence alone. *"Knowing this first, that no prophecy of the scripture is of any private interpretation"* (2 Peter 1:20). God Himself will reveal His secrets: *"But there is a God in heaven that revealeth secrets"* (Dan 2:28; also 2:22,47). Since the Scriptures have been inspired by the Holy Spirit, they can best be explained by Him. *"Howbeit when he, the Spirit of truth, is come, he will guide you into all truth: for he shall not speak of himself; but whatsoever he shall hear, that shall he speak: and he will shew you things to come"* (John 16:13; also Eph 3:5; 1 Cor 2:10,12).

God usually reveals secrets – to enable men to do His will. *"The secret things belong unto the LORD our God: but those things which are revealed belong unto us and to our children for ever, that we may do all the words of this law"* (Deut 29:29). Or to warn us about coming judgments. *"Surely the Sovereign LORD does nothing without revealing his plan to his servants the prophets"* (Amos 3:7, NIV).

The secrets of God will continue to be revealed until the end of the present world order at the Second Coming of Christ. *"But in the days of the voice of the seventh angel, when he shall begin to sound, the mystery of God should be finished, as he hath declared to his servants the prophets"* (Rev 10:7).

Only for a few?

God reveals His secrets only to the worthy: *"So then, men ought to regard us as servants of Christ and as those entrusted with the secret things of God"* (1 Cor 4:1-2, NIV; also Ps 25:14; Prov 3:32). Christ revealed secrets to only a few of His closest disciples, not to all people. *"He answered and said unto them, Because it is given unto you to know the mysteries of the kingdom of heaven, but to them it is not given"* (Matt 13:11). Why? *"Because narrow is the gate and difficult is the way which leads to life, and there are few who find it"* (Matt 7:14, NKJV).

Biblical prophecies

Many of God's secrets are in the form of prophecy. Prophecies are found in just one holy book: the Bible. They are absent from the texts of other religions. This sets the Judeo-Christian faith apart from all others.

Bible scholar Wilbur Smith, wrote about the Bible: "It is the only volume ever produced by man, or a group of men, in which is to be found a large body of prophecies relating to individual nations, to Israel, to all the peoples of the earth, to certain cities, and to the coming of One who was to be the Messiah."[56] Bible prophecies primarily concern God's chosen people, Israel, but many times include the whole world.

Nature of prophecy.

Most people are under the impression that prophecies are purely predictions of future events. Those are predictive prophecies, which are simply the best known kind. Basically, a prophecy is any Spirit-inspired utterance of God's divine will by a prophet. Some prophecies may be past events in retrospect. For instance, Isaiah 14:9-15 and Ezekiel 28:12-19 speak of Lucifer's corruption in a much earlier time.

There are straightforward prophecies, framed in plain language, and "veiled" prophecies, couched in symbols and mysterious metaphors.

Prophecies are usually "in context," that is, part of a prophet's discourse on a given topic. Other times, though, prophecy may be "out of context" – distantly or even totally unrelated to the subject spoken about. In Isaiah and Ezekiel's prophecies above, the subjects are the kings of Babylon and Tyre, when almost unnoticeably the message shifts to Lucifer's sins and judgment.

Predictive prophecies.

It is predictive prophecies that conclusively prove the omniscience of God. The all-knowing Creator declared some 2,750 years ago: *"Behold, the former things are come to pass, and new things do I declare: before they spring forth I tell you of them"* (Isa 42:9; also 46:10). Predictive prophecy is "history told in advance." Since God is outside space-time, He knows the beginning and the end, and everything in-between.

The Holy Scriptures contain at least 1,817 predictions concerning 737 topics in 8,352 verses.[57] These prophecies represent 27% of the 31,093 verses in the Bible. Some prophecy teachers used to think that the Bible was around 33% prophecy. Around the end of the 20th century, the estimate rose to 50%. Today, some prophecy analysts claim the Bible is likely 75% prophecy, since many actual historical incidents and stories in the Bible are "types" or prophetic models of future events.

A predictive prophecy is fulfilled in several ways. It may occur as plainly foretold. Or it may have a partial or staggered fulfillment -- with one or several parts of the prophecy occurring first, then the other parts later. Daniel's prophecy of the 70 "weeks" of years (490 years -- Dan 9:24-27) is a well-known example. The first 483 years had been fulfilled precisely until Christ, but the last 7 years are still in abeyance. There may also be multiple fulfillment – with the same prophecy coming true several times at various periods under different circumstances. Hosea 11:1-2, which predicted Israel's fall into idolatry, also came true in the Holy Family's flight to Egypt and return to Nazareth (Matt 2:14-21). Jeremiah 31:15-16 foretold the Jews' return from Babylonian captivity, but it also prefigured Herod's slaughter of innocent children (Matt 2:18).

Fulfilled prophecies

A prophecy cannot be true unless fulfilled. Although most Biblical prophecies foretold events far beyond the lifetimes of the prophets -- hundreds, even thousands of years in advance, many prophecies, astonishingly, have already been fulfilled! Authors Norman Geisler and William Nix wrote: "No unconditional prophecy of the Bible about events to the present day has gone unfulfilled... As a result, fulfilled prophecy is a strong indication of the unique, divine authority of the Bible."[58] Let us examine a few fulfilled Biblical prophecies.

Egyptian bondage.

The LORD told Abraham on the 14th day of the first month (Abib) in 1921 B.C. that his descendants would be persecuted in a foreign land for some 400 years. *"And he said unto Abram, Know of a surety that thy seed shall be a stranger in a land that is not theirs, and shall serve them; and they shall afflict them four hundred years"* (Gen 15:13). The Israelites left Egypt in the Exodus led by Moses in 1491 B.C. *"And it came to pass at the end of the four hundred and thirty years, even the selfsame day it came to pass, that all the hosts of the LORD went out from the land of Egypt"* (Ex 12:41).

Babylonian captivity.

God had said the Jews would be held captive in Babylon for 70 years. *"For thus saith the LORD, That after seventy years be accomplished at Babylon I will visit you, and perform my good word toward you, in causing you to return to this place"* (Jer 29:10-11). History recorded that in 606 B.C. Nebuchadnezzar invaded Judea for the first time and took Jews captive to Babylon. About 100 years earlier, Isaiah had prophesied that Jerusalem and the Temple would be rebuilt at the command of a certain Cyrus. *"That saith of Cyrus, He is my shepherd, and shall perform all my pleasure: even saying to Jerusalem, Thou shalt be built; and to the temple, Thy foundation shall be laid* (Isa 44:28). Amazingly, after Babylon fell to Media-Persia, Cyrus the Great issued a decree for the Jews to rebuild Jerusalem in 536 B.C. – precisely 70 years after the first Babylonian captivity of the Jews!

Some skeptics say these ancient events are false history made up by biased writers to affirm the veracity of the Bible. Let us consider one of the greatest prophecies in the OT that, although highly improbable, has been fulfilled beyond any shadow of doubt in our very own time.

Diaspora and regathering.

God many times foretold that, as a punishment for their sins, He would disperse the Israelites across the face of the earth (the *Diaspora*). *"And the LORD shall scatter thee among all people, from the one end of the earth even unto the other"* (Deut 28:64a,25; Jer 8:3,34:17; Ezek 4:13; Mic 5:7; etc.). Moreover, their land of "milk and honey" would become desolate. *"And I will bring the land into desolation: and your enemies which dwell therein shall be astonished at it. And I will scatter you among the heathen, and will draw out a sword after you: and your land shall be desolate, and your cities waste"* (Lev 26:32-33; etc.).

In 70 and 135 A.D. Roman legions suppressing Jewish revolts razed Jerusalem About a million Jews were massacred, over 100,000 were taken as slaves, while other survivors fled to far-flung places. Rome gave Judea the new name *Palaestina*, and Jerusalem, *Aelia Capitolina*. They plowed the city with salt before bringing in new settlers to the land.

Over 1,800 years of successive Roman, Arab, Crusader, Mameluke, Turkish, and British rules, the once flourishing Holy Land truly became desolate. In 1267, Jewish philosopher Nachmanides saw Jerusalem as "deserted and laid waste."[59] The Turks taxed trees, so the Bedouin inhabitants, who hated any form of tax, cut down the remaining trees.[60] British author George Sandy counted less than 1,000 trees in the whole land in 1610, noting that, "The country is a vast empty ruin."[61] In the 1880s Mark Twain described Palestine as a "a blistering, naked, treeless land."[62] Rainfall had dwindled. Abraham Kuyper (1837-1920), Dutch minister of state, said: "Only God can check the blight of the incoming desert. Only a miracle can save the Holy Land!"[63]

Regathering. Yet, God had also promised to regather Israel. *"But, The LORD liveth, that brought up the children of Israel from the land of the north, and from all the lands whither he had driven them: and I will bring them again into their land that I gave unto their fathers"* (Jer 16:15; Ezek 39:25-28; 37:21; Deut 30:4; Isa 43:5-6; etc.).

After centuries of persecution and *pogroms* (massacres) in their host countries, the Jews began to dream of *aliyah* ("ascent") or return to the land. In 1882 Jewish youths in Russia formed the *Hoveve-Zion* ("Lovers of Zion") promoting *aliyah*. In 1897, Austrian journalist Theodor Herzl organized the First Zionist Congress in Basel, Switzerland. Soon, Jewish settlements of returnees began sprouting in Palestine.

At the end of the 15th century, there were just about 4,000 families in Jerusalem, 70 of them Jewish "of the poorest class, lacking even the commonest necessities."[64] In 1845, around 12,000 Jews resided in all of Palestine. The number rose to 47,000 in 1908. In 1914, the Jews nearly doubled to 85,000. By 1948, immigrants from some 70 countries had swelled the Jewish population to 670,000. On May 14 that year, the modern state of Israel declared its independence – fulfilling Biblical prophecy. The following year, the Jews numbered over 1,000,000. The figure kept rising. In late 2010, with a growth rate of 1.8% for the 7th consecutive year, the population of Israel (including Arabs) stood at 7,645,000[65] – with over 40% (6 million plus) of the estimated 15 million Jews in the world. No less than 50,000 continue to arrive each year. Today, however, 71.7% of Israelis are native-born *sabras*, including 161,042 babies born in 2009.[66]

Restoration. The Lord had also sworn: *I will also cause you to dwell in the cities, and the wastes shall be builded. And the desolate land shall be tilled, whereas it lay desolate in the sight of all that passed by. And they shall say, This land that was desolate is become like the garden of Eden; and the waste and desolate and ruined cities are become fenced, and are inhabited* (Ezek 36:33-35, Amos 9:14, etc.).

The Jews built new homes and buildings outside the old walls of Jerusalem. Incredibly, the configurations of the new city followed the lines prophesied in Jeremiah 31:38-40![67] Along the Mediterranean coast, beaches became the streets of modern Tel Aviv.

Millions of trees were planted. The swamps of Galilee were drained to become tropical farms that made Israel the "California of the Middle East." As the new trees grew, rainfall increased over 10% every decade (Joel 2:23; Isa 35:7).[68] By the end of the 20th century, Israel had 350 million plus fully grown trees.[69] More than 80% of Israel's fruits and vegetables are exported to neighboring Arab and European nations (Isa 27:6). Israeli factories manufacture chemicals, fertilizer, processed food, textiles, paper, plastics, electronic and military equipment, scientific instruments. From just $6 million in 1948, exports have risen to over $80.5 billion in 2010, 35% of which are high tech and R&D products. Cut diamonds, a traditional industry, grew from $2.8 million to $8.9 billion in the same period. In all, Israeli exports multiplied by 13,400%![70]

The dispersion and regathering of the Jews after some 1,800 years is Biblical prophecy fulfilled right before our parents' and our very own eyes. It constitutes an astounding miracle that proves beyond any doubt that the Bible is truly the Word of an eternal and all-knowing God.

Messianic prophecies.

No prophecies presaged the coming of any of the founders of other religions in their holy books. On the other hand, hundreds of prophecies foreshadowed the birth, death, resurrection, and ascension to heaven of the Messiah (including His yet future Second Coming). Christ had been so clearly foretold in the Scriptures that the people expected Him long before He was born. Christ, unlike the founders of other religions, did not create a new calling for Himself. He came to assume a calling that had been described much earlier by the prophets.

Inventor-evangelist Martin Hunter observes that "Christ fulfilled 333 prophecies out of 333 prophecies in the Old Testament... According to the theory of probability in mathematics... Christ overcame mathematical odds of 1 over 84 as a fraction with 97 zeros then following that 84. That means it required odds of infinity... certifying that Jesus Christ is the authentic Son of God."[71] Let us take a look at a few of those 333 OT prophecies that the Messiah fulfilled in the NT:

From the tribe of Judah: *"The sceptre shall not depart from Judah, nor a lawgiver from between his feet, until Shiloh ('peace-maker'/'Prince of peace') come; and unto him shall the gathering of the people be"* (Gen 49:10/Matt 2:2; Heb 7:14).

From the family of David: *"And when thy days be fulfilled, and thou shalt sleep with thy fathers, I will set up thy seed after thee, which shall proceed out of thy bowels, and I will establish his kingdom. He shall build an house for my name, and I will stablish the throne of his kingdom for ever"* (2 Sam 7:12-13/Luke 1:32).

Born of a virgin: *"Therefore the Lord himself shall give you a sign; Behold, a virgin shall conceive, and bear a son, and shall call his name Immanuel ('God with us')"* (Isa 7:14/Matt 1:18).

Born in Bethlehem: *"But thou, Bethlehem Ephratah, though thou be little among the thousands of Judah, yet out of thee shall he come forth unto me that is to be ruler in Israel; whose goings forth have been from of old, from everlasting"* (Mic 5:2/Matt 2:1).

Sold for 30 pieces of silver: *"And I said unto them, If ye think good, give me my price; and if not, forbear. So they weighed for my price thirty pieces of silver"* (Zech 11:12/Matt 26:14-15).

Money paid for potter's field: *"And the LORD said unto me, Cast it unto the potter: a goodly price that I was prised at of them. And I took the thirty pieces of silver, and cast them to the potter in the house of the LORD"* (Zech 11:13/Matt 27:5-7).

Nailed to the cross: *"For dogs have compassed me: the assembly of the wicked have inclosed me: they pierced my hands and my feet"* (Ps 22:16/John 20:25; Luke 24:39).

Counted among criminals: *"...and he was numbered with the transgressors; and he bare the sin of many, and made intercession for the transgressors"* (Isa 53:12b/Matt 27:38).

Lots cast for His garments: *"They part my garments among them, and cast lots upon my vesture"* (Ps 22:18/John 19:23-24a).

Gall and vinegar to drink: *"They gave me also gall for my meat; and in my thirst they gave me vinegar to drink"* (Ps 69:21/Matt 27:34).

Darkness at noon: *"And it shall come to pass in that day, saith the Lord GOD, that I will cause the sun to go down at noon, and I will darken the earth in the clear day"* (Amos 8:9/Matt 27:45).

No bones broken: *"He keepeth all his bones: not one of them is broken"* (Ps 34:20; Ex 12:46b/John 19:33)

Buried in rich man's tomb: *"And he made his grave with the wicked, and with the rich in his death"* (Isa 53:9a/Matt 27:57-60a).

Raised from the dead: *"For thou wilt not leave my soul in hell; neither wilt thou suffer thine Holy One to see corruption"* (Ps 16:10/Luke 24:4-6a).

Incredibly, for every prophecy about Christ's first advent, there are approximately eight more predicting His Second Coming. The Messianic prophecies yet to be fulfilled are those about the "Rapture" (catching up of the elect); His victory at the last great battle on earth at Armageddon; His reign as King of kings during the Millennium; His role in the Last Judgment and the Kingdom of God -- some 2,345 prophecies more (2,025 in the OT and 320 in the NT).[72]

Symbols and similes

Many times, Biblical prophecies are clothed in symbolic language – to conceal their meanings from the profane. The interpretive method Jewish sages, Bible scholars, mystics, and other researchers use is called "hermeneutics," the science of explaining hidden meanings in Scripture.

As we know, no man can interpret prophecy on his own (2 Peter 1:20-21). That is probably why God placed many of the keys and clues to interpreting prophecy in the Scriptures themselves! In short, the Bible interprets itself.

Below are some of the most significant similes and metaphors in both the OT and NT, together with their meanings. Although they often have several meanings, this list is limited to the few prophetic ones:

Metaphors and meanings.

Beast: kingdom, government (Dan 7:3-7; Rev 13:1-18).
Blood: life, death (Lev 17:11; Deut 12:23: Isa 34:3; Ezek 14:19).
Cloud: multitude, angels (Ezek 38:9; Matt 24:30; Heb 12:1; etc.).

Dogs: wicked men (Ps 22:16; Matt 7:6; Rev 22:15; etc.).
Dragon: Satan (Rev 12:3-4,7-9,13-17; 13:2,4,11; 16:13; etc.).
Earth: mankind (Gen 6:11; etc.); desolate land (Rev 13:11).
Field: the world (Matt 13:38).
Fig tree: Israel (Jer 24:1; etc.; Nah 3:12; Matt 21:19; etc.).
Fire: destruction (Ps 18:8; etc.); Holy Spirit (Matt 3:11; etc.).
Fish: the Church, believers (Matt 13:47-48).
Flood: invaders (Isa 8:7-8; Jer 46:7; Dan 11:22, etc.).
Garments: salvation (Ecc 9:8; Isa 52:1; Luke 24:4; Rev 3:4; etc.).
Grass: people, mortality (Isa 40:6-7; Ps 103:14-15; 90:5-6).
Hail: God's wrath (Isa 28:2; Ezek 13:13; Hag 2:17; Rev 8:7; etc.).
Hand: labor, work (Prov 10:4; Ecc 9:10).
Head: mountain, kingdom (Dan 2:38-41; Rev 17:9).
Horn: king (Rev 17:12).
Lamp: guide (2 Sam 22:29; Ps 18:28; 119:105; Prov 6:23).
Light: truth, holiness (Rom 13:12; 2 Cor 4:6; Eph 5:14; 1 Peter 2:9).
Moon: idolatry (Deut 4:19; Job 31:26-28; etc.).
Mountain: kingdom (Isa 2:2; Jer 51:25; Zech 4:7; etc.).
Oil: God's Name (Song 1:3); Spirit (1 Sam 10:1,6; Isa 61:1; etc.).
Rock/stone: God (Deut 32:4; Ps 18:2; etc.); Christ (1 Cor 10:4; Ps
    118:22; Eph 2:20; 1 Pet 2:4-8, etc.).
Sea/waters: multitudes, nations (Rev 17:12).
Star: angel (Judg 5:20; Job 38:7; Ps 147:4; Rev 1:20; etc.).
Sun: glory (Ps 84:11; Matt 17:2; Rev 1:16; etc.).
Sword: war (Lev 26:25; etc.); Word of God (Eph 6:17; Heb 4:12).
Tree: enemy of Israel (Ezek 31:3,18; Dan 4:20-22).
Wilderness: place of refuge (Ex 15:22; Isa 35:1; Rev 12:14).
Wind/whirlwind: war (Jer 18:17; Dan 11:40; Amos 1:14).
Woman: church, religion (Jer 6:2; 2 Cor 11:2; Rev 17:5; etc.).

Nebuchadnezzar's dream.

Let us examine one famous prophecy filled with symbols. Babylon's king Nebuchadnezzar dreamt of a strange image: *"This image's head was of fine gold, his breast and his arms of silver, his belly and his thighs of brass, His legs of iron, his feet part of iron and part of clay. Thou sawest till that a stone was cut out without hands, which smote the image upon his feet that were of iron and clay, and brake them to pieces. Then was the iron, the clay, the brass, the silver, and the gold, broken to pieces together, and became like the chaff of the summer threshingfloors; and the wind carried them away, that no place was found for them: and the stone that smote the image became a great mountain, and filled the whole earth"* (Dan 2:32-35).

Daniel, then a Jewish captive in Babylon, explained the meaning of the king's dream (Dan 2:38-44). The first four parts of the image signify four successive kingdoms that subjugated the Jews, as history bears out. The *"head of gold"* stands for Nebuchadnezzar and his wealthy kingdom of Babylon. The *"breast and arms of silver"* mean the unified kingdoms of Media-Persia. The *"belly and thighs of brass"* correspond to Alexander's homeland Macedonia and Greece, famous for its brass artifacts. The *"legs of iron"* symbolize Rome, which conquered the then known world with its iron implements of war; the two legs portending the empire's later division into the Western and Eastern halves. The *"feet, part of iron and part of clay"* with their ten toes seem to be an end-time coalition of ten nations that once belonged to the Roman Empire, united with peoples denoted by clay. (These look like the ten kings in league with the Antichrist in Rev 17:12.) The *"stone cut out without hands"* is Christ, who will defeat the forces of Antichrist (*"smote the image upon his feet that were of iron and clay, and brake them to pieces"*) at Armageddon. That *"the wind carried them away"* means war would expunge all these kingdoms. The eternal kingdom of God (*"great mountain"*) will then reign over the world (*"filled the whole earth"*).

Biblical "types"

Closely related to prophetic symbols are "types" in the Scriptures. Persons, objects, places, and incidents serve as prophetic models that foreshadow future events. Hundreds of "types" are in the stories of Adam, Noah, Abraham, Isaac, Jacob, Joshua, Caleb, Job, Joseph, Ruth, David, Solomon, Elijah, Samuel, Samson, and many other Biblical personages, including objects and articles in the text of the Bible.

Abraham sacrificing Isaac.

A most detailed example of Biblical "typology" is when God tested Abraham by asking him to sacrifice his son Isaac to Him: *"And he said, Take now thy son, thine only son Isaac, whom thou lovest, and get thee into the land of Moriah; and offer him there for a burnt offering upon one of the mountains which I will tell thee of"* (Gen 22:2). Abraham as a "type" personifies God, who sacrificed His Only Begotten Son, typified by Isaac, nearly two thousand years later at Golgotha.

"And Abraham rose up early in the morning, and saddled his ass, and took two of his young men with him, and Isaac his son, and clave the wood for the burnt offering, and rose up, and went unto the place of which God had told him" (Gen 22:3). The two young men represent two groups of spiritually saved people God will take with Him.

"*Then on the third day Abraham lifted up his eyes, and saw the place afar off. And Abraham said unto his young men, Abide ye here with the ass; and I and the lad will go yonder and worship, and come again to you*" (Gen 22:4-5). The "*third day*" means Christ would be crucified in the third millennium from God's first covenant with Abraham. Abraham's instruction for the young men to wait prophesies Christ's return (Second Coming) to His waiting followers.

"*And Abraham took the wood of the burnt offering, and laid it upon Isaac his son; and he took the fire in his hand, and a knife; and they went both of them together*" (Gen 22:6). As Isaac carried the wood for the sacrifice up Mount Moriah, so would Christ later carry a wooden cross to Golgotha (the same hill?) to be crucified. The "*knife*" and the "*fire*" suggest the wars and destruction that God would inflict upon the Jews for rejecting and killing His Only Begotten Son.

"*And Isaac spake unto Abraham his father, and said, My father: and he said, Here am I, my son. And he said, Behold the fire and the wood: but where is the lamb for a burnt offering? And Abraham said, My son, God will provide himself a lamb for a burnt offering: so they went both of them together*" (Gen 22:7-8). Indeed, God Himself would provide the "*lamb*" for the offering – Christ, "the Lamb of God."

"*And they came to the place which God had told him of; and Abraham built an altar there, and laid the wood in order, and bound Isaac his son, and laid him on the altar upon the wood. And Abraham stretched forth his hand, and took the knife to slay his son*" (Gen 22:9-10). Isaac's quiet acquiescence prefigured Christ's stoic acceptance of His death on the cross.

"*And the angel of the LORD called unto him out of heaven, and said, Abraham, Abraham: and he said, Here am I. And he said, Lay not thine hand upon the lad, neither do thou any thing unto him: for now I know that thou fearest God, seeing thou hast not withheld thy son, thine only son from me. And Abraham lifted up his eyes, and looked, and behold behind him a ram caught in a thicket by his horns: and Abraham went and took the ram, and offered him up for a burnt offering in the stead of his son*" (Gen 22:11-13). The thicket around the ram's horns presaged the crown of thorns on Christ's head. The ram that replaced Isaac was a "type" of the Lamb of God who substituted His life for sinful humanity. Isaac was spared from death on the third day, prophetic of Christ's resurrection from the dead on the third day.

Objects and things.

On occasion, inanimate objects may prophetically represent persons, things, even units of time. Such is one prophecy of "types" in an incident that took place nearly 3,500 years ago: *"And they commanded the people, saying, When ye see the ark of the covenant of the LORD your God, and the priests the Levites bearing it, then ye shall remove from your place, and go after it. Yet there shall be a space between you and it, about two thousand cubits by measure: come not near unto it, that ye may know the way by which ye must go: for ye have not passed this way heretofore"* (Josh 3:3-4).

The *"ark of the covenant"* is a "type" for Christ, whom the people must follow *"two thousand cubits"* behind. "Cubit" is a "type" for "year," the veiled prophecy connoting that after 2,000 years faithful believers are to follow Christ to where He went (*"ye have not passed this way heretofore"*). Where? Paradise! Several other veiled prophecies in the Bible strongly suggest that the elect would go to meet Christ some 2,000 years after His ascension (Hos 6:2; Est 5:1; John 2:1; 2 Pet 3:8; etc.).

Prophetic Psalms

Editor-publisher J.R. Church (*Prophecy in the News*) revealed in his 1983 book *Hidden Prophecies in the Psalms* his startling discovery that the Psalms, besides poetry and wisdom, contain year-to-year messages to the Jews. He had realized that in the Psalms, the 19th book of the Bible, Psalm 1 is a prophecy for the year 1901 (19+1=1901), Psalm 2 for 1902, and so on. Each psalm prophesies events in the national life of the Jews or simply reflects their sentiments for a given year. Let us take a closer look at two of the most telling prophetic psalms.

Liberation of Jerusalem.

Psalm 17 seems to picture events in Jerusalem in late 1917, towards the end of World War I. *"Keep me as the apple of Your eye; Hide me under the shadow of Your wings, From the wicked who oppress me, From my deadly enemies who surround me"* (Ps 17:8-9, NKJV).

The Turks, who ruled over Jerusalem, were surrounded by the big guns of the British forces under Gen. Allenby. It looked like most of the holy places in the Holy City would be destroyed. Asking London for instructions, Allenby received a verse from the Bible: *"As birds flying, so will the LORD of hosts defend Jerusalem; defending also he will deliver it; and passing over he will preserve it"* (Isa 31:5). The general had the verse read to his troops in the hills around Jerusalem.

On Dec. 10, Allenby had all available aircraft do a reconnaissance flight over Jerusalem. The Turks, many of whom had never seen a plane before, were terrified by the flying machines, which dropped a note from General Allenby demanding their surrender. The Turks were further frightened by the name Allenby; they thought they were being asked to give up by Allah-beh, the son of God! (*beh* is Arabic for "son.") The Turks abandoned the city without firing a single shot.[73,74] Quite literally, God saved Jerusalem from destruction, *"under the shadow of Your wings"* – the wings of the British planes, as prophesied in Psalm 17.

Rebirth of Israel.

The rebirth of Israel in 1948 – a major world event of the 20th century – is in Psalm 48:4-8. (Note the numbers.)

On May 14, 1948, as the British mandate over Palestine expired at midnight, the Jews unilaterally declared an independent state of Israel. From here on, Psalm 48:4-8 reads like a newspaper report: *"When the kings joined forces, when they advanced together..."* (Ps 48:4). Within 24 hours, neighboring Arab countries -- Egypt, Syria, Lebanon, Iraq, and Transjordan (three of them ruled by kings) – with Palestinian guerillas, attacked the tiny newly born state.

"...they saw [her] and were astounded; they fled in terror" (Ps 48:5, NIV). One interesting anecdote tells of how the ragtag, ill-equipped Israeli fighters overcame the numerically superior and heavily equipped Arab forces. At one point, when the odds looked formidable, the Israelis gathered all available motor vehicles – cars, taxis, buses – and removed the exhaust manifolds that kept the engines quiet. At dusk, they drove their clattering vehicles toward the enemy lines. In the half-dark, the Arabs thought the Israelis had launched a massive armored attack and fled, abandoning their modern tanks.

"Trembling seized them there, pain like that of a woman in labor" (Ps 48:6, NIV). The verse speaks of childbirth -- the rebirth of Israel.

"You destroyed them like ships of Tarshish shattered by an east wind" (Ps 48:7, NIV). *"Tarshish"* means the lands at and beyond the western end of the Mediterranean Sea: the British Isles among them. The *"ships"* were thus those of the Royal Navy, which transported British troops to war zones. The British, their resolve broken by years of war and Arab-Jewish terrorist activities (*"shattered by an east wind"*), had earlier turned over the Palestine problem to the United Nations in 1947 and preferred not to intervene in the new conflict.

"As we have heard, so have we seen in the city of the LORD Almighty, in the city of our God: God makes her secure forever" (Ps 48:8, NIV). The verse affirms the permanent establishment of the state of Israel, with the holy city of Jerusalem as its eternal capital.

Fig tree prophecies

The number "48" seems to be a Biblical milestone not only in the OT, but also in the NT, wherein Christ strangely demonstrated the likeness of Israel to a fig tree: *"Now in the morning as he returned into the city, he hungered. And when he saw a fig tree in the way, he came to it, and found nothing thereon, but leaves only, and said unto it, Let no fruit grow on thee henceforward for ever. And presently the fig tree withered away"* (Matt 21:18-19).

The fig tree was like Israel, which produced no fruit for the Messiah. Apart from a little over a hundred disciples, the Jews as a nation rejected Christ. Thus, the Jews, like the accursed fig tree, were destined to wither away as a people. It came to pass in 70 A.D. and 135 A.D. in the hands of the rampaging Roman legions.

In three gospels, Christ spoke metaphorically of the rebirth of Israel – as a fig tree coming back to life with new leaves: *"Now learn a parable of the fig tree; When his branch is yet tender, and putteth forth leaves, ye know that summer is nigh"* (Matt 24:32; Mark 13:28; Luke 21:29). If we add the chapter and verses numbers, divide the sums by 3 to get the averages, round them up, then add the quotients, the prophetic number "48" comes up again!

Book	Chapter		Verse	Total
Matthew	24	:	32	
Mark	13	:	28	
Luke	21	:	29	
	58		89	
Divide by:	3		3	
	19*	+	29*	= 48

*(Rounded)

Biblical landmark.

Furthermore, the significance of the number "48" is manifest not only in the book of Psalms and the Gospels, but is also apparently a landmark for the entire Bible itself.

The Open Scroll writer-publisher Bob Schlenker points out that the book of Psalms is the 19th book from the beginning of the Bible, Genesis. Counting backward from the last book of the Bible, Revelation, we find that Psalms is the 48th book. Put the two numbers together (19+48), and we get "1948" – the year the nation of Israel was reborn!

The Bible Code

Scholars, mathematicians, and computer scientists are discovering hidden messages in the Bible that leave them stunned. Secret words, phrases, and even whole sentences appear to be encoded in the original Hebrew text of the Scriptures. The codes can be read by taking letters at regular intervals: every 7th letter, 49th, 153rd, 862nd, name it. Researchers call the arrangement "Equidistant Letter Sequencing" (ELS).

Centuries-old technique.

Jewish mystics are known to have painstakingly extracted messages encrypted in the *Torah* letter-by-letter since the 12th century. Rabbi Moses Cordevaro wrote in the 16th century: "The secrets of the Torah are revealed... in the skipping of the letters."[75]

Early in the 20th century, as a 13-year-old lad in Slovakia, Rabbi Michael Ber Weissmandl, guided by a 13th-century book by Rabbeynu Bachayah ben Asher of Saragossa, Spain, began looking for words hidden in the Hebrew Scriptures. He found that from the first letter *tav* (ת, "T") in Genesis, thence every 49th letter, *Torah* ("TORH," תורה) is spelled out. In Exodus, the 2nd book of the Bible, *Torah* is again found at the same interval. The phenomenon does not repeat in Leviticus, the 3rd book, but instead the Name of God ("YHWH," יהוה) appears every 7th letter. In Numbers and Deuteronomy, the 4th and 5th books, *Torah* appears again, although spelled backwards ("HROT," הרות).[76] It is as though the *Torahs* in the 1st, 2nd, 4th, and 5th books, two on each side, are paying homage to the Name of God in the 3rd and middle book (TORH > TORH > **YHWH** < HROT < HROT)![76]

The 18th century *Gaon* (Genius) of Vilna, Lithuania (Eliyyahu ben Shelomoh Zalman), regarded as a master of the code, taught: "The rule is that all that was, is, and will be unto the end of time is included in the *Torah*, from the first word to the last word. And not merely in a general sense, but as to the details of every species and each one individually, and details of details that happened to him from the day of his birth until his end."[77] That means everything and everyone, even you and I, are secretly encoded in the first five books of the Bible!

Faster with computers.

The advent of computers has exponentially expedited the search for encoded words in the Bible. A computer program capable of millions of calculations per second can examine millions of possible combinations of the 304,805 Hebrew characters of the Torah in minutes, something no man can accomplish manually even in a lifetime.

The Torah codes first attracted widespread attention in August 1994 with the article "Equidistant Letter Sequences in the Book of Genesis" by Israeli scientists Doron Witztum, Eliyahu Rips, and Yoav Rosenberg in the *Statistical Science Journal*. Six years earlier, the authors had submitted the work featuring the names of 34 prominent 9th-18th century

Jewish men, encoded in the Torah with their respective dates of birth or death. The editors were incredulous and demanded that the authors add 32 more Jews from the same period. The scientists complied and came up with the same results -- for a total of 66 Jewish personages, complete with their dates of birth or death![78] The editors subjected the data and methodology to rigorous and repeated peer reviews and analyses, and eventually printed the article. The authors ended their article with these words: "We conclude that the proximity of ELS's with related meanings in the Book of Genesis is not due to chance."[79]

Bible Code: the book.

Michael Drosnin, a former reporter for the *Washington Post* and *Wall Street Journal*, following interviews with Eliyahu Rips, conducted his own computer search and in early 1997 came out with a book, *The Bible Code*, which became an instant best-seller. The popularity of the book has led countless other investigators of diverse backgrounds to join the hunt for hidden messages in the Scriptures.

To date, thousands of encrypted messages have been brought to light, about such varied topics as: World Wars I and II; Hitler and the Holocaust; the atomic bomb; the Lincoln, Gandhi, Kennedy, Sadat, Rabin assassinations; Apollo moon-landing; Watergate and Nixon; Saddam Hussein and the Gulf War; the American Revolution; the Napoleonic wars; Shakespeare; Bach, Mozart, Beethoven; Rembrandt, Picasso; Edison, Marconi, the Wright brothers; Newton, Einstein; terrorist activities; and untold others.

Rips speculates: "Theoretically, there is no limit to the amount of information that could be encoded... In the end, the amount of information is incalculable, and probably infinite."[80]

Unbiblical codes.

Equidistantly spelled words have also been found in other lengthy texts, such as the Hebrew translations of *War and Peace, Moby Dick,* the penal code. And even in short ones: "Rabin" is seen in the software license on envelopes of Microsoft software products.[81]

However, the words found in secular works are scattered in no particular order, whereas in the Torah the words are clustered. It is only in the Bible codes that related words and phrases about the same topics are grouped together in close proximity, showing coherent relationships.

God's own code?

Some people say the Bible Code is the discovery of the millennium. The system is so simple, yet so comprehensive that it is beyond Moses, or any man, no matter how intelligent, to have woven hidden messages about the future into the narrative text of the Torah. Investigator Jeffrey Satinover remarks, "The code points to one thing and one thing only: the authorship of a document in which it is found."[82] The Code looks like God's own handiwork – undeniable proof that the Creator is truly the Author of the Bible.

Rips observes that ELS "is only the first, crudest level of the Bible code... It is almost certainly more levels deep, but we do not yet have a powerful enough mathematical model to reach it... It is probably less like a crossword puzzle, and more like a hologram. We are only looking at two-dimensional arrays, and we probably should be looking at three dimensions, but we don't know how to."[83]

Ancient Jewish tradition tells of seventy gates of wisdom or methods of deciphering the Torah. The Bible Code, according to *Sefer HaZohar* ("Book of Splendor"), is only one of those – in fact, the fiftieth.[84]

Unpredictable future.

The Bible Code cannot be used for predicting the future. Doron Witztum, creator of the ELS mathematical model, says: "It is impossible to use Torah codes to predict the future." Rips adds: "All attempts to extract messages from Torah codes or to make predictions on them are futile and are of no value."[85]

For instance, Drosnin in his 1997 book showed two future years linked to an atomic holocaust: 2000 and 2006. There were jitters when the second *intifada* or Palestinian revolt erupted in 2000. Next, heavy fighting between Israel and Hezbollah in Lebanon, and Hamas in the Gaza Strip broke out in 2006. Yet, none of these sparked the much-dreaded nuclear war. Drosnin notes: "The Bible Code may be a set of probabilities. Every future event appears to be encoded with at least two probabilities."[86] One message he found declares, "Five roads, five futures."[87] He concludes: "There are many possible futures, and the Bible Code can reveal each one of them. It is up for us to choose."[88]

Drosnin's remark echoes ancient Jewish wisdom. "Everything is foreseen, but freedom of action is given," thus intones the Talmud, the medieval commentary on the Torah.

Altered letter spacing

The original script of the Hebrew Scriptures consisted mostly of consonants – with no vowel markers, upper case (capital) or lower case (small) letters, punctuation marks, and even spaces between words. The reader himself had to mentally provide the missing indicators to make sense of the text. According to mystical tradition, secret messages can be brought to light by altering the spaces between the letters of the text.

Rabin assassination.

On Nov. 4, 1995, as part of their annual Torah reading schedule, Jews in their synagogues around the globe read Genesis 15:17-18, wherein God gave Abraham and his descendants all the land from the Nile in Egypt to the Euphrates in modern Iraq. God and Abraham sealed their covenant or agreement with the sacrifice of several animals cut into pieces: *"And it came to pass, that, when the sun went down, and it was dark, behold a smoking furnace, and a burning lamp that passed between those pieces. In the same day the LORD made a covenant with Abram, saying, Unto thy seed have I given this land, from the river of Egypt unto the great river, the river Euphrates."*

When the spaces between the letters in the passage are altered every second or third letter, *"lamp that passed between those pieces"* can be read as "A fire, an evil fire into Rabin, decreed by God."

In the evening of that fateful day, a gunman assassinated Israeli Prime Minister Yitzhak Rabin. The Jewish leader was killed at night -- *"when the sun went down, and it was dark"*. Prophecy analyst Bob Schlenker noted that the mention of the word "fire" twice foretold the two bullets that were fired into Rabin.[89]

The tragedy seems to have stemmed from the "land-for-peace" deal Rabin forged with then U.S. President Bill Clinton and Palestinian leader Yasser Arafat on Sept. 13, 1993. The Palestine Liberation Organization (PLO) would recognize the state of Israel in return for the creation of autonomous Palestinian enclaves within Israel. The pact divided Israel: some hailed Rabin as a peacemaker, others labeled him a traitor for handing over parts of their God-given land to the enemy.

Watergate and Nixon.

Another example of a hidden prophecy found through altered letter-spacing is the infamous Watergate scandal involving then U.S. President Richard Nixon. The encrypted prediction is in Numbers 3:24 – *"And the chief of the house of the father of the Gershonites shall be Eliasaph the son of Lael."*

According to Drosnin, in the entire Bible the word "Watergate" in Hebrew characters can be found only in this passage. When the spacing is rearranged between the letters of the Hebrew words *"And the chief of the house of the father of the Gershonites..."* the clause can be read in English as: "President, but he was kicked out."[90]

Biblical numerics

Many believe that the study of symbolic or mystical use of numbers originated with the Jews. Some experts on Bible numerics note that one out of every five verses in the Scriptures contains a number.[91] Christ Himself spoke of numbers a number of times. For instance... *"But the very hairs of your head are all numbered"* (Matt 10:30).

Greek philosopher-mathematician Pythagoras (ca. 580-500 B.C.) adopted the Jewish tradition to explain the origin and phenomena of the universe.[92] He and his followers taught that numbers were the essence of all things – the universe was built on and could be explained by numbers. (Incidentally, that is exactly what theoretical physicists are doing today.)

In the Bible, numbers have spiritual meanings attached to them. Multiples – by doubling, tripling, squaring, etc. – usually have the same meanings of the cardinal numbers, but intensified.[93]

Meanings of numbers.

Let us look at the meanings of some numbers in the Bible. Caution: Biblical numerics should not be confused with occult numerology, a form of divination that is abominable to God (Deut 18:10-12).

1 – "oneness, beginning": one God; one body, one Spirit, one Lord, one faith, one baptism; creation; Only Begotten Son; one lost sheep; etc.

2 – "division/opposition": heaven and earth; light and darkness; man and woman; good and evil; heaven and hell; Old and New Testaments.

3 -- "completeness": Father, Son, and Holy Spirit; Christ is the way, the truth, and the life; who is, was, and is to come; crucifixion in the third hour: three hours of darkness; resurrection on the third day; etc.

4 -- "the world": north, south, east, west; spring, summer, fall, winter; four rivers in Eden;. clean animals for sacrifice (bullock, sheep, goat, turtledove); four gospel portrayal of Christ (king, servant, man, God); four soils (wayside, stony places, thorns, good ground); peoples, kindreds, tongues, nations; four horsemen; etc.

5 -- "grace of God": for atonement of sin (burnt offering, peace offering, sin offering, trespass offering, meat offering); five ministries for God's grace (apostles, prophets, evangelists, pastors, teachers); etc.

6 -- "man/weakness": man created on sixth day; six days of work; the land planted for six years; Hebrew slaves served for six years; etc.

7 -- "fullness/perfection": the Creation week; seven Spirits of God; seven colors of the rainbow; seven holy days; seven branches of the lampstand; seven gifts of the Spirit; seven last years before the end; etc.

8 -- "new beginning": eight persons in Noah's Ark; male infants circumcised on the eighth day; Christ resurrected on the eighth day (first day of the following week); in music, eighth note begins new octave, etc.

9 – "finality/fruition": nine fruits of the Spirit; nine gifts of the Spirit; nine beatitudes; Israel ate of the new harvest in the ninth year; etc.

10 – "law/responsibility": ten patriarchs before the Flood (Adam to Noah); Ten Commandments; tithe is one-tenth of a man's increase; high priest uttered God's Name ten times on Day of Atonement; ten virgins; the universe was created with ten words, according to the rabbis;[94] etc.

12 – "organizational completion": twelve months in a year; twelve signs of the *Mazzaroth* (Zodiac); twelve tribes of Israel; twelve judges who ruled Israel; twelve apostles; twelve foundations and twelve gates of New Jerusalem; twelve kinds of fruit of the tree of life; etc.

13 – "disobedience": man's life span decreased to 1/13th (900+ to 70 years) after the Flood; Nimrod, who defied God, was 13th man from Ham, son of Noah; "dragon" is found 13 times in Revelation; the 13th sin of Israel in the Exodus was their refusal to possess the land; etc.

14 – "salvation": events on the 14th day of the month -- God made His covenant with Abraham; the Passover lamb that saved the Israelites from the last plague in Egypt was killed; Christ was crucified; Paul and others on the ship were saved from the storm; etc.

17 – "triumph": Noah's Ark landed in the mountains of Ararat and the Israelites crossed the Red Sea on the 17th day; Jacob lost his 17-year-old son Joseph, who later cared for him 17 years in Egypt; etc.

18 – "oppression": years Israelites served Moab and Israel oppressed by the Philistines and Ammonites; sum of the number of the beast (6+6+6), who will oppress the saints at the time of the end; etc.

24 – "priesthood": David divided priesthood among 24 descendants of Aaron; 24 elders around God's throne; Christ, as High Priest in heaven, will do 24 things for the saints (Ps 72 = 24 x 3); etc.

40 – "trials/testing": 40 days and nights of rain at the start of the Flood; Moses spent 40 years in Egypt, 40 in Midian, and 40 in the wilderness; he was 40 days with God on Mt. Sinai; God gave Nineveh 40 days to repent; the devil tempted Christ 40 days; etc.

42 – "the coming of Christ": 42 generations from Abraham to Christ; the beast will continue in power 42 months; Jerusalem will be trodden by Gentiles 42 months; the "woman," (remnant of Israel) will hide from the dragon 1,260 days or 42 months; the end will come after "*a time, times, and an half*" (3-1/2 years or 42 months); etc.

70 – "probation": average life span of man is 70 years; Israel's council of 70 elders since Moses; Jews captive in Babylon for 70 years; Jews given 70 "weeks" of years to restore relationship with God; etc.

Biblical alphanumerics

Interestingly, the Hebrew letters were first used as numerals before they were used to sound words. Sages and mystics have gained new insights on the holy Scriptures from the numerical values of the letters. The Hebrew alphabet has 22 letters, most of which are consonants. The first nine letters have values of 1 to 9, the next nine 10 to 90, and the last four 100 to 400. (See Hebrew alphabet, with symbols and values, in the Appendix.) Later, when *sofits* or word-ending forms for five letters came into use, the Hebrew numerals increased from 22 to 27 characters, with the five new letter-numbers having values of 500 to 900.

Similarly, the Greeks and the Romans used the characters of their alphabets for both numbers and letters. The Romans, however, used only six letters: I, V, X, L, C, and D for 1, 5, 10, 50, 100 and 500, respectively. (Incidentally, the six letter-numbers add up to 666.) The use of M for 1,000 came much later.

Exegetical methods.

Jewish mystics and rabbis use four major methods of exegesis or interpretation of the numerical values of the Hebrew Scriptures[95]:

1. Gematria. A corruption of Greek *geometria* or *grammateia*, this entails the substitution of numbers for letters. The values of letters in a word are added up to arrive at a total with a meaning.[96]

Hebrew words with the same values are considered identical to each other. For instance, in the mystical term for God, *Ein Sof*, *Ein* has a total of 61 (1+10+50), which is also the value of *Adon* (1+4+6+50), "Lord" or "Master." *Sof* (60+6+80) has a value of 146, the selfsame total of *Olam* (6+30+70+40), "world" or "universe." Thus, *Ein Sof* ("Without End") is synonymous to *Adon Olam* ("Lord of the World" or "Master of the Universe")! In addition, *Ein Sof* refers to God's "light." *Ein Sof* has a total of 207 (61+146), which is also the numerical value of *Ohr* (1+6+200=207), which means "light."

In another example, the coming of the Messiah in Genesis 49:10 is cryptically phrased as "Shiloh come" (*yabo Shiloh*), with a gematria of 358. The Hebrew word for Messiah (*Mashiach*) has the same value (358). *Shiloh*, therefore, refers to no one else but the Messiah.

In this connection, the name "Jesus" in Greek, Ιησουσ ("Iesous"), has a gematria of "888" (10+8+200+70+400+200). This inevitably brings to mind the number of the name of the end-time "beast" (the so-called "Antichrist") in Revelation 13:18, which is "666."

Gematria has seven variations of increasing complexity:

> *Ragil*, the simplest, is what we have just discussed, the substitution of numbers for each of the letters.

Kolel is basically *ragil*, plus the number of letters in a word.

Katan means "small" or reduced value -- all tens and hundreds are added until they are reduced to a single digit (1-9).

Hakadmi consists of the *ragil* values, with the value of each preceding letter added.

Hameruba haklali means the total value of a word squared.

Hameruba haperati, a more complex variant of *hameruba haklali*, is the sum of the squares of each individual letter.

Miluy means the sum of the values of the names of each letter that forms part of the word (also called "filling").

2. *Notarikon* involves acronyms in two ways. In the first, each letter in a word is taken as the initial letter of another word, so a word can be interpreted as a sentence. An example is the word *Bereshith* ("In the beginning"). From every letter (בראשית, b-r-'-sh-y-t) a new word is created, thus forming *Bereshith Ra Elohim Sheyequebelo Israel Torah* ("In the beginning God saw that Israel would accept the law").

The second kind is the reverse of the first: the initial, or sometimes final, letters of words in a sentence are taken to form just one word.

3. *Timurah* means the substitution of a letter for another. Following certain special rules, each letter is replaced with another that follows or precedes it in the Hebrew alphabet, thus forming an entirely new word.

A variation of *timurah* is *atbah,* permutation of letters, wherein the first letter of the Hebrew alphabet is replaced by the last, the second letter is replaced by the second to the last, and so on.

4. *Tziru* is a more complicated process. It entails the transposition or changing of the places of the letters in the Hebrew words of the Torah.

The power of God.

Mystics believe that squaring a key number is specially meaningful. The Hebrew word for God, *El* (אל), has a value of 31 (1+30). The first chapter of the Bible has 31 verses. The number 31 squared produces 961 – a number considered representing the power of God.

The letter ה (*hey.* "H," 5) is at times used as a single-letter Name for God. God added *hey* to the names Abram and Sarai. Their new names, taken together with that of their son Isaac, who had been miraculously given to them by God in their old age, point to the power of God:

AbraHam	(1+2+200+5+40)	=	248
SaraH	(300+200+5)	=	505
Isaac	(10+90+8+100)	=	208
			961 (Power of God)

3

Conundrums
of Creation

*Of old hast thou laid the foundation of the earth:
and the heavens are the work of thy hands"*

-- Psalm 102:25.

Have you, like countless others, ever wondered how the world began? Stephen Hawking, the famous British theoretical physicist, wrote: "We find ourselves in a bewildering world. We want to make sense of what we see around us and to ask: What is the nature of the universe? What is our place in it and where did it and we come from?"[1]

Practically all cultures on earth have a cosmogony -- a creation myth of how the world came into being. These traditions present a broad variety of scenarios that range from the death of a god or animal, whose body parts became the land, sea, and sky; to a primordial sea, from which gods and the world emerged; to eggs that hatched creator-gods; to struggles among gods, who produced offspring through incest or self-fertilization; to men springing forth from the tears of gods or even fleas from the skin of a dead god. The numerous tableaux had been limited only by the ancients' imaginations.

Under scrutiny, however, all of these stories of origin are nothing but continuations of previous circumstances, built on things that already existed. On the other hand, the Genesis account of creation in the Bible tells of a universe that emerged from nothing.

Science confirms Scripture

In great steps, advances in modern science are confirming the Biblical account. While science textbooks have to be revised or updated from time to time in the past 200 years to accommodate new discoveries and theories, in 3,500 years nothing ever needed to be changed in the Bible. Rather, many mysteries in the Sciptures have become clear and well established facts in the light of increasing scientific knowledge.

Astronomer Hugh Ross remarks: "Instead of another bizarre creation myth, here (in the Bible) was a journal-like record of the earth's initial conditions – correctly described from the standpoint of astrophysics and geophysics – followed by a summary of the sequence of changes through which Earth came to be inhabited by living things and ultimately by humans. The account was simple, elegant, and scientifically accurate."[2]

Science writer Fred Heeren notes: "Hebrew revelation is the only religious source coming to us from ancient times that fits the modern cosmological picture. And in many cases, 20th-century archeology and myth experts have also been forced to turn from older views that treated the Bible as myth to ones that treat it as history."[3]

The convergence of Biblical teachings and scientific findings is truly amazing. Let us begin with the first few words and verses of the Bible to see for ourselves this growing harmony between science and Scripture.

A beginning

"In the beginning ..." (Gen1:1).

The Judeo-Christian Scriptures unfold with the story of the birth of the universe. Ancient men generally believed in so such thing. The Greek philosopher Aristotle taught around 2,300 years ago that the world was eternal – it had always existed. Indeed, the starry sky we see on a clear night seems to be unchanging. Albert Einstein, considered one of the most brilliant scientific minds in modern times, tried to prove that we live in a static, unchanging universe. As late as the early 1960s, two-thirds of the leading American scientists surveyed professed their belief in the steady-state theory of the cosmos.[4]

In 1917, though, after Einstein published his theories of special and general relativity (1905 and 1915), Dutch astronomer Willem de Sitter saw an oversight in Einstein's equations. He pointed out that if the density of the universe were low enough, it would not be static, but expanding at nearly the speed of light.[5] In 1922, Russian astronomer Alexandr Friedmann found a hidden mathematical prediction in Einstein's equations: The universe was finite, not infinite. Anything that is not infinite must have had a beginning.

In 1927 American astronomer Edwin Hubble discovered that, based on the observed redshift (wavelengths of light lengthening or turning red when moving away from the observer), all the other galaxies were speeding away from the Earth. The farther away they were, the higher their velocity – as fast as about 25,000 miles per second![6]

The law of inertia states that a body at rest remains at rest and a body in motion remains in motion unless acted upon by some outside force. Hence, the galaxies have once been close together before a force caused them to move away from each other. Ergo, the universe had a beginning. The editors of the *Encyclopedia Britannica* express their agreement: "The observed expansion of the universe immediately raises the spectre that the universe is evolving, that it had a beginning..."[7]

In addition, the science of thermodynamics dictates that heat must flow from a warm body to a cold one. If the universe has always existed, its temperature should be uniform throughout. However, observations indicate that the cosmic temperature is still cooling down. Therefore, the universe has not always existed – it had a starting point.

Robert Jastrow, founder and former director of NASA's Goddard Institute for Space Studies, concludes that "the astronomical and biblical accounts of Genesis are alike in one essential respect. There was a beginning, and all things in the Universe can be traced back to it."[8]

A Beginner?

"In the beginning God..." (Gen1:1).

The law of causality, or cause and effect, declares that nothing can happen or exist without a cause. The universe, being an effect, must have had a cause. What caused the universe to come into existence?

Scientists are able to analyze and explain the observable universe; but they remain in the dark as to its cause. Paul Dirac, the Nobel laureate from Cambridge University, said: "It seems certain that there was a definite time of creation."[9] Aside from accepting a cosmic beginning, Dirac implies, by the word "creation," the hand of a creator.

The *Encyclopedia Britannica* admits the implication: "...the notion that the Cosmos had a beginning, while common in many theologies, raises deep and puzzling questions for science, for it implies a creation event -- a creation not only of all the mass-energy that now exists in the universe but also perhaps of space-time itself."[10] Stephen Hawking is of the same mind: "So long as the universe had a beginning, we could suppose it had a creator."[11]

Empty space created

"In the beginning God created the heaven..." (Gen 1:1).

If the universe had a beginning, then "space" has not always been there. There was once a state or condition when the emptiness of space did not exist at all.

As most people today know, "heaven" is the empty space above and surrounding Earth in all directions, where the stars and the planets are. How did space come into being? Jewish mystics have long been familiar with this mystery: The *Ein Sof* (the "Infinite Nothingness") contracted Itself to make room for space. The "contraction" is known in Kabbalistic terms as the *tzimtzum*.

Can you imagine what empty space is like? It contains nothing, not even light or darkness. Yet, surprisingly, scientists have discovered that the vacuum of "empty space" is not absolutely empty. Space possesses electromagnetic qualities, dielectric permittivity, intrinsic impedance, and immense "zero-point" energy that helps keep all the electrons in the cosmos in their orbits around atomic nuclei![12]

A cosmic "air pocket"?

Perhaps we can use an analogy, although inadequate, to imagine the relationship between the *Ein Sof* and space: If the *Ein Sof* were the atmosphere that is everywhere around us, then space would be an "air pocket" (which air travelers are quite familiar with). An air pocket forms when a mass of air cools, becomes heavier, and sags as one distinct body. The air pocket is still very much a part of the atmosphere, but for the time being has acquired a separate identity of its own.

Matter materializes

"In the beginning God created the heaven and the earth" (Gen1:1).

After creating "heaven" (space), God went on to create the "earth" in the emptiness He had just brought forth. Here, *"earth"* may mean something else other than the planet Earth, because the next passage says that the earth was still *"without form, and void."* The Hebrew word used was *'erets* (from a root meaning "to be firm"). We could thus take *"earth"* in the passage to mean "solid matter."

The first law of thermodynamics states that matter can neither be created nor destroyed. Something cannot be created from nothing. If so, how did the first speck of matter materialize? Paul says God created the physical universe from invisible materials: *"...what is seen was not made out of things which are visible"* (Heb 11:3b, NASU).

A medieval Jewish sage in Spain, Moses Ben Nachman, also known as Naḥmanides or Ramban, wrote: "In the beginning, from total and absolute nothing, the Creator brought forth a substance so thin it had no corporeality, but that substanceless substance could take on form."[13]

All things from "nothing."

Cosmologists generally believe that in the beginning there was nothing. Then, all of a sudden, from out of that nothing, the universe was born. Jewish sages are in complete agreement. They just differ in their concept of "nothing."

Scientists arrive at a mathematical "zero." Stephen Hawking says that "the total energy of the universe is exactly zero."[14] Paul Davies wonders: "Astronomers can measure the masses of galaxies, their average separation, and their speeds of recession. Putting these numbers into a formula yields a quantity which some physicists have interpreted as the total energy of the universe. The answer does indeed come out to be zero within the observational accuracy. The reason for this distinctive result has long been a source of puzzlement to cosmologists. Some have suggested that there is a deep cosmic principle at work which requires the universe to have exactly zero energy."[15]

In contrast, by "nothing" Jewish philosophers mean the *Ein Sof* – the "Infinite Nothingness" -- God. It appears He was that "deep cosmic principle at work" in the beginning.

A thought in God's mind?

In *Space-Time and Beyond,* Fred Alan Wolf wrote: "The quantum physicist calls the 'pre-matter' phase, the quantum wave function. The quantum wave function is very well calculated, but it is not matter! It is not anything, really… As fantastic as it sounds, the mathematical models for such things are very well defined and, mathematically at least, well understood… the quantum wave represents where and when something is likely to occur; in other words, it is a measure of the probability of an event taking place… this probability not only *exists* in our minds, but also *moves* in space and time. In other words this wave is both in our minds and out there in the world."[16]

Before matter first appeared, was it merely a probability in the mind of God? Paul Davies muses, "it seems that the entire universe may be nothing more than a thought in the mind of God."[17] James Jeans, the knighted British mathematician, says: "The world looks more like a great thought than a great machine"[18] and adds: "If the universe is a universe of thought, then its creation must have been an act of thought."[19]

From wave to particle?

In 1906 English physicist J.J. Thomson won the Nobel Prize for demonstrating that electrons were particles. In 1924 French physicist Louis de Broglie (who won the Nobel Prize in 1929) proposed that all matter, including light, possessed a quality called "wave-particle duality"

– that is, they can appear as either waves or particles.[20] J.J. Thomson's only son, George Paget Thomson, likewise became a Nobel laureate in 1937 by proving that electrons were waves! Both father and son, as well as de Broglie, were correct – they established the wave-particle duality common to all subatomic entities.

Quantum physicists now know that when an atom is broken down to its subatomic components, particles like protons, neutrons, and electrons surprisingly lose their characteristics as particles. They may sometimes still behave like particles, but they no longer have dimensions. Thus, a subatomic entity, such as an electron, can appear as a particle or a wave. Amazed physicists found that if we assume that a quantum entity is a particle, it will appear as a particle. Assume it is a wave, and we will observe it as a wave! We see matter the way we believe it exists. In theory, all matter, including humans, has this property of duality.[21]

Was the wave-particle duality principle responsible for a thought of God morphing from a wave into the first particle of matter?

Infinitesimal speck.

Advocates of the Big Bang Theory hold that the universe began as an infinitesimally small, infinitely hot, and incredibly compact point called a "singularity." It contained all the matter of the universe. This hews closely to what Jewish sages have taught for centuries.

In his exegesis of Genesis in the 12th century, Moses Maimonides said that the entire universe had been created from something smaller than a mustard seed.[22] Nachmanides corroborated that: "Now this creation was a very small point and from this all things that ever were or will be formed."[23] Later, in 1930, Belgian astronomer Georges Lemaitre described the primal atom as a super dense "cosmic egg."

Astronomer Edwin Hubble's discovery of an expanding universe implies that all the particles that make up the universe were indeed once tightly packed together. The supremely hot and compact speck suddenly exploded and dispersed at close to the speed of light, eventually forming the stars and the galaxies.

Fellow astronomer John D. Barrow of the University of Sussex, in England, speculates: "If the universe is expanding, then when we reverse the direction of history and look in the past we should find evidence that it emerged from a smaller, denser state – a state that appears to have once had zero size. It is the apparent beginning that has become known as the big bang."[24] Advocates of the Big Bang Theory are fond of saying: "First, there was nothing. Then it exploded."

"Quantum fluctuation."

The NASA posits that the creation of the universe was the result of a "quantum fluctuation." Quantum what?

Edward Tryon first proposed the idea in a *Nature* magazine article in 1973: "Is the Universe a Vacuum Fluctuation?"[25] Scientific writer Andrew Chaikin remarks: "Quantum mechanics says that matter and energy can appear spontaneously out of the vacuum of space, thanks to something called a quantum fluctuation, a sort of hiccup in the energy field thought to pervade the cosmos."[26]

Physicists have realized that even the supposedly empty vacuum of space has "things" swarming in it. As author Richard Morris (*The Edges of Science*) points out: "In modern physics, there is no such thing as 'nothing.' Even in a perfect vacuum, pairs of virtual particles are constantly being created and destroyed. The existence of these particles is no mathematical fiction. Though they cannot be directly observed, the effects they create are quite real. The assumption that they exist leads to predictions that have been confirmed by experiment to a high degree of accuracy."[27] The spontaneous appearance and disappearance of virtual particles in space is what scientists call a "quantum fluctuation."

Law of parity. An article in *The New York Times* (August 21, 1990), entitled "New Direction in Physics: Back in Time," explains that "the vacuum's totally empty space is actually a seething turmoil of creation and annihilation, which to the ordinary world appears calm because the scale of fluctuations in the vacuum is tiny and the fluctuations tend to cancel each other out."[28]

In other words, as soon as a virtual particle appears, its closely following antiparticle twin collides with it, destroying both of them. The process of mutual destruction is part of the "law of parity." (The "virtual particles" are pairs of matter and antimatter, such as quarks and antiquarks, which form the atoms that make up all things in the universe. An antiparticle is identical to its particle partner in every way, except that its charge or spin is the exact opposite.)

The *Encarta Encyclopedia* sheds further light on the matter: "In physics, the seemingly inviolable law of parity holds that the conversion of energy into matter produces equal amounts of matter and antimatter that then annihilate each other."[29]

A quark of nature.

Until the 1950s physicists believed there was always perfect balance and symmetry in the creation and mutual annihilation of matter and antimatter. Yet, if that was the case, the universe could never have materialized. All matter would have vanished almost as soon as it had appeared. But a quirk of nature happened. Every so many collisions left one extra particle or quark surviving intact.

Matter-antimatter imbalance. In 1964, James W. Cronin of the University of Chicago and Val L. Fitch of Princeton did experiments which showed that every so often an extra particle survived the matter-antimatter annihilation: two in each 1,200 decays of a particle produced a survivor that violated the law of parity. For their achievement, Cronin and Fitch shared the Nobel Prize in physics in 1980.[30]

Physicist Gerald Schroeder speaks of even greater odds: In the first 1/100,000 of a second of the Big Bang, more quarks than antiquarks were produced – 10,000,000,001 particles for every 10,000,000,000 antiparticles -- establishing a numerical edge of matter over antimatter. Nobel laureate Steven Weinberg wrote: "The one part in ten billion excess of matter over antimatter is one of the key initial conditions that determined the future development of the universe."[31]

The extra quarks left by the matter-antimatter imbalance in the quantum fluctuations accumulated and bonded together to form the elements that gave birth to the stars and the galaxies, and, later, all living organisms. What caused the imbalance?

Astrophysicist John Gribbin comments that, although scientists can describe in detail what happened *after* the creation, they cannot explain what started it all. The "instant of creation remains a mystery... maybe God did make it, after all."[32]

Gases and dust

"And the earth was without form, and void..." (Gen1:2a)

Scripture suggests and science affirms that the primeval particles of matter were in the form of gases and dust before they bonded together to form the celestial bodies and all things else in the universe.

In 1796, French astronomer Pierre Laplace advanced the "nebular hypothesis" in his book *Exposition of the System of the Universe*. He proposed that the stars, the sun, and the planets formed from nebulae – swirling clouds of interstellar gases, dust, and minerals

According to the theory, refined over the past 200 years, dynamic interactions cause a spinning cloud to flatten into a disk as gravity pulls much of the materials into the center, which begins to contract. The contraction raises the pressure and temperature at the core until it develops into a "protosun." The outer parts of the disk, on the other hand, cool down. Mutual attraction causes solid pieces and ice crystals to agglomerate and form asteroids, planetesimals, and rocky inner planets like Mercury, Venus, Earth, and Mars, while farther out gases and dust freeze into great ice balls that become outer gaseous planets, such as Jupiter, Saturn, Uranus, and Neptune.

"Blackbody" of space

"...and darkness was upon the face of the deep" (Gen1:2b).

Space, at the outset, was simply an empty darkness. Did God create darkness? Or was darkness the mere absence of light? The Scriptures tell us that the Creator also made darkness: *"I form the light, and create darkness: I make peace, and create evil: I the LORD do all these things"* (Isa 45:7).

Towards the end of the 1800s, physicists observed that, at very low temperatures, efficient emitters and absorbers of radiation appeared black. They thus called a perfect emitter or absorber of radiation a "blackbody."[33]

The rate of absorption depends on the size of the exposed surface area – the larger the area, the greater the absorption. The immense darkness of space therefore is the ultimate "blackbody."

The Spirit of God

"And the Spirit of God moved..." (Gen1:2c)

The presence of physical space presented a medium for motion to take place in. The first recorded motion in space is that of God's Spirit.

What, daresay, is Spirit? The Spirit of God moved, so It must have possessed energy. Or was It itself energy?

And what in turn is energy? Physicists say energy can be scientifically detected, measured, and managed, but nobody really knows what it is. Yet, everything in the universe is energy. In fact, energy fills the entire universe. Scientists generally accept the existence of an "energy field thought to pervade the cosmos."[34]

Matter, moreover, is simply congealed or solidified energy.

Energy into matter.

Albert Einstein's famous formula ($E=mc^2$) for his theory of relativity equates energy *"E"* to mass *"m"* (matter). In short, energy and matter are interchangeable. Energy can be transformed into matter, and vice-versa. Perhaps, not too surprisingly, the psalmist knew this in spiritual terms 3,000 years ago: *"Thou sendest forth thy spirit, they are created"* (Ps 104:30). Did God's Spirit, which is energy, produce matter?

A *New York Times* article of Aug. 21, 1990, concurs: "According to quantum theory... potential existence can be transformed into real existence by the addition of energy. (Energy and matter are equivalent, since all matter ultimately consists of packets of energy.)"[35]

Hawking elaborates: "There are something like ten million million million million million million million million million million million million million million (1 with 85 zeroes after it) particles in the region of the universe that we can observe. Where did they all come from? The answer is that, in quantum theory, particles can be created out of energy in the form of particle/antiparticle pairs."[36]

Particles of matter are created from energy. Or, perhaps we should say, Divine Energy?

God entered space-time?

Did God enter the space-time domain in the form of His Spirit? How can the Infinite Nothingness be inside the finite space-time framework?

God apparently manifested an essence of Himself as the Spirit in the material universe. The Infinite Nothingness, having no physical form or dimensions, would not have entered the limitations of space-time that He had created. Doing so would have subjected Him to the laws of nature that He Himself had set in operation.

A part, such as space-time, cannot possibly contain the whole, in this case the Infinite Nothingness. It would have been like trying to put a tree into its seed.

Electromagnetic properties.

Eliphaz, Job's friend, encountered a spirit: *"Then a spirit passed before my face; the hair of my flesh stood up"* (Job 4:15). Since the passing spirit caused the hair on the body of Eliphaz to stand, the unseen entity must have had the effect of static electricity.

Is an ordinary spirit similar to the Spirit of God? God is the Father of spirits: *"...shall we not much rather be in subjection unto the Father of spirits..."* (Heb 12:9b). It follows, then, that the Spirit of God, the spirits of His sons, the angels, and the spirits of men are similar in nature -- energy with electromagnetic properties.

Water in space

"And the Spirit of God moved upon the face of the waters" (Gen1:2c).

Water in space before the creation of the earth? Aristotle recorded in his book, *Metaphysics,* that Thales, the earliest Greek philosopher, believed that the source of all things was water.[37]

Elementary element.

A molecule of water (H_2O), as we learned in school, is made up of two hydrogen atoms and one oxygen atom. Hydrogen, which means "water-maker" (*hydro-gen*) in Greek, is the most abundant element in the universe. A hydrogen atom is the lightest, simplest, and most basic of all atoms, consisting of just one proton as the nucleus and one electron orbiting around it.

In 1948, Russian-born physicist George Gamow, who produced the first evidences for the Big Bang with his students Alpher and Herman, worked out the nuclear reactions that could have occurred during the first few minutes of the explosion.[38] They found that, after about one second, protons would have formed. In the next three minutes, when the temperature of the universe was about 300 million degrees Kelvin,[39] protons and neutrons would have formed hydrogen, as well as the other light elements -- primarily helium, and some lithium, beryllium, boron.[40] The initial nucleosynthesis stopped when there were approximately 78% hydrogen and 22% helium by weight, or 93% hydrogen and 7% helium abundances.[41]

Their calculations have since been confirmed through spectroscopic observations. "Atomic hydrogen clouds are the most widely distributed in interstellar space and, together with molecular hydrogen clouds, contain most of the gaseous and particulate matter of interstellar space..."[42] Hydrogen today comprises some 73% of the visible mass of the universe,[43] while helium constitutes approximately 23%.[44] The Sun alone burns about 40 million tons of hydrogen per second.

Most abundant element.

How did Moses, who wrote the book of Genesis around 3,500 years ago, know that water, or at least its main component hydrogen, was the very first and most abundant element in the universe? Peter reiterated this scientific fact in his general epistle about 1,500 years later: *"But they deliberately forget that long ago by God's word the heavens existed and the earth was formed out of water and by water"* (2 Peter 3:5-6, NIV).

Just as the Bible says, science has discovered that there were "waters" (hydrogen) in space before the earth took shape!

Curiously, this information is in the Hebrew word for "heavens" – *shamayim*. The Hebrew term for "waters" is *mayim*, while *sham* means "there" or "in it." Hence, *shamayim* can be read as: "there (*sham*) are waters (*mayim*) -- in the heavens (*shamayim*)"! Could this be a mere coincidence?

Light created

"And God said, Let there be light: and there was light" (Gen 1:3).

In the deep darkness of the "blackbody" of space, the Creator next brought into existence... light!

An unimaginably brilliant flash of light must have burst forth, filling all of primordial space. George Gamow was led to say: "One may almost quote the Biblical statement, In the beginning there was light, and plenty of it."[45]

Early men knew the sun lighted up the world. It was inconceivable to have light in the heavens without the sun, as well as the moon and the stars. So, even as late as at the time of Moses, to be told that light was created before the sun must have stretched their imaginations to the brink of incredulity; or, worse, unbelief.

Light from "water."

Scientists know all too well that hydrogen atoms are typical sources of photons -- light. When four hydrogen atoms combine into a helium atom through the process of thermonuclear fusion, the energy released is transformed into light and heat.

Thus, the Sun generates radiant energy -- light – through the nuclear conversion of hydrogen into helium. In a hydrogen bomb explosion, hydrogen atoms fuse to produce a blinding blast of light and energy.

Science once again confirms the truth of the Biblical account. But… just what is light?

Electromagnetic radiation.

Technically, "light" is the generic term used for any and all kinds of electromagnetic radiation. In waves of electric and magnetic energy consisting of elementary particles called photons, light results when atoms gain surplus energy by absorbing photons from other sources or by being struck by other particles. As the atoms give up the extra energy, photons are emitted as light.[46]

There are many forms of radiant energy, but seven forms are well known: radio waves, microwaves, infrared rays, visible light, ultraviolet rays, x-rays, gamma rays. Radio waves have the longest wavelengths, measured in meters; gamma rays shortest at 0.000000001 cm. In the color spectrum, red has the longest wavelengths at 0.000075 cm, with violet the shortest at 0.000035 cm. Regardless of their wavelengths and frequencies (number of times waves are repeated within a given period), all forms of electromagnetic radiation travel at the speed of light.

Gottfried Leibniz, 17th century German philosopher-mathematician, observed that a ray of light always chose a path that took it fastest to a destination,[47] a phenomenon known as the "principle of least action." Why do they do that when they can just, let us say, drift? Max Planck, the eminent German physicist, could not help saying, "Photons… behave like intelligent human beings."[48]

The speed of light.

Men had always believed that light was instantaneous. In 1676 Danish astronomer Olaf Roemer announced that the irregular behavior of the eclipse times of Io, Jupiter's inner moon, could be accounted for by a finite speed of light. The English astronomer James Bradley independently confirmed in 1729 the finite speed of light. In 1983, the speed of light was officially declared a universal constant of nature at 299,792.458 kilometers (about 186,282 miles) per second.

According to Albert Einstein's special theory of relativity, the velocity of light is the ultimate speed limit. Only objects without mass can travel at that speed. Photons, having no mass, traverse space without any loss of energy. Changes in their wavelengths or frequencies do not affect their velocity. At the speed of light, time stops. Light, including all forms of electromagnetic energy, thus exists in a timeless state. The fact that light is outside the realm of time has been proven in thousands of experiments at hundreds of universities.[49]

Light speed decelerating? From 1929 to 1940, Raymond Birge, physics department chairman at the University of California, Berkeley, and arbiter of atomic constants (such as the speed of light), several times recommended decreasing the value for the speed of light.[50] In 1979, an Australian college student, Barry Setterfield, charted 163 measurements of the speed of light using 16 different methods since Roemer. He found that in general the older the observation, the faster the speed of light.[51]

Measurements of the Speed of Light

Year	Experimenter	Speed (km/s)	(+/- km/s)
1657	Roemer	307,600	
1738	(Not named)	303,320	310
1861	(Not named)	300,050	60
1875	Harvard	299,921	13
1880	Michelson	299,910	50
1883	Newcomb	299,860	30
1883	Michelson	299,853	60
1926	Michelson	299,796	4
1950	Bergstrand	299,792.7	.25
1952	Froome	299,792.6	.7
1967	Grosse	299,792.5	.050
1974	Blaney et al.	299,792.459	.0006
1976	Woods et al.	299,792.4588	.0002
1977	Monchalin et al.	299,792.457.6	.00073

With statistician Dr. Trevor Norman, Setterfield showed that, even with the technical crudeness of early experiments, the speed of light was discernibly higher 100 years ago, and as much as 7% higher in the 1700s. Canadian mathematician Alan Montgomery has published a computer analysis backing the Setterfield-Norman findings, indicating that the decay of the speed of light "closely follows a cosecant-squared curve, and has been asymptotic since 1958. If he is correct, the speed of light was 10-30% faster in the time of Christ; twice as fast in the days of Solomon; four times as fast in the days of Abraham, and perhaps more than ten million times faster prior to 3000 B.C." In 1987, Russian cosmologist V.S. Troitskii calculated that the speed of light was originally about 10^{10} (ten billion) times faster at time zero.[52]

Other scientists have published works asserting that light speed was as much as 10 to the 10th power faster in the early stages of the Big Bang than it is today.[53] For his part, Setterfield estimates that the speed of light was infinite 6,000 years ago.

Light speed accelerated! The *London Sunday Times* reported on June 4, 2000: "In research carried out in the United States, particle physicists have shown that light pulses can be accelerated to up to 300 times their normal velocity of 186,000 miles per second… The work was carried out by Dr. Lijun Wang of the NEC research institute in Princeton, who transmitted a pulse of light towards a chamber filled with specially treated cesium gas. Before the pulse had fully entered the chamber it had gone right through it and traveled a further 60 (feet) across the laboratory. In effect it existed in two places at once, a phenomenon that Wang explains by saying it traveled 300 times faster than light." In effect, light leaped forward in time!

The Italian National Research Council has reportedly approximated Wang's results by making microwaves travel 25% faster than light.[54] In fine, all the studies agree: the speed of light is not constant. Light can travel slower or faster than the presently accepted "speed of light."

Many are excited over the possibilities. Others are bothered. If the findings hold true, they would shatter Einstein's theory of relativity, which states that the speed of light is an inviolable universal constant.

The Big Bang

The "Big Bang" is the most widely accepted theory of the origin of the universe. After the Hubble discovery in 1927 that all the other galaxies were speeding away from the Earth, George Gamow proposed in the 1940s that all matter in the universe was once compressed in an extremely hot and compact point that suddenly exploded, with the expanding matter forming the galaxies. (The Bible depicts that event in more unequivocal terms: *"I am the LORD, who makes all things, Who stretches out the heavens..."* -- Isa 44:24a, NKJV.)

In early 2006 NASA announced the findings of a team of U.S. and Canadian scientists indicating an exceedingly rapid inflation at the birth of the universe. "Data collected from a new satellite map of the 13.7 billion-year-old universe backed the concept of inflation, which poses that the universe expanded many trillion times its size in less than a trillionth of a second."[55]

Only photons could have traveled at that incredible speed. The Big Bang was an immense explosion of photons – light. Robert Jastrow wrote: "Now we see how the astronomical evidence leads to a biblical view of the origin of the world. The details differ, but the essential elements in the astronomical and biblical accounts of Genesis are the same: The chain of events leading to man commenced suddenly and sharply at a definite moment in time, in a flash of light and energy."[56]

Light into matter.
The rapidly dispersing light (photons) transformed into matter in accordance to Einstein's equation $(E = mc^2)$! Just how did it happen?

Schroeder points out that "as long as radiant energy *(E)* is more powerful than a specific threshold needed to make a particle of matter, that energy can change spontaneously and become a particle of nuclear matter *(m)*." ("Threshold" refers to the minimum temperature of "quark confinement," "approximately a million million times hotter than the current 3°K black of space," when quarks bond together to form protons and neutrons, converting energy into matter.)[57]

Science writer George Sim Johnston is amazed: "Twentieth-century physics... describes the beginning of the universe in virtually the same cosmological terms as Genesis. Space, time and matter came out of nothing in a... burst of light entirely hospitable to carbon-based life."[58]

Surprisingly, the Jews in olden times knew this: *"Mehitabut ha'orot, nithavu hakelim"* ("From the condensation of the lights, were the vessels brought into being") – an old Jewish saying.[59]

Lab-created matter. The title of an article in the 1997 *Encarta Yearbook* is a grabber: "Scientists Create Matter Out of Light." It tells of experimental physicists bombarding heavy atoms (made up of many protons and neutrons) with high-energy radiation in the form of X-rays. Collisions between the X-ray beam and the atoms created pairs of electron (matter) and positron (antimatter) particles.

In other trials at the Stanford Linear Accelerator Center (SLAC) in Palo Alto, California, scientists accelerated a beam of electrons at close to the speed of light, then directed a pulse of high-energy laser light at the electron beam. When a photon collided with an electron, the photon ricocheted onto other photons from the laser with such force that the ensuing energy produced an electron-positron (matter-antimatter) pair. The physicists recorded over 100 pairs in several months.

Big Bang problems.

The Big Bang Theory violates many laws of physics. For instance, the second law of thermodynamics (entropy) states that all systems proceed from an orderly state to one of disorder. In short, all things break down and deteriorate. How could the orderly universe be the result of the Big Bang -- an explosion, which is a form of destruction?

It was highly improbable for the rapidly expanding universe to have produced highly concentrated and rotating bodies, as well as solar systems and clusters of galaxies. Moreover, can fast-moving objects accompany slow-moving objects? Many quasars with very high redshifts cluster with galaxies having low redshifts. Apparently moving at different velocities, they should have dispersed a long, long time ago.

In the disorder of the Big Bang, something (or, perhaps, Someone?) introduced order so that the universe could form.

An orderly universe

Astrophysicist Paul Davies marvels that "the universe conforms to an orderly scheme and is not an arbitrary muddle of events"[60] But of course. The world was not created in a random manner. Albert Einstein once sagely said: "God does not play dice with the universe." That truth has been in Scripture for some 3,000 years: *"The lot is cast into the lap; but the whole disposing thereof is of the LORD"* (Prov 16:33).

A new field of mathematics called "Chaos Theory" is devoted to the study of random effects. "Mathematicians, however, have been unable to prove the physical existence of randomness," according to author Chuck Missler (*Cosmic Codes*, 2004). The search for randomness may prove to be a futile pursuit. The apostle Paul tells us: *"For God is not a God of disorder…"* (1 Cor 14:33-34a, NIV).

Solomon knew that heaven and earth had been intelligently created and arranged in certain ways for certain reasons. *"By wisdom the LORD laid the earth's foundations, by understanding he set the heavens in place…"* (Prov 3:19, NIV).

Size of the universe

On a clear night, a person with good eyesight may be able to count about 1,029 stars in the sky. With a pair of binoculars or a low-power telescope, he or she can raise the number to some 3,300 stars. As late as

1915, astronomers thought the Milky Way made up the entire universe. Then, in 1925, Edwin Hubble, using his new 100-inch mirror telescope, reported there were as many galaxies as there were stars in the Milky Way, our home galaxy. Current observations indicate there are at least 100 billion galaxies in observable space – each having no less than 100 billion stars – totaling some 10,000 billion billion stars in the universe.

Estimates place the diameter of the cosmos at no less than 40 billion light years; the Milky Way, 80-100 thousand light years wide and 6,000 light years thick. Earth is 25,000-30,000 light years from the galactic center and about 100,000 light years from the center of the universe.

However, University of Arizona astronomer Chris Impey says there are parts of the universe that we cannot observe, because light from extremely distant areas has not yet reached Earth. "We know that our own physical universe is substantially, maybe enormously larger, than the visible universe," he says.[61]

Cosmic shape.

Most scientists assume that after the Big Bang matter agglomerated into stars and galaxies, forming an "island universe" in a "sea" of space.

In Einstein's general theory of relativity, the universe is spherical in shape and finite, with boundaries. He had built his concept around a system by German mathematician Georg Riemann, who said that three-dimensional space curved in every direction in a constant curvature. Thus, a ray of light always curved back on itself over the same path, endlessly. Could there be anything "outside" that spherical universe?

Other cosmological models assume that the universe has no edges. D. Russell Humphreys explains: "In the big bang's mathematical model, *space itself* expanded outward with the ball of hot matter, with the matter completely filling space at all times. There would never be a large empty part. In the most favored version of the big bang, if you traveled very fast in any given direction, you would arrive back at your starting point without ever encountering a large region of empty space. That makes it impossible to define a boundary around the matter."[62] Hence, a border cannot outline the shape of the universe because, without any space around it, the universe has no outer edges.

How many dimensions?

The Bible says God can do many things with the heavens (space): "*I am the LORD that maketh all things; that stretcheth forth the heavens…*" (Isa 44:24b); "*Which alone spreadeth out the heavens*" (Job 9:8a); "*He bowed the heavens…*" (2 Sam 22:10a); "*the heavens shall be rolled together as a scroll…*" (Isa 34:4b); "*Oh that thou wouldest rend the* heavens..." (Isa 64:1a); "*I will shake the heavens...*" (Hag 2:6b); "*And as a vesture shalt thou fold them up...*" (Heb 1:12a); "*The sky was split apart like a scroll when it is rolled up...*" (Rev 6:14, NASU).

If all those things can be done to the "heavens," there must be some sort of "room" around space wherein it can be manipulated – another dimension or dimensions conjoined to space! There are several known, as well as theorized, numbers of dimensions:

3 dimensions. Greek mathematician Euclid (d. 270 B.C.), the "father of geometry," measured objects according to length, width, and height or depth. Paul named these three dimensions in an epistle: "*That Christ may dwell in your hearts by faith; that ye, being rooted and grounded in love, May be able to comprehend with all saints what is the breadth, and length, and depth, and height...*" (Eph 3:17-18a).

4 dimensions. In 1854, Georg Riemann proposed that "forces" were the result of a distortion of geometry. Almost sixty years later, Albert Einstein published his famous Theory of Relativity, making use of a four-dimensional Riemannian geometry, with "time" as the fourth physical dimension.

5 dimensions. Scientists seek a "theory of everything" (General Unified Theory) that would integrate all the forces in the cosmos. Albert Einstein tried, but failed to unify gravity and electromagnetism. About 1915 the German-Polish mathematician Theodor Kaluza and Swedish physicist Oskar Klein proposed that the two could be mathematically unified if the universe had five dimensions. As a result, many particle scientists now treat light as a vibration in the fifth dimension.

6 dimensions. Philosophers during the Middle Ages taught their students that there were no less than six visually perceptible physical dimensions: before, behind, left, right, above, and below.

10 dimensions. Thirteenth century Jewish sage Nachmanides concluded from his study of Genesis chapter 1 that the universe had ten dimensions – four are knowable, six indiscernible. Quantum scientists arrived at the same numbers after British physicist Paul Dirac developed the "string theory" in 1950. Quantum particles like quarks, electrons, and neutrinos, usually considered "points" without length, width, or height, are more easily described when viewed as "strings," which have only one dimension -- length. Their particular vibrations give different particles their appearances. But strings are said to occur outside the four dimensions of space-time, curled up within themselves, so at least six additional dimensions are needed to detect them.

Interestingly, the number "10" is the *gematria* or numerical value of the Hebrew letter *yod* ("Y"), the initial of the sacred Name of God.

26 dimensions. The addition of "supersymmetry" to the String Theory has led to even more novel "superstring" theories, which are now the frontrunners in the quest to unify the four fundamental forces of nature. Some variations of "superstring" theories require as many as 26 dimensions to explain particle properties and interactions.

Coincidentally, "26" is also the sum of the four Hebrew letters that spell the Tetragrammaton ($Y/10+H/5+W/6+H/5=26$).

First day of Creation

"And God saw the light, that it was good: and God divided the light from the darkness. And God called the light Day, and the darkness he called Night. And the evening and the morning were the first day" (Gen 1:4-5).

The phrase "first day" was translated from the Hebrew *yom echad*, which literally signifies "day one" or "one day." ("First day" is *yom hari'shon.*) The succeeding days of creation, though, have been written in Hebrew as "second day," "third day," and so forth.

The course of the first day is exactly the opposite of the way we reckon the passage of a day today, which begins in the morning. The first day began in the evening. For this reason, and in obedience to the commandments of God (Lev 23:32; Ex 12:18), Jews have always marked the start of a 24-hour day at sunset, ending at sunset of the following day.

However, the first day, if we reread the passage, ended in the morning. It did not continue through noon and finally come to a close at the start of another evening. So, the first "day" was just a 12-hour period from evening to morning, a time of darkness. It is logical that God did His first creative act in darkness, because there was darkness before light, but did He also work in darkness for the next several days of the Creation "week"? Scripture suggests that ever since He created light, God has always worked in the light (1 John 1:5-7).

Period of inactivity?

Ralph Woodrow's research clarifies things for us: "The word that is translated *'were'* in the expression *'the evening and the morning were the first day'*, the second day, the third day, etc., is *hayah* (*Strong's Concordance*, #1961). It appears many times in the Bible and has been translated a variety of ways. In the references (that follow) it is translated *'follow'* or *'followed'*: Ex 21:22 – *'yet no mischief follow'*; 21:23 – *'if any mischief follow'*; 23:2 – *'thou shalt not follow a multitude'*; Deut. 18:22 – *'if the thing follow not'*; 2 Sam. 2:10 – *'Judah followed David'*; 1 Kings 16:21 – *'the people followed Tibni.'*

"If we apply this translation in Genesis 1, we would have: '*And the evening and the morning followed the first day... and the evening and the morning followed the second day... and the evening and the morning followed the third day.*' This would give a good sense to the passage and allow it to flow in a logical sequence."[63]

It becomes clear as day, pardon the expression, that the phrase "*the evening and the morning*" does not denote a full Creation "day," but instead indicates an inactive second period following the active first half of each of God's creative "days." Thus, the creation of light made up the daylight half of the first day, followed by a second half of darkness – a time of inactivity. The next five "days" apparently followed this pattern: God worked during daylight, then stopped when evening came.

When was the first "day"?

According to some Jewish rabbis, Adam was created on the first day of Tishri -- the first month of the Jewish civil year, which begins in the evening of the first new moon of autumn in late September or early October.

Archbishop James Ussher (1581-1656) of Armagh, Ireland, regarded as the preeminent Bible chronologist to this day, drew up a timeline based on the Biblical genealogy of the first men, starting from Adam. He pinpointed the actual time of the beginning of creation to have been in autumn, in the morning of October 23, 4004 B.C.[64] The astronomer Johannes Kepler disagreed, he believed creation began in the spring.

In 1654 John Lightfoot refined Archbishop Ussher's calculation of the first day of creation to an extreme degree of precision: 9:00 A.M., October 26, 4004 B.C. in the Julian calendar, in Mesopotamia.[65]

In 2005, *Prophecy in the News* editor-publisher J.R. Church used a *Starry Night Pro* astronomy computer program to search for the first new moon in the fall of 4004 B.C., which ushered in *Rosh HaShanah*, the start of the civil new year in the Jewish calendar. He saw that the year, and perhaps creation, astronomically began on September 25, 4004 B.C., a Sunday, the first day of the week.[66]

How long is a "day"?

The Genesis account narrates that God began to create heaven and earth on the first "day." However, interpretations of the word "*day*" vary considerably. The *International Standard Bible Encyclopaedia* informs us, "the word is used in several different senses in the English Bible...

"(1) It sometimes means the time from daylight till dark...

"(2) Day also means a period of 24 hours, or the time from sunset to sunset... (...where night is put before day)...

"(3) The word 'day' is also used of <u>an indefinite period</u>, e.g 'the day' or 'day that' means in general 'that time' (see Gen 2:4; Lev 14:2); 'day of trouble' (Ps 20:1); 'day of his wrath' (Job 20:28); 'day of (the LORD,' Isa 2:12); 'day of the Lord' (1 Cor 5:5; 1 Thess 5:2; 2 Peter 3:10); 'day of salvation' (2 Cor 6:2); 'day of Jesus Christ' (Phil 1:6).

"(4) It is used figuratively also in John 9:4, where 'while it is day' means 'while I have opportunity to work, as daytime is the time for work'...

"(5) We must also bear in mind that with God time is not reckoned as with us (see Ps 90:4; 2 Peter 3:8).

"(6) The apocalyptic use of the word 'day' in Dan 12:11; Rev 2:10, etc., is difficult to define. It evidently <u>does not mean a natural day</u>...

"(7) On the meaning of 'day' <u>in the story of Creation</u> we note (a) the word 'day' is used of <u>the whole period of creation</u> (Gen 2:4); (b) these days are days of God... the <u>whole age or period</u> of salvation is called 'the day of salvation'; see above. So we believe that in harmony with Bible usage we may understand <u>the creative days as creative periods</u>..."[67] (Underscoring by the author.)

The wise men of Israel are said to have known that the six "days" of creation were not literal 24-hour days. Nachmanides, the 13th century Jewish philosopher, cryptically said that the six "days" contain "all the secrets and ages of the universe."[68]

Over the last two hundred years, differing schools of thought have polarized believers concerning the actual length of each "day" of the Creation "week," leading to the formation of separate camps: Young Earth and Old Earth Creationists, and even Framework Hypothesists.

Young Earth Creationism

Young Earth Creationists are traditionalists who believe that, based on the Biblical narrative, the universe today is no older than a little over 6,000 or 12,000 years. They advocate two different interpretations of Creation "days": Literal 24-Hour Days and Thousand-Year "Days."

Literal 24-Hour Days.

Adherents of this belief hold that each set of *"evening and morning"* in the Genesis account constituted one literal 24-hour day. Hence, if we add the six days of creation to the time that has elapsed from 4004 B.C. until the present, the universe today is just a little over 6,000 years old.

No sunset, no sunrise. Detractors argue that the *"evening and morning"* cannot possibly be literal, since they are characterized by the setting and rising of the sun, which had not yet been created on the first "day." The rotation of the earth around its axis cannot be cited, either, because Genesis 1:6-8 infers that the Earth's sphere formed only on the second "day," with the appearance of the firmament or vault of the sky. Besides, the earth has not always rotated around its axis in 24 hours. In conformity with the laws of nature, after gravitational attraction caused the gases and dust that would form the Earth to agglomerate, the planetesimals rotated very slowly at first, before gradually gaining momentum as the new planet solidified.

Further, if those were literal 24-hour days, why were no parts of the day ever mentioned when several entities were created in succession – say, grass in the morning, herbs at noon, trees in the afternoon?

Thousand-Year "Days."

A second Young Earth belief holds that each creation "day" is one millennium, or a period of 1,000 years, based on two passages in the Bible: (1) *"For a thousand years in thy sight are but as yesterday when it is past, and as a watch in the night"* (Ps 90:4); and (2) *"But, beloved, be not ignorant of this one thing, that one day is with the Lord as a thousand years, and a thousand years as one day"* (2 Pet 3:8).

If we add the 6,000 years of the first six "days" to the 6,000 years that have gone by since the creation of Adam in 4004 B.C., the universe would be about 12,000 years old today, as illustrated below:

Thousand-Year "Days" Chronology
(1 Creation "Day" = 1,000 Years)

Day	Years ago	Period (approx.)/Entity(ies) created
1	12,000-11,000	10,000-9000 B.C.; light
2	11,000-10,000	9000-8000 B.C.; firmament, waters above/below
3	10,000-9,000	8000-7000 B.C.; grass, herbs, trees
4	9,000-8,000	7000-6000 B.C.; sun, moon, stars
5	8,000-7,000	6000-5000 B.C.; sea creatures, flying creatures
6	7,000-6,000	5000-4000 B.C.; land animals, creeping things, man
7	6,000-5,000	4000-3000 B.C. (God's day of rest)
8	5,000-4,000	3000-2000 B.C.
9	4,000-3,000	2000-1000 B.C.
10	3,000-2,000	1000-1 B.C.
11	2,000-1,000	1-1000 A.D.
12	1,000-recent	1000-2000 A.D.
	Total: 12,000	
13	Present-	2000-3000 A.D. (man's Millennium rest)
14		3000-4000 A.D. (God's next day of rest)

NOTE: God created Adam in 4004 B.C., part of Day 6 (Ussher's Chronology).

Out-of-place Sabbath. The Thousand-Year "Days" Chronology entails at least one major difficulty: God's Sabbath rest on the seventh "day" (the seventh 1,000 years after the first six "days" or 6,000 years). During that supposed period of rest, God actively interacted with Cain and Abel, Enoch, and others. God's seventh-day Sabbath thus appears out-of-place in the Thousand-Year "Days" timeline. Further, God's next Sabbath rest would not coincide with man's coming Millennial rest (about 2000-3000 A.D.). God's rest would be in the next 1,000-year period yet (around 3000-4000 A.D.). This means God would not have any active dealings with man during that 1,000-year period, contrary to Biblical prophecy.

Light from the stars. If the Earth is only 6,000–12,000 years old, we cannot see light from stars hundreds of thousands or millions of light-years away. Although light is the fastest thing in the universe, it covers less than 6 trillion miles (10 trillion km.) in one year (1 light-year). Light from a star that is, say, one million light-years away will become visible on Earth only after one million years. In 1987, astronomers spotted a supernova (exploding star, SN 1987A) about 170,000 light-years away. That means the explosion took place 170,000 years ago, something they could not have seen if the Earth is just 6,000-12,000 years old.

"Time dilation." In 1994, nuclear physicist D. Russell Humphreys, a Young Earth Creationist, published his book *Starlight and Time* to prove otherwise. He built his case around "an effect in general relativity called gravitational time dilation..." He explains: "Experiment and Einstein's theory agree that time and all physical processes run more slowly in areas which are lower in a gravitational field than in areas which are higher... the expanding universe was at a critical size (about fifty times smaller than it is now)... during the fourth day of Creation Week. While one ordinary day was elapsing on earth, billions of years worth of physical processes were taking place in distant parts of the universe." Humphreys postulates that time elapsed very rapidly at the outer edges, but was virtually at a standstill at and near the center.[69] "This allows starlight from even the most distant star to arrive during or soon after the fourth day, the same day God created all the stars."[70]

Bottom line: Relativity allows us to choose by which clock to tell the age of the universe, as well as the time events occurred in it. Humphreys chose the one that tells time in terms of the "earth's frame of reference, not some other frame." He concludes that "the universe is young as measured by clocks on earth."[71]

One problem with the Humphreys scenario is its having two different locales. The six 24-hour "days" transpired on Earth, while the billions of years elapsed in the outermost reaches of the universe. The *Starlight and Time* hypothesis falls short of explaining the apparent old age of fossils and the Earth's geological rock layers.

Billions of years?

Some 300 years ago, the new science of geology began shaking the foundations of Young Earth Creationism by stating that the Earth is much older than 6,000 years, or even 12,000 years. Two landmark books were at the frontline: *A New Theory of the Earth* (1696) by William Whiston and *Theory of the Earth* (1785) by James Hutton, called the father of modern geology. By the end of the 1800s, estimates of the age of the Earth were in hundreds of millions of years.[72]

Catastrophism vs. Uniformitarianism.

Until the 19th century, most geologists explained the origins of rock layers and other geological formations by saying that the earth had gone through many sudden catastrophes -- the most recent being the Biblical Flood. The doctrine was called "catastrophism." In line with this view, the majority of fossilized plants and animals being unearthed today were buried during the Deluge about 4,350 years ago.

In 1830-1833, Scottish lawyer-turned-geologist Charles Lyell formed the idea of "uniformitarianism," explained in his *Principles of Geology*. Based on the concepts he laid out, the Earth's surface is constantly changing, and geological features are the result of natural forces working slowly, but uniformly, over vast ages. The idea has since become the cornerstone of the modern science of geology.

"Stones and bones."

By the 20th century, cosmologists theorized, based on the estimated age of the oldest rocks, that the Earth and its moon came from the same materials that formed the solar system around 4.6 billion years ago.

In addition, paleontologists have unearthed numerous petrified plants and animals estimated to be millions and even billions of years old. Some of the most spectacular bones are those of dinosaurs, which are thought to have dominated the planet for some 120 million years before becoming extinct approximately 65 million years ago.

And then there are the manlike remains in the fossil collection. If God created the perfect man Adam on the sixth "day," just 6,000-7,000 years ago, did He create the evidently inferior subhumans just a few hours, or even a few hundred years, earlier on the same "day"?

Sheep and dinosaurs. The first land animal specifically mentioned in the Bible is the sheep: *"And Abel was a keeper of sheep..."* (Gen 4:2b). If God created all land animals on the same "day" 6,000-7,000 years ago, sheep and dinosaurs would have lived alongside each other. But while there are still millions of sheep today, dinosaurs (which should have devoured the sheep) have disappeared long ago. And, because they have proven to be the more durable species, more sheep than dinosaurs should be in the fossil record. But no sheep fossil has been reported vis-à-vis numerous dinosaur remains.

Besides, God gave all animals plants for food (Gen 1:30), allowing flesh-eating only after the Flood (Gen 9:3). When did some reptiles develop sharp teeth, claws, and other predatory features to become carnivorous dinosaurs? Were some 1½ thousand years from Creation enough for all those physical changes to develop before the dinosaurs supposedly became extinct in the Flood? In contrast, there is no record of the sheep ever having changed in the last 6,000 years. It looks clear the dinosaurs appeared long before the sheep.

Old Earth Creationism

Scientific estimates pointing to an old Earth that was billions of years old divided Bible-believers. Many worried 19th century churchmen felt the pressing need to harmonize the Biblical six-day creation story and the scientifically reckoned ancient age of the Earth.

Old Earth Creationism emerged from the confusion. Its advocates hold that God created the universe over immense ages spanning billions of years. By 1852, American commentator William Hayden estimated that about 50% of all Christians, to accept an old Earth without giving up their faith in the Bible, had adopted either one of two teachings: (1) the "Gap Theory"; and (2) the "Day-Age Theory."[73]

The "Gap Theory."

"Gappists" claim there is a "gap" or time interval between the first two sentences of the Bible: *"1 In the beginning God created the heaven and the earth"* and *"2 And the earth was without form, and void…"* (Gen 1:1-2a). Their theory hinges upon one simple word in verse 2, *"was,"* the past tense of the verb "to be" (Hebrew *hayah*). They argue that *"hayah"* can also be translated "became." Thus, verse 2 should read, *"And the earth became without form, and void…"* In short, the earth was created in verse 1, but after an untold period was found in a ruined state in verse 2. The unspecified span of time between verses 1 and 2 are taken to be the geological ages arrived at by scientists. God then recreated the earth in the next verses.

The recent popularity of the Gap Theory is credited to 19th century Scotsman Thomas Chalmers, who wrote about it in 1814. The concept, though, has been around as early as the 2nd century A.D. when the

Hebrew scribes who composed the *Onkelos Targum* translated Genesis 1:2 as *"and the earth was laid waste."*[74] Church theologian Origen (186-254) wrote in his commentary *De Principiis* that in Genesis 1:2 the original earth had been "cast downwards."[75] Medieval scholars, such as Dionysius Peavius and Pererius, also seriously considered a time gap between Genesis 1:1 and 1:2."[76] *The New Schaff-Herzog Encyclopedia of Religious Knowledge* states that "the Dutch scholar Simon Episcopius (1583-1643) taught that the earth had originally been created before the six days of creation described in Genesis. This was roughly 200 years before geology discovered evidence for the ancient origin of earth."[77] In 1876, George Pember further publicized the theory in his book, *Earth's Earliest Ages*.

Cyrus Scofield (1843-1921), in his Scofield Reference Bible, said the verb "*was*" in Genesis 1:2 can also be written as "became." The 1973-79 New International Version (NIV) had a note in the margin saying, *"Now the earth was* (or possibly *became*) *formless and empty..."* The inclusion of a hint supporting the Gap Theory in Bibles used by millions all over the world facilitated the widespread acceptance of the theory.

Many scenarios. The Gap scenario has many versions. For lack of any proof text in the Bible, anyone can come up with his or her own story of what happened. The Gappists have conjured many fantastic tableaux. The freewheeling models present a world that pre-existed in the distant, dateless past before verse 2, inhabited by manlike, but soul-less beings whose fossils are being unearthed today. One elaborate narrative tells of a technologically advanced civilization of angels and supermen who became evil under the influence of Satan. After many ages, God destroyed their world in a cataclysm called "Lucifer's Flood." The destruction is said to have produced the earth's geological strata and all the plant and animal fossils.

No Biblical basis. Hebrew expert Charles Taylor, in an article entitled "The First 100 Words," explains that the word "*was*" has been translated from the Hebrew verb form *haythah*. According to the rules of Hebrew grammar, the word cannot be correctly rendered "*became*" as in the Gap version. For *haythah* to be translated as "became" it must be preceded by a Hebrew preposition meaning "to."[78]

Further, *The Complete Word Study: Old Testament, KJV* says that the Hebrew construction of "verse two is disjunctive and is describing the result of the creation described in verse one. It is not describing the result of any judgment."[79]

The Gap Theory, based on a single presumed word ("became"), requires God to recreate everything from light to stars to man. If a prior and original Creation truly took place, does not such a grand act of the

Creator deserve a richly detailed account? Evidently, all the bizarre scenarios engendered by the Gap Theory have no Biblical basis.

"Day-Age" Theory.

In 1823, Anglican theologian George Stanley Faber introduced the Day-Age Theory, which proposed that, while the creation account in the Bible is true, the "days" were mere figures of speech and not ordinary 24-hour days – because the Hebrew word for "day" (*yom*) can be interpreted to mean an "age" or a long stretch of time. As the theory's name suggests, each "day" was an "age."

Day-Agers claim that the sequence of events during the six Biblical "days" of Creation generally match the cosmic and terrestrial stages that scientists today theorize occurred during the birth and early development of the universe. The Genesis account, they contend, is a simplified summary of the discoveries of modern science, written in advance for an ancient, pre-scientific audience.

No death before sin? Some of the most telling evidences cited for an old Earth are the fossilized plants and animals estimated to be tens, hundreds of thousands, and even millions of years old. Young Earthers reject the age estimates for fossils on the belief that death was unknown before Adam sinned, based on Paul's epistles: *"Wherefore, as by one man sin entered into the world, and death by sin; and so death passed upon all men, for that all have sinned"* (Rom 5:12). He even stressed: *"For the wages of sin is death..."* (Rom 6:23a). Adam's disobedience was the sin that brought death into the world. Since then, sinners must pay for their sins with their lives. Even plants and animals, which cannot sin, supposedly started dying only after sin came in about 6,000 years ago. Hence, no fossils are supposed to be older than 6,000 years.

Two kinds of death. Let us examine the context of Romans 5:12 in a following verse: *"Nevertheless, death reigned from the time of Adam to the time of Moses, even over those who did not sin by breaking a command, as did Adam..."* (Rom 5:14a, NIV). If *"death reigned from the time of Adam to the time of Moses"* death should have ceased when Moses came! Yet, men continued to die even after Moses, who himself died. What "death" was Paul talking about?

Christ clarifies things for us: *"And fear not them which kill the body, but are not able to kill the soul: but rather fear him which is able to destroy both soul and body in hell"* (Matt 10:28). So, men can die two kinds of death. Paul was talking about spiritual death, not physical death! Plants and animals, which have no spirits and cannot sin, are exempt from spiritual death. Author Hugh Ross (*The Fingerprint of God,*

1989) notes that by the word "death" Paul meant human spiritual death; not biological death of either of humans or animals.[80]

A fact of life. God gave Adam and the animals *"every herb bearing seed"* and *"fruit of a tree yielding seed"* (Gen 1:29-30) for food. What are the implications? When man and animals ate herbs, the plants they ate died. And why did God tell man and the animals to eat in the first place? Was not the reason for them to become strong and healthy, and live long? Without eating they would, according to the laws of nature God Himself had established, grow weak, become sickly, and eventually die. Otherwise, God would not have told them to eat at all. Plants also have to "eat" moisture and nutrients from the soil, and light from the sun, or they, too, would waste away, wither, and die.

Furthermore, why did God plant the tree of life in Eden? After Adam sinned, he had to be cast out of the Garden, *"lest he put forth his hand, and take also of the tree of life, and eat, and live for ever"* (Gen 3:22). This reveals Adam had not been created immortal; he would have to eat from the tree of life to avoid dying. Death appears to have been a fact of life from the very beginning -- even in Paradise.

Natural cycle. Birth and death, growth and decay, creation and destruction seem to be the natural rhythmic cycle of the universe. Matter and antimatter appear and mutually annihilate. Stars are born and die. Oxford scholar Arthur Peacocke wrote: "Biological death was present on the earth long before human beings arrived. It is the prerequisite of our coming into existence through the creative processes of biology which God himself has installed in the world... God had already made biological death the means of his creating new forms of life. This has to be accepted, difficult though it may be for some theologies."[81]

The wisdom of the Holy Scriptures declares: *"To every thing there is a season, and a time to every purpose under the heaven: A time to be born, and a time to die..."* (Eccl 3:1-2a).

Non-salvation issue

Belief in either a Young Earth or an Old Earth is a non-salvation issue. Charles Hodge (1779-1878), Presbyterian theologian at Princeton Seminary, taught that one's belief in the age of the earth was of no consequence to spiritual salvation. He first embraced the Gap Theory, then shifted to the Day-Age doctrine towards the end of his life.[82] Therefore, you may believe that the universe has been created in just six 24-hour days, or 6,000 years, or over millions and billions of years, and still be saved spiritually. Whatever timeline we believe in, at the end of the day, no pun intended, we are saved if we *"keep the commandments of God, and have the testimony of Jesus Christ"* (Rev 12:17; cf. 14:12).

The two camps, and their sub-groups, should not be regarded as adversaries. They are actually on the same side – defending the faith in one God who created heaven and earth.

Same timeline from Adam. Actually, the Young Earthers and Old Earthers, particularly Day-Agers, hold the same Biblical chronology for mankind. Both groups generally believe that God created Adam 6,000 years ago, as calculated from the life spans of his descendants. The dispute lies in the length of time involved in the other Creation events before Adam. It just so happened that Archbishop Ussher and the other Bible chronologists thought the "days" were 24-hour periods.

Age of the world

The French scientist Comte de Buffon theorized in his 1779 book *Epochs of Nature* that the Earth was once a hot molten ball that took around 75,000 years to cool down (the figure was 3 million years in his unpublished manuscript).[83] In 1899. Lord Kelvin calculated the age of the earth, based on the cooling rate of a molten sphere, at 20 to 40 million years (revised from his 1862 computation of 100 million years). With the advent of radiometric dating, in 1913 Arthur Holmes made an estimate of 1.6 billion years in his book *The Age of the Earth*. In 1956, Claire Patterson published her calculations for a 4.5-billion-year age of the earth, extremely close to the 4.6 billion years widely acknowledged in the scientific community today.[84]

Cosmological calculations. When Edwin Hubble discovered in the mid-1920s that the universe was expanding, he suggested that finding out how fast the universe was expanding and how large it was would reveal its age.

The density of the mass or quantity of matter the cosmos contains determines how the gravitational force slows down the expansion rate, which in turn depends on the age and density of the universe. Cosmologists measure the cosmic expansion rate by establishing the relationship between the distance of an object from Earth and the rate at which it is moving away, revealed by redshift (stretched wavelengths of light). They then assess the density of the universe to calculate its age.[85]

14-16 billion years?

Scientists have variously placed the age of the universe at between 10 to 20 billion years. The wide range is the result of the uncertain expansion rate of the universe and the age of the oldest stars. Both depend on the extrapolation of available data, which are inadequate. Astronomers use the Hubble constant, a measure of the expansion rate of the universe, whose value scientists have not agreed on.[86]

The NASA has nonetheless officially placed the age of the universe at 16 billion years, with a potential error of plus or minus 15%. Thus, the universe could be at least 13.5 billion years old, or 18.5 billion years old at the most. Some scientists use a figure of 12-18 billion years, but the most common estimate is 14-16 billion years.[87]

Big Bang "echo." In the 1940s George Gamow and his students Ralph Alpher and Robert Herman formed a theory that, since elements heavier than hydrogen can be formed only at a high temperature, the universe must have been supremely hot at its birth.[88] Their calculations showed temperatures of billions of degrees around one second after the Big Bang. After a few hundred thousand years of expansion, the radiant heat would have gone down to just thousands of degrees.[89]

They concluded that the Big Bang produced a blackbody or thermal radiation and predicted that a trace or "echo" left by the blast still exists, pervading the universe. In 1965 American physicists Arno Penzias and Robert Wilson detected by radio telescopes a uniform background of microwave radiation in space, which has since been called "cosmic microwave background radiation" (CMBR). Coming from all directions, the CMBR's temperature is almost the same everywhere, approximately 2.7° Celsius above absolute zero (-459.67 °F, or -273.15 °C) -- very close to what Gamow and his students had calculated.[90]

15 billion years?

According to the *World Book*: "Observations of supernovae and the CMB radiation suggest that the present age of the universe is about 13.7 billion years. This estimate agrees with studies of the ages of stars in groups called globular star clusters, which contain the oldest stars found in the Milky Way."[91]

A news report in early 2006 stated: "The latest data from NASA's Wilkinson Microwave Anisotropy Probe is based on three years of continuous observations of the cosmic microwave background (CMB), the afterglow light produced when the universe was less than a million years old."[92] If the CMBR appeared sometime during the first million years of the Big Bang, the universe may be somewhat older than 13.7 billion years. The *Encyclopedia Britannica* notes: "The discovery of the 2.7 K background radiation... is regarded as convincing evidence that the universe originated approximately 15 billion years ago..."[93]

The shape of time

In a novel concept, M.I.T. physicist and author Gerald Schroeder (*Genesis and the Big Bang, The Science of God, God According to God,* etc.) equates the six "days" of Creation to some 15 billion years.

The "cosmic clock."

Schroeder based his calculations on the CMBR, which he calls the "clock" of the cosmos. He explains that about "0.00001 seconds after the big bang... (t)he universe was approximately a million million times smaller and hotter than it is today... the temperature... is not a value extrapolated or estimated from conditions in the distant past or far out in space. It is measured right here on Earth in the most advanced physics laboratories and corresponds to a temperature approximately a million million times hotter than the current 3°K black of space. That radiant energy had a frequency a million million times greater than the radiation of today's cosmic background radiation."[94] This translates to a ratio of 1,000,000,000,000 to 1 in the perception of earth time vis-à-vis cosmic time. Thus, at the Big Bang, one second in cosmic time was equivalent to about one trillion seconds in Earth time.

However, he points out that as the universe rapidly expanded and cooled, cosmic time would have slowed down. Frequency, wavelength, and temperature are all directly related: when temperature goes down, so too the frequency, and wavelength becomes longer (and vice-versa). So, as the radiant energy cooled, its wavelengths were stretched and its frequency became lower – as measured today in light coming from the Sun. "Waves of sunlight reaching Earth are stretched longer 2.12 parts in a million relative to similar light waves generated on Earth. This stretching of the light waves means that the rate at which they reach us is lowered by 2.12 parts per million. This lowering of the light wave frequency is the measure of the slowing of time. For every million Earth seconds, the Sun's clock would 'lose' 2.12 seconds relative to our clocks here on Earth. The 2.12 parts per million equals 67 seconds per year, exactly the amount predicted by the laws of relativity."[95]

The CMBR reveals how much cosmic time has slowed down since the Big Bang. "The radiation... has been stretched a million million fold... That stretching of the light waves has slowed the frequency of the cosmic clock – expanded the perceived time between ticks of that clock – by a million million."[96] In simple terms, time passed at a much slower rate at the edges of the expansion compared to time on Earth. Whereas an imaginary clock at the edge of the cosmos would have shown only days, a clock on earth would have already recorded billions of years. (It is the exact opposite of Humphreys's *Starlight and Time* hypothesis.)

Exponential regression.

The redshift observed in galaxies suggests an expansion factor of 10^{12} or 1,000,000,000,000 (1 trillion).[97] As the universe expanded, the waves of radiant energy stretched in the same ratio as the expansion.[98]

"Each doubling in size 'slowed' the cosmic clock by a factor of 2."[99] In the mathematical equations Schroeder presented, each succeeding Creation "day" was equivalent to just a half-period.[100] "Each successive Genesis day exponentially represents fewer years as perceived from our earthly vantage…"[101] In other words, each "day" following Day One was only one-half the length of the "day" immediately preceding it.

Schroeder noted that the "opening chapter of Genesis acts like the zoom lens of a camera. Day by day it focuses with increasing detail on less and less time and space. The first day of Genesis encompasses the entire universe. By the third day, only earth is discussed. After day six, only that line of humanity leading to the patriarch Abraham… This narrowing of perspective… each successive day presents in greater detail a smaller scope of time and space…"[102]

In Schroeder's calculations, Day One was 8 billion years long, Day Two 4 billion years, Day Three 2 billion years, Day Four 1 billion years, Day Five ½ billion years, Day Six ¼ billion years – for a total of 15.75 billion years – *i.e.*, the age of the universe.[103] This closely matches a 16-billion-year age estimate for the oldest stars. Schroeder suggests a plus or minus 20% margin of error.[104]

Spiral structure.

We usually think of time as a straight line, proceeding from the past through the present to the future. However, it looks like the Designer of the universe had drawn up a Creation scheme of time that is much more elegant than just a simple straight line.

The exponentially regressing scenarios of Creation, diminishing day after day, seem to display a structural design. Schroeder notes: "Genesis has chosen a base that occurs throughout the universe, a base known in mathematics as the natural log *e*."[105] He is referring to a figure that occurs more often in nature than any other shape: the spiral.[106] We see it from the macrocosm to the microcosm -- in the shape of galaxies, hurricanes and tornados, whirlpools, breaking waves, animal horns, snail shells, seahorses' tails, mammalian ears, human cochleae, flower seed-heads, emerging fern leaves, DNA molecules. The spiral, Schroeder hypothesizes, was the structure of time at the Creation.

In a simplified version of Schroeder's CMBR-based timeline, we can see an intriguing "day"-by-"day" correspondence between the Biblical account of creation and the scientific version of the birth of the universe.[107] (Schroeder notes that if corrections are made based on the recently observed increase in the rate of expansion of the universe, the start of Day One would be approximately 15 billion years ago.)[108]

Schroeder's CMBR-Based Timeline
(6 "Days" of Creation = 15.75 Billion Years)

Day	Start b.p.*	Duration	End b.p.	Bible	Science
1	15¾billion	8 billion	7¾billion	Light	Big Bang, light, electrons, atoms, galaxies
2	7 ¾ billion	4 billion	3¾billion	Firmament	Milky Way, Sun
3	3 ¾ billion	2 billion	1¾billion	Oceans, dry land, plants	Earth cooled, bodies of water, bacteria, algae
4	1 ¾ billion	1 billion	¾ billion	Sun, moon, stars	Clear, oxygen-rich atmosphere
5	¾ billion	½billion	¼ billion	Aquatic animals, reptiles, winged animals	Multi-cellular, aquatic animals, winged insects
6	¼ billion	¼ billion	ca. 6,000	Land animals, mammals, humankind	90% extinction, hominids, humans
		15¾billion			

*before present

Science-Scripture match-up.

In Schroeder's timeline, the scientific data basically parallel the day-by-day Genesis account from Day One to Day Four; but the match-up is broken on Day Five, when reptiles and insects appeared. His Day Five supposedly began 750 million years ago and ended 250 million years ago. It agrees with the fossil record, which places the age of amphibians at 417 million years, insects 350 million years, and reptiles 323 million years; but it does not conform with the Bible, which says God created "creeping things" (amphibians, reptiles, insects) on Day Six.

Moreover, God's "seventh-day" Sabbath rest does not form part of the timeline after Day Six, which he says ended about 6,000 years ago. Did the "days" stop their exponentially regressing rate? How long was God's Sabbath? Did it suddenly shorten to a 24-hour day?

Framework Hypothesis.

A third theory, unconnected to either Young Earth Creationism or Old Earth Creationism, does not involve any timeline of "days" at all. Known as the Framework Hypothesis (also "framework interpretation" or "literary framework view"), it proposes that the six "days" of creation in Genesis are neither literal nor figurative "days," but literary or symbolically artistic descriptions of the origin of the universe.

The idea first appeared in the writings of the early Church father Augustine (354-430). It has gained acceptance among many theistic evolutionists and some progressive creationists through the works of modern scholars like Meredith Kline, Henri Blocher, Bruce Waltke, and Gordon Wenham, who contend that the Genesis account is so full of repetitive formulas and figurative language that the wording of the text cannot be taken literally.[109]

For instance, they say the first and fourth "days" of creation closely resemble each other, like two descriptions of just one event. On the first day God "*divided the light from the darkness*" and "*called the light day and the darkness... night.*" This is repeated on the fourth "day" when God created two great lights "*to divide the light from the darkness*" and "*the day from the night.*" The Genesis writer is said to have used the literary device of parallelism. The only difference is the introduction of "*two great lights... to rule*" over the realm or dominion of light on the fourth "day." The same realm-ruler relationship pattern recurs between the second and fifth "days," and the third and sixth "days."

Thus, Framework theologians divide the six "days" of Creation into two triads. The first three "days" depict the creation of the first triad of realms: (1) darkness and light, night and day; (2) the firmament, waters under and above; and (3) dry land, grass, herbs, trees. The next three "days" portray the creation of the second triad of rulers: (4) the sun, moon, and stars to rule the day and the night; (5) living creatures in the waters and fowl that fly in the firmament; and (6) beasts of the earth, cattle, creeping things, and man on dry land.

Hence, the six "days" of Creation advanced according to topics, instead of chronological sequence, as illustrated in the table below:

Framework Hypothesis
(Creation "days" not literal; but figurative literary devices)

Day	First Triad: "<u>Realms</u>"	Second Triad: "<u>Rulers</u>"	Day
1	Darkness and light, night and day	Sun, moon, and stars – to rule the day and the night	4
2	The firmament, waters under and above	Creatures in the waters, fowl that fly in the firmament	5
3	Waters and dry land; grass, herbs, trees	Beasts of the earth, cattle, creeping things, man	6

4

Primordial Planet Puzzles

*hese are the generations of the heavens and
of the earth when they were created, in the day that
the LORD God made the earth and the heavens"*

-- Genesis 2:4.

The scenarios of Creation events appeared smaller and smaller in
scope with each new "day." Time seems to have advanced on a
similarly decreasing scale during Creation "week." It has been likened to
a spiral, a frequently occurring figure in nature, to demonstrate the
diminishing rate. An exponential spiral can be graphically derived from
and illustrated in a golden rectangle.

The golden rectangle

The "golden rectangle" has intrigued artists, philosophers, and
mathematicians since ancient times with its special beauty, which, for
inexplicable reasons, is tantalizingly pleasing to the eye. The longer side
of a golden rectangle is to the shorter side as the sum of the two short
sides is to the longer side. The figure has a 1-to-0.618 length-to-width
ratio, known as the "golden ratio," also called "divine proportion,"
"golden section," "magic ratio," "golden mean," "Fibonacci series," and
"Phi," after the classical Greek sculptor Phidias, who made use of it. In
his work *Timaeus,* Plato described the Phi as the most binding of all
mathematical relations, calling it the key to the physics of the cosmos.

The golden ratio has served as the magical framework of many great masterpieces. Whether by design or intuition, artists Leonardo da Vinci, Michelangelo, Raphael became famous for it. Great composers like Bach, Mozart, Beethoven used it to divide musical time.[1] The golden rectangle can be seen in many ancient and modern structures: the Parthenon, the Great Pyramid, the United Nations Building. It is also in similarly proportioned credit cards, playing cards, photograph prints, postcards, business cards, light switch plates, PC monitors, iPods. But the most holy object in the form of a golden rectangle is the Biblical Ark of the Covenant, being 2.5 cubits wide and 1.5 cubits high (Ex 25:10).

To form a golden spiral: Mark off a perfect square on one side of a golden rectangle, a smaller golden rectangle will then remain. Mark out another square from the left-over rectangle, and a still smaller golden rectangle will be left, *ad infinitum*. In the Creation narrative, the first and biggest square represents Day One; the second, smaller square Day Two; the next square Day Three, and so on.

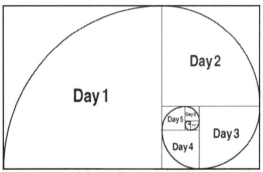

A golden spiral formed within a golden rectangle, analogous to the structure of time during Creation, with each "day" exponentially diminishing in scope.

A more exact chronology?

We have seen that Schroeder's CMBR-based timeline of 15.75 billion years, though evidently a stroke of genius, does not perfectly correspond to the six "days" of Creation. Would other estimates result in a more exact chronology? What about the oft-mentioned 15-billion-years? Surprisingly, a little pencil-pushing is quickly rewarded.

As it turned out, 15 billion years produce a near-perfect match with the six "days" of Creation, God's seventh-day rest, the ensuing 6,000 years from Adam, and the prophesied seventh Millennium! The order of the diminishing day-ages in the successively contracting squares of a golden rectangle correctly correspond to the sequence of events that scientists theorize took place in the young universe – precisely agreeing with Scripture, cosmology, paleontology and, yes, even prophecy.

The shorter 15-billion-year timeline even has an extra factor in its favor. The *gematria* of the number 15 spells out the short form of the Name of God [YH = 10+5). It is assuring to think that God has both initiated and initialed His creation. Below is that timeline:

Diminishing Day-Ages Chronology*
(7-"Day" Creation "Week" until 3000 A.D. = 15 Billion Years)

Day-Age	Length in Yrs.	Start, Yrs. Ago	End, Yrs. Ago
1	7,500,000,000	15,000,000,000	7,500,000,000
2	3,750,000,000	7,500,000,000	3,750,000,000
3	1,875,000,000	3,750,000,000	1,875,000,000
4	937,500,000	1,875,000,000	937,500,000
5	468,750,000	937,500,000	468,750,000
6**	468,735,694	468,750,000	13,306
7	7,153	13,306	6,153
Sub-total	14,999,992,847		
4000 B.C.-3000 A.D.	7,153	6,000	on-going
Total:	15,000,000,000		

*Figures are approximate. **Day 6 made up of several successive exponentially regressing segments also (explained in succeeding sections).

Using the above "Diminishing Day-Ages" figures, let us make a side-by-side comparison with the other interpretations of the six "days" of Creation by Young Earth Creationists ("Literal 24-Hour Days" and "Thousand-Year Days").

Day 1: Light, night and day
"And God said, Let there be light: and there was light. And God saw the light, that it was good: and God divided the light from the darkness. And God called the light Day, and the darkness he called Night. And the evening and the morning were the first day" (Gen 1:3-5).

Interpretations of Day 1:
- Literal 24-Hour Days: 5 days before man was created circa 6,000 years ago
- Thousand-Year Days: circa 12,000-11,000 years ago
- Diminishing Day-Ages: circa 15,000,000,000-7,500,000,000 years ago (Duration: approximately 7,500,000,000 years)

As interpreted by Young Earth Creationists, light was created as recently as 6,000 years ago (in 4004 B.C.) or sometime between 12,000-11,000 years ago.

On the other hand, in the Diminishing Day-Ages timeline, God created light between 15 billion to 7.5 billion years ago (bya). The Day-Ages estimate accommodates scientific estimates that the Big Bang took place about 13.7 to 15 billion years ago. (Particles that survived from quantum fluctuations could have accumulated prior to the explosion.)

The divine word.

The Creator's first words were probably *"Yehi 'or!"* ("Let there be light!"). A psalmist memorialized the event around 3,000 years ago: *"The entrance of thy words giveth light"* (Ps 119:130). God sounded the words -- and light, from which the cosmos would form, came into being.

Some people are surprised to learn that the "Word" of God is a Person: *"In the beginning was the Word, and the Word was with God, and the Word was God. The same was in the beginning with God. All things were made by him; and without him was not any thing made that was made"* (John 1:1-3). The Word is the Son of God, who created heaven and earth in behalf of Father God – the *Ein Sof* or "Infinite Nothingness," who is outside the space-time domain.

The power of sound.

The Jewish sages knew that sound possesses great power. It can lull a baby to sleep, or incite mobs to violence. The "Word" created the universe by sound: *"By the word of the LORD were the heavens made; and all the host of them by the breath of his mouth"* (Ps 33:6).

Rabbi Eleazar ben Judah (1165-1230) of Worms, Germany, taught that the creation of the universe had been wrought with the 22 letters of the Hebrew alphabet.[2] Other teachings involve less. According to the *Sefer Yetzirah*: "The manipulation of the sacred letters forming the divine names (of God) was the means used to create the world."[3] Only three letters make up the sacred Names of God. These are:

Hey. The sound of *hey* (ה/"H") is produced by simply exhaling, almost effortlessly, with no movement of the lips or tongue. In the book *The Wisdom in the Hebrew Alphabet*, Rabbi Michael Munk says, "This effortless enunciation symbolizes the effortless creation of the world."[4]

Symbolizing "wind," *hey* is an abbreviation for *Ruach* ("breath" or "spirit") – the Spirit of God.[5] In the esoteric technique of altering the spaces between Hebrew letters, in the verse *"These are the generations of the heavens and of the earth when they were created..."* (Gen 2:4a), the phrase *"when they were created"* is *bahibaram* in Hebrew. If the compound word is divided into two as *bahi baram*, it can be translated as: "With (the letter) *hey* (He) created them."[6] *Hey* has a value of "5," the number of "grace" or "favor."

Yod. With the "Y" sound, *yod* (י) is actually the first letter of God's Sacred Names. Every Hebrew letter is a symbol for something, and *yod*, signifies a "hand." It alludes to the unseen "hand" of God when He created heaven and earth. Its value of "10" stands for "law." At the Creation, it probably meant the laws of nature the Creator established.

Waw. The letter *waw* (ו), sounded as "W" or "V," represents a hook, peg, or nail, and has a numerical value of "6." Rabbi Munk explains the use of *waw* in the Creation: "The physical world was completed in six days and a complete self-contained object consists of six dimensions: above and below, right and left, before and behind."[7]

During the Middle Ages, tales spread about wise men who could bring a dummy or mannequin to life (*golem*) by combining letters to form a sacred word or one of the Names of God.[8]

Day 2: Firmament, waters under and above

"And God said, Let there be a firmament in the midst of the waters, and let it divide the waters from the waters. And God made the firmament, and divided the waters which were under the firmament from the waters which were above the firmament: and it was so. And God called the firmament Heaven. And the evening and the morning were the second day" (Gen 1:6-8).

Interpretations of Day 2:
- Literal 24-Hour Days: 4 days before man was created circa 6,000 years ago
- Thousand-Year Days: circa 11,000-10,000 years ago
- Diminishing Day-Ages: circa 7,500,000,000-3,750,000,000 years ago (Duration: approximately 3,750,000,000 years)

A firmament, the arch or vault of the sky, can be seen only from the surface of a planet. That means planet Earth, our home world's sphere, formed on the second "day" of Creation. Astronomer Hugh Ross says: "From what I understood to be the stated viewpoint of an observer on Earth's surface, both the order and the description of creation events perfectly matched the established record of nature."[9]

Young Earth Creationists say the "firmament" appeared just 5,000 or 11,000 to 10,000 years ago.

In the Diminishing Day-Ages timeline, Earth took shape sometime between 7.5 billion to 3.750 billion years ago. Squarely fitting into this time span is the scientific estimate that, based on the age of the oldest rocks, the Earth was formed approximately 4.6 billion years ago.[10]

A nebulous hypothesis?

The *Encarta Encyclopedia* tells us that Earth and the "planets reached their present sizes and arrangement probably within 10 million to 50 million years after the Sun's ignition."[11]

The Nebular Hypothesis, which posits that solar systems formed from nebulae, swirling clouds of gases and dust in space, has raised many questions that remain unanswered. For instance, if all the planets had formed from one spinning disk, why are the inner planets much smaller than the outer ones? It should be the other way around.

The sun has 99.86% of all the mass of the solar system, but only 1.9% of the angular momentum. The planets have 98.1%.[12] Why?

All the planets should spin in the same direction, but Venus, Uranus, and Pluto rotate in reverse. Some planetary orbits are tilted. One of Saturn's 60 moons, Phoebe, has a tilted orbit nearly perpendicular to the planet's equator. Of the nearly 200 moons in the solar system, more than 30 orbit in the opposite direction. Jupiter, Saturn, Uranus, and Neptune have moons orbiting in both directions.[13]

Why did colliding particles adhere rather than destroy each other? Science writer Erik Asphaug points out: "It turns out to be surprisingly difficult for planetesimals to accrete mass during even the most gentle collisions."[14] Even if a planet did manage to form through collisions, it would be nearly non-rotating, because the spins imparted by many small impacts would have been largely self-canceling.

Concerning gas planets, Boyle's Law states that gas clouds dissipate, they do not agglomerate. Gases disperse rapidly in the vacuum of space, specially the two lightest gases, hydrogen and helium, which compose most of the mass of the giant gaseous planets.[15]

If the solar system had formed from a cloud of dust, particles that did not become part of planets, according to the Poynting-Robertson Effect, should still be falling into the sun today, burning up and giving off a measurable infrared glow. No such glow has ever been detected.

Author Stephen G. Brush observes: "Attempts to find a plausible naturalistic explanation of the origin of the Solar System began about 350 years ago but have not yet been quantitatively successful, making this one of the oldest unsolved problems in modern science."[16]

Waters under and above.

The *"waters under the firmament"* we understand as the oceans, as well as underground water, including the waters beneath the continental shelves and tectonic plates, evidenced by the formation of the Mid-Ocean Ridge stretching under both the Atlantic and Pacific Oceans. But what were the *"waters above the firmament"*?

The psalmist affirms there were waters above the firmament or sky: *"Praise him, ye heavens of heavens, and ye waters that be above the heavens"* (Ps 148:4).

Ice crystal canopy? Researcher Dr. Joseph Dillow speculates that the high-altitude waters may have been water vapor[17] above the atmosphere, forming a protective canopy around the planet. Extremely low temperatures in the Earth's upper atmosphere could have frozen much of the water vapors. In the early 1900s Isaac Vail theorized that the *"waters above the firmament"* might have been an ice-crystal canopy.[18] Dr. Larry Vardiman thought of the ice particles as equatorial rings surrounding the Earth similar to those around Venus.[19] Recent studies by Donald Cyr on light patterns that could have been produced by a crystal veil fifty miles above the Earth where noctilucent clouds form, showed a correlation with patterns in archeological artifacts (pottery, woven materials, temple construction). These relationships have reportedly been confirmed in computer simulations.[20]

There seems to be a hint about this in the Biblical text: *"Spread out above the heads of the living creatures was what looked like an expanse, sparkling like ice, and awesome"* (Ezek 1:22, NIV).

A hanging "circle."

The ancients thought the world was flat. The first Greek philosopher Thales believed the world was a flat disk floating on water. Later, men realized that the circular shadow which covered the moon during lunar eclipses was that of planet Earth. World-circling sea voyages during the Age of Exploration provided additional proof that the world is a globe. With the coming of the space age, photographs from manmade satellites captured the curvature of the Earth's horizon. Finally, men first saw the Earth as a complete orb floating in space in December 1968 as the Apollo 8 spacecraft carried astronauts around the Moon.

Yet, the prophet Isaiah knew more than 2,750 years ago that the earth was a circle, or what we call today a globe or sphere: *"It is he that sitteth upon the circle of the earth, and the inhabitants thereof are as grasshoppers; that stretcheth out the heavens as a curtain, and spreadeth them out as a tent to dwell in"* (Isa 40:22).

Earth's support. The cosmogonies or legends of the origin of the world of various cultures have different things supporting the Earth -- twelve pillars, four huge elephants, three great fish, a great bull, a giant tortoise, the god Atlas, etcetera.

Around 4,000 years ago, Job already knew that the earth hung in the emptiness of space: *"He stretcheth out the north over the empty place, and hangeth the earth upon nothing"* (Job 26:7).

Empty north.

Job cryptically said that the north was over the empty place. Incredibly, astronomers have discovered that the area north of the axis of the Earth, toward the pole star, is indeed nearly empty – unlike the rest of the star-filled sky! An article in the November 27, 1981, issue of *Science* magazine reported: "The recently announced 'hole in space,' a 300 million-light-year gap in the distribution of galaxies, has taken cosmologists by surprise… But three very deep core samples in the Northern Hemisphere, lying in the general direction of the constellation Bootes, showed striking gaps in the red shift distribution."[21]

Center of the universe?

Jewish tradition has it that God formed the earth and the entire universe from a single piece of rock. In the pseudepigraphal Book of Enoch, the man saw the rock holding up the world: "*I then surveyed the receptacles of all the winds, perceiving that they contributed to adorn the whole creation, and to preserve the foundation of the earth. I surveyed the stone which supports the corners of the earth*" (Enoch 18:1-2).

The rock is said to be the same block on Mount Moriah upon which Abraham laid his son Isaac as a sacrifice to God. It was also the room-sized rock inside the Holy of Holies of the Temple that King Solomon built. Falling under different hands since 70 A.D., when the Romans destroyed Jerusalem, the rock is today the centerpiece of the Temple Mount's Dome of the Rock, Islam's third holiest shrine.

The Temple Mount is in Jerusalem, which pious Jews in all ages have regarded as the center of universe. God Himself spoke of the city as being centrally located: "*This is what the Sovereign LORD says: This is Jerusalem, which I have set in the center of the nations, with countries all around her*" (Ezek 5:5, NIV).

Nelson's Illustrated Bible Dictionary tells us there are also historical reasons for this: "The medieval concept that Palestine was the center of the earth is not as farfetched as one might expect. This tiny strip of land not only unites the peoples and lands of Asia, Africa, and Europe but also the five seas known as the Mediterranean Sea, the Black Sea, the Caspian Sea, the Red Sea, and the Persian Gulf. Palestine was sandwiched in between two dominant cultures of the ancient world – Egypt to the south and Babylon-Assyria-Persia between the Tigris and Euphrates Rivers to the northeast."[22]

Cartography and calligraphy. Mapmakers and scribes confirmed the idea. Gentile cartographers traditionally drew their world maps with the Holy Land at the center. On the next page is a simplified 11th century world map depicting the world as a disk surrounded by water, with the east on top (a common practice for many centuries). Paradise (Eden) is in the east, as part of Asia, with the two other known continents then,

Europe and Africa, occupying the northwest and southwest, respectively. Jerusalem lay in the center of the disk of the Earth.[23]

In addition, the handwritings of nations west of Jerusalem – Greek, Latin, French, German, English, and others -- are written from left to right. On the other hand, the scripts of countries east of Jerusalem are written from right to left – Hebrew (Abraham came from the east), Aramaic, Chaldean, Arabic,

Simplified 11th century world map,

Sanskrit, Chinese, etc. It is as though the calligraphies of all the other peoples to the east and to the west of the Holy Land are pointing to Jerusalem as the center!

Cosmological confirmation. Dr John Hartnett, in his book *Starlight, Time and the New Physics*, refers to "recent observational data that overwhelmingly leads to the conclusion that the universe must have a centre, with our galaxy somewhere near it… Observations also indicate that we are in a galactocentric universe."[24]

D. Russell Humphreys notes: "The quantized redshift data imply that we are within about 100,000 light-years of the center, a very small distance compared to the diameter of all the matter in the cosmos, at least 40 billion light-years. The probability of us being so close to the center by accident is less than one out of a quadrillion, implying we are where we are as a result of purposeful design."[25]

Galaxies are moving away from the Earth in every direction. The CMBR comes to us from all directions. These strongly indicate that we are indeed in a central location.

God's throne nearby?

As the Creator of the universe, God must have placed His throne at the very center of His creation. Ellen G. White, the 19th century Seventh Day Adventist leader and prophetess, wrote about "suns and stars and systems, all in their appointed order circling the throne of Deity."[26]

Interestingly, according to the *World Book*, "radio telescopes and infrared telescopes have shown that a powerful gravitational force comes from the exact center of the galaxy… so strong that the mass responsible for it must be about 3 million times as great as the mass of the sun… packed into a volume of space smaller than our solar system."[27] Could God's throne be there? Earth is very near the center of the Milky Way.

No wonder the psalmist was inspired to write: *"And He has exalted the horn of His people, The praise of all His saints -- Of the children of Israel, A people near to Him"* (Ps 148:14, NKJV). The nearness may be more than just figurative, it may actually be physical.

Divine arrangement?

Did the arrangement of the solar system simply happen by chance? David sings of God arranging the celestial lights in the heavens: *"When I consider your heavens, the work of your fingers, the moon and the stars, which you have set in place..."* (Ps 8:3, NIV).

As any school-age child knows, the sun is much bigger than the moon. Yet, the sun and the moon, viewed from the Earth, appear to be of the same size. The impression is reinforced during solar eclipses when the moon covers the sun. That is because the sun, whose diameter of about 1,390,000 km, which is around 400 times bigger than the moon (3,480 km), is approximately 400 times farther away from the earth (149,600,000 km) than the moon (384,467 km). Incidentally, the size of the moon is just over ¼ that of the earth (12,756 km). Are not the ratios uncanny? (Notice the recurring number "4," the Biblical number for the world. The numbers "4," "40," and "400" are associated with the Son of God, God's hands-on co-Creator. Is it any wonder these numbers figure in the relationships among the Earth, the sun, and the moon?)

Moreover, the moon revolves around the Earth every 29.5 days. At the same time, it completes one rotation around its axis every 29.5 days. Thus, we always see the same side of the moon. How did the numbers happen to be identical to produce that extraordinary effect? It is too improbable to be simply the product of chance!

"Oddball" planet Earth. The distances of the seven major objects closest to the sun, excluding planet Earth, have an exponential ratio. Starting from Mercury, the distances from the Sun of Venus, Mars, the Asteroid Belt (materials that failed to become a planet), Jupiter, Saturn, and Uranus approximately double from one object to the next.[28]

In the table

Mean Distances from the Sun*

Object	Miles	Kilometers
Mercury	35,980,000	57,910,000
Venus	67,240,000	108,210,000
Earth	**93,000,000**	**150,000,000**
Mars	141,620,000	227,920,000
Asteroid Belt	275,000,000	440,000,000
Jupiter	483,780,000	778,570,000
Saturn	890,750,000	1,433,530,000
Uranus	1,784,860,000	2,872,460,000

*Approximately doubling, excluding planet Earth.

shown here, Earth is an out-of-place oddball in the solar system! It looks like it had been plucked from somewhere and inserted into the system's arrangement.

(The two outermost objects, Neptune and Pluto, do not form part of the equation. They occasionally switch places, owing to Pluto's eccentric orbit. Astronomers suspect an outside force had perturbed their orbits in the past. Pluto came closer to the Sun than Neptune in 1979 and stayed that way for the next twenty years.)

Day 3: Seas, dry land, vegetation

"And God said, Let the waters under the heaven be gathered together unto one place, and let the dry land appear: and it was so. And God called the dry land Earth; and the gathering together of the waters called he Seas: and God saw that it was good" (Gen 1:9-13).

Interpretations of Day 3:
- Literal 24-Hour Days: 3 days before man was created circa 6,000 years ago
- Thousand-Year Days: circa 10,000-9,000 years ago
- Diminishing Day-Ages: circa 3,750,000,000-1,875,000,000 years ago (Duration: approximately 1,875,000,000 years)

Young Earth Creationists say God separated the seas and the dry land either around 6,000 years ago or 10,000-9,000 years ago.

In the Diminishing Day-Ages chronology, God gathered the seas for the dry land to appear between 3.75 billion and 1.875 billion years ago. The scientific estimate for the appearance of the oceans falls exactly within this period. The *Encyclopaedia Britannica* says that "the oceans have been present for at least three billion years."[29]

One supercontinent.

As the waters came together, the exposed dry surface of the planet became one vast supercontinent surrounded by an immense ocean.

Scientists confirmed the Scriptures early in the 20th century. German geophysicist Alfred Wegener, intrigued by the matching contours of the coastlines of eastern South America and western Africa, postulated in 1912 that all the continents were once part of just one land mass that slowly drifted apart over millions of years. This was called "continental drift," which became part of the theory of plate tectonics in the 1960s.

Canadian geologist John Tuzo Wilson posits that the continents have been repeatedly breaking up and rejoining ("Wilson cycle"). As evinced by the rocks, about 800 million years ago all the continents were joined together in one supercontinent called Rodinia, with what is now North America in the middle. The movement of the Earth's mantle caused Rodinia to break up into North America, Europe, and Africa. Then, 250 million years ago, the continents reassembled to form another supercontinent – Pangaea, surrounded by a single, worldwide ocean, Panthalassa. About 200 million years ago, Pangaea broke apart into two large land masses: Gondwanaland and Laurasia. Gondwanaland then broke up to form Africa, Antarctica, Australia, South America, and India. Laurasia split apart into Eurasia and North America.[30]

The plant kingdom

"And God said, Let the earth bring forth grass, the herb yielding seed, and the fruit tree yielding fruit after his kind, whose seed is in itself, upon the earth: and it was so. And the earth brought forth grass, and herb yielding seed after his kind, and the tree yielding fruit, whose seed was in itself, after his kind: and God saw that it was good. And the evening and the morning were the third day" (Gen 1:9-13).

God created the first living things on Earth – plants – on Day 3. The *World Book* says the oldest fossils are those of bacteria that lived about 3.5 billion years ago.[31] Paleobiologists say these organisms (microscopic plants) appeared as soon as there was water on Earth. The timing is again a perfect match, because Day 3 in the Diminishing Day-Ages was from 3.75 billion to 1.875 billion years ago.

Cells to grass to trees.

The bacteria were one-celled prokaryotes (no nuclei). Cyanobacteria (blue-green algae) with chlorophyll were capable of photosynthesis. They were followed by unicellular organisms with nuclei (eukaryotes); then multi-celled vegetation like moss, grass, herbs, trees.

The Jewish sage Nachmanides said the creation of grasses, plants, and trees actually transpired over a protracted period.[32] The Genesis writer simply had the tendency to summarize a string of events in one or two sentences, rather than make a long-winded, detailed narration. After all, even if he did lengthily describe a bacterium that could not be seen by the unaided eye, would he have been understood and, more importantly, believed by his fellow desert nomads 3,500 years ago?

Prefab components?

God said, *"Let the earth bring forth…"* The wording implies that the elements that would constitute the grass, herbs, and trees had been laid down in the earth earlier. The various "prefabricated" components were just waiting to combine into specific forms at God's command.

Note that each type of plant life reproduced *"after his kind,"* showing that the Creator had set the fixed laws of genetics in operation.

Plants without a sun?

At this point, there was still no mention of the sun. How did the first plants manage to survive without sunlight for photosynthesis? We get the answer from prophecy. In Acts 3:21 (NIV) Paul speaks of *"the time... for God to restore everything,"* which infers that former conditions (in the beginning) will be reestablished in the future.

We are told that in the future Kingdom of God there will be *"no need of the sun, neither of the moon, to shine in it: for the glory of God did lighten it, and the Lamb is the light thereof* (Rev 21:23,22:5; also Isa 60:19). If this is a glimpse of the restored conditions in the future, then in the beginning it was light from the glory of God and His Son that enabled the first plants on earth to survive and even thrive.

Day 4: Sun, moon, and stars

"And God said, Let there be lights in the firmament of the heaven to divide the day from the night; and let them be for signs, and for seasons, and for days, and years: And let them be for lights in the firmament of the heaven to give light upon the earth: and it was so. And God made two great lights; the greater light to rule the day, and the lesser light to rule the night: he made the stars also. And God set them in the firmament of the heaven to give light upon the earth, And to rule over the day and over the night, and to divide the light from the darkness: and God saw that it was good. And the evening and the morning were the fourth day" (Gen 1:14-19).

Interpretations of Day 4:
- Literal 24-hour Days: 2 days before man was created 6,000 circa years ago
- Thousand-Year Days: circa 9,000-8,000 years ago
- Diminishing Day-Ages: circa 1,875,000,000-937,500,000 years ago (Duration: approximately 937,500,000 years)

Young Earth Creationists hold that the sun, moon, stars, and other heavenly bodies were created either just 6,000 years ago or 9,000-8,000 years ago at the most.

In the Diminishing Day-Ages, the celestial lights first shone on Earth sometime between 1.875 billion and 937.5 million years ago (mya).

"Made" or "had made"?

The Creator used the words *"let there be"* and *"let them be,"* which could mean that the heavenly bodies were already in existence before Day 4. In the phrase *"And God made…"* the word translated *"made"* is from the Hebrew *asah*, ("to do or make"), which can be translated into several words in English, but "to create" is not one of them.

The verb form in English is in the simple past tense ("made"). However, the pluperfect or past perfect tense "had made," indicating a prior act, could have also been used to translate *asah* (ex.: Gen 1:31, 2:2, 3:1, etc.). Hence, the verse could also be rendered as: *"And God had made two great lights…"* Gen 1:16a), implying God had earlier created the sun, moon, and stars before they became visible on earth.

Gas clouds thinned?

Possibly, after the Earth had formed, the lighter gases which did not become part of the solid sphere continued to surround the planet – the way some planets, like Venus, Jupiter, Saturn, Uranus, and Neptune, are still shrouded with gas clouds today. Venus is covered by a gaseous canopy so thick that astronomers cannot see its surface. Saturn's largest moon, Titan, is also veiled by a thick blur of gases.

The Earth's cloudy atmosphere could have thinned and become clear sometime between 1,875,000,000 and 937,000,000 years ago. From a viewpoint on the surface of the planet, that would have been the first time the sun, moon, and stars shone from the sky.

Moreover, according to ScienceDaily, "The primitive sun did not use to shine as brightly as it does at present. Four billion years ago the solar output was only about 60% of what it is today."[33] The weak rays of the young sun would not have been able to penetrate Earth's dense gaseous atmosphere, which might have been merely translucent.

Signs in the stars.

The Bible says God arranged the celestial bodies in certain ways for particular reasons: *"And God said, Let there be lights in the firmament of the heaven to divide the day from the night; and let them be for signs…"* (Gen 1:14, cf. Dan 6:27).

The sun, moon, stars, and other celestial objects bear messages from God! *"The heavens declare the glory of God; and the firmament sheweth his handywork. Day unto day uttereth speech, and night unto night sheweth knowledge. There is no speech nor language, where their voice is not heard. Their line is gone out through all the earth, and their words to the end of the world…"* (Ps 19:1-4a). To communicate His messages, God uses a heavenly language that can be understood by all peoples.

The Mazzaroth. Men in Mesopotamia first visualized the shapes of the constellations, or clusters of stars, around 2700 B.C.[34] Collectively, they were called the *Mazzaroth*, which means "high ones"[35] or "scattered ones."[36] *"Canst thou bind the sweet influences of Pleiades, or loose the bands of Orion? Canst thou bring forth Mazzaroth in his season? or canst thou guide Arcturus with his sons?"* (Job 38:31-32).

The constellations seem to have been named at the time of the Tower of Babel[37] circa 2000 B.C., and arranged in groups around 700 B.C.[38] The earliest known zodiac with all 12 signs dates from the 400s B.C.[39] At least one fragment of the Dead Sea Scrolls, from the 200s B.C., lists the signs of the Zodiac.[40] Adopting the Babylonian symbols that mostly represent animals, the Greeks called them *ta zōdia*, "the little animals," or *zōdiakos kyklos* ("circle of animals").[41] The Egyptians and the Chinese also used the 12 divisions, but gave other names and symbols to them.[42]

The Magi. Some Biblical personages appear to have been astrologers: *"And the king communed with them; and among them all was found none like Daniel, Hananiah, Mishael, and Azariah: therefore stood they before the king. And in all matters of wisdom and understanding, that the king inquired of them, he found them ten times better than all the magicians and astrologers that were in all his realm"* (Dan 1:19-20).

Daniel was made the king's top astrologer: *"There is a man in your kingdom who has the spirit of the holy gods in him. In the time of your father he was found to have insight and intelligence and wisdom like that of the gods. King Nebuchadnezzar your father -- your father the king, I say -- appointed him chief of the magicians, enchanters, astrologers and diviners"* (Dan 5:11, NIV).

Daniel probably passed on his knowledge to his assistants, especially fellow-Jews in Babylon, which lay east of Judea. Some 600 years later *"wise men from the east,"* apparently astrologers who knew the star signs, came to Jerusalem looking for the newly born Messiah, *"Saying, Where is he that is born King of the Jews? for we have seen his star in the east, and are come to worship him"* (Matt 2:1-2). Christ had been prophesied as the coming "King of the Jews." The wise men must have been Jews; else, why would they worship the King of the Jews if they were not themselves Jewish?

Starry story.

First century Jewish historian Flavius Josephus wrote of an ancient belief that Adam's son Seth and great-great grandson Enoch saw a drama inscribed in the starlit night sky. The starry story is said to be the salvation of man by a coming Messiah. How do we read the story? Where does it start? The constellations in the celestial circle have no apparent beginning or end. Ancient astrologers started the year from Aries, where the sun was at the spring equinox. Should we do likewise?

Egyptologist Frances Rolleston found the key in the 4,000-year-old zodiac of Denderah on the ceiling of the portico of the temple of Esneh in Egypt. She discovered a picture of the Sphinx just below and between the figures of Virgo and Leo.[43] In Greek, *Sphinx* means "to bind tight" (also the root-word of "sphincter," a ring of muscle around a body opening). The Sphinx, with the head of a woman and the body of a lion, "tightly binds" the two together. Thus, Virgo is the "head," or start of the story, and Leo, the rear, or "ending."

Gospel in the stars. Interpretations of the 12 constellations slightly vary, but the overall picture they paint is the same: the Gospel is in the stars! Below is a synthesis of the basic meaning of each sign:

1. Virgo, the Virgin: a sinless woman (the pure faith, church, or religion) carrying an infant and holding a branch (the Messiah);

2. Libra, the Weighing Scales: purchase and judgment -- the son of the woman will pay the price (for sin) and act as the coming judge;

3. Scorpio, the Scorpion (formerly the snake Serpens battling the eagle Aquila): Satan opposing the Messiah, the Redeemer of men;

4. Sagittarius, the Archer or mighty hunter: the Antichrist defying God and attempting to kill His Only Son, the Savior of mankind;

5. Capricorn, the Goat-Fish or wounded scapegoat: the sacrificial offering was pierced (His blood as atonement for the sins of the world);

6. Aquarius, the Water-Bearer: God pouring His Holy Spirit (water) upon the earth, baptizing the body of believers during the Church Age;

7. Pisces, the Fishes (a small one and a big one): the Judeo-Christian faith, made up of two groups of people who will be saved;

8. Aries, the Ram: the sacrificed Lamb of God, the Messiah, who has grown greater and more powerful through His death on the cross;

9. Taurus, the Bull: the power and longsuffering of God, patiently waiting for men to repent of their sins before rendering judgment;

10. Gemini, the Twins: two children of the same woman (faith), also symbolic of the Bridegroom (the Messiah) and His bride (the Church);

11. Cancer, the Crab (formerly a sheepfold): the ingathering of the flock at the "Rapture" or first resurrection at Christ's Second Coming;

12. Leo, the Lion: the return of Christ as Lion of Judah, pouncing on the serpent Hydra (Satan) stretching over a third of the stars (angels).

Do you see the complete story?

Horoscopes? Horrors!

The *Mazzaroth* reveals God's plan for His chosen people. But Gentile stargazers began making predictions for their countrymen – such as national prosperity or disaster. ("Dis-aster" comes from the Latin words *dis* ["reverse"] and *aster* ["star"], a reversal or disarrangement of the stars.) The Greeks and Romans started casting personal horoscopes sometime between 600 and 200 B.C.[44] Fortune-telling, however, including horoscopes, is detestable to God: *"There shall not be found among you any one that maketh his son or his daughter to pass through the fire, or that useth divination, or an observer of times, or an enchanter, or a witch, Or a charmer, or a consulter with familiar spirits, or a wizard, or a necromancer. For all that do these things are an abomination unto the LORD"* (Deut 18:10-12).

Jeremiah told the Jews: *"Thus says the LORD: "Do not learn the way of the Gentiles; Do not be dismayed at the signs of heaven, For the Gentiles are dismayed at them. For the customs of the peoples are futile..."* (Jer 10:2-3a, NKJV).

Day 5: Water creatures, fowl

"And God said, Let the waters bring forth abundantly the moving creature that hath life, and fowl that may fly above the earth in the open firmament of heaven. And God created great whales, and every living creature that moveth, which the waters brought forth abundantly, after their kind, and every winged fowl after his kind: and God saw that it was good. And God blessed them, saying, Be fruitful, and multiply, and fill the waters in the seas, and let fowl multiply in the earth. And the evening and the morning were the fifth day" (Gen 1:20-23).

Interpretations of Day 5:

- Literal 24-Hour Days: 1 day before man was created circa 6,000 years ago
- Thousand-Year Days: circa 8,000-7,000 years ago
- Diminishing Day-Ages: circa 937,500,000-468,750,000 years ago (Duration: approximately 468,750,000 years)

According to Young Earth Creationists, aquatic creatures and birds first appeared no later than 6,000 years ago, but no earlier than 8,000-7,000 years ago, either.

In the Diminishing Day-Ages timeline, God created the first marine animals during Day-Age 5, sometime between 937.5 million and 468.75 million years ago. This corresponds precisely to the oldest known animal fossils, about 700 million years old, that the *Encyclopedia Britannica* identifies as *Ediacara fauna*, small wormlike creatures with soft bodies.[45]

Oxygen-breathing animals.

Until about 700 million years ago, there was a negligibly low amount of oxygen available. (The estimated threshold or minimum amount of oxygen needed for animal life to begin and multiply on earth is 1-10% of the present atmospheric level.)[46] Photosynthesizing bacteria then began oxygenating the oceans to produce the oxygen needed by new marine animals that derived energy through respiration.

Do you see the thoughtful planning involved? God created plants on Day 3 to produce oxygen. After an adequate supply had been assured, He proceeded to create oxygen-breathing animals on Day 5.

The Cambrian "explosion."

Approximately 544 million years ago, new forms of life with various anatomical structures appeared in rapid succession.[47] Writer Leslie Orgel said in the *New Scientist*: "Beginning at the base of the Cambrian period and extending for about 10 million years, all the major groups of skeletonized invertebrates made their first appearance in the most spectacular rise in diversity ever recorded on our planet."[48]

All the basic shapes and features of multi-cellular organisms living today first appeared during that period: mouths, eyes, gills, intestines, shells, bones, spines, appendages, joints. The seas teemed with a great variety of invertebrates: sponges, worms, bryozoans ("moss animals"), hydrozoans (jellyfish), brachiopods (clams), mollusks (snails), arthropods (trilobites), echinoderms (starfish).[49]

Sir Jonathan Sacks wonders, "Something' happened to cause an 'explosion' of complex multi-cellular body forms. Scientists have long been puzzled about why this burst of diversity occurred... How did life evolve at such speed that even Francis Crick, co-discoverer of DNA, was forced to suggest that it came from Mars?"[50]

Gerald Schroeder suggests the increased supply of oxygen resulted in a tenfold improvement in the conversion of food to energy. With the new energy, organisms were able to develop more complex structures.[51] These were the "abundant moving creatures in the waters" (Gen 1:20).

The first fish.

Fish appeared 490 million years ago. The presence of a backbone differentiates the fish, a vertebrate, from invertebrates. But where it came from remains a mystery.

Author Arthur Strahler wrote: "Origin of the vertebrates is obscure -- there is no fossil record preceding the occurrence of fishes in the late Ordovician time."[52] Writer Francis Downes Ommanney says, "How this earliest chordate stock evolved, what stages of development it went through to eventually give rise to truly fishlike creatures we do not know. Between the Cambrian when it probably originated, and the Ordovician when the first fossils of animals with really fishlike characteristics appeared, there is a gap of perhaps 100 million years which we will probably never be able to fill."[53] The *Readers Digest* sums it up: "To our knowledge, no 'link' connected this new beast to any previous form of life. The fish just appeared."[54] But, of course. God created the fish.

Dragonflies and dragons?

God also said: "*Let the waters bring forth... fowl that may fly above the earth... And... great whales*" (Gen 1:20-21). "*Fowl*" from the waters? Were these the first birds? Did they precede the land animals? Let us take a closer look.

"*Fowl.*" The word is translated from the Hebrew *owph*, meaning "to cover with wings or obscurity." "Bird" is *tsippor* in Hebrew. In its commentary on Genesis 1:20, *Barnes' Notes* explains: "[Bird of wing] Here the wing is made characteristic of the class, which extends beyond what we call birds." The commentator points out that *owph* ("fowl") means more than just "birds."[55]

The idea is demonstrated in Leviticus 11:13-20: "*And these are they which ye shall have in abomination among the fowls; they shall not be eaten, they are an abomination: the eagle, and the ossifrage, and the ospray, And the vulture, and the kite after his kind; Every raven after his kind; And the owl, and the night hawk, and the cuckow, and the hawk after his kind, And the little owl, and the cormorant, and the great owl, And the swan, and the pelican, and the gier eagle, And the stork, the heron after her kind, and the lapwing, and the bat. All fowls that creep, going upon all four, shall be an abomination unto you.*"

God enumerated birds under the word "*fowls*," but also included a flying mammal – the bat! Let us grant that in that pre-scientific time the Israelites did not know the difference between a true bird and a bat. Yet, in the last line we read a stranger thing: "*fowls that creep, going upon all four.*" Four-footed fowl? No member of the avian family creeps, much less on all fours, because birds have only two legs. The NKJV renders the verse in a more contemporary language: "*All flying insects that creep on all fours...*" (Lev 11:20, NKJV; also NIV and NASU).

It becomes clear that the word "*fowls*" lumps together true birds, a flying mammal, and flying insects -- even if they are biologically unrelated. It shows that *owph* refers to any creature that flies! Science asserts: "There is no fossil evidence of primitive wings prior to the appearance of fully developed winged insects..."[56]

Thus, the "fowl" from the waters in Genesis 1:20-22 may have actually been winged insects, prehistoric predecessors of modern dragonflies, mosquitoes, and similar insects which lay their eggs and spend the larval stages of their lives in the water!

Great whales. The *"great whales"* God created, rendered *"great sea creatures"* in NKJV and NIV, and *"great sea monsters"* in NASU and ASV, are *hataninim hagadolim* in the original Hebrew text.

In other Bible verses, the translation is "dragons": *"Praise the LORD from the earth, ye dragons (taninim)…"* (Ps 148:7a); *"Thou shalt tread upon the lion and adder: the young lion and the dragon (tanin)…"* (Ps 91:13; Ps 74:13, Deut 32:33, Jer 9:11). Elsewhere, the translation is "serpents": *"And Moses and Aaron went in unto Pharaoh, and they did so as the LORD had commanded: and Aaron cast down his rod before Pharaoh, and before his servants, and it became a serpent (tanin)… For they cast down every man his rod, and they became serpents (taninim)…"* (Ex 7:10,12a).

"Dragons" and "serpents" are both reptiles. Hence, the Hebrew *taninim hagadolim* ("great whales") must have actually been huge sea reptiles -- marine dinosaurs – the sea serpents of ancient legends!

Day 6: Mammals, creeping things, man

"And God said, Let the earth bring forth the living creature after his kind, cattle, and creeping thing, and beast of the earth after his kind: and it was so. And God made the beast of the earth after his kind, and cattle after their kind, and every thing that creepeth upon the earth after his kind: and God saw that it was good" (Gen 1:24-25).

Interpretations of Day 6:
- Literal 24-hour Days: the day man was created circa 6,000 years ago
- Thousand-Year Days: circa 7,000-6,000 years ago
- Diminishing Day-Ages: circa 468,750,000-13,306 years ago (Duration: approximately 468,735,694 years)

Young Earth Creationists claim land animals and man first walked on earth some 6,000 years ago, or 7,000-6,000 years ago at the earliest.

In the Diminishing Day-Ages timeline, God created land animals and hominids during Day-Age 6, 468,750,000 to 13,306 years ago (kya).

A multi-segmented Day 6?

In the Diminishing Day-Ages timeline, the sixth segment should be Day-Age 6, ending about 234,375,000 years ago after the creation of land animals (amphibians, insects, reptiles, mammals). But it cannot be the Biblical Day 6, because it ended before man could be created.

However, if we continue with the exponentially regressing pattern, we see the coming of hominids in the succeeding segments until around 28,611 years ago. For still unclear reasons, it appears that the time segments after Day-Age 5 are not individual day-ages, but parts of a multi-segmented Day-Age 6! There is no apparent basis, but the time segments match the scientific estimates accurately.

There is a clue in the Bible, though. More time and words were used to relate the events of Day 6, because more things happened and more entities were created on that last creative "day." Moreover, there is a textual parallel in the next chapter, where one "day" is used to mean several days: *"These are the generations of the heavens and of the earth when they were created, in the day that the LORD God made the earth and the heavens"* (Gen 2:4). We know that the *"the earth and the heavens"* were not created in one single "day,' but over several "days."

Did God (*Elohim*) use more segments of time for Day-Age 6 to create animals of a higher order, as well as to perfect man -- the prime paradigm of His creative work? Let go through those time segments.

Day-Age 6-a
- Circa 468,750,000 to 234,375,000 years ago (Duration: approximately 234,375,000 years)

First of worst extinctions. Paleontologists have identified at least 17 mass extinctions since life began on earth. Eight are major, all of which took place in the last 500 million years. However, five events are the most devastating: the first took place around 438 million years ago during Day-Age 6-a. Over 85% of species became extinct.[57]

Amphibians created. God created land animals and "creeping things" on Day 6. Fossil remains show that amphibians, a kind of creeping creature, crawled onto dry land around 417 million years ago during Day-Age 6-a.

Second of worst extinctions. The second of the five worst mass extinction events also happened during Day-Age 6-a, approximately 367 million years ago. This time, 82% of all species were lost.[58]

Insects created. God created insects approximately 350 million years ago during Day-Age 6-a. Scientists are puzzled why insects, comprising 80% of all living and extinct animal species, have no known evolutionary ancestors.

A U.S. government reference (*Insects,* 1952) states: "There is... no fossil evidence bearing on the question of insect origin; the oldest insects known show no transition to other arthropods."[59]

Reptiles created. God created more "creeping things" – reptiles. The record of the rocks reveals that cold-blooded saurians, the forerunners of modern lizards, arose on the face of the planet starting approximately 323 million years ago during Day-Age 6-a.

Mammals created. God created warm-blooded mammals -- the "beasts of the earth" (wild animals) and "cattle" (domestic animals).

The fossil record shows that the mammals first walked upon the earth 248 million years ago during Day-Age 6-a.

Third of worst extinctions. The third and most devastating of the five worst mass extinctions also occurred during Day-Age 6-a, some 245 million years ago. As many as 96% of all species were wiped out.

The destruction was so great paleontologists use this event to mark the end of the ancient or Paleozoic Era and the beginning of the middle or Mesozoic Era, when many new groups of animals arose.[60]

Day-Age 6-b
- Circa 234,375,000 to 117,187,500 years ago (Duration: approximately 117,187,500 years)

Fourth of worst extinctions. The fourth of the five worst mass extinctions transpired some 208 million years ago, claiming about 76% of all species at the time, including many reptiles.[61]

Archaeopteryx appeared. A chimeric creature appeared 150 million years ago. Scientists say it was the first true bird – with feathers and wings, and a "wishbone" (the fused collarbones underpinning wing muscles). However, it also had jaws with teeth, claws on its wings, and a long tail like dinosaurs. It was half-bird, half-reptile – the archaeopteryx!

It seems to be alluded to in Scripture. Leviticus 11:18 (NKJV) lists birds: "*the white owl, the jackdaw, and the carrion vulture.*" The "while owl" is *tanshemeth* in the Hebrew original. Several verses later, 11:30 lists reptiles: "*the gecko, the monitor lizard, the sand reptile, the sand lizard, and the chameleon.*" Strangely, "chameleon" is also *tanshemeth* in the original. The word *tanshemeth*, applicable to both a bird and a reptile, perfectly describes the archaeopteryx! Was *tanshemeth* the Scriptural term for the archaeopteryx?

Day-Age 6-c
- Circa 117,187,500 to 58,593,750 years ago (Duration: approximately 58,593,750 years)

Fifth of worst extinctions. The fifth and most recent of the five worst mass extinctions occurred more or less 65 million years ago, with the death of 76% of all species, most notably the dinosaurs.[62]

Primates created. Around the time that "terrible lizards" (dinosaurs) became extinct, primates – animals that resemble modern lemurs, monkeys, and apes – came onto the scene some 65,000,000 years ago during Day-Age 6-c.

Day-Age 6-d
- Circa 58,593,750 to 29,296,875 years ago (Duration: approximately 29,296,875 years)

Rise of mammals. As the level of atmospheric oxygen continued to rise from 10% to 17% about 50 million years ago, then 23% some 40 million years ago, mammals dominated the planet.

Paul Falkowski, a marine science professor, explains: "In the fossil record, we see that this rise in oxygen content corresponds exactly to a really rapid rise of large, placental mammals... The more oxygen, the bigger the mammals... the rise in oxygen content allowed mammals to become very, very large – mammals like 12-foot-tall sloths and huge saber-toothed cats."[63] Some hornless rhinoceroses measured about 30 feet long and stood 18 feet high at the shoulder.

Day-Age 6-e
- Circa 29,296,875 to 14,648,437 years ago (Duration: approximately 14,648,437 years. From here on, fractions are added to succeeding numbers to keep figures rounded.)

Day-Age 6-f
- Circa 14,648,437 to 7,324,218 years ago (Duration: approximately 7,324,218 years)

Manlike creatures.

The Jewish philosopher Maimonides said in his exegesis of Genesis that there were manlike creatures before Adam.[64] Similarly, the Talmud and other ancient Jewish commentaries mention pre-Adamic animals with human forms but without the *neshamah* or God-given spirit.[65] How did they know that before fossils were discovered?

Anthropologists call manlike creatures thought to be ancestors of man "hominids." They call living apes "hominoids," because they are only similar to humans, but not man's supposed ancestors.

Ramapithecus, 14-8 mya. Found in 1932 in northern India (now part of Pakistan), parts of a fossilized jaw and some teeth, dated about 14-8 million years old, were named *Ramapithecus* -- "Rama's ape," after Rama, a mythical prince of India, combined with *pithekos*, Greek for "ape." In 1976, a complete jaw was discovered. With a distinctly simian V shape, it differs markedly from the parabolic shape of hominid jaws.[66] More complete fossils have been found in China and Pakistan, confirming that *Ramapithecus* was not a hominid, but a true ape.[67]

<u>Day-Age 6-g</u>
- Circa 7,324,218 to 3,662,109 years ago (Duration: approximately 3,662,109 years)

Sahelanthropus tchadensis, 7-6 mya. In 2001 the fossils of the supposedly oldest hominid species, estimated at 7-6 million years old, were found in the north central African nation of Chad.[68] Dubbed *Sahelanthropus* ("Sahel man," after the semi-arid region and the Greek word *anthropos*, meaning "human"), it has an apelike skull. The fossil pieces are so few, it is uncertain if *Sahelanthropus* walked bipedally.[69]

Orrorin tugenensis, 6 mya. Found in the Tugen Hills of central Kenya in 2000, the fossils received the name *Orrorin tugenensis*, which means "original man in the Tugen region." Thought to be 6 million years old,[70] the fossilized skeleton has simian features, including long, curved finger bones for grasping and movement in trees, and apelike canine and premolar teeth.[71]

Ardipithecus, 4.4 mya. Unearthed in Ethiopia in 1994, this fossil find dated to be 4.4-million years old has been named *Ardipithecus*, from words in the Afar and Greek languages meaning "ground ape."[72] "Ardi," however, has apelike teeth and skeleton, suggesting its ability to walk upright might not have been well developed.[73]

Australopithecus, 4-1 mya. In 1924, a fossilized skull was dug up in Taung, South Africa. It was named *Australopithecus,* which means "southern ape." Thought to be man's ancestor, six species have since been identified. An almost complete 3,200,000-year-old skeleton of a female unearthed in 1974 by Donald Johanson at Hadar, Ethiopia, was nicknamed "Lucy," after the Beatles song "Lucy in the Sky with Diamonds," which played on the night of the find.[74]

Australopithecines, some 3½ to 5 feet tall, had a brain (390-550 cu cm) about one-third of that of a modern human; a low cranium behind a projecting face; small canine teeth like those of humans, but large cheek teeth (molars) like apes. Although Lucy had arms proportionally longer than those of modern people, she is said to have walked upright,[75] based on a knee joint. (Johanson later said the knee fragment was discovered a mile and a half away in a rock layer 200 feet deeper, but was included due to "anatomical similarity.")[76]

Bruce Bower, in the *Science News* of 2 June 2001, reported that, in one study, Australopithecine inner ear bones used to maintain balance were found to be greatly similar to those of chimpanzees and gorillas, but markedly different from those of humans.[77] Mark Cartmill et al. wrote in the July-August 1986 issue of *American Scientist*: "At present we have no grounds for thinking that there was anything distinctively human about australopithecine ecology and behavior... they were surprisingly apelike in skull form, premolar dentition, limb proportions, and morphology of some joint surfaces, and they may still have been spending a significant amount of time in the trees."[78]

Anatomist Sir Solly Zuckerman and Dr. Charles Oxnard, in contrast to anthropologists using subjective and less analytical visual techniques, developed a multivariate analysis technique with computers performing millions of analyses on homologous Australopithecine, simian, and human bones. Their finding: *Australopithecus* is *not* a missing link between ape and man.[79] Sir Solly observed: "When compared with human and simian skulls, the Australopithecine skull is in appearance overwhelmingly simian – not human... Our findings leave little doubt that... *Australopithecus* resembles not *Homo sapiens* but the living monkeys and apes."[80]

Paleontologist Richard Leakey said in his book *Origins* (1977) that it is "unlikely that our direct ancestors are evolutionary descendants of the australopithecines."[81] James Shreeve remarked in the *Science* magazine issue of May 3, 1996: "The proportions calculated for (*Australopithecus*) *africanus* turned out to be amazingly close to those of a chimpanzee, with big arms and small legs... One might say we are kicking Lucy out of the family tree..."[82] As their family name *pithecus* ("ape") denotes, these prehistoric pithecoid creatures were just apes.

Day-Age 6-h
• Circa 3,662,109 to 1,831,054 years ago (Duration: approximately 1,831,054 years.)

Kenyanthropus platyops, 3.5 mya. A fossilized cranium and other bones, estimated to be 3.5 million years old, were found in 1999 in northern Kenya. The creature had a mixture of features not seen in earlier hominid fossils: a much flatter face and smaller molars; the cheekbone joined the rest of the face in a forward position; and the region beneath the nose opening was flat. Researchers placed it under a new genus and species: *Kenyanthropus platyops*. In Greek *anthropos* means "humen being," while *platyops* means "flat" – combined to mean "flat-faced human from Kenya."[83]

Homo habilis, 2.8-1.5 mya. So named for the primitive stone tools found with its fossilized skull in 1960, *Homo habilis* means "handy man" -- from Latin words meaning "human" (*homo*) and "able or skillful" (*habilis*). The first to be classified under the genus *Homo*, the species had a bigger braincase of about 600 cu cm.[84] It was also taller.

The fossil had been found beneath volcanic ash dated at about 2.6 million years, pushing back the presumed origin of man by millions of years. Its discoverer, Richard Leakey, says: "Either we toss out this skull or we toss out our theories of early man." He adds that "it leaves in ruins the modern notion that all early fossils can be arranged in an orderly sequence of evolutionary change."[85]

The first confirmed limb bones of *Homo habilis* were discovered in 1986. They showed the creature clearly had apelike proportions and should never have been classified as human. Hugh Ross comments on the web: "Starting about 2-4 million years ago, God began creating man-like mammals or 'hominids.' These creatures stood on two feet, had large brains, and used tools. Some even buried their dead and painted on cave walls... God replaced them with Adam and Eve."[86]

Homo rudolfensis, 1.9 mya. In 1972, more than 150 fragments of bone fossils were discovered in eastern Kenya. As the size of the skull and several anatomical features differed from those of earlier finds, scientists classified it under a new species named *Homo rudolfensis*, after Lake Rudolf (now Lake Turkana). Its best-known fossils from the lake area date from about 1.9 million years ago.[87]

Richard Leakey notes: "This Australopithecine material suggests a form of locomotion that was not entirely upright nor bipedal. The Rudolf Australopithecines, in fact, may have been close to the 'knuckle-walker' condition, not unlike the extant African apes."[88]

Day-Age 6-i
* Circa 1,831,054 to 915,527 years ago (Duration: approximately 915,527 years)

Homo erectus, 1.5 mya. A skullcap and tooth found in 1891 by Eugene Dubois in the Dutch East Indies (now Indonesia) was first named *Pithecanthropus erectus* ("erect ape-man"). Popularly known as "Java man," it is dated about 1,500,000 years old. It had a larger brain (about 850 cc) and a rounder cranium than earlier species.[89]

In China, at a site known as Chou K'ou Tien (Dragon-Bone Hill), 25 miles from Peking, from 1921 to 1934 a total of 14 skull fragments, 11 jawbones, 7 thigh pieces, 2 arm bones, a wrist bone, and 147 teeth similar to Java Man were found. Called *Sinanthropus pekinensis* – "Peking Man" – its composite skull was named "Nellie."[90]

Forty years after finding "Java man," Dubois conceded it was a big ape. "Pithecanthropus was not a man, but a gigantic genus allied to the Gibbons, superior to its near relatives on account of its exceedingly large brain volume, and distinguished at the same time by its erect attitude."[91] He admitted withholding parts of four simian thigh bones found in the same area.

The *World Book* states: "Modern humans could not have evolved from these late populations of *H. erectus*, a much more primitive type of human."[92]

Day-Age 6-j:
- Circa 915,527 to 457,763 years ago (Duration: approximately 457,763 years)

Homo heidelbergensis, 600-300 kya. In 1907 a fossilized manlike jaw was discovered 16 kilometers southeast of Heidelberg, Germany. It had no chin, but was unusually thick and broad, as well as long, suggesting the individual had a projecting lower face. The teeth also were too small for the massive mandible.

Other specimens from Africa (Ethiopia, Zambia, Tanzania), Europe (Greece, France), and possibly Asia (China) have been dated at from approximately 600 to 300 thousand years ago (kya).[93] Their craniums have heavy browridges, long and low braincases, and thick vault bones like *H. erectus*, but larger.

The image of God

"And God said, Let us make man in our image, after our likeness: and let them have dominion over the fish of the sea, and over the fowl of the air, and over the cattle, and over all the earth, and over every creeping thing that creepeth upon the earth" (Gen 1:26).

Science and Scripture are again in complete agreement: human beings were the last form of living creatures to appear on earth.

A "plural" God?

Oddly, God spoke in the first person plural: *"let us... in our image... after our likeness..."* Apart from the verse above, God's reference to Himself in the plural is seen in a few other Biblical verses: Genesis 3:22 (*"And the LORD God said, Behold, the man is become as one of us..."*);

Genesis 11:7 ("*Come, let us go down and confuse their language...*"); Isaiah 6:8 ("*Also I heard the voice of the Lord, saying, Whom shall I send, and who will go for us?*").

Some scholars say God referred to Himself in the plural, because the Godhead is said to have three Persons – the Father, the Son, and the Holy Spirit. Others suggest the way He spoke was "*communicative* (including the attendant angels),"[94] that is, God was speaking for both Himself and the angels in His presence. In Genesis 3:22, the phrase "*one of us*" in both Hebrew and the literal English translation, clearly means one among many. We can only conclude that by "us" God means Himself plus others who were with Him.

God and "gods." In the Scriptures, the word "God" is usually translated from the Hebrew *elohim* ("gods"), the plural form of *El* and its variants *Elah, Eloah, Eloha*. Scholars "interpret the –im ending as an expression of majesty (*pluralis majestatis*) or excellence (*pluralis excellentiae*), expressing high dignity or greatness..."[95] Others disagree. "Theologians who dispute this cite the hypothesis that plurals of majesty came about in more modern times. Richard Toporoski, a classical scholar, asserts that plurals of majesty first appeared in the reign of Diocletian (284-305 CE)... The use of the plural as a form of respectful address is quite foreign to Hebrew."[96]

In Psalm 82, the angels are called "gods" (*elohim*): "*God (Elohim) standeth in the congregation of the mighty (el); he judgeth among the gods (elohim)... I have said, Ye are gods (elohim); and all of you are children of the most High*" (Ps 82:1,6).

In Psalm 149:2, the English word "Maker" was actually "Makers" in the Hebrew original, as indicated by the plural verb. It thus should read: "*Let Israel rejoice in their Makers; Let the children of Zion be joyful in their King.*" Similarly, in Ecclesiastes 12:1, "Creator" was "Creators" in the original: "*Remember now thy Creators in the days of thy youth...*" The pluralization of words in Hebrew requires correct spellings that differ markedly from the singular, so the plurals could not have been mere scribal "slips of the pen." The plurals had been deliberately written.

God showed Himself to Abraham as three angels. "*And the LORD appeared unto him in the plains of Mamre: and he sat in the tent door in the heat of the day; And he lift up his eyes and looked, and, lo, three men stood by him: and when he saw them, he ran to meet them from the tent door, and bowed himself toward the ground*" (Gen 18:1-2).

In view of the above, did God have angels acting for Him during the Creation? The Angel of the LORD? Moreover, do the terms "*image*" and "*likeness*" imply that the Angel of the LORD and the angels have a physical form after which they fashioned man?

Physical resemblance?

The terms "*image*" and "*likeness*" may have two implications: First, they could signify that man, or at least a part of him, has been made a spirit like God and the angels. Second, they could mean that man has been patterned after the physical configurations of the Creator (the Angel of the LORD) and the angels, literally.

The terms are used at least once in the Bible in the physical sense: "*And Adam lived an hundred and thirty years, and begat a son in his own likeness, after his image; and called his name Seth*" (Gen 5:3). *The Interpreter's Dictionary of the Bible* explains: "Man's resemblance to God is analogous to Seth's resemblance to his father Adam. This makes it certain that physical resemblance must not be excluded."[97]

The form of angels. If God and the angels were spirits, why did God create the physical universe? Of what use would it be to them? God also planted a garden in Eden, but it was not for Adam, whom He made only to be its gardener (Gen 2:5,8,15). Did God create the material world for His own and the angels' enjoyment? That is what we are told in Revelation 4:11 – "*Thou art worthy, O Lord, to receive glory and honour and power: for thou hast created all things, and for thy pleasure they are and were created.*" That being the case, the Spirit of God, and those of His angels, needed physical bodies to experience and enjoy the delights of the material universe. Indeed, we read about "*the LORD God walking in the garden in the cool of the day*" (Gen 3:8).

The Scriptures hint angels can change their physical forms. In Psalm 68:17 ("*The chariots of God are twenty thousand, even thousands of angels [shin'an]...*"), the Hebrew word used for angels is *shin'an*, the root meaning of which is "to change or alter." This strongly suggests angels can change or alter their forms at will.

As we know, God and the angels descended to earth from time to time in physical form. Of all organic structures, the human figure appears to be the most suitable and most efficient design for the terrestrial setting. James, Christ's own brother, reiterates that the human form has been patterned after that of God: "*Therewith bless we God, even the Father; and therewith curse we men, which are made after the similitude of God*" (James 3:9).

One kind, several forms. If man was created in the "*image*" and "*likeness*" of God, how can the appearance of various manlike creatures before Adam be explained?

The Torah account tends to skip over some details to simplify the narrative, as we have seen earlier. On Day 6 amphibians, reptiles and insects are lumped together under just one term: "*creeping things*" (Gen

1:24-25). It is the same in Leviticus 11:13-23, where true birds, the bat, and flying insects are all bunched in just one word, *"fowl."*

Similarly, it looks like Genesis 1:26 has grouped together in one word – *"man"* – all the different species of subhumans and hominids, different versions and "likenesses" of the same type which eventually culminated in Adam, the crowning glory of God's creation.

Day-Age 6-k:
- Circa 457,763 to 228,882 years ago (Duration: approximately 228,882 years)

Homo Neanderthalensis, 300 kya. In 1856 workmen found fossil bones in a limestone cave in the Neander valley (*thal*), near Dusseldorf, Germany. Anatomist Prof. Schaafhausen declared the bones were human.[98] The remains were named Neanderthal man.

Over 60 more similar fragments have since been unearthed in other parts of Europe, as well as Asia and Africa. Undoubtedly human, the "Neandertals were larger and more muscular than modern humans and are believed to have lived in Europe and western Asia from 300,000 years ago to as recently as 30,000 years ago."[99] The bones indicate a powerful body, though of short stature -- males averaged 1.7 m (5' 5") tall and 84 kg (185 lb), females 1.5 m (5') tall and 80 kg (176 lb).[100] The cranial capacity was about 1,500 cu cm (90 cu in), around 10-15% larger than that of modern men! (The larger brain is thought to be in correlation to the greater muscle mass of the Neanderthals.)

At first scientists thought Neanderthals had a crouching and apelike posture. They later realized some of the bones bore signs of arthritis and rickets. They concluded that Neanderthals actually walked upright, not stooped on bent knees. Recent dental and x-ray studies suggest they matured at a slower rate, but lived longer than people today.

Neanderthals used fire, made stone tools and leather, played music (indicated by a wooden flute), cared for the injured and elderly (bones show survival to old age after suffering wounds, fractures, diseases, even blindness).[101] They seemed to have worshipped bears and buried their dead, covering them with flowers.

In 1997, researchers announced they had extracted a small amount of DNA from a Neanderthal fossil. They "compared the Neandertal DNA sequence to sequences in the same region of DNA for 994 modern human lineages, which included Australians, Pacific Islanders, Africans, Asians, Native Americans, and Europeans. The Neandertal DNA sequence differed from all the modern human DNA by either 27 or 28 base pairs. In comparison, modern human sequences in this region of

DNA differ from each other on average by 8 base pairs."[102] The DNA evidence, the *World Book* says, supports the belief that the Neanderthals were a separate species and not ancestors of modern humans.[103]

Day-Age 6-l:
- Circa 228,882 to 114,441 years ago (Duration: approximately 114,441 years)

Day-Age 6-m:
- Circa 114,441 to 57,221 years ago (Duration: approximately 57,221 years.)

Homo sapiens, 200-100 kya. In 1868, fossilized human bones were discovered in the Cro-Magnon cave in southwestern France. Anthropologists have classified the evidently more advanced species, which appeared between 200,000 and 100,000 years ago,[104] as *Homo sapiens* – Latin for "wise human being."

Also called "Cro-Magnon man," more than 100 specimens have since been found. A population appears to have lived in Europe from about 40,000 to 10,000 years ago. Cro-Magnon bones closely resemble those of modern men. They indicate a powerfully muscled body of about 166-171 cm (5" 5" to 5' 7") tall. They were distinguished from Neanderthals by a high forehead with a slight browridge, a short wide face, and a prominent chin (the first specimen with a well-defined chin). The *H. sapiens* brain volume was about 1,600 cc (100 cu in), bigger than that of modern men.[105]

Finely shaped artifacts reveal the Cro-Magnons had mastered the techniques of making useful objects from stone, bone, shell, and clay, such as tools, trinkets, lamps, needles. They wore fitted clothes, jewelry, and other ornaments.[106] Most notably, they produced beautiful paintings of animals in the caves of southwestern France and northern Spain.

Like Neanderthals, Cro-Magnons buried their dead. This suggests they believed in an other world of spirits. After all, the Creator had spoken to them: *"And God blessed them, and God said unto them, Be fruitful, and multiply, and replenish the earth, and subdue it: and have dominion over the fish of the sea, and over the fowl of the air, and over every living thing that moveth upon the earth"* (Gen 1:28).

No relation. Remains of Cro-Magnons and the older Neanderthals overlap in the fossil record, showing the two species lived alongside each other for a long period of time – no less than 70,000 years. This precludes any notion that Cro-Magnons evolved from Neanderthals.

Neither did modern man. Neanderthals had an ear canal (labyrinth, three hollow rings involved in balance) that was distinctly different in size and location from that of people today. The *Word Book* notes: "Because the features of the Neandertal's labyrinth do not exist in modern humans, the scientists believe that the muscular hominid belongs to a separate species, or at least is not an ancestor of modern humans."[107]

Researchers have extracted DNA samples from a 40,000-year-old human skeleton (from the Cro-Magnon era) found at Lake Mungo in Australia. The DNA differs from that of living people.[108] The findings reinforce the belief that the earlier species were not ancestors of modern humans. (Of course we know Adam had none, do we not?)

A vegetarian world

"And God said, Behold, I have given you every herb bearing seed, which is upon the face of all the earth, and every tree, in the which is the fruit of a tree yielding seed; to you it shall be for meat. And to every beast of the earth, and to every fowl of the air, and to every thing that creepeth upon the earth, wherein there is life, I have given every green herb for meat: and it was so" (Gen 1:29-30).

Were plants and fruits alone sufficient to have kept the first men in the excellent health necessary for long and active lives?

A well-rounded diet? Nutritionists name six kinds of nutrients: water, carbohydrates, fats, proteins, vitamins, and minerals. The first four are "macronutrients" we must have in large amounts. Much water is needed, since the body is 50-75% water. A lot of carbohydrates and fats are a must for energy; proteins for body tissues. Vitamins and minerals, the "micronutrients," are taken in minute quantities, but are vital for growth and organ functions.

Plants and fruits have high water contents. Grains, legumes, and rootcrops are mostly carbohydrates. Oil sources, like coconut, olive, corn, soybean, sunflower, supply fats. Fruits and vegetables are rich in vitamins and minerals. But proteins are best obtained from animals as milk, eggs, meat, fish. These are complete proteins containing all the essential amino acids. Cereals, nuts, and vegetables, lacking one or more essential amino acids, are incomplete proteins. A primeval vegetarian diet would not have been well-rounded. Or was it?

Were all the nutrients that the first men and animals needed in the right amounts in the plants and fruits that have since become extinct? The herbivorous dinosaurs were the biggest creatures on earth and lasted for millions of years. The biggest and strongest land animals today are the plant-eating elephants, giraffes, rhinoceroses, buffaloes. Part of the dinosaurs' diet 248-65 million years ago were leaves of the ginkgo tree, today a "living fossil" in China and Japan. Used for centuries as a medicine, ginkgo is reputed to help improve memory and concentration

among those with Alzheimer's disease. It calls to mind the *"tree of life...
the leaves of the tree were for the healing of the nations"* (Rev 22:2).

Flesh-eating creatures

In many paleontological digs around the globe, animal bones have
been found with manlike fossils. Java and Peking man sites yielded
remains of bats, monkeys, rhinoceroses, elephants, wild cats. Hominids
ate many herbivores like deer, goats, and oxen, but their diet included
carnivorous predators and scavengers such as lions, wolves, bears.

Traders or raiders? Archeologists believe, based on mixed artifacts
found, that primitive Neanderthals may have traded with the more
modern Cro-Magnons. The May 16, 1996, issue of *Nature* reported the
discovery southeast of Auxerre, France, of Neanderthal fossils with bone
and ivory jewelry nearly identical to those of Cro-Magnons. The find
suggested that Neanderthals probably bartered with Cro-Magnons.[109]

Did they trade with each other or raid one another? Skeletal remains
show that Neanderthals and Cro-Magnons lived in a brutal period.
There were signs of violence in the form of broken bones, scars, and
healed-over bone growths. In particular, there was a high incidence of
neck and head injuries. The artifacts could have been spoils of war.

Man-eating men. A French-American team has unearthed
evidence of cannibalism at a Neanderthal site in France. The *Encarta
Encyclopedia* tells of hominid and animal fossils that had been
butchered the same way: "faunal and hominid remains were subjected
to similar treatment. In the case of Moula-Guercy, crania and limb bones
of both taxa are broken... Bone fracture is presumably related to
processing for marrow and brains in both *Homo* and *Cervus*."[110]

Other *Homo erectus*, Neanderthal, and early *Homo sapiens* (Cro-
Magnon) sites piece together the same grisly picture: With sharp stone
tools, hominids dismembered and defleshed their kills. They used stone
hammers and anvils to break open the big bones for the marrow. Many
skulls had been bashed open to extract the brains. Evidence indicates
some Neanderthals may have done the same to their relatives.

Signs of cannibalism are present in only a few sites, but because the
total number of sites is small, it was statistically a widespread practice.

Day-Age 6-n:
- Circa 57,221 to 28,611 years ago (Duration: approximately
  28,611 years)

Day-Age 6-o:
- Circa 28,611 to 13,306 years ago (Duration: approximately
  14,306 years)

End of Day 6

"And God saw every thing that he had made, and, behold, it was very good. And the evening and the morning were the sixth day" (Gen 1:31-2:1).

Day-Age 6 Summary:
- Total duration (Day-Age 6-a to 6-o): circa 468,735,694 years. (To round figures, 0.8858 remainder from the exponential regression has been added to the remaining 14,305.1142 years, for a full 14,306 years. See table at the end of this chapter.)

Day 7: Day of rest

"Thus the heavens and the earth were finished, and all the host of them. And on the seventh day God ended his work which he had made; and he rested on the seventh day from all his work which he had made. And God blessed the seventh day, and sanctified it: because that in it he had rested from all his work which God created and made" (Gen 2:1-3).

Interpretations of Day 7:
- Literal 24-Hour Days: 1 day after man was created circa 6,000 years ago
- Thousand-Year Days: circa 6,000-5,000 years ago
- Diminishing Day-Ages: circa 13,306 to 6,153 years ago (Duration: approximately 7,153 years)

Shift to 1,000-year "days"?

After the seven-"day" Creation "week," the flow of time appears to have shifted inexplicably to a dual mode for all, as laid down in 2 Peter 3:8 (*"one day is with the Lord as a thousand years, and a thousand years as one day"*; cf. Ps 90:4): literal 24-hour days from man's standpoint, and prophetic 1,000-year "days" from God's viewpoint.

Thus, both Young and Old Earth Creationists now reckon days as 24-hour periods, but at the same time are subject to God's 1,000-year "days" in the prophetic countdown.

Countdown to completion.

In the Diminishing Day-Ages timeline, some 7,153 years were still remaining in 4004 B.C. at the creation of modern man's ancestor, Adam, before the full 15 billion years could be completed.

Homo sapiens sapiens. The subspecies *Homo sapiens sapiens,* whose first specimen was Adam, includes all people living today. The braincase of modern man ranges from about 1,000 to 2,000 cu cm (60 to 120 cu in), averaging around 1,350 cu cm (80 cu in),[111] slightly smaller than those of Neanderthals and Cro-Magnons, but proportional to a less massive muscular build.

The *World Book* reports that, after scientifically comparing DNA samples of modern men with those of Neanderthals and other extinct hominids, many scientists conclude that the results indicate all people today form a separate species distinct from prehistoric humans.[112] (The scientists, however, fell short of saying how the first man came about.)

Homo sapiens sapiens timeline.

- Circa 6,000-5,000 years ago. God created Adam some 6,000 years ago (4004 B.C.) The wheel was invented around 5,500 years ago (3500 B.C.) in Sumer, Mesopotamia,[113] where an early writing system in the form of pictographs also appeared at about the same time; followed 5,300 years ago by Egyptian hieroglyphics (3300-3200 B.C.).[114]

- Circa 5,000-4,000 years ago. The Bronze Age began some 5,000 years ago (3000 B.C.) in Greece and China.[115] Noah was born around the same time (2948 B.C.). The Flood took place in 2348 B.C.

- Circa 4,000-3,000 years ago. Abraham was born about 4,000 years ago (1996 B.C.) The Iron Age began sometime around 1500-1000 B.C., with the use of iron for tools and weapons.[116]

- Circa 3,000-2,000 years ago. David lived and died about 3,000 years ago (1015 B.C.), followed by his son Solomon (975 B.C.). Rome was founded in 753 B.C., made a republic in 509 B.C., and became an empire in 27 B.C.[117]

- Circa 2,000-1,000 years ago. Christ was born about 2,000 years ago (5 B.C.). The eastern Roman Empire fell in 476 A.D.; the Dark Ages (early Middle Ages) began, ending in the 900s; the Medieval Period (late Middle Ages) lasted until the 1400s.

- Circa 1,000 years ago-present. Christians launched Crusades from 1096 to 1396 to regain the Holy Land from the Muslims. The Renaissance, an era of learning and cultural revival, lasted from about 1450 to 1600. In the Age of Enlightenment, from the 1600s to the late 1700s, philosophers held reason as the best tool for finding truth. The modern age began in the 1700s.

- Next 1,000 years. The Millennium, the prophesied 1,000-year era of peace (mankind's great Sabbath of rest), during which Christ will reign on earth as King of Kings (Rev 20:1-7).

Diminishing Day-Ages Chronology
(7-"Day" Creation "Week" until 3000 A.D. = 15 Billion Years)

Day-Ages	Scriptures	Beginning, circa years ago	Science/History	Occurrence, circa years ago
Day 1	Light	15,000,000,000	Big Bang	13,700,000,000
			Milky Way	8,000,000,000
Day 2	Firmament	7,500,000,000	Sun, Earth, Moon	4,600,000,000
Day 3	Seas, dry land, vegetation	3,750,000,000	Oceans; bacteria/ cells w/out nuclei	3,500,000,000
Day 4	Heavenly lights	1,875,000,000	Atmosphere thinned	
			Cells with nuclei	1,800,000,000
Day 5	Sea creatures,	937,500,000	Animal life forms	700,000,000
	flying creatures		Cambrian Explosion	544,000,000
			Chordates, fish	490,000,000
Day 6-a		468,750,000	85% extinction	438,000,000
	Land animals		Amphibians	417,000,000
			82% extinction	367,000,000
	Creeping		Insects	350,000,000
	things		Reptiles	323,000,000
	Beasts, cattle		Mammals	248,000,000
			96% extinction	245,000,000
6-b		234,375,000	76% extinction	208,000,000
			Archaeopteryx	150,000,000
6-c		117,187,500	76% extinction	65,000,000
			Primates (lemurs,	"
6-d		58,593,750	monkeys,	
6-e		29,296,875	apes)	
6-f		14,648,437	Ramapithecus	14,000,000
6-g		7,324,218	Sahelanthropus	7,000,000
			Orrorin tugenensis	6,000,000
			Ardipithecus	4,400,000
			Australopithecus	4,000,000
6-h		3,662,109	Kenyanthropus	3,500,000
			Homo habilis	2,800,000
			Homo rudolfensis	1,900,000
6-i		1,831,054	Homo erectus	1,500,000
6-j		915,527	H. heidelbergensis	600,000
6-k	Man	457,763	H. Neanderthalensis	300,000
6-l		228,882	Homo sapiens	200,000
6-m	"	114,441		
6-n		57,221		
6-o		28,611		
Day 7	Day of rest	14,306		
Day 8	Adam	6,000	Wheel, writing	5,500
Day 9	Noah, Flood	5,000	Bronze Age	5,000
Day 10	Abraham	4,000	Iron Age	3,500
Day 11	David, Solomon	3,000	Rome	2,750
Day 12	Christ	2,000	Dark/Middle Ages	1,600
Day 13	(Crusades)	1,000	Modern Age	250
Day 14	Millennium/rest	(near future)		

5

Early Earth Enigmas

I *have made the earth, and created man upon it:*
I, even my hands, have stretched out the heavens,
and all their host have I commanded"

-- Isaiah 45:12.

The universe appears to have been mathematically designed. Greek mathematician Pythagoras, who taught that the universe was built upon numbers, is known to have said: "Nature geometrizes."[1]

Sir Jonathan Sacks, Chief Rabbi, United Hebrew Congregations of the Commonwealth, is awed: "The believer might wonder, as does Lord Rees, president of the Royal Society, in his Just Six Numbers, at the extraordinary precision of the six mathematical constants that determine the shape of the Universe, such that if even one were fractionally different neither we nor the Universe would exist."[2]

Nobel laureate for physics Steven Weinberg concurs: "Life as we know it would be impossible if any one of several physical quantities had slightly different values... One constant does seem to require incredible fine tuning." He quantifies the tuning as one part in 10^{120}![3]

Sir James Jeans, knighted British physicist, once remarked: "From the intrinsic evidence of His creation, the Great Architect of the Universe now begins to appear as a pure mathematician."[4]

Isaiah expresses the same thought in enigmatic terms: *"Who has measured the waters in the hollow of His hand, Measured heaven with a span And calculated the dust of the earth in a measure? Weighed the mountains in scales And the hills in a balance?* (Isa 40:12, NKJV).

"Anthropic" planet

Earth, a tiny planet, is just one of the countless objects in the vastness of space, yet it is the only one known to support life. Scientists are puzzled by the numerous "accidents" that favor life on earth. Many conclude the Earth is "anthropic" -- that is, "specially made for man."

Size of the Earth.

The scientific data suggest that the Earth did not randomly come into existence. It has precise measurements that look like the product of careful planning and design. So said God to Job: "*Where were you when I laid the foundations of the earth? Tell Me, if you have understanding. Who determined its measurements? Surely you know! Or who stretched the line upon it?*" (Job 38:4-5, NKJV).

If the Earth were larger, gravity would be stronger. Hydrogen would be unable to escape from the surface and collect in the atmosphere, rendering the planet inhospitable to life. If the Earth were smaller, gravity would be weaker. Oxygen would escape into space, and animals could have never emerged on the planet.

Location and motion.

Astrophysicist Paul Davies, in his book *The Goldilocks Enigma* (2007), nicknamed the Earth "the Goldilocks Planet." It has just the right temperature, neither too hot nor too cold.[5]

Distance from the sun. The Earth lies at an ideal distance from the Sun: 93,000,000 miles (150,000,000 km) away. If the distance changed by as little as 2%, all life on Earth would perish. If the Earth were a bit farther from the sun, water would freeze; a little closer, water would evaporate. Consider our neighbors: Venus, closer to the Sun, is too hot; while Mars, farther away, is too cold.

Earth's orbit. The Earth's orbit around the Sun is just about 3% off a perfect circle – just right to keep water liquid. If its orbit were as elliptical as that of Mars, water would alternately boil when we are nearest to the Sun and freeze when we are farthest.

The Earth orbits the sun at a speed of about 66,600 miles per hour. That velocity is perfect to offset the gravitational pull of the sun, as well as keep the earth at an ideal distance. If the speed were slower, the Earth would be gradually pulled toward the sun, eventually having all life scorched to extinction. If faster, the Earth would move farther and farther away from the sun, and eventually become a frozen wasteland.

Rotation and axis. The Earth's rotation period cannot be changed by even just a few percent. Too slow, the temperature differences between night and day would be too great. Too fast, wind velocities would become disastrous.

The tilt of the Earth's axis is at a 23.5° angle relative to the sun. Greater, summers would be much hotter and winters much colder, wreaking havoc on plant cycles and agriculture.

Neighboring objects. For a satellite, the moon is too big for the Earth. And, yet, it is just the right size. Its gravitational pull produces the tides that prevent the oceans from either boiling or freezing. Coastal waters are cleansed, oxygen and nutrients which sustain marine life are replenished, and the tilt of the Earth is stabilized.

The gargantuan planet Jupiter, with its massive gravitational force, occupies a nearby location that is favorable to our planet. Otherwise, Earth would be struck about a thousand times more frequently by asteroids, comets, and space debris.

Atmosphere and magnetosphere.

Oxygen. This life-sustaining gas comprises 21% of the Earth's atmosphere. Much more than that would be harmful – oxygen could be toxic if breathed too long, as well as make the environment fire-prone.

Ozone, an unstable oxygen molecule, forms a layer in the top level of the atmosphere. The ozone layer blocks most of the sun's ultraviolet radiation that can burn sensitive skin, damage eyes, and cause cancer.

Nitrogen. This constitutes 78% of the gases surrounding the planet. It dilutes the oxygen, serving as a fertilizer for plant life. Lightning bolts around the world mix nitrogen with oxygen each day, producing compounds that come down to earth with rain and enrich the soil.

Carbon dioxide. The amount of this gas in the atmosphere (3/100 of 1%) is just right – less would not be enough to keep vegetation thriving; more, say 10%, would be fatal to both animals and humans.

All the other necessary elements are present – carbon, hydrogen, phosphorous, sulfur, as well as liquid water -- in the right proportions, as though deliberately combined. Science writer Stuart Clark wonders: "Chemically speaking, Earth is simply better set up for life than its neighbors. So how come we got all the good stuff?"[6]

Magnetosphere. The Earth has just enough internal radioactivity to maintain its iron core in a molten state,[7] thus creating a protective force field surrounding the planet as far as 40,000 miles out. The magnetosphere protects the Earth against cosmic radiation.

Isaiah tells us why God did all these: *"For this is what the LORD says -- he who created the heavens, he is God; he who fashioned and made the earth, he founded it; he did not create it to be empty, but formed it to be inhabited..."* (Isa 45:18a, NIV).

The air we breathe

When the Earth became a solid body, about 4.6 billion years ago, the atmosphere is believed to have consisted solely of volcanic emissions -- a mixture of water vapor (85%), carbon dioxide (10%), sulfur dioxide, and nitrogen, with almost no oxygen.[8]

Rise of oxygen.

Around 2.4 billion years ago, new marine microorganisms capable of photosynthesis (primitive plants) began splitting water molecules to produce oxygen using the sun's energy.[9]

Subsequently, oxygen escaped from the oceans to the atmosphere, starting the formation of the ozone layer, which acted as a sunscreen that reduced harmful ultraviolet rays striking the oceans. This allowed photosynthetic bacteria that previously lived in the depths to move up to the surface and increase the output of oxygen.[10]

About 100 million years later, organisms with 2-3 different cell types and deriving energy from oxygen appeared. Then followed more complex cells equipped with mitochondria (sausage-shaped structures that produce energy in cells).[11] Further increases of oxygen in the air led to the emergence of new air-breathing marine animals approximately 570 million years ago.[12]

Bigger creatures.

The availability of more oxygen greatly enhanced the metabolic efficiency of organisms in extracting nutrients from food and converting them to energy. Many marine creatures grew to enormous sizes. Chambered nautiluses that are eight inches wide today measured nine feet across.[13] On land, cockroaches were about a foot long. Dragonflies had wings almost three feet in span.[14]

Air bubbles in amber (fossil resin from trees) strongly suggest that oxygen in the atmosphere might have been as high as 25%.[15] Then, in the last 10 million years, atmospheric oxygen went down to its present level of 21%. Why?

Some scientists speculate that great fires burned over the earth about 10 million years ago, reducing the number of trees and, consequently, the amount of photosynthesis and oxygen.[16]

The wonders of water

Earth is the only planet positively known to have liquid water. The most abundant substance on earth, water covers approximately 71% of the planet's surface.

Water is essential to life. Combined with carbon and certain other key elements, water is the basis of almost all the molecules of living organisms. Fluids primarily made up of water, like sap and blood, carry the vital materials that plants, animals, and humans need to live. Water is an ideal solvent for metabolism as it dissolves the food that sustains living organisms.

Where all the water came from remains an enigma. If the solar system and the Earth had formed from clouds of gases and dust, hardly any water would be found on Earth. Any water this close to the Sun would have been vaporized and blown away by the solar wind, like water vapor in the tails of comets.

Law of nature altered?

Most liquids contract as their temperature goes down. So, too, water. As it gets colder, water in rivers, lakes, and seas becomes denser and heavier, sinking and forcing the lighter, warmer water beneath to rise to the top. Yet, on reaching precisely 7°F (4°C) above zero, the process is inexplicably reversed! Water begins to expand until frozen into ice, its volume increasing by 10%. Being lighter, ice floats above liquid water.

The ice on the surface serves as an insulator that keeps the water below from freezing, protecting organisms beneath. If water did not stop contracting just before freezing point, ice would be heavier and sink to the bottom, where the sun's heat could not melt it. Eventually, layers upon layers of ice would pile up, turning the Earth into an ice planet.

Did God recalibrate a law of nature to make Earth hospitable to life? This reminds us of what He said through Jeremiah: *"For I know the plans I have for you," declares the LORD, "plans to prosper you and not to harm you, plans to give you hope and a future"* (Jer 29:11, NIV).

First life forms

Scientists believe life on earth began in the water. Charles Darwin, who advanced the theory of evolution in his 1859 book *On the Origin of Species*, once wrote to a friend that life might have begun in "some warm little pond." His evolutionary theory assumes that, billions of years ago, microscopic life spontaneously appeared.

Spontaneous generation?

Richard Dawkins, an atheist, summarizes the idea in his book, *The Selfish Gene* (1976): "The newly formed Earth had an atmosphere made up of carbon dioxide, methane, ammonia, and water. These simple compounds were broken up by energy from sunlight, lightning, and exploding volcanoes, then reformed into amino acids. These accumulated in the sea and combined into protein-like compounds, producing a potentially 'organic soup.' Then, 'a particularly remarkable molecule was formed by accident' – a molecule that had the ability to reproduce itself." (The accident, the author admitted, was exceedingly improbable.) Similar molecules clustered together, and then, by an exceedingly improbable accident again, wrapped a protective barrier of other protein molecules around themselves as a membrane. Thus, it is thought, the first "living" cell generated itself. (In the preface to his book, Dawkins says: "This book should be read almost as though it were science fiction.")[17]

The first organic molecules are said to have been simple sugars and amino acids, the building blocks of proteins. Proteins, in turn, are the building blocks of living cells. The first living cell is presumed to have been anaerobic (surviving without oxygen), using methane for energy.[18]

The sudden appearance of life all by itself from non-living matter is called "spontaneous generation" or *abiogenesis*, which comes from the Greek words *a* ("without"), *bio* ("life") and *genesis* ("birth"). However, this theory violates the law of biogenesis, which states that all life must come from preceding life of its kind.

Spontaneous dissolution. "Spontaneous generation" has serious problems. First, the same energy from sunlight, lightning, and volcanic explosions that split up the compounds in the atmosphere would have even more quickly destroyed any amino acids that formed. So, the amino acids had to reach the oceans quickly for protection. However, science writer George Wald observes that in the water "spontaneous dissolution is much more probable, and hence proceeds more rapidly, than spontaneous synthesis."[19] Mike Riddle, a creationist, explains that water immediately destroys amino acids by *hydrolysis* ("water splitting"). The entry of a water molecule between two bonded molecules (such as amino acids) causes them to split. The "water tends to break chains of amino acids apart. If any protein had formed in the oceans 3.5 billion years ago, they would have quickly disintegrated."[20]

"Catch 22" situation. If there was no oxygen in the atmosphere, there would have been no ozone layer, and the ultraviolet rays from the sun would have instantly destroyed any newly forming amino acids. If there was oxygen, it would have soon oxidized and destroyed any self-organizing amino acids. Either way, the emergence of life was doomed from the start. Author Michael Denton notes in his book *Evolution: A Theory in Crisis* (1985): "What we have is a sort of a 'Catch 22' situation. If we have oxygen we have no organic compounds, but if we don't have oxygen we have none either"[21] It was a no-win situation. But then something, or Someone, intervened.

Biogenesis vs. Abiogenesis

In the 1600s scientists believed life could arise from decaying matter, because maggots and flies emerged from dung, rotting meat, and garbage. Italian biologist Francesco Redi demonstrated in 1668 that maggots did not appear in meat if kept away from flies.[22] In 1768 another Italian, naturalist Lazzaro Spallanzani, proved that substances originally containing microorganisms, when boiled and then sealed, remained microbe-free.[23]

It did not keep German biologist Ernst Haeckel (1834-1919), a rabid Darwinian, from promoting abiogenesis. Biochemist Michael Behe says: "From the limited view of cells that microscopes provided, Haeckel believed that a cell was a 'simple little lump of albuminous combination of carbon,' not much different from a piece of microscopic Jell-O. So it seemed to Haeckel that such simple life, with no internal organs, could be produced from inanimate material."[24]

Famous French microbiologist Louis Pasteur refuted abiogenesis in 1862 in his "On the Organized Particles Existing in the Air." He showed that microbes would grow only if a solution was exposed to air with spores of bacteria. In 1869, British physicist John Tyndall demonstrated that when dust was present putrefaction occurred; in the absence of dust, no decay took place.[25]

Lab-created "life"?

In 1953 chemist Stanley Miller, a graduate student at the University of Chicago, and Nobel laureate Harold Urey, put a mixture of gases through heat and electricity and produced a tar-like substance with some amino acids in it. The Miller-Urey result rocked the world: the "building blocks of life," it was claimed, could be produced in the laboratory!

However, the experiment used a man-made "atmosphere" that did not include oxygen, which would have produced a different result. The process also had "unnatural" components such as a "trap" (which quickly removed chemical products from the destructive energy sources that made them). Further, biologist Gary Parker notes: "The molecules Miller made did not include only the amino acids required for living systems; they included even greater quantities of amino acids that would be highly destructive to any 'evolving' life."[26]

Besides, half the amino acids produced were chemically "right-handed." Every living protein, whether in animals, plants, molds, bacteria, and even viruses -- except in some diseased or aging tissue – is made up of at least 300 amino acids, practically all of them structurally "left-handed." Hence, the probability of a living protein being formed through sheer chance is equal to unerringly getting 300 "heads" in a row from the toss of a coin.

Co-authors Sir Fred Hoyle and Chandra Wickramasinghe calculated the odds for a living protein to form solely by chance in one place as just one chance in $10^{40,000}$. In comparison, statisticians regard a probability of less than 1 in 10^{50} to be an absolute impossibility. They concluded that it was "an outrageously small probability that could not be faced even if the whole universe consisted of organic soup."[27]

The Miller-Urey experiment (and all other experiments after it) failed to produce even one single living protein – never mind that a protein still has a long, long way to go before becoming a complete living cell.

Enough time and chance?

Some scientists argue that, given enough time, as well as chance, all things are possible – even the emergence of the first living things from inanimate matter. Writer C. Folsome asked them in the magazine *Scientific American*: "Can we really form a biological cell by waiting for chance combinations of organic compounds? Harold Morowitz, in his book *Energy Flow and Biology*, computed that merely to create a bacterium would require more time than the Universe might ever see if chance combinations of its molecules were the only driving force."[28]

Chemist Ilya Prigogine, 1977 Nobel Prize laureate, sums it up in *Physics Today*: "The idea of the spontaneous genesis of life in its present form is therefore improbable, even on the scale of billions of years."[29] Gerald Schroeder informs us that: "Since 1979, articles based on the premise that life arose through chance random reactions over billions of years are not accepted in reputable journals."[30]

The "simple" cell.

Charles Darwin believed that single-celled organisms were most primitive. Until the first half of the 20th century, scientists called the most basic living unit the "simple cell" -- made up of nothing more than a jelly-like "protoplasm."

In 1963 Dr. George Palade of the Rockefeller Institute discovered a complex network of minuscule tubes and sacs within the protoplasm, now called the "endoplasmic reticulum."[31] It became evident that there is no such thing as a "simple" cell. Even the earliest unicellular organisms on earth were unimaginably complex. Molecular biologist Jonathan Wells and mathematician William Dembski concur that "the simplest life forms we know, the prokaryotic cells (such as bacteria, which lack a nucleus), are themselves immensely complex. Moreover, they are every bit as high-tech as the eukaryotic cells..."[32] Single-celled animals can "catch food, digest it, get rid of wastes, move around, build houses, engage in sexual activity... with no tissues, no organs, no hearts and no minds..."[33] They even communicate with each other using chemicals.

We read in the *National Geographic*: "Each cell is a world brimming with as many as two hundred trillion tiny groups of atoms called molecules."[34] *Newsweek* is quite graphic: "Each of those 100 trillion cells functions like a walled city. Power plants generate the cell's energy. Factories produce proteins, vital units of chemical commerce. Complex transportation systems guide specific chemicals from point to point within the cell and beyond. Sentries at the barricades control the export and import markets, and monitor the outside world for signs of danger. Disciplined biological armies stand ready to grapple with invaders. A centralized genetic government maintains order."[35]

In addition, the "simple" cell has one capability not even today's most advanced machines can do: It can replicate its entire structure within a matter of a few hours.

The theory of evolution

The roots of the theory of evolution goes back many years before Charles Darwin. In the 17th century, scientists like Francis Bacon and William Harvey recognized it. Darwin's own grandfather, Erasmus Darwin (d. 1802), wrote about it. The French naturalist Chevalier de Lamarck proposed a similar theory in 1809. In 1835 and 1837, Edward Blyth, a creationist, published a treatise on natural selection.[36]

In 1855, Alfred Russel Wallace published the theory of evolution in a brief note in the *Annals and Magazine of Natural History*. On March 9, 1858, he explained the theory in a letter to Charles Darwin.[37] Twenty months later, in 1859, Darwin published a more detailed version of the theory in his book that he had been at work on earlier: *On the Origin of Species by Means of Natural Selection, or the Preservation of Favoured Races in the Struggle for Life*. It became an instant sensation.

The Theory of Evolution posits that all living things changed through the ages into all the life forms today. From the first living cell, "simple" organisms evolved into fish, then into amphibians, then into reptiles, then into birds and mammals, then into primates and, eventually, man.

Darwin speculated that similarities in different species, such as the five digits of a man's hand, a bat's wing, and a dolphin's flipper, which he called "homology," constituted evidence for a common ancestry. He capitalized on the idea of "natural selection" or "survival of the fittest" –

that is, nature selected the fittest organisms to survive. The "fittest" individuals supposedly had traits that enabled them to fare better than other members of their groups.

Darwin's book led many Christians to abandon their belief in the Biblical creation by God. Almost all universities and public schools today teach Darwinian evolution, which holds that the ten million-plus species on earth evolved from a single cell that suddenly came to life around 3.5 billion years ago. We must give credit to Darwin for honesty, though, because he admitted that his theory needed to be proven.

"Ontogeny recapitulates phylogeny"?

Ernst Heinrich Haeckel helped spread Darwin's theory of evolution through lectures and books. He popularized the catchphrase "Ontogeny recapitulates phylogeny." Accordingly, every animal's embryonic stages (ontogeny) replicate in just a few weeks its species' evolutionary history (phylogeny) which took millions of years. Thus, a human fetus begins life as a single cell, just like the first organisms on earth. Next, the cell multiplies as a hollow ball similar to sponges. The embryo then folds in to form a cuplike structure like jellyfish and corals. It afterward lengthens, passing through phases with gill slits, fin-like limbs, and a tail typical of fish and amphibians. The embryo then takes on a basic mammalian form, before finally assuming the shape of a primate.

Haeckel, however, cheated. He altered illustrations to fit his theory when the similarity of embryos was not satisfactory. He was found out, charged with fraud, and convicted by a university court at Jena, Germany. Eventually, "The theory of recapitulation was destroyed in 1921 by Professor Walter Garstang in a famous paper. Since then no respectable biologist has ever used the theory of recapitulation, because it was utterly unsound, created by a Nazi-like preacher named Haeckel."[38] Co-authors George Gaylord Simpson and William S. Beck (*Life: An Introduction to Biology*, 1965) confirm this: "It is now firmly established that ontogeny does not repeat phylogeny."[39]

Surprisingly, many modern textbooks still include the disproved idea as proof for evolution.

Mutation: engine of evolution?

Evolutionists claim that mutation, a change in the genetic material (DNA) inside the cells of plants and animals, is the engine of evolution. Mutational changes are said to be passed on to descendants – producing "improved" new members of the species, which gradually turn into a new distinct species.

Harmful, not helpful. For mutation to happen, new information has to be introduced in the genes of the organism. Yet, practically all mutations showed a loss, rather than a gain, of genetic information – resulting in missing eyes, limbs, wings, tails, etc. Author Lee Spetner (*Not by Chance*, 1996) reports: "All point mutations that have been studied on the molecular level turn out to reduce the genetic information and not to increase it."[40]

In any case, slight mutational changes are usually insignificant, but major genetic mutations, instead of producing improved organisms, are generally harmful to the species. Author Peo C. Koller (*Chromosomes and Genes*, 1971) tells us: "The greatest proportion of mutations are deleterious to the individual who carries the mutated gene. It was found in experiments that, for every successful or useful mutation, there are many thousands which are harmful."[41] The *Encyclopedia Americana* says that "mutants illustrated in biology textbooks are a collection of freaks and monstrosities, and mutation seems to be a destructive rather than a constructive process."[42]

Author G. Ledyard Stebbins (*Processes of Organic Evolution*, 1971) relates that in laboratory experiments, mutated insects were kept with normal members of their species. "After a greater or lesser number of generations the mutants are eliminated."[43] They were unable to compete and died off, because they had become less adapted for survival than their normal fellows.

Statistically improbable. Researchers often conduct experiments with fruit flies, chosen for their short life spans. Gordon Rattray Taylor, former chief science advisor of BBC TV (*The Great Evolution Mystery*, 1983), observed: "It is a striking, but not much mentioned fact that, though geneticists have been breeding fruit-flies for sixty years or more in labs all round the world -- flies which produce a new generation every eleven days -- they have never yet seen the emergence of a new species or even a new enzyme."[44] Although fruit flies can be made to mutate into deformed specimens, they are all still fruit flies.

Co-authors P. Moorhead and M. Kaplan ("Mathematical Challenges to the Neo-Darwinian Interpretation of Evolution," 1967) report: "The Wistar Institute symposium in 1967 brought together leading biologists and mathematicians in what turned out to be a futile attempt to find a mathematically reasonable basis for the assumption that random mutations are the driving force behind evolution. Unfortunately, each time the mathematics showed the statistical improbability of a given assumption..."[45]

Pierre-Paul Grasse, former French Academy of Sciences president and an evolutionist, admits: "No matter how numerous they may be, mutations do not produce any kind of evolution."[46]

Anti-mutation mechanisms.

Two British scientists, Dr. A.R. Fersht and Dr. G.R. Lambert, made an important "discovery that enzymes exist within living cells that have just one assignment in nature. They find and correct any errors in the genetic code. These errors can creep into the code because of radiation, some chemicals, or for other reasons. However, these enzymes faithfully correct any errors, preventing mutations."[47] Francis Hitching (*The Neck of the Giraffe*, 1982) adds: "Genes are a powerful stabilizing mechanism whose main function is to prevent new forms evolving."[48]

The law of genetics dictates that the offspring of the parent organism shall be of the same species. This is exactly what the Bible teaches: *"But God giveth it a body as it hath pleased him, and to every seed his own body. All flesh is not the same flesh: but there is one kind of flesh of men, another flesh of beasts, another of fishes, and another of birds"* (1 Cor 15:38-39).

Microevolution vs. macroevolution

Pierre-Paul Grasse, as a zoologist, observed that adaptations within species have nothing to do with evolution. They are just minor changes around a stable genotype. For example, there are no less than 200 breeds of dog today, descended from just a few ancient dogs and wolves. They range from tiny Chihuahuas to burly St. Bernards, from cuddly Pomeranians to vicious pit bulls. Yet, they are all still dogs. Citrus fruits vary greatly – from sweet nectarines to sour lemons, little limes to large pomelos -- but each one is still a citrus. They are examples of "microevolution." What Darwin "discovered" – such as the variations in the beaks of finches in the Galapagos Islands -- were limited biological principles that govern microevolution (change within a species), not those governing "speciation" or "macroevolution" (change from one species to another).

In breeding experiments, scientists have tried to keep modifying selected plants and animals indefinitely by crossbreeding to see if they could develop new species. Result? "Breeders usually find that after a few generations, an optimum is reached beyond which further improvement is impossible, and there has been no new species formed... Breeding procedures, therefore, would seem to refute, rather than support evolution."[49]

Microevolution in reverse. In the 1930s brothers Heinz and Lutz Heck, Munich Zoo and Berlin Zoo directors, respectively, recreated extinct animals. First was the tarpan, a Stone Age horse whose drawings were on the walls of caves in France and the last of which died in captivity in 1887. They crossed stallions known to have descended from the tarpan with modern mares. After just two breedings, a foal with all the tarpan characteristics was born.

They had actually followed their father, who, while running the Berlin Zoo, crossed the ibex (a wild goat) with domesticated goats. The older Heck produced animals with the exact color of the bezoar, the Middle Eastern wild goat that was the progenitor of all goats today.

The Heck brothers also recreated the auroch, the ancestor of modern cattle. The last of the huge auroch, which weighed up to a ton, died in a game preserve in Poland in 1627. After ten years of crossbreeding, they obtained a calf with all the traits of an auroch.[50]

Problems with evolution

There were a few gaps in the "evolutionary tree" when Darwin published *On the Origin of Species* in 1859. Believers in the theory expected these gaps to be filled as fossil finds increased.

We read in the *Newsweek* magazine issue of March 29, 1982: "Darwin, and most of those who followed him, believed that the work of evolution was slow, gradual and continuous and that a complete lineage of ancestors, shading imperceptibly one into the next, could in theory be reconstructed for all living animals... But a century of digging since then has only made their absence more glaring."[51]

Evolutionary gaps.

David B. Kitts of the School of Geology and Geophysics, University of Oklahoma, said in the September 1974 issue of the journal *Evolution*: "Despite the bright promise that paleontology provides a means of 'seeing' evolution, it has presented some nasty difficulties for evolutionists the most notorious of which is the presence of 'gaps' in the fossil record. Evolution requires intermediate forms between species and paleontology does not provide them."[52]

Norman D. Newell, former Curator of Historical Geology at the American Museum of Natural History, wrote in *Adventures in Earth History* (1970) that "the gaps which separate the highest categories may never be bridged in the fossil record. Many of the discontinuities tend to be more and more emphasized with increased collecting."[53]

In Darwin's time, all living things fell under two kingdoms: plant and animal. As science progressed and scientists recognized finer distinctions between organisms, the number of kingdoms rose to the five that we have today: Prokaryotae, Protista, Fungi, Plantae, and Animalia. As the groupings increased, the "missing links" multiplied.

No transitional forms.

Many one-celled life forms exist, but there are no known forms of life with 2, 3, 4, or 5 cells. Multi-celled organisms with 6–20 cells are parasites that depend on complex animals as hosts to perform functions such as respiration and digestion for them. If evolution is true, there should be transitional forms with 2–5 cells even as fossils.

Plants. Some 375,000 species of plants exist on earth today, and most have not changed from the way they first appeared as fossils. Geneticist Jerry Bergman notes in the *Technical Journal* (Internet): "A major problem for Neo-Darwinism is the complete lack of evidence for plant evolution in the fossil record. As a whole, the fossil evidence of prehistoric plants is actually very good, yet no convincing transitional forms have been discovered in the abundant fossil record."[54]

If plants evolved, nonvascular plants should have preceded vascular plants (with sap-carrying channels). However, there are no fossilized nonvascular plants in the rock layers formed before the earliest vascular plants appeared. Further, no traces of stages leading to the development of seeds and fruits have been found. Darwin wrote to his friend, botanist Joseph Hooker, that the sudden appearance of flowering plants in the fossil record was an "abominable mystery."[55]

Arthropods. Of creatures with jointed legs, the U.S. government handbook *Insects* states: "There is, however, no fossil evidence bearing on the question of insect origin; the oldest insects known show no transition to other arthropods"[56] like spiders, scorpions, centipedes, crustaceans, etc.

Vertebrates. A backbone distinguishes the fish, the first vertebrate, from invertebrates. For the fish to evolve into an amphibian, it had to develop a pelvic bone for legs to be attached to; but no fossil fish with an emergent pelvis has ever been found, not even the coelacanth. The fish has a heart with two chambers, an amphibian heart has three. The lungfish, which has gills plus a swim bladder it uses for breathing out of water, is often said to be the link between fish and amphibians. But the skull is entirely different. David Attenborough (*Life on Earth*, 1979) says that "the bones of their skulls are so different from those of the first fossil amphibians that one cannot be derived from the other."[57] Apparently, neither the lungfish nor the coelacanth evolved into amphibians.

Richard Milton (*Shattering the Myths of Darwinism*, 1997) notes: "Although each of these classes (fishes, amphibians, reptiles, mammals, and primates) is well represented in the fossil record, as of yet no one has discovered a fossil creature that is indisputably transitional between one species and another species. Not a single undisputed 'missing link' has been found in all the exposed rocks of the Earth's crust despite the most careful and extensive searches."[58]

A "missing link"? Just a second. Have we not earlier seen the archaeopteryx, which looks like the link between reptiles and birds?

Some scientists believe birds evolved from theropods (dinosaurs that walked on hind legs). However, theropods had tiny "arms," compared to the large wings of early birds. Moreover, their "hands" differed. Ann C. Burke and Alan Feduccia tell us in *Science* magazine (October 24, 1997): "Theropods have 'fingers' I, II, and III (having lost the 'ring finger' and little finger), while birds have fingers II, III, and IV."[59] In the same issue, Richard Hinchliffe notes that "most theropod dinosaurs and in particular the birdlike dromaeosaurs are all very much later in the fossil record than Archaeopteryx (the supposed first bird)."[60] In a subsequent issue (November 14, 1997), John Ruben et. al. argue that "a transition from a crocodilian to a bird lung would be impossible, because the transitional animal would have a life-threatening hernia or hole in its diaphragm."[61]

While the archaeopteryx appears like half-reptile and half-bird, no fossil remains look like an intermediate between a reptile and the archaeopteryx, or between the archaeopteryx and a true bird. W.E. Swinton ("The Origin of Birds," *Biology and Comparative Physiology of Birds*, 1960) concluded: "The origin of birds is largely a matter of deduction. There is no fossil evidence of the stages through which the remarkable change from reptile to bird was achieved."[62]

Hybrids? There are other creatures that look like crosses between species, but are not. Whales, porpoises, dolphins, and manatees live in the water and look like fish, but they are mammals that suckle their young. Of course, the most enigmatic hybrid-looking animal is the platypus. It has a bill like a duck, feeds underwater like a fish, and lays eggs like a bird or reptile, but is actually a mammal that produces milk for its offspring. The only member of the Ornithorhynchidae ("bird-snout") family, the platypus has neither "evolutionary" ancestors nor descendants even vaguely resembling it.

Charles Darwin had agonized: "Why, if species have descended from other species by fine gradations, do we not everywhere see innumerable transitional forms?... Why do we not find them imbedded in countless numbers in the crust of the earth?[63]

And why, if evolution is true, does it seem to have stopped?

Vestigial organs?

Several seemingly useless parts of the human body, presumed to be evolutionary "leftovers," are cited as proofs for the theory of evolution. Are they? Here are some of the best known.

Appendix. It is most often mentioned by evolutionists as one of the so-called "vestigial organs." But it has been found that the appendix is part of the lymphatic system, which, especially in early life, produces antibodies that fight infections in the digestive system.[64]

Tonsils (adenoids). These used to be removed from children when inflamed, but are now medically known to protect the nose and throat from infection against invading bacteria and viruses. They also filter out harmful substances that could pass into the digestive system. There are indications that people who have had their tonsils removed experience more problems in the upper respiratory tract.[65]

Thymus. An organ in the chest cavity that shrinks from childhood until maturity, the thymus is now recognized as the control center of the body's defense system against germs.

Coccyx. Better known as the "tailbone," it supposedly shows man evolved from monkeys. However, patients who have had their tailbones removed have difficulty sitting. The coccyx also holds the muscles for bowel and childbirth movements, supports internal organs, and keeps the end of the alimentary canal closed. It anchors the gluteus maximus, the large muscle along the back of the thigh, which enables us to walk upright (something monkeys cannot do).

Writers Mario Seiglie et al. tell us in *The Good News* magazine (November-December 2006): "The list of what were once considered vestigial organs in our body has gone down from 100 in the early 20th century to virtually zero…"[66]

"Irreducible complexity."

All organisms, from cells to humans, are "irreducibly complex" – all their basic components have to be in place before they can function. Thus, all species, extinct or extant, appear fully developed. There is no known partially-developed species.

Evolution, though, is believed to work through small, gradual steps, keeping new traits that it finds functional. Will it keep in reserve anything that does not work, even if potentially useful? There are no instances of half-developed appendages or organs in any fossilized or living organism – no budding eyes that could not see or partial wings that could not fly.

Blood clotting. Vital to healing wounds, blood-clotting in animals and man involves 20–30 complex chemical steps. Omission of one step, inclusion of an abnormal step, or alteration of the timing of a step will prevent blood from clotting and lead to death. If the first few of the many blood clotting factors were not immediately useful, the body would not have kept them, unaware that the rest of the factors would also form. How did such a complex, yet precise, process fully develop?

Charles Darwin had confessed in his famous book: "If it could be demonstrated that any complex organ existed which could not possibly have been formed by numerous, successive, slight modifications, my theory would absolutely break down."[67]

The eye. As a human embryo develops in its mother's womb, some one million optic nerves start to grow from the back of each eye, simultaneous with a corresponding one million nerves from the brain. Each of the millions of nerves from both sides has to make its way through the tissues in between and connect to its counterpart – much like two work teams digging a tunnel from opposite sides of a mountain must meet precisely at the center according to the engineer's plan.

Most animals, invertebrates as well as vertebrates, have eyes. Even the sea wasp, a jellyfish, has eyes. Among of the strangest are multiple-lensed, compound eyes found in fossilized worms![68]

Did the eye evolve? Darwin admitted the failure of his theory to explain the development of the eye. "To suppose that the eye with all its inimitable contrivances for adjusting the focus to different distances, for admitting different amounts of light, and for the correction of spherical and chromatic aberration, could have been formed by natural selection, seems, I freely confess, absurd in the highest degree."[69]

Solomon understood the matter quite well. *"The hearing ear, and the seeing eye, the LORD hath made even both of them"* (Prov 20:12).

In the sixth edition of his book, Darwin junked the idea of natural selection or "survival of the fittest" as the driving force behind the theory of evolution: "Natural selection is incompetent to account for the incipient stages of useful structures," he said.[70]

Genetic pre-programming.

How does evolution explain metamorphosis -- the form-changing stages in the life cycles of insects, amphibians, and crustaceans? Most of them hatch from eggs as larvae. Were they once all larvae before they evolved into more advanced forms? One may say larvae, just like some worms, reproduced sexually in the distant past. But there is no trace of reproductive organs in any type of larva. And, if a larva could not reproduce, how could it have evolved?

Some insect larvae pass through a cocoon stage when their brains, nerves, muscles, eyes, and other organs dissolve into goo. Does it mean some larvae evolved into goo before becoming, say, butterflies? How did they survive as goo for thousands or even millions of years?

Metamorphosis exemplifies genetic pre-programming. Similarly, ants and termites have the ability to grow wings in order to migrate when their colonies become overpopulated or destroyed. The insects use their wings for just one short flight, before shedding them to seek mates.[71] Obviously, these are not cases of biological evolution.

The Cambrian "explosion."

For nearly 3 billion years since life first appeared on earth, organisms remained microscopic in size: bacteria, protozoan, Ediacaran spheres and discs without mouths and appendages.[72] Then, suddenly: the Cambrian "explosion." *Time* magazine's cover story in its Dec. 4, 1995, issue tells us in graphic terms: "Creatures with teeth and tentacles and claws and jaws materialized with the suddenness of apparitions. In a burst of creativity like nothing before or since, nature appears to have sketched out the blueprints for virtually the whole of the animal kingdom. This explosion of biological diversity is described by scientists as biology's Big Bang"[73]

All anatomical designs. In a quantum leap, life advanced from microbial, amorphous organisms to complex multi-cellular life forms: rotifers, annelids (worms), arthropods, fish – equipped with jointed, food-gathering appendages, intestines, notochords, gills, eyes – all the anatomical designs found in the animal phyla existing today. Oddly, no new phylum has appeared since the Cambrian Explosion. Succeeding developments have been confined to variations within each phylum.[74]

In fact, says Paul Chien, Biology Dept. Chair of the University of San Francisco, the number of phyla has even decreased! "A simple way of putting it is that currently we have about 38 phyla of different groups of animals, but the total number of phyla discovered during that period of time (Cambrian) adds up to over 50 phyla. That means more phyla in the very, very beginning, where we found the first fossils, than exist now... The theory of evolution implies that things get more complex and get more and more diverse from one single origin. But the whole thing turns out to be reversed -- we have more diverse groups in the very beginning, and in fact more and more of them die off over time, and we have less and less now."[75]

He adds: "Also, the animal explosion caught people's attention when the Chinese confirmed they found a genus now called Yunnanzoon that was present in the very beginning. This genus is considered a chordate, and the phylum Chordata includes fish, mammals and man. An evolutionist would say the ancestor of humans was present then. Looked at more objectively, you could say the most complex animal group, the chordates, were represented at the beginning, and they did not go through a slow gradual evolution to become a chordate."[76]

No ancestors. For new life forms to appear, it would have taken hundreds of millions of years for the thousands of mutations needed to alter existing genes. Yet, the fossil record indicates that the Cambrian Explosion transpired in 5 million years or less.[77] Further, there is no evidence of mutational evolution within the 5-million-year span of the Cambrian explosion.[78,79] Colin Patterson (*Evolution*, 1978) avers: "Most of the major groups of animals (phyla) appear fully fledged in the early Cambrian rocks and we know of no fossil forms linking them."[80]

Paleontologist Alfred S. Romer corroborates that: "Below this (Cambrian period), there are vast thicknesses of sediments in which the progenitors of the Cambrian forms would be expected. But we do not find them; these older beds are almost barren of evidence of life, and the general picture could reasonably be said to be consistent with the idea of a special creation at the beginning of Cambrian times."[81]

Surprisingly, even staunch evolutionist Richard Dawkins seems to agree: "If progressive evolution, from simple to complex is correct, the ancestors of these full-blown creatures in the Cambrian should be found; but they have not been found and scientists admit there is little prospect of their ever being found. On the basis of the facts alone, on the basis of what is actually found in the earth, the theory of a sudden creative act in which the major forms of life were established fits best."[82]

Darwin had acknowledged the possibility of his theory's demise: "If numerous species... have really started into life at once, the fact would be fatal to the theory of evolution."[83]

Sudden entry and exit. Many scientists have arrived at that conclusion. David M. Raup (*Field Museum of Natural History Bulletin*, January 1979): "Species appear in the sequence very suddenly, show little or no change during their existence in the record, then abruptly go out of the record."[84] Steven M. Stanley (*The New Evolutionary Timetable*, 1981): "The record now reveals that species typically survive for a hundred thousand generations, or even a million or more, without evolving very much... After their origins, most species undergo little evolution before becoming extinct."[85] Harvard University paleontologist Stephen Jay Gould ("Evolution's Erratic Pace," *Natural History*, May 1977): "The history of most fossils includes two features particularly inconsistent with gradualism: (1) *Stasis*. Most species... appear in the fossil record looking pretty much the same as when they disappear... (2) *Sudden appearance*. In any local area, a species does not arise gradually by the steady transformation of its ancestors: it appears all at once and 'fully formed'."[86]

George Sim Johnston ("An Evening with Darwin in New York," *Crisis*, April 2006) sums it all up: "This is the verdict of modern paleontology: The record does not show gradual, Darwinian evolution. Otto Schindewolf, perhaps the leading paleontologist of the 20th century, wrote that the fossils 'directly contradict' Darwin."[87]

Darwin confessed to fellow-scientists in his letters: "It (the theory of evolution) is a mere rage of a hypothesis with as many flaws and holes as sound parts..." He considered the possibility that, "I... have devoted my life to a fantasy."[88]

Unscientific theory.

C.F. Morgan ("Evolution Not Based on Fact," 1998) points out that "true science is limited to observable phenomena. To be truly scientific, something must be observable, documentable, repeatable, experimentally verifiable, and testable, among other things. Conversely, evolution is a philosophical belief about the past based upon subjective interpretations and opinions of scientific data which exists in the present... Evolution is not a fact. It is not even a good theory. It has never been observed, and there is no direct evidence that it has ever occurred. It is no more than a religious or philosophical belief based upon choice, not science."[89]

Mathematician I.L. Cohen (*Darwin Was Wrong: A Study in Probabilities*, 1984) confirms that "every single concept advanced by the theory of evolution (and amended thereafter) is imaginary as it is not supported by the scientifically established facts of microbiology, fossils, and mathematical probability concepts. Darwin was wrong... The theory of evolution may be the worst mistake in science."[90]

Arthur L. Bruce ("Evolution Is a Creation Myth," 1998) comments: "Actually, evolution is not even a scientific theory because it cannot be tested by the scientific method. It is an unscientific hypothesis or speculation about origins that contradicts the basic laws and facts of science. It is the 'creation myth' upon which the religion of secular humanism is founded. Its proper place for study in the public schools is not the science classroom but the social studies or humanities classroom where it should be examined in comparison with the classical myths and other religions of the world."[91] (In the late 1990s the states of Alabama, Arizona, and New Mexico declared that the subject of evolution can only be taught as one theory of origins and not as fact.)

Austin H. Clark ("Animal Evolution," *Quarterly Review of Biology*, December 1928) concedes: "Thus so far as concerns the major groups of animals, the creationists seem to have the better of the argument. There is not the slightest evidence that any one of the major groups arose from any other. Each is a special animal complex related, more or less closely, to all the rest, and appearing, therefore, as a special and distinct creation."[92]

Sir Fred Hoyle and N. Chandra Wickramasinghe (*Evolution from Space: A Theory of Cosmic Creationism,* 1981) conclude: "The speculations of *The Origin of Species* turned out to be wrong... It is ironic that the scientific facts throw Darwin out..."[93]

Divinely designed DNA?

When the cell of a bacterium divides, it becomes two bacteria, not two amoebae. Apple trees bear apples, not oranges. A smooth-coated Siamese cat cannot give birth to thick-furred Persian kittens, although they belong to the same feline family. All living species, as well as varieties within them, stay the same from one generation to the next.

The Creator had apparently intended it to be that way from the very beginning: "*And God said, Let the earth bring forth the living creature after his kind, cattle, and creeping thing, and beast of the earth after his kind: and it was so*" (Gen 1:24).

Physically responsible for this biological order is a chemical molecule called deoxyribonucleic acid (DNA), which forms part of threadlike chromosomes inside all living cells (except red blood cells and some viruses). In the form of two intertwined chains in a double helix (spiral), like a twisted ladder, each DNA comprises thousands of encoded genes that govern heredity, the transmission of physical characteristics from parent to offspring.

"Chicken or egg" paradox.

Proteins depend on DNA for their formation. Yet, DNA cannot form without pre-existing protein. Which came first?

Chemistry lecturer John C. Walton further lamented: "The origin of the genetic code presents formidable unsolved problems. The coded information in the nucleotide sequence is meaningless without the translation machinery, but the specification for this machinery is itself coded in the DNA. Thus without the machinery the information is meaningless, but without the coded information the machinery cannot be produced! This presents a paradox of the 'chicken and egg' variety, and attempts to solve it have so far been sterile."[94]

Stored genetic information.

DNA is stored information written in a genetic language with a four-letter (nucleotide) alphabet and grammatical rules, telling the cells how to function and reproduce. Despite having only four letters, through their various combinations DNA is able to maintain the distinctions not only among all species, but also between individuals of each species. The language components in the human gene are identical to that of other organisms, say, a snail. Only the sequence is different.[95]

One of the tiniest one-celled organisms is the bacterium *R. coli*. Scientists estimate it has about 2,000 genes, with some 1,000 enzymes each. Every enzyme contains roughly one billion nucleotides or letters of the chemical alphabet, comparable to bytes in computer language.

Physicist Jonathan Sarfati reckons that the "amount of information that could be stored in a pinhead's volume of DNA is equivalent to a pile of paperback books 500 times as high as the distance from Earth to the moon, each with a different, yet specific content. Putting it another way, while we think that our new 40 gigabyte hard drives are advanced technology, a pinhead of DNA could hold 100 million times more information."[96]

Information from intelligence.

Information is nonmaterial and, therefore, could not have originated from matter. Information can only come from intelligence. Co-authors L. Lester and R. Bohlin tell us: "Intelligence is a necessity in the origin of any informational code, including the genetic code..."[97] The vast amounts of information in the DNA can only have come from an intelligent source.

1962 Nobel Prize winner Francis Crick, co-discoverer of the DNA structure, had said that the more he studied the DNA double-helix, the more he became convinced that it could not have evolved by chance. In his book *Life Itself*, he wrote: "An honest man, armed with all the knowledge available to us now, could only state that, in some sense, the origins of life appears at the moment to be almost a miracle."[98]

On December 16, 2010, the History Channel aired interviews with scientists who admitted that evolution of the DNA molecule by chance or accident is totally impossible.[99]

Designed on purpose. Biochemist Michael Behe of Lehigh University in Pennsylvania (*Darwin's Black Box: The Biochemical Challenge to Evolution*, 1996) construes that "the straightforward conclusion is that many biochemical systems were designed. They were designed not by the laws of nature, not by chance and necessity; rather they were *planned*. The designer knew what the systems would look like when they were completed, then took steps to bring the systems about... Life on earth at its most fundamental level, in its most critical components, is the product of intelligent design."[100]

Natural processes, such as mutation, cannot alter the DNA. I.L. Cohen says that "any physical change of any size, shape or form is strictly the result of purposeful alignment of billions of nucleotides (in the DNA). Nature or species do not have the capacity to rearrange them nor to add to them... The only way we know for a DNA to be altered is through a meaningful intervention from an outside source of intelligence – one who knows what it is doing, such as our genetic engineers are now performing in the laboratories..."[101]

Every living cell (except a few highly specialized ones) carries in its DNA all the information needed reproduce a new, identical organism. To clone an entire human being, the scientist needs just one cell.

Alternative theories

The absence in the fossil record of transitional forms that would prove the Theory of Evolution has led many frustrated evolutionists to consider alternative theories for the development of life forms on Earth.

Theistic Evolution.

In the late 19th and early 20th centuries, many Catholics and Protestants accepted Theistic Evolution, the belief that the process of biological evolution was divinely supervised. Theistic evolutionists believe that God created the first cell, then afterward allowed evolution to proceed, intervening only occasionally. He waited for primitive man to evolve into the first perfect human being before endowing him with a soul. The hybrid doctrine is a combination of divine creation and Darwinian evolution.

Botanist Asa Gray (d. 1888), one of Darwin's leading American disciples, embraced a variant of the concept. He argued that, only in special cases like those of human beings and complex organs such as the eye, did God carry out direct special creation.

Geologist Arnold Guyot, a staunch anti-Darwinist, advocated at least three interventions by the Creator: first, when He created matter; second, when He created life; and, third, when He created man.[102]

Punctuated Equilibrium.

In an attempt to explain the absence of transitional forms, Stephen Jay Gould and Niles Eldredge, American Museum of Natural History curator, jointly proposed the theory of Punctuated Equilibrium in several articles in scientific publications (*Mammals in Paleontology*, 1972; *Nature*, 1993; *Paleontology*, 2007).[103,104,105] *Newsweek* magazine reported on March 29, 1982: "In 1972 Gould and Niles Eldredge collaborated on a paper intended... to resolve a professional embarrassment for paleontologists: their inability to find the fossils of transitional forms between species, the so-called 'missing links'." Their concept: "Instead of changing gradually as one generation shades into the next, evolution as Gould sees it, proceeds in discrete leaps. According to the theory of punctuated equilibrium there are no transitional forms between species, and thus no missing links!"[106]

Gould and Eldredge speculate that speciation (the change from an old species to a new one) usually occurs in small, isolated, peripheral groups rather than in the main populations of species, making their fossilized remains harder to find. Fossils of the general population are usually found, which creates the impression of the unchanging nature or stasis of most species over millions of years.[107]

Panspermia (spores from space).
Sir Fred Hoyle mused that "life could not have originated here on the Earth. Nor does it look as though biological evolution can be explained from within an earth-bound theory of life."[108] Earlier, in 1908, Svante Arrhenius theorized that spores could have drifted to Earth from other star systems. These gave rise to the first living cells that later evolved into more complex organisms.[109]

Nobel laureate Francis Crick similarly proposed that "life on earth may have sprung from tiny organisms from a distant planet, sent here by space ship as part of a deliberate act of seeding"[110] Crick gave the old theory, known as "panspermia" (from Greek *pan*, "of all," and *sperma*, "seed"), a new twist: "directed panspermia." Some people find this plausible. J. Horgan wrote in the *Scientific American* (February 1992): "Given the weaknesses of all theories of terrestrial genesis (the origin of life on Earth), directed panspermia (the deliberate planting of life on Earth) should still be considered a serious possibility."[111]

Panspermia, though, fails to answer the question of life's origin. It merely takes the problem of creation out to space. Just how life arose on a planet many light years away is not explained.

Progressive Creation
In the 1930s Russell L. Mixter, a Wheaton College graduate, formed the concept that God created the universe and the various forms of life on earth gradually, over millions and billions of years. Creation was accomplished in progressive steps -- hence the name of the doctrine: Progressive Creationism. In 1954 theologian Bernard Ramm wrote *The Christian View of Science and Scripture*, popularizing the idea which no longer demanded a young Earth and the recent creation of man.[112]

Progressive Creationism is thus a form of Old Earth creationism, accepting geological and cosmological estimates for the age of the Earth and the universe, while teaching that the successive species of plants and animals in the fossil record were the products of divine creation, not Darwinian evolution. As earlier organisms died off and became extinct, God created new species to replace them.

Most of God's replacements were typically improved models. Each time, the basic forms or "templates" of previously existing life are used -- with just a few minor adjustments. For instance, the DNA of a gorilla has been found to be 97.8% similar to a man's; the chimpanzee's DNA resembles that of a human being by 98.2%.

The leading proponents of Progressive Creationism are Reasons To Believe, organized by astronomer Hugh Ross, and Answers in Creation, another organization set up in 2003 to publish rebuttals to Young Earth Creationists' scientific claims, which are regarded as pseudoscience.[113]

Spurious specimens

Of all fossilized organisms discovered about 95% are those of marine invertebrates. Around 4.7% consist of the older algae and primitive plants. About 0.2% are insects and other invertebrates. Only some 0.1% are vertebrates. And just a very tiny fraction of these represents primates (lemurs, monkeys, apes, and humans).[114] Nicholas Wade said in *The New York Times* of October 4, 1982: "The known fossil remains of man's ancestors would fit on a billiard table. That makes a poor platform from which to peer into the mists of the last few million years."[115]

Hominid fossils are so rare paleoanthropologists are overly eager to declare almost every promising find a hominid. For that reason we hardly hear about anybody unearthing the fossilized ancestors of modern monkeys and apes.

One of the most archaic mammals scientists say was an ancestor of both apes and humans was a small rodent-like animal that died around 70 million years ago. In the book *Lucy: The Beginnings of Humankind* (1981), authors Donald C. Johanson and Maitland A. Edey described the species as "insect-eating quadrupeds about the size and shape of a squirrel."[116] Richard Leakey called the animal a "rat-like primate."[117]

Harvard zoology professor emeritus Ernst Mayr, former American Museum of Natural History curator and lifelong evolutionist, fears that the origin of the human species is a "puzzle" that may never be solved. No link leading directly to *homo sapiens* has ever been found.[118]

Pre-Adamic pictures.

The majority of scientists who write about the evolution of man have never actually seen a hominid fossil, much less examined one up close. Most scientific papers on evolution are based on published photos and descriptions; a rare few on casts of the original finds. Access to the fossils is usually restricted to the discoverer and a few favored individuals.[119]

Donald Johanson, Lucy's discoverer, averred: "No one can be sure just what an extinct hominid looked like."[120]

What about the pictures and reconstructions of "ape-men" that we see in books, magazines, and scientific publications? According to Francis Hitching (*The Neck of the Giraffe*, 1982), the portrayals of "ape-men" are "pure fiction in most respects… sheer invention."[121] *Science Digest* concurs: "The vast majority of artists' conceptions are based more on imagination than on evidence… Artists must create something between an ape and a human being; the older the specimen is said to be, the more apelike they make it."[122] James C. King (*The Biology of Race*, 1971) elaborates: "The flesh and hair on such reconstructions have to be filled in by resorting to the imagination… Skin color; the color, form, and distribution of the hair; the form of the features; and the aspect of the face – of these characters we know absolutely nothing for any prehistoric men."[123]

Stephen Jay Gould (*Hen's Teeth and Horse's Toes*, 1983) recounts that in one instance an apelike "missing link" was drawn and presented to the media. It was later revealed that the "evidence" consisted of only one tooth that turned out be that of an extinct form of pig![124]

The perfected paradigm

The Creator appears to have given man the most efficient physical design suitable to conditions on Earth – the form He Himself and His angels make use of. Modern man, *Homo sapiens sapiens*, is the highest form of life on the planet – the perfected paradigm of God's creation.

David sang: *"What is man, that thou art mindful of him? and the son of man, that thou visitest him? For thou hast made him a little lower than the angels, and hast crowned him with glory and honour"* (Ps 8:4-5).

Just the right size?

What is the right size for man? Why not as small as an ant or as tall as a giraffe? This quizzical thought probably led Jonathan Swift to write the novel *Gulliver's Travels* (1726), wherein the hero met men just 1/12 his size in Lilliput and people 12 times bigger than him in Brobdingnag.

Let us consider one vital factor: body temperature. If man were twice as tall, his body mass would increase eight times, while the surface of the skin would only increase fourfold. The rate of heat loss from the body would be cut in half, and the body would overheat. The bigger the body, the slower the heat loss.[125] That is why in humid central Africa, where perspiration does not easily evaporate, Pygmies with small bodies do well. The Masai in the arid savannas of east Africa are tall, but they make up for it with slender bodies and long extremities that allow larger areas of skin to sweat.

On the other hand, a much smaller man half the size of the average person would lose body heat twice as fast. For this reason, the Inuit (Eskimos) tend to have short, stout bodies that conserve heat in the extreme cold of the Arctic region. This also proves Santa Claus cannot have elves working for him in the North Pole. The diminutive elves would quickly succumb to the frigid temperatures.

There is an optimum value for perfection. The size range of humans seems to be just perfect.

The "divine proportion."

Other than in a golden rectangle, the golden ratio can be made out in any straight line divided into two sections with the 1-to-0.618 ratio. Awed Renaissance writers were the first to name it "divine proportion."

Curiously, everything in the universe seems to be based on the divine proportion – from space to nature, from inanimate objects to living things. The physicist sees it in the behavior of light and atoms. A mathematician can discover it in the dimensions of the pentagram. A botanist finds it in the growth patterns of flowers. An entomologist analyzes it in the anatomy of an ant. The zoologist can graph it in the genealogy of guinea pigs. An analyst observes it in a bulls-and-bears chart of the stock market.[126]

Man, too, has been genetically encoded with the divine proportion. There exists a universal standard for physical beauty that applies to every person, with the divine proportion as its basis.

A standard for beauty. The Creator gave Adam and Eve physical bodies patterned after His own image. That divine image is divinely proportioned. The human anatomical structure has been discovered to be configured according to the divine proportion – inside and out, from top to bottom. Some experts say there are "millions, possibly billions," of examples of the divine proportion all over the human body.

Starting with the human stature, if top of head to navel = 1, then navel to soles of feet = 1.618. If shoulder to opposite fingertip = 1, then the ideal height (male or female) = 1.618. The human head reveals countless divine proportions, whether frontally or in profile. Faces that conform to the divine proportion, regardless of race, sex, age, and other variables, are intuitively perceived to be beautiful. A beautiful face is enclosed by a golden rectangle formed by the hairline, the cheeks and the chin, with the most prominent features -- the eyes, nose, and mouth – characterized by divine proportion. If height of the face = 1.618, then distance of chin to the eyes = 1, mouth to eyes = .618, top of eyes to hairline = .618; right eye corner/cheek to left eye corner/cheek = 1; midpoint of nose at eye level to either cheek = .618. If mouth to eyes = 1, then mouth to chin = .618. If width of nose = 1, then width of mouth = 1.618.[127] The many incidences of divine proportion in the human figure is irrefutable proof that man is truly the product of divine design, the perfect image of the Grand Designer of the cosmos.

As David sang to God about a thousand years ago, *"I will praise thee; for I am fearfully and wonderfully made: marvellous are thy works; and that my soul knoweth right well"* (Ps 139:14).

Below are some examples of the divine proportion in man. (Other examples occurring in nature and man-made objects in the Appendix.)

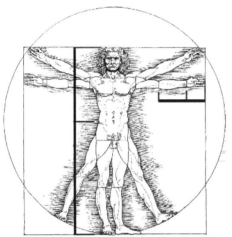

Divine proportions in the "Vitruvian Man," a famous drawing by Leonardo da Vinci.

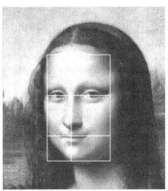

Divine proportions in a beautiful face, like *Mona Lisa*'s by da Vinci.

Divine proportions in human teeth, as examined by an orthodontist.

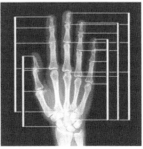

Divine proportions in the human hand and fingers.

6

First Family
Foibles

This is the book of the generations of Adam. In the day that God created man, in the likeness of God made he him; Male and female created he them; and blessed them, and called their name Adam, in the day when they were created"

-- Genesis 5:1-2.

The Hebrew word for earth, soil, or ground is *adamah*. It came from the root-word *adam*, which means "ruddy" or "reddish," owing to the earth's general redness. The Hebrew term for "man," a human being (whether male or female), is also *adam*, as, according to the Genesis account, the first human was formed from the "dust of the ground." Accordingly, the first personal name given to a human was "Adam." Hence, *adam* is the generic Hebrew word for a human being, while *Adam* was the first person given a name in the Bible.

Science confirms the Bible story that man came from the ground. Writer George Sim Johnston said in the *Readers Digest* (May 1991): "The book of Genesis has held up well under the scrutiny of modern geology and archeology... A growing number of chemists and biologists agree that life had its beginning from clay templates."[1] An earlier article in the same magazine (Nov. 1982) reported the findings of scientists at NASA's Ames Research Center: Every single element in the human body can be found in the soil.[2] Chemically, human beings are made up of the same 17 elements found in the dust of the ground.[3]

God created Adam 6,000 years ago as the first of the subspecies *Homo sapiens sapiens,* after a succession of earlier hominid species.

A latter creation?

The Jewish sages knew it, writes Gerald Schroeder: "Nahmanides, seven hundred years ago, Maimonides over eight hundred years ago, and the Talmud, dating back some sixteen hundred years, discuss the existence of beings living before and alongside Adam. They were described as human in shape and intelligence but lacking the soul, the *neshama,* to make them human."[4] He explains: "It is our *neshama,* the spirit of the Eternal placed within us, not our physical attributes, that uniquely sets us apart from all other life, making us moral beings rather than amoral animals."[5]

Maimonides said that the pre-Adamic manlike creatures "were not human in the true sense of the word. They had not the spirit of God... It is acknowledged that a being who does not possess this spirit is not human but *a mere animal in human shape and form...* For those gifts of *intelligence and judgment* with which he has been endowed for the purpose of acquiring perfection... are used by him for wicked and mischievous ends."[6]

Rav Rick Aharon Chaimberlin, editor-publsher of *Petah Tikvah* (Door of Hope), writes that "according to many rabbis, there was more than one earlier creation (of human beings), and that the current Creation is actually the 6th or 7th creation."[7]

How the medieval Jewish sages knew there were manlike creatures that predated Adam hundreds of years before hominid fossils were discovered is, to say the least, a profound mystery.

Two creation accounts?

There is a little-known theory that the first two chapters of Genesis contain a doublet that relates the creation of man twice – one in verse 1:27 and another in 2:7, the online Christian Answers Network avers. David T. Tsumura, a professor of the Old Testament at the Japan Bible Seminary, Tokyo, mentions two studies (Kikawada 1983; and Kikawada and Quinn 1985), which concluded that Genesis 1 refers to "the first creation of man," while Genesis 2 refers to "the second creation of man," namely, Adam and Eve.[8]

There are strong reasons for this theory, and a detailed scrutiny of the Biblical account yields several circumstances that appear to substantiate the belief. Let us go over them one by one.

Barren earth.

God finished the Creation by Genesis 2:1-2 -- *"Thus the heavens and the earth were finished, and all the host of them..."* God then rested on the seventh day (Gen 2:3). But, two verses later, we see a barren earth: *"...and no shrub of the field had yet appeared on the earth and no plant of the field had yet sprung up, for the LORD God had not sent rain on the earth and there was no man to work the ground"* (Gen 2:5, NIV). No vegetation was growing. There were no animals or humans around, either. It looks as though the earth had become desolate while the Creator rested. If plants and animals, as well as men, had been created earlier, did a worldwide cataclysm cause a mass extinction that wiped out living things from the face of the planet?

New term for God.

In Genesis chapter 1, the Creator had been referred to as "God" (*Elohim*). Starting Genesis 2:4, He is called by a different name: "the LORD God" (*YHWH Elohim*). This points to two distinct stories, not one, according to the article "Genesis and ancient Near Eastern stories of Creation and the Flood" on ChristianAnswers.Net.[9]

The angels are called *elohim* (Ps 82), as we have seen in a previous chapter. Was God (*Elohim*) in Genesis 1 the angels, and now the LORD God (*YHWH Elohim*) Himself had come forward to perform acts of creation personally?

Man formed first.

In Genesis chapter 1, man was created last. In Genesis 2, however, the LORD God formed man first before plants and animals. Moreover, it appears the latter man was endowed with an additional component. *"And the LORD God formed man of the dust of the ground, and breathed into his nostrils the breath of life; and man became a living soul"* (Gen 2:7).

Given "neshamah." Nahmanides pointed out that the clause *"and man became a living soul"* in the Hebrew text is actually *"and man became to a living soul."* The extra word "to" might have been inserted to suggest a progression – i.e., from spiritless creatures to a spirit-filled human being.[10]

Furthermore, the word "formed" when the LORD God made man in Genesis 2:7 is in Hebrew *yiytser*, but *yitser* when the LORD formed the animals in verse 2:19. The structure and grammar are the same in both verses. Yet, in forming man *yiytser* is spelled with two Hebrew letters *yod* ("y"); while in forming animals, the word is spelled with just one *yod*. Three Jewish sages (Rashi, Maimonides, and Nahmanides) gave identical explanations for this: *Yod* is both the initial and abbreviation of the Creator's personal name. With a double *yod* for man, Scripture is intimating to us that there was an additional divine input in man.[11]

Man was thus given a *neshamah*, the animals were not. Neither were the pre-Adamic manlike creatures.

Plants after man.

In Genesis chapter 1, plants were the first living things to appear. In Genesis chapter 2, the LORD God grew plants after forming man. *"And the LORD God planted a garden eastward in Eden; and there he put the man whom he had formed. And out of the ground made the LORD God to grow every tree that is pleasant to the sight, and good for food…"* (Gen 2:8-9a).

In Genesis 1, God simply created man, with no mention of any particular place for him. As we have just read in Genesis 2, the LORD put the man He had formed in a special place: the garden east of Eden.

Animals after man.

In the first creation story (Gen 1), God created man last, almost like an afterthought. In the second creation account (Gen 2), man was the LORD God's first priority – almost like a necessity, for taking care of the forthcoming Garden of Eden. It was only sometime later that the LORD God formed the land animals: *"And the LORD God said, It is not good that the man should be alone; I will make him an help meet for him. And out of the ground the LORD God formed every beast of the field, and every fowl of the air; and brought them unto Adam to see what he would call them: and whatsoever Adam called every living creature, that was the name thereof"* (Gen 2:18-19).

Did you notice anything amiss? Only land animals (*"beast of the field"*) and birds (*"fowl of the air"*) were formed – no water creatures and creeping things! If there had been a mass extinction, some water creatures and creeping things could have survived, and there was no need to form more of them.

"Formed" or "had formed"? Although the KJV and many other English translations of the Bible use the simple past tense *"formed"* in Genesis 2:19, the NIV translates it differently: *"Now the LORD God had formed out of the ground all the beasts of the field and all the birds of the air…"* (Gen 2:19a, NIV). Just one word, "had," has been added, but the meaning has been reversed. The verb form *"had formed"* (pluperfect or past perfect tense) indicates that God had created the animals earlier -- before man, not after.

Considering the number of translations using the simple past tense "formed" and the antiquity of the KJV (1611) vis-à-vis the recency of the NIV (1979), it seems that the pluperfect tense *"had formed"* in the NIV was introduced to resolve the difficulty surrounding Genesis 2:19.

Why animals came later. The reason why the LORD God formed the animals after man is right there in the preceding passage: *"Then the LORD God said, 'It is not good for the man to be alone; I will make him a helper suitable for him'"* (Gen 2:18, NAS).

The LORD God formed the animals to find a "suitable helper" and companion for man. If some of the animals formed earlier had survived, there would have been no need to form new ones again.

Adam on the 8th day?

We have seen in the Diminishing Day-Ages Chronology in Chapter 4 that God, in consonance with the Biblical account, created "man" (the various hominid species before Adam) on the sixth "day" of the Creation week. Adam, the perfected paradigm, appears to have been formed on the first "day" of the following "week" -- Day 8. In the Bible, "8" is the number of new beginnings.

Just as the last Adam, Christ, would later rise from the dead to new life on the 8th day (Sunday, following Saturday, the seventh day), the first Adam could have also begun life as the first of the subspecies *Homo sapiens sapiens* at the beginning of the 8th "day."

Adam created a grown-up?

In the traditional interpretation of the story of creation that we see in religious paintings, the LORD God formed Adam as a grown-up man.

God was impatient?

Why would the LORD form Adam as an adult who did not need to go through the normal growing process? Was He in a hurry to populate the earth? If He was, why did He wait for Adam to reach the age of 130 years before giving him another son, Seth, to replace the slain Abel and castaway Cain? If God was impatient, He would have created the heavens and the earth and everything in them fully formed, instantly, instead of patiently going through the seven-day creation week, paying great attention to details. The Scriptures say He is a patient God. *"God waited patiently in the days of Noah while the ark was being built"* (1 Pet 3:20, NIV) to give men the chance to repent. Other passages attest to His patience (Ex 34:6, Ps 86:15, Rom 9:22, etc.).

No time interval?

It seems that the early readers of Genesis jumped to the conclusion that Adam was created a fully grown man, because there is no apparent time interval between the time God created the first man and woman and the time He instructed them to multiply. *"So God created man in his own image, in the image of God created he him; male and female created he them. And God blessed them, and God said unto them, Be fruitful, and multiply, and replenish the earth, and subdue it: and have dominion over the fish of the sea, and over the fowl of the air, and over every living thing that moveth upon the earth.* Gen 1:27-28).

But that was simply the literary style of the Genesis writer. For the sake of conciseness, he dispensed with details, such as time intervals. For instance, in just one verse (Gen 1:12) the earth brought forth grass, herbs, and trees – giving the impression that they were all created at the same time, or at least in rapid succession. The Jewish sages, though, taught that long periods elapsed between the appearance of each kind of vegetation. Same with the creation of man. As we have seen earlier, only one word – "man" – was used, when actually several progressive versions of similar species had been created one after another.

Adult male or simply human being?

As explained in the beginning of this chapter, the English word "man" (Gen 1:26) has been translated from *adam*, which is the generic Hebrew term for a human being. It does not always mean a male person, for which another Hebrew word is used – *ish*, as in Genesis 2:22-23 -- *"And the rib, which the LORD God had taken from man ('adam'), made he a woman ('ishah'), and brought her unto the man ('adam'). And Adam ('Adam') said, This is now bone of my bones, and flesh of my flesh: she shall be called Woman ('ishah'), because she was taken out of Man ('ish')."*

Ishah, the feminine of *ish*, means "woman, female, wife." Thus, in Genesis 2:25 (*"And they were both naked, the man and his wife ['ishah'], and were not ashamed"*) *"his wife"* can also be rendered as "his female (partner)."

Later, Eve gave birth to their firstborn: *"And Adam knew Eve his wife; and she conceived, and bare Cain, and said, I have gotten a man ("ish") from the LORD"* (Gen 4:1). Note that Eve said she had acquired *"a man"* (*ish*, male person), not an infant (*uwl* or *olel* in Hebrew). Obviously, Eve could not have given birth to a full-grown man.

Newly formed Adam was also called a "man" (*adam*, human being). This no doubt led to the notion that he was created a full-grown "man."

Adam created an infant?

If God formed Adam as a fully grown man who did not pass through the normal developmental stages of living organisms, He disregarded the laws of nature He had established. On the other hand, there is ample circumstantial evidence in the Bible for the notion that God might have created Adam as an infant – not as the grown-up man we see in religious paintings and illustrations.

Christ grew up.

Christ, God's Only Begotten Son, came to earth in human form. More than Adam, it was important for Christ to have entered the world instantly as a fully grown man – souls were getting lost because of sin. The sooner He came, the more souls would have been saved. Besides, coming as a grown-up would have ensured his spotlessness by not incarnating through a sin-tainted human parent (Ecc 7:20, Rom 3:23). God could have sent Him as an adult into the world, coming out of nowhere, just like Melchizedek. *"Without father, without mother, without descent, having neither beginning of days, nor end of life; but made like unto the Son of God; abideth a priest continually"* (Heb 7:3).

Yet, God patiently waited for His Only Son to grow in the womb of a woman for nine months before being born, then go through the normal growing up process. *"And the child grew, and waxed strong in spirit, filled with wisdom: and the grace of God was upon him"* (Luke 2:40). Christ even had to wait until He turned 30, the legal age to serve in the Tabernacle (Num 4), before He could begin His earthly ministry.

If Christ, the last Adam (1 Cor 15:45), had to go through the natural process of biological growth from infancy to maturity, why not the first Adam, who was lesser as the prototype of the species?

Parts of man.

Paul, in 1 Thessalonians 5:23, names three parts of man: *"And the very God of peace sanctify you wholly; and I pray God your whole spirit and soul and body be preserved blameless unto the coming of our Lord Jesus Christ."* The first two parts are non-physical (spirit and soul), while the third part is physical, the body.

Most people think the soul and the spirit are identical. If you have noticed, the Jewish sages, as well as Gerald Schroeder, had used "soul" and "spirit" synonymously. *The New Unger's Bible Dictionary* tells us this is quite common. "The two terms (soul and spirit) are often used interchangeably, the same functions being ascribed to each..."[12] But we have an advantage over the Jewish sages: the New Testament.

In the NT, Paul demonstrates that the soul and the spirit are different from each other. *"For the word of God is quick, and powerful, and sharper than any twoedged sword, piercing even to the dividing asunder of soul and spirit..."* (Heb 4:12). He says the soul and the spirit can be separated, so that means they are really two distinct entities.

What makes them different? Let us learn more about the soul and the spirit of man.

The soul. As defined by *Fausset's Bible Dictionary*: "The soul is the seat of the appetites, the desires, the will; hunger, thirst, sorrow, joy; love, hope, fear, etc..."[13] In short, the soul possesses and manifests the human instincts, basic drives, and emotions. The soul feels the need to eat and drink (Isa 29:8, Ps 107:9, Prov 25:25, etc.), sorrow (Matt 26:38, etc.), joy (Ps 86:4, etc.), love (Song 1:7, etc.), fear (Acts 2:43, etc.), hate (Lev 26:11, etc.) -- the whole spectrum of human desires and emotions.

The spirit. The *International Standard Bible Encyclopaedia* gives one shade of meaning of spirit, "generally for all the manifestations of the spiritual part in man, as that which thinks, feels, wills..."[14] Along the same vein Roberto Assagioli, an Italian Jew regarded as the father of transpersonal psychology, defined the spirit as the personal "I" or "conscious self."[15]

Based on these, the spirit is the seat of consciousness and intelligence in man. The Hebrew word for spirit (*ruach*) is translated "mind" in several verses (Gen 26:34-35, Prov 29:11, Ezek 11:5, Dan 5:20, Hab 1:11, etc.). The spirit can be full of knowledge and wisdom (Dan 5:12), make decisions (Deut 2:30, Matt 26:41), be troubled (Gen 41:8, Dan 2:1, John 13:21), be patient or proud (Ecc 7:8), etc. – in sum, have all the possible thoughts that can enter a man's mind.

God is a spirit (John 4:24), and so are His angels (Ps 104:4, Heb 1:7). The angels, unless they materialize, have neither bodies nor souls. But, as we know, God is the all-knowing Cosmic Intelligence, while the angels, although incorporeal, have minds of their own. This goes to show that the mind or consciousness is in the spirit.

Parts of Adam.

We see two parts of man in Adam after he was formed. *"And the LORD God formed man of the dust of the ground, and breathed into his nostrils the breath of life; and man became a living soul"* (Gen 2:7).

Adam had a physical body, though only inferred – that which had been formed from the *"dust of the ground."* Then, after receiving the LORD's breath (*neshamah*), he suddenly had a soul. But one part seems to be missing. Adam had no spirit! What could be the reason for this?

Zechariah gives us a hint: "*The burden of the word of the LORD for Israel, saith the LORD, which stretcheth forth the heavens, and layeth the foundation of the earth, and formeth the spirit of man within him*" (Zech 12:1). The prophet says God forms the spirit inside the human body, evidently after the birth of the individual.

In Adam's case, after his physical body was formed, he acquired a soul that gave him the instincts to eat and drink in order to survive. But he had as yet no spirit or mind necessary for intelligent thought! It looks like the LORD forms the spirit or mind within the person as his or her body grows. This explains why we cannot converse with infants. Their spirits or minds are not yet formed.

Conclusion: The LORD formed Adam as an infant or a little baby, with a still undeveloped spirit or mind.

Without a navel?

Inquisitive minds have long wondered if Adam had a navel, since he was not born of a woman. The opinion tends to lean on the negative, as he did not grow in a mother's womb attached to an umbilical cord for nourishment, the terminal of which in the fetus is the navel.

Author Philip Henry Gosse, however, elaborated in his 1857 book *Omphalos* (Greek for "navel") that Adam had been created with a navel.[16] Gosse reasoned that, for the world and all things in it to be functional, God must have created them fully formed to the minutest details. Thus, even trees believed to have been created instantly, he wrote, had annual growth rings.

"Babe in the woods"

Could a helpless baby without an adult to care for it have survived on its own in the wild? Gosse argued in *Omphalos* that if Adam had been created as a newborn infant or even a child, it was less likely for him to have survived, than if he had been created as an adult, or at least a teenager.[17] But legend has it that the founders of Rome, the castaway twin brothers Romulus and Remus, had been found and nursed by a she-wolf. In more recent times, cases of feral children growing up with wild animals have been documented and studied. These inspired popular novels such as Rudyard Kipling's *The Jungle Book* (1894) and Edgar Rice Burroughs' *Tarzan* (1914).

Were conditions better or worse in the primordial world? Do you imagine a harsh land teeming with reptilian predators and alternately at the mercy of thunderstorms, hurricanes, blizzards, erupting volcanoes, earthquakes, tsunamis, heat waves? The Bible assures us that there were no such things in the very beginning.

To view the past, let us peer into the future. Luke says God will return all things to their former state. *"He must remain in heaven until the time comes for God to restore everything, as he promised long ago through his holy prophets"* (Acts 3:21-22, NIV). Surely, "everything" includes the Garden of Eden.

Pictures of Paradise.

Isaiah gives us snapshots of a restored Paradise in the Millennium -- the thousand-year era of peace following the Second Coming of Christ. These visions mirror scenes in the Garden of Eden: *"The wolf will live with the lamb, the leopard will lie down with the goat, the calf and the lion and the yearling together; and a little child will lead them. The cow will feed with the bear, their young will lie down together, and the lion will eat straw like the ox. The infant will play near the hole of the cobra, and the young child put his hand into the viper's nest"* (Isa 11:6-8, NIV).

The prophet says peace will reign among all animals and men. There will be no predators in the restored Paradise, so it will be as safe as a playpen – just like the original Garden of Eden might have been if Adam had been formed as a baby!

Ideal climate. The sages of Israel referred to the Garden of Eden as Paradise, a beautiful pleasure park or resort where the environmental conditions were simply perfect.

By what we can glean from the Biblical narrative, Eden had ideal weather conditions. As we know, Adam and Eve did not have to wear any clothing. There was also no mention of a house or whatever kind of shelter; they must have lived in the open, under the sky. It is doubtful if they even caught a cold. There was no fire, since they did not need to cook anything or light up a place at night.

Josephus recounted the popular concept of Paradise as held by the Essenes, members of an ascetic Jewish sect: A place " beyond the ocean, in a region that is neither oppressed with storms of rain, or snow, or with intense heat, but that this place is such as is refreshed by the gentle breathing of a west wind, that is perpetually blowing from the ocean."[18]

No rain before the Flood? Between the lines of Scripture, it seems it did not rain before Noah's Flood. We read in Genesis 2:5-6 that *"...the LORD God had not caused it to rain upon the earth... But there went up a mist from the earth, and watered the whole face of the ground"* (Gen 2:5-6).

When the LORD told Noah about the coming Deluge, *"By faith Noah, being divinely warned of things not yet seen..."* (Heb 11:7a, NKJV). The line can mean Noah had never seen rain before in his life, much less a flood brought about by heavy rains.

The idea is further bolstered by the Biblical account that the first rainbow appeared in the sky only after the Flood (Gen 9:11-17). A rainbow is the product of the refraction and reflection of sunlight on raindrops. If there are no raindrops, no rainbow. The absence of a rainbow before the Flood makes for strong proof that it did not rain in the antediluvian world.

What could have been the reason for those wonderful pre-Flood atmospheric conditions?

No tilt in Earth's axis? The Earth's rotational axis is tilted at a 23.5° angle toward the sun. If the tilt of the Earth's axis was less than 5°, evenly rotating all year, the planet's more upright position would have caused different air flow patterns. Warm air from the equator would have flowed all the way to the poles, while cold polar air would have blown towards the equatorial zone. Result: a narrow tropical zone, small arctic zones, and broad temperate zones, with no scorchingly hot summers and bitterly cold winters.[19]

There could have been a pleasant subtropical-to-temperate climate worldwide, encouraging the growth of lush vegetation all over the globe. Some coal seams discovered in Antarctica contain fossilized plants that do not presently grow in the polar region – indicating they grew at or near the pole under warmer conditions.[20]

The Earth must have been a wholesome and hospitable paradise even for homeless babies wearing nothing, not even diapers.

Two is company

"So Adam gave names to all cattle, to the birds of the air, and to every beast of the field. But for Adam there was not found a helper comparable to him" (Gen 2:20, NKJV). None of the animals the LORD had formed proved to be a suitable companion for Adam.

World's first clone.

"And the LORD God caused a deep sleep to fall on Adam, and he slept; and He took one of his ribs, and closed up the flesh in its place. Then the rib which the LORD God had taken from man He made into a woman, and He brought her to the man" (Gen 2:21-23, NKJV).

In these two verses we see several firsts in human history: The first ever use of anesthesia ("*deep sleep*"); the first ever surgery ("*took one of his ribs, and closed up the flesh*"); and the first ever cloning procedure ("*the rib... taken from man... made into a woman*").

A missing rib? Folklore has it that because God took one of Adam's ribs to make Eve, men today must have one less rib than women. Or, conversely, women ought to have one or two ribs more than men. However, as medical practitioners know, men and women have exactly the same number of ribs – 12.

But there is a part of the human body where there is a difference of one or two bones between the two sexes – the coccyx or tailbone. The coccyx consists of three to five successively smaller coccygeal vertebrae below the sacrum (compound bone) at the lower end of the spine. In early adulthood the three lowest of these bones usually fuse to form a single curved, beaklike bone. Sometimes the coccyx fuses entirely with the sacrum. The bone fusion occurs more often among women than men. Thus, instead of having one surplus bone, women often have one or two bones less than men.[21]

No *neshamah*?

Did you notice something different with Eve? Unlike Adam, she was not given the breath of life from the LORD. Does it mean that she did not have the *neshamah*? Let us delve more deeply into the matter.

Same as the soul and spirit, the *neshamah* is incorporeal, invisible, and imperceptible. They may be similar in other ways. According to *The New Unger's Bible Dictionary:* "The origin of man's immaterial nature is subject to three theories: (1) The creational, maintaining that soul and spirit are created at birth. (2) Traducian. Soul and spirit are generated the same as the body. (3) The soul is preexistent, embracing the idea of transmigration of souls."[22] Which one is correct?

We now know that, based on Zechariah 12:1, the spirit is not created at birth, it is formed by the LORD (as the body grows). Neither is the spirit preexistent nor does it migrate from one body to another. As Paul makes it clear: *"And as it is appointed for men to die once, but after this the judgment"* (Heb 9:27, NKJV). Man dies only once, so this closes the door to the New Age belief in reincarnation

That leaves us with just one theory: the Traducian. The *Merriam-Webster's Dictionary and Thesaurus* gives the root-word of "traduce" as the Latin *traducere*, meaning "to lead across, transfer, degrade." The *World Book Dictionary* shows the obsolete meanings of "traduction" as: "4. a transmission by generation. 5. a bringing over, transferring, or transmitting." Thus, just as the genetic code carrying hereditary traits is transmitted physically from parents to offspring, the non-physical soul and spirit (or parts thereof) are similarly passed on to the children.

If this is also true for the *neshamah*, then Adam's rib already had it and the LORD God did not have to breathe into Eve's nostrils.

Clothed with light?

While the climate in Eden may have been ideal so that no article of clothing was necessary, the Genesis writer believed an innate factor in human nature dictated Adam and Eve should have worn clothes -- shame. *"And they were both naked, the man and his wife, and were not ashamed.* Gen 2:25).

Yet, Adam and Eve felt no shame toward each other (even if they might still have been pre-pubescent children). Some Bible teachers think Adam and Eve needed no clothing in the Garden, because they were clothed with light. Let us search the Bible for evidence on this notion.

Light of holiness.

In Psalm 104:1-2, we read that the Creator is clothed with light: *"Bless the LORD, O my soul. O LORD my God, thou art very great; thou art clothed with honour and majesty. Who coverest thyself with light as with a garment..."* On at least one occasion, so was Christ: *"And after six days Jesus taketh Peter, James, and John his brother, and bringeth them up into an high mountain apart, And was transfigured before them: and his face did shine as the sun, and his raiment was white as the light"* (Matt 17:1-2). God's angels are arrayed similarly: *"And it came to pass, as they were much perplexed thereabout, behold, two men stood by them in shining garments"* (Luke 24:4). So is spiritual Israel, personified by a "woman": *"And there appeared a great wonder in heaven; a woman clothed with the sun, and the moon under her feet, and upon her head a crown of twelve stars"* (Rev 12:1).

God, Christ, angels, spiritual Israel – they were all clothed with light. Is there a common denominator among them? Yes, they are similarly pure, sinless, and holy. It seems that those who are pure and sinless are covered by a "light of holiness" like a garment.

Righteousness and salvation.

White garments appear to be a metaphor for both righteousness and salvation. Solomon admonished men: *"Let thy garments be always white..."* (Eccl 9:8). Christ figuratively said: *"Thou hast a few names even in Sardis which have not defiled their garments; and they shall walk with me in white: for they are worthy"* (Rev 3:4), referring to the spiritual clothing of believers.

Job likens righteousness to a garment: *"I put on righteousness, and it clothed me: my judgment was as a robe and a diadem"* (Job 29:14). Isaiah equates righteousness to salvation: *"I will greatly rejoice in the LORD, my soul shall be joyful in my God; for he hath clothed me with the garments of salvation, he hath covered me with the robe of righteousness..."* (Isa 61:10). (Righteousness means living according to God's will.)

Salvation through Christ can likewise be worn, says Paul: *"For as many of you as have been baptized into Christ have put on Christ"* (Gal 3:27). *"But put ye on the Lord Jesus Christ, and make not provision for the flesh, to fulfil the lusts thereof"* (Rom 13:14). *"And that ye put on the new man, which after God is created in righteousness and true holiness"* (Eph 4:24).

Christ told His followers how to be clothed with the light of holiness: *"The light of the body is the eye: if therefore thine eye be single, thy whole body shall be full of light"* (Matt 6:22, *cf.* Luke 11:34). The believer's entire being will be covered with holy light if his eye is "single" – that is, single-mindedly focused on God and His righteousness.

Does it look like Adam and Eve had been clothed with light?

Garden of delights

"Eden" in Hebrew means "pleasure" or "delight." For that reason, Eden is thought to be the land of delights. It is synonymous to Paradise (Hebrew *pardes*), which stands for an "orchard,"[23] "a wooded park," or "a garden with fruit trees."[24]

"And out of the ground made the LORD God to grow every tree that is pleasant to the sight, and good for food; the tree of life also in the midst of the garden, and the tree of knowledge of good and evil" (Gen 2:9). The LORD planted many ornamental and fruit-bearing trees in the Garden of Eden. Only two trees in the Garden, however, are specifically mentioned by name in the Scriptures -- the tree of life and the tree of the knowledge of good and evil.

Surprisingly, in the Hebrew text of Genesis chapter 2, which relates the creation of the Garden of Eden and events that took place in it, Bible Code researchers making use of the Equidistant Letter Sequencing (ELS) technique have found encrypted in Hebrew the names of 25 plants and trees. All 25 presumably grew in the Garden.[25]

No sex in the Garden.

In Genesis 1:28, God commanded man to *"be fruitful and multiply."* Not to do so would have been disobedience to the LORD. Yet, Adam did not lie down with Eve in the Garden. The first time we learn Adam slept with Eve was after they had been driven out. *"And Adam knew Eve his wife; and she conceived, and bare Cain ..."* (Gen 4:1a).

Why did not Adam sleep with Eve in the Garden? As we have seen earlier, Adam and Eve might have been formed as infants. If so, then they were still sexually immature. Either one or both of them did not reach puberty while still in the Garden. Adam and Eve probably attained sexual maturity only after they had been cast out of Paradise.

Where was the Garden?

Was the Garden of Eden simply a Biblical story, or did it actually exist? If it did, where was it located?

North Pole? Some scholars speculated that the Garden might have existed in pre-Ice Age times in the North Pole, when the climate was uniform throughout the year. They pointed to numerous fossil plants in Northern Greenland and Spitzbergen Island, indicating a polar climate similar to that of Southern Europe and southern USA today. The problem is, it is now generally known that there is no land within several hundred miles of the ice-covered waters of the North Pole.[26]

Missouri, USA? Mormons (Latter-Day Saints) thought the Garden of Eden was in Jackson County, Missouri – based on their mythology, which described it as the "center place" of Zion and the original home of Adam and Eve. Its location in America is explained by their belief that the supercontinent Pangaea split apart only after the Flood, when the earth was "divided" in the days of Peleg (Gen 10:25, 1 Chron 1:19). As for the names of the lands and rivers, their book *Pearl of Great Price* says in the footnotes that these had later been given to other places.[27]

East of the Red Sea? In the pseudepigraphal Book of Enoch, the author supposedly had a vision of the place, referred to as the "garden of righteousness": *"From there I passed on above the summits of those mountains to some distance eastwards, and went over the Erythraean sea (Red Sea). And when I was advanced far beyond it, I passed along above the angel Zateel, and arrived at the garden of righteousness"* (Enoch 31:2a). From this account, we get the idea that the Garden of Eden was some distance east of the Red Sea.

River with four heads.

The location of the Garden is marked by waterways: *"And a river went out of Eden to water the garden; and from thence it was parted, and became into four heads. The name of the first is Pison: that is it which compasseth the whole land of Havilah, where there is gold; And the gold of that land is good: there is bdellium and the onyx stone. And the name of the second river is Gihon: the same is it that compasseth the whole land of Ethiopia. And the name of the third river is Hiddekel: that is it which goeth toward the east of Assyria. And the fourth river is Euphrates"* (Gen 10-14).

We now have two clues: First, Eden might have been somewhere east of the Red Sea; and, second, the river that flowed out of the Garden split apart into four streams.

Central Asia? Some naturalists named one of the world's highest mountain ranges -- the Pamir in Central Asia, where the Himalaya, Hindu Kush, Kunlun, and Tian Shan mountains meet. Also called *Bam i Dunya* ("roof of the world"), the area is the source of four great rivers: the Indus, Tarim, Sur Daria (Jaxartes), and Ainu Daria (Oxus). Further, three races can be found in the vast region – white, yellow, and black – fueling the notion that it was the original cradle of mankind.[28]

Euphrates and Hiddekel.
The identity of the fourth river is a give-away: the Euphrates bears the same name to this day. The longest river in southwestern Asia (2,736 km), the Euphrates begins in the mountains of eastern Turkey, flows southwest through Syria, then turns southeast across Iraq, finally joining the Tigris to form the Shatt al-Arab waterway before emptying into the Persian Gulf.

The third river, called Hiddekel in the KJV, is positively identified as the Tigris by the NIV: *"The name of the third river is the Tigris; it runs along the east side of Asshur…* (Gen 2:14).

So we have now identified the third and fourth rivers. The names of the first two, Pison and Gihon, are unknown today and pose a puzzle.

Armenia? Other researchers believe the Euphrates and the Tigris originate in Armenia, where two other rivers, the Aras (Araxes) emptying into the Caspian Sea and the Phasis (Choruk?) spilling into the Black Sea, could be the Gihon and the Pison. Havilah could then be Colchis, now part of Georgia, which anciently supplied the Greeks with gold. Yet, locating Ethiopia (Cush) in the region exhausts the imagination.[29]

Eastern Turkey? The Canadian *National Post* reported in its Jan. 11, 2001, issue that the Garden of Eden had been located in eastern Turkey. Michael Sanders, expedition leader of the Mysteries of the Bible Research Foundation, based in Irvine, California, announced he found the site after a meticulous study of satellite photographs taken by NASA. He said the Garden used to be in the region where the Euphrates and the Tigris rise in the mountains of eastern Turkey. Sanders identified the four rivers in the area as the Murat, the Tigris, the Euphrates, and the north fork of the Euphrates. Aside from the presence of four rivers, though, there is little further evidence to support his claim.

Pison and Gihon.
In the *Smithsonian* magazine (May 1987), writer Dora Jane Hamblin cited archeologist Juris Sarins, who noted that Pison was in the "land of Havilah," listed in the table of nations as northern Arabia. "Havilah" means "sandy" or "land of sand," from the Hebrew root-word *chuwl*

("sand"). Landsat satellite images show a large riverbed in the Arabian desert that is now known as the Wadi (dry riverbed) Batin,[30] Also called the Kuwait River, 2,500-3000 years ago it drained the central part of the Arabian Peninsula from the Hijaz Mountains 600 miles southwest.[31]

Gihon is more problematical. It is said to have flowed around Ethiopia; but Ethiopia is in east Africa, about 1,500 miles away! The NIV, however, uses the name "Cush" for Ethiopia (Gen 2:13-14). According to Ms. Hamblin, Biblical scholar Ephraim Speiser "suggested that the mysterious Gush or Kush should be correctly written as Kashshu and further, that it refers to the Kashites, a people who, in about 1500 B.C., conquered Mesopotamia and prevailed until about 900 B.C."[32] In Genesis 2:13 and 10:8, there is a reference to an earlier Asiatic (Mesopotamian) Cush, who may have been the Kassites (Cossaeans).[33] Isaiah associated Cush with Elam (Isa 40:11), Ezekiel with Persia (Ezek 38:5) -- both of which now constitute modern Iran.[34]

Juris Zarins, using various data, including Landsat images from space, concluded that the Gihon corresponds to the Karun River, which originates from west central Iran and flows southwesterly into the Shatt al-Arab channel formed by the merger of the Euphrates and the Tigris near the head of the Persian Gulf. The episode "Mysteries of the Garden of Eden" of History Channel's "Decoding the Past" series showed that, near the Persian Gulf where the Euphrates and Tigris met, there are geological traces of two fossil rivers that flowed from the east and the west, possibly the Pison and the Gihon.[35]

Southern Iraq? "Eden" may have originally meant "plain." In ancient Assyrian inscriptions *idinu* (*edin* in Accadian) signifies "plain."[36] In the older Sumerian writings, the term *edin* means "steppe, plain, desert, or wilderness."[37] Thus, *"eastward in Eden"* could mean "east of the plain or desert," which would be Arabia. The *"four heads"* of the river of Eden, then, could have been the Euphrates, Tigris (Hiddekel), Wadi Batin or Kuwait River (Pison), and Karun (Gihon), which converged into one at the Shatt al-Arab in southern Iraq near the northern end of the Persian Gulf.

The river that *"went out of Eden to water the garden"* of Eden could have been the Persian Gulf itself, called *Nar Marratum* ("bitter river") by the Babylonians. According to cuneiform inscriptions, Eridu, the oldest settlement in Mesopotamia, had a garden, "a holy place" with a sacred palm tree ("tree of life"?) with two guardian spirits on either side.[38]

Bahrain? For thousands of years, Arab folklore has placed the location of the Garden of Eden along the western or Arabian coast of the Persian Gulf. Native epics named it "Dilmun." Some local traditions even pinpoint its location in the island of Bahrain.[39]

Persian Gulf? History Channel's "Mysteries of the Garden of Eden" narrator said that around 6000 B.C. the ocean levels rose, and the area

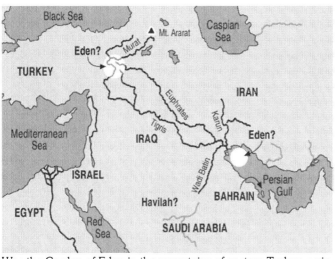

thought to be the site of the Garden of Eden went underwater when the rising seas entered through the lowest passes of the mountains near the Strait of Hormuz, submerging low-lying valleys. The episode ended with the conjecture that

Was the Garden of Eden in the mountains of eastern Turkey, or in a lowland now under the northwestern end of the Persian Gulf?

the Garden of Eden may now be at bottom of the Persian Gulf.[40]

The "Fertile Crescent."

Incidentally, the Shatt al-Arab delta, where four ancient rivers converged, was the scene of some of the most bitter fighting in the eight-year Iran-Iraq War (1980-88). The delta is at the southeastern tip of the so-called Fertile Crescent arching from the northern part of Syria southeast through Mesopotamia, between the Euphrates and the Tigris, the "cradle of civilization" that gave rise to Sumer, Assyria, Babylonia, Phoenicia. The region is also known as the birthplace of organized warfare.

The outline of the Fertile Crescent shown here (based on an image from the *Encarta Encyclopedia*) has a familiar shape. Does it remind you of a Biblical creature that figured prominently in an incident in the Garden of Eden?[41]

The Fertile Crescent arching from Syria to Mesopotamia -- the "cradle of civilization."

The forbidden tree

In Genesis ch. 1, God gave man all seed-bearing plants and fruits for food without any restriction. In chapter 2, the LORD planted all kinds of ornamental and fruit-bearing trees in the Garden of Eden, but then told Adam he could not eat from a specific tree.

"And the LORD God commanded the man, saying, Of every tree of the garden thou mayest freely eat: But of the tree of the knowledge of good and evil, thou shalt not eat of it: for in the day that thou eatest thereof thou shalt surely die" (Gen 2:16-17). The prohibition to eat of that tree was a matter of life and death. Disobedience meant death.

Knowledge of all things?

Not only was eating of the tree of knowledge forbidden, but Eve also said they may not even touch the tree! *"And the woman said unto the serpent, We may eat of the fruit of the trees of the garden: But of the fruit of the tree which is in the midst of the garden, God hath said, Ye shall not eat of it, neither shall ye touch it, lest ye die"* (Gen 3:2-3).

What was that curious tree? Some theologians called it "the tree of conscience," which conferred the wisdom of distinguishing between right and wrong. In *The Bible and the Ancient Near East*, co-authors Cyrus Gordon and Gary Rendsburg suggest that the phrase "good and evil" is a "merism," a figure of speech wherein a pair of opposites is used to mean *all* or *everything*. This is seen in such English phrases as "search high and low" (look everywhere), "through thick and thin" (in all kinds of situation), "creatures great and small" (all animals). Thus, "knowledge of good and evil" means "knowledge of all things."[42,43]

The Book of Enoch confirms the idea: *"In this garden I beheld, among other trees, some which were numerous and large, and which flourished there. Their fragrance was agreeable and powerful, and their appearance both varied and elegant. The tree of knowledge also was there, of which if any one eats, he becomes endowed with great wisdom"* (Enoch 31:2b-3).

Gift of free will.

Why, if the tree of the knowledge of good and evil was so reprehensible, did the LORD plant it at all in the Garden? And, of all places, at the very center – the most conspicuous spot!

As always, we can find a clue in the Scriptures. Thousands of years after Adam, the LORD would tell the Israelites through Moses: *"I call heaven and earth to witness against you today, that I have set before you life and death, the blessing and the curse. So choose life in order that you may live, you and your descendants"* (Deut 30:19, NASU).

In the same way that He would later give the Israelites the freedom to choose between life and death, it seems that from the very beginning the LORD had given man, through Adam and Eve, the gift of free will. He had granted them the privilege of charting their own destinies – whether eventually rewarding or damning.

The LORD may have planted the tree of knowledge in the middle of the Garden to more readily test the couple's obedience to Him. The choice was then left to Adam and Eve.

Immortality missed.

According to Jewish tradition, Adam and Eve would have attained absolute perfection and immortality had they succeeded in resisting the temptation to eat of the fruit of the "untouchable" tree.[44]

It looks like the LORD had created them with the intention of making them live forever. Also in the Garden was the tree of life, whose fruit they could eat, presumably when they would have grown old and weak. Evidently, the fruit of the tree of life was also the antidote to the threat of death arising from any cause, including eating the fruit of the forbidden tree. Adam and Eve could have eaten of the fruit of the tree of life to prevent death and live forever. But it appears from the context that the LORD had not told them about the immortality bestowed by the tree of life. In any case, Adam and Eve brought to naught the wonderful future the LORD had intended for them and their offspring.

It is mankind's misfortune that Adam and Eve, in exercising their God-given free will, made the faulty and fatal choice.

A walking, talking snake

Long before Walt Disney's Mickey Mouse, the Looney Tunes, or even Aesop's Fables, the first talking animal appeared right at the unfolding of mankind's history in the Bible: a snake. Sounds like a comic character. Yet, there was nothing funny concerning its intentions.

"Now the serpent was more cunning than any beast of the field which the LORD God had made. And he said to the woman, 'Has God indeed said, "You shall not eat of every tree of the garden"?' And the woman said to the serpent, 'We may eat the fruit of the trees of the garden; but of the fruit of the tree which is in the midst of the garden, God has said, "You shall not eat it, nor shall you touch it, lest you die." ' Then the serpent said to the woman, 'You will not surely die'." (Gen 3:1-4, NKJV).

Practically all people who know the story of Adam and Eve believe that the serpent was the devil. Can we be sure?

Slanderer and deceiver.

The word "devil" comes from the Greek *diabolos*, which *Strong's Concordance* says is also translated as "slanderer," "false accuser." The ways of the serpent identify him as no one else but the devil.

He slandered God: "*And the serpent said unto the woman, Ye shall not surely die*" (Gen 3:3-4). The devil brazenly insinuated that God lied to Adam and Eve when He told them they would die if they ate of the tree of the knowledge of good and evil.

The devil also slanders man: "*So Satan answered the LORD and said, 'Does Job fear God for nothing? Have You not made a hedge around him, around his household, and around all that he has on every side? You have blessed the work of his hands, and his possessions have increased in the land. But now, stretch out Your hand and touch all that he has, and he will surely curse You to Your face!*'" (Job 1:9-11, NKJV). The devil said Job remained faithful to God only because He kept on blessing him.

The devil accuses faithful believers nonstop, according to John: "*And I heard a great voice in heaven, saying, Now is come the salvation, and the power, and the kingdom of our God, and the authority of his Christ: for the accuser of our brethren is cast down, who accuseth them before our God day and night*" (Rev 12:10, ASV).

The serpent has a forked tongue, the metaphor for "double-talk" – that is, to speak insincerely with the intent to deceive. The devil, also known as Satan, is the great deceiver: "*So the great dragon was cast out, that serpent of old, called the Devil and Satan, who deceives the whole world...*" (Rev 12:9a, NKJV). His first victim was innocent Eve.

The forbidden fruit

Was the forbidden fruit an actual fruit or merely a symbol of sin, as some commentators contend? A partly bitten apple is today widely regarded as the symbol of illicit sex. If it was an actual fruit, what was it? We are not told in the Genesis story what sort the tree of the knowledge of good and evil was, yet its fruit is traditionally pictured as an apple.

An apple or a fig?

Early Church writers began the apple tradition as an offshoot of a Latin pun: "By eating the *malum* (apple), Eve contracted *malus* (evil)." (The word *malus* also means apple tree in Latin.) Thus, by the 12th century, the apple was the favorite of French and German artists as the forbidden fruit. However, Byzantine and Italian painters were inclined to show the fig. Come the Renaissance, renowned painters depicted either of the two: Albrecht Dürer, an apple in the years 1504 and 1507; and

Michelangelo, a fig on Rome's famous Sistine Chapel ceiling around 1510.[45] Just the same, it is the image of the more popular apple that has made a lasting impression on the minds of the laity.

The problem is, the apple, which originated from central Asia, does not easily ripen to perfection in the hot and dry places of the Middle East. (Of course, the climate in the Garden of Eden may have been totally different 6,000 years ago.)

Other likely fruits.

A strange fruit is described in Enoch 31:14, "It was like a species of the tamarind tree, bearing fruit which resembled grapes extremely fine; and its fragrance extended to a considerable distance." However, the rabbis believe that the forbidden fruit was one that we still know and enjoy today.

In the Talmud, Rabbi Meir claimed the fruit was a grape, suggesting Eve made and drank wine. Rabbi Nechemia asserted that it was a fig. Rabbi Yehuda argued it was wheat. Others suggest the fruit was a pomegranate, which is indigenous in western Asia.[46] Those were some of the choice foods God told the Israelites abounded in the Promised Land. "*For the LORD thy God bringeth thee into a good land, a land of brooks of water, of fountains and depths that spring out of valleys and hills; A land of wheat, and barley, and vines, and fig trees, and pomegranates; a land of oil olive, and honey*" (Deut 8:7-8).

These were also the fruits the Israelites longed for in the wilderness after the Exodus (Num 20:5). The twelve spies Moses sent out to scout Canaan brought back grapes, pomegranates, and figs (Num 13:23).

Fig, olive, or pomegranate?

Since the other fruits named do not come from trees, we can trim down the list to three -- the fig, the olive, and the pomegranate.

If it was the fig, Adam and Eve would not have made coverings for themselves from fig leaves (Gen 3:7). That would have been a telltale sign that they had been tampering with the tree they were not even supposed to "touch."

So, was it the olive or the pomegranate? Perhaps we can gather clues from what went through Eve's mind that eventually moved her to savor the forbidden fruit: "*And when the woman saw that the tree was good for food, and that it was pleasant to the eyes, and a tree to be desired to make one wise, she took of the fruit thereof, and did eat...*" (Gen 3:6a).

"**Good for food**." Figs, Pliny the Elder (d. 79 A.D.) wrote, made up a large portion of the food of Roman slaves. Today, in Mediterranean countries where the fig is widely eaten, either fresh or dried, it is called "the poor man's food."[47] Could a fruit that supposedly conferred great wisdom go down to a level fit only for the lowest classes?

As regards olives, the fresh fruit is almost inedible because of its extremely bitter taste. That is why olives are traditionally pressed into oil or pickled in brine before consumption. Does this eliminate the olive from our list of candidates?

As for the pomegranate (Latin *pomum granatum*, "grainy fruit"), its numerous juice-covered seeds are enjoyed fresh; as a sweet, sometimes somewhat tart, refreshing drink; or as fermented wine (Song 8:2).

"Pleasant to the eyes." Figs, depending on the variety, have green, yellow, pink, purple, brown, or black skins.

The olive fruit, as it ripens, turns from green to yellow to red to purple-black.

The pomegranate is typically golden brown with a blush of red. King Solomon likened the temples (upper cheeks) of the maiden he was wooing to pomegranates (Song 4:3). Her orchard had only one kind of fruit-bearing tree -- the pomegranate; the rest were spices (Song 4:13).

The "Mother of Knowledge."

In his book *The Two Babylons*, Alexander Hislop wrote: "Astarte, or Cybele, was also called Idaia Mater, and the sacred mount in Phrygia, most famed for the celebration of her mysteries, was named Mount Ida – that is, in Chaldee, the sacred language of these mysteries, the Mount of Knowledge. 'Idaia Mater,' then signifies 'the Mother of Knowledge' – in other words, our Mother Eve, who first coveted the 'knowledge of good and evil,' and actually purchased it at so dire a price to herself and to all her children. Astarte, as can be abundantly shown, was worshipped not only as incarnation of the Spirit of God, but also the mother of mankind."[48]

He added: "When, therefore, the mother of the gods, and the mother of knowledge, was represented with the fruit of the pomegranate in her extended hand, inviting those who ascended the sacred mount to initiation in her mysteries, can there be a doubt what that fruit was intended to signify? Evidently, it must accord with her assumed character; it must be the fruit of the 'Tree of Knowledge'... whose mortal taste brought death into the world, and all our woe."[49]

Idaia Mater – the "Mother of Knowledge" and "Mother of Mankind" – was Eve, offering knowledge symbolized by the pomegranate in her extended hand.

Symbol of plenty, marriage. The pomegranate was regarded as a symbol of plenty and fertility in the ancient world. Topped by a crown-like calyx, the fruit seems to have an air of sanctity around it. The LORD commanded Moses to embroider two rows of pomegranates around the hem of the high priest's robe (Ex 28:33-35). Hundreds of pomegranates adorned the capitals of the two columns in front of the Holy Temple in Jerusalem (1 Kings 7:18, 20). The Hebrew word for pomegranate, rimmon, formed part of several place-names in Israel.

In Greek mythology, the pomegranate was the symbol of marriage. By eating the seeds, the gods entered into wedded union.[50] Did the myth begin when Adam and Eve shared the forbidden fruit?

Same fate shared

Eve *"gave also unto her husband with her; and he did eat"* (Gen 3:6b). Was it out of love? Did Eve want to share her pleasure from eating the forbidden fruit with Adam? Quite the opposite may have been her motive. According to some rabbis in antiquity, she might have wanted him to suffer the same fate she realized awaited her.

A widower remarrying?

A legend in the Talmud says that, after having eaten the forbidden fruit, it dawned upon Eve that she might indeed die. That meant Adam would go on living without her and, sooner or later, look for another companion, probably a new wife. Eve could not bear the thought and persuaded Adam to eat of the fruit, too, so he would die with her.[51]

Where did Eve get the idea that Adam would find another woman? As we now know, the Talmud and other ancient Jewish commentaries told of creatures with human form and intelligence, but without the God-given *neshamah*. Were these primitive beings the Neanderthals and the Cro-Magnons (*Homo sapiens*)? Did some of them survive to the time of Adam and Eve (*Homo sapiens sapiens*)?

At first glance, Eve's prophetic name appears to belie the existence of other men in their time. *"Adam named his wife Eve, because she would become the mother of all the living"* (Gen 3:20, NIV). "Eve" in the Hebrew original was *Chavah*, which means "life-giver." The name implies all people living today are descended from Eve.

However, the prophecy in her name would still hold true even though there might have been manlike creatures before and during her time. If those pre-Adamic subhumans died out in a mass extinction event or perished in Noah's Flood, Eve would still be the mother of all people living today.

Shameful situation

"And the eyes of them both were opened, and they knew that they

were naked; and they sewed fig leaves together, and made themselves aprons" (Gen 3:7). It seems that, soon after Adam and Eve committed the sin of disobedience, the light of holiness covering them like garments dimmed. Stripped of their innocence, they realized they were naked! In shame they made coverings for their private parts.

Sin equals nakedness.

Sin appearss to be denoted by nakedness. Ezra laments: *"For the LORD brought Judah low because of Ahaz king of Israel; for he made Judah naked, and transgressed sore against the LORD"* (2 Chron 28:19). Jeremiah told the king: *"If you say in your heart, 'Why have these things happened to me?' Because of the magnitude of your iniquity Your skirts have been removed And your heels have been exposed"* (Jer 13: 22, NASU). According to *The Wycliffe Bible Commentary,* *"heels"* are a euphemism signifying "secret parts," that is, the genitals.[52]

Christ warns: *"Behold, I come as a thief. Blessed is he that watcheth, and keepeth his garments, lest he walk naked, and they see his shame"* (Rev 16:15). Paul rephrases it: *"For in this we groan, earnestly desiring to be clothed upon with our house which is from heaven: If so be that being clothed we shall not be found naked"* (2 Cor 5:2-3).

Finger-pointing brats.

"And they heard the voice of the LORD God walking in the garden in the cool of the day: and Adam and his wife hid themselves from the presence of the LORD God amongst the trees of the garden. And the LORD God called unto Adam, and said unto him, Where art thou? And he said, I heard thy voice in the garden, and I was afraid, because I was naked; and I hid myself. And he said, Who told thee that thou wast naked? Hast thou eaten of the tree, whereof I commanded thee that thou shouldest not eat?" (Gen 3:8-11). Adam and Eve could not avoid facing the music.

"And the man said, The woman whom thou gavest to be with me, she gave me of the tree, and I did eat. And the LORD God said unto the woman, What is this that thou hast done? And the woman said, The serpent beguiled me, and I did eat" (Gen 3:12-13). Like little children caught red-handed in an act of mischief, Adam and Eve resorted to finger-pointing. Adam told the LORD that Eve was to blame. In turn, Eve pointed to the serpent as the culprit.

Sentences pronounced

The LORD God pronounced sentences on each of the guilty parties -- from the most to the least responsible for the transgression.

"And the LORD God said unto the serpent, Because thou hast done this, thou art cursed above all cattle, and above every beast of the field; upon thy belly shalt thou go, and dust shalt thou eat all the days of thy life" (Gen 3:14).

Snake had legs!

It seems snakes originally had legs. Why would the LORD sentence the serpent to creep on his belly for life if he had already been doing that before? Some modern snakes, notably the python or boa constrictor, have vestigial limbs – shrunken leg and feet bones that form part of their skeletal systems.

In December 2000, the *National Geographic* casually mentioned on the Internet the discovery of a fossil snake with legs in Israel: "Before the 'Ein Yabrud quarry, located 12 miles north of Jerusalem, was closed in 1985, quarry workers brought several hundred fossil specimens to the late George Haas of Hebrew University. The fossils include plants, bony fish, a shark with the outline of its skin preserved, turtles, lizards, a pterosaur foot, snakes with legs, and others."[53]

Earlier, the *SMU News,* a university publication, had made a more detailed report in its March 16, 2000, issue: "Researchers from Southern Methodist University have described an intriguing new species of fossil snake with legs that was found in a limestone quarry north of Jerusalem... named *Haasiophis terrasanctus* after a Hebrew professor named George Haas who obtained it from quarry workers more than 20 years ago."[54]

According to the *Encyclopaedia Britannica,* two other fossil snakes with short rear legs have been discovered in the Middle East: the *Podophis* and the *Pachyrhachis.* The finds have reportedly sparked renewed scientific controversy over the origin of snakes.[55]

So, the serpent in the Garden not only talked, it also walked! Can you imagine the elongated creature waddling vertically on two stumpy hind legs? It must have been a funny sight. The effect on us of what it did, though, is not something we can laugh about.

"Missing link" from lizards? The *Encyclpaedia Britannica* says there are at least three theories concerning the origin of two-legged snakes. First, they are a "missing link" between lizards and snakes.[56] However, Hussam Zaher, a snake expert and member of a University of Sao Paulo (Brazil) research team, reported that the strange creatures form a branch of the snake family that is closely related to modern boas and pythons, not to prehistoric marine lizards called *mosasaurs.* Similarly, the Vidal and Hedges study, using statistical methods that compared differences in the sequences of two genes -- RAG1 and C-mos

– in DNA samples, established that monitor lizards, which also have forked tongues, are not related to snakes.[57]

The second theory posits that the two-legged serpents make up a separate species that never lost their legs. The third theory proposes that the bipedal animals were more advanced relatives of boas and pythons that re-grew legs! The uncertainty regarding the origin of snakes, researchers say, is due to the poor and fragmentary fossil record of snakes, compared with other vertebrates.[58]

If there are hardly any snake fossils, have paleontologists ever considered the possibility that the snake may actually be a relatively new animal? Unless they change their mindset, they may never learn where to look for the right answer. But, of course, we do, do we not?

Snakes eat dust. The LORD had told the serpent: *"...and dust shalt thou eat all the days of thy life"* (Gen 3:14b). From what a prophet later said in Micah 7:17, this may truly have become second nature to snakes: *"They shall lick the dust like a serpent..."*

Snakes seem to deliberately lick and eat dust. Why? Because God said so. But let us hear biologists explain the matter scientifically: In the roof of a snake's mouth is a pair of tiny chemically sensitive cavities called "Jacobson's organ." It complements the snake's nostrils, enabling the animal to heighten its sense of smell. The snake flicks out its forked tongue to get samples of dust in the air or on the ground on the points of the fork, then retracts it across the two cavities, where nerve endings lining the tissues assess the dust molecules for odors. The dust is left in the mouth so the tongue can come out clean to repeat the process. Thus, snakes truly lick and eat dust![59]

The author personally saw proof that snakes do eat dust. He once found a small black snake dead at the bottom of a closet with a clump of half-swallowed cobweb in its mouth. It looked like the snake died of starvation, but tried eating the cobweb shortly before death.

End-time prophecy.

The LORD also told the serpent: *"And I will put enmity between thee and the woman, and between thy seed and her seed; it shall bruise thy head, and thou shalt bruise his heel"* (Gen 3:15). The statement is a veiled prophecy of Armageddon, the final battle between Satan and Christ, a descendant of Eve, at His Second Coming.

As a "woman" in prophecy represents a church or faith, *"enmity between thee and the woman"* means the struggle between Satan (the serpent or dragon, Rev 12:9) and the true faith (the woman, Rev 12:1) for supremacy. *"Thy seed"* points to the "beast" (Antichrist), who derives its power from the "dragon" (Rev13:4), while *"her seed"* is

Christ (the son of the "woman," Rev 12:4a-5). Note that Christ is not called the "seed of man," because He would not have an earthly father.

Sentenced to "hard labor"

The LORD God next pronounced two different kinds of "hard labor" on Adam and Eve.

Labor at childbirth. *"Unto the woman he said, I will greatly multiply thy sorrow and thy conception; in sorrow thou shalt bring forth children…"* (Gen 3:16).

Human mothers experience the most intense pains in delivering their babies, compared to other creatures on earth. You have probably seen on the National Geographic, Discovery, Animal Planet, and other cable television channels how birthing female animals, even the big ones like the buffalo and whales, deliver their young without the least sign of pain or discomfort. On the other hand, women as a rule find childbirth as a most painful and laborious process.

Labor on the ground. *"And unto Adam he said, Because thou hast hearkened unto the voice of thy wife, and hast eaten of the tree, of which I commanded thee, saying, Thou shalt not eat of it: cursed is the ground for thy sake; in sorrow shalt thou eat of it all the days of thy life; Thorns also and thistles shall it bring forth to thee; and thou shalt eat the herb of the field; In the sweat of thy face shalt thou eat bread, till thou return unto the ground…"* Gen 3:17-19a).

Whereas before Adam and Eve simply plucked any plant or fruit they desired to eat, after being driven out of the Garden the man had to laboriously till the ground to produce the food they ate. This situation has remained true for humankind to this day.

Death on the same "day"?

Adam did not die on the day he ate of the forbidden fruit. Was the LORD's warning merely meant to instill fearful obedience in him?

There are actually two profound reasons why Adam and Eve did not die within the next 24 hours.

A prophetic "day."

Adam lived another 900 years, more or less, after he sinned: *"And all the days that Adam lived were nine hundred and thirty years: and he died"* (Gen 5:3-5). Adam died at the extremely old age of 930 years. Does that make God a liar?

As we have seen earlier, it seems that from the creation of Adam, God's way of reckoning time shifted to a new mode, based on two key verses: *"For a thousand years in thy sight are but as yesterday when it is past, and as a watch in the night"* (Psalm 90:4) and *"But, beloved, be not ignorant of this one thing, that one day is with the Lord as a thousand years, and a thousand years as one day"* (2 Peter 3:8). In God's eyes, one day is equivalent to 1,000 years, and vice-versa.

So, the LORD's words truly came to pass. Adam died within the "day" he ate of the forbidden fruit – a "day" that was 1,000 years long!

Spiritual death.

The second reason is in one of Paul's epistles: *"For the wages of sin is death"* (Rom 6:23). Whoever sins will die. But what, exactly, is sin? John defines it pithily: *"Whosoever committeth sin transgresseth also the law: for sin is the transgression of the law"* (1 John 3:4). Sin is the violation of God's commandments. Because Adam violated the LORD's instruction not to eat of the tree of knowledge, he had to die.

Yet, as we have learned, there are two kinds of death: physical and spiritual. It now becomes evident that the LORD meant not only physical death, but spiritual death as well! For that reason, Adam did not die physically on that same day. That is also why many sinful people in the world today go on living.

Adam's disobedience has far-reaching consequences. *"Wherefore, as by one man sin entered into the world, and death by sin; and so death passed upon all men, for that all have sinned"* (Rom 5:12). Adam passed on his sinful nature to his descendants.[60] So all of them, including us, became subject to both physical and spiritual deaths.

An escape clause

The LORD, in His great love and mercy, had inserted an escape clause in His law. As the wise woman told King David: *"'For we will surely die and are like water spilled on the ground which cannot be gathered up again. Yet God does not take away life, but plans ways so that the banished one will not be cast out from him"* (2 Sam 14:14, NASU). God has provided a way for sinners to avert spiritual death!

A means for atonement.

God would tell Moses: *"For the life of a creature is in the blood, and I have given it to you to make atonement for yourselves on the altar; it is the blood that makes atonement for one's life"* (Lev 17:11, NIV). Paul reiterates the concept in the NT: *"In fact, the law requires that nearly everything be cleansed with blood, and without the shedding of blood there is no forgiveness"* (Heb 9:22, NIV). The sinner can atone for his sin, be forgiven, and save his spirit from death with blood!

In Hebrew, "atonement" comes from the root *kaphar*, meaning "to cover." Figuratively, the blood "covers" sin from the LORD's sight. But whose blood – the sinner's? He might die just the same!

Sacrificial substitutes.
The LORD replaced the fig leaves with which Adam and Eve had made coverings for themselves. *"Unto Adam also and to his wife did the LORD God make coats of skins, and clothed them"* (Gen 3:21). Many people familiar with the story think God simply made more durable garments for Adam and Eve from animal skins. Yes, indeed, but it is now obvious there was a second, more important reason: God shed the blood of animals to show them how to atone for their sin!

Apparently, sinners do not necessarily have to shed their own blood, they can "cover" their sins with the blood of sacrificial substitutes. That first animal sacrifice was the precursor of the sacrificial system that the LORD would institute through the Mosaic Law and which Christ would later replace with His own holy blood on the cross at Golgotha.

The symbol of sin. Writers have sometimes wondered which animals provided the garments of skin for Adam and Eve. Some thought the coats were made from sheepskin – because the sheep was one of the "clean" animals God would tell the Israelites to sacrifice to Him. But would God have given sinners coats of "clean" sheepskin? A white, spotless lamb symbolizes sinlessness.

Conversely, spots and blemishes are strongly associated with sin. Paul wrote: *"That he might present it to himself a glorious church, not having spot, or wrinkle, or any such thing; but that it should be holy and without blemish"* (Eph 5:27). Peter shares the same idea: *"Wherefore, beloved, seeing that ye look for such things, be diligent that ye may be found of him in peace, without spot, and blameless"* (2 Peter 3:14).

Jeremiah likens evil, or sinfulness, to the spots of the leopard: *"Can the Ethiopian change his skin or the leopard its spots? Then may you also do good who are accustomed to do evil"* (Jer 13:23, NKJV).

Leopard skin coats? Did the LORD sacrifice spotted leopards to "cover" the sin, as well cover the nakedness, of Adam and Eve? It would have been most fitting. The apocryphal Book of Jasher (7:24-26) says Adam had leopard skin coats, which he gave to his great great great great grandson Enoch, his 7th generation descendant, who passed on the garments to his own son Methuselah, whose grandson Noah took them with him into the Ark. Noah's son Ham stole the coats after the Flood and later gave them to his firstborn son Cush, who bequeathed them to his youngest and favorite son, Nimrod.[61]

Alexander Hislop wrote in *The Two Babylons* that Nimrod means "subduer of the leopard" (*namer* in Hebrew) and was depicted as a god wearing leopard skin. The case for God having sacrificed leopards to make garments for Adam and Eve is quite strong.

Mortal son of God

Most people are under the impression that God cast Adam and Eve out of the Garden as punishment for their disobedience. But Adam had already been sentenced – he and his descendants would have to till the ground for their food all their lives. Let us examine the real reason.

"And the LORD God said, Behold, the man is become as one of us, to know good and evil: and now, lest he put forth his hand, and take also of the tree of life, and eat, and live for ever: Therefore the LORD God sent him forth from the garden of Eden, to till the ground from whence he was taken" (Gen 3:22-23). Adam and Eve were driven out of the Garden to prevent them from gaining undeserved immortality!

Interestingly, despite having banished the man and woman from the Garden of Eden, the LORD apparently still considered Adam His son. Luke, in his gospel, said so in the genealogy of Christ: *"...Adam, which was the son of God"* (Luke 3:38b).

The "first" family

"This is the book of the generations of Adam. In the day that God created man, in the likeness of God made he him; Male and female created he them; and blessed them, and called their name Adam, in the day when they were created" (Gen 5:1-2). Not all of the descendants of Adam are named – only the firstborn or the most prominent son in each generation from whom the lineage continues. Ordinarily, daughters are not named, or even mentioned at all, except in a few special cases.

Descriptive, prophetic names.

Their names were apparently inspired by the LORD. They were descriptive of the person, even prophetic of future events.

Adam. As we have learned previously, his name means "ruddy" or "reddish" in Hebrew, owing to the general redness of the earth, from which he came. *"And the LORD God formed man of the dust of the ground..."* (Gen 2:7).

Created in 4004 B.C., Adam lived a total of 930 years. *"And all the days that Adam lived were nine hundred and thirty years: and he died"* (Gen 5:5). Thus, Adam died in 3074 B.C.

Eve. We have seen earlier that her name, meaning "life-giver" in the Hebrew original, was *Chavah*, which came from the root *chayah*, signifying "life" or "to live." *"Adam named his wife Eve, because she would become the mother of all the living"* (Gen 3:20, NIV). There is no mention in the Scriptures of how long Eve lived or when she died.

Cain. The name of Adam's firstborn came from Eve's words at his birth: *"And Adam knew Eve his wife; and she conceived, and bare Cain, and said, I have gotten a man from the LORD"* (Gen 4:1). "Cain" may have come from either or both of two Hebrew roots: *qanah* meaning "to procure, obtain"; or *qayin* meaning "spear," "smith," or "weapon-maker." It is possible Cain dabbled in weapon-making, As a future castaway, Cain does not have the years of his life in the Scriptures.

Abel. The name of Adam's second son' came from *hebel*, a root signifying "emptiness, vanity, futility" or "something transitory and unsatisfactory." "Abel" was prophetic of his brief life. As his line would be cut short, there is no timeframe for his abbreviated existence.

There is an inkling in the Scriptures that Cain and Abel might have been twins. We read in Genesis 4:2a – *"And she again bare his brother Abel."* Eve had conceived Cain, but the absence of the verb *harah* ("conceive") in the case of Abel gives occasion to the conjecture that perhaps Cain and Abel were conceived simultaneously as twins.[62]

Bad blood between brothers

According to the *World Book*, most scientists believe agriculture began in the Middle East. "The first farmers lived in a region called the Fertile Crescent, which covers what is now Lebanon and parts of Iran, Iraq, Israel, Jordan, Syria, and Turkey."[63]

A farmer and a shepherd.

Adam was probably both a farmer and a herdsman. His first two sons divided the two occupations between them: *"And Abel was a keeper of sheep, but Cain was a tiller of the ground"* (Gen 4:2b).

"And in process of time it came to pass, that Cain brought of the fruit of the ground an offering unto the LORD. And Abel, he also brought of the firstlings of his flock and of the fat thereof" (Gen 4:3-4a). The Biblical text suggests there was a regular place for worship, probably an altar, where the two brothers brought their offerings.

From the specific mention of *"fat,"* which fuels fire, it looks like Abel burned his animal offerings, after shedding their blood. Cain's offerings, presumably grain, vegetables, and fruits, had neither blood nor fat. It is not known if Cain burned them. *"And the LORD had respect unto Abel and to his offering: But unto Cain and to his offering he had not respect. And Cain was very wroth, and his countenance fell"* (Gen 4:4b-5).

God counseled Cain: *"Then the LORD said to Cain, "Why are you angry? Why is your face downcast? If you do what is right, will you not be accepted? But if you do not do what is right, sin is crouching at your door; it desires to have you, but you must master it"* (Gen 4:6-7, NIV). There is a hint in God's words that Satan continued to hound their family beyond the confines of the Garden.

The first murder.
Instead of doing what was right, Cain vented his bitterness on his younger sibling: *"Now Cain said to his brother Abel, 'Let's go out to the field.' And while they were in the field, Cain attacked his brother Abel and killed him"* (Gen 4:8, NIV).

It appears Cain used an object to kill Abel, because the latter's blood flowed out of his body. *"The LORD said, "What have you done? Listen! Your brother's blood cries out to me from the ground. Now you are under a curse and driven from the ground, which opened its mouth to receive your brother's blood from your hand"* (Gen 4:10-12, NIV). Did Cain use a spear in fulfillment of a prophecy in his name?

There might have been a second, little-known motive for Cain to end his younger brother's life. Seth, the alleged author of the 3rd century pseudepigraphal Testament of Adam, was supposedly told by Adam: "You have heard, my son Seth, that a Flood is coming and will wash the whole earth because of the daughters of Cain, your brother, who killed your brother Abel out of passion for your sister Lebuda..."[64]

If the account has any shred of truth in it, it shows the brothers had at least one female sibling before the murder took place, and that sister Lebuda might have favored Abel over Cain. Cain's lust for his sister could have been one sin the LORD spoke to him about.

A curse on Cain. The LORD put a curse on Cain. *"When you work the ground, it will no longer yield its crops for you. You will be a restless wanderer on the earth"* (Gen 4:12, NIV). Cain would no longer be blessed as a farmer. He would become a nomad constantly in search of food.

"Cain said to the LORD, "My punishment is more than I can bear. Today you are driving me from the land, and I will be hidden from your presence; I will be a restless wanderer on the earth, and whoever finds me will kill me" (Gen 4:13-14, NIV). His banishment would keep him away from God's presence and the blessings and protection it provided. Cain now also feared being killed himself.

Who would kill Cain? It seems that, apart from their sister Lebuda, Adam and Eve had already begotten other unnamed children who had grown up or were still growing up when the murder of Abel took place.

Vengeance to the Lord.

Despite Cain's evil deed, God assured him of his safety. *"And the LORD said unto him, Therefore whosoever slayeth Cain, vengeance shall be taken on him sevenfold. And the LORD set a mark upon Cain, lest any finding him should kill him"* (Gen 4:15). We are not told what the "mark" was. It could have been an actual mark on the skin, or an unusual appearance that distinguished Cain. In any case, it served its purpose of preserving his life, as his great great great grandson Lamech would later imply (Gen 4:17-24). But why would the LORD want to preserve Cain's life?

After that first murder in recorded history, the only motive anyone would have to kill Cain would have been revenge. But as we read in the Bible, *"To me belongeth vengeance, and recompence..."* (Deut 32:35a); *"O LORD God, to whom vengeance belongeth..."* (Ps 94:1a). Revenge is the prerogative of the LORD. For any man to take revenge is to commit sin. It seems the LORD did not want any more sins incurred in addition to what Cain had already committed.

Whence came Cain's wife

As his parents had been cast out of the Garden, Cain was cast out of Eden. *"And Cain went out from the presence of the LORD, and dwelt in the land of Nod, on the east of Eden. And Cain knew his wife; and she conceived, and bare Enoch..."* (Gen 4:16-17a). Where did Cain's wife come from?

A mixed marriage?

In 1655, Frenchman Isaac La Peyrère published his theory that Cain's wife came from a prehistoric race that had existed long before Adam.[65] Was that pre-Adamic race that of the Neanderthals or the latter Cro-Magnons, or a mixture of both?

But the more plausible explanation is, Cain married one of his own sisters. It is reasonable to assume that Adam and Eve had other children as Cain and Abel were growing up, as well as during the hundreds of years that they continued to live and procreate after Cain's banishment. We cannot say if Cain eventually took as wife Lebuda or one of his other sisters, or a niece, or even a grandniece. He might not even have taken a wife soon after arriving in the land of Nod.

Today, sexual relations between close relatives are called incest, which is socially and legally prohibited. It usually produces offspring with defects as a result of inbreeding. Yet, the human genetic pool was much more robust in the days of the patriarchs. Close relatives married each other without fear of having abnormal children. Eve was Adam's clone.

Even 2,000 years later, Abram's wife Sarai was his half-sister by his father. His son Isaac took Rebekah, daughter of his (Isaac's) first cousin Bethuel. Isaac's son Jacob married his first cousins Leah and Rachel, daughters of his mother's brother Laban.

The city of Cain.
After the birth of his son, Cain founded a city: *"...and he builded a city, and called the name of the city, after the name of his son, Enoch"* (Gen 4:17b). How was Cain able to build a city so soon?

According to La Peyrère, members of the pre-Adamic stock (Neanderthals or Cro-Magnons, or both) made up the inhabitants of the city.[66] However, it is equally possible that the dwellers of the city were all descendants of Adam and Eve. It is amazing how fast humans can multiply. Consider the birth of the nation of Israel:

Jacob, who had been renamed Israel, went with his 70 descendants (Ex 1:1-5) and their families to Egypt in 1706 B.C.[67] during a famine in Canaan. The clan swelled in Egypt. *"And the children of Israel were fruitful, and increased abundantly, and multiplied, and waxed exceeding mighty; and the land was filled with them"* (Ex 1:7). After only 215 years, when they departed from Egypt in 1491 B.C. in the Exodus led by Moses, the Israelites had 600,000 men (Ex 12:37) twenty years old and above (Num 1:20). If we add the women and children (1-19 years old), assuming each couple had on average at least two offspring, as well as the elderly, we find that from only 70 persons Israel had grown to well over 2,000,000 people in just 215 years!

Conditions were even more favorable during the time of Cain. With men and women living close to a thousand years and begetting children for hundreds of years in an ideal environment, it would not have taken long for Cain to gather many people around him and build a city.

Adam's grave

Adam missed his chance at immortality and eventually died. *"And all the days that Adam lived were nine hundred and thirty years: and he died"* (Gen 5:5). The Bible does not say if Adam was buried. But if the primitive Neanderthals and Cro-Magnons buried their dead, there were more reasons for Adam, a son of God, to have been buried.

There is a pre-Christian Jewish tradition that the skull of Adam had been found in Golgotha. The early Church theologian Origen (d. 254), who lived in Jerusalem for twenty years, wrote: "I have received a tradition to the effect that the body of Adam, the first man, was buried upon the spot where Christ was crucified."[68]

"Place of a skull."

John 19:17 says: *"And he bearing his cross went forth into a place called the place of a skull, which is called in the Hebrew Golgotha."* "Golgotha" came from the Aramaic *gulgaltha* and Hebrew *gulgoleth*, meaning "skull." The alternative name "Calvary" came from the Latin *calvaria*, which also means "skull" (*calvus* means "bald").

Latter Christian writers, such as Athanasius, Epiphanius, Basil of Caesarea, Chrysostom, and others quoted Origen. According to the *International Standard Bible Encyclopedia*, the tomb and skull of Adam are still "in an excavated chamber below the traditional Calvary."[69] It is probably for that reason that the place called "Golgotha" or "Calvary" was given its name. That the site of the crucifixion hill derived its name from its resemblance to a skull is said to be a modern idea.

Christ was crucified and buried in that location. *"At the place where Jesus was crucified, there was a garden, and in the garden a new tomb, in which no one had ever been laid. Because it was the Jewish day of Preparation and since the tomb was nearby, they laid Jesus there"* (John 19:41-42, NIV). Is it not simply amazing that the first Adam with a God-given spirit might have been buried in the exact place where Christ, "the "last Adam" with a life-giving spirit (1 Cor 15:45), would likewise be buried some 4,000 years later?

7

Wonderful World Wasted

nd God looked upon the earth, and, behold,
it was corrupt; for all flesh had corrupted
his way upon the earth"

-- Genesis 6:12.

After Cain killed Abel, he was no longer worthy to continue the line of Adam leading to the promised "seed of the woman" (Gen 3:15). He was banished from Eden, and Adam and Eve produced another son.

Antediluvian ancestors

The new son would take the place of the righteous, but now dead Abel in the genealogy of man. The lineage from Adam to Noah to Abraham to David and, eventually, to the Messiah would now be traced from this third addition to the family.

Seth. His name came from the words Eve uttered at his birth. *"Adam had relations with his wife again; and she gave birth to a son, and named him Seth, for, she said, "God has appointed me another offspring in place of Abel, for Cain killed him"* (Gen 4:25, NASU).

Seth was born in 3874 B.C. His name came from the Hebrew root *shiyth,* which means "put, placed, substituted." Indeed, the LORD had placed Seth as a substitute for both Cain and Abel. Although actually Adam's third son, he became the patriarch of the second generation.

"And all the days of Seth were nine hundred and twelve years: and he died" (Gen 5:8). Seth died in 2962 B.C.

Enos. Seth fathered a son: *"And Seth lived an hundred and five years, and begat Enos"* (Gen 5:6). Enos was born in 3769 B.C.

The third generation man from Adam, Enos had a name that came from *anash*, meaning "to be frail, feeble, melancholy." Scripture is silent on how Enos fulfilled the prophecy in his name. He might have been an infirm, introverted person for much of his life.

We read earlier that *"And to Seth, to him also there was born a son; and he called his name Enos: then began men to call upon the name of the LORD"* (Gen 4:26). Perhaps Seth started calling on the name of God to pray for the good health of his son; then Enos himself and others followed Seth's example. Incidentally, the word "men" infers there were already many people in the third generation from Adam.

Perhaps due to a weak constitution, Enos had a shorter life than both his father and grandfather. *"And all the days of Enos were nine hundred and five years: and he died"* (Gen 5:11). He died in 2864 B.C.

Cainan. Enos sired his own son, despite his presumed infirmity: *"And Enos lived ninety years, and begat Cainan"* (Gen 5:9).

Born in 3679 B.C., in the fourth generation from Adam, Cainan had a name with the same root as Cain, so his name denoted a "possessor" or "weapon-maker." Cainan lived at the dawn of the Bronze Age, which developed around 3000 B.C.[1] He might have been a smith.

"And all the days of Cainan were nine hundred and ten years: and he died" (Gen 5:14). He lived longer than his father, dying in 2769 B.C.

Mahalaleel. Cainan had a son. *"And Cainan lived seventy years, and begat Mahalaleel"* (Gen 5:12). Mahalaleel was born in 3609 B.C.

Cainan must have been a pious person, unlike his granduncle and namesake Cain, because he gave his son a godly name: Mahalaleel, a compound of the Hebrew words *halal* ("to shine, be clear" or "fame, praise") and *el* ("mighty one or strong one"), thus denoting "God shines forth"[2] or "praise of God."[3] Mahalaleel was the fifth generation patriarch from Adam. *"And all the days of Mahalaleel were eight hundred ninety and five years: and he died"* (Gen 5:17). He died in 2714 B.C.

Jared. Mahalaleel had a son born to him in 3544 B.C. *"And Mahalaleel lived sixty and five years, and begat Jared"* (Gen 5:15).

Mahalaleel gave his son, the sixth generation man, an odd name: "Jared." It came from the root *yarad*, meaning "to descend." Jared thus means "descent." According to an ancient tradition, Jared's name prophesied the descent to earth of angels during his lifetime!

Jared lived longer than any man before him. *"And all the days of Jared were nine hundred sixty and two years: and he died"* (Gen 5:19-20). He died in 2582 B.C.

Descent of angels

"And it came to pass, when men began to multiply on the face of the earth, and daughters were born unto them, That the sons of God saw the daughters of men that they were fair; and they took them wives of all which they chose" (Gen 6:1-2).

Some commentators think the "sons of God" were men from the godly line of Seth who intermarried with women from the ungodly line of Cain. Others speculate they were earthly rulers who established harems from among the daughters of commoners. The growing consensus, though, is that the "sons of God" were actually angels.

Enamored with women.

It appears that, as the human population increased, angels noticed that the female children grew up to be attractive. Some of the angels were fascinated by the young women's charms. A more detailed account is in the Book of Enoch, a 2nd-1st century B.C. pseudepigraphal work.

(A brother of Christ himself quoted from it [Jude 14], and the early Church leaders used it. The book had been lost until 1773, when James Bruce found three Ethiopic copies written in Geez [an ancient Semitic dialect] in Abyssinia. An English translation was published by Richard Laurence in 1821; a second in 1912 by R.H. Charles, the source of quotations here.)[4]

We read in Enoch 7:1, "It happened after the sons of men had multiplied in those days, that daughters were born to them, elegant and beautiful. And when the angels, the sons of heaven, beheld them, they became enamoured of them, saying to each other, Come, let us select for ourselves wives from the progeny of men, and let us beget children."

However, it seems that the LORD had previously assigned specific places for them in heaven, as we see in Jude 6a: *"And the angels which kept not their first estate, but left their own habitation..."* By descending to earth the angels would go against the will of God!

From heaven to highest peak.

The angels feared God would punish them for abandoning their appointed places in heaven. "Then their leader Samyaza said to them; I fear that you may perhaps be indisposed to the performance of this enterprise; And that I alone shall suffer for so grievous a crime. But they answered him and said; We all swear; And bind ourselves by mutual execrations, that we will not change our intention, but execute our projected undertaking. Then they swore all together, and all bound themselves by mutual execrations" (Enoch 6:3-7a).

The unfaithful angels had the odd idea that if they did it as a group, they could somehow escape the punishment of God.

"Their whole number was two hundred, who descended upon Ardis, which is the top of mount Armon. That mountain therefore was called Armon, because they had sworn upon it, and bound themselves by mutual execrations" (Enoch 6:7b-8).

They landed on the highest peak of the mountains whose melting snows in the north of present-day Israel, on its border with Lebanon and Syria, feed the Jordan River and the Sea of Galilee. The name of the highest peak, "Ardis," is the Greek form of Jared ("descent"). Armon is today Mount Hermon, derived from the Hebrew word *cherem* ("curse" or "oath").[5]

"These are the names of their chiefs: Samyaza, who was their leader, Urakabarameel, Akibeel, Tamiel, Ramuel, Danel, Azkeel, Saraknyal, Asael, Armers, Batraal, Anane, Zavebe, Samsaveel, Ertael, Turel, Yomyael, Arazyal. These were the prefects of the two hundred angels, and the remainder were all with them" (Enoch 6:9-10). An older Aramaic text lists the of names of other angels not mentioned in the more recent Greek text: Semihazah, Artqoph, Ramtel, Kokabel, Ramel, Danieal, Zeqiel, Baraqel, Asael, Hermoni, Matarel, Ananel, Stawel, Samsiel, Sahriel, Tummiel, Turiel, Yomiel, Yhaddiel.[6]

The first polygamists?

The angels carried out their intention of having relations with earthly women. "Then they took wives, each choosing for himself; whom they began to approach, and with whom they cohabited..." (Enoch 7:10a). The Bible text tells us: "...*and they took them wives of all which they chose*" (Gen 6:2b). It appears the angels lay down with all the women they took a liking for. They thus introduced polygamy to men.

The 7th generation man

Jared became a father in 3382 B.C. "*And Jared lived an hundred sixty and two years, and he begat Enoch*: Gen 5:18).

Enoch. The seventh man from Adam, Enoch's name came from the Hebrew root *chanak*, meaning "to initiate, dedicate, consecrate" – hence, "dedicated to God."

He fulfilled the prophecy of his name, becoming the most godly of all the antediluvian patriarchs. "*And all the days of Enoch were three hundred sixty and five years: And Enoch walked with God: and he was not; for God took him* (Gen 5:23-24). Enoch was so pious he did not die. He was "translated" -- God physically took him to heaven alive. Paul explains: *"By faith Enoch was translated that he should not see death; and was not found, because God had translated him: for before his translation he had this testimony, that he pleased God"* (Heb 11:5). God took Enoch to heaven when he was 365 years old in 3017 B.C.

Enoch was a prophet. He voiced a prophecy about the coming of the Lord. *"And Enoch also, the seventh from Adam, prophesied of these, saying, Behold, the Lord cometh with ten thousands of his saints, To execute judgment upon all, and to convince all that are ungodly among them of all their ungodly deeds which they have ungodly committed, and of all their hard speeches which ungodly sinners have spoken against him"* (Jude 14-15).

Fausset's Bible Dictionary tells of a Phrygian named Annakos, who lived more than 300 years(!) in Iconium in Asia Minor and foretold a coming Flood that would destroy the earth.[7] That prophet Annakos was in all likelihood Enoch.

God took Enoch more than 400 years before his father Jared died, so it is possible Enoch saw the angels who descended to earth during his father's lifetime. If their presence had been a great trial for him, he evidently overcame their influence.

Hidden wisdom revealed

The angels shared their secret arts with their wives, "teaching them sorcery, incantations, and the dividing of roots and trees" (Enoch 7:10b). "Amazarak taught all the sorcerers, and dividers of roots: Armers taught the solution of sorcery" (Enoch 8:3-4). These arts were magic, witchcraft, herbal medicine. They also revealed the mysteries of the heavenly bodies: "Barkayal taught the observers of the stars, Akibeel taught signs; Tamiel taught astronomy; And Asaradel taught the motion of the moon" (Enoch 8:5-8).

Ancient Persian and Arabic traditions attribute the invention of astronomy to Adam, Seth, and Enoch.[8] Flavius Josephus wrote that Adam's son, Seth, and his sons "were the inventors of that peculiar sort of wisdom which is concerned with the heavenly bodies and their order."[9] Adam died in 3074, when Jared was already 470 years old; Seth died in 2962 B.C., when Jared was aged 582 years. When Enoch was translated in 3017 B.C., Jared was 524 years old. Hence Adam, Seth, and Enoch all lived hundreds of years with Jared during whose lifetime angels descended to earth. Did they meet the angels or, at least, hear about the esoteric wisdom they imparted to men?

Violence and vanity.
The angels taught men how to make implements of war. "Moreover Azazyel taught men to make swords, knives, shields, breastplates..." (Enoch 8:1a). Lamech, a descendant of Cain, and his son Tubal-cain ("smith" or "forger") lived during that period. Tubal-cain taught others. *"And Zillah, she also bare Tubal-cain, an instructer of every artificer in brass and iron..."* (Gen 4:22a).

Many artifacts made with advanced technology in ancient times, but with no discernible periods of development leading to them, have been found around the world, The Bronze Age suddenly began 5,000 years ago. A 4,500-year-old metal factory, unearthed in 1968 at Medzamor, Armenia, near Mount Ararat, had more than 200 furnaces that produced weapons and ornaments of copper, lead, zinc, iron, gold, tin, manganese, and 14 different kinds of bronze around 2500 B.C.,[10] shortly after Jared's death in 2582 B.C.

In 1936, a hammer embedded in sandstone was found near the Llano River in Texas. Analyzed at the Battelle Labs in Columbus, Ohio, the metal was determined to be 96.6% iron, 2.6% chlorine, and 0.74% sulfur. It had no carbon used to harden iron today. Moreover, perplexed metallurgists said it is not possible to fabricate an alloy of iron with chlorine in modern-day atmospheric conditions.[11] Was that hammer made with angelic technology before Noah's Flood?

The angels also influenced men and women to become vainglorious by teaching them "the fabrication of mirrors, and the workmanship of bracelets and ornaments, the use of paint, the beautifying of the eyebrows, the use of stones of every valuable and select kind, and all sorts of dyes, so that the world became altered. Impiety increased; fornication multiplied; and they transgressed and corrupted all their ways" (Enoch 8:1b-2). The new arts and crafts gave rise to ungodly sex and all sorts of wickedness. The secrets of the angels corrupted the once wonderful world the LORD had created for mankind.

Worship of false gods.
The angels led the people into worshipping false gods. "And being numerous in appearance (able to assume many forms) made men profane, and caused them to err; so that they sacrificed to devils as to gods. For in the great day there shall be a judgment, with which they shall be judged, until they are consumed; and their wives also shall be judged, who led astray the angels of heaven that they (the people) might salute (revere) them (the angels)" (Enoch 19:2). It seems that the angels' wives influenced their husbands to use their powers in order to appear as gods to be worshipped by the people.

Ardis, Mount Hermon's highest peak, where the renegade angels landed, was highly venerated. There, Baal-worshippers erected the *Quibla*, their chief sanctuary, which they faced when worshipping in the many shrines around the mountain. Mount Hermon was so closely identified with the false god it was also called Baal-hermon (Judges 3:3).

The Israelite tribe of Dan settled at the foot of the mountain, where some of them adopted the Baal religion. Sometime in the 8th century B.C., they became one of the "Ten Lost Tribes" of Israel. Still later, the Danaans (Spartans) of Greece established a religion identical to that of the Danites. They had a "messenger of the gods" called Hermes (Hermon), called Mercury by the Romans.[12]

Mutant giant offspring

With physical bodies, the runaway angels were able to procreate with their mortal wives. *"And the women conceiving brought forth giants"* (Enoch 7:11). The Bible confirms this: *"There were giants in the earth in those days; and also after that, when the sons of God came in unto the daughters of men, and they bare children to them, the same became mighty men which were of old, men of renown"* (Gen 6:4).

The NIV has it somewhat differently: *"The Nephilim were on the earth in those days -- and also afterward -- when the sons of God went to the daughters of men and had children by them. They were the heroes of old, men of renown"* Gen 6:4, NIV). The word translated "giants" in the KJV is *nephilim* in Hebrew, from the root *naphal* ("to fall")· Thus, *nephilim* is descriptive of both the fathers (the "fallen" angels) and their sons (gigantic men who can make others fall).

Gods in Greek mythology.

The memory of the giants apparently survived in Greek culture and formed a basic part of the Grecian pantheon. The *Nephilim* became the gods called "Titans" in Greek mythology. They were gigantic children of Uranus (heaven) and Gaea (earth). The Nephilim were indeed the offspring of heavenly angels and earthly women.

Josephus confirms that "many angels of God accompanied with women, and begat sons that proved unjust, and despisers of all that was good, on account of the confidence they had in their own strength, for the tradition is that these men did what resembled the acts of those whom the Grecians call giants."[13] The gigantic sons of the fallen angels became abusive, cruel bullies and tyrants.

Man-eating monsters.

The Nephilim demanded enormous amounts of food that the people could hardly give them. "These devoured all which the labor of men produced; until it became impossible to feed them" (Enoch 7:12b). They then broke God's commandment of eating only plants and fruits. "And began to injure birds, beasts, reptiles, and fishes, to eat their flesh one after another, and to drink their blood" (Enoch 7:14). They even gorged on blood, the Creator's strictest dietary prohibition (Gen 9:4; Lev 7:26).

The giants then started eating the people themselves. "When they turned themselves against men, in order to devour them" (7:13).

God acted to stop the Nephilim. "To Gabriel also the Lord said, Go to the biters (bastards), to the reprobates, to the children of fornication; and destroy the children of fornication, the offspring of the Watchers, from among men; bring them forth, and excite them one against another. Let them perish by mutual slaughter; for length of days shall not be theirs" (Enoch 10:13). Unwittingly incited by angels carrying out God's command, the voracious monsters began killing and feasting on their fellows. Their race came to a distasteful end by their own hands.

Renegades rounded up

God ordered the arrest of the fallen angels' ringleader. "Again the Lord said to Raphael, Bind Azazyel hand and foot; cast him into darkness; and opening the desert which is in Dudael, cast him in there. Throw upon him hurled and pointed stones, covering him with darkness; There shall he remain for ever; cover his face, that he may not see the light. And in the great day of judgment let him be cast into the fire. Restore the earth, which the angels have corrupted; and announce life to it, that I may revive it. All the sons of men shall not perish in consequence of every secret, by which the Watchers have destroyed, and which they have taught, their offspring. All the earth has been corrupted by the effects of the teaching of Azazyel. To him therefore ascribe the whole crime" (Enoch 10:6-12).

The account is repeated twice in the Bible. *"And the angels who did not keep their proper domain, but left their own abode, He has reserved in everlasting chains under darkness for the judgment of the great day"* (Jude 6, NKJV); *"For if God spared not the angels that sinned, but cast them down to hell, and delivered them into chains of darkness, to be reserved unto judgment"* (Peter 2:4).

The word translated "hell" in the last verse is the Greek "*Tartarus*" -- the "deep" or "abyss" (Luke 8:31) or "bottomless pit" (Rev 9:11), where the rebel angels are imprisoned, awaiting the Last Judgment.

The story passed on to Greek mythology, with some distortions. The Titans (giants) rebelled against their father Uranus (heaven) and made their leader Cronus the ruler of the universe. Zeus, one of Cronus's sons, defeated him, and cast him and the Titans who had supported him into Tartarus, a deep pit surrounded by a river of fire beneath the earth.

Gigantic gays?

There is a hint in Scripture that the fallen angels might have also led ancient men to commit sexual perversions, *"just as Sodom and Gomorrah and the cities around them, since they in the same way as these indulged in gross immorality and went after strange flesh..."* (Jude 6-7a, NASU).

Jude likened the homosexuals of Sodom and Gomorrah to the Nephilim. Did the fallen angels practice sodomy, too?

The 8th and 9th generations

Enoch had a son before the LORD took him alive to heaven: *"And Enoch lived sixty and five years, and begat Methuselah"* (Gen 5:21).

Methuselah. Born in 3317 B.C., the eighth generation patriarch Methuselah had a strange name. Formed by the root-words *muwth* ("to die") and *shalach* ("to send"), "Methuselah" thus means "he dies, it is sent."[14] His name prefigured that his death would bring something momentous upon the world – a great blessing... or a great cataclysm.

"And all the days of Methuselah were nine hundred sixty and nine years: and he died" (Gen 5:27). Methuselah lived the longest any man ever lived, before or since. The LORD may have added many years to his life in order to delay whatever it was that was forthcoming. He eventually died in 2348 B.C. -- the year of the Flood!

Some writers think Methuselah died in the Deluge. We get a clue from Josephus in *The Antiquities of the Jews*: "Now this Seth, when he was brought up, and came to those years in which he could discern what was good, became a virtuous man; and as he was himself of an excellent character, so did he leave children behind him who imitated his virtues. All these proved to be of good dispositions. They also inhabited the same country without dissensions, and in a happy condition, without any misfortunes falling upon them till they died."

Accordingly, Seth's descendants were all as righteous he was and died natural deaths. Methuselah therefore did not drown in the Flood. Some Jews believe that Methuselah died one week before the Flood, giving Noah time to mourn his grandfather before boarding the Ark.[15]

Lamech. Methuselah became a father at a very advanced age. *"And Methuselah lived an hundred eighty and seven years, and begat Lamech"* (Gen 5:25).

Born in the ninth generation, in 3130 B.C., Lamech might have been renowned for his physical prowess. His name, from the Hebrew *lemekh*, means "strong youth."[16] Yet, Lamech lived a much shorter life than his predecessors. *"And all the days of Lamech were seven hundred seventy and seven years: and he died"* (Gen 5:31). Lamech died at the interesting and mysterious age of 777 years in 2353 B.C., five years before the Flood.

Monuments of wisdom

God might have told Adam about His coming judgments upon the world, and Adam had in turn shared these prophecies with his sons.

Destruction by fire and water.

In *The Antiquities of the Jews,* Josephus wrote about Seth and his sons: "They also were the inventors of that peculiar sort of wisdom which is concerned with the heavenly bodies, and their order. And that their inventions might not be lost before they were sufficiently known, upon Adam's prediction that the world was to be destroyed at one time by the force of fire, and at another time by the violence and quantity of water, they made two pillars; the one of brick, the other of stone: they inscribed their discoveries on them both, that in case the pillar of brick should be destroyed by the flood, the pillar of stone might remain, and exhibit those discoveries to mankind; and also inform them that there was another pillar of brick erected by them. Now this remains in the land of Siriad to this day."[17] Peter wrote about the same twin destructions by fire and water some 3,000 years later: *"For this they willingly are ignorant of, that by the word of God the heavens were of old, and the earth standing out of the water and in the water: Whereby the world that then was, being overflowed with water, perished: But the heavens and the earth, which are now, by the same word are kept in store, reserved unto fire against the day of judgment and perdition of ungodly men"* (2 Peter 3:5-7).

Pillars of brick and stone.

Seth and sons determined to preserve their store of knowledge for posterity by building two "pillars" containing their discoveries. The word "pillar" in Hebrew is *matsebah,* which means a "column" or "memorial stone." Thus, a "pillar" may not look like a stone post at all.

Some writers say Seth and his sons built the pillar of brick in Mesopotamia,[18] but this might have been destroyed in the Flood. Josephus, who wrote in Greek, said one "pillar" still stood in *Siriad* in his time, the 1st century A.D. Where was Siriad?

Siriad, it turns out, was anciently a Greek name for the land of the people who venerated *Sirius*, the Dog Star in the constellation *Canis*

Major. Next to the planets, Sirius is the brightest star in the sky. Its annual heliacal (near the sun) rising, after disappearing for several months, heralded the yearly flooding of the Nile River and ensuing good harvest. The Egyptians built many temples in such a way that Sirius shone into their inner chambers. Siriad, therefore, was Egypt.

At the center and border, too?

Curiously, a Biblical verse could be an allusion to one of the pillars: *"In that day shall there be an altar to the LORD in the midst of the land of Egypt, and a pillar at the border thereof to the LORD"* (Isa 19:19).

Although the passage gives the impression that the "altar" and the "pillar" are two different structures located in separate places in Egypt -- one at the center and the other at the border -- the two might just be one and the same object. Is that possible?

The "border" between the two ancient kingdoms of Lower and Upper Egypt was called by the old Semitic word *gizeh* and is today a suburb of the city of Cairo known as Giza, where the world-famous Great Pyramid and the Sphinx stand. Gizeh, the "border," became the center of the land in 3100 B.C., when King Menes of Upper Egypt conquered Lower Egypt, unifying the two kingdoms.

The Great Pyramid

The Great Pyramid of Cheops (Khufu) in Giza, said to have been built around 2600 B.C., is the only one remaining among the Seven Wonders of the Ancient World. Except for the loss of much of its white limestone casings removed by the Arabs to build mosques and palaces starting about 600 years ago, the Great Pyramid alone, of about 90 pyramids in Egypt, stands in its near-original condition.[19]

The largest and most precisely constructed structure in the world, the Great Pyramid exhibits highly advanced mathematical, optical, geodetic, and engineering know-how that far surpasses the techniques used in all other pyramids. The blocks fit together so precisely that a sheet of paper cannot be inserted between them. The Pyramid has cornerstones with built-in "ball-and-socket" devices used today in modern bridges as a safeguard against movements due to temperature changes, earthquakes, and ground settling.[20]

As tall as a modern 45-story building, the Great Pyramid has been made with about 2.3 million quarried blocks of stone weighing 2.5-20 tons each – more stone than all the churches and cathedrals in England,[21] Its nearly 90 million cubic feet of masonry are enough to build 30 Empire State Buildings.[22]

Not Khufu's tomb.

The Great Pyramid may not have been built as a tomb, nor by Khufu. It has air passages not needed for tombs, since air hastens the decay of dead bodies. Khufu's body, or anybody else's, has not been found there. (Herodotus said he was buried elsewhere.) And, unlike the other Egyptian pyramids with hundreds of official hieroglyphics and wall paintings, the Great Pyramid has none.

George Riffert, in his book *Great Pyramid: Proof of God*, wrote that "while it stands in Egypt, it is not of Egypt. The pyramid is intensely religious in symbolism, purpose, and themes, but carries no religious marks or signs of any kind."

In 1857, an "inventory stele" or inscribed stone slab attributed to Khufu himself was found near the front paws of the Sphinx. Featured in a recent documentary by filmmaker Ken Klein, the inscription recorded that Pharaoh Khufu visited the "Temple of Isis" (the Great Pyramid) and ordered repairs made to it and the Sphinx, as well as the construction of three smaller pyramids as tombs for himself and his family. (These are obviously the three undersized, crumbling pyramidal heaps of rubble today beside the Great Pyramid.)

The stele proves Khufu did not build the Great Pyramid. It is dated circa 2600 B.C. only because Khufu is thought to have built it. But if he ordered repairs to it, then the Pyramid was already aging in his time – and was therefore built earlier.

Center of the earth's landmass.

At the center of the Nile delta quadrant, in a precise north-south and east-west orientation, the Great Pyramid is also located at the exact center of the Earth's land mass. An imaginary line over the pyramid in a north-south direction, extending through Asia, Africa, Europe, and Antarctica produces the longest land meridian. A transverse east-west line, cutting across Africa, Asia, and America results in the longest parallel over land.[23]

The massive weight of the Great Pyramid requires an extraordinarily firm base to prevent it from sinking or tilting. The shifting sands of the desert were certainly not it. Yet, amazingly, a solid granite mountain has been detected directly beneath the Pyramid![24] The builders evidently knew this and erected the structure on top of that practically immovable foundation right at the center of the planet's landmass.

Databank of knowledge.

The Great Pyramid is a rich databank of advanced mathematical, geographical, and astronomical information concerning the earth's sphere, curvature, latitude, longitude, equator-pole relationship, mass (weight), as well as the value of *pi* (3.14159265), sun-earth distance, solar and sidereal time, and others too many to enumerate here.

For instance, the four sides of the Pyramid are not perfectly flat, but slightly concave. The curved sides exactly duplicate the curvature of the Earth! The elevated entrance on the north side leads into a descending passage that is perfectly aligned to the polestar, the true north, not the magnetic north. The Paris Observatory has the closest modern-day alignment at six minutes of a degree off true north; but the Great Pyramid is just three minutes off after more than 4,600 years -- the result of slight land shifting, not an error of the builders.

The length of the Pyramid's base, on each side, measures 9,131 inches, for a total of 36,524 inches. Adding a decimal point results in 365.24 – the exact number of days in a solar year. The height of the Pyramid is 5,449 inches. That is also the average elevation of land above sea level, as measured by satellite and computer technologies.[25]

The rich lode of many other bits of scientific information found in the Great Pyramid is discussed in detail in many books.

"Prophecy in Stone."
The builders of the Great Pyramid built into it not only scientific knowledge, but prophecies of mankind's destiny as well. For that reason, the Great Pyramid is also called the "Prophecy in Stone." John and Morton Edgar, in their book *Great Pyramid Passages*, discussed the puzzling implications of its interior design. Investigators have found that if they counted every inch as one year, the various shapes and sizes, angles and directions of the passages and chambers inside the pyramid match events in human history and Biblical prophecy.[26]

Various measurements. On either wall of the pyramid's descending passage, some distance from the elevated entrance on the north side, are scored lines, suggesting a starting point. Author Peter Lemesurier (*Nostradamus: The Final Reckoning*, 1995) assumes it marks 2623 B.C., when Khufu became pharaoh.[27] Farther down the slope, an ascending passage suddenly branches up at a point thought to be about 1453 B.C., supposedly the year the Israelites left Egypt in the Exodus (actually, 1491 B.C.). But Patrick Robinson, a pyramid researcher on the Internet, tells us that there are only 688 inches from the scored lines to the junction.[28] So, the year should be 1925 B.C. instead. Still, in prophetic terms, this year draws a blank. It is a little bit past 2000 B.C., around which several Biblical milestones and turning points took place (e.g., the Tower of Babel and the birth of Abram).

Considering the conflicting measurements, which cannot possibly be reconciled at this point, let us tentatively assume that the junction where the descending and ascending passages part ways is 2000 B.C.

Planning and construction? Now, 688 inches from the junction (2000 B.C.) back to the scored lines take us to around 2688 B.C. The *Encyclopedia Britannica* states that pyramid-building in Egypt began at the start of the Old Kingdom,[29] which the *World Book* says arose with the Third Dynasty in 2686 B.C. -- a near-perfect match with 2688 B.C. From the scored lines, there are 482 inches more to the entrance,[30] taking us all the way back to about 3170 B.C. Does this point to the year construction of the Great Pyramid began?

If we use the scale in the cross section of the Great Pyramid on the next page, we will see that every 10 meters correspond to about 500 years – a ratio we can use henceforth.

Timeframe for the world? Halfway up the ascending passage, a grand gallery opens up with an abrupt rise in ceiling level, at the same time branching to a horizontal passage leading to the Queen's Chamber. The ascending passage continues to the end of the grand gallery, where the ceiling drops back to its former level before the antechamber of the King's Chamber. The floors of the first half of the ascending passage and the horizontal passage to the interior of the Queen's Chamber, and the ceiling of the grand gallery to the floor of the King's antechamber are of approximately the same length -- about 40 meters (hence, equivalent to some 2,000 years each).

This brings to mind a prophecy by Rabbi Elias about 200 years before Christ: "The world endures six thousand years: two thousand years before the law, two thousand years under the law, and two thousand years under Messiah."[31] Thus, the creation of Adam in 4004 B.C. to the birth of Abraham in 1996 B.C. were the 2,000 years before the law. From Abraham, to whom God gave his first commandments, to the birth of Christ in 5 B.C. were the 2,000 years under the law. From Christ to about 1997 A.D. were the 2,000 years under Messiah.

Rise and fall of spirituality? The sudden rise in ceiling level that opens up to the grand gallery likely stands for a sudden rise in spirituality, with the crucifixion and ascension to heaven of Christ in 30 A.D. The drop in ceiling level at the end of the gallery may symbolize the decline in morality and spirituality in the last days (2 Tim 3:1-5). The horizontal passage to the Queen's Chamber probably represents the Church Age (the queen being the king's "bride"). The continuation of the descending passage, which is about as long as the ascending passage (4,000 years, both ending shortly after points corresponding to 2000 A.D.), is perhaps indicative of the continuing degeneration of mankind after the dispersion at the Tower of Babel in 2008 B.C.

Ordeal and destruction. The descending passage ends and levels off underground as a subterranean passage, entering a "chamber of ordeal" characterized by irregularities on the rough floor, said to signify end-time troubles, such as superquakes, tsunamis, wars, food shortages and famines, oil crises, terrorist activities, pandemics, severe weather disturbances, recessions and economic meltdowns. The floor then plunges into a "pit of destruction" a short distance from a point corresponding to about 2000 A.D.

Overhead is the King's Chamber, with its antechamber and five more chambers above it – making seven chambers in all. Do they represent the seven heavens in Jewish mystical tradition? Paul wrote having been to the third heaven (2 Cor 12:2). Incidentally, the King's Chamber has exactly the same dimensions as the "Holy of Holies" of the Temple in Jerusalem,[32] which is an exact copy of the original in heaven (Ex 25:9; Heb 8:5).

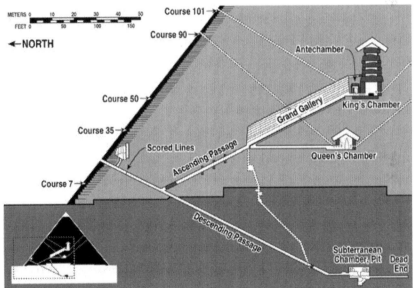

Cross-section of the Great Pyramid showing prophetic passages and chambers.

Builders' identities?

Herodotus wrote that strangers supervised the construction of the Great Pyramid. Were they Seth and his sons? If they were, then Seth, Enos, Cainan, Mahalaleel, and Enoch would have been no longer around when the Great Pyramid was finished in 2688 B.C. Only Jared and his grandson Methuselah would have stood before their superb masterwork – probably with great awe and admiration.

What role could have Jared played in the Pyramid's construction?

His name means "descent." Why does entry into the Great Pyramid begin with a descending passage? Why not a regular, level passage? Even though the slope of the passage is prophetic, it could have been placed elsewhere. Was the descending passage the builder's mark?

There is a legend that Enoch, Jared's son, built the Great Pyramid with the help of angels using techniques unknown to men. The ancient Egyptians and latter people of the area called the Great Pyramid "the Pillar of Enoch." Supposedly, holy angels before the "fall" of rebel angels built "a 500-foot high pyramid as an altar to the Creator." The Great Pyramid's height of 5449 inches (454 feet) does not include the missing capstone. With the capstone, it would have attained a full height of 500 feet, which translates to 6,000 inches[32] (prophetically equivalent to 6,000 years – the time God has allotted to man).

As we have seen, the sum of the base on all four sides is 36,524 inches, pointed as 365.24 – the number of days in a solar year. Is it any coincidence God "translated" Enoch at the age of 365 years? Is that number a clue that Enoch built the Great Pyramid?

The Flood generations

Two generations of patriarchs, the 10th and the 11th, were born shortly before the great Flood and survived through that unprecedented and unparalleled global cataclysm.

Noah. *"And Lamech lived an hundred eighty and two years, and begat a son: Now he called his name Noah, saying, "This one shall give us rest from our work and from the toil of our hands arising from the ground which the LORD has cursed"* (Gen 5:28-29, NAS).

Noah's birth in 2948 B.C. must have brought great joy to the antediluvians. His name prophesied men's emancipation from their labors. It came from either the Hebrew *nuwach* ("rest, quiet") or *nacham* ("comfort, ease"). His father obviously thought they would finally find rest from tilling the soil. Little did they suspect that it was going to be another kind of "rest."

Noah was born exactly 600 years before the Flood. *"And Noah lived after the flood three hundred and fifty years. And all the days of Noah were nine hundred and fifty years: and he died"* (Gen 9:28-29). He passed away in 1998 B.C.

Shem, Ham, and Japheth. Noah fathered three sons. *"And Noah was five hundred years old: and Noah begat Shem, Ham, and Japheth"* (Gen 5:32). Either they were triplets, or the first of the first three siblings was born in 2448 B.C.

Shem's name is the Hebrew *shem*, denoting "name" or "fame." Ham's name came from the root-word *cham*, meaning "hot or warm."

Japheth's name, derived from the word *pathah*, signifies "to expand, be spacious" or "broad, wide-spreading."

The sequence of their names seems to suggest their birth order. Shem is presumed to be the eldest, but this is not so. We find clues a few chapters later: "*Ham, the father of Canaan, saw his father's nakedness and told his two brothers outside... When Noah awoke from his wine and found out what his youngest son had done to him*" (Gen 9:22, 24; NIV). Here, we learn that Ham was actually the youngest.

In the next chapter, we read; "*Sons were also born to Shem, whose older brother was Japheth...*" (Gen 10:21a, NIV). Shem was actually younger than Japheth and, thus, second born. Therefore, the sequence should be: Japheth, Shem, and Ham. If they were not triplets, this identifies Japheth as Noah's first son born in 2448 B.C.

The next chapter reveals the birth year of Shem. "*These are the generations of Shem: Shem was an hundred years old, and begat Arphaxad two years after the flood*" (Gen 11:10). If Shem reached the age of 100 years in 2346 B.C., two years after the Flood, it follows he was born in 2446 B.C., two years after Japheth. No clue has been found concerning the year Ham, the youngest, was born.

Shem died in 1846 B.C. at the age of 600 years (Gen 11;11). As for Japheth and Ham, no dates for their deaths are known. The table below summarizes the lives of the first 11 generations, with their respective years of birth and death, as well as the age each patriarch sired a son.

Antediluvian Patriarchs*
(Adam to Shem, 4004-1846 B.C.)

Gene-ration	Name	Born (B.C.)	Age Had Son:	Age Died	Died (B.C.)
1	Adam	(4004)[a]	130	930	3074
2	Seth	3874	105	912	2962
3	Enos	3769	90	905	2864
4	Cainan	3679	70	910	2769
5	Mahalaleel	3609	65	895	2714
6	Jared	3544	162	962	2582
7	Enoch	3382	65	365	(3017)[b]
8	Methuselah	3317	187	969	2348
9	Lamech	3130	182	777	2353
10	Noah	2948	500	950	1998
11	Shem	2446	100	600	1846
	FLOOD	(2	3	4	8)

*Years in bold letters from Archbishop James Ussher, first printed in Bible margins in 1701. [a]Created. [b]Translated.

Antediluvian longevity

The pre-Flood patriarchs enjoyed prodigiously long lives. Except the translated Enoch, who did not die a natural death, the average life span of the ten antediluvian patriarchs, from Adam to Noah, was 912 years.

Long lives only legends?

Many people today find it hard to believe that the first men before the Flood lived close to a thousand years. One Bible commentator even speculated that the names and life spans of the patriarchs had been fabricated: "It is in accord with what we find in the earliest legend of most races that in these chapters a great length of life is ascribed to these (patriarchs)... It is possible that, in the case of the Hebrew record, the names of certain pre-Abrahamic patriarchs were derived from an ancient tradition, and that in the desire to fill up the chronology of the period before the call of Abraham, these names were inserted and the time which was supposed to have elapsed was divided among them..."[33]

It seems the commentator was thinking the antediluvians lived one after another. But, the fact is, until around 3100 B.C., some 900 years from the creation of Adam, the first nine generations lived alongside each other, as well as with their descendants. When Adam died in 3074 B.C., Lamech, Noah's father, was already 56 years old. The only antediluvian patriarchs who did not know Adam personally were Noah, born 126 years after Adam died, and his sons Shem, Ham, and Japheth.

Reasons for longevity.

Josephus shrugs off the doubts of skeptics and offers explanations for antediluvian longevity in his *Antiquities of the Jews*: "Now when Noah had lived three hundred and fifty years after the Flood, and that all that time happily, he died, having lived the number of nine hundred and fifty years. But let no one, upon comparing the lives of the ancients with our lives, and with the few years which we now live, think that what we have said of them is false; or make the shortness of our lives at present an argument, that neither did they attain to so long a duration of life, for those ancients were beloved of God, and made by God himself; and because their food was then fitter for the prolongation of life, might well live so great a number of years: and besides, God afforded them a longer time of life on account of their virtue, and the good use they made of it in astronomical and geometrical discoveries, which would not have afforded the time of foretelling unless they had lived six hundred years; for the great year is completed in that interval."[34]

Some of the reasons Josephus gave for the incredibly long lives of the pre-Flood patriarchs were: (1) The LORD loved them; (2) They ate better food; (3) They were godly, thus receiving the promise of long life (Ps 91:16); (4) They needed long lives to make scientific discoveries, such as the cycles of stars, which took centuries to complete.[35]

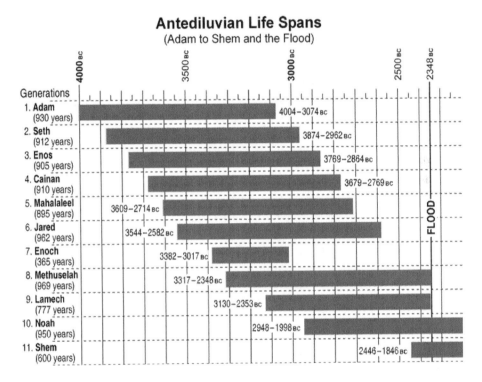

Antediluvian Life Spans
(Adam to Shem and the Flood)

A "hyperbaric chamber"?

As we have considered earlier, an ice crystal canopy might have formed above the Earth when God separated the waters above and below the firmament. Aside from screening out harmful radiations from space, a layer of ice in the sky could have prevented gases accumulating near the surface from dissipating higher and beyond the atmosphere. Result: the air pressure below the canopy would have steadily built up, and an effect similar to that of a "hyperbaric chamber" (with a higher-than-normal air pressure) would have developed on Earth.

There seems to be some evidence for this. Some fossilized pterosaurs had wingspans about 40 feet wide. If the atmospheric pressure they lived in was like ours (14.5 pounds per square inch at sea level), they would have had great difficulty taking off from the ground. A higher air pressure of about 30 p.s.i. would have made life easier for the flying reptiles.[36]

A denser atmosphere would have had a higher amount of oxygen, greatly benefiting breathing organisms. We saw earlier that the oxygen level in the earth's atmosphere could have been as high as 25%, instead of the 21% we have today. Some paleontologists have noted that the chest cavities of many huge dinosaurs were too small for the big lungs needed to supply the oxygen their massive frames required. However, if the air had a higher level of oxygen, more could have been inhaled with each breath and supplied to the circulatory system.[37] Today, injured patients placed in hyperbaric chambers heal much faster. Some professional sports teams even maintain their own for their players.[38]

The rise of oxygen in the air resulted in bigger animals. Says marine scientist Paul Falkowski: "The more oxygen, the bigger the mammals."[39] The same applies to reptiles, which do not stop growing until they die. And, as growth requires time, the reptiles must have lived much longer in order to grow into the much bigger dinosaurs.

Mammals must have lived longer, too. The oxygen-rich atmosphere could have lasted until the Flood. And, for the antediluvians, it looks like it contributed to extraordinarily long life spans.

The pre-Flood population.

How many people were there before Noah's Flood? The Genesis account simply tells us that other sons and daughters were born to the patriarchs. But, with human life spans close to a thousand years, it might have been common for antediluvian women to bear children until the age of 700 or 800 years. Many pre-Flood mothers could have had dozens, scores, even hundreds of children in each generation!

Author Dennis Petersen (*Unlocking the Mysteries of Creation*, 2002) hazards a guesstimate that the population of the earth by the time of the Flood could have possibly numbered three billion people.[40]

The divine decision

The fallen angels had corrupted the world. *"And GOD saw that the wickedness of man was great in the earth, and that every imagination of the thoughts of his heart was only evil continually... The earth also was corrupt before God, and the earth was filled with violence. And God looked upon the earth, and, behold, it was corrupt; for all flesh had corrupted his way upon the earth"* (Gen 6:5,11-12).

Some people cried out to God: *"You have seen what Azazyel has done, how he has taught every species of iniquity upon earth, and has disclosed to the world all the secret things which are done in the heavens. Samyaza also has taught sorcery, to whom you have given authority over those who are associated with him. They have gone together to the daughters of men; have lain with them; have become polluted; And have discovered crimes* (revealed sins) *to them. The women likewise have brought forth giants. Thus has the whole earth been filled with blood and with iniquity. And now behold the souls of those who are dead, cry out. And complain even to the gate of heaven. Their groaning ascends; nor can they escape from the unrighteousness which is committed on earth. You know all things, before they exist. You know these things, and what has been done by them; yet you do not speak to us. What on account of these things ought we to do to them?"* (Enoch 9:5-14).

The LORD decided to destroy the earth! *"And it repented the LORD that he had made man on the earth, and it grieved him at his heart. And the LORD said, I will destroy man whom I have created from the face of the earth; both man, and beast, and the creeping thing, and the fowls of the air; for it repenteth me that I have made them"* (Gen 6:5-7). Animals, too, were to be destroyed. Was it because many creatures God had told to eat plants also became flesh-eaters?

Soul-saver, sole survivor?

Happily for humanity, one godly man deserved to be spared. *"But Noah found grace in the eyes of the LORD... Noah was a just man and perfect in his generations, and Noah walked with God"* (Gen 6:8,9b). Only one other man also "walked with God"– his great grandfather Enoch, who did not see death. Noah must have actively tried to save many of his fellow antediluvians, because he was a preacher, a soul-saver. For his godliness, the LORD *"protected Noah, a preacher of righteousness..."* (2 Peter 2:5b, NIV).

God warned Noah through an angel. *"Then the Most High, the Great and Holy One spoke, And sent Arsayalalyur to the son of Lamech (Noah), Saying, Say to him in my name, Conceal yourself. Then explain to him the consummation which is about to take place; for all the earth shall perish; the waters of a deluge shall come over the whole earth, and all things which are in it shall be destroyed. And now teach him how he may escape, and how his seed may remain in all the earth."* (Enoch 10:1-5).

No rain before the Flood.

If it never rained before the Flood, Noah would not have known what "rain" was, much less a "flood." The book of Hebrews seems to imply this: *"By faith Noah, when warned about things not yet seen, in holy fear built an ark to save his family"* (Heb 11:7a, NIV). So, there could have been no water cycle before the Flood. No excessive heat from the sun, no evaporation, no clouds, no rains or storms, no thunder and lightning. That spells an ideal temperate weather all year round.

Faithful family favored.

Noah's family was to be saved with him, along with pairs of every kind of animal. *"But with thee will I establish my covenant; and thou shalt come into the ark, thou, and thy sons, and thy wife, and thy sons' wives with thee. And of every living thing of all flesh, two of every sort shalt thou bring into the ark, to keep them alive with thee; they shall be male and female. Of fowls after their kind, and of cattle after their kind, of every creeping thing of the earth after his kind, two of every sort shall come unto thee, to keep them alive"* (Gen 6:18-20). The men and the animals were to repopulate the earth after the Flood.

In His goodness and mercy, the LORD did not immediately execute His judgment, but gave men a lengthy "grace period," one last chance for some to repent and be saved: *"And the LORD said, My spirit shall not always strive with man, for that he also is flesh: yet his days shall be an hundred and twenty years"* (Gen 6:3). God gave men 120 long years to, as we say today, "shape up or ship out." (Or, should we say, "miss the boat"? Because, actually, all the others did.) Anyway, since the Deluge came in 2348 B.C., God must have said it in 2468 B.C.

A box or a boat?

God instructed Noah: *"Make thee an ark of gopher wood; rooms shalt thou make in the ark, and shalt pitch it within and without with pitch. And this is the fashion which thou shalt make it of: The length of the ark shall be three hundred cubits, the breadth of it fifty cubits, and the height of it thirty cubits. A window shalt thou make to the ark, and in a cubit shalt thou finish it above; and the door of the ark shalt thou set in the side thereof; with lower, second, and third stories shalt thou make it"* (Gen 6:14-16). The English word "ark" came from the Latin *arca* ("chest"), translated from the Hebrew *tebah*, meaning "box." Curiously, the ratio of the width and height of the Ark (50:30) is approximately in the shape of a golden rectangle (1.618:1).

How big was the Ark in modern terms? The cubit, the oldest unit of length believed to have originated in Egypt around 3000 B.C., is the distance from the elbow to the tip of the middle finger, or roughly 18 inches. However, since men, even within the same race, differ in size and proportions, several values developed for the cubit: a commercial or Roman cubit of 17.5 inches; an Egyptian royal cubit of 20.6 inches; a construction cubit of 22 inches; and a sacred cubit of 25.5 inches, which Solomon used for the Temple. If Noah used the sacred cubit, then the ark was truly of gargantuan dimensions: 637½ feet long (longer than two regular soccer fields), 106 ¼ feet wide (wider than two basketball courts), and 63 ¾ feet high (six stories tall).

In comparison, Roman galleys in the time of Julius Caesar were just about 150 feet long (less than ¼ the length of the Ark). Lord Nelson's 18th century flagship, the *Victory*, measured only 186 feet from bow to stern (less than 1/3 as long).

A "floating coffin."

The Ark had a width-to-length ratio of 1:6 (50 cubits to 300 cubits). Incredibly, in the modern shipbuilding industry, as a rule it is also the most stable proportion for an ocean-going vessel! With this particular configuration, ships can easily ride over even the tallest waves. This design made the Ark almost impossible to capsize.

According to *Fausset's Bible Dictionary*: "Augustine (*de Civ. Dei*, 15) notices that the ark's proportions are those of the human figure, the length from sole to crown six times the width across the chest, and ten times the depth of the recumbent figure measured from the ground."[41] The Ark had the dimensions of a sarcophagus – a stone coffin used for the mummified bodies of pharaohs, kings, and other important people. Paradoxically, the vessel that would save the lives of Noah and his family was a colossal "floating coffin"!

Tall order at short notice.

Was it possible for just four men – Noah and his three sons – to build such a big vessel in just 120 years? A tall order at short notice.

Actually, Noah and his three sons had even less than 120 years to work on the Ark together. The LORD gave Noah a 120-year advance warning in 2468 B.C., but Noah's first son Japheth was born 20 years later in 2448 B.C., 100 years before the Flood (2348 B.C.). His second son Shem was born in 2446 B.C. Hence, Noah must have labored alone on the Ark for some 40 years before his eldest son Japheth, became able-bodied at the age of 20 years (Num 1:3) to start helping him full time. That would have been just 80 years before the Flood.

Landlubbers and lumberjacks.

As instructed, Noah built the ark with "gopher wood" – cypress, a light but hard and durable wood that abounded in Mesopotamia. Phoenicians also used cypress, sometimes called "box tree" (Isa 41:10; 60:13), for their ships. Alexander the Great likewise used it for his fleet.

For its size, the Ark would have required no less than 380,000 cubic feet of wood. Tim LaHaye and John Morris in their book *The Ark on*

Ararat (1976) estimate that four men could have felled, dressed, and installed 15 cubic feet of lumber per day.[42] Thus, working 6 days a week, Noah and his three sons could have fitted around 4,680 cubic feet of timber per year and finished the Ark in a little over 81 years. But, since Noah must have obediently begun building the Ark even before his sons were born, the construction period could have been shorter. There would have been time remaining to waterproof the Ark with pitch (asphalt), which oozed from the ground in the oil-rich region (Gen 14:10). The finished Ark was a long wooden box with a flat bottom, not intended to sail, but merely to float on water, without even a rudder for steering. It probably looked more like a building than a boat.

As Noah was a preacher, he must have preached to the curious and amused kibitzers as he and his sons built the Ark – evidently to no avail.

"Clean" and "unclean" creatures

The Ark was that big, because it was meant to hold thousands of pairs of animals. In addition: *"You shall take with you seven each of every clean animal, a male and his female; two each of animals that are unclean, a male and his female; also seven each of birds of the air, male and female, to keep the species alive on the face of all the earth"* (Gen 7:2-4, NKJV).

And then… boarding time. *"The LORD then said to Noah, "Go into the ark, you and your whole family, because I have found you righteous in this generation… Seven days from now I will send rain on the earth for forty days and forty nights, and I will wipe from the face of the earth every living creature I have made… And Noah and his sons and his wife and his sons' wives entered the ark to escape the waters of the flood"* (Gen 7:1,4,7, NIV).

Noah and his family did not spend the next 7 days cooped up in darkness inside the Ark. They likely became busy receiving the animals and guiding them to their respective berths on board.

Herdsmen from heaven?

"They had with them every wild animal according to its kind, all livestock according to their kinds, every creature that moves along the ground according to its kind and every bird according to its kind, everything with wings" (Gen 7:14, NIV).

Did Noah and his family gather all the animals and guide them up a ramp into the Ark? It was a task no small group of only 8 people could have done in just 7 days. The animals themselves came! *"Pairs of clean and unclean animals, of birds and of all creatures that move along the ground, male and female, came to Noah and entered the ark, as God had commanded Noah"* (Gen 7:8-9, NIV). How did the animals know what to do? There can only be one answer: angelic guidance.

"Watchers" around throne.

The Bible gives us inklings as to who might have been involved. The first clue is in Daniel: *"I saw in the visions of my head upon my bed, and, behold, a watcher and an holy one came down from heaven"* (Dan 4:13). What is a "watcher"? It was probably "watchers" that John saw around the throne of God. *"...and around the throne, were four living creatures full of eyes in front and in back. The first living creature was like a lion, the second living creature like a calf, the third living creature had a face like a man, and the fourth living creature was like a flying eagle"* (Rev 4:6b-7, NKJV). The four creatures with many eyes must be the "watchers." Who or what could they be watching?

Each of the four creatures has a different head – that of a lion, a calf, a man, and an eagle. Interestingly, they represent four of the six kinds of creature God created on the fifth and sixth days of creation: fowl (winged creatures), beasts (wild animals), cattle (domesticated animals), and man. Are they the "watchers" who oversee the creatures that look like them? These heavenly "watchers" could have guided the respective groups of creatures under their care into the Ark.

"King of the creeps"?

What about "creeping things," such reptiles, amphibians, and insects – who could have guided them? There is no "watcher" around God's throne that resembles any of them. But, wait. Yes, there is someone elsewhere who does look like them: *"And the great dragon was cast out, that old serpent, called the Devil, and Satan, which deceiveth the whole world..."* (Rev 12:9a).

The devil or Satan is called the "great dragon" and "old serpent," which are reptiles -- creeping things! What is more, Satan is also known as Baalzebub (2 Kings 1:2-3,16) or Beelzebub (Matt 10:25, etc.), meaning "Lord of the flies." Flies are insects, which are also creeping things. It seems Satan was the overseer of creeping things! Did he use to be the fifth watcher? If he was, the book of Habakkuk gives us the impression that he no longer is: *"Why do You make men like fish of the sea, Like creeping things that have no ruler over them?"* (Hab 1:14, NKJV). For some still unclear reason, Satan might have lost his authority over those cold-blooded creatures.

Incidentally, fish and other sea creatures were not among those God said He would destroy from the face of the earth (Gen 6:7).

What about dinosaurs? In a cover story of *Time* magazine ("Did Comets Kill the Dinosaurs?", 5/6/85), the writer quipped: "Maybe there just wasn't enough room for them on the ark." But we know that those terrible lizards became extinct millions of years before the Flood, so it goes without saying that there were no dinosaurs on Noah's Ark.

Boatful of beasts, birds, bugs

How many animals in all could Noah's Ark have accommodated? Authors Morris and Whitcomb, in their book *The Genesis Flood*, give an estimate of approximately 35,000 animals. John Woodmorappe, in his *Noah's Ark – A Feasibility Study*, puts it at a low of only about 2,000 animals. (He later revised the figure to 16,000 animals, which he said could have easily been cared for on the Ark.) Let us count all the species that would have taken up floor space on the Ark.

Class		Number	
Mammals	--	3,700	species
Reptiles	--	6,500	"
Amphibians	--	2,500	"
		12,700	species

The number could be less if the animals came by genus representing several species, instead of by individual species. (Not counted are the birds, which would have had roosts on the walls and ceilings, except for the few flightless ones like the dodo, ostrich, emu, rhea, kiwi. Similarly, the insects could have just clung to the walls or rested on the animals.)

If a pair of each kind boarded the Ark, we simply multiply 12,700 species by 2, for a total of around 25,400 animals. Taking into account the few flightless birds and the additional 6 pairs of each "clean" animal and bird that the LORD told Noah to take in (like the cloven-hoofed, cud-chewing sheep and goats, various cattle and deer species, chickens, ducks, geese, doves, pigeons and turtledoves, quail, sparrows), it may be safe to say that all the animals on the Ark numbered no more than 26,000. Was Noah's Ark big enough for all of them?

Bedspacers and hangers-on.

If Noah used the sacred cubit each of the three decks would have had 67,734.38 square feet of floor space, or a total of 203,203 square feet. If we take away 10% of the floor space for, say, a 10-foot-wide central aisle on all three decks and eight 20-foot-long ramps just as wide amidships at 100-foot intervals, there would still be no less than 182,883 square feet of bedspace left for both people and animals.

Dividing the available bedspace by 26,000 we get an average of at least 7 square feet for each animal. Was that amount of space adequate? Apart from the few large animals such as elephants, giraffes, camels, horses, oxen, most other animals are small, like rodents, cats, rabbits. It is also possible that the animals on board were small juveniles that would not reach maturity until after the Flood. The average size of the animals on board could have been that of sheep and dogs, which would fit snugly into 7 square feet. The divinely planned capacity of Noah's Ark ought to have been just right for all the creatures on board.

Diluvian destruction

At the end of the 120-year reprieve He had given man, God brought about an end to the world by water. *"In the six hundredth year of Noah's life, in the second month, the seventeenth day of the month, the same day were all the fountains of the great deep broken up, and the windows of heaven were opened. And the rain was upon the earth forty days and forty nights. In the selfsame day entered Noah, and Shem, and Ham, and Japheth, the sons of Noah, and Noah's wife, and the three wives of his sons with them, into the ark"* (Gen 7:11-13). Noah's hecklers must have been thrown into chaotic panic. Can you imagine great numbers of them trying to get into the Ark? But it was too late.

God made use of two geophysical means to bring in the great Flood: the *"fountains of the great deep"* and the *"windows of heaven."*

"Fountains of the deep"

The third of the LORD's Ten Commandments contains a strange phrase that theologians often just gloss over: *"Thou shalt not make thee any graven image, or any likeness of any thing that is in heaven above, or that is in the earth beneath, or that is in the waters beneath the earth"* (Deut 5:8). There are waters beneath the earth. Nothing unusual about that, is there? People have been drawing water from underground for ages. What may be quite startling was the amount involved.

The Mid-Ocean Ridge. In the 1950's oceanographers discovered an underwater ridge system in the Atlantic Ocean that forms the longest chain of mountains on Earth, winding around the globe for some 46,000 miles (73,000 km). Resembling the seam on a baseball, the Mid-Ocean Ridge extends southward all the way from the Arctic to the Antarctic, turning east below the tip of Africa, branching in a Y-shape in the Indian Ocean northward to the Middle East and southward to Australia, then northeastward across the Pacific Ocean, eventually ending off Alaska.[43,44] The image on the nest page is from NOAA, the U.S. National Oceanographic and Atmospheric Administration.

The Mid-Ocean Ridge, encircling Earth like the seam on a baseball.

The Mid-Ocean Ridge is a long crack encircling the Earth's shell! The *Encarta Encyclopedia* says the ridge formed when pressure forced molten rock up between tectonic plates, pushing the oceanic crust upward.[45] Walt Brown, in his book *In the Beginning: Compelling Evidence for Creation and the Flood* (2008), suggests that a vast subterranean ocean once existed beneath the Earth's crust. Tremendous pressure building up in the trapped water "ruptured the crust, breaking it into plates."[46] The subterranean waters thus squeezed out could have formed fountain-like jets thousands of feet high from openings along the crustal crack encircling the globe. Were these the "fountains of the deep"?

"Windows of heaven."

The "*windows of heaven were opened*" at the onset of the Flood. Movement of the tectonic plates that created the Mid-Ocean Ridge would have also triggered massive volcanic eruptions. These would have belched immense amounts of dust into the atmosphere, causing the water vapor to collect around the dust particles and produce rain.[47]

If indeed it did not rain for 1,656 years since the creation of Adam, vast amounts of water vapor probably accumulated slowly, but steadily in the sky. Additionally, if the hypothetical ice crystal canopy was true, it could also have precipitated. So, when it finally rained, the downpour lasted many days, in such a volume that inundated the entire planet.

"*For forty days the flood kept coming on the earth, and as the waters increased they lifted the ark high above the earth. The waters rose and increased greatly on the earth, and the ark floated on the surface of the water. They rose greatly on the earth, and all the high mountains under the entire heavens were covered*" (Gen 7:17-19, NIV).

Provender for passengers

The LORD had told Noah to stock up on food for his family and the animals. "*And take thou unto thee of all food that is eaten, and thou shalt gather it to thee; and it shall be for food for thee, and for them*" (Gen 6:21). The stored food would have consisted mostly of grains, hay, dried fruits, and other provender.

Logistical and manpower problems.

Providing for all the beasts, birds, and bugs, as well as for his own family, must have been a terrible logistical headache for Noah. Some animals consume the equivalent of their own weight in a month's time – others in a week or even just a day! For example, a duck weighing 1½ kg, eats nearly ¼ kg of feed per day. Hence, it consumes more than the equivalent of its own weight in a week! A year's supply of feed for just one duck weighs more than 50 ducks. What about that for elephants?

Noah was not told they would be on the Ark for more than a year. If he knew, he might have filled the Ark to the roof with food! That would have left many animals out for lack of space. But if his store was less than that, some animals would have starved to death.

And how did eight people manage their time to feed all the 26,000 animals? Not to mention the collection of dung and droppings. Some writers have done manpower studies to arrive at the man-hours needed for the animal husbandry. One reported that 8 people working 60 hours a week each could have "easily" cared for all the animals, and still had time to keep the weekly Sabbath day of rest. That means 10 hours of work per day six days a week for each member of the family. Still, with 3,250 creatures under the care of each person, he or she could have fed and cleaned up after every 540 of them on only one day per week!

Beauty sleep and the beasts

The chore of feeding the animals could have been a nightmare. But not if they went to sleep. (It was no beauty sleep, but one for survival.) God has implanted a mechanism for survival in the physiological systems of animals. Under adverse conditions, such as lack of food, many animals – including amphibians, reptiles, mammals, birds, even insects -- can go into either hibernation (in extreme cold) or aestivation (in intense heat). These are states of suspended animation called torpor. The torpid condition in some species may simply be prolonged rest, usually with short periods of wakefulness at intervals.

A hibernating animal's blood circulation, digestion, and breathing slow down to barely perceptible levels, and body temperature drops several degrees to as low as 0° C (32° F). The animal may look dead, but is kept alive by the fat stored in its body. (Appropriately enough, the Ark was shaped like a sarcophagus – a coffin!)

The animals on Noah's Ark may have hibernated from weeks to months at a time, depending on their body sizes relative to the outside temperature. None of the animals on board had probably hibernated before in the wonderful antediluvian environment. Their descendants today, though, regularly use that ability in order to survive.

Prayer power.

What about Noah and his family – were they able to store enough food for themselves? Probably not. Yet, although they could not hibernate, they could have resorted to something similar that is even more suited to humans: meditation. The LORD told Joshua to meditate on His law (Josh 1:8). Isaac meditated. David (Ps 143:5, etc.) and other psalmists (Ps 104:34, etc.) likewise practiced meditation.

Physiologically, meditation also slows down body functions to a state resembling deep sleep. Psychologically, it helps the meditator to develop a positive attitude in the face of adversities. One form of meditation: intense prayer. Noah and the members of his family might have prayed intensely and constantly on the Ark while the great Flood lasted.

Symbol of salvation

"The waters rose and covered the mountains to a depth of more than twenty feet. Every living thing that moved on the earth perished -- birds, livestock, wild animals, all the creatures that swarm over the earth, and all mankind. Everything on dry land that had the breath of life in its nostrils died. Every living thing on the face of the earth was wiped out; men and animals and the creatures that move along the ground and the birds of the air were wiped from the earth. Only Noah was left, and those with him in the ark" (Gen 7:18-23, NIV).

As Noah evidently lived in Mesopotamia, before the Flood the highest peak within sight, some 15,000 feet above sea level, was the Zagros mountain range in southwestern Iran.

Noah and his family were saved from physical death. At the same time, their passage through floodwaters symbolizes spiritual salvation. It prefigured the future system of baptism (Greek *baptizo,* "to immerse, submerge"), which metaphorically illustrates the washing of sinners in order to be saved from spiritual death.

Peter affirms the principle: *"God waited patiently in the days of Noah while the ark was being built. In it only a few people, eight in all, were saved through water, and this water symbolizes baptism that now saves you also -- not the removal of dirt from the body but the pledge of a good conscience toward God. It saves you by the resurrection of Jesus Christ"* (1 Pet 3:20-22, NIV).

The waiting gamekeeper

"And God remembered Noah, and every living thing, and all the cattle that was with him in the ark: and God made a wind to pass over the earth, and the waters asswaged; The fountains also of the deep and the windows of heaven were stopped, and the rain from heaven was

restrained; And the waters returned from off the earth continually: and after the end of the hundred and fifty days the waters were abated. And the ark rested in the seventh month, on the seventeenth day of the month, upon the mountains of Ararat" (Gen 8:1-3).

The Ark ran aground after exactly 5 months. ("Ararat" is Hebrew for Urartu, the Assyro-Babylonian kingdom that held sway from the 9th to the 7th century B.C. between the Upper Tigris River and the Aras River Valley at the boundaries of eastern Turkey, southwestern Armenia, West Azerbaijan, and northern Iran today.)[48]

"And the waters decreased continually until the tenth month: in the tenth month, on the first day of the month, were the tops of the mountains seen" (Gen 8:5). The floodwaters subsided slowly. After only another 134 days were the surrounding peaks revealed. Patiently, Noah waited over a month more.

"And it came to pass at the end of forty days, that Noah opened the window of the ark which he had made: And he sent forth a raven, which went forth to and fro, until the waters were dried up from off the earth. Also he sent forth a dove from him, to see if the waters were abated from off the face of the ground; But the dove found no rest for the sole of her foot, and she returned unto him into the ark, for the waters were on the face of the whole earth: then he put forth his hand, and took her, and pulled her in unto him into the ark" (Gen 8:6-9). The raven Noah loosed never returned. (The black bird is a scavenger that feeds even on dead bodies.) He had also let a dove out, which came back, finding no place to alight upon.

"And he stayed yet other seven days; and again he sent forth the dove out of the ark; And the dove came in to him in the evening; and, lo, in her mouth was an olive leaf pluckt off: so Noah knew that the waters were abated from off the earth" (Gen 8:10-11). A hardy tree, the olive survives in watery conditions longer than most. Theophrastus (*Hist. Plant.* 4:8) and Pliny (*H.N.* 50) wrote of olive trees by the Red Sea.[49]

"And he stayed yet other seven days; and sent forth the dove; which returned not again unto him any more. And it came to pass in the six hundredth and first year, in the first month, the first day of the month, the waters were dried up from off the earth: and Noah removed the covering of the ark, and looked, and, behold, the face of the ground was dry" (Gen 8:12-13). The dove that did not return probably found food from new growth on the now dry ground.

Noah did not dare leave the Ark without God's permission. *"And in the second month, on the seven and twentieth day of the month, was the earth dried. And God spake unto Noah, saying, Go forth of the ark, thou, and thy wife, and thy sons, and thy sons' wives with thee. Bring forth with thee every living thing that is with thee, of all flesh, both of fowl, and of cattle, and of every creeping thing that creepeth upon the earth; that they may breed abundantly in the earth, and be fruitful, and multiply upon the earth"* (Gen 8:14-17). They had been on the Ark for one whole year and 17 days. Noah was now 601 years old.

Anchors aweigh!

In 1959, American explorers found twelve stone anchors in eastern Turkey, about 20 miles southwest of Mount Ararat and 14 miles west of the ruins of Naxuan, known locally as the ancient city of Noah. The size

of the anchors, taller than a man, indicates they had been used in an unusually big vessel. Each had a hole near the top, where a stout rope could have been tied. Eleven of the stones had eight crosses carved on them, obviously made later during the Byzantine or Crusader period and likely standing for the eight members of Noah's family.

The anchors were scattered over a wide area of the countryside, suggesting Noah had cut off a stone anchor from time to time to keep the Ark's bottom afloat above the rugged terrain as the floodwaters subsided.[50]

Anchor stone of Noah's Ark? Twelve pieces found scattered 20 miles southwest of Mt Ararat and 14 miles west of Naxuan, ruins of the so-called City of Noah.

High-altitude harbor

Most people think the Ark landed on Mount Ararat in today's modern Turkey. However, the plural *"mountains"* does not seem to pinpoint that mountain, which acquired its name in relatively recent times. (Ararat also means "holy ground" in Sanskrit, a branch of the Indo-European language family tree.)[51] The *"mountains of Ararat"* can also refer to the range at the northeastern slopes of the mountain overlooking the Aras River Valley.

Alexander Polyhistor (1st century) cited the earliest mention of the Ark by the Greek historian Berosus the Chaldean (*History of Babylonia*, circa 275 B.C.): "But of this ship that grounded in Armenia some part still remains in the mountains of the Gordyaeans in Armenia, and some still get pitch from the ship by scraping it off and use it for amulets."[52]

Berosus pointed to the Kurdistan mountains, on the southern frontier of Armenia, as the Ark's resting place.[53] Epiphanius of Salamis (A.D. 315-403) wrote: "Do you seriously suppose that we are unable to prove our point, when even to this day the remains of Noah's ark are shown in the country of the Kurds?"[54] The highest mountain in the range, called Massis by the Armenians, was known to the Persians as *Kuh-i-Nuh*, that is, "Noah's mountain."[55]

An Armenian tradition says Noah founded the city of Nakhichevan (or Naxcivan) in the Aras Valley.[56] Josephus wrote in *The Antiquities of the Jews* (1:3) that Noah was buried in Nachdjevan.[57] The Aras Valley was once the dominion of the Urartu kingdom called Van, which may have anciently meant "city."[58] Hence, Nakhichevan, Naxcivan, Nachdjevan, and Naxuan all probably mean "Noah's city."

The *Encyclopaedia Britannica* states that Armenians, who consider Ararat sacred, believe they were be the first race of men after the Flood. A Persian legend referred to Ararat as the cradle of humanity.[59]

Site sighted?

Reports of the Ark having been sighted, examined up close, and even inspected inside and out, have been the subject of many books and magazine articles. Let us examine two of them.

By an American in Iran. In 1943, a U.S. Army Corps engineer named Ed Davis, helping build a water system in northern Iran, made a three-day trip with a village man to the secret resting place of Noah's Ark. He saw the Ark and many of the tools that had been taken from the vessel over the years. He reported seeing ancient vineyards (Noah had planted grapevines), smelling sulfur from springs (Ararat is part of an extinct volcanic massif), and other details that he could not have known without actually going to the site.

Years later, investigators subjected Davis to lengthy interviews and a lie detector test, which he passed without any difficulty.[60]

By Chinese in Turkey. In 2004, the Hong Kong-based Noah's Ark Ministries International (NAMI), led by evangelical Christian billionaire Thomas Kwok, formed a Chinese team to search for the Ark on Mount Ararat. In October 2008, after several unfruitful years, a Turkish guide who knew of a wooden structure high up on the mountain took a NAMI climber, Panda Lee, and a group of Turkish mountaineers to the site. Lee reported: "At an elevation of more than 4,000 meters, I saw a structure built with plank-like timber. Each plank was about eight inches wide. I could see tenons, proof of ancient construction predating the use of metal nails. We walked about 100 meters to another site. I could see broken wood fragments embedded in a glacier, and some 20 meters long. I surveyed the landscape and found that the wooden structure was permanently covered by ice and volcanic rocks."

In October 2009, a 15-member NAMI team and Chinese film crew, reportedly reached the site at a 13,000-foot level. Through tunnels in the ice, they entered a massive wooden structure at least 150 meters long, which had small doors linking compartments. One room had stairs leading to an upper level; another, a wooden hatch in the ceiling. The NAMI team, together with Turkish climbers and authorities, announced their discovery of what they believed was Noah's Ark in a news conference on April 24, 2010. To back their claim, they displayed photographs and video footage showing various compartments of the vessel, as well as shelves, pottery, pieces of rope, and close-ups of frozen white pellets, possibly grain, littering the floor. They also brought back wood samples they said had been verified to be about 4,800 years old through carbon-14 testing.

NAMI said no images of the Ark's exterior were shown to safeguard its location until protective measures would have been taken.[61]

Flood: fact or fiction?

Was there really a Flood in Noah's time? If there was, was it truly worldwide? Many people still doubt the veracity of the Genesis account, in part or in full. Yet, Christ confirmed the historicity of the event: *"And as it was in the days of Noe, so shall it be also in the days of the Son of man. They did eat, they drank, they married wives, they were given in marriage, until the day that Noe entered into the ark, and the flood came, and destroyed them all"* (Luke 17:26-27; also Matt 24:37-39).

In history, mythology, paleontology.

Traces of the Flood are found in the traditions of ancient cultures, as well as in the disciplines of the modern world.

History. In lower Mesopotamia, accounts of the Flood have been preserved through oral tradition and inscriptions. The oldest record is on a Sumerian cuneiform tablet from ancient Nippur in north central Babylonia, dating before the second millennium B.C.[62] The Sumerian Kings List, after listing eight antediluvian kings, interrupts the sequence with a reference to the Flood before proceeding to the postdiluvian rulers: "(Then) the Flood swept over (the earth). After the flood had swept over (the earth) and when kingship was lowered (again) from heaven..."[63,64]

Mythology. Events similar to the Biblical Flood are in the Gilgamesh Epic, a Babylonian legend dating from 2000 B.C. and in the story of Deucalion, the "Noah" of Greek mythology.[65] In the Greek myth, Zeus decided to destroy the human race by a flood because of their corruption in the "brazen age" (Pindar, Ol. 9:37),[66] (The Bronze Age began in 3000 B.C., some 500 years before the Deluge.) Other cultures whose folklore contains accounts of a devastating deluge are those of southern Asia (China and Japan), North, Central and South America, and Polynesia.[67]

Paleontology. In England and Western Europe, particularly at the Rock of Gibraltar and Santenay, central France, piles of animal bones have been found in rock fissures some 1,000 feet above sea level, similar to those discovered in a cave at San Ciro. The bones were those of wolves, bears, horses, oxen. None showed signs of having been the victims of predators. They were randomly commingled as though swept in by torrents of towering waters.[68] Similarly, in the 19th century trees with fruit on them were found under frozen gravel in the New Siberian and Spitsbergen Islands within the Arctic Circle.[69]

Global or local?

Some incredulous Christians want to compromise. They say that the Flood really took place, but it was just a local or regional disaster. They contend that Genesis 7 does not really say that the Deluge inundated the whole earth. Congregational theologian John Pye Smith (d. 1851) promoted the notion that the Deluge occurred only in the plains of Mesopotamia.[70] If the Flood was merely local, consider the following:

God's word. The LORD vowed "to destroy all flesh, wherein is the breath of life, from under heaven; and every thing that is in the earth shall die" (Gen 6:17). If the Flood was local, people and animals in other areas would not have been affected, making God a liar.

God later promised "never again shall there be a flood to destroy the earth" (Gen 9:11-12, NKJV). There are still local floods wreaking havoc today. Does that mean the LORD repeatedly breaks His promise?

Advance warning. Noah did not have to build the Ark. God could have simply told him to migrate to some faraway place. Same with the animals. Both man and beast would have had 120 years to look for a refuge far removed from the coming Flood.

All animals? Mesopotamia did not have too many species of birds and beasts. Noah did not have to build such a huge vessel. And God did not have to send local animals to board the Ark in order to survive. There were others of their kinds in other places to continue reproducing. The birds could have simply flown to nearby mountains.

The floodwaters. Water seeks its own level. Several mountains in Mesopotamia (modern Iraq) are over 10,000 feet above sea level. The Flood could not have risen 15 cubits (22 feet) above their peaks and still have left the rest of the planet dry. Fossilized seashells found on mountaintops, including Mount Everest, evidence a worldwide Flood.

Scattered bits and pieces.
Bits and pieces of the story of Noah's Flood are told separately in various parts of the world. The aborigines of America, like the Aztecs, Mixtecs, Zapotecs, Plascaltecs, and Mechoacans, have the legend of Coxcox, with elements like a man with a woman in a boat, a mountain, a dove, and a vulture.[71] Other fragments are: the divine warning in Babylonian, Hindu, and Cherokee myths; the construction of a boat in Greek, Chinese, and Central American folklore; eight people saved in Chinese and Fijian stories; caring for the animals in Babylonian, Indian, and Polynesian versions; birds sent forth in Babylonian and Erech (Uruk/Iraqi) tales; the dove in Greek and Mexican narratives; the olive leaf in Phrygian account; the pitch (asphalt), seven days, mountain, raven escaping and dove returning in Erech tradition.[72]
The widely scattered components of the story point to a common source. The dispersion of people after the Flood no doubt corrupted the story as new groups of people formed ideas about their origins.

Where the water went
Where did all the waters of the Flood go? The psalmist gives us a good idea: *"Thou coveredst it with the deep as with a garment: the waters stood above the mountains. At thy rebuke they fled; at the voice of thy thunder they hasted away. They go up by the mountains; they go down by the valleys unto the place which thou hast founded for them. Thou hast set a bound that they may not pass over; that they turn not again to cover the earth"* (Ps 104:6-9).
Authors Ken Ham, Jonathan Sarfati, and Carl Wieland (*The Revised and Expanded Answers Book*) tell it to us in more scientific terms. They speculate that, in the initial stages of the Flood, the movements of tectonic plates would have pushed up the ocean basins until water covered everything. Then the ocean floor would have subsequently sunk, allowing water to cascade off the continents, pressing down the seabed and resulting in the further deepening of the oceans.[73] Around 71% of the earth's surface is covered by water. Evidently, the waters of Noah's Flood are in today's ocean basins.

Chinese characters and customs
Isaiah prophesied that among those who will be regathered to the LORD in the last days will be a people from a distant country called

Sinim. *"Behold, these shall come from far: and, lo, these from the north and from the west; and these from the land of Sinim"* (Isa 49:12).

Where or what is Sinim? The *New Exhaustive Strong's Numbers and Concordance* says Sinim is a distant Oriental region.[74] An inhabitant of Sinim must be called a Sinite, a descendant of Canaan, the fourth son of Ham and a grandson of Noah. *"And Canaan begat Sidon his firstborn, and Heth, And the Jebusite, and the Amorite, and the Girgasite, And the Hivite, and the Arkite, and the Sinite"* (Gen 10:15-17).

As defined by the Merriam-Webster Dictionary, the prefix Sino-, probably of Indo-Aryan origin and akin to the Sanskrit *Cīnā*, means "Chinese." Is Sinim China, and the Sinites, the Chinese people?

The Miautso people of China called their ancestor *Nuah* (Noah?), and his three sons *Lo Han* (Ham?), *Lo Shen* (Shem), and *Japhu* (Japheth?).[75] In a Chinese legend, a man named Fahe, said to be the founder of Chinese civilization, escaped from the Flood, and was the first man with his wife, three sons and three daughters, in the renewed world.[76] The Chinese ideograph or character for "boat" depicts a vessel with eight mouths or persons in it!

| Vessel | Eight | Mouths/People | **BOAT** |

Chinese character for "boat" is made up of a "vessel," the number "eight" and a "mouth" or "person," that is, "eight persons in a vessel"!

For some 4,000 years, even before the first Chinese emperors took power before 2000 B.C. until the overthrow of the Manchu empire by the Communists in 1911, China's emperors traveled yearly to the border of the realm, or at least to the border of the capital, to perform what was called the "Border Sacrifice." The ritual mainly consisted of the sacrificial burning of a bullock as an offering to God.[77] Accounts in the *Shu Jing* (Book of History), compiled by Confucius, recorded that Emperor Shun, when the first dynasty began, worshipped and sacrificed a bull to *ShangDi* (literally, "Heavenly Ruler"), Creator-God of the Chinese. Linguists point out that *ShangDi* is the phonetic equivalent of *Shaddai* (Hebrew "Almighty"). About 700 B.C., the Zhou pronunciation of ShangDi was "djanh-tigh" (Zhan-dai).[78] Before Moses, God was known to the patriarchs as *El Shaddai*. *"And I appeared unto Abraham, unto Isaac, and unto Jacob, by the name of God Almighty (El Shaddai)..."* (Ex 6:3a).

The Chinese pictograph for "border" is made up of a square (an enclosed garden?) divided by a cross (4 rivers flowing from the center?) beside three curved lines (the three Persons?) symbolizing Shang Ti (the Creator), with the bent figure of a worshipper bowing. It seems to picture Adam worshipping the LORD at the border of the Garden of Eden!

Garden & 4 Rivers   God   Worshipper   **BORDER**

Chinese character for "border" consists of an enclosed "garden" divided by "four rivers" plus "God" plus a bowing "worshipper."

Sole surviving structure

The only man-made structure to have survived Noah's Flood is the Great Pyramid. That it was built before the Flood is evidenced by sea salt, as much as an inch thick, found on the floors and walls inside the Great Pyramid, specially in the Queen's Chamber. It was discovered in 820 A.D., when Abdullah Al Mamoun, son of the Caliph of Baghdad, broke into the Great Pyramid. The limestone casings that used to cover the pyramid had been marked with several levels of waterline as high as halfway up the sides, or about 250 feet above the ground. At the base of the pyramid was 14-foot-deep silt with seashells and other marine fossils. The nearby Sphinx, sitting like a guard of the Great Pyramid, showed a considerable amount of vertical erosion apparently caused by a continuous heavy downpour.[79] How that happened in a desert area such as Giza is a mystery to many. Is it to you?

8

Full Circle
to Square One

nd God blessed Noah and his sons,
and said unto them, Be fruitful, and multiply,
and replenish the earth"

-- Genesis 9:1.

True to his godly character, the first act of Noah upon disembarking from the Ark was to give thanks to the LORD with animal sacrifices for delivering him and his family from the destruction brought about by the Flood. *"And Noah builded an altar unto the LORD; and took of every clean beast, and of every clean fowl, and offered burnt offerings on the altar"* (Gen 8:20).

It now becomes clear why the LORD had told Noah to take into the Ark 7 pairs of each "clean" animal and bird, but only a pair each of the "unclean" ones.

After being cooped up in the dark bowels of the Ark for more than a year, Noah and his family must have felt strange to be out in the open. Except for a few signs of renewed plant growth, the earth was desolate. Many things must have changed – the land, the air, the sky…

Earth's axis tilted?!

At the Third International Conference on Creationism in 1994, the team of S.A. Austin, J.R. Baumgardner, D.R. Humphreys, A.A. Snelling, L. Vardiman, and K.P. Wise proposed a Catastrophic Plate Tectonics theory to explain turbulences in the Earth's core.[1] One such turbulence resulted in the formation of the Mid-Ocean Ridge. At the Twin-Cities Creation Conference in 1992, earth scientist Bill Overn of St. Paul, Minnesota, speculated that a turbulence would have caused a sudden change in the tilt of the Earth's axis.[2]

Author Peter Lorie explains that "a massive weight on the planet's surface would potentially cause a 'wobble' in the movement of the natural axis, that the Earth would slip into a different axis... Evidence indicates that the polar ice-caps have moved from their present position in the past billion years... In his book *Earth's Shifting Crust*, Charles Hapgood, Professor of Science at Keene College, New Hampshire, theorizes that polar shifts have happened three times in the past one hundred thousand years..."[3] The upsurge of subterranean waters, combined with an immensely voluminous rainfall worldwide could have brought on an imbalance enough to make the Earth's axis tilt!

The Dodwell discovery.

At the 1983 National Creation Conference in Minneapolis, Barry Setterfield gave a report on the planetary axial change, as documented by a fellow-Australian astronomer.[4] George Dodwell was doing a study of winter/summer solstice shadow measurements recorded by ancient astronomers as far back as 3,000 years ago when he noticed that, although the shadow lengths were right in relation to latitude, they were incorrect vis-à-vis the alignment of the Earth's axis with the sun.

Graphing the ancient measurements by means of reverse projections from present-day planetary alignments and motions, Dodwell compared them with assumptions of modern astronomers. He saw a pattern of increasing discrepancy as he went further back in time. Dodwell also discovered that the data corresponded to the curve of recovery of a spinning top struck by an outside force. He began to suspect that the problem lay not in the accuracy of the ancient records, but in the current idea of earth-sun alignment in the past. A change must have occurred.

Dodwell likewise saw a correlation of the anomaly with three well-documented cases of dating discrepancies -- namely, those of Eudoxus, the Stonehenge, and the Temple of Amen-Ra.

Eudoxus. This Greek astronomer (ca. 400-347 B.C.) described the North Celestial Pole (point in the sky around which the stars appear to rotate, marking the position of the earth's axis). Yet, results of reverse projections from modern measurements of the earth's axis, orbit, etc., date the observations at around 1900 B.C. -- some 1,500 years before Eudoxus was born -- not in 350 B.C. when he recorded the data.

Stonehenge. Huge stone slabs arranged in circles on the Salisbury Plain in southern England, these were anciently used for astronomical observations that formed part of religious ceremonies. Associated with the Druid cult, Stonehenge had been dated at around 350 B.C.

Modern-day astronomers, however, have revised its age to 1500-1900 B.C. Per reverse projections the solstitial formations, which Stonehenge was built to observe, would have only been possible at the earlier period. Archeologists, though, insist on its younger age.

Temple of Amen-Ra. Built in Karnak, Egypt, around 2000 B.C., it was the site of a religious rite called the "manifestation of Ra" (sun-god). At the summer solstice, the longest day of the year, as the sun reached its most northerly point, the setting sun shone down a long corridor and flooded the innermost sanctuary with light, bathing the seated Pharaoh with brilliance, and making the god-king and the sun-god one.

The problem is, modern astronomical calculations show that the sun would not have reached far enough north to shine down the corridor at the time recorded in the ancient hieroglyphics. The plausible period is around 4000 B.C.

There was obviously something wrong with the process of projecting back from current astronomical alignments to determine those in the past. Dodwell constructed a mathematical curve to fit the observations, and made important discoveries. (1) It had a point of origin from about 2345 B.C. (2) It tallied with the archeological dates for Eudoxus, Stonehenge, and the Temple of Amen-Ra. (3) The curve matched the recovery path of a spinning top that is struck by an outside force and returns to a new position of spinning equilibrium.

Dodwell's findings indicate that something happened to planet Earth around 2345 B.C. The globe wobbled like a spinning top, but gradually stabilized to a new axis with a tilt. The time closely coincides with the year of Noah's Flood – 2348 B.C.[5]

Paradise past

Scripture infers and the fossil record corroborates that the Earth was once a paradise. If the Earth's axis used to be fully or nearly vertical, there would have been little or no temperature changes worldwide. For instance, fossilized palm trees have been found in the sub-Arctic region of northern Vancouver Island in Canada.[6] Climatic variations would have begun if the axis of the Earth tilted. Seasonal extremes in the world today, such as scorching summers and freezing winters, are the effects of a 23° tilt in the axis of the Earth towards the Sun.

Noah made a burnt offering to God. *"And the LORD smelled a sweet savour; and the LORD said in his heart, I will not again curse the ground any more for man's sake; for the imagination of man's heart is evil from his youth; neither will I again smite any more every thing living, as I have done. While the earth remaineth, seedtime and harvest, and cold and heat, and summer and winter, and day and night shall not cease"* (Gen 8:21-22). Did the LORD reaffirm the environmental and ecological cycles of the Earth, as well as ordain new ones?

License to kill.

"And God blessed Noah and his sons, and said unto them, Be fruitful, and multiply, and replenish the earth. And the fear of you and the dread of you shall be upon every beast of the earth, and upon every fowl of the air, upon all that moveth upon the earth, and upon all the fishes of the sea; into your hand are they delivered. Every moving thing that liveth shall be meat for you; even as the green herb have I given you all things. But flesh with the life thereof, which is the blood thereof, shall ye not eat" (Gen 9:1-4). In addition to plants, the LORD gave man all moving things for food. The only thing forbidden to man is blood, which has the life in it.

But why was man, after being a vegetarian for over 1,600 years, suddenly being allowed to become an omnivore?

Less healthful plants?

The fossil record indicates that plants grew to enormous sizes before the Flood. Mosses, which normally grow to about one inch today, were 2-3 feet high in the antediluvian world. Present-day horsetail reeds, which are typically 5-6 feet tall, attained heights of up to 50 feet.[7] Surely, the bigger prehistoric plants were more robust and healthier, and probably much more healthful, than their modern-day counterparts. The leaves of the ginkgo tree, a "living fossil" mentioned earlier that is the only survivor of a group that flourished 286-245 million years ago, have been used as medicine for centuries in China. Ginkgo extract has become a much sought dietary supplement based on research findings that, among other things, it may help improve short-term memory and concentration among those with Alzheimer's disease.[8]

If the Earth's axis was more upright before the Flood, plants would have received a uniform amount of sunlight with the same temperature throughout the year. With the tilting of the planetary axis, plants were subjected to the stresses of uneven periods of light and darkness, extreme heat or cold, drought or flooding, not to mention destructive strong winds. No wonder the plants grew smaller.

But did the downsizing directly result in a decrease of the nutritional values of plants? If so, then the proteins that plants might have provided antediluvians were no longer available in the usual amounts. It would have become necessary for men to get their complete proteins from animals in the form of meat, milk, eggs. God forestalled nutritional deficiencies that would have inevitably led to illnesses, and ultimately death, by allowing men to eat "moving things."

The first rainbow?

"And I will establish my covenant with you; neither shall all flesh be cut off any more by the waters of a flood; neither shall there any more be a flood to destroy the earth. And God said, This is the token of the covenant which I make between me and you and every living creature that is with you, for perpetual generations: I do set my bow in the cloud, and it shall be for a token of a covenant between me and the earth. And it shall come to pass, when I bring a cloud over the earth, that the bow shall be seen in the cloud" (Gen 9:11-14).

The LORD promised to never again destroy the earth by water. The sign of His vow: a rainbow in the sky. The bow, with an arrow, is an instrument of death. Yet, the rainbow, with no visible string from both ends on the ground, became a symbol of peace between God and man.

The first rainbow was the proof that it did not rain before the Flood. The colors of the rainbow are formed by the refraction and reflection of sunlight on raindrops.

The rainbow has all 7 primary colors of the visible spectrum: violet, indigo, blue, green, yellow, orange, and red. Violet has the highest frequency and shortest wavelengths (0.000035 cm), while red has the lowest frequency and longest wavelengths (0.000075 cm). The colors form a "color wheel," wherein each color is formed by the combination of two colors on either side of it. White light, such as sunlight, with wavelengths of from 35 to 75 millionths of a centimeter, has all the colors of the spectrum.

A chronicle of creation.

Unknown to many, the LORD has imprinted the story of creation in the rainbow. Each color represents an event during those six "days" – in the correct order! Let us examine the colors and their meanings:

White, which is not part of the color wheel and thus placed above it, has all the colors and symbolizes the Creator.

Pink, which can be formed from a combination of white and red or white and violet, personifies the Son of God – the Creator's surrogate, hands-on factotum in creating heaven and earth (John 1:3, etc.). It is midway between white (the Creator) and the seven primary colors (the created universe), Christ being the only mediator between God and men

(1 Tim 2:5). Pink hints of tender emotions, such as love and mercy.

Violet, having the highest frequency among all the colors, signifies "light" itself, which was created on Day 1 of the "creation week."

Indigo, a deep violet-blue, represents the "firmament" or vault of the sky extending towards the darkness of space, created on Day 2.

Blue embodies the *"waters above"* and the *"waters below"* (the oceans) separated by the firmament on Day 2.

Green stands for the plant life (bacteria, grass, herbs, and trees) that the Creator brought forth from the earth on Day 3.

Yellow indicates the sun, moon, and stars that God caused to start shining upon the earth on Day 4.

Orange, paler than red, denotes the cold-blooded aquatic animals (fish, etc.) and "fowl" (winged insects) that God created on Day 5.

Red corresponds to the warm-blooded land animals and the human beings God created in His image on Day 6.

The Story of Heaven and Earth in the Colors of the Rainbow

WHITE — Father

PINK — Son

Warm-blooded Animals, Man (5th–6th Day) — RED — VIOLET — Light (1st Day)

Cold-blooded Creatures (5th Day) — ORANGE — Clockwise: Order of Creation / Counterclockwise: Material Hierarchy — INDIGO & BLUE — Sky & Waters (2nd Day)

Heavenly Bodies (4th Day) — YELLOW — GREEN — Plants (3rd Day)

Material Hierarchy.

Counterclockwise, the color wheel portrays the material hierarchy of the universe. Warm-blooded man and animals (red) are superior to cold-blooded creatures like fish and "creeping things" (orange), which are higher in order than the lifeless elements of the sun, moon, and stars (yellow) that nonetheless give off light needed for life by plants (green), which are above the inert elements of water (blue) and the sky (indigo). At the base of all these is light (violet), whose photons are the building blocks from which all matter originated.

The village drunk?

"And Noah began to be a farmer, and he planted a vineyard" (Gen 9:20, NKJV). The Encyclopaedia Britannica says that, according to a local tradition, there was once a village on the slopes of the Ararat above the Aras River Valley, at the place where Noah built an altar and later on planted a vineyard.[9]

"Then he drank of the wine and was drunk, and became uncovered in his tent" (Gen 9:21, NKJV). Noah was a righteous man who "walked with God." Did he become a drunkard? Rather, the grape juice he might have used to drink before the Flood probably fermented in the new hot and humid weather conditions conducive to the growth of fungi, like the yeast that turns grape juice into wine.

"And Ham, the father of Canaan, saw the nakedness of his father, and told his two brothers outside. But Shem and Japheth took a garment, laid it on both their shoulders, and went backward and covered the nakedness of their father. Their faces were turned away, and they did not see their father's nakedness" (Gen 9:22-23, NKJV).

The curse on Canaan.

"And Noah awoke from his wine, and knew what his younger son had done unto him. And he said, Cursed be Canaan; a servant of servants shall he be unto his brethren. And he said, Blessed be the LORD God of Shem; and Canaan shall be his servant. God shall enlarge Japheth, and he shall dwell in the tents of Shem; and Canaan shall be his servant" (Gen 9:24-27). Was Ham's unintentional offense of seeing his father's nakedness that grievous? And, if Ham had wronged his father, why did Noah put a curse on Canaan, Ham's fourth and youngest son and not on Ham himself?

Some writers link the incident to one of God's commandments in Leviticus: "The nakedness of thy father's wife shalt thou not uncover: it is thy father's nakedness" (Lev 18:8). Based on the meaning of the passage, Noah's nakedness was figuratively also that of his wife.

Researcher Tim Osterholm explains: "According to many of the ancient scholars, the wife who accompanied Noah in the ark was Naamah, the last-named in the genealogy of Cain. It was through her that the Serpent's seed lineage continued on this side of the Flood (Serpent's Seed, 27:197-198)."[10] Naamah, it is said, was not the mother of Shem, Ham, and Japheth. She supposedly became drunk with Noah; and Ham, seeing her nakedness, lay down with her. Naamah conceived a bastard son, Canaan. Noah realized what Ham had done and cursed the bastard son-to-be. Bastards are accursed (cherem, Josh 6:17, etc.) under the Mosaic law (Deut 23:2).

Post-Flood generations

Noah lived a total of 950 years (Gen 9:28), passing away in 1998 B.C., 350 years after the Flood. He was the third longest living antediluvian patriarch, after his grandfather Methuselah (969 years) and great great grandfather Jared (962 years).

Shem, Ham, and Japheth fathered their own sons after the Flood, and their descendants began to replenish the earth. Shem died in 1846 B.C. at the much younger age of 600 years (Gen 11:11). *"These are the generations of Shem: Shem was an hundred years old, and begat Arphaxad two years after the flood"* (Gen 11:10).

Arphaxad. Born 2346 B.C., his name may have meant "one who heals."[11] It seems injuries and diseases had become common after the Flood. He died when he was 438 years old (Gen 11:13) in 1908 B.C.

Salah. Born 2311 B.C. (Gen 11:12). *Salah* came from *shelach*, which means "spear, sprout, branch." His name boded both good and bad tidings. "Spear" suggests fighting had become rampant. "Sprout" and "branch" imply some men lived peacefully as farmers. Salah lived to be 433 years old (Gen 11:15), expiring in 1878 B.C.

Eber. Born 2281 B.C. (Gen 11:15). *Eber* means "region across, opposite side." It is the root-word of "Hebrew," meaning the people who came "from the other side (of the river)." The term applied to Abraham (Gen 14:13), after he and his household crossed the Euphrates River from Haran (Gen 11:31) on their way to Canaan.[12] Eber lived a total of 464 years (Gen 11:17), expiring in 1817 B.C. Perhaps owing to a pious nature, Eber lived the longest among the patriarchs born after the Flood.

Peleg. Born 2247 B.C. (Gen 11:16). *"And unto Eber were born two sons: the name of one was Peleg; for in his days was the earth divided..."* (Gen 10:25a). Peleg's name, which came from *palag*, meaning "to split, divide," prophesied the division or dispersion of the human race at the Tower of Babel during his lifetime. Peleg passed away in 2008 B.C., having lived just 239 years (Gen 11:19). He was the first patriarch whose life span did not exceed 300 years.

Reu. Born 2217 B.C. (Gen 11:18). *Reu* is from the root-word *re'uw*, which carries the meaning "friend, companion." Reu died in 1978 B.C. at an age identical to that of his father Peleg – 239 years (Gen 11:21).

Serug. Born 2185 B.C. (Gen 11:20). *Serug* was derived from *sarag*, which means "to entwine; thus, shoot, tendril, branch." The significance of his name could have been figurative – connoting continued clinging to his homeland and branching out into many Semitic tribes. Serug died in 1955 B.C. in the 230th year of his "short" life (Gen 11:23).

Nahor. Born 2155 B.C. (Gen 11:22). *Nahor* came from the root-word *nachar*, meaning "to snort, snore." People who snore usually have respiratory problems. When one snores, less air gets in and out of the lungs, decreasing oxygen while increasing carbon dioxide in the blood. This can lead to high blood pressure and related heart ailments. Nahor's snoring must have really been a symptom of health problems, because he lived "only" 148 years (Gen 11:25), dying at an age younger than those of his son, grandson, and great grandson, in 2007 B.C.

Terah. Born 2126 B.C. (Gen 11:24). Terah's name came from the Akkadian *turahu*, which means "ibex," a wild goat with long horns (50-60") that curve backward.[13] A *shofar*, or trumpet, made from an ibex's horn is highly prized. Terah passed away in 1921 B.C., when he was 205 years old (Gen 11:32).

Birth of a rebel

Noah's youngest son, Ham, had a grandson who stood out over his contemporaries. *"And the sons of Ham; Cush, and Mizraim, and Phut, and Canaan. And the sons of Cush; Seba, and Havilah, and Sabtah, and Raamah, and Sabtecha: and the sons of Raamah; Sheba, and Dedan. And Cush begat Nimrod: he began to be a mighty one in the earth"* (Gen 10:6-8). Based on the dates (ff.) for the Tower of Babel (Stone Chumash), his reign in Nineveh and assassination (Book of Jasher), Nimrod appears to have been born in 2037 B.C.,

The Bible is brief about Nimrod, but the apocryphal Book of Jasher (cited in Joshua 10:13; 2 Samuel 1:18) gives us more details. "And Cush, the son of Ham, the son of Noah, took a wife in those days in his old age, and she bare a son, they called his name Nimrod, saying, At that time the sons of men again began to rebel and transgress against God, and the child grew up, and his father loved him exceedingly, for he was the son of his old age" (Jasher 7:23). Because of what his parents said at his birth, some writers say Nimrod means "rebel,"[14] a title likely given to him also by his followers.

Scripture says: *"He was a mighty hunter before the LORD: wherefore it is said, Even as Nimrod the mighty hunter before the LORD"* (Gen 10:9). Why is the statement made twice in a single verse? Why the special emphasis? The word "before" has been translated from the Hebrew root *neged*, meaning "in front," "opposite," or "against." The Septuagint translated the phrase in Greek as *"against the Lord."* Hence, the phrase *"before the Lord"* can also mean "against" or "in defiance of the Lord." Medieval rabbi Eleazar noted: "He was called Nimrod for the reason that he rebelled against the most high King above, against the higher angels and against the lower angels."[15] Nimrod is said to have replaced the traditional patriarchal hierarchy by appointing chieftains based on bravery and aggressiveness.[16] Josephus adds: "Now it was Nimrod who excited them to such an affront and contempt of God."[17]

A leopard-tamer.

Nimrod, though, may have come from *namer*, Hebrew for the leopard, which used to roam Canaan, according to *Fausset's Bible Dictionary*. "The prevalence of leopards anciently in Palestine is marked by the many places named from them: *Nimrah, Nimrim, Beth Nimrah*."[18] According to Alexander Hislop (*The Two Babylons*), Persian legends attribute to Nimrod the development of hunting with dogs and leopards. "Now the name Nimrod signifies 'the subduer of the leopard.' This name seems to imply, that as Nimrod had gained fame by subduing the horse, and so making use of it in the chase, so his fame as a huntsman rested mainly on this, that he found out the art of making the leopard aid him in hunting other wild beasts. Kitto has the following remarks: 'The swiftness of the leopard is proverbial in all countries where it is found... it is in India that the cheetah, or hunting leopard, is most frequently employed, and is seen in the perfection of his power'."[19]

Great size and strength.

According to legend, Nimrod had a gigantic size and extraordinary strength. Josephus says: "He was the grandson of Ham, the son of Noah, -- a bold man, and of great strength of hand."[20]

Hislop, quoting historical authorities, identifies a certain "Bel," the founder of Babylon, as none other than Cush. His son, Ninus, known in the Bible as Nimrod, was the first ruler of Babylon. He was said to have claimed some connection with the power of the giants (*Nephilim*), who had corrupted mankind before the Flood.

Rabbi Eleazar wrote: "Truly he was a man of might, because he was clad in the garments of Adam, and was able by means of them to lay snares for mankind and beguile them."[21] The secret of Nimrod's power was in Adam's garments that he wore!

Adam's garments

The Book of Jasher relates: "And the garments of skin which God made for Adam and his wife, when they went out of the garden, were given to Cush. For after the death of Adam and his wife, the garments were given to Enoch, the son of Jared, and when Enoch was taken up to God, he gave them to Methuselah, his son. And at the death of Methuselah, Noah took them and brought them to the ark, and they were with him until he went out of the ark. And in their going out, Ham stole those garment from Noah his father, and he took them and hid them from his brothers" (Jasher 7:24-26). Ham, in the hubbub of the mass disembarkation from the Ark, stole Adam's garments!

"And when Ham begat his first born Cush, he gave him the garments in secret, and they were with Cush many days. And Cush also concealed them from his sons and brothers, and when Cush had begotten Nimrod, he gave him those garments through his love for him, and Nimrod grew up, and when he was twenty years old he put on those garments" (Jasher 7:28-29).

Source of strength.

"And Nimrod became strong when he put on the garments, and God gave him might and strength, and he was a mighty hunter in the earth, yea, he was a mighty hunter in the field, and he hunted the animals and he built altars, and he offered upon them the animals before the Lord" (Jasher 7:30). Nimrod was at first pictured as a godly man who offered his kills to God.

The *International Standard Bible Encyclopaedia* tells us: "In the primitive days of Mesopotamia, as also in Palestine, wild animals were so numerous that they became a menace to life and property (Ex 23:29; Lev 26:22); therefore the king as benefactor and protector of his people hunted these wild beasts. The early conquest of the cities of Babylonia, or their federation into one great kingdom, is here ascribed to Nimrod."[22] He was acclaimed leader for his prowess as a hunter.

"And the beginning of his kingdom was Babel, and Erech, and Accad, and Calneh, in the land of Shinar" (Gen 10:10). *Fausset's Bible Dictionary* says, "Nimrod, a Hamite, intruded into Shem's portion, violently set up an empire of conquest, beginning with Babel, ever after the symbol of the world power in its hostility to God."[23]

"And Nimrod strengthened himself, and he rose up from amongst his brethren, and he fought the battles of his brethren against all their enemies round about. And the Lord delivered all the enemies of his brethren in his hands, and God prospered him from time to time in his battles, and he reigned upon the earth" (Jasher 7:31-32).

Leopard skins.

What were the garments of Adam? Ancient inscriptions depict Nimrod arrayed in leopard skins or other garments adorned with leopard-like spots.[24] Rabbi Eleazar said: "Nimrod used to entice people into idolatrous worship by means of those garments, which enabled him to conquer the world and proclaim himself its ruler, so that mankind offered him worship."[25] Adam's attire made Nimrod seem so powerful and invincible the people started to worship him as a god! Hislop wrote that "Osiris, the grand god of Egypt, under different forms, was thus arrayed in a leopard's skin or spotted dress... The rites of Osiris and Bacchus are the same..." In the Greek rite of Bacchus, leopards pulled his carriage, and Bacchus was clothed in leopard skin.[26] "Now, as the classic god bearing the lion's skin is recognized by that sign as Hercules, the slayer of the Nemean lion, so in like manner, the god clothed in the

leopard's skin would naturally be marked out as Nimrod, the 'leopard-subduer'."[27]

The ancient priests likewise wore garments of leopard skins or fabrics with imitation leopard spots. We learn that "on all occasions when the Egyptian high priest was called to officiate, it was indispensable that he should do so wearing, as his robe of office, the leopard's skin... it is a universal principle in all idolatries that the high priest wears the insignia of the god he serves, this indicates the importance which the spotted skin must have had attached to it as a symbol of the god himself."[28] The Greek priests of Bacchus also wore leopard skins.[29] Nimrod might have been worshipped as Osiris in Egypt and Bacchus in Greece.

Egyptian priest attired in ceremonial leopard skin.

Adam's, and later Nimrod's, garments of leopard skin started a tradition that has gone down through history. Leopard skin, specially the rare and valuable snow leopard skin in latter times, was a symbol of power and wealth worn only by members of royalty and aristocracy.

Unregenerate generations

"And the whole earth was of one language, and of one speech. And it came to pass, as they journeyed from the east, that they found a plain in the land of Shinar; and they dwelt there" (Gen 11:1-2). The Stone edition of the Chumash (annotated Torah) relates that "All the national families were concentrated in present day Iraq (Babel) and they all spoke one language, the Holy Tongue, the language with which the world was created." Noah and his three sons were all still living.

Josephus wrote: "God also commanded them to send colonies abroad, for the thorough peopling of the earth... but they were so ill instructed, that they did not obey God... when they flourished with a numerous youth, God admonished them again to send out colonies; but they, imagining the prosperity they enjoyed was not derived from the favor of God, but supposing that their own power was the proper cause of the plentiful condition they were in, did not obey him. Nay, they added to this their disobedience to the divine will, the suspicion that they were therefore ordered to send out separate colonies, that, being divided asunder, they might the more easily be oppressed."[30]

The new generations after the Flood refused to obey God, believing the abundance they enjoyed were the fruits of their own efforts, not blessings from the LORD. Worse, they suspected God wanted them to disperse, so He could more easily control them in small groups.

War against God.

The people at the time, called "the generation of secession" in Jewish commentaries, supposedly said: "God has no right to choose the upper world for Himself, and to leave the lower world to us; therefore we will build us a tower, with an idol on the top holding a sword, so that it may appear as if it intended to war with God." The *Mishnah*, a collection of Jewish traditions (c. 200 A.D.), describes the Tower of Babel as a rebellion against God.[31]

"And they said one to another, Go to, let us make brick, and burn them throughly. And they had brick for stone, and slime had they for morter. And they said, Go to, let us build us a city and a tower, whose top may reach unto heaven; and let us make us a name, lest we be scattered abroad upon the face of the whole earth" (Gen 11:3-4).

Josephus tells us more: *"He (Nimrod) also said he would be revenged on God, if he should have a mind to drown the world again; for that he would build a tower too high for the waters to be able to reach! And that he would avenge himself on God for destroying their forefathers!"*[32] One of Nimrod's alleged reasons for building the Tower of Babel was revenge against God!

Nimrod led the people in building the Tower of Babel. According to commentaries in the Stone edition of the *Chumash*, "The year of the... narrative is 1996 from Creation, 340 years after the Flood." The year, therefore, was 2008 B.C.

The tower builders

Tradition has it that seventy families joined Nimrod in Shinar (future site of Babylon) to build the tower. Those families represented most of the clans descended from Shem, Ham, and Japheth. *"Now these are the generations of the sons of Noah, Shem, Ham, and Japheth: and unto them were sons born after the flood. The sons of Japheth; Gomer, and Magog, and Madai, and Javan, and Tubal, and Meshech, and Tiras. And the sons of Gomer; Ashkenaz, and Riphath, and Togarmah. And the sons of Javan; Elishah, and Tarshish, Kittim, and Dodanim"* (Gen 10:1-4).

Families descended from Japheth (14)

Sons		Grandsons	
Gomer	Javan	Ashkenaz	Elishah
Magog	Tubal	Riphath	Tarshish
Madai	Meshech	Togarmah	Kittim
	Tiras		Dodanim

"And the sons of Ham; Cush, and Mizraim, and Phut, and Canaan. And the sons of Cush; Seba, and Havilah, and Sabtah, and Raamah, and Sabtecha: and the sons of Raamah; Sheba, and Dedan... And Mizraim begat Ludim, and Anamim, and Lehabim, and Naphtuhim, And Pathrusim, and Casluhim, (out of whom came Philistim,) and Caphtorim. And Canaan begat Sidon his firstborn, and Heth, And the Jebusite, and the Amorite, and the Girgasite, And the Hivite, and the Arkite, and the Sinite, And the Arvadite, and the Zemarite, and the Hamathite..." (Gen 10:6-7,13-18a). (The 30 families do not include Nimrod, the leader of the tower-building enterprise, in the count.)

Families descended from Ham (30)

Sons	Grandsons			Great grandsons
Cush	Seba	Lebabim	Amorite	Sheba
Mizraim	Havilah	Naphtuhim	Girgasite	Dedan
Phut	Sabtah	Pathrusim	Hivite	Philistim
Canaan	Raamah	Casluhim	Arkite	(Nimrod)
	Sabtecha	Caphtorim	Sinite	
	Ludim	Sidon	Arvadite	
	Anamim	Heth	Zemarite	
		Jebusite	Hamathite	

"The children of Shem; Elam, and Asshur, and Arphaxad, and Lud, and Aram. And the children of Aram; Uz, and Hul, and Gether, and Mash. And Arphaxad begat Salah; and Salah begat Eber. And unto Eber were born two sons: the name of one was Peleg; for in his days was the earth divided; and his brother's name was Joktan. And Joktan begat Almodad, and Sheleph, and Hazar-maveth, and Jerah, And Hadoram, and Uzal, and Diklah, And Obal, and Abimael, and Sheba, And Ophir, and Havilah, and Jobab: all these were the sons of Joktan. And their dwelling was from Mesha, as thou goest unto Sephar a mount of the east. These are the sons of Shem, after their families, after their tongues, in their lands, after their nations. "These are the families of the sons of Noah, after their generations, in their nations: and by these were the nations divided in the earth after the flood" (Gen 10:22-32).

Families descended from Shem (26)

Sons	Grand-sons	Great grandsons	Great^2 grandsons	Great^3 grandsons	
Elam	Uz	Eber	Peleg	Almodad	Dildah
Asshur	Hul		Joktan	Sheleph	Obal
Arphaxad	Gether			Hazar-maveth	Abimael
Lud	Mash			Jerah	Sheba
Aram	Salah			Hadoram	Ophir
				Uzal	Havilah
					Jobab

The total of 70 families listed were those who helped Nimrod build the tower. However, there were other families which did not participate in erecting the tower. They had the good sense, decency, and fear of God to dissent from Nimrod's ignominious enterprise.

Decent dissenters.

Mysteriously missing from the Biblical lists of the 70 families are the descendants of Peleg and their families – Reu, Serug, Nahor, and Terah, the father of Abraham, who were all born before Nimrod, (Please see Life Spans of the Patriarchs table near the end of this chapter).

Writer Brian Allen enlightens us: "There was a group of people that were not interested in helping Nimrod build the tower of Babel, these faithful few did not get their language confounded! Who was that? It was the righteous line from which our Saviour came."[33]

The "earth divided"

Josephus narrates: "Now the multitude were very ready to follow the determination of Nimrod, and to esteem it a piece of cowardice to submit to God: and they built a tower, neither sparing any pains nor being in any degree negligent about the work: and by reason of the multitude of hand employed in it grew very high sooner than anyone could expect."[34] It is not clear when the tower-building actually started, but the construction was well underway in 2008 B.C.

"And the LORD came down to see the city and the tower, which the children of men builded. And the LORD said, Behold, the people is one, and they have all one language; and this they begin to do: and now nothing will be restrained from them, which they have imagined to do. Go to, let us go down, and there confound their language, that they may not understand one another's speech" (Gen 11:5-7).

According to the apocryphal Greek Apocalypse of Baruch, "they had built the tower to the height of four hundred and sixty-three cubits (about

695 feet). And they took a gimlet, and sought to pierce the heavens, saying, Let us see (whether) the heaven is made of clay, or of brass, or of iron. When God saw this He did not permit them, but smote them with blindness and confusion of speech, and rendered them as thou seest" (Apocalypse of Baruch, 3:5-8).

Tower-builders' tongues twisted.

"So the LORD scattered them abroad from thence upon the face of all the earth: and they left off to build the city. Therefore is the name of it called Babel; because the LORD did there confound the language of all the earth: and from thence did the LORD scatter them abroad upon the face of all the earth" (Gen 11:8-9).

Was there really a "confusion" of the original language – so that each family began speaking in a totally different tongue? Some people think the "division" meant a sudden geophysical splitting of the continents, caused by movements of the earth's tectonic plates. But such a cataclysmic event would have produced great earthquakes, tsunamis, or another global flood. The "earth," meaning the people (as in Genesis 6:11 and 11:1), was "divided" when God caused the people to speak in different languages. Proof that it can really happen was when God did it again, for a more positive reason, a little over 2,000 years later: "All of them were filled with the Holy Spirit and began to speak in other tongues as the Spirit enabled them" (Acts 2:4, NIV). God's Spirit caused the first Christians to speak in different languages, too!

Accounts about a tower and the sudden emergence of various languages are found in the legends of peoples in Mesopotamia, eastern Europe, Asia, Polynesia, and the Americas.[35] "Babel" has come to mean "confusion" in Hebrew. But the *International Standard Bible Encyclopaedia* states that, "written in the cuneiform script of the Babylonians, *bab-ili*... means in Sem, 'the gate of god'."[36] Was the Tower of Babel also a portal for angels from heaven descending to earth? Scripture says "The Nephilim ("fallen ones") were on the earth in those days, and also afterward..." (Gen 6:4a, NASU).

New cities built.

Nimrod, says *Fausset's Bible Dictionary*, "abandoned Babel for a time after the miraculous confusion of tongues, and went and founded Nineveh."[37] Yet, Scripture relates that it was Asshur who founded Nineveh. "Out of that land went forth Asshur, and builded Nineveh, and the city Rehoboth, and Calah, And Resen between Nineveh and Calah: the same is a great city" (Gen 10:11-12). So, which is correct -- was the founder Nimrod or Asshur?

Some scholars read Genesis 10:11 as *"Out of that land (he/Nimrod) went forth (into) Asshur (Assyria) and built Nineveh..."* Alternatively, others render the verse, *"Out of that land, he went forth, being made strong (ashur) and built Nineveh..."* That city's name was *Ninua* in ancient Assyrian, coming from two of Nimrod's other names – Ninua and Ninus. Nineveh rose on the east bank of the Tigris River,

Nimrod was therefore the first king of Nineveh (later, capital of Assyria, which fell under Babylon). As *Fausset's Bible Dictionary* bears out, "The later Babylonians spoke Semitic, but the oldest inscriptions are Turanian or Cushite,"[38] the language of Nimrod, son of Cush.

Arrival of a rival

"And Terah lived seventy years, and begat Abram, Nahor, and Haran" (Gen 11:26). The verse seems to say that Abram was Terah's oldest son, but he was not nor was he born when Terah was 70 years old. He was named first, being the most prominent of the three sons. Haran appears to be the oldest because both Nahor and Abram married his daughters (Gen 11:29). One of them, Iscah, according to Josephus (Ant. 1:6, section 5), was Sarai,[39] who was only 10 years younger than Abram (Gen 17:17). Hence, her father Haran could not have been younger than Abram. Terah died in Haran at the age of 205 (Gen 11:32), after which Abram, 75, left on God's call (Gen 12:4). Evidently, Terah was 130 years old when he sired Abram. So, if Terah's birth year was 2126 B.C., then Abram was born in 1996 B.C.

Abram. Abram's name is a compound made up of *ab* ("father") and *ruwm* ("to be high, rise, raise"), together meaning "exalted father."

The Book of Jasher relates that "a bright star in the sky announced the birth of Abram during the reign of Nimrod" (Jasher 8:2). "Wise men went to Nimrod telling him about the star, and that a son had been born to Terah who would 'possess all the earth' and that his seed would slay great kings" (Jasher 8:4).[40] Nimrod then dreamt that a descendant of the prophesied sovereign killed him.[41]

A well-known folksong in Ladino (Judeo-Spanish language), "Quando el Rey Nimrod" ("When King Nimrod"), begins with the words "When King Nimrod went out to the fields/Looked at the heavens and at the stars/He saw a holy light in the Jewish quarter/A sign that Abraham, our father, was about to be born." The song is a poetic account of the cruelty of Nimrod and the miraculous birth and deeds of Abraham.[42]

Son of a sinner.

Nimrod sought to kill the future sovereign. Abram's mother escaped into the fields, where she gave birth secretly.[43] "Nimrod killed the child of one of Terah's servants, thinking it was Abram. Then Terah took Abram and concealed him in a cave, where he lived for ten years. Then Abram was taken out, and brought to the home of Noah... Abram lived in the home of Noah for 39 years, where Shem taught him the ways of the Lord" (Jasher 8:33-34).[44] (Noah had died in 1998 B.C., two years before Abraham was born.) Thanks to Shem, at a young age Abraham knew God and learned to worship Him.[45]

Abram's father Terah made idols for a living (Josh 24:2). When Abram was 50 years old, he went to live with his father. One night, "after Terah went to bed, Abram took a hatchet and destroyed all the idols except the biggest idol. He then put the hatchet in the hands of the biggest idol. Terah heard the noise, and entered the idol shop. He saw Abram in the shop, and asked Abram why he destroyed the idols. Abram told him that the big idol had destroyed all the other idols. Terah answered, 'Thou speakest lies to me. Is there in these gods spirit, soul or power to do all thou has told me? Are they not wood and stone which I myself have made?' So Abram asked his dad why he worshipped and manufactured such idols that have no power."[46] Probably incensed by his son's insolence, Terah told Nimrod that the child Nimrod killed 50 years earlier was not Abram, and that Abram was still alive.[47]

Foes face off.

Brought before Nimrod, Abram fearlessly debated with Nimrod against idolatry. "Haran [Abraham's brother] was standing there. He said: what shall I do? If Abraham wins, I shall say: 'I am of Abraham's,' if Nimrod wins I shall say 'I am of Nimrod's'."

Nimrod told Abram: "Worship the Fire! Abraham said to him: Shall I then worship the water, which puts off the fire? Nimrod told him: Worship the water! (Abraham) said to him: If so, shall I worship the cloud, which carries the water? (Nimrod) told him: Worship the cloud! (Abraham) said to him: If so, shall I worship the wind, which scatters the clouds? (Nimrod) said to him: Worship the wind! (Abraham) said to him: And shall we worship the human, who withstands the wind? Said (Nimrod) to him: You pile words upon words, I bow to none but the fire -- in it shall I throw you, and let the God to whom you bow come and save you from it!" Nimrod ordered Abram burned. Yet, from the midst of the fire, Abraham walked out unscathed. "Haran was asked: 'Whose are you?' and he answered: 'I am Abraham's!' (Then) they took him and threw him into the furnace, and his belly opened and he died and predeceased Terach, his father."[48]

The Bible notes Haran's death. *"And Haran died before his father Terah in the land of his nativity, in Ur of the Chaldees"* (Gen 11:28).

Departure from Ur.

"And Terah took Abram his son, and Lot the son of Haran his son's son, and Sarai his daughter in law, his son Abram's wife; and they went forth with them from Ur of the Chaldees, to go into the land of Canaan; and they came unto Haran, and dwelt there" (Gen 11:31).

Presumably distressed by the death of Haran, Terah left Ur with his family. Abram's departure from Mesopotamia is sometimes interpreted as an escape from Nimrod's revenge.[49] *"And the days of Terah were two hundred and five years: and Terah died in Haran"* (Gen 11:32). Terah died around 1921 B.C. (He had named the place they settled in "Haran," after his deceased oldest son.)

The Promised Land

"Now the LORD had said unto Abram, Get thee out of thy country, and from thy kindred, and from thy father's house, unto a land that I will shew thee: And I will make of thee a great nation, and I will bless thee, and make thy name great; and thou shalt be a blessing: And I will bless them that bless thee, and curse him that curseth thee: and in thee shall all families of the earth be blessed" (Gen 12:1-3).

The godly Abram obeyed. *"So Abram departed, as the LORD had spoken unto him; and Lot went with him: and Abram was seventy and five years old when he departed out of Haran. And Abram took Sarai his wife, and Lot his brother's son, and all their substance that they had gathered, and the souls that they had gotten in Haran; and they went forth to go into the land of Canaan; and into the land of Canaan they came... And the LORD appeared unto Abram, and said, Unto thy seed will I give this land: and there builded he an altar unto the LORD, who appeared unto him"* (Gen 12:4-5,7).

Science teacher?

"And there was a famine in the land: and Abram went down into Egypt to sojourn there; for the famine was grievous in the land" (Gen 12:10). Josephus wrote that Abram, who came from the technologically advanced city of Ur in Mesopotamia, taught the Egyptians mathematics and astronomy. He "communicated to them arithmetic, and delivered to them the science of astronomy; for before Abram came into Egypt they were unacquainted with those parts of learning; for that science came from the Chaldeans into Egypt."[50]

Abram grew wealthy in Egypt. *"And Abram went up out of Egypt, he, and his wife, and all that he had, and Lot with him, into the south. And Abram was very rich in cattle, in silver, and in gold"* (Gen 13:1-2).

Battle with Amraphel.

In about 1913 B.C., Abram engaged Nimrod, although perhaps not directly, in battle. Nimrod was also known as Amraphel. "Nimrod king of Babel, the same was Amraphel..." (Jasher 27:2).

"And it came to pass in the days of Amraphel king of Shinar, Arioch king of Ellasar, Chedorlaomer king of Elam, and Tidal king of nations; That these made war with Bera king of Sodom, and with Birsha king of Gomorrah, Shinab king of Admah, and Shemeber king of Zeboiim, and the king of Bela, which is Zoar... And they took all the goods of Sodom and Gomorrah, and all their victuals, and went their way. And they took Lot, Abram's brother's son, who dwelt in Sodom, and his goods, and departed" (Gen 14:1-2,11-12).

"And when Abram heard that his brother was taken captive, he armed his trained servants, born in his own house, three hundred and eighteen, and pursued them unto Dan. And he divided himself against them, he and his servants, by night, and smote them, and pursued them unto Hobah, which is on the left hand of Damascus. And he brought back all the goods, and also brought again his brother Lot, and his goods, and the women also, and the people" (Gen 14:13-16).

Amraphel, a.k.a. Nimrod, and his allies fled before Abram, the baby he had failed to kill many years earlier. Nimrod was then 124 years old, Abram 83.

The first covenant.

Around 1912 B.C., when Abram was 84 years old, he lamented that, despite God's promises, he was still childless. His servant would probably inherit God's blessings to him. But God reassured him. *"Then He brought him outside and said, 'Look now toward heaven, and count the stars if you are able to number them.' And He said to him, 'So shall your descendants be'."* (Gen 15:5, NKJV).

"And he said unto him, I am the LORD that brought thee out of Ur of the Chaldees, to give thee this land to inherit it... In the same day the LORD made a covenant with Abram, saying, Unto thy seed have I given this land, from the river of Egypt unto the great river, the river Euphrates" (Gen 15:7,18).

"Then He said to Abram: "Know certainly that your descendants will be strangers in a land that is not theirs, and will serve them, and they will afflict them four hundred years. And also the nation whom they serve I will judge; afterward they shall come out with great possessions. Now as for you, you shall go to your fathers in peace; you shall be buried at a good old age. But in the fourth generation they shall return here" (Gen 15:13-16, NKJV).

Family flourishes

"Now Sarai Abram's wife bare him no children: and she had an handmaid, an Egyptian, whose name was Hagar. And Sarai said unto Abram, Behold now, the LORD hath restrained me from bearing: I pray thee, go in unto my maid; it may be that I may obtain children by her" (Gen 16:1-2a). Sarai was then 75 years old, Abram 85.

Ishmael. *"So Hagar bore Abram a son, and Abram gave the name Ishmael to the son she had borne. Abram was eighty-six years old when Hagar bore him Ishmael"* (Gen 16:15-16, NIV). Born in 1910 B.C., Ishmael had a name derived from the roots *shama* ("to hear, listen") and *El* ("mighty one, God"), hence, "God hears." An angel had told Hagar, *"the LORD hath heard thy affliction"* (Gen 16:11). Enmity had developed between her and Sarai during her pregnancy (Gen16:4-6).

Sign of the covenant.

Around 1897 B.C., God told Abram: *"This is my covenant with you and your descendants after you, the covenant you are to keep: Every male among you shall be circumcised. You are to undergo circumcision, and it will be the sign of the covenant between me and you. For the generations to come every male among you who is eight days old must be circumcised, including those born in your household or bought with money from a foreigner--those who are not your offspring"* (Gen 17:10-12, NIV). God instituted circumcision as the token of the agreement between Him and Abram, and all of his descendants! *"On that very day Abraham took his son Ishmael and all those born in his household or bought with his money, every male in his household, and circumcised them, as God told him. Abraham was ninety-nine years old when he was circumcised, and his son Ishmael was thirteen"* (Gen 17:23-25).

But why on the 8th day for male infants? Medical science has found the answer. Surprisingly, the levels of Vitamin K and prothrombin, both blood-clotting agents, are highest on the 8th day of a person's life!

New, prophetic names.

"Neither shall thy name any more be called Abram, but thy name shall be Abraham; for a father of many nations have I made thee. And I will make thee exceeding fruitful, and I will make nations of thee, and kings shall come out of thee" (Gen 17:5-6). Abraham means "father of a multitude."

"And God said unto Abraham, As for Sarai thy wife, thou shalt not call her name Sarai, but Sarah shall her name be. And I will bless her, and give thee a son also of her: yea, I will bless her, and she shall be a mother of nations; kings of people shall be of her?" (Gen 17:15-16).

Sarai means "domineering," from the Hebrew *sar*, meaning "head person, ruler." The new name Sarah, from the same root, means "lady, princess, queen."

A laughing matter? *"Then Abraham fell upon his face, and laughed, and said in his heart, Shall a child be born unto him that is an hundred years old? and shall Sarah, that is ninety years old, bear?"* (Gen 17:17). Sarah also laughed. *"So Sarah laughed to herself as she thought,'After I am worn out and my master is old, will I now have this pleasure?' Then the LORD said to Abraham, 'Why did Sarah laugh and say, "Will I really have a child, now that I am old?" Is anything too hard for the LORD? I will return to you at the appointed time next year and Sarah will have a son.' Sarah was afraid, so she lied and said, 'I did not laugh.' But he said, 'Yes, you did laugh.'"* (Gen 18:12-15, NIV).

The promised son.

God named the promised son even before he was conceived. *"But my covenant will I establish with Isaac, which Sarah shall bear unto thee at this set time in the next year"* (Gen 17:21).

Isaac. *"And Abraham was an hundred years old, when his son Isaac was born unto him"* (Gen 21:5). The boy was born in 1896 B.C.

"And Abraham called the name of his son that was born unto him, whom Sarah bare to him, Isaac. And Abraham circumcised his son Isaac being eight days old, as God had commanded him" (Gen 21:3-4). "Isaac" means "laughter," from the Hebrew root *tsachaq* ("to laugh").

Deaths and births.

Sarah died in 1860 B.C. *"And Sarah was an hundred and seven and twenty years old: these were the years of the life of Sarah"* (Gen 23:1).

About three years later, Abraham sent his servant to Mesopotamia to find a wife for Isaac from his relatives there. The servant came back with Rebekah, the granddaughter of his brother Nahor (Gen ch. 24). *"And Isaac brought her into his mother Sarah's tent, and took Rebekah, and she became his wife; and he loved her: and Isaac was comforted after his mother's death"* (Gen 24:67). *"And Isaac was forty years old when he took Rebekah to wife, the daughter of Bethuel the Syrian of Padan-aram, the sister to Laban the Syrian"* (Gen 25:20). It was 1857 B.C.

Abraham, who seems to have acquired new vigor, married again. *"Then again Abraham took a wife, and her name was Keturah. And she bare him Zimran, and Jokshan, and Medan, and Midian, and Ishbak, and Shuah"* (Gen 25:1-2). Aged 136-plus, he sired six more sons.

In 1846 B.C. Shem, Noah's second son and Abraham's spiritual mentor in his youth, died at the age of 600 years.

Abraham's grandsons.

"Isaac prayed to the LORD on behalf of his wife, because she was barren. The LORD answered his prayer, and his wife Rebekah became pregnant" (Gen 25:21, NIV). Rebekah conceived after almost 20 years.

"The babies jostled each other within her, and she said, "Why is this happening to me?" So she went to inquire of the LORD. The LORD said to her, 'Two nations are in your womb, and two peoples from within you will be separated; one people will be stronger than the other, and the older will serve the younger' (Gen 25:22-23, NIV).

Esau, 1837 B.C. *"When the time came for her to give birth, there were twin boys in her womb. The first to come out was red, and his whole body was like a hairy garment; so they named him Esau"* (Gen 25:24-25, NIV). Esau means "hairy" or "rough (to the touch)" from the Hebrew root *asah* ("to do, make"), in the original sense of handling.

Jacob. *"After this, his brother came out, with his hand grasping Esau's heel; so he was named Jacob. Isaac was sixty years old when Rebekah gave birth to them"* (Gen 25:26, NIV). Jacob, from the Hebrew root *aqeb* ("heel"), means "heel-catcher" or, by extension, "supplanter" (one who follows the footsteps, succeeds, or takes the place of another).

Some Hebrew scholars say the name Jacob used to be "Jacobel." "In the list of places in Palestine conquered by the Pharaoh Thutmose III appears a certain J'qb'r, which in Egyptian characters represents the Semitic letters ya`aqobh-'el..." Jacob-el "belongs to that large class of names consisting of a verb with some Divine name or title (in this case 'El) as the subject." "Jacob" is the abbreviated form derived by dropping the subject, e.g., "Nathan" from Nathanael ("God hath given"). The noun 'eqebh means "consequence, recompense" (whether as reward or punishment), so the name is interpreted as "God rewardeth."[51] Other researchers give a somewhat different meaning: "Jacob, which stands evidently for Ya'qub-'el, 'May El protect,' occurs in tablets of the eighteenth century B.C. from Chagar Bazar in N Mesopotamia..."[52]

Monarch meets match

"And the boys grew: and Esau was a cunning hunter, a man of the field; and Jacob was a plain man, dwelling in tents" (Gen 25:27). Esau, like Nimrod, became a skillful and clever hunter. Jacob apparently grew up as a shepherd.

Death of Abraham.

Abraham, the twin brothers' grandfather, died in 1822 B.C. at the age of 175 years, when they were 15 years old. "And Esau at that time, after the death of Abraham, frequently went in the field to hunt. And

Nimrod king of Babel, the same was Amraphel, also frequently went with his mighty men to hunt in the field, and to walk about with his men in the cool of the day. And Nimrod was observing Esau all the days, for a jealousy was formed in the heart of Nimrod against Esau all the days" (Jasher 27:1-3). Nimrod presumably disliked the idea that there was a hunter as good as, or even better than, he was.

End of the road for Nimrod.

"And on a certain day Esau went in the field to hunt, and he found Nimrod walking in the wilderness, but they (Nimrod's men) removed at a distance from him, and they went from him in different directions to hunt, and Esau concealed himself for Nimrod, and he lurked for him in the wilderness. And Nimrod and his men that were with him did not know him (where Esau was), and Nimrod and his men frequently walked about in the field at the cool of the day, and to know where his men were hunting in the field" (Jasher 27:4-5).

"And Nimrod and two of his men that were with him came to the place where they were, when Esau started suddenly from his lurking place, and drew his sword , and hastened and ran to Nimrod and cut off his head. And Esau fought a desperate fight with the two men that were with Nimrod, and when they called out to him, Esau turned to them and smote them to death with his sword. And all the mighty men of Nimrod, who had left him to go to the wilderness, heard the cry at a distance, and they knew the voices of those two men, and they ran to know the cause of it… they found their king and the two men that were with him lying dead in the wilderness" (Jasher 27:6-8,9b).

Stolen garments restolen.

"And when Esau saw the mighty men of Nimrod coming at a distance, he fled, and thereby escaped, and Esau took the valuable garments of Nimrod, which Nimrod's father had bequeathed to Nimrod, and with which Nimrod prevailed over the whole land, and he ran and concealed them in his house" (Jasher 27:10).

"And when Nimrod the son of Cush died, his men lifted him up and brought him in consternation, and buried him in his city, and all the days that Nimrod lived were two hundred and fifteen years and he died. And the days that Nimrod reigned upon the people of the land were one hundred and eighty-five years; and Nimrod died by the sword of Esau in shame and contempt, and the seed of Abraham caused his death as he had seen in his dream" (Jasher 27:15-16).

It seems Esau had planned the ambush. He knew the places the king and his men frequented. The *Jewish Encyclopedia* states Esau slew

Nimrod because a rivalry existed between them as to who was the better hunter. Yet, Esau may have slain Nimrod for another reason. Ham had stolen Adam's garments from Noah. Esau might have thought that the garments rightfully belonged to his line, since Shem, Noah's favored son, was his direct ancestor, whose lineage extended to his grandfather Abraham, his father Isaac, and himself as the firstborn son.

Birthright for a bowl of stew.

"And Esau took those garments and ran into the city on account of Nimrod's men, and he came unto his father's house wearied and exhausted from fight, and he was ready to die through grief when he approached his brother Jacob and sat before him. And he said unto his brother Jacob, Behold I shall die this day, and wherefore then do I want the birthright? And Jacob acted wisely with Esau in this matter, and Esau sold his birthright to Jacob, for it was so brought about by the Lord" (Jasher 27:11-12).

Let us compare the Bible version: *"Now Jacob cooked a stew; and Esau came in from the field, and he was weary. And Esau said to Jacob, 'Please feed me with that same red stew, for I am weary.' Therefore his name was called Edom* ("red"). *But Jacob said, "Sell me your birthright as of this day." And Esau said, "Look, I am about to die; so what is this birthright to me?" Then Jacob said, "Swear to me as of this day." So he swore to him, and sold his birthright to Jacob. And Jacob gave Esau bread and stew of lentils; then he ate and drank, arose, and went his way. Thus Esau despised his birthright"* (Gen 25:29-34, NKJV).

Esau's words were those of a man thinking he was about to die. He probably believed Nimrod's men would track him down shortly to avenge their master. He thus no longer had any need for his birthright.

A Jewish tradition says it was Shem who slew Nimrod. However, Ussher's chronology shows that Shem died in 1846 B.C. at the age of 600 years, That was 24 years before Nimrod's death in 1822 B.C. Ussher and the Book of Jasher show the lives of Nimrod and Esau overlapped. (Summary of Key Events related to Abraham and Nimrod in Appendix.)

The beginnings of Israel

About 1760 B.C. Jacob, 77, on his mother's bidding, tricked his blurry-eyed father, 136, into thinking he was Esau, thus receiving the prophetic blessing of the firstborn. Learning about it, Esau was enraged and determined to kill Jacob as soon as their father died. Alarmed, Rebekah advised Jacob to go to her brother Laban in Haran. Isaac told Jacob to marry one of his mother's nieces there (Gen 27:1-28:5).

Jacob arrived empty-handed in Haran (some Jewish writers say

Esau's eldest son, Eliphaz, robbed Jacob of the money and jewels for his bride that Rebekah had given him).[53] He served 7 years for Rachel, Laban's younger daughter, until 1753 B.C. Laban held a wedding feast, but in the evening brought his elder daughter Leah instead to Jacob. When Jacob complained in the morning, Laban said he would also give him Rachel after the week-long feast, if Jacob would serve him another 7 years. Thus, Jacob, at the age of 84, had two brides within a period of two weeks (Gen 29:1-30). Some commentators believe that, since men at that time lived about twice longer than today, Jacob's physical condition may have been just half as old as his actual age.

First 11 sons. During the next 7 years, between 1752 and 1745 B.C., Jacob sired the first eleven of his twelve sons, whose names reflect Leah's longing for Jacob's affection and Rachel's frustration over her infertility. In the sisters' contest to produce children, they also gave their respective maids to Jacob (Gen 29:32-30:24). The sons were:

By Leah: 1. Reuben ("Behold, a son") from Hebrew root-words *ra'ah* ("to see") and *ben* ("son"). 2. Simeon ("hearing") from *shama* ("to hear"). 3. Levi ("joined") from *lavah* ("to adhere, join together, attach"). 4. Judah ("the LORD be praised") from *yadah* ("to use the hand," e.g., in worship).

By Bilhah, Rachel's maid: 5. Dan ("judge") from *din* or *dun* ("to rule, judge"). 6. Naphtali ("my wrestling.") from *pathal* ("to twine, struggle").

By Zilpah, Leah's maid: 7. Gad ("good fortune") from *gud* ("to crowd upon, attack"). 8. Asher ("happy.") from *ashar* ("to be straight, level, right, happy").

Probable Birth Years of Jacob's Sons

B.C.	Leah	Bilhah	Zilpah	Rachel
1752	Reuben			
1751	Simeon			
1750	Levi			
1749	Judah	Dan		
1748		Naphtali	Gad	
1747	Issachar		Asher	
1746	Zebulun			
1745				Joseph
1729				Benjamin

By Leah again: 9. Issachar ("hired worker") from *nasa'* ("to lift, accept," etc.) and *sakar* ("payment"). 10. Zebulun ("dwelling.") from *zabal* ("to inclose, reside").

By Rachel: 11. Joseph ("may [God] add") from *yacaph* ("to increase"). Joseph was born when Jacob was 92 years old, at the end of his 14th year of service to Laban, about 1745 B.C.

Extremely wealthy. Jacob wished to return to Canaan, but Laban offered to pay the wages he wanted if he stayed. Through cleverness

(Gen 30:31-42) and hard work (Gen 31:38-41), Jacob grew exceedingly wealthy with *"large flocks, maidservants and menservants, camels and donkeys"* (Gen 30:43). Laban's benign attitude to him changed. In 1739 B.C. God spoke to him, and Jacob left after 20 years in Haran with his household and belongings, and returned to Canaan (Gen 31:2-55).

Renamed Israel. Along the way, an angel wrestled with Jacob all night, then told him, *"'Your name shall no longer be called Jacob, but Israel; for you have struggled with God and with men, and have prevailed'"* (Gen 32:22-28, NKJV). "Israel" is a compound name made up of *sarah* ("to prevail, have power") and *El* ("mighty one, God") – thus meaning "prince or ruler with God," "having power with God," "contender with God," "soldier or fighter of God."

Reconciled with Esau. Jacob sent ahead hundreds of goats, sheep, camels, cattle, and asses as peace offerings to Esau (Gen 32:3-21). Coming with 400 men, Esau declined to accept the gifts, but on Jacob's insistence, took them. After their emotional reconciliation, Esau returned to Seir, while Jacob went on to settle at Succoth (Gen 33).

Birth of 12th son, death of Rachel. On a journey around 1729 B.C., when Jacob was 98 years old, Rachel gave birth to her second child, Jacob's 12th son. As she lay dying, she named the infant "Ben-Oni" ("son of my pain," from *'aven*, "to pant, exert oneself"). Jacob, however, renamed him "Benjamin" ("son of my right hand," from *yamin*, "right hand or side"), (Gen 35:16-19). Jacob's twelve sons would become the patriarchs of the "twelve tribes of Israel."

Death of Isaac. Around the year 1716 B.C. Jacob went to see his father Isaac at Mamre (present-day Hebron), where Abraham used to live. Isaac died, being 180 years old. Esau and Jacob together buried their father (Gen 35:27-29).

Joseph, dream master

Joseph was Jacob's favorite son, for whom he made a coat of many colors. Joseph had dreams wherein sheaves of grain, the sun, moon and stars, representing his parents and brothers, bowed down to him. His dreams incensed his envious brothers (Gen 37:2-11).

Slave and prisoner. In 1728 B.C., when Joseph was 17 years old and Jacob was 109, his brothers, who had wanted to kill him, sold him to a caravan of merchants. They dipped his coat in kid's blood, leading Jacob to think a wild animal had killed Joseph (Gen 37:12-35).

In Egypt, the captain of Pharaoh's guard bought Joseph and shortly made him overseer of his properties. Falsely accused by his master's wife, whose advances he had repudiated, Joseph was thrown into prison (Gen 39:2-20). Soon, the warden put him in charge of all the prisoners, including the king's cupbearer and baker. The two had cryptic dreams, which Joseph interpreted as the return of the cupbearer to his royal position and the hanging of the baker. Both came to pass in three days, on Pharaoh's birthday (Gen 37:21-40:23).

Pharaoh's vicegerent. Two years later, Pharaoh dreamt of 7 fat cows eaten by 7 thin cows; and 7 full heads of grain eaten by 7 thin heads of grain. None of the wise men could explain the dreams. On his cupbearer's suggestion, Pharaoh sent for Joseph, who told Pharaoh that the dreams were portents of an impending 7 years of plenty and 7 years of famine. Joseph advised the king to store a fifth of the harvest in the 7 years of plenty in reserve for the 7 years of famine (41:1-37).

Pharaoh made Joseph vicegerent, next only to him in power, and gave him an Egyptian name "Zaphnath-paaneah" (several meanings are suggested: "revealer of secrets,"[54] "savior of the world,"[55] "food of life or of the living"[56]) and a wife, Asenath, daughter of Poti-pherah priest of On. Joseph was 30 years old (Gen 41;46), around 1716 B.C.

Joseph then went throughout Egypt, gathering up a fifth of all the food produced in Egypt during the 7 years of plenty (Gen 41:38-49).

Two sons. Joseph fathered two sons. He named his firstborn "Manasseh" ("causing to forget," from *nashah*, "to forget"), because *"God has made me forget all my trouble and all my father's household."* He named his second son "Ephraim" ("doubly fruitful," from *parah*, "to bear fruit"), because *"God has made me fruitful in the land of my suffering"* (Gen 41:50-52). (The tribe of Joseph would later be divided into the two half-tribes of Ephraim and Manasseh.)

Fateful famine. The famine began around 1709 B.C. *"There was famine in all the other lands, but in the whole land of Egypt there was food... And all the countries came to Egypt to buy grain from Joseph, because the famine was severe in all the world"* (Gen 41:54b,57, NIV).

Jacob sent his ten older sons to buy grain in Egypt. They did not recognize Joseph, who cleverly made them bring Benjamin to Egypt. Joseph next framed Benjamin to keep him in Egypt, but his brothers pleaded to him for the sake of Jacob. Joseph then tearfully revealed he was their brother they had sold into slavery. He told them to bring Jacob and their families to Egypt, where he would provide for them during the five remaining years of the famine (Gen 42-45).

Settlers in Egypt. Jacob came to Egypt when he was 130 years old (Gen 47:8-9) and Joseph was 39, around 1706 B.C. *"All those who went to Egypt with Jacob -- those who were his direct descendants, not counting his sons' wives -- numbered sixty-six persons. With the two sons who had been born to Joseph in Egypt, the members of Jacob's family, which went to Egypt, were seventy in all"* (Gen 46:26-27, NIV).

Pharaoh told Joseph, *"The land of Egypt is before you. Have your father and brothers dwell in the best of the land; let them dwell in the land of Goshen..."* (Gen 47:6a, NKJV). Goshen was a fertile region northeast of the Nile delta, where Egypt's farmlands were located. Although ideal for pasture, Goshen had little value to the Egyptians, who were mainly farmers and dreaded being polluted by herdsmen who slaughtered cows, which were sacred in Egypt.

Joseph settled his father and his brothers in Rameses, a district in Goshen (Gen 47:11). *"And Israel dwelt in the land of Egypt, in the country of Goshen; and they had possessions therein, and grew, and multiplied exceedingly"* (Gen 47:27).

Jacob's death. *"And Jacob lived in the land of Egypt seventeen years: so the whole age of Jacob was an hundred forty and seven years"* (Gen 47:28). Jacob died and was brought back to Canaan for burial around 1689 B.C., when Joseph was 56. *"So Joseph went up to bury his father. All Pharaoh's officials accompanied him -- the dignitaries of his court and all the dignitaries of Egypt... Chariots and horsemen also went up with him. It was a very large company"* (Gen 50:7,9,11, NIV). It was as if Pharaoh himself had died!

Joseph's death. Joseph died 54 years later around 1635 B.C. *"So Joseph died, being an hundred and ten years old: and they embalmed him, and he was put in a coffin in Egypt"* (Gen 50:26). Moses would later take his bones from Egypt to Canaan (Gen 40;24-25; Ex 13:19).

(Note about Joseph's birth: Joseph was 30 years old when he interpreted Pharaoh's dreams at the start of the 7 years of plenty, so he was 39 when Jacob came to Egypt in 1706 B.C. in the second year of the famine. If we count back 39 years, Joseph was born in 1745 B.C.)

The "Shepherd-Kings"

From very early times, shepherds and herdsmen from Palestine and Edom had been allowed into the region of Zoan in Egypt.[57] According to the *World Book*, invaders from Palestine and nearby areas settled in ancient Egypt in the 1700's B.C.[58] The Semitic settlers from the east spread in the Nile River delta and eventually gained control of Egypt around 1670 B.C.[59]

The *Encyclopaedia Britannica* says the settlers were called *Hyksos* "by the Egyptian historian Manetho (fl. 300 BC), who, according to the Jewish historian Josephus (fl. 1st century AD), translated the word as 'king-shepherds' or 'captive shepherds.' Josephus... identified the Hyksos with the Hebrews of the Old Testament." "'Hyksos' may have been an Egyptian term for 'rulers of foreign lands' (*heqa-khase*)." Most of the Hyksos names appear to have been Semitic.[60]

From herdsmen to horsemen?

In battle, "the immigrants used horse-drawn chariots, improved bows, and other war implements unknown to the native Egyptians."[61] When Joseph became vicegerent of Egypt, it seems Pharaoh had only two chariots (Gen 41:43).

Did the Israelites have horses? As herdsmen, they kept sheep, goats, and oxen, as well as asses and camels, but no horses. However, Joseph did acquire horses in Egypt. *"And they brought their cattle unto Joseph: and Joseph gave them bread in exchange for horses..."* (Gen 47:17a). Joseph accumulated horses used to pay him with during the famine.

It looks like the Israelites bred horses while in Egypt. Moses told them, *"'you shall surely set a king over you whom the LORD your God chooses; one from among your brethren you shall set as king over you; you may not set a foreigner over you, who is not your brother. But he shall not multiply horses for himself, nor cause the people to return to Egypt to multiply horses, for the LORD has said to you, 'You shall not return that way again'"* (Deut 17:15-17, NKJV).

More Egyptians began riding in horse-drawn chariots when they became common in the 1600's B.C.[62] This was after the 7-year famine beginning in 1709 B.C. and Israel's immigration in 1706 B.C.

From sanctuary to stronghold?

The Hyksos captured Memphis, the Egyptian capital, and set up a stronghold at Avaris, on the northeastern border of the Nile delta.[63]

Avaris was originally *Ha-Awar* or *Pa-Awar* ("the house of going out").[64] Another version is *Ha-uar-t,* meaning "the city of movement" or "flight."[65] The Hyksos named the city Zoan, from a Hebrew root-word signifying "moved tents" or "place of departure."[66] In Arabic, it is Tsan, which means "migration"[67] or "departing."[68] The ancient Greeks called it Tanis.[69] (In the Greek translation of the OT, Zoan is identified with Tanis.)[70] It is the present-day village of San in Egypt.[71]

Monuments in Zoan show its plain was the "land of Rameses" given to the Israelites.[72] According to *Nelson's Illustrated Bible Dictionary,* during its long history Rameses had at least three other names: Avaris, Zoan, and Tanis.[73]

Rameses and Pithom were the two principal cities of Goshen.[74] In Psalm 78:12,43 the "field of Zoan" is synonymous to the land of Goshen.[75] Pharaoh and Joseph referred to Goshen and Rameses interchangeably (Gen 47:6,11).

Clearly, the Israelites settled in Goshen, specifically in Rameses, which was also Avaris that became the capital of the Hyksos, who gave it the Hebrew name Zoan (called San or Tsan by the Arabs and Tanis by the Greeks). Some historians claim the "shepherd-kings" came to Egypt earlier than the Israelites. If they did, they would have taken the choicest pastureland. But it looks like Goshen was idle when Jacob came.

"Many scholars place Joseph's rise to power much later, during the Hyksos Period, c. 1700 B.C... Consistent with this is the fact that the Israelites were settled about the Hyksos capital of Egypt in the 'plain of Tanis' called 'the field of Zoan' (Ps 78:12)."[76]

From refugees to rulers?

The Hyksos kings ruled Egypt for about 100 years – having gained control around 1670 B.C.[77] and dominating the land until 1570 B.C.[78] (Jacob and his family arrived in 1706 B.C.; Joseph died in 1635 B.C.)

According to the *International Standard Bible Encyclopaedia*, the "claims of Rameses II, that he built Pithom, compared with the stele of 400 years, which he says he erected in the 400th year of King Nubti, seems to put Joseph about the time of the Hyksos king."[79]

From Avaris the Hyksos ruled through vassals over most of Lower and Upper Egypt.[80] *The New Unger's Bible Dictionary* says power became centralized in Egypt during Joseph's premiership. "The Middle Kingdom began with the nobles enjoying considerable power as feudal lords. However, the pharaohs were able to reestablish the absolute power over Egypt that they had enjoyed during the Old Kingdom period (the pyramid age) at just about the time Joseph as prime minister would have been enslaving the people in return for food,"[81] *"So Joseph bought all the land of Egypt for Pharaoh, for every Egyptian sold his field, because the famine was severe upon them. Thus the land became Pharaoh's... So they said, "You have saved our lives! ...we will be Pharaoh's slaves."* (Gen 47:20,25, NASU).

More clues on the Hyksos.

Fausset's Bible Dictionary tells us: "On the tomb of Chnumhotep at Benihassan, under the 12th dynasty, the Semitic visitors are represented in colored robes, of pieces sewn together."[82] Their garments sound quite similar to Joseph's coat of many colors.

Furthermore, "Osirtasin I, the second king of the 12th dynasty, was perhaps Joseph's Pharaoh. This dynasty was especially connected with On... Chnumhotep, Osirtasin's relative and favorite, is described upon the tombs of Benihassan... 'When years of famine occurred he plowed all the lands producing abundant food.'"[83] Joseph was not a relative of Pharaoh, but he had said, *"God... hath made me a father to Pharaoh"* (Gen 45:8b). Was Pharaoh a weak figurehead, with Joseph as the real power behind the throne? Was Joseph, Chnumhotep?

Also, the *International Standard Bible Encyclopaedia* says that "a Pharaoh of the Hyksos period bears a name that looks like ya`aqobh-'el" ("Jacobel").[84] Was it the patriarch of Israel, Jacob?

Isaiah seems to say that the rulers of Zoan were the sons of "ancient kings" – *"Surely the princes of Zoan are fools; Pharaoh's wise counselors give foolish counsel. How do you say to Pharaoh, "I am the son of the wise, The son of ancient kings?"* (Isa 19:11, NKJV). Joseph was once Pharaoh's counselor. Did other Israelites later succeed him?

Experienced fighters? We are under the impression that Jacob was a simple and timid man. But, in his deathbed blessings on his sons, Jacob told Joseph, *"Moreover I have given to thee one portion above thy brethren, which I took out of the hand of the Amorite with my sword and with my bow"* (Gen 48:21-22). His statement reveals Jacob was an expert with the sword, as well as with the bow and arrow, seizing land from his enemies in Canaan, before coming to Egypt!

And when Israel left Egypt in the Exodus, *"The Israelites went up out of Egypt armed for battle"* (Ex 13:18b, NIV). Fourteen months later, the LORD told Moses: *""Take a census of all the congregation of the children of Israel, by their families, by their fathers' houses, according to the number of names, every male individually, from twenty years old and above -- all who are able to go to war in Israel. You and Aaron shall number them by their armies"* (Num 1:2-3, NKJV). The passages show they were ready for war, and were presumably trained for such.

In Scripture, very little is written about the period between the death of Jacob and the birth of Moses. *The New Unger's Bible Dictionary* says "the period 1780-1546 B.C. is one of great obscurity in Egypt, and the Hyksos conquest is as yet imperfectly understood. Although the history of Joseph cannot yet be placed in the frame of known Egyptian history, Israel was in Egypt during this period of confusion and turmoil..."[85] If the Israelites were in Egypt at the time of the Hyksos, were they the shepherd-kings? Or were they allies, if not merely bystanders?

A nation of slaves

"And the children of Israel were fruitful, and increased abundantly, and multiplied, and waxed exceeding mighty; and the land was filled with them" (Ex 1:7). *"Then a new king, who did not know about Joseph, came to power in Egypt. 'Look,' he said to his people, 'the Israelites have become much too numerous for us. Come, we must deal shrewdly with them or they will become even more numerous and, if war breaks out, will join our enemies, fight against us and leave the country.'"* (Ex 1:8-10, NIV). The Egyptians forced the Israelites into slave labor for them. However, it did not stop the Israelites from multiplying (Gen 1:11-12).

Levi's descendants.

Levi, Jacob's third son, had three sons, the second of whom was Kohath, who had four sons – the eldest being Amram (Ex 6:18a). *"And Amram took him Jochebed his father's sister to wife; and she bare him Aaron and Moses..."* (Ex 6:20a). They also had a daughter, Miriam (Num 26:59; 1 Chron 6:3). Moses, Amram's second son, was therefore the great grandson of Levi, being in the fourth generation from him. According to Josephus, magicians foretold his birth as that of a destroyer to Pharaoh; Amram saw in a dream the coming of a deliverer.[86] Moses is said to have been born at Heliopolis ("city of the sun") near the Nile.[87]

Before Moses was born in about 1571 B.C., Pharaoh had ordered all newborn Hebrew male infants killed. His mother hid him for 3 months, then put him in a papyrus basket in the reeds along the bank of the Nile, within sight of his sister. Pharaoh's daughter found the baby and raised him, unwittingly with the help of his own mother (Ex 2:1-9).

Moses. *"And the child grew, and she brought him unto Pharaoh's daughter, and he became her son. And she called his name Moses: and she said, Because I drew him out of the water"* (Ex 2:10). In Hebrew, *mosheh* is "drawn out." The Egyptian forms *mose, meses,* and *mes* mean the same and, by extension, "born of"[88] -- thus, "child, son."[89] These often occur in Egyptian royal names, such as Thutmose or Thothmes ("son or born of Thoth"), Rameses or Ramses ("son or born of Ra"), Ahmose or Ahmes, etc. Moses was not born of Pharaoh's daughter, so only the primary meaning "drawn out" applied to him.

In 1531 B.C., when Moses was 40 years old, he killed an Egyptian beating an Israelite. When it reached Pharaoh, Moses had to flee into the wilderness (Ex 2:11-15; Acts 7:23-29). Jethro, the priest of Midian, gave him shelter and one of his daughters, Zipporah, as wife. He fathered two sons, Gershom ("outcast," from *garash,* "to cast out") and Eliezer ("help of God," from *azar,* "to help"), (Ex 2:16-22; 18:3-4; Acts 7:23-29).

Moses was a shepherd for 40 years (Acts 7:30; Ex 3:1-2). God then spoke to him from a burning bush, commanding him to lead his people from bondage in Egypt to Canaan, the land God had promised to Abraham. God also revealed to him a new Name that was unknown to Abraham, Isaac, and Jacob; and gave him power to perform miracles. Moses protested that he was "slow of speech," but the LORD appointed his older brother Aaron to be his spokesman. God said that all those who wanted to kill Moses in Egypt were dead (Ex 3:1-4:19).

Ten plagues of Egypt.

"Moses was eighty years old and Aaron eighty-three when they spoke to Pharaoh" (Ex 7:7, NIV). "Let my people go," Moses told

Pharaoh, who refused. And, to show his contempt for the God of Moses, he made the labor of the Israelites even harder (Ex 5:1-19).

The LORD inflicted ten plagues on Egypt, with Pharaoh hardening his heart each time: (1) the Nile turned into blood; (2) frogs covered the land; (3) dust turned into lice on the Egyptians and their animals; (4) flies filled the Egyptians' houses; (5) a pestilence killed all livestock, except those of Israel; (6) boils broke out on all Egyptians and their animals; (7) hail rained on trees and plants, except in Goshen; (8) locusts ate all remaining plants and fruits; (9) three days of darkness (Ex 7:14-12:28). The 10th plague killed all the firstborn in Egypt, from that of Pharaoh to those of prisoners and all livestock (Ex 12:29-30). The LORD passed over the homes of the Israelites, who marked their doorframes with the blood of the Passover lamb – foreshadowing the saving blood of Christ, the Lamb of God, "our Passover" (1 Cor 5:7). It is also a prophecy of the end-time Armageddon, when "houses" (physical bodies, 2 Cor 5:1) with the blood of Christ will be spared from the passing destruction.

In the middle of the night, Pharaoh told Moses to leave Egypt with all the Israelites and their flocks and herds at once. The Israelites asked the Egyptians for jewelry and clothing, a custom among freed slaves (Deut 15:13). The Egyptians readily granted their requests to get rid of the Israelites as quickly as possible. Departing so suddenly, the Israelites had no time to leaven their dough and so ate unleavened bread for seven days after they left Egypt (Ex 12:31-36).

The Exodus

Israel left Egypt after midnight on the 14th day of Abib (March-April) in the spring of 1491 B.C. *"Now the length of time the Israelite people lived in Egypt was 430 years. At the end of the 430 years, to the very day, all the LORD's divisions left Egypt"* (Ex 12:40-41, NIV).

430 or 400 years?

There is a little problem here. God had told Abraham that *"thy seed shall be a stranger in a land that is not theirs, and shall serve them; and they shall afflict them four hundred years"* (Gen 15:3). There is a 30-year discrepancy. Were the numbers simply rounded? Besides, if Jacob arrived in Egypt in 1706 B.C., then the Exodus in 1491 B.C. marked the end of only 215 years! Let us reread the line in the KJV, a word-for-word translation: *"Now the sojourning of the children of Israel, who dwelt in Egypt, was four hundred and thirty years"* (Ex 12:41).

The phrasing and punctuation are such that the line can mean the Israelites truly lived in Egypt, but not necessarily for 430 years. Let us go to the Hebrew original:

"Uwmowshab	bᵃney	Yisra'el	'ᵃsher	yashᵃbuw
And the sojourning	(of the) children	(of) Israel,	who	dwelt

bᵃ'erets Kᵃna`an	uwb'erets	bᵃ-Mitsrayim	shᵃloshiym	shanah
		in Egypt,	thirty	years

wᵃ'arba	me'owt	shanah"
(was) four and	hundred	

The Hebrew words *bᵃ'erets Kᵃna`an uwb'erets* ("in the land of Canaan and the land...") had not been translated into English! The complete line therefore should read as: *"Now the sojourning of the children of Israel, who dwelt* (in the land of Canaan and the land) *in Egypt, was four hundred and thirty years"* (Ex 12:41). The 430 years include the period their forefathers stayed in Canaan!

When did they arrive in Canaan? After Terah died in 1921 B.C., God told Abram to go to Canaan, which he did. From 1921 B.C. to 1491 B.C. were exactly 430 years! So, the 430-year period began with the call of Abram and ended with the Exodus. But what about the prophesied 400 years of affliction? ("Affliction" is translated from the Hebrew *anah*, which connotes "to eye, look down, browbeat, bully.") In 1891 B.C. Isaac, the son of Abraham in his old age, was weaned at the age of 5 years. *"And Sarah saw the son of Hagar the Egyptian, which she had born unto Abraham, mocking"* (Gen 21:9). From 1891 B.C. to 1491 B.C. are fully 400 years. Evidently, the years of "affliction" began when Ishmael, the son of the Egyptian, mocked Isaac. (Please see the Appendix for a more comprehensive chronicle of events.)

Two million Israelites?

Jacob and his descendants numbered 70 when he came to Egypt in 1706 B.C. Just 215 years later, in the Exodus of 1491 B.C., *"There were about six hundred thousand men on foot, besides women and children..."* (Ex 12:37, NIV). An Israelite male person was considered a "man" at the age of 20 years and older, according to Hebrew standards (Num 1:20, etc.). If we add to 600,000 an equal number of women, there would have been 1.2 million adult individuals. If half of them were married couples with an average of 2-3 children (1-19 years old), the minors would have been 600,000-900,000. The Israelites could thus have totaled between 1,800,000 and 2,100,000 individuals!

Only 4 generations? Skeptics think two million are too many for Israel after only 4 generations from Levi to Moses. They overlook the fact that, from Joseph, Levi's brother, to Joshua, Moses's right hand man, there were 11 generations (1 Chron 7:22-27). Those in Levi's line begot sons at more advanced ages, while their relatives from the other tribes apparently married earlier and had children at much younger ages. Thus, just as God had told Abram that *"in the fourth generation"* his descendants would return to Canaan (Gen 15:16), Moses, of the 4th generation of his line in Egypt, led Israel in the Exodus to Canaan.

Logistical problems. Some writers cite logistical problems such as the amount of food and water needed for such a multitude. One mini-study calculated the time involved in fetching water from a single pool or well in the wilderness (Ex 15:23-25). Assuming 1 person filled one water bag for 20 others, and it took 1 minute to fill the bag, even if 10 people could draw water at the same time, only 200 people could have drunk per minute (1x20x10), and it would have taken 9,000 minutes for 1,800,000 persons to drink. Since there are only 1,440 minutes in a day, the last person would have been able to drink after 6¼ days![90]

"Thousands" or "families"? To solve the problems, it has been pointed out that the Hebrew word for "thousand," *eleph*, can also mean "family." Thus, instead of *"six hundred thousand"* the phrase can also be rendered as "six hundred families" (or clans), which were logistically more manageable.

However, just 14 months after Israel left Egypt, God had a census taken of *"all the men in Israel twenty years old or more who are able to serve in the army... The total number was 603,550. The families of the tribe of Levi, however, were not counted along with the others"* (Num 1:46-47, NIV). The able-bodied Israelite men totaled slightly more than the 600,000 reckoned when they left Egypt a year earlier. The count did not even include the men from the tribe of Levi, whose only duties were to care for the Tabernacle (Num 1:4,48-50). The census conclusively proves that Israel had truly multiplied many times over into a great multitude within only 215 years in Egypt.

Census of Israel

Tribe	No. of men*
Reuben	46,500
Simeon	59,300
Gad	45,650
Judah	74,600
Issachar	54,400
Zebulun	57,400
Ephraim	40,500
Manasseh	32,200
Benjamin	35,400
Dan	62,700
Asher	41,500
Naphtali	53,400
Total:	603,550

*20 years old and above

Wilderness wandering

"And the LORD went before them by day in a pillar of a cloud, to lead them the way; and by night in a pillar of fire, to give them light; to go by day and night" (Ex 13:21).

Red Sea parted. After the Israelites left, Pharaoh changed his mind and went after them. He found them encamped by the Red Sea. The

LORD, through Moses, parted the waters of the sea so the Israelites could escape to the other side. When the Egyptian army tried to follow, the waters closed over them (Ex 14).

The Reed Sea crossing prefigured baptism ("immersion" or burial of the old self and subsequent rebirth to a new spiritual life). Paul says: *"Moreover, brethren, I do not want you to be unaware that all our fathers were under the cloud, all passed through the sea, all were baptized into Moses in the cloud and in the sea"* (1 Cor 10:1-2, NKJV).

Quail and manna. In the wilderness of Sin, the Israelites grumbled for food. God gave them quail in the evening and, in the morning, manna that continued six days a week for the next 40 years until they entered Canaan (Ex 16). The psalmist sings, *"Men ate the bread of angels; he sent them all the food they could eat"* (Ps 78:25, NIV).

Paul adds that *"all ate the same spiritual food"* (1 Cor 10:3, NKJV) – manna, a "type" or prophetic symbol of Christ, who said: *"Our fathers did eat manna in the desert; as it is written, He gave them bread from heaven to eat... Moses gave you not that bread from heaven; but my Father giveth you the true bread from heaven"* (John 6:31,32b). *"I am the living bread which came down from heaven: if any man eat of this bread, he shall live for ever: and the bread that I will give is my flesh, which I will give for the life of the world"* (John 6:51).

Water from the rock. Encamping at Rephidim, the thirsty Israelites clamored for water. The LORD told Moses to strike the rock at Horeb, from which water flowed out (Ex 17:1-7), *"and all drank the same spiritual drink. For they drank of that spiritual Rock that followed them, and that Rock was Christ"* (1 Cor 10:4, NKJV). The water represented eternal life through Christ! *"But whosoever drinketh of the water that I shall give him shall never thirst; but the water that I shall give him shall be in him a well of water springing up into everlasting life"* (John 4:14).

The word "strike" (or "smite") is translated from the Hebrew *nakah*, which means "to beat, wound, kill," etc. Hence, Moses's act of striking the rock stood for Christ's death on the cross at Golgotha.

Covenant and Commandments.

In the wilderness of Sinai, Israel encamped before the "mountain of God." They entered into a covenant or agreement with the LORD: He would make them His chosen people, and they would obey His words. God gave them the first of His laws, which Moses recorded in the "Book of the Covenant." The laws defined the Israelites' relationship with each other and with God. They were to be a holy people separate from the immorality and idolatry of the nations around them (Ex 19-23).

Moses spent 40 days and nights with God on the mount, receiving the instructions for the Tabernacle and the priesthood, and two stone tablets inscribed by God Himself with the Ten Commandments. Seeing the people dancing before a golden calf they had made while he was gone, Moses smashed the stone tablets in anger. Three thousand Israelites were killed in punishment. God told Moses to make two new stone tablets, on which he wrote the commandments anew (Ex 24-34).

Generation condemned.
The LORD told Moses to send 12 spies, one from each tribe, to scout the land of Canaan. After 40 days, the spies returned with huge grapes, pomegranates, and figs, proof of the fertility of the land. But ten of the spies said they could not take the land, because the cities were fortified and the inhabitants, some of them giants, were much stronger. Only two of the spies, Caleb and Joshua, urged the people to go at once and conquer the land. The fearful Israelites agitated for a new leader who would take them back to Egypt (Num 13-14:1-10).

The LORD condemned their generation for their lack of faith. All of them, from 20 years old and above, except Caleb and Joshua, would die wandering in the wilderness for 40 years, equivalent to the number of days the spies scouted the land. Only their children would enter the Promised Land (Num 14:26-35).

Barred from the land. In the wilderness of Zin, the Israelites again clamored for water. The LORD told Moses, "*Speak to the rock before their eyes, and it will yield its water; thus you shall bring water for them out of the rock, and give drink to the congregation and their animals*" (Num 20:8b, NKJV). "*Then Moses lifted his hand and struck the rock twice with his rod; and water came out abundantly, and the congregation and their animals drank*" (Num 20:11, NKJV).

Displeased, "*the LORD said to Moses and Aaron, "Because you did not trust in me enough to honor me as holy in the sight of the Israelites, you will not bring this community into the land I give them.*" (Num 20:12, NIV). Why? God told Moses to speak to the rock, but he struck the rock twice with his rod. For that mistake, Moses was barred from entering the Promised Land. Was his error that grave? As we have seen earlier, Moses's act of striking the rock the first time stood for Christ's saving death on the cross, which needed to be done only once. Thereafter, believers could seek forgiveness of sin and eternal life by simply calling on or speaking with Him. By striking the rock again, Moses illustrated a second crucifixion, ruining the prophetic picture.

A peek from the peak. After 40 years of wandering in the wilderness, including battles with hostile inhabitants, the Israelites neared Canaan. "*And Moses went up from the plains of Moab unto the* *mountain of Nebo, to the top of Pisgah, that is over against Jericho. And the LORD shewed him all the land of Gilead, unto Dan, And all Naphtali, and the land of Ephraim, and Manasseh, and all the land of Judah, unto the utmost sea, And the south, and the plain of the valley of Jericho, the city of palm trees, unto Zoar"* (Deut 34:1-3).

The LORD gave Moses a glimpse of the Promised Land from the peak of Pisgah (now in Jordan) before he died. *"Then the LORD said to him, 'This is the land of which I swore to give Abraham, Isaac, and Jacob, saying, "I will give it to your descendants." I have caused you to see it with your eyes, but you shall not cross over there.' So Moses the servant of the LORD died there in the land of Moab, according to the word of the LORD. And He buried him in a valley in the land of Moab, opposite Beth Peor; but no one knows his grave to this day. Moses was one hundred and twenty years old when he died. His eyes were not dim nor his natural vigor diminished"* (Deut 34:4-7, NKJV).

Before he died, Moses had turned over the leadership of Israel to Joshua (Num 27:12-22).

Decline of human longevity

Did you notice? Man's longevity declined drastically after the Flood. From an antediluvian average of 912 years, life spans had shortened to less than 150 by Jacob's time, going down further to 70 by David's time. As life spans decreased, many men lived longer than their sons and grandsons. Shem had a shorter life than his forefathers, yet outlived 7 generations after him! His son Arphaxad and grandson Salah both lived longer than 5 younger generations, including Abram's father Terah. Eber outlived 6 generations after him, including Abraham.

In the following table of life spans and corresponding longevity graph are the years of birth and death of patriarchs in the line leading directly to the Messiah: 11 from Adam to Shem before the Flood; 11 from Arphaxad after the Flood to Jacob, founder of Israel; 2 in David and Solomon (33rd and 34th generation, respectively); plus two other persons whose times are recorded in the Bible.

70- to 80-year life spans.

Strangely, even if Moses lived to be 120 years old, he wrote about a much shorter life expectancy for man: *"The days of our lives are seventy years; And if by reason of strength they are eighty years, Yet their boast is only labor and sorrow; For it is soon cut off, and we fly away"* (Ps 90:10, NKJV). It appears, however, to have become the norm by the time of David and Barzillai, one of his supporters, about 400 years later.

Life Spans of the Patriarchs*

Gen. No.	Name	Born (B.C.)	Age Had Son:	Age Died	Died (B.C.)
1	Adam	4004**	130	930	3074
2	Seth	3874	105	912	2962
3	Enos	3769	90	905	2864
4	Cainan	3679	70	910	2769
5	Mahalaleel	3609	65	895	2714
6	Jared	3544	162	962	2582
7	Enoch	3382	65	365	(3017)***
8	Methuselah	3317	187	969	2348
9	Lamech	3130	182	777	2353
10	Noah	2948	500	950	1998
11	Shem	2446	100	600	1846
	FLOOD				(2348)
12	Arphaxad	2346	35	438	1908
13	Salah	2311	30	433	1878
14	Eber	2281	34	464	1817
15	Peleg	2247	30	239	2008
16	Reu	2217	32	239	1978
17	Serug	2185	30	230	1955
18	Nahor	2155	29	148	2007
19	Terah	2126	130	205	1921
20	Abraham	1996	100	175	1822
21	Isaac	1896	60	180	1716
22	Jacob/Israel	1837		147	1689
23	Joseph	1745		110	1635
23	Levi			137	
24	Kohath			133	
25	Amram			137	
26	Moses	1571		120	1451
	Joshua			110	
	Barzillai			80	
33	David	1085		70	1015
34	Solomon	1033		58	975

*Years in bold figures from Archbishop Ussher, 1650-1654, (Old Testament Chronology, *Treasury of Biblical Information*, 1952). **Created. ***Translated.

Solomon, David's son, died young. According to Archbishop James Ussher's Chronology, Solomon was born in 1033 B.C. and died in 975 B.C. – living just 58 years (1 Kings 3:7; 11:42-43). Despite his renowned wisdom, Solomon was unable to prolong his life. (Did his 700 wives and 300 concubines [1 Kings 11:3] have something to do with it?)

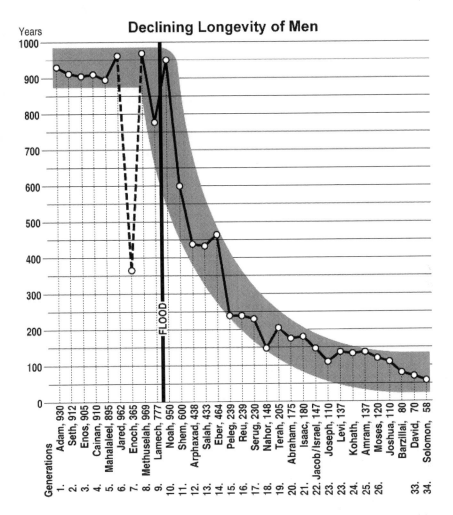

Declining Longevity of Men

Years

Generations

1. Adam, 930
2. Seth, 912
3. Enos, 905
4. Cainan, 910
5. Mahalaleel, 895
6. Jared, 962
7. Enoch, 365
8. Methuselah, 969
9. Lamech, 777
10. Noah, 950
11. Shem, 600
12. Arphaxad, 438
13. Salah, 433
14. Eber, 464
15. Peleg, 239
16. Reu, 239
17. Serug, 230
18. Nahor, 148
19. Terah, 205
20. Abraham, 175
21. Isaac, 180
22. Jacob/Israel, 147
23. Joseph, 110
23. Levi, 137
24. Kohath, 137
25. Amram, 137
26. Moses, 120
26. Joshua, 110
33. Barzillai, 80
33. David, 70
34. Solomon, 58

FLOOD

Besides 70 being 1/13 (number of disobedience) of the antediluvian average (912 years), what factors may have caused human life to suddenly shorten after the Flood? Let us consider possible causes.

A harsher environment? As we have seen earlier, the theorized tilting of the Earth's axis and disappearance of the hypothetical ice crystal or water vapor canopy above the atmosphere could have brought about extreme weather variations that men, animals, and plants had not been used to. Plants presumably became less nutritious, so God allowed men and animals to eat all kinds of moving things.

And, with the seasonal increase of sunlight and heat in many places, bacteria would have begun to proliferate, becoming agents of infection spreading various diseases. This is reflected in the name of the son of Shem, the first patriarch born after the Flood – Arphaxad ("healer").

Shorter life spans actually began with Shem, who was born *before* the Flood, but died living less than two-thirds (600 years) of his father Noah's life (950 years) after the Flood. Was he the first to be affected by the new, harsher environment?

"Population bottleneck"? When a sizable population suddenly shrinks and becomes isolated due to natural disasters, epidemics, wars, etc., the wide variety of genes previously present among the people is drastically reduced to those of just a few survivors. The loss of genetic diversity is aggravated by the inbreeding that naturally follows. Since a child gets 50% of its genes from the father and 50% from the mother, genes that remain with the parents die without being passed on. With each successive generation, more and more genes are lost.

The genetic loss is equated to loss of physical fitness. Similar effects of population bottlenecks have been observed on animal species in modern times. Today, marriages between close relatives often result in genetic loss that affects the immune system of the children, making them vulnerable to diseases. Conditions seem different in Biblical times.

After the Flood, the world population restarted from just eight people: Noah, his three sons, and their wives. But the extreme example of inbreeding are Adam and Eve, whose genetic make-ups were identical, as she was his clone, coming from one of his ribs. Still, eight generations of their descendants averaged 912 years in longevity.

And, though life spans shortened after the Flood, Abram married his half-sister Sarai and fathered a physically perfect son, Isaac. Isaac wed Rebekah, the daughter of his first cousin Bethuel, yet sired two excellent specimens in Esau and Jacob. Jacob had his first cousins Leah and Rachel, who gave birth to eight robust sons between them. Amram, Moses's father, took his father's sister Jochebed to wife. It was only at the time of Moses, in the 26th generation from Adam, that the LORD forbade His people from marrying close relatives.

Genetic mutations? Mutations cause a loss of information in the DNA, leading to the deterioration of the defense, maintenance, and repair systems of the body. It has been suggested that the rate at which all types of mutations occur per generation is higher than 1,000. The offspring inherit these mutations from their parents, develop additional mutations of their own, and pass them on to their own children. It is thought that, from Adam to Noah, large numbers of mutations have accumulated, manifesting in the shorter lives of men after the Flood.[91]

According to science writer Wendy Wippel: "Human lifespan has been demonstrated to be both pre-determined and programmed into the DNA itself, through a mechanism involving a repetitive DNA sequence at the end of each chromosome called a telomere."[92] Telomeres shorten with each cell division, owing to the failure of enzymes that copy DNA to reach the end of the chromosomes. When telomeres become too short, the cell stops dividing. The cessation of cell division results in aging and eventual death.

If man's life span is programmed in the DNA, the LORD might have simply reprogrammed human genes after the Flood. After all, He has the power to lengthen or shorten men's lives. *"He shall call upon me, and I will answer him: I will be with him in trouble; I will deliver him, and honour him. With long life will I satisfy him, and shew him my salvation"* (Ps 91:15-16; also Kings 3:11; 2 Chron 1:11; Pr 3:2; Eph 6:2-3).

The Bible also tells us that God set a limit on men's life span. *"Man's days are determined; you have decreed the number of his months and have set limits he cannot exceed"* (Job 14:5, NIV).

Man's "piece of mind"

Speculation began in the late 19th and early 20th centuries that people use only about 10% of their full mental potential. Some early neurologists based the notion on the observed proportion of neurons in the brain that "fired" at any given time.[93] Thus, about 90% of man's mental potential remains unused for the rest of his life. He is able to use just a piece of his mind! According to author Richard M. Restak (*The Brain: The Last Frontier*): "Behind Darwin's discomfiture was the dawning realization that the evolution of the brain vastly exceeded the needs of prehistoric man. This is, in fact, the only example in existence where a species was provided with an organ that it still has not learned how to use."[94] Why did God give man the full 100% of his mind power – if 90% of it would just remain dormant throughout his lifetime? Or did God really intend for man to use all 100% of his intellectual prowess?

Intelligence grows with age?

Job asked rhetorically, *"Is not wisdom found among the aged? Does not long life bring understanding?"* (Job 12:12, NIV). Job said that a man became wiser, or more intelligent, as he grew older. Elihu, a young sympathizer of Job, echoed his thoughts: *"Age should speak; advanced years should teach wisdom"* (Job 32:7, NIV). A direct relation seems to exist between intelligence and age. Wisdom increases as age advances.

Bildad, one of Job's three friends, spoke of earlier generations. *"Ask the former generations and find out what their fathers learned, for we were born only yesterday and know nothing, and our days on earth are but a shadow"* (Job 8:8-9, NIV). His words suggest their forefathers knew more than they did, because they had shorter lives (*"our days on earth are but a shadow"*) compared to earlier generations.

Your slightly used brain.

If a man grows more intelligent with age, then the antediluvians who lived close to a thousand years must have been able to use nearly 100% of their brain potential! When human life span decreased to less than 10% of its pre-Flood length, man's use of his mental capacity likewise stopped short at around 10%! Even in this modern age of countless discoveries and inventions, we are still only slightly using our brains!

Consider some of the most brilliant men in history, in the likes of Leonardo da Vinci (1452-1519), William Shakespeare (1564-1616), Isaac Newton (1642-1727), Wolfgang Mozart (1756-1791), Thomas Edison (1847-1931), Albert Einstein (1879-1955). Living only some 35-85 years, they made their most important achievements between the ages of 20 and 50 years, a productive period of around 30 years or less. If these relatively short-lived men accomplished so much in their 30-year or so prime, what could the antediluvians have accomplished with 25-30 times more productive years in their hands, er, heads?

So many ideas must have entered their minds. Testing concepts, they had so much time for trial and error. If they did not get things right the first time, they could have made all the corrections and adjustments they wanted until an idea worked. Moreover, they probably exchanged ideas and compared experiences gained over hundreds of years. (Plus, some of them might have had an added boost in the form of hidden knowledge from the fallen angels.)

9

Recurring Riddles Reexamined

ut God hath revealed them unto us by his Spirit:
for the Spirit searcheth all things, yea, the deep things of God"

-- 1 Corinthians 2:10.

Many mysteries which continue to puzzle people today are either directly mentioned or hinted at in Scriptures. Some of these are the so-called "crypto-creatures." Let us try to learn more about them.

Dinosaurs after the Deluge?

The Bible tells us that all land animals which were not with Noah in the Ark died in the waters of the Flood (Gen 7:21-22). Aquatic creatures were spared. A number of reptiles, including some dinosaurs, were sea-dwellers. They were cold-blooded creatures whose body temperatures rose and fell with that of the environment. Thus, reptiles live unusually long. Some turtles today are said to live around 100 years in their natural habitat; tortoises in captivity have lived over 200 years! If the warm-blooded antediluvian humans had life spans close to a thousand years, many reptiles could have lived just as long, or even longer! Some dinosaurs might have even survived the Deluge.

Two dinosaurs seem to be described in the book of Job, who lived sometime between Noah and Moses. His book was written after the Flood, but is the only one in the Bible that does not mention God's law, so Job must have died before God gave the commandments to Moses.

Job may have been a contemporary of Peleg or Reu (2247-1978 B.C.), when the decreasing longevity of men was at the 240-year level. Peleg and Reu both lived to be 239 years old, and saw four generations after them. When Satan unjustly persecuted Job, he was already a very wealthy man, *"the greatest of all the men of the east"* (Job 1:3b), and maybe 50-100 years old. All his seven sons were apparently grown up and also well-to-do, because they *"feasted in their houses, every one his day; and sent and called for their three sisters to eat and to drink with them"* (Job 1:4). After God restored him, Job lived another *"hundred and forty years, and saw his sons, and his sons' sons, even four generations"* (Job 42:16). Thus, Job may have lived some 200-240 years – around 100-400 years after the Flood.

Behemoths and leviathans. God told Job: "*Look at the behemoth, which I made along with you and which feeds on grass like an ox. What strength he has in his loins, what power in the muscles of his belly! His tail sways like a cedar; the sinews of his thighs are close-knit. His bones are tubes of bronze, his limbs like rods of iron. He ranks first among the works of God, yet his Maker can approach him with his sword. The hills bring him their produce, and all the wild animals play nearby. Under the lotus plants he lies, hidden among the reeds in the marsh. The lotuses conceal him in their shadow; the poplars by the stream surround him*" (Job 40:15-22, NIV).

It sounds like the herbivorous Apatosaurus, the largest dinosaur with powerful hips and legs, a large belly, and a huge tail like the trunk of a tree. It measured up to 90 feet long and weighed as much as 80 tons, thus ranking *"first among the works of God"*! Living near the water, it lay among the water plants and nearby trees. When God said to "look at" it, did He mean the *behemoth* still lived in Job's time?

God next said: "*Can you draw out Leviathan with a hook, Or snare his tongue with a line which you lower? Can you put a reed through his nose, Or pierce his jaw with a hook?... Can you fill his skin with harpoons, Or his head with fishing spears? Lay your hand on him; Remember the battle -- Never do it again! Indeed, any hope of overcoming him is false; Shall one not be overwhelmed at the sight of him?... Who can open the doors of his face, With his terrible teeth all around? His rows of scales are his pride, Shut up tightly as with a seal... When he raises himself up, the mighty are afraid; Because of his crashings they are beside themselves. Though the sword reaches him, it cannot avail; Nor does spear, dart, or javelin. He regards iron as straw, And bronze as rotten wood. The arrow cannot make him flee; Slingstones become like stubble to him. Darts are regarded as straw; He laughs at the threat of javelins... He makes the deep boil like a pot; He makes the sea like a pot of ointment. He leaves a shining wake behind him; One would think the deep had white hair* (Job 41: 1-32, NKJV).

Although some commentators say the leviathan was a whale, the combination of "tongue," "nose," "skin," "face," "teeth" and "scales" suggests a sea serpent or marine dinosaur like the plesiosaur, a 50-foot-long fish-eating dinosaur that became extinct 70 million years ago,.

Fire-breathing dragons. Did those saurian stragglers become the stuff of myths and legends in the arts and literature of many cultures in Asia, the Middle East, Europe, and the Americas?

Some tales tell of incredible fire-breathing dragons. Strangely, such a creature is described in the Bible: *"His snorting throws out flashes of light; his eyes are like the rays of dawn. Firebrands stream from his mouth; sparks of fire shoot out. Smoke pours from his nostrils as from a boiling pot over a fire of reeds. His breath sets coals ablaze, and flames dart from his mouth"* (Job 41:18-21, NIV). It must be true, it was God Himself speaking. Besides, there are creatures today that produce similar fiery effects. Fireflies generate a blinking light in their abdomens. Bombardier beetles shoot a scorching substance at would-be predators. Electric eels shock enemies with 600 volts of electricity.

Oriental depiction of a ferocious dragon.

Sea serpent sightings. Marine dinosaurs could have given birth to stories about sea serpents. Sightings have been reported over the last 1,500 years. In the 4th century B.C. Aristotle wrote about huge sea serpents off the coast of Libya. "Mariners sailing along the coast have told how... the serpents came to attack them, some of them throwing themselves on a trireme and capsizing it."

In 1555, the Archbishop of Uppsala in Sweden wrote about a sea serpent about 200 feet long and 20 feet wide. It reportedly had sharp scales and hair hanging from its neck. In 1734, Norwegian missionary Hans Egede described a "terrible sea monster" he saw near Greenland. "It had a long, sharp snout, and blew like a whale, had broad, large flippers, and the body... was very wrinkled... formed like a snake, and when... it raised its tail above the water, a whole ship-length from its body." In 1848, Captain Peter M'Quhae and his crew of HMS *Daedalus* spotted an enormous serpent off the African coast in the Atlantic. "It had no fins, but something like a mane of a horse, or rather a bunch of seaweed, washed about its back."

In 1905, British Royal Zoological Society member Meade Waldo, on the steamship *Valhalla* off the coast of Brazil, saw "a large fin or frill sticking out of the water, dark seaweed brown in color, somewhat crinkled at the edge... under the water to the rear of the frill, the shape of a considerable body. A great head and neck rose out of the water in front of the frill. The neck appeared to be the thickness of a man's body. The head had a very turtle-like appearance, as had also the eye."[1]

Most popular monster. One similar creature became a modern legend because it was often seen in a relatively small area frequented by people. In the last 1,400 years, there have been some 3,000 sightings and even some vague photographs of a "beastie" in Loch Ness, Britain's largest lake in northern Scotland. First known as the Loch Ness Monster, it is now fondly called "Nessie" by believers.

In 565 A.D., the Irish saint Columba spotted the monster as one of his disciples swam across the mile-wide lake to fetch a boat from the opposite shore. It reared to the surface "with a great roar and open mouth." St. Columba prayed for the man, and the monster went away.

In 1933, a London surgeon on holiday had the first picture of the creature published in the London *Daily Mail*. The photograph agreed with the description by many witnesses, among them schoolmasters, naval officers, Benedictine monks, one Nobel prize-winner, two town clerks, and Scottish professionals.

"Nessie" was about 20 feet long with a serpentine neck and stout torso with flippers. In 1951, a forester who lived beside the loch saw three humps in the water moving towards the shore. He managed to take a shot before the camera's shutter jammed. In 1960, aviation engineer Tim Dinsdale took the first moving pictures of something that might have been "Nessie."

Famous first photograph of Loch Ness Monster ("Nessie") taken by a surgeon on a holiday in 1933.

In November 1975, a team from the Massachusetts Academy of Applied Sciences lowered a 16-mm motor-driven camera 45 feet below the surface to take shots with a searchlight every 75 seconds. Several pictures taken appeared to show a reddish brown animal about 12 feet long, with a "hideous" head and an arching neck around 8 feet long. The images convinced naturalist Sir Peter Scott that a family of plesiosaurs had survived in Loch Ness.[2]

Crypto-creature cousins. Creatures resembling "Nessie" have been sighted in other lochs in the Western Highlands. In 1527, in Gairloch in Ross and Cromarty, Scottish historian Hector Boece saw "a terrible beast as big as a greyhound, struck down great trees and slew three men with three strokes of his tail." Likewise, Loch Morar was said to be the lair of a creature locally called "Mhorag," described variously as "about the size of an Indian elephant," "about 30 feet long with four humps," and "with snake-like head and four legs."

Outside Scotland, similar lake monsters have been reported in Ireland, Scandinavia, Iceland, Canada, the United States. In British Columbia, a long-necked creature known as "Ogopogo" was said to inhabit Lake Okanagan. The Indian tribes that inhabited the area made crude drawings on stone of the creature they called "Naitaka," which remarkably looked like "Nessie."[3] In Lake Champlain between New York and Vermont, bordering Canada, a similar crypto-creature has been nicknamed "Champ."

Thunderbirds and swamp-dwellers. Other prehistoric stragglers may have lived farther inland. A news item in *The Tombstone Epitaph* of April 26, 1890, reported two ranchers startled by a gigantic flying reptile with huge leathery wings, a long slim body, and claws on its feet and at the joints of its wings. Its 8-foot head was like an alligator's, with a mouth full of teeth and large protruding eyes. They killed it, cutting off the tip of the wing for a trophy.[4] It could have been the legendary creature Native American tribes called the "thunderbird," whose powerful wings made thunderous sounds when they flapped.

In the Jiundu swamps in northwest Rhodesia (now Zambia), near the Belgian Congo, there was a much-feared giant animal called "Kongamato." Said to be a bird, it was more like a lizard with wings like those of a bat. When explorer Frank Melland showed natives pictures of dinosaurs, they excitedly pointed to a pterodactyl.[5]

The February 13, 1910, issue of the *The New York Herald* featured an article entitled, "Is a Brontosaurus Roaming Africa's Wilds?" A giant animal with a small head, long neck, and massive tail was said to inhabit the unexplored Likouala swamps around Lake Tele in the Congo. The pygmies called it "mokele-mbembe." In 1960, they speared one and cooked it. Tribe members who ate the creature died shortly afterward. Seeing pictures of prehistoric animals, the pygmies said it most closely resembled the brontosaurus.[6]

In Peru, Dr. Javier Cabrera of the University of Lima and his father have since the 1930s collected over 11,000 engraved burial stones of the ancient Ica culture from 500-1500 A.D. Amazingly, almost a third of the stones depict dinosaurs like triceratops, stegosaurus, pterosaurs, diplodocus. Modern drawings of these dinosaurs based on fossil remains were made beginning only in the 1880s![7]

Deceased dinosaurs? Some specimens have been examined up close -- although lifeless. In 1883, *Scientific American* reported a 39-foot long "extraordinary saurian" killed in Bolivia. "The legs, belly, and lower part of the throat appear defended by a kind of scale armor, and all the back is protected by a still thicker and double cuirass, starting from behind the ears of the anterior head, and continuing to the tail. The neck is long, and the belly large and almost dragging on the ground."[8]

In 1925, the carcass of a 34-foot creature, with a yard-wide body and duck-billed head the size of a barrel, washed ashore at Santa Cruz (Moore's Beach), north of Monterey Bay, California. President Wallace of the Natural History Society of B.C., Canada, recorded: "It had no teeth. Its head is large and its neck fully 20 feet long. The body is weak and the tail is only three feet in length from the end of the backbone. These facts do away with the whale theory (which had been proposed by a handful of other authorities, as the backbone of a whale is far larger than any bone in this animal... I would call it a type of plesiosaurus."[9]

In 1937, a 10-foot long cadborosaurus juvenile, was found in the belly of a sperm whale. It belonged to a species with a head like a horse, a long neck, short front flippers, and a body up to 50 feet long. It had often been sighted off the coast of British Columbia, Canada.[10]

In 1977, a Japanese fishing crew netted a decomposing 30-foot giant carcass weighing about 4,000 pounds off the coast of New Zealand. Before it was dumped back into the sea, a zoologist on board photographed the dead creature, noting its long neck, flippers, and other features, which showed it was a reptile, not a fish of some kind.[11]

Decomposing carcass netted by crew of a Japanese fishing boat.

Manlike apes or apelike men?

In many mountainous areas around the world are stories about manlike creatures bigger than men. In the Himalayas, the natives call the creature "Yeti" – known to Western mountaineers as the "Abominable Snowman." Sherpas, an ethnic group living near Mount Everest, regale foreign visitors with stories of these apemen. In 1832, B.H. Hodson, the first British Resident in Nepal, told of an unknown creature that "moved erectly, was covered in long, dark hair and had no tail."[12]

In other parts of Asia, from the Gobi Desert in the north to Assam in the south, similar beings go by a variety of names: "Meti," "Shookpa," "Migo," "Kang-Mi." In the Rocky Mountains of the American northwest, the counterpart is called "Bigfoot" and, in the nearby Canadian Rockies, "Sasquatch." Hundreds of sightings have been reported to newspapers and broadcast stations in Canada. Eyewitness accounts have also been recorded in some regions of Africa and South America. In spite of the differences in name, the portrayal is the same: hairy and apelike, yet walking erect, as tall as 10 feet, weighing about 300 pounds.

Encounters and evidences. Monks around the Himalayas keep what they claim to be *yeti* scalps, skins, and bones. In 1948, Jan Frostis, a Norwegian uranium prospector, said his shoulder was badly mauled in an attack by two yetis near Zemu Gap in Sikkim. In 1951, British mountaineer Eric Shipton published photos of humanoid footprints 13 inches long and 8 inches wide, taken in the Gauri Sankar range. A few years later, the mummified joint of an index finger and a thumb were found at Pangboche, Nepal. Some anthropologists thought they were "similar in some respects to that of Neanderthal man." In 1957, Thomas Slick, a Texas oilman on a yeti-hunt, learned from Nepalese villagers that *yetis* had battered to death at least five people in the past 4 years.

In 1967, near Eureka, California, rancher Roger Patterson captured

in 29 feet of 16-mm film a tall, hairy female creature, with pendulous breasts, walking upright with long strides and swinging arms, turning cautiously to look at him before disappearing among the trees.[13]

Is this the Bigfoot or Sasquatch of the U.S. and Canada?

At midnight on June 25, 1973, a teenage couple sitting in a parked car in Murphysboro, in southern Illinois, was startled by an 8-foot-tall shrieking figure, with thick light-colored hair covered in slime, lumbering towards them from Big Muddy River. They sped away and alerted the police. Sometime later, workers on a nearby fairground saw the same "Murphysboro Mud Monster" staring at some tethered ponies.[14]

Some people theorize these creatures may be descendants of *Gigantopithecus*, a prehistoric giant ape whose teeth had been found being sold as "dragon teeth" in Chinese apothecary shops in the 1930s. *Gigantopithecus* is estimated to have stood at 11 to 13 feet tall.[15]

Giants after the Flood?

"There were giants in the earth in those days; and also after that..." (Gen 6:4a). Little noticed is the short phrase *"and also after that."* Giants (*Nephilim*) reappeared after the Flood!

Biblical record. Accounts about giants are found in many places in the OT. *"And there we saw the giants, the sons of Anak, which come of the giants..."* (Num 13:33). The twelve spies of Moses saw giants in Canaan in 1451 B.C. *"The Emim had dwelt there in times past, a people as great and numerous and tall as the Anakim. They were also regarded as giants, like the Anakim, but the Moabites call them Emim"* (Deut 2:10-11, NKJV). *"That also was accounted a land of giants: giants dwelt therein in old time; and the Ammonites call them Zamzummims"* (Deut 2:20). *"(Only Og king of Bashan was left of the remnant of the Rephaites. His bed was made of iron and was more than thirteen feet long and six feet wide. It is still in Rabbah of the Ammonites.)"* (Deut 3:11, NIV). *"A people great and tall, the children of the Anakims, whom thou knowest, and of whom thou hast heard say, Who can stand before the children of Anak!"* (Deut 9:2). *"A champion named Goliath, who was from Gath, came out of the Philistine camp. He was over nine feet tall"* (1 Sam 17:4-5, NIV). David slew Goliath, the most famous giant in the Bible, in 1063 B.C. *"And yet again there was war at Gath, where was a man of great stature, whose fingers and toes were four and twenty, six on each hand, and six on each foot: and he also was the son of the giant"* (1 Chron 20:6, 2 Sam 21:20-21).

Just tall stories? Traces of this race of giants have been found throughout history. Sometime between 600 and 200 B.C., two 36-foot human skeletal remains were separately discovered in Carthage.[16] A 23-foot tall skeleton was reportedly found in 1456 beside a river in Valence, France. In 1577, a human skeleton measuring 19 feet, 6 inches was discovered beneath a fallen oak tree in the canton of Lucerne, also in France.[17] In 1613, a 25-foot, 6-inch skeleton was excavated near the castle of Chaumont in France.[18]

In 1833, soldiers digging a pit at Lompock Rancho, California, unearthed a 12-foot giant with a double row of teeth.[19] In 1846, Joseph Henry, first secretary of the

Giant's skull unearthed by workmen.

Smithsonian Institution, estimated that in Ohio alone, there were over 10,000 burial mounds of giant humans. Unfortunately, the pioneers destroyed most of them. At least one burial mound has been reconstructed in Adams County, Ohio. It stretches across the meadow in the form of a serpent (the god of this ancient race of giants?). In 1872, the *Historical Collections of Noble County Ohio* (pp. 350-351) reported the discovery under a mound of "the remains of three skeletons whose size would indicate they measured in life at least eight feet in height. The remarkable feature of these remains was they had double teeth in front as well as in back of mouth and in both upper and lower jaws. Upon exposure to the atmosphere the skeletons crumbled back to mother earth."

Mutant man-mountains? We read in *Giants: Master Builders of Prehistoric and Ancient Civilizations* that in the late 1950s workmen constructing a road to the Euphrates Valley in southeastern Turkey uncovered a grave containing a human skeleton about 15 feet in length. Several more graves containing skeletons of giants were unearthed in the same area.[20]

Recently, one Jonathan Grey wrote: "On May 13, 2004, a Muslim newspaper in Bangladesh reported that the skeletal remains of a giant human were found by ARAMCO petroleum explorers in Saudi Arabia... Saudi religious officials were concerned that the discovery could somehow contradict part of the Koran, thereby helping propagate Christianity, so they sent in the Muawwain, their notorious religious police to silence the matter... I received an e-mail from a person in the Saudi oil industry who wishes to remain nameless. He told me that he was working as a technician with the team that found the skeleton. The

skeleton was indeed of a giant human, and there was a police cover-up. He managed to copy one of the photos taken at the excavation site from a digital camera to his laptop just before the police came and took all the cameras... (he wants the world to see the truth of what was found in the desert... the skeleton in this photo stood between 15 and 20 feet tall – in line with what we would expect from Biblical research..."[21]

The giant's skull is bigger than the body of the man sitting beside it.

Were these giants mutant humans, or were they the offspring of the Biblical "giants after the Flood"?

Giant steps for men? In the ruins of Tiahuanaco, an ancient city 13,000 feet high in the Andes Mountains of Bolivia, visitors can still see enormous stone stairways that appear to have been made for a people of gigantic stature. We read in *The World's Last Mysteries*, "it is easy to believe in the Indian legend that the city was built by a race of giants."[22]

One Semitic legend says Adam stood over 15 feet tall. In this modern-day, we still have a few giants in out midst. Are they somehow related to the Nephilim?

Capt. Martin Bates and wife Anna, then the world's tallest married couple, posed for a photograph with a friend in 1878.

Chang, the Chinese giant, towers over his wife and a Western visitor.

DNA-determined descent

Are all human beings descended from just one man and one woman? Genetic anthropology seems to have found the answer. This new field stirred the public mind in 1987, when scientists announced that mitochondrial DNA analysis showed that all living people today came from the same woman. Similar analysis of Y-chromosome DNA demonstrated that all human males are also descended from one male person. Did that conclusively prove that all people on earth came from Adam and Eve? No. The tests showed that the human male lived much later than the female. So, news headlines around the world bannered: "Adam and Eve Never Met!"

However, science writer Wendy Wippel put things in their proper perspective with her article "The History of the World in the Molecules of Life" in *Prophecy in the News* (December 2006). She explained: "Y-chromosome DNA is passed only from father to son; similarly, mitochondrial DNA is passed only from the mother to her offspring... What 'mitochondrial Eve' and 'Y-chromosome Adam' really represented are statistical entities called the Most Recent Common Ancestor, or MRCA, meaning the last shared relative... Since the males on the ark were Noah and his sons, all should have had identical Y-chromosomes. The four women, however (Mrs. Noah, Ham, Shem, and Japheth), ostensibly not related, would therefore trace their maternal lineages back to the Biblical Eve. The MRCA of the men, then, was Noah; but the MRCA of the maternal lineage was NOT Mrs. Noah, but Eve..."[23] The genetic tests, therefore, do not contradict, but actually reinforce the Biblical story! She added: "Y-chromosome studies proved conclusively that Arab and Jewish populations shared a MRCA, who, by genetic dating, lived about 4,000 years ago."[24] Abraham was born about 1996 B.C., and he fathered both Ishmael, the forefather of the Arabs, and Isaac, the ancestor of the Jews.

Curiously, Scripture seems to refer to DNA, on which the genetic code is written: *"Thine eyes did see my substance, yet being unperfect; and in thy book all my members were written, which in continuance were fashioned, when as yet there was none of them"* (Ps 139:16).

Peopling the planet

The Bible says that all the people in the world are descended from Noah's three sons – Shem, Ham, and Japheth. *"These are the families of the sons of Noah, after their generations, in their nations: and by these were the nations divided in the earth after the flood"* (Gen 10:32).

In accord with this, *Fausset's Bible Dictionary* says the human race consists of three great ethnological divisions: Semites, Aryans, and Turanians.[25] The Semites came from Shem, the Aryans from Japheth, and the Turanians from Ham. (In Persian, "Turan" refers to Turkestan, a vast region in Asia with no definite boundaries, stretching from Siberia in the north to Iran, Pakistan, India, and Tibet in the south.)

Genetic and linguistic data indicate one group of people (Semites) remained mostly in the Middle East. Another group (Japhethites) migrated west to Europe, as well as east to Central and Northeast Asia. A third group (Hamites) went south and westward into Africa and east along the coasts of Asia into the South Pacific.[26]

The Semites.

"These are the sons of Shem, after their families, after their tongues, in their lands, after their nations" (Gen 10:31). The name of Shem means "name" or "renown". His progeny mostly stayed in the East and Middle East, giving rise to the Semitic nations. The *Encarta Encyclopedia* tells us: "Semites, a term first used toward the end of the 18th century for peoples listed in the Bible (see Genesis 10:21-32) as descended from Shem, the eldest son of the biblical patriarch Noah... Ancient peoples grouped under this term include those who inhabited Aram, Assyria,

Babylonia, Canaan (including the Hebrews), and Phoenicia. Among modern peoples speaking Semitic languages are the Arabs and Jews, particularly in Israel."[27]

Apparently, only descendants who had been born and lived nearby were known to the Biblical writers and thus named in the Biblical record. The descendants of Shem remained in the areas around their homeland and are listed down to the great great great grandsons. The offspring of Ham who settled farther away are named down to the great grandsons with whom the enumeration stops. The children of Japheth, who strayed farthest from Mesopotamia, are named down to the grandsons only.

The Aryans.

"The sons of Japheth... By these were the isles of the Gentiles divided in their lands; every one after his tongue, after their families, in their nations..." (Gen 10:2a,5). Japheth's prophetic name means "to expand," thus "widespreading." This is amplified in Noah's prayer: *"May God extend the territory of Japheth"* (Gen 9:27, NIV). The *Encarta Encyclopedia* plainly states: "Japhetites, formerly a loose ethnographic designation for the Caucasian peoples of Europe and certain parts of Asia, supposed to be descended from Japheth, a son of the Old Testament patriarch Noah."[28]

According to researcher Tim Osterholm: "The Japhetic people are, in general, the peoples of India and Europe (Indo-European stock)... The descendants of Japheth migrated into Europe and parts of Central Asia. The Greeks, Romans, Spaniards, Celts, Scythians, and Medes were Japheth's descendants."[29] Nennius, an 8th century Roman historian, constructed a table of nations showing the descent of many European peoples from Japheth: Gauls, Goths, Bavarians, Saxons, Romans, Medes, Thracians, Scythians, Franks, Britons, Albans, Vandals, Burgundians, Lombards.[30]

Osterholm further explains: "The early Aryans knew Japheth as Djapatischta (chief of the race); Greeks referred to Japheth as Iapetos or Japetos; East Indians called him Iyapeti or Pra-Japati; Romans deified him by the name Ju-Pater or Jupiter. The Saxons perpetuated his name as Iafeth, subsequently transliterated as Sceaf... and recorded in their early genealogies as the son of Noah the forebear of their various peoples (Anglo-Saxon Chronicles). The variant Seskef was used by the early Scandinavians."[31]

The Turanians.

"These are the sons of Ham, after their families, after their tongues, in their countries, and in their nations..." (Gen 10:20). Ham's name

means "hot," "passionate," "burnt," or "dark." He is regarded as the ancestor of the Negroid, Australoid, and Mongoloid groups. The first Hamitic peoples were the Egyptians, Ethiopians, Canaanites, Phoenicians and Hittites. Hamites, according to the *World Book,* "are certain African peoples who live mainly in eastern, northern, and northeastern Africa, including parts of Eritrea, Ethiopia, the Sahara, and the Sudan."[32] Ham's other descendants appear to be the first to fill the earth. Tribes in Africa, Arabia and Asia, aboriginal groups in Australia, native Pacific Islanders, American Indians and Eskimos came from the children of Canaan, Cush, Mizraim and Phut.

Ham's eldest son Cush ("black") was the progenitor of the Cushites, Nubians, Ethiopians, Ghanaians, Africans, Bushmen, Pygmies, Australian Aborigines, New Guineans, and related groups. His second son Mizraim ("double straits") produced the Egyptians, Khemets, Copts, and related groups. His third son, Phut ("a bow"), sired the Libyans, Cyrenacians, Tunisians, Berbers, Somalians, Sudanese, North Africans, and related groups. His fourth son Canaan ("down low") begot the Mongols, Chinese, Tibetans, Japanese, Inuit or Eskimos, Native Americans, Vietnamese, Thais, Laotians, Khmers, Burmese, Malays, Indonesians, Filipinos, Polynesians, Melanesians, Chamorros, and other related groups.[33]

All the racial divisions and subdivisions from Noah, including their respective territories, Bible historian Luke tells us, had been preordained by God: *"And He has made from one blood every nation of men to dwell on all the face of the earth, and has determined their preappointed times and the boundaries of their dwellings"* (Acts 17:26, NKJV).

Many-hued humans

Scholars once believed that humans could be classified into three main races: Caucasoid; Negroid; and Mongoloid. These divisions roughly corresponded to Europe, Africa, and Asia, respectively. In the late 1700s German physician Johann Blumenbach proposed five varieties: Caucasian, Mongolian, Malayan, Ethiopian, and American. These races were identified with Europe, Asia, Australia and Oceania, Africa, and the Americas, respectively. Later, the groupings became popularly known as white, yellow, brown, black, and red races.[34]

Skin color is determined by the amount of melanin -- a black, dark brown, reddish-brown, or yellow pigment -- in the skin. The more melanin present, the darker the complexion. Melanin absorbs ultraviolet rays from the sun, leading many scientists to believe that skin color is an environmental adaptation that serves to protect the individual from sunburn and skin cancer caused by solar radiation.

The white men. The Japhethites were said to be specially noted for their fairness of skin. They inhabited the hill country east of the Tigris River before the construction of the Tower of Babel.[35] Skin color is lightest among northern Europeans, specially those who live around the Baltic Sea, becoming gradually darker toward southern Europe, the Mediterranean, the Middle East, and northern Africa.

The blacks. The descendants of Ham migrated to Africa and other hot countries, and became dark-skinned.

The skin is darkest in people who live in the tropical savannahs or treeless plains and deserts, where solar radiation is most intense. For this reason, indigenous peoples in tropical Africa, Australia, parts of India, and the South Pacific have very dark skin. On the other hand, African Pygmies and, to a lesser extent, other Africans living in forested areas have lighter skin color.

The yellow race. Evidence suggests that Ham's grandsons, Heth (Hittites/Cathay) and Sin (Sinites/China), were the ancestors of Chinese and Mongoloid stocks. "Hittite" in cuneiform appears as "Khittae," preserved in "Cathay" -- the old term for China north of the Yangtze River. Marco Polo called the country "Khitai."[37] Hittites from what is now central Turkey trekked eastward and settled among the Sinites. Together, they became the ancestors of the Asiatic peoples. Craniologists note that their skulls and high cheekbones are characteristically Mongoloid. Other links between the Hittites and Cathay include modes of dress, shoes with turned-up toes, and the custom of wearing their hair in a pigtail.[38]

Migrating all over the region and beyond, their descendants make up the present-day Mongoloid races in Asia and the Americas.

The brown people. The natives of the South Pacific islands have their roots in southern China. Before the Mongols became dominant in northern China, Negroid peoples had come in earlier from east Africa and the Sahara. A number of African cultures had ancient texts, as well as oral history and legends, of migrations to ancient China.

When Mongol groups migrated into southern China, an admixture of races and cultures resulted. Thus, the original population of the region is thought to have been a blend of Mongoloids and Negroids. Becoming skilled seafarers, they sailed into Polynesia and the surrounding areas, populating the islands of the South Pacific.

The "redskins." The aborigines of America were of only one stock: the Turanian. These include the Aztecs, the Mixtecs, the Zapotecs, the Plascaltecs, and the Mechoacans of Mexico.[39] Christopher Columbus recorded details about the Taíno people of the Caribbean islands, describing their olive- to copper-colored skin.

Native Central and South American populations lived in forest areas, where shadows from the trees considerably reduced their exposure to solar radiation. They thus have much lighter skin than other Turanians.

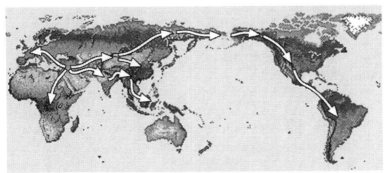

Migration paths of the descendants of brothers Japheth and Ham.

What was the original tongue?

There are today over 6,900 languages spoken in the world, not including dialects or regional variations. Philology, the science of the structure and development of language, identifies three parent groups of languages: Aryan, Semitic, and Turanian. The Aryan group is made up of all Indo-European languages. The Semitic group includes Hebrew, Arabic, Aramaic or Chaldean, Syriac, Ethiopic, Phoenician or Canaanite. The Turanian group comprises all Asiatic languages that are neither Semitic nor Indo-European.

Did languages evolve?

In his book *The Descent of Man* (1871), Charles Darwin linked the evolution of languages to biological evolution. It has not been proven. Today, most linguists reject the idea that simple languages evolve into more complex ones.[40] If languages evolve, the earliest languages ought to be the simplest. But studies reveal that ancient languages were more complex in syntax, case, gender, mood, voice, tense, verb form, inflection. Examples are Vedic Sanskrit, Linear B (early Greek), Greek, Latin. Evidently, languages tend to become simpler instead of more complex over time.[41]

Besides, children do not spontaneously learn to speak. Case studies of 36 children who grew up without human contact ("feral children") showed they only learned to speak a language later from other humans.[42] Animals also communicate, but not with language as we know it. Language must have a vocabulary and grammar. With grammar, a vocabulary of just a few words can express a variety of ideas. It thus looks like language did not develop among the first humans. Rather, they had been *taught* to speak a language.

The written word.

Archaeological discoveries suggest Sumerian word-pictures made about 3500 B.C. in Mesopotamia are the oldest form of writing.[43] After this, the earliest Egyptian hieroglyphics are believed to have been inscribed from around 3300 or 3200 B.C.[44] Hebrew letters have been patterned after a proto-Semitic alphabet, Phoenician, which appeared in the early 15th century B.C. All other alphabets currently in use, Semitic and non-Semitic, have been similarly derived from Phoenician.[45]

Elsewhere, other early forms of writing were Chinese ideographs incised on ox bones or tortoise shells -- oracular sayings by court diviners of the Shang dynasty dating from the 14th century B.C.[46] European writing systems also developed: Greek in approximately 1400 B.C.; but Latin came much later, sometime around 500 B.C.[47]

The original language.

The Creator and Adam, as well as Eve, spoke with each other using one language. The name of Adam ("reddish") came from the Hebrew word *adamah* ("red earth"), referring to the fact that the LORD created him from the earth. Adam called Eve by two "names": Woman (*ishah*) and Eve (*chavah*, "to live"). Each of the two words makes perfect sense only in Hebrew. Moreover, the Name of God that the first men knew (a short sentence in Hebrew) was also in the Hebrew tongue (Gen 4:26).

Hence, from Adam and Eve until the Tower of Babel, all the people spoke one common language – Hebrew, the original language.

Death of Hebrew. Isaiah had foretold the death of the Hebrew language. *"And thou shalt be brought down, and shalt speak out of the ground, and thy speech shall be low out of the dust, and thy voice shall be, as of one that hath a familiar spirit, out of the ground, and thy speech shall whisper out of the dust"* (Isa 29:4).

When Jews returned from Babylonian Exile in 536 B.C., they spoke a new language they had adopted during their captivity: Aramaic (Chaldee). When the first *Targums* (Aramaic translations of the Hebrew Scriptures) were written, Hebrew was called *leshon kodesh* ("the sacred tongue"), in contrast to Aramaic, which was used in ordinary speech.[48,49] Scholars and rabbis continued to use Hebrew until about 200 A.D., as evidenced in the Dead Sea Scrolls from the 200s B.C. and the *Mishnah*, a collection of Jewish laws written between 70 and 200 A.D.[50]

Revival of Hebrew. Two other prophets, though, prophesied the revival of Hebrew. God said through Zephaniah: *"For then I will restore* to the peoples a pure language, That they all may call on the name of the LORD, To serve Him with one accord" (Zeph 3:9, NKJV). And Jeremiah: "Thus says the LORD of hosts, the God of Israel: "They shall again use this speech in the land of Judah and in its cities, when I bring back their captivity: 'The LORD bless you, O home of justice, and mountain of holiness!" (Jer 31:23, NKJV).

Late in the 19th century, Lithuanian-born Jewish scholar Eliezer ben-Yehuda (d. 1922) began efforts to revive the "dead" Hebrew language. Starting with some 7,000 words originally used by the priests in Temple worship, he had to coin about 4,000 new words from Biblical roots for modern terms, such as fountain pen, airplane, etc.[51] In 1881 ben-Yehuda immigrated to Palestine, where four years later he published a magazine dedicated to the revival of Hebrew. In 1910 he began work on his *Complete Dictionary of Ancient and Modern Hebrew*. Its 17 volumes were posthumously completed in 1959.[52]

The revived Hebrew language serves as a powerful unifying factor for the millions of Jews, speaking many different languages, who have returned, and are still returning, to Israel after nearly 2,000 years of *diaspora* all over the globe. In 1948 *Ivrit*, or modern Hebrew, became the official language of Israel.

Remains of the tower

Was there really a Tower of Babel? The *Atlas of the Bible* states that the name of the tower in Sumerian was *Etemenanki*, meaning the "building of the foundation-platform of heaven and earth." This was identified with the temple of the Babylonian god Marduk Esagila, "the building whose top is in heaven." In Iraq, archeologist Robert Kodewey excavated a structure believed to be the foundation of the Tower of Babel. It lies beneath a more recent ziggurat supposedly built by Hammurabi in the 19th century B.C.[53]

Author Grant Jeffrey says the tower, whose base was 460 feet by 690 feet, reached a height of some 275 feet (27 stories) in its unfinished state. "The remains of the Tower of Babel are vitrified (melted to form a kind of rough glass) which indicates that God used a huge amount of heat to destroy this tower." Some of the clay bricks are still visible, but the ruins have been reduced to some 150 feet above the plain, with a circumference of about 2,300 feet.[54]

There are records of the tower's restoration by Esarhaddon in 681-665 B.C. Cuneiform inscriptions found in the ruins of Babylon recorded that Nebuchadnezzar (630?-562 B.C.) rebuilt the base of the tower in honor of the gods. He referred to it in Chaldean as *Barzippa*, meaning "tongue-tower," but also called it the "temple of the spheres." He resurfaced the lowest platform with gold, silver, cedar, and fir on top of clay bricks with his royal seal. Cuneiform inscriptions read in part: "...this edifice, the house of the seven lights of the earth, the most ancient monument of Borsippa. A former king built it (they reckon 42 ages), but he did not complete its head. Since a remote time, people had abandoned it, without order expressing their words."[55]

Herodotus visited the site in 460 B.C.: "The temple is a square

building, two furlongs each way, with bronze gates, and was still in existence in my time; it has a solid central tower, one furlong square, with a second erected on top of it and then a third, and so on up to eight. All eight towers can be climbed by a spiral way running round the outside... On the summit of the topmost tower stands a great temple..."[56] Iraqi president Saddam Hussein also

Aerial view of the remains of the supposed Tower of Babel near Babylon in present-day Iraq.

restored the ancient ziggurat as a symbol of the neo-Babylonian character of his regime.

Chinese memories.

Memory of the Tower of Babel is preserved in Chinese characters. The ideograph for "united" is made up of the symbols for "man," "one," and "mouth" (language?). When "grass" (or "hay" for strengthening bricks) is attached to these, the word "undertake" results. Adding "clay" (the basic component for brick), we get the character for "tower."

Mankind	One	Mouth	**United**	Grass	**Undertake**	Clay	**TOWER**

人 + 一 + 口 = 合 + 卄 = 荅 + 土 = 塔

Characters "man," "one" and "mouth"/"person" mean "united." With "grass," meaning becomes "to undertake." "Clay" added (to make brick) forms "tower."

The World Population

Did all the people in the world today – some 7 billion – come from just three couples after the Flood: Shem, Ham, Japheth, and their respective wives? (Excluded from the reckoning are Noah and his wife, to whom no further children are attributed in Scripture.)

Prof. Henry M. Morris (*The Biblical Basis for Modern Science,* 1984) did a study, based on the following assumptions:

- Mankind made a fresh start from just one couple about 4,300 years ago. (Actually four couples.)
- They and their descendants produced an average of only 2.5 children per family per generation, taking into account deaths from diseases, accidents, violence, famine, etc. (The average number of children per family cannot be 2 or less, as it would result in zero growth or even a decrease.)
- There was a new generation every 43 years, on the notion that there were 10 generations from Ephraim to Joshua over 430 years (1 Chron 7:20-27). (We now know, however, that human life spans were on a diminishing scale from Shem to Joshua. Besides, there were only 225 years from 1716 B.C., when Joseph, Ephraim's father, had a wife, to 1491 B.C., when Joshua left Egypt with Moses in the Exodus.)

Despite the inaccurate premises on at least three points, Morris's calculations show that the world population, over the next 100 generations from Noah (4,300 years), would have grown to roughly 5.5 billion by the mid-1990s.[57] Surprisingly, the result is a near-perfect match to the world population estimate for 1993: 5,436,358,000.

Morris's study indicates a world population growth rate of ½% per year.[58] Statistics show that the world population posted a 2% annual increase in the 1970s (average of 3.6 children per family). This has dropped to 1.3% in the early 2000s.[59]

World population growth.

On the next page is a World Population Growth graph, based on data from various sources, from 1700 B.C. to 2011.

In the graph, the line starting from 1700 B.C. (120 million people) rises gently through 1 B.C./1 A.D. to 1500 A.D. Then, suddenly, it curves steeply upward like a jet plane climbing in the sky through the 1700s, 1800s, 1900s, to 2011 (7 billion people), depicting the so-called "population explosion."

When the initial line is extended backward from the starting point in 1700 B.C., we go back to zero population (or just slightly above it) in or very close to the year 2348 B.C., the year of the Flood! It graphically illustrates that all the people in the world today descended from a very small group who survived the Deluge.

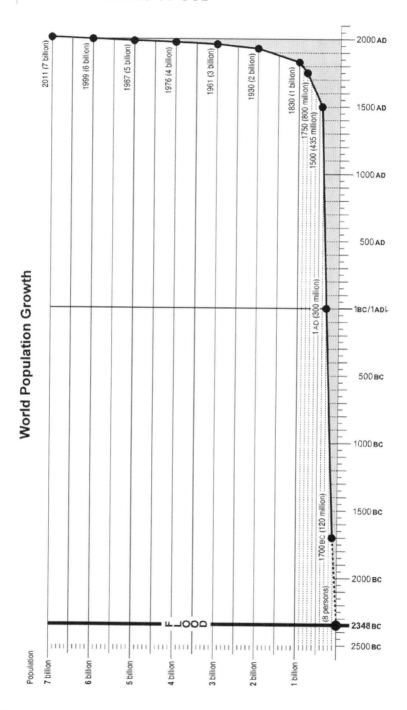

The nearly vertical line from 1830 (1 billion people) to 2011 (7 billion people), resembling the sheer wall of a cliff, gives one the uneasy feeling that it cannot continue rising at the same rate indefinitely -- a downturn seems inevitable, as well as imminent. When that happens, Biblical prophecy will be fulfilled.

World Population Estimates

Year	Years Elapsed	World Pop.	Increase
2348 BC		8	
1700 BC	648	120,000,000[1]	120,000,000
1 AD	1,700	300,000,000[2]	180,000,000
1500	1,500	435,000,000[3]	135,000,000
1750	250	800,000,000[4]	365,000,000
1830	80	1,000,000,000[5]	200,000,000
1880	50	1,500,000,000[6]	500,000,000
1930	50	2,000,000,000[4]	500,000,000
1950	20	2,406,000,000[5]	406,000,000
1961	11	3,000,000,000[5]	594,000,000
1971	10	3,706,000,000[5]	706,000,000
1976	5	4,000,000,000[6]	294,000,000
1982	6	4,585,000,000[7]	585,000,000
1987	5	5,000,000,000[7]	415,000,000
1993	6	5,436,358,000[2]	436,358,000
1999	6	6,000,000,000[8]	563,642,000
2004	5	6,350,480,000[9]	350,480,000
2011	7	7,000,000,000[10]	649,520,000

[1]*BHS Bible Study Aids*; [2]*Encarta Encyclopedia* 2004; [3]*Dorling-Kindersley Encyclopedia* 1999; [4]*Encyclopedia Britannica* 2009; [5]*Collier's Year Book* 1999/United Nations; [56]*Prophecy in the News*, Aug. 2005, p.3; [7]Population Reference Bureau; [8]*Encarta Encyclopedia* 2004/U.N.; [89]*World Book* 2005; [910]U.N. 2011.

Man-made marvels

How the Great Pyramid and other enormous structures had been built remains some of the greatest unsolved mysteries of the world. Even with the most advanced machinery and state-of-the-art engineering know-how, experts claim no construction company today can duplicate the feats of the ancient builders.

The Great Pyramid. Giza was far from the known quarries of the period. How were over two million blocks of stone weighing 2.5-20 tons each transported? It has been suggested that logs were used as rollers under the stone blocks. But there were no wooded areas near the desert site. Hundreds of thousands of workers would have been needed to build the Pyramid over many years. (In comparison, Solomon built the much smaller Temple in Jerusalem with 183,859 workers in 7½ years.) Yet, under the hot sands around the Great Pyramid, no dried up human wastes have been found.

The penchant for pyramid-building spread after the Tower of Babel as the people dispersed in all directions to fill the earth. Egypt has about 90 pyramids, but several hundred smaller pyramids can be found across Central and South America.[60]

Colossal constructions. In Lebanon's Bekaa Valley near Beirut, the ruins of the huge temples at Baalbek have 70-foot-high columns, some of the biggest ever used. The local people have an oral tradition that, in pre-Roman times the stones were quarried in Egypt, floated across the Mediterranean, then hauled over the mountains to

A leftover block of temple stone at Baalbek near Beirut. A man sits atop the edge of the block, while another leans on it below.

the site. How did the builders do it? One leftover block measures 14 feet by 13 feet by 70 feet, weighing over 1,000 tons!

A world away, in the ruined city of Tiahuanaco in the Bolivian Andes, stands the massive Gateway to the Sun, hewn from a single piece of rock! Other blocks of stone measure more than a foot thick and as large as 26 feet by 26 feet, weighing up to 100 tons apiece. These had been transported from a quarry almost 100 kilometers (60 miles) away, over mountainous terrain without roads, and without the use of wheels. A priest who had lived with the local people wrote: "The great stones one sees at Tiahuanaco were carried through the air to the sound of a trumpet."[61]

Sound levitation? In the book *The Cycles of Heaven*, authors Playfair and Hill wrote about Tibetan monks levitating blocks of stone in a ceremony performed with drums and trumpets.[62] Tibetan experts Linaver, Spalding, and Huc also wrote about sound levitation. Engineer Henry Kjelson, in his book *The Lost Techniques,* reported an eyewitness account complete with geometric and geodetic measurements by a Swedish doctor who then worked for the English Scientific Society – a Dr. Jarl, who reportedly went to Tibet in 1939 to treat a high-ranking lama. His account:

About 250 meters up a cliff, monks on a platform in front of a cave were building a wall. In the meadow below, 250 meters from the cliff, lay a 1 meter by 1½ meters polished stone slab, with a bowl-like cavity in the middle, about 1 meter across and 15 cm deep. A block of stone drawn by yaks was placed in the cavity. Nineteen musicians around the stone slab, in an arc of 90° and a distance of 63 meters, began playing their drums and trumpets. The other monks present sang and chanted prayers, gradually increasing the tempo. In 5 minutes, as the din heightened, the stone block began to rock and sway, then floated in the air towards the platform up the cliff, landing on the platform after 3 minutes. The monks brought new blocks and repeated the process again and again, raising 5 to 6 blocks per hour on a parabolic flight track approximately 500 meters long and 250 meters high.

Fearing he was a victim of mass-psychosis, Dr. Jarl twice filmed the process. Unfortunately, his employer, the English Scientific Society, confiscated the films and declared them classified.[63]

The walls of Jericho. The Israelites, too, were able to move large blocks of stone by the power of sound. Laying siege to the walled city of Jericho in 1451 B.C., they received instructions from the LORD on how to use this power to conquer the city. *"'Have seven priests carry trumpets of rams' horns in front of the ark. On the seventh day, march around the city seven times, with the priests blowing the trumpets'... When the trumpets sounded, the people shouted, and at the sound of the trumpet, when the people gave a loud shout, the wall collapsed; so every man charged straight in, and they took the city"* (Josh 6:1-5,20; NIV). The elements are almost exactly the same: trumpet blasts and loud voices, but without drums. However, in Jericho, instead of making the stone blocks rise in the air, the Israelites made them fall to the ground.

"Acoustic levitation." The same principle, scientifically called "acoustic levitation," is now being tested in laboratories for research and industrial purposes. Objects are suspended by means of acoustic radiation pressure from intense sound waves. The Otsuka Lab even demonstrated that materials can be levitated acoustically without sounds audible to humans. In 1987 Dr. David Deak built an acoustic levitation chamber for NASA that successfully simulated the micro-gravity conditions inside the space shuttle during orbit.[64]

Some levitators are now commercially available, being particularly useful in containerless processing, in view of the small size and resistance of microchips, as well as the necessity for extremely high purity in some materials and precision in chemical reactions not possible in containers.

Although the heaviest object lifted by acoustic levitation weighed no more than a few kilos, theoretically there is no limit to what the power of sound can raise, given the necessary amount of sound vibrations.

Did the ancient builders of the Great Pyramid and other pyramids, the temples at Baalbek, the city of Tiahuanaco, and other enormous edifices, know the incredible power of sound?

Technologically advanced ancients

Many ancient artifacts being found today display startling, yet unmistakable signs of advanced scientific know-how in the distant past. They look like prehistoric prototypes of technologically sophisticated systems modern man has developed only recently in many fields.

Astronomy. Around 4,000 years ago, the Mayans of Central America built astronomical observatories, such as the one that can still be seen in Chichen Itza in the Yucatan Peninsula. These ancient people of Mexico calculated the length of the solar year as 365.242 days (modern datum: 365.2422 days).[65] They also devised a mechanism that accurately forecast astronomical events, such as solstices and equinoxes.

Book printing. Job, who lived about 4,000 years ago, gives us ideas on how knowledge was preserved and disseminated in his time. *"Oh that my words were now written! oh that they were printed in a book! That they were graven with an iron pen and lead in the rock for ever!"* (Job 19:23-24). From the verse we learn that people wrote with iron pens and lead. Books with printed pages seem to be well-known.

Electrical power. In 1936 near Baghdad, Iraq, workers dug up a small 2,000-year-old Parthian earthenware vase with a copper cylinder containing an iron rod soldered with a tin-lead alloy and bonded together with asphalt. German archeologist Wilhelm Konig speculated:

 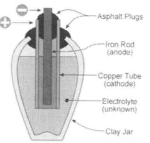

Filled with an acidic solution, the artifact had served as a rudimentary electric battery! In 1940 Willard Gray, an engineer

"Baghdad Battery": a 2,000-year-old clay jar with copper cylinder containing an iron rod soldered with a tin-lead alloy and bonded with asphalt. It was able to generate electricity with grape juice.

with General Electric in the U.S., made a replica that when filled with a copper sulfate solution easily produced half a volt of electricity. In the 1970s, West German Arne Eggebrecht made his own "Baghdad battery" filled with fresh grape juice. He was able to electroplate a silver statuette with gold![66,67]

Aeronautics. In 1898 a small winged object made of wood was found in a 2,100-year-old tomb near Saqqara, Egypt. It was stored with other "wooden bird models" in the basement of the Cairo Museum of Antiquities. In 1969, Egyptologist Khalil Messiha realized that its slightly curved 7-inch overhead wing, tapered body, and vertical tailfin were those of a model airplane called a push-glider. He said: "It still sailed easily through the air with only the slightest flick of the hand." A committee created by the Egyptian Ministry of Culture reported that the design incorporated concepts used by modern aviation engineers. A fully-loaded aircraft with the same proportions could stay airborne at speeds as slow as 45 mph.

Halkatha, a Babylonian text, recorded: "To operate a flying machine is a great privilege... Knowledge of flying is most ancient, a gift of the gods of old for saving lives." *Sifr'ala of Chaldea*, another ancient text, contains a fragmentary, but detailed instructions on how to build and operate a flying machine. It provides specific information on copper and graphite parts, and describes the effects of wind resistance on stability.

Chinese records dated around 2258 B.C. tell of how Emperor Shun built an aircraft and used a parachute to escape an attempt on his life. Some 450 years later, another Chinese emperor, Chen Tang, made and successfully flew a "flying chariot," but had it destroyed after the flight to keep its secrets from falling into the wrong hands.[68]

Computer technology. In 1900 archeologists salvaged artifacts from a Greek ship that sank around 65 B.C. near the Mediterranean island of Antikythera. Half a century later, a Yale University professor realized that one puzzling piece of instrument was actually a 2,000-year-old mechanical computer – fitted

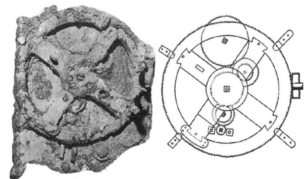

A 2,000-year-old mechanical computer, salvaged from a Greek ship that sank about 65 B.C. Fitted with dials, brass instruction plates, and bronze gears, it appears to have been used to compute the motions of the sun, moon, and stars.

with dials, brass instruction plates, and some 20 bronze gears. The device appears to have been used to compute the motions of the sun, moon, and stars![69]

Radio communication. A 1,000-pound slab of solid crystalline rock, found in a tower in the ruins of the ancient Mayan city of Palenque in Mexico, is said to have been used by the priest-kings of the lost civilization to send and receive messages.[70] A simple crystal radio receiver, such as those boys used to assemble in school, consists of a piece of silicon crystal, a small metal wire to detect radio waves, and an earphone. Though able to produce only a low volume sound, a crystal radio works on just the power of the radio waves it receives, with no need for electric power.

The breastplate God commanded the Israelite high priest to wear, serving as a pouch for the oracular Urim and Thummim used for making decisions, had 12 gemstones, many of which were crystalline. *"Then mount four rows of precious stones on it. In the first row there shall be a ruby, a topaz and a beryl; in the second row a turquoise, a sapphire and an emerald; in the third row a jacinth, an agate and an amethyst; in the fourth row a chrysolite, an onyx and a jasper"* (Ex 28:17-20a NIV). Josephus believed the answers to the high priest's questions were indicated by the precious stones in the breastplate.[71] Was it a crystal radio set that received messages from God?

Medical sciences. Trepanning, or brain surgery by cutting a hole in the cranium, seems to have been practiced by medicine men of the ancient Inca civilization. Skulls with small partially healed circular incisions have been found in the remains of their jungle-covered cities.

In dentistry, the "lost wax" method used by modern-day dentists for making artificial tooth crowns, appears to have been employed by the ancient Aztecs of Mexico at least 500 years ago.

"Nothing new under the sun."

Solomon said around 1,000 years ago that all things had already been thought of and made before his time. *"What has been will be again, what has been done will be done again; there is nothing new under the sun. Is there anything of which one can say, "Look! This is something new"? It was here already, long ago; it was here before our time"* (Eccl 1:9-10, NIV). What we think are modern discoveries and inventions are probably just recycled concepts from antiquity.

The standards of Israel

In the wilderness after the Exodus, the LORD told Moses: *"The Israelites are to camp around the Tent of Meeting some distance from it, each man under his standard with the banners of his family."* (Num 2:2, NIV). God divided the twelve tribes into four groups of three tribes each, with a lead tribe heading each group. Thus, although each tribe had a standard of its own, they gathered around the standards of their respective lead tribes. The three-tribe group led by Judah was assigned in the east (Num 2:3-9); the group of Reuben, in the south (Num 2:10-16); that of Ephraim (who had replaced his father Joseph), in the west (Num 2:18-24); and that of Dan in the north (Num 2:25-31). (The tribe of Levi, which served in the Tabernacle at the center of the camp, was replaced in the groupings by that of Manasseh, Joseph's other son.)

Prophetic positions. Some eschatology teachers suspect that the Antichrist might come from the tribe of Dan, because it traditionally occupied the north in the wilderness, as well as in the land of Israel. The Israelites named directions from a position facing the rising sun in the east, regarding the north to the left as the seat of gloom and darkness, in contrast to the bright and sunny south to the right. So, the hand of strength and blessing, the right, indicated the south, but the hand of deception and treachery (Judg 3:15,21), the left, designated the north.[72]

In the end-time prophecy of the Son of God judging the nations, He will gather the sheep, the righteous ones, at His right hand -- the place of honor – but the goats, the unrighteous ones, at His left -- the place of condemnation [Matt 24:31-46].) In an apocalyptic event wherein the servants of God are sealed in their foreheads, the tribe of Dan is mysteriously missing from the list of the tribes of Israel (Rev 7:1-8).

Emblems of the 4 lead tribes.

Each tribal standard had an emblem based on Jacob's deathbed prophecies to his twelve sons. Let us scrutinize those of the four lead tribes. Jacob described Reuben as *"unstable as water"*; Judah as *"a lion's whelp"*; Dan as *"a serpent by the way"*; and Joseph as *"a fruitful bough"* (Gen 49:3-4,9,17,22). Accordingly, the ancient emblem of the standard of Judah was a lion; that of Reuben, a man; that of Ephraim, an ox; and that of Dan, an eagle.[73,74]

Except for the emblem of Judah, the others need to be explained. The man's head on the standard of Reuben was that of a water-bearer. The ox or bull on Ephraim's banner implied fruitfulness, based on the saying "let out freely the ox" (Isa 32:20) – that is, let the ox roam freely in a land of abundance, where there is no worry about the ox foraging in the grainfields.[75] The eagle on Dan's standard was formerly depicted in a life-and-death battle with a serpent. The serpent had been removed, leaving only the eagle. In fulfillment of prophecy, however, over time the eagle was replaced with a serpent.

Angels around the Almighty. Incredibly, the four emblems were also the faces of the angels Ezekiel saw with God about 900 years after the Exodus. *"Also out of the midst thereof came the likeness of four living creatures. And this was their appearance; they had the likeness of a man. And every one had four faces... As for the likeness of their faces, they four had the face of a man, and the face of a lion, on the right side: and they four had the face of an ox on the left side; they four also had the face of an eagle.* (Ezek 1:5-6,10).

And some 1,000 years later, near the end of the 1ˢᵗ century A.D., John saw angels with the same four faces around the throne of God in heaven! *"And before the throne there was a sea of glass like unto crystal: and in the midst of the throne, and round about the throne, were four beasts full of eyes before and behind. And the first beast was like a lion, and the second beast like a calf, and the third beast had a face as a man, and the fourth beast was like a flying eagle.* (Rev 4:6-7).

Quadrants of the zodiac. The four figures are also in the four quadrants of the zodiac, the great circle of constellations in the sky. Aquarius, the water-bearer, and Leo, the lion, were anciently the zodiacal constellations of the winter and summer solstices; Taurus, the ox or bull, was that of the spring equinox; and Aquila, the eagle, is by the autumnal equinox, with Serpens, the snake it is battling.[76] They occupy the same celestial quarter as Scorpio, the scorpion, which is Biblically paired with the serpent in terms of deadliness (Deut 8:15; Luke 10:19).

Precession of the equinoxes

Every 2,150 years or so, the sun's position at the spring equinox appears to retrograde or move backward into a different sign of the *Mazzaroth*, beginning a new age. The 25,800-year cycle is called the "precession of the equinoxes." (An *equinox* [Latin for "equal night"] is one of the two times each year when the sun is precisely above the equator, and day and night are of equal length all over the globe – around March 21 [spring equinox] and September 23 [autumn equinox].) We are now in transition from the Age of Pisces to the Age of Aquarius. Let us review the ages from the creation of Adam.

Age of **Taurus** the Bull (ca. 4000-2000 B.C.). The bull or ox left a strong imprint on men in the form of the winged bull of Nineveh; the bull-god Apis of Egypt; the sacred bull of Mithra in Persia; the bull-headed Minotaur in Crete; the first letter *aleph* of the Semitic alphabet, from the hieroglyph for a bull. The astrological symbol for Taurus is a circle with a crescent on top. The crescent resembles a boat (Noah's Ark) on the circular figure of the earth. (Noah's Flood occurred during the

Age of Taurus.) The memory of the bull lingered among the Israelites, who made the golden calf at Mount Sinai.

Age of **Aries** the Ram (ca. 2000-1 B.C.). During this period, Amun was the ram-god of the leading Egyptian cult. When Abraham was to sacrifice his son Isaac on God's command, a substitute ram appeared. Animal sacrifices, sheep and rams foremost among them, were instituted at the Tabernacle in the wilderness and, later, at the Temple in Jerusalem. At the end of this age Christ, the Lamb of God, was born.

Age of **Pisces** the Fish (ca. 1 A.D.-2000 A.D.). Christ made disciples of fishermen to become fishers of men. He miraculously fed 5,000 men with two fish, and 4,000 more with a few small ones. The fish was the secret sign of the early Christian church; its password was the Greek word for fish, *ICHTHUS*, also an acronym for *Iesou Christou Theou Huios Soter* ("Jesus Christ, God's Son, Savior"). Christian bishops adopted the miters worn by the priests of Dagon (sun-fish god of the Philistines and Assyrians), a hat in the shape of a fish head with its mouth open. Pisces, depicted as two fish, a big one and a small one, prefigures the spiritual salvation of two groups of people.

Age of **Aquarius** the Water-Bearer (ca. 2000-4000 A.D.). We are now at its threshold. Astrologer Cheiro said the first vibrations of the Aquarian Age commenced about 1762 A.D., but the "cusp" or transition may last some 700 years.[77] The French National Observatory announced in the late 1990s that the Age of Aquarius would begin in 2011. Aquarius, portraying God pouring His Spirit on earth, will rule over the Millennium – the 1,000-year period of peace on earth.

Star of apostate Israelites?

In both the OT and the NT, it looks like some Israelites worshipped stars. The LORD said through Isaiah: *"But ye have borne the tabernacle of your Moloch and Chiun your images, the star of your god, which ye made to yourselves"* (Amos 5:26). When invaders took the Israelites to Assyria and Media in 721 B.C., they brought along the star of their god.

"You have lifted up the shrine of Molech and the star of your god Rephan, the idols you made to worship" (Acts 7:43a, NIV).

Chiun and Rephan were one and the same.[78] The two names came from the same word, the difference probably due to a transcription error. *Kaph* (כ, K), the initial of the word "Chiun" (KVN) might have been read as *resh* (ר, R), resulting in "Rephan" (RVN). The word should have been transliterated *Kaivan*, which was planet Saturn among the ancient Arabs and Syrians.[79] In Persia, Saturn was called Kaivan or Kevan.[80]

The star-god Saturn? The Phoenicians worshipped Saturn as their chief god. Eusebius quoted Philo, in his redaction of the lost Phoenician

History of Sanchuniathon, that "Kronos (*El*) was deified in the star Saturn."[81] Amos and Stephen linked the star to the worship of Moloch ("king"), god of the Ammonites and Phoenicians. In turn, Moloch is intimately connected to sun-worship and the golden calf. The sun rose in the sign of Taurus, the solar bull, at the spring equinox. According to the rabbis, Moloch's brass statue had a human body with the head of an ox. And, since the sun was the king star, Moloch the "king" was himself the sun. In Carthage, Moloch was known as Saturn. The correlation between the sun and Saturn (Kronos) probably arose from the two being both regarded as symbols of time.[82]

Saturday and the Sabbath. The weekly seventh-day Sabbath falls on Saturday, named after the planet Saturn. Conversely, the Jews anciently called Saturn *Shabbatai*, after the Sabbath.[83] Probably for this reason, the Greeks and Romans identified Israel with the mythological god Kronos and Saturn, respectively.[84]

In Chaldee, Saturn is pronounced "Satur," but is written with only four letters: S-T-U-R. The name, spelled thus, contains exactly the dreaded number in the Apocalypse.[85]

$$
\begin{array}{rcl}
S &=& 60 \\
T &=& 400 \\
U &=& 6 \\
R &=& \underline{200} \\
&& 666
\end{array}
$$

The Star of David. A hexagram or six-pointed star, formed by two intertwined equilateral triangles, first appeared in the 960s B.C. in the time of Solomon.[86] It was called the "Seal of Solomon" and was used in occult practices.[87] It was also known as the "Talisman of Saturn."[88] In the late 200s A.D., a six-pointed star became known as the "Star of David" or "Shield of David" (*Magen David*).[89] It began to be identified with Judaism in the 14th century.[90,91]

The Star of David has become the universal symbol of Judaism since the 17th century, as well as the emblem of Zionism since 1897.[92] The six-pointed star is today on the flag of Israel, in synagogues, on Jewish ritual objects, and on insignias of various organizations.

Constellations coming closer

If the universe is expanding and the galaxies are racing away from each other, why do some stars and constellations appear to be actually coming closer to Earth? One well-known example is the Andromeda Galaxy in Pisces, the secret symbol of the Christian church.

Arcturus the Bear, the fourth brightest star in the night sky, is part of Bootes the Herdsman or Shepherd, a constellation in Virgo, the Virgin. Just 36 light-years away, Arcturus is moving towards our planet at a rate of 3 miles (5 km) per second[93] – that is over 30 million miles or more than 50 million kilometers per year!

The Pleiades is a cluster of seven stars on the shoulder of Taurus the Bull. Before the invention of the telescope, only six stars could be seen clearly with the naked eye. Incredibly, the ancients knew that the constellation had seven stars! *"Seek him that maketh the seven stars and Orion..."* (Amos 5:8a). The brightest star in the Pleiades is Alcyone, which means "the center." Some ancient astronomers thought that the Pleiades, and particularly Alcyone, was the center of the universe.[94] Johann Heinrich von Mädler (1794-1874), German astronomer at the University of Dorpat, Estonia, proposed the central-sun theory of our galaxy, with the Pleiades as the center of the Milky Way.[95] He "discovered that the whole solar system is moving forward round Alcyone, the brightest star in Pleiades... they draw our whole planetary system and sun round them at the rate of 422,000 miles a day..."[96] That is 154 million miles or 246 million km per year, nearly 5 miles or 8 kilometers per second!

Curiously, some of the constellations approaching Earth are those named specifically in the Bible. *"Which maketh Arcturus, Orion, and Pleiades, and the chambers of the south"* (Job 9:9). (Orion, "the hunter," is in Taurus the Bull.) Are the seven heavens in the seven stars of the Pleiades? Is the seventh heaven, the heaven of heavens, where God's throne is, in the brightest star Alcyone – "the center"?

Visitors from the stars?

Are there humans, humanoids, or even other forms of intelligent life out there in the vastness of space? Servants of pharaohs and soldiers of Alexander told of "shields" in the sky. Medieval monks reported flying vessels. In modern times, H.G. Wells' book, *The War of the Worlds,* perked public interest in 1898. Its radio dramatization caused panic in 1938, when many Americans thought Martians had actually invaded New Jersey. Since then extraterrestrial life has become de rigueur in popular science fiction books, comics, TV series, movies, video games.

UFOs and ETs.

Countless news reports, articles, and books about close encounters -- sightings, communication, even abductions – with unidentified flying objects (UFOs) and extraterrestrials (ETs) have been written since the mid-20th century. The first widely publicized UFO sighting was in 1947, when American businessman Kenneth Arnold, flying a small plane near Mount Rainier in Washington, claimed seeing nine crescent-shaped objects flying at the incredible speed of several thousand mph. In the newspaper report, Arnold said they moved "like saucers skipping on water," giving birth to the term "flying saucer."[97]

Over 90% of reported UFO's have been dismissed as bright planets, stars, meteors, aircraft, missiles, satellites, weather balloons, auroras, peculiar clouds, searchlights, aerial flares, kites, birds, insect swarms. Radar sightings are more reliable, but they do not distinguish between artificial objects and meteor trails, ionized gas, rain, or thermal discontinuities in the atmosphere.[98] Recollections of abductions are highly doubtful, because of the use of hypnosis to obtain forgotten, or probably imaginary, information.[99] Many psychologists suggest that the temporary immobility and sensation of being watched experienced by "abductees" are the effects of a common occurrence called "sleep paralysis."[100]

Close encounter of the dead kind. The most celebrated close encounter with UFOs and ETs is the alleged crash of an alien spacecraft in New Mexico and the retrieval of the vessel and its dead crew.

The crash allegedly took place on July 3, 1947. Rancher Mac Brazel found the wreckage a few days later and notified Sheriff Geo. Wilcox. Irrigation water surveyor Grady Barnett, as well as a group of archeologists and their students, also saw the debris field. A detail from the nearby Roswell Army Air Field, led by intelligence officer Major Jesse A. Marcel, recovered the partially-crushed saucer-shaped vehicle and four lifeless non-human bodies in and around it. The July 8, 1947, issue of the *Roswell Daily Record* blared: "RAAF Captures Flying Saucer on Ranch in Roswell Region." However, the newspaper made an abrupt turnaround the following day: "Gen. Ramey Empties Roswell Saucer." The news read: "An examination by the army revealed last night that the mysterious object found on a lonely New Mexico ranch was a harmless high altitude weather balloon – not a grounded flying disk."

Case closed? UFO researchers later pieced together an incredible picture: The creatures, with large hairless heads, huge slanted eyes, and long arms with hands of just four fingers, were wearing skin-tight suits with no visible fasteners. At the airfield, dozens of witnesses saw the actions taken to examine and preserve the bodies. Dr. Jesse Johnson, Roswell base pathologist, revealed the bodies weighed about 40 pounds each. They had heavy brow ridges; almond-shaped eyes without pupils; mere slits for ears, mouths, and noses unconnected to internal organs. They had no teeth, gastrointestinal tracts and alimentary canals, showing they did not eat to stay alive. Their skin, pinkish-gray with a mesh-like appearance, was tough and leathery. In lieu of blood, there was only a clear liquid. The bodies were packed in ice and flown to Fort Worth, Texas; later, to Wright Field in Dayton, Ohio.

Major Marcel is said to have brought home several broken parts of the saucer, which his wife and son handled -- a small construction beam with unknown purple lettering; a metal foil that returned to a smooth, flat shape after being crumpled; a paper-thin metal sheet that could not be bent or dented even with a hammer.[101]

"Project Blue Book." As sightings increased, in 1948 the U.S. Air Force initiated an investigation called "Project Sign." "Project Grudge" followed within a year. In 1952, "Project Blue Book" began at Wright-Patterson Air Force Base in Dayton, Ohio, to determine if UFOs posed a threat to national security. Out of 12,618 UFO cases, 701 (5.6%) were classified as "unexplained." The USAF also commissioned a study at the University of Colorado from 1966 to 1968. Scientists concluded that further study of UFOs would not produce any useful information about a security threat, and Project Blue Book ended in 1969.[102,103,104] In 1997 the Central Intelligence Agency (CIA) admitted hiding information about high-altitude spy planes -- the U-2A and SR-71. These had accounted for over 50% of the UFO sightings in the late 1950s and 1960s.[105]

From CETI to SETI.

In September 1971, 84 of the world's leading authorities in various fields converged at the Byurakan Astrophysical Observatory in Yerevan, Armenia, for a conference jointly sponsored by the U.S. National Academy of Sciences and the USSR's Akademiia nauk SSSR. The meet, called "Communication with Extraterrestrial Intelligence" (CETI), aimed to solve the Green Bank formula proposed by Frank Drake of Project Ozma, which attempted to detect radio signals from extraterrestrial civilizations in 1960. The formula was $N = R_* f_p n_e f_l f_i f_c L$, where:

N is the product showing the number of extant civilizations in the Milky Way Galaxy at or beyond our level of technological development;

R_* is the rate of star formation, averaged over the lifetime of the galaxy, in units of number of stars per year (astrophysics);

f_p is the fraction of stars which have planetary systems (astrophysics);

n_e is the mean number of planets within such planetary systems which are ecologically suited for life (astronomy and biology);

f_l is the fraction of such planets on which origin of life actually occurs (organic chemistry and biochemistry);

f_i is the fraction of such planets on which, after life arises, intelligence in some form develops (neurophysiology and evolution of advanced organisms);

f_c is the fraction of such planets on which the intelligent beings advance to a communicative stage (anthropology, archaeology, and history); and

L is the mean lifetime of such technical civilizations (psychology, psychopathology, history, politics, sociology, etc.).

Result? The world's best minds in their respective fields arrived at the consensus that there is only one technical civilization in the Milky Way Galaxy – the one on planet Earth.[106] As astronomer Carl Sagan once said, life on Earth is unique, "a miracle rather than a statistic."[107]

Despite the conclusion reached by CETI, a project called Search for Extraterrestrial Intelligence (SETI) at Palo Alto, California, continued. Clearly, however, the once highly confident "communication" plan (CETI) has been downgraded to "search" mode (SETI). Undeterred, astronomers at the Harvard/Smithsonian observatory began using the Million-channel Extra-Terrestrial Assay (META), a 26-meter, steerable Cassegrainian radio telescope, in 1985.[108]

Exercise in futility? What are the prospects of SETI? The nearest star system is Alpha Centauri, some 4.3 light years away. In the remote event that radio signals transmitted by intelligent beings are actually received from that sector of space, communication between them and us would require patience. An exchange of a "hi" and "hello" by radio signals traveling at the speed of light would take 8.6 years, assuming both parties respond promptly. Fair enough. However, farther out from the Earth the conversation could bore the parties to death, literally, since introductions alone would take hundreds or even thousands of years. Aldebaran, the brightest star in the constellation Taurus, is 130 light years away. Regulus, the brightest star in Leo, 150 light years. Spica, the brightest star in Virgo, more than 500 light years. Pleiades, nearly 800 light years. Orion, 3,000 light years. The Crab Nebula, 12,000 light years. And these handful are the nearest.

Space travel beyond our solar system may simply be no more than a pipe dream. Intergalactic journeys would have to be made at the speed of light, which is physically impossible. Light travels at the speed of, well, light, because photons have no mass. Hence, no physical object with mass, such as a spacecraft, can travel at the speed of light.

Referring to man, the Bible says God has *"appointed his bounds that he cannot pass"* (Job 14:5b) and has fixed *"the bounds of their habitation"* (Acts 17:26b). Job, in the first verse, speaks of time limits, while Luke, in the second, those of space. In the theory of relativity, time and space are interchangeable. So, the message is clear: there are space-time limits man cannot go beyond.

Demonic deception?

There is no reference to UFOs in Scriptures. The closest things to flying disks from outer space in the Bible are the flaming wheels that the prophets Daniel (Dan 7:9) and Ezekiel (Ezek 10:1-17) saw beneath the throne of God. If Medieval men saw ETs, what would they have called them? They did, and called them elves, gnomes, trolls, imps, etc.

Many reports describe UFOs as strange lights racing across the sky. Biblically, angels are lights (Jas 1:17, Heb 1:17). Satan can manifest as *"an angel of light"* (2 Cor 11:14). UFOs reportedly execute improbable aerial maneuvers, such as blinding acceleration to vanishing point and right-angle turns at fantastic speeds. According to the Bible, Satan is *"the prince of the power of the air"* (Eph 2:2), able to perform seemingly miraculous feats: *"Even him, whose coming is after the working of Satan with all power and signs and lying wonders"* (2 Thess 2:9).

Alien anatomy. Although humanoid, the Roswell ETs differed anatomically from humans -- with slits for ears, mouths, and noses unconnected to internal organs; and without respiratory, digestive, and excretory systems. How could any living organism live without breathing and eating? Alleged victims of abductions say ETs act like droids without minds of their own. Could they have a connection to the cases of mysterious cattle mutilations in the American West, where the eyes, tongues, genitals, and other organs of cows appear surgically removed with some kind of laser? Are the little gray aliens simply organically stuffed dummies or droids made from animal parts?

Occasionally reported directing the little ETs are reptilian or tall, blond-haired, Nordic-looking masters of seemingly great intelligence and beauty. This brings to mind the reptilian form of Satan, *"the dragon, that old serpent"* (Rev 20:2), formerly an angel whose *"heart became proud on account of your beauty, and you corrupted your wisdom because of your splendor"* (Ezek 28:17, NIV).

The image of God. Christ, on the other hand, *"is the image of the invisible God, the firstborn of every creature"* (Col 1:15; cf. 2 Cor 4:4, Heb 1:3). Man has also been created in the *"image"* and *"likeness"* of God (Gen 1:26-27). That image, as we have seen earlier, has countless instances of the divine proportion (1.618). ETs, from the way they look, do not have the divine proportion. This is of utmost importance, *"For whom he did foreknow, he also did predestinate to be conformed to the image of his Son, that he might be the firstborn among many brethren"* (Rom 8:29). God made Christ and man look alike, because the spiritually saved will become the younger brothers and sisters of His firstborn Son! Obviously, the strange looking ETs are unlikely candidates to become brethren of Christ.

Besides, without blood in their systems, the aliens cannot possibly be among the sinners for whom Christ substituted His own blood on the cross as a ransom or payment for sin.

Invaders or saviors? The ETs allegedly belong to two categories. One group consists of invaders who want to take over Earth and even the bodies of its human inhabitants. The second group is made up of do-gooders with a mission to save mankind from destroying itself in a nuclear holocaust, ecological devastation, or some other global calamity. Thus, if or when they eventually reveal themselves, they would be hailed as saviors! They would pre-empt the anticipated return of the Messiah. *"For false Christs and false prophets shall rise, and shall shew signs and wonders, to seduce, if it were possible, even the elect"* (Mark 13:22).

Some New Age cults nurture the idea that every inhabited planet in the cosmos has its own avatar or incarnated savior. Accordingly, Christ's mission of redemption is only for planet Earth. The Scriptures, though, declare that salvation through Christ is universal: *"And, having made peace through the blood of his cross, by him to reconcile all things unto himself; by him, I say, whether they be things in earth, or things in heaven"* (Col 1:20). The phrase *"things in heaven"* evidently means matters pertaining to God and the angels.

Extraterrestrial creators? Others, including prominent scientists like Francis Crick, believe that the seed of life came to Earth through ancient alien astronauts. ETs are therefore man's creators, just visiting the planet occasionally to check on the condition of their creation. In 1968, writer Erich Von Daniken (*Chariots of the Gods, Gods from Outer Space*) started broaching the idea that aliens must be the God of the Old Testament and man the product of an intergalactic experiment.

One self-declared contactee, Frenchman Claude Vorilhon (*Space Aliens Took Me to Their Planet*, 1975), allegedly renamed "Rael" ("light of the Elohim" or "Ambassador of the Elohiim"?), claims to have been told: "There is no God and no soul." With a following of 55,000 in 84 countries, he recently established an "embassy" in Israel in preparation for the return of their "creators" from outer space.

What does the Bible have to say about this? *"The fool hath said in his heart, There is no God"* (Ps 14:1a). *"And every spirit that confesseth not that Jesus Christ is come in the flesh is not of God: and this is that spirit of antichrist, whereof ye have heard that it should come; and even now already is it in the world"* (1 John 4:3).

10

Personal Names of God

*𝒯his is my name for ever,
and this is my memorial unto all generations"*

-- Exodus 3:15.

Do you pray to God? If you do, by what name do you invoke Him? The vast majority of people who worship the Judeo-Christian God or the "God" of a different religion simply call on "God."

The word "God" can be seen 4,442 times in the King James Version of the Bible – 3,089 in the OT and 1,353 in the NT. It came from the Teutonic *guth gut, gud;* Scandinavian *gudd;* Germanic *gott;* Dutch and Anglo-Saxon *gōd,* meaning "good" – denoting the divine beneficence to men of an unseen, but powerful supernatural Being. "God" is English for the Hebrew word *el,* which actually means "Strong or Mighty One." The term is sometimes extended as *elah, eloah,* or *eloha.* The plural form *elohim* is often rendered in English as the singular "God." *El* has been translated as *Theos* in Greek, *Deus* in Latin, *Dios* in Spanish, *Dio* in Italian, *Dieu* in French, *Duw* in Welsh, *Dia* in Scottish and Irish. Yet, like its various versions in other languages, "God" is not a name, but a title that can be used for different deities.

Many "Gods"

Surprisingly, in the Bible itself many entities are called "God" or "god." Paul makes it quite clear: ""*For though there be that are called* gods, whether in heaven or in earth (as there be gods many, and lords many)" (1 Cor 8:5). Anciently, Hebrew had no capital letters; so, in Hebrew, "God" and "god" looked the same. The capitals have been supplied in the English translations as suggested by the context. Called "God" or "god" in the Bible are the following:

The Creator. The first and foremost God in Scriptures, of course, is the Creator of heaven and earth. *"Hast thou not known? hast thou not heard, that the everlasting God, the LORD, the Creator of the ends of the earth..."* (Isa 40:28a).

Christ. The Messiah or Christ, the Son of God, is Himself God. *"But unto the Son he saith, Thy throne, O God, is for ever and ever: a sceptre of righteousness is the sceptre of thy kingdom"* (Heb 1:8).

Angels. In several passages in Scriptures, angels are referred to as "gods." *"Confounded be all they that serve graven images, that boast themselves of idols: worship him, all ye gods"* (Ps 97:7).

Moses. The LORD designated Moses a "god," as His emissary to the king of Egypt. *"And the LORD said unto Moses, See, I have made thee a god to Pharaoh..."* (Ex 7:1a).

Prophets. The witch of Endor called the prophet Samuel a "god." *"And the woman said unto Saul, I saw gods ascending out of the earth. And he said unto her, What form is he of? And she said, An old man cometh up; and he is covered with a mantle. And Saul perceived that it was Samuel..."* (1 Sam 28:13b-14).

Judges. The magistrates, who held the power of life and death in their hands, were also considered "gods." *"I have said, Ye are gods; and all of you are children of the most High"* (Ps 82:6).

The stomach. Humorous as it may seem, even the stomach is figuratively regarded as a "god" when people make material possessions their top priority in life. *"(For many walk, of whom I have told you often, and now tell you even weeping, that they are the enemies of the cross of Christ: Whose end is destruction, whose God is their belly, and whose glory is in their shame, who mind earthly things.)"* (Phil 3:18-19).

Satan. The devil as *"the god of this world hath blinded the minds of them which believe not, lest the light of the glorious gospel of Christ, who is the image of God, should shine unto them"* (2 Cor 4:4b).

Demons. The devil's minions who inveigle people into worshipping them are also called "gods." *"They sacrificed unto devils, not to God; to gods whom they knew not, to new gods that came newly up, whom your fathers feared not"* (Deut 32:17).

Idols. Graven images are regarded as "gods." *"For all the gods of the nations are idols: but the LORD made the heavens"* (Ps 96:5). Demons are specially fond of inhabiting graven images, because it is they who are worshipped and glorified when the people pray, kneel down, and offer sacrifices to the idols.

Other "Gods," other names.

Although people of various faiths usually speak of one "God," they refer to different deities. Hindus worship God as a universal spirit they call Brahman ("strong"), a trinity (Brahma, Vishnu, Shiva) over 33 million lesser gods. Parsis in India, descendants of Zoroastrians from Persia, venerate Ahura Mazda ("wise lord") as the God who created all things. Shinto reveres Amaterasu Omikami ("great spirit illuminating the heavens"), sun goddess and legendary ancestor of Japan's emperors. Muslims pray seven times a day to Allah (al'illah, "the God"), formerly the supreme deity of Muhammad's once polytheistic Quraysh tribe. Voodoo has a God called Bon Dieu ("the good god"). Santeria pays homage to a supreme God called Olodumare. Deists defer to the Supreme Being as God and Divine Providence, among other terms. Freemasons bow to the "Great Architect of the Universe." Some present-day philosophers refer to God as the "First Cause." Many liberal theologians prefer to use gender-neutral and impersonal names for God, such as "the unconditioned ultimate" and "the wholly other."

There were many names for "God" even in the days of the prophet Micah, about 2,700 years ago. *"For all people will walk every one in the name of his god, and we will walk in the name of the LORD our God for ever and ever"* (Mic 4:5).

Other names taboo.

Jews and Christians worship the same God, who had revealed His personal name to Moses, commanding His people to *"make no mention of the name of other gods, neither let it be heard out of thy mouth"* (Ex 23:13b). Why? *"(For the LORD thy God is a jealous God among you) lest the anger of the LORD thy God be kindled against thee, and destroy thee from off the face of the earth"* (Deut 6:15).

But the danger in saying the names of other Gods may be graver from the other side. Rabbi Yeshayahu Heiliczer wrote in an article in the Summer 1999 issue of the *Messianic Home* that "when the Yisraeli came out of Babylonian captivity, they brought along with them the Babylonian culture, and along with it Babylonian beliefs and superstitions... One of these pagan Babylonian practices or beliefs was called 'ineffability.' This was the superstition against using the name of a deity for fear of something happening to them... The idea was that if you said the name of a deity he or she would notice you."[1]

In our modern day, the principle is known as the "cocktail party effect." At a noisy party, you can usually hear your name if someone mentions it, even in the other side of the room. We are so familiar with our respective names that we hear it over the other noises.[2]

Only one true God

There is only one true God. *"Thus saith the LORD the King of Israel, and his redeemer the LORD of hosts; I am the first, and I am the last; and beside me there is no God"* (Isa 44:6). As the Creator of all things, including space and time, nothing preceded the one true God. *"For thus saith the LORD that created the heavens; God himself that formed the earth and made it; he hath established it, he created it not in vain, he formed it to be inhabited: I am the LORD; and there is none else"* (Isa 45:18). Furthermore, *"Ye are my witnesses, saith the LORD, and my servant whom I have chosen: that ye may know and believe me, and understand that I am he: before me there was no God formed, neither shall there be after me"* (Isa 43:10).

The LORD wants His chosen people to know and call on His Name. *"Therefore my people shall know my name: therefore they shall know in that day that I am he that doth speak: behold, it is I"* (Isa 52:6). Because His name is in Hebrew, He will restore the single universal language. *"For then will I turn to the people a pure language, that they may all call upon the name of the LORD, to serve him with one consent"* (Zeph 3:9). *"And the LORD shall be king over all the earth: in that day shall there be one LORD, and his name one"* (Zech 14:9).

Need we know God's Name?

Many people say it is not necessary to find out and call on the true Name of God, because, whatever name we use, God will know it is He we are addressing our prayers to. How about you – would you rather be called by your own name or something else?

Let us take a mundane example. Say you put up a business and hired some people. At first they called you "boss," but, being a friendly person, you told them to just call you "Robert," your actual name. Most cheerfully complied, but some persisted in calling you "boss." As the business grew, you appointed managers, who were also called "boss" by their subordinates. Sometimes, you and a manager would be talking about something and somebody would come along and say, "Hey, Boss!" and both of you would turn to look. The employee would say, "Oh, not you, I mean him." Another employee would call you "Albert," instead of "Robert." How would you feel?

Names have meanings. As we have seen earlier, in Biblical times the name given to a newborn child was typically about the circumstances surrounding its birth or a prophecy that foretold the character, mission, destiny, or events that would mark the person's life. Needless to say, if the names of those Biblical characters were important, the importance of the Creator's Name is inestimably far greater.

One highly important reason God revealed His personal Name to men is for us not to confuse Him with false gods. *"I am the LORD: that is my name: and my glory will I not give to another, neither my praise to graven images"* (Isa 42:8).

Sound waves and frequencies.

Jewish sages taught that the letters of the Hebrew alphabet each have their own distinctive values and qualities. Letters are sounded through vibrations made with the vocal chords, lips, tongue, teeth, throat, nasal cavity, lungs. Sound travels in waves, with varying wavelengths and frequencies. Thus, every letter and every word made up of a certain combination of letters have their own unique vibrations. So, too, names, which are words.

Every name therefore is one of a kind. The personal Name of God, with its own unique set of wavelengths and frequencies, is the one that resonates in perfect harmony with His Being. By revealing His sacred Name to men, the LORD has given us, as it were, His direct line. He has taught us how to precisely tune in to His personal frequency. When we use a common word or a different name to call on God, we are tuning in to a different frequency and, thus, could be communicating with an entity entirely different from the one true God.

The "Book of Life."

If you do not value the Name of God, He may not value yours, either. God has special books wherein your very own name may be written. *"Then they that feared the LORD spake often one to another: and the LORD hearkened, and heard it, and a book of remembrance was written before him for them that feared the LORD, and that thought upon his name"* (Mal 3:16). That "book of remembrance" is called the "Book of Life" in the NT. *"And I saw the dead, small and great, stand before God; and the books were opened: and another book was opened, which is the book of life: and the dead were judged out of those things which were written in the books, according to their works"* (Rev 20:12). If your name has been written in the Book of Life, a place is reserved for you for an infinite holiday in the Kingdom of Heaven.

The bookings, though, are not confirmed; they can be canceled by the Proprietor. *"He that overcometh, the same shall be clothed in white raiment; and I will not blot out his name out of the book of life, but I will confess his name before my Father, and before his angels"* (Rev 3:5). *"And there shall in no wise enter into it any thing that defileth, neither whatsoever worketh abomination, or maketh a lie: but they which are written in the Lamb's book of life"* (Rev 21:27). If your name is removed from the Book of Life, you can look forward to a sure future of nothing but fries and toast. *"And whosoever was not found written in the book of life was cast into the lake of fire"* (Rev 20:15).

See how important names can be?

Christ taught the Name

Christ taught His disciples to honor the Father's holy Name. *"After this manner therefore pray ye: Our Father which art in heaven, Hallowed be thy name..."* (Matt 6:9).

He said, *"I am come in my Father's name"* (John 5:43), because on top of being the Father's representative on earth, He literally has the Father's Name as part of His own personal Name (explained later).

Christ taught the Name to His disciples. *"I have manifested thy name unto the men which thou gavest me out of the world: thine they were, and thou gavest them me; and they have kept thy word... And I have declared unto them thy name, and will declare it: that the love wherewith thou hast loved me may be in them, and I in them"* (John 17:6,26).

Blessings of the Name

God made promises for those who will know and call on His holy Name. *"Our help is in the name of the LORD, who made heaven and earth"* (Ps 124:8). He will not abandon believers who come to Him for help. *"And they that know thy name will put their trust in thee: for thou, LORD, hast not forsaken them that seek thee"* (Ps 9:10). Calling on His true Name is comparable to being enclosed by the thick walls of an impregnable fortress. *"The name of the LORD is a strong tower: the righteous runneth into it, and is safe"* (Prov 18:10).

Honors, long life, salvation.

God promises to answer and grant protection, honors, long life, and salvation to those who will call on His Name. *"Because he hath set his love upon me, therefore will I deliver him: I will set him on high, because he hath known my name. He shall call upon me, and I will answer him: I will be with him in trouble; I will deliver him, and honour him. With long life will I satisfy him, and shew him my salvation"* (Ps 91:14-16).

His Name can save the faithful, even from the brink of death. *"The sorrows of death compassed me, and the pains of hell gat hold upon me: I found trouble and sorrow. Then called I upon the name of the LORD;*

O LORD, I beseech thee, deliver my soul. Gracious is the LORD, and righteous; yea, our God is merciful. The LORD preserveth the simple: I was brought low, and he helped me. Return unto thy rest, O my soul; for the LORD hath dealt bountifully with thee. For thou hast delivered my soul from death, mine eyes from tears, and my feet from falling. I will walk before the LORD in the land of the living" (Ps 116:3-9).

End-time survival. Come the wars and disasters prophesied in the Bible, God's Name will save the faithful from destruction. "And it shall come to pass, that whosoever shall call on the name of the LORD shall be delivered: for in mount Zion and in Jerusalem shall be deliverance, as the LORD hath said, and in the remnant whom the LORD shall call" (Joel 2:32). Even if mankind is decimated, those who invoke His true Name will survive. "And it shall come to pass, that in all the land, saith the LORD, two parts therein shall be cut off and die; but the third shall be left therein. And I will bring the third part through the fire, and will refine them as silver is refined, and will try them as gold is tried: they shall call on my name, and I will hear them: I will say, It is my people: and they shall say, The LORD is my God" (Zech 13:8-9).

Sadly, God's promises exclude the wretched multitudes who do not know or neglect to call on His Name. "Pour out thy fury upon the heathen that know thee not, and upon the families that call not on thy name: for they have eaten up Jacob, and devoured him, and consumed him, and have made his habitation desolate" (Jer 10:25).

"The LORD" is His Name?

Several passages in Scripture seem to proclaim the Name of God. "Seek him that maketh the seven stars and Orion, and turneth the shadow of death into the morning, and maketh the day dark with night: that calleth for the waters of the sea, and poureth them out upon the face of the earth: The LORD is his name" (Amos 5:8)

The prophets declared it, too. "Therefore, behold, I will this once cause them to know, I will cause them to know mine hand and my might; and they shall know that my name is The LORD" (Jer 16:21; Isa 42:8). The Israelites invoked it in praise and worship. "Let them know that you, whose name is the LORD -- that you alone are the Most High over all the earth" (Ps 83:18, NIV).

However, "the LORD" is obviously not a name, it is a title.

Revealed to Moses

Forty years year after Moses escaped from Egypt and became a shepherd in the wilderness of Midian, God spoke to him from a burning bush at Horeb, the "mountain of God." The LORD commanded him to bring out the Israelites from slavery in Egypt. Moses was at first hesitant, unsure of who was speaking to him. *"And Moses said unto God, Behold, when I come unto the children of Israel, and shall say unto them, The God of your fathers hath sent me unto you; and they shall say to me, What is his name? what shall I say unto them?*

"And God said unto Moses, I AM THAT I AM: and he said, Thus shalt thou say unto the children of Israel, I AM hath sent me unto you. And God said moreover unto Moses, Thus shalt thou say unto the children of Israel, the LORD God of your fathers, the God of Abraham, the God of Isaac, and the God of Jacob, hath sent me unto you: this is my name for ever, and this is my memorial unto all generations" (Ex 3:13-15).

Hebrew original.

God's name is "I AM THAT I AM"? In Hebrew it is *Eheyeh Asher Eheyeh. Eheyeh* is the first-person singular imperfect form of the verb *hayah* ("to be"), OT:1961 in *Strong's Greek/Hebrew Definitions*. It is usually translated "I will be," because the imperfect tense denotes actions that are not yet completed (e.g., "Certainly I will be *(ehyeh)* with thee." -- Ex 3:12).[3] The second word, *Asher,* OT:834, is a relative pronoun of every gender and number ("who, which, what, that"), which also functions as an adverb and conjunction ("when, where, how, because, in order that," etc.).[4]

Other renditions. Thus, "I AM THAT I AM" (KJV) can also be rendered alternatively as "I am who I am" (NKJV, NIV, *et al.*); "I am what I am"; "I am because I am"; "I will be who I will be"; "I will be what I will be"; "I will be because I will be"; "I will be that I will be" (Leeser). The New Jerusalem Bible has "I am he who is."[5] Other renditions include: "I will become whatsoever I please" (Rotherham); "I am the Being"; "I am the Existing One."[6]

Etymological explanation. The *Encyclopaedia Judaica* points out that *"Eheyeh-Asher-Eheyeh,* 'I-Am-Who-I-Am,' offers a folk etymology, common in biblical explanation of names..."[7] *Smith's Bible Dictionary* agrees: "This passage is intended to indicate the etymology of (God's Name), as understood by the Hebrews..."[8] Sacred Name proclaimer B. Earl Allen adds: "It is the interpretation, definition, explanation, translation, or meaning of the sacred name."[9] The real Name of the LORD has a specific spelling and pronunciation in Hebrew.

The Tetragrammaton

The LORD gave the true pronunciation of His Name to Moses. *"And God spoke to Moses and said to him: "I am the LORD. I appeared to*

Abraham, to Isaac, and to Jacob, as God Almighty, but by My name, LORD, I was not known to them" (Ex 6:2-3, NKJV). (In the KJV and ASV, the word "LORD" is translated "JEHOVAH.")

"LORD" and "JEHOVAH," however, are mere substitutes for the four original Hebrew consonants *yod-hey-waw-hey* (יהוה), written from right to left in both the ancient paleo-Hebrew characters and the more recent "square" Aramaic Hebrew letters. Depending on the transliteration method, Sephardic (Spanish-Portuguese) or Ashkenazic (German-eastern European) Hebrew, the four letters may be written in English as "YHWH," "YHVH," or "JHVH."

God's Name has come down to us spelled only with consonants, because in ancient times the Hebrew alphabet did not have a system to indicate vowels. The reader had to mentally supply the missing vowels as he or she read, much as today when we see "MR" we pronounce it as "Mister," "BLDG" as "building," "LTD" as "limited," etc.

Four-Lettered Name. *The Jewish Encyclopedia* states: "The name Yhwh is considered as the Name proper; it was known in the earlier rabbinical works simply as the Name; also as *Shem ha-Meyuhad* ('The Extraordinary Name'); as *Shem ha-Meforash* ('The Distinguished Name'); as *Shem ben Arba' Otiyyot* ('the Tetragrammaton' or 'the Quadriliteral Name'); and as *Yod He Waw He* (spelling the letters of Yhwh)."[10] "Tetragrammaton" is Greek for "four-lettered." It was used in the 1st century A.D. by the Jewish philosopher Philo of Alexandria.[11]

The Four-Lettered Name is also used in combination with many titles. (Please see list of "YHWH Titles" in the Appendix.)

Many times more than any other name, the Tetragrammaton is found 6,823 times in the Hebrew text of the Bible. Earlier, some 134 occurrences of the Name had been removed by the scribes, according to Ginsburg's *Massorah*. The abbreviated, two-letter form of the Name appears 49 times. In all, therefore, the number of instances that the Name of God had originally been written in the Hebrew Scriptures totals 7,006.[12]

YHWH

Tetragrammaton YHWH written in various forms of Hebrew characters (read right to left) and English.

Root-word. Alexander MacWhorter of Yale University, in his book *Memorial Name* (1857), said the Name originated from *havah*, the old form of *hayah*, meaning "to exist."[13] The *Scofield Bible* footnote on Gen 2:4 confirms that the Name is from *havah*, but more accurately from *hawah*. *Young's* and *Strong's* Concordances, as well as *Funk & Wagnall's Encyclopedia*, agree that the Name derived from *hawah*. *Gesenius' Hebrew-English Lexicon* states the root-word is *hawah* or *hayah*, meaning "to exist, self-existing."

The verb "to be" or "to exist" thus had several forms in Hebrew: *havah*, *hawah*, and *hayah* -- the consonants V, W, and Y having been used in place of one another.

Shades of meaning. The *Encyclopedia Judaica* notes that "in the opinion of many scholars, YHWH is a verbal form of the root *hwh*, which is an older form of the root *hyh* 'to be.' The vowel of the first syllable shows that the verb is used in the form of a future-present causative *hiph'il*, and must therefore mean 'He causes to be, He brings into existence'."[14]

The Jewish Encyclopedia observes: "In appearance, YHWH (יהוה) is the third person imperfect '*kal*' of the verb הוה ('to be'), meaning, therefore, 'He is,' or 'He will be,' or, perhaps, 'He lives'... The meaning would, therefore, be 'He who is self-existing, self-sufficient,' or, more correctly, 'He who lives'."[15]

Researcher Choon-Leong Seow wrote in the December 1991 issue of *Bible Review*: "The tetragrammaton is understood by scholars to be related to the root *HWH* (originally *HWY*, later *HYY/HYH*) 'to be, exist, be present.' The name YHWH is, in any case, a verb form, commonly believed to be a causative meaning 'he (God) causes to be' – that is, 'he creates,' or 'he brings to pass (promises),' or the like."[16]

Archeological evidences.

One of the most famous archeological evidences for the Tetragrammaton is a black basalt monument about 3½ feet high and 2 feet wide, erected around 830 B.C. some 13 miles east of the Dead Sea: the Moabite Stone. It memorialized the victory of King Mesha of Moab in his revolt

The Moabite Stone, a 9th century B.C. monument to King Mesha's victory over Israel, with the Name YHWH in line 18.

against Israel. (His army was shortly destroyed by the combined forces of Israel, Judah, and Edom -- 2 Kings ch. 3). Discovered by a missionary in 1868, then cut up by Bedouins who sold the pieces, the Moabite Stone contains the sacred Name spelled in paleo-Hebrew letters. Line 17-18 reads: "I took from thence the vessels of YHWH and dragged them before Chemosh" (the Moabite god).

Other artifacts with the Four-Lettered Name are the Lachish Letters, *ostraca* (inscribed potsherds) written between 589-587 B.C., unearthed in 1935 in the ancient walled city of Lachish 30 miles southwest of Jerusalem. In several pieces the Tetragrammaton was used as part of the greeting: "YHWH give you to hear peaceable tidings."

Facsimile of a Lachish Letter on an *ostracon or* potsherd circa 589-587 B.C., with YHWH inscribed on it.

The Tel Arad Ostraca, pottery fragments dated about 580 B.C., were found in Arad, a city in southern Israel, in 1966. The inscriptions detail the transactions of Eliashib, an official in charge of the kingdom's local stores of oil, wine, and grain. The Four-Lettered Name is in the salutation: "May YHWH ask for your peace."

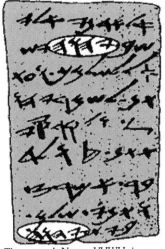

The Khirbet Beit Lei burial cave, uncovered by road construction workers in 1961 five miles east of Lachish, has carved figures and inscriptions on the walls, estimated to have been made around 500-400 B.C. by the writing style and letter formation. The most legible inscriptions declare: "YHWH is the (mighty one) of all the earth" and "The mount of Moriah thou has favored, the dwelling of YHWH."

The sacred Name YHWH in a copy of a Tel Arad *ostracon* pottery fragment, ca .580 B.C.

In 1975-76, archeologists in the Negev discovered Hebrew and Phoenician inscriptions on plaster walls, as well as stone vessels and storage jars. Portions of the writings show the Tetragrammaton in ancient Hebrew characters.

God's Nickname

In the book of Psalms, we find another personal Name of God. "*Sing unto God, sing praises to his name: extol him that rideth upon the heavens by his name JAH, and rejoice before him"* (Ps 68:4). From this one precious verse we learn that "JAH" is also a Name of God! However, there are several ways "JAH" may be pronounced. Is it "Djah," as English-speakers would articulate it; "Hah," as Spanish language users would enunciate it; or "Yah," as Germanic peoples would vocalize it?

"Praise ye Jah!"

For a clue, let us search the Scriptures for other verses that may also contain the word "Jah." It turns out we need not do much searching. The word is part of a Hebrew phrase thousands of years old, yet still one of the most popular praise and worship expressions today: "Hallelujah!" "Hellelujah" literally means "Praise ye *(Hallelu-)* Jah." So, here we learn that "JAH" is actually sounded as "Yah." But how come the "Y" is spelled with the letter "J"?

Youngest letter. "J" is the youngest letter in the English alphabet. It first appeared in Roman times, when it was used interchangeably with "I."[17] Both "I" and "J" were used as substitutes for *yod* ("Y"), the tenth letter in the ancient Semitic alphabet. Both had the consonantal sound of "Y" (as in "year"). The 1560 Geneva Bible has "Iah" in Psalm 68:4.[18] Other examples are "Jesus" and "judge," which appeared as "Iesus" and "iudge" in the 1611 King James Bible.[19] Similarly spelled were "Ierusalem," "Iudah," "Ieremiah," which should have been "Yerusalem," "Yudah," "Yeremiah."

Ornamental "tail." In the late Middle Ages, when two "I's" were written together, scribes often added a tail to the last "I." In the 1600s, it was the "I" at the beginning of a word that was written with a tail.[20] The elongated form ("J") was at first used simply as an ornamental device.[21]

In the 17th century, the development of the dictionary by Dutch printers demanded consistent spellings for the alphabetical listing of entries.[22] "I" became a standard vowel, while **"J"** (as in "joy") became a consonant permanently.[23] The younger "J" was positioned after the older "I" in the alphabet, with the lower case "j" retaining the dot over it, similar to its precursor, the small letter "i."

Two-Lettered Name.

When God told Moses His personal Name, He also mentioned a short form of His Name. *"And God said unto Moses, I AM THAT I AM: and he said, Thus shalt thou say unto the children of Israel, I AM hath sent me unto you"* (Ex 3:14). "I AM," evidently, is an abbreviation of "I AM THAT I AM."

The Bible reference *Insight on the Scriptures* (1988) confirms this: "Hebrew scholars... point out that the abbreviated form of the name is Yah (Jah in the Latinized form), as at Psalm 89:8 and in the expression *Hallelu-Yah* (meaning 'Praise Jah, you people!'), (Ps 104:35; 150:1,6)."[24] *New Exhaustive Strong's Numbers and Concordance* states that "Jah," OT:3050 Yah, is a contraction of OT:3068 (YHWH) and has the same meaning.[25] The *Encyclopedia Judaica* says the pronunciation "is confirmed, at least for the vowel of the first syllable of the name, by the shorter form Yah, which is sometimes used in poetry..."[26] The *Jewish Encyclopedia* concludes: "The name Yah (יה) is composed of the first letters of Yhwh."[27]

To summarize, "YHWH" (meaning "I AM THAT I AM") is the Four-Lettered Name of God, and "YH" (meaning "I AM"), pronounced "Yah," is its short form – the Two-Lettered Name.

Scriptural confirmation. In the Gospel of John, we read: *"Then said the Jews unto him, Thou art not yet fifty years old, and hast thou seen Abraham? Jesus said unto them, Verily, verily, I say unto you, Before Abraham was, I am. Then took they up stones to cast at him..."* (John 8:57-59b). The NT was written in Greek, but Christ must have uttered the short form of the Name in Hebrew, *Yah* ("I AM"). The Jews perceived He was claiming to be God and picked up stones to stone Him to death – the Mosaic punishment for blasphemy (Lev 24:16).

Theoporic names. The names of many persons in the Bible are "theoporic" (bearing the Name of God) – with the Two-Lettered Name ("Yah") as a suffix. The better known are: Jeremiah ("exalted by Yah"), Zechariah ("remembered by Yah"), Zephaniah ("hidden or treasured by Yah"), Nehemiah ("consoled by Yah"), Zedekiah ("just or righteous is Yah"). The spelling of the theoporic suffix "Yah" is usually "-iah," but in a few cases "-jah" -- as in Elijah ("my God is Yah"), Adonijah ("my Lord is Yah"), Ahijah ("my brother is Yah"). The suffix seems to have been known before Moses, as in the name Moriah ("seen of Yah").

Tetragrammaton forgotten

The Name of God used to be part of daily greetings. *"And behold, Boaz came from Bethlehem, and said unto the reapers, The LORD (YHWH) be with you. And they answered him, The LORD (YHWH) bless thee"* (Ruth 2:4). Boaz, who lived in the 11th century B.C., was the great grandfather of David,

Five centuries later, though, Jeremiah said the people had forgotten God's Name. *"How long shall this be in the heart of the prophets that prophesy lies? yea, they are prophets of the deceit of their own heart; Which think to cause my people to forget my name by their dreams which they tell every man to his neighbour, as their fathers have forgotten my name for Baal"* (Jer 23:26-27).

The *Jewish Encyclopedia* informs us that in "former times the Name was taught to all; but when immorality increased it was reserved for the pious"[28] The *Encyclopedia Judaica* marks the last time God's Names was spoken freely: "At least until the destruction of the First Temple in 586 B.C.E., this name was regularly pronounced with its proper vowels, as is clear from the *Lachish Letters, written shortly before that date."[29]

Utterance forbidden.

The priests and scribes invoked a number of seemingly legal reasons for forbidding the utterance of the Tetragrammaton by the people.

Third commandment. The prohibition against pronouncing the Name of God carelessly is embodied in the third commandment: *"Thou shalt not take the name of the LORD thy God in vain; for the LORD will not hold him guiltless that taketh his name in vain"* (Exodus 20:7).

The *Jewish Encyclopaedia* notes: "According to Dalman... the Rabbis forbade the utterance of the Tetragrammaton to guard against desecration of the Sacred Name."[30] To keep the people from desecrating the sacred Name, wittingly or unwittingly, the rabbis instructed them never to pronounce God's Name at all!

Too sacred. In the Second Temple period (5th century B.C.), the Tetragrammaton came to be regarded as too sacred to be spoken. The practice of substituting other terms to refer to God became common.[31]

The *Jewish Encyclopedia* says: "Awe of the sacredness of the names of God and eagerness to manifest respect and reverence for them... in the Targumim the name Yhwh was replaced by two 'yods' with a 'waw' over them... which letters are equal in value to Yhwh (=26)."[32]

God of all peoples. The *Encyclopaedia Britannica* tells us that "As Judaism began to become a universal religion, the proper name (YHWH) tended to be replaced by the common noun Elohim, meaning 'God,' which could apply to foreign deities and therefore could be used to demonstrate the universal sovereignty of Israel's God over all others."[33]

Solomon Zeitlin wrote in the *Jewish Quarterly Review* of April 1969: "In the biblical period (YHWH) was a proper name, for the G-d of Israel, an ethnic G-d. After the Restoration (of the Temple) those who adhered to the view of the universality of G-d maintained that (YHWH) is not an ethnic G-d but is the G-d of all the universe, the G-d of all peoples. To propagate this view they declared that the word (YHWH) in the Pentateuch should be pronounced *Adonai* to signify that He is the L-rd, Master, of the universe."[34]

Clerical caveats.

Some passages in Scripture had been reinterpreted to ensure that the people would avoid uttering the sacred Name of God.

To be concealed. Exodus 3:15a reads: *"And God said moreover unto Moses, Thus shalt thou say unto the children of Israel, The LORD God of your fathers, the God of Abraham, the God of Isaac, and the God of Jacob, hath sent me unto you: this is my name for ever..."*

According to *Mackey's Revised Encyclopedia of Freemasonry*, "The word *forever* is represented in the original by *l'olam;* but the Rabbis... by the change of a single letter, made *l'olam, forever,* read as if it had been written *l'alam,* which means *to be concealed,* and hence the passage was translated *'this is my name to be concealed,'* instead of *'this is my name forever'.*"[35]

Death for uttering. Leviticus 24:16 declares: *"And whoever blasphemes the name of the LORD shall surely be put to death. All the congregation shall certainly stone him, the stranger as well as him who is born in the land. When he blasphemes the name of the Lord, he shall be put to death"* (NKJV).

In the original Hebrew text, "the word *nokeb,* here translated *to blaspheme,* also means *to pronounce distinctly, to call by name."* It could be and was thus retranslated as *"'whosoever shall pronounce the name (YHWH) shall suffer death."*[36]

God's Name taken back

The rabbis and scribes gave reasons for concealing the Name. Little did they know that it was actually the LORD who took back His Name from them! God retracted His Name from the Jews in three distinct steps. The retractions occurred roughly over 600 years.

First time taken back.

In 586 BC, King Nebuchadnezzar of Babylon invaded Judah for the second time, destroyed the Temple, and took most of the Jews captive. He appointed one of the remaining Jews, Gedaliah, as governor of the land. But some defiant men, egged on by the king of the Ammonites, murdered Gedaliah. The other Jews prepared to escape to Egypt for fear of reprisal from the Babylonians (Jer ch. 39-41). Before fleeing, they requested Jeremiah to ask God on what to do (Jer 42:2-3).

Ten days later, Jeremiah met with them. *"And said unto them, Thus saith the LORD, the God of Israel, unto whom ye sent me to present your supplication before him; If ye will still abide in this land, then will I build you, and not pull you down, and I will plant you, and not pluck you up: for I repent me of the evil that I have done unto you. Be not afraid of the king of Babylon, of whom ye are afraid; be not afraid of him, saith the LORD: for I am with you to save you, and to deliver you from his hand"* (Jer 42:9-11). Their worst fears would follow them in Egypt if they persisted. *"If ye wholly set your faces to enter into Egypt, and go to sojourn there; Then it shall come to pass, that the sword, which ye feared, shall overtake you there in the land of Egypt, and the famine, whereof ye were afraid, shall follow close after you there in Egypt; and there ye shall die"* (Jer 42:15b-16).

Abandoned the land. Yet, instead of obeying, the Jews accused Jeremiah of lying and conniving with the followers of the Babylonians (Jer 43:2-3). They pushed through with their plan to escape to Egypt and abandoned the land the LORD had given their fathers (Jer 43:7).

The Jews forgot a prohibition the LORD told Moses some 900 years earlier: *"Moreover, he shall not multiply horses for himself, nor shall he cause the people to return to Egypt to multiply horses, since the LORD has said to you, 'You shall never again return that way'"* (Deut 17:16, NASU). God had warned the Israelites never to return to Egypt.

God's Name profaned. The Jews put God's Name to shame by leaving the Promised Land. *"And when they entered unto the heathen, whither they went, they profaned my holy name, when they said to them, These are the people of the LORD, and are gone forth out of his land. But I had pity for mine holy name, which the house of Israel had profaned among the heathen, whither they went"* (Ezek 36:20-21).

God had given them their own land – a "land of milk and honey." Abandoning the land for another country was an embarrassment and a shame to God. It made the LORD look like a deceiver and a liar, or a weak God who could not keep His promises. His Name or reputation as an all-powerful God was tarnished, even ruined.

Name lost in Egypt. God said through Jeremiah: *"Therefore hear ye the word of the LORD, all Judah that dwell in the land of Egypt; Behold, I have sworn by my great name, saith the LORD, that my name shall no more be named in the mouth of any man of Judah in all the land of Egypt, saying, The Lord GOD liveth"* (Jer 44:26).

Moreover, as God had said, many of the Jews died just the same when Nebuchadnezzar invaded Egypt. *"And when he cometh, he shall smite the land of Egypt, and deliver such as are for death to death; and such as are for captivity to captivity; and such as are for the sword to the sword"* (Jer 43:11).

Lost, too, in Babylon. Hebrew fell into disuse in Babylon among the captive Jews, who spoke the language of the land, Aramaic or Syriac, sometimes called Chaldee.[37] The Jews also stopped saying the Name of God. *The Jewish Encyclopedia* avers: "The avoidance of the original name of God both in speech and, to a certain extent, in the Bible was due according to Geiger... to a reverence which shrank from the utterance of the Sublime Name; and it may well be that such a reluctance first arose in a foreign, and hence in an 'unclean' land, very possibly, therefore, in Babylonia."[38] In Judea, the poorest Jews who had been left behind adopted the language of their conquerors, too.[39]

Only 3 times a year. Rabbi Yeshayahu Heiliczer wrote: "After the return from Babylon we find that 'The Name' was totally suppressed by the P'rushim (Pharisees), who had removed the sons of Aharon from Moshe's seat. They forbade the use of 'The Name' and limited its use to temple services held on the 'Shalosh Regalim,' the three pilgrimage festivals of Pesach, Shavuot, and Sukkot. The rest of greater Isra'el had no permission to use 'The Name'."[40]

Thus, the sacred Name of the LORD could be uttered only three times a year -- during Temple services on Passover (Pesach) and the Feast of Unleavened Bread; Pentecost (Shavuot, Feast of Weeks or Harvest); and Feast of Tabernacles (Sukkot, Booths) or Ingathering.

Second time taken back.

The next retraction of God's Name took place during the inter-Testamental period -- the so-called "400 silent years" in the Bible, between Malachi, the OT's last book, and Matthew, the NT's first book.

Alexander arrived. Daniel, as a Jewish captive in Babylon, had visions of a powerful two-horned ram that was later destroyed by a one-horned he-goat (Dan 8:3-8). The angel Gabriel explained: "The ram which thou sawest having two horns are the kings of Media and Persia. And the rough goat is the king of Grecia: and the great horn that is between his eyes is the first king" (Dan 8:21). As history recorded, the unified kingdom of Media-Persia conquered Babylon, while Greece, under Alexander the Great ("the first king"), defeated Media-Persia.

In 332 B.C. Alexander entered Judea, where the Jews led by the high priest ceremoniously welcomed him. "Josephus (Ant. 11:8, section 5) says that Alexander meeting the high priest Jaddua (Neh 12:11,22) said that at Dium in Macedonia he had a divine vision so habited, inviting him to Asia and promising him success. Jaddua met him at Gapha (Mizpeh) at the head of a procession of priests and citizens in white. Alexander at the sight of the linen arrayed priests, and the high priest in blue and gold with the miter and gold plate on his head bearing (YHWH's) name, adored it, and embraced him; and having been shown Daniel's prophecies concerning him, he sacrificed to God in the court of the temple, and granted the Jews liberty to live according to their own laws, and freedom from tribute in the sabbatical years."[41]

Jews Hellenized. As the Greeks conquered southwestern Asia, the Greek language and Hellenistic thought spread throughout the occupied lands. "Greek became the language of literature and commerce from the shores of the Mediterranean to the banks of the Tigris."[42]

The Jews were greatly impressed by the sophistication of the Greek culture. The Greek way of life became established in Judea. Many Jews abandoned the Mosaic laws for Greek customs. At a gymnasium in Jerusalem, some Jews tried to hide their circumcision when competing naked in games. Greek names became fashionable. Two high priests of the Second Temple, Jesus (Jeshua) and Onias (son of High Priest Jaddua and father of High Priest Simon the Just) adopted the Greek names "Jason" and "Menelaus," respectively.[43]

A foreign king. The Jews ignored an express commandment of the LORD by welcoming and acknowledging a foreign king over them! God had said: *"When you enter the land the LORD your God is giving you and have taken possession of it and settled in it, and you say, 'Let us set a king over us like all the nations around us,' be sure to appoint over you the king the LORD your God chooses. He must be from among your own brothers. Do not place a foreigner over you, one who is not a brother Israelite"* (Deut 17:14-16, NIV).

Only once a year. The *Jewish Encyclopedia* informs us: "At the beginning of the Hellenistic era… the use of the Name was reserved for the Temple… it appears that the priests were allowed to pronounce the Name at the benediction only in the Temple." Later, "from the time Simeon the Just died (this is the traditional expression for the beginning of the Hellenistic period), the priests refrained from blessing the people with the Name…"[44] Question: When did Simeon the Just die?

There were two Simeons the Just, who were both high priests and sons of men named Onias: Simeon I (310-291 or 300-270 B.C.), son of Onias I and grandson of Jaddua, and Simeon II (219-199 B.C.), son of Onias II.[45] The better match, though, is Simeon I.

After his death, the utterance of the Sacred Name even by the priests was further restricted. We learn from the *Encyclopedia Judaica* that the Tetragrammaton was "pronounced by the high priest only once a year on the Day of Atonement in the Holy of Holies… and in the Temple by the priests when they recited the Priestly Blessing."[46]

The Name mumbled. The priests also "pronounced it indistinctly, or they mouthed or mumbled it. Thus says Tosef… Formerly they used to greet each other with the Ineffable Name; when the time of the decline of the study of the Law came, the elders mumbled the Name. Subsequently also the solemn utterance of the Name by the high priest on the Day of Atonement, that ought to have been heard by the priests and people... became inaudible or indistinct." "R. Tarfon (or Tryphon) relates...: 'I was standing in the row of young priests, and I heard the high priest mumbling the Name, while the rest of the priests were chanting'."[47]

Adonai and Kyrios substituted. When the Jews stopped uttering the Tetragrammaton, they started using the Hebrew term Adonai to refer to the LORD. (Adonai is plural ["my Lords"], but is regarded as a plural of respect. Jews only use the singular form Adoni ["my lord"] to refer to a distinguished person. It is the source of the Greek name "Adonis.")

From the 3rd century B.C. onward, when a Jewish reader came across the sacred Name YHWH in the Biblical text, he pronounced it as Adonai. The Babylonian Talmud teaches: "The Holy One, blessed be He, said, 'I am not pronounced as I am written; I am written with (the letters) yod he, but I am pronounced by alef daleth' (Kiddushin 71a). That is to say, although the name was written as YH(WH), it was pronounced as 'd(wny) (Adonay), 'Lord'."[48]

In addition to the Hebrew term Adonay it became a custom among the Jews from the Second Temple period onward to say the Greek word Kyrios, which also means "Lord," whenever they encountered God's personal name YHWH in the Scriptures.[49]

Third time taken back

The third and last retraction came after a little over 300 years. "When Simeon the Righteous died, with many indications that such glory was no more enjoyed, his brethren no more dared utter the Ineffable Name."[50] When did Simeon the Righteous die?

The historical marker for his death was the loss of the Temple. "After the death of the high priest Simeon the Righteous forty years prior to the destruction of the Temple, the priests ceased to pronounce the Name (Yoma 49b). From that time, the pronunciation of the Name was prohibited"[51] Next question: When was the Temple destroyed?

The Temple, also called the Second Temple or Herod's Temple, was razed to the ground by Roman legions commanded by Titus, son of Emperor Vespasian, in 70 AD. According to the International Standard Bible Encyclopedia: "The prediction (of Luke 21:5) was fulfilled to the letter in the destruction of the temple by the Romans in 70 AD."[52] So, forty years before the destruction of the Temple was in 30 A.D. This was the year the priests in the Temple stopped uttering the Tetragrammaton altogether! Why did the use of the Name cease in that particular year?

The crucifixion. Nelson's Illustrated Bible Dictionary narrates: "During the week before Passover in A.D. 30, Jesus taught each day in the Temple area, debating with other teachers of differing beliefs... To block the possibility of an uprising among the people, the priestly party decided to arrest Jesus as soon as possible... Arrested on Passover Eve, Jesus was brought first before a Jewish court of inquiry, over which the high priest Caiaphas presided."[53] The rest of the story is in the Bible. Christ was crucified the following day in 30 A.D.

Christ had foretold his death in the parable of a landowner who planted a vineyard, then rented it out to some farmers. At harvest time, he sent servants several times to collect his share, but the tenants beat up the servants and even killed some of them. Finally, the landowner sent his son. When the tenants saw him, they thought the vineyard could be theirs by killing the heir, which they did (Matt 21:33-41; Luke 20:9-16). *"What then will the owner of the vineyard do? He will come and kill those tenants and give the vineyard to others"* (Mark 12:1-10, NIV). Apparently, the landowner personifies God; the tenants, the Jews; the servants, prophets; and the son, Christ, who spelled out the consequence for the Jews: *"Therefore say I unto you, The kingdom of God shall be taken from you, and given to a nation bringing forth the fruits thereof"* (Matt 21:43).

If some people are cast out of a kingdom, it follows the king would no longer be their king – and they would be stripped of all benefits and protection they used to enjoy under the king's name.

Never uttered again. God took back His Name completely, including all the promises that come with it after the Jews killed His Only Begotten Son. It was the proverbial last straw! *The Jewish Encyclopedia* avers: "After the destruction of the Second Temple there remained no trace of knowledge as to the pronunciation of the Name."[54]

The number "40" has long been known as the Biblical number of trial and testing. It looks like God tested the Jews for 40 years after the crucifixion – to see if they would still accept Christ as their long-awaited Messiah. When they did not, He allowed the full force of His judgment to fall upon them. The Romans destroyed Jerusalem and the Temple in 70 A.D. Over one million Jews died during the war, while 97,000 were sold into slavery throughout the Roman Empire.

Christian era developments

The use of *Kyrios* as a substitute for the Tetragrammaton in speech extended to the written translations of the Scriptures.

Lost in translation.

Author P. Kahle (*The Cairo Geniza*, 1959) says it was the Christians who replaced the Tetragrammaton with *kyrios* in manuscripts when the divine name in Hebrew characters was no longer understood.[55] "In later copies of the Septuagint, God's name was removed and words like 'God' (The-os') and 'Lord' (Ky'ri-os) were substituted... (there are) early fragments of the Septuagint where God's name was included and later copies of those same parts of the Septuagint where God's name has been removed."[56]

Choon-Leong Seow confirms this: "The Greek codices of the Bible of the early Christian Church in the 4th and 5th centuries A.D. had Kyrios ('Lord') in practically all the places where the Tetragrammaton used to be in the original Hebrew texts."[57]

Vowel indicators.

The second half of the first Christian millennium saw the emergence of the Masoretes, Jewish scribes who compiled the *Masorah*, a body of notes on the textual traditions of the Hebrew Scripture. The Masoretes introduced the use of vowel points to indicate vowel sounds in Hebrew. It was "the 8th century rabbis who compiled the most widely read and studied *Chumash* (annotated Torah) existing today. The Masoretic text is famous for adding the 'vowel points' under all the consonants in the Torah so as to assist readers in pronouncing the words correctly."[58]

Sound changes. The *Encyclopedia Americana* observes: "The occurrence of the four sacred letters in the text of the Bible itself could not be thus replaced, but the same fear of profanation caused the Masoretes (6-8 centuries C.E.) to change the pronunciation by replacing the vowels (which in Hebrew are marked beneath or above the consonants, if not omitted altogether) with the vowels of *Adonai* (or, more rarely, the vowels of *Elohim*)."[59] *Sacred Name Broadcaster* writer-publisher Jacob O. Meyer explains: "The technical term for this practice is called Kethiv-Qere. This means – it is written one way, but read or pronounced another. The Talmud says, '*It is written* יה *yothe hay (YHWH), but it was pronounced* אד *aleph daleth, (Adonai)'*."[60]

Other substitutes.

Orthodox Jews deemed even the substitute title *Adonai* too close to the actual Name of the LORD that they began using, and even coining, still other terms when referring to God.

HaShem. The body of Jewish traditional or oral laws, *Halakha*, requires secondary rules around the primary law to reduce the chance of its being broken. Thus, besides saying *Adonai* in place of the Four-Lettered Name, the Jews came up with still another word to say in place of *Adonai*, whose use was restricted to prayer. In ordinary speech, most Jews call God "*HaShem*" (השם), literally, "the Name."[61]

Adoshem. A combination of *Adonai* and *HaShem*, *Adoshem* was quite common until the mid-20th century. . It took a few centuries for the word to fall out of usage. Rabbi David HaLevi Segal (known as the Taz) discouraged its use in his commentary to the *Shulchan Aruch*. He said that it was disrespectful to combine a Name of God with another word. Some Orthodox Jews, though, still use it occasionally in conversation in place of *Adonai*.[62]

Kel, Elokim. Many Jews sometimes altered the original sound or attached additional sounds to a title of God to alter its pronunciation when using it outside religious ceremonies -- such as adding a "k" to *El* or replacing the "h" with a "k" in *Elohim*, producing contrived titles such as *Kel* and *Elokim*.[63]

Amonai, Abonai Elokenu. Although Orthodox Jews generally substitute *HaShem* for *Adonai* when making audio recordings of prayer services, other Jews say *Amonai*. On other occasions, similar sounding words are used for authenticity, as in the movie *Ushpizin*, where *Abonai Elokenu* (for "the Lord, our God") was used throughout.[64]

Permutations of "YHWH." Jewish mystics have for centuries dabbled in various arrangements of the letters representing the Name of God – from the One-Lettered Name to the 216-Lettered Name. (Please see the Appendix for a comprehensive enumeration.)

"LORD" and "Lord GOD."

"Many English translations of the Bible, following the tradition started by William Tyndale, render *YHWH* as 'LORD' (all capitals) or 'LORD' (small capitals) and *Adonai* as 'Lord' (upper & lower case)."[65] In a few cases where *Adonai YHWH* ("Lord YHWH") appears, the combination is written as "Lord GOD" (*Adonai Elohim*) – not as the unlikely *Adonai Adonai* ("Lord LORD"). Each time the words "LORD" and "GOD" are spelled with capital letters in the Biblical text, it means the original Name of God ("YHWH") has been replaced.

We see this in the following verses: *"The LORD said unto my Lord, Sit thou at my right hand, until I make thine enemies thy footstool"* (Ps 110:1). And, *"Behold, the Lord, the LORD of hosts..."* (Isa 10:33).

Pronunciation lost forever?

In Scripture, Christ never pronounced the Father's Name publicly. Neither did the apostles and the other New Testament writers. As devout Jews, they apparently followed the practice of avoiding the casual utterance of the Four-Lettered Name of God.

Practitioners of the Jewish Kabbalah claim that the true sound of *YHWH* is known to a few, but so strong is the power of the spoken word that the Tetragrammaton is never pronounced by devout Jews. "He who can rightly pronounce it, causeth heaven and earth to tremble, for it is the name which rusheth through the universe."

Jewish denominations teach that, since the Temple where the Name could be uttered only by the High Priest no longer exists, the sacred Name of God should never be spoken, even if one knew how. Hence, Orthodox and some Conservative Jews never attempt to pronounce it for any reason. Some non-Orthodox Jews are willing to say it for educational purposes, but not in casual conversation or even in prayer.[66]

Has the pronunciation of the Tetragrammaton been lost to the world forever? Since the beginning of the Christian era, over 100 presumed pronunciations have been proposed. (Please see list in the Appendix.)

Micah the prophet assures us that *"the man of wisdom shall see thy name..."* (Mic 6:9b). God promises through Isaiah that His chosen people, the elect, will know His true Name. *"Therefore my people shall know my name: therefore they shall know in that day that I am he that doth speak: behold, it is I"* (Isa 52:6).

Safeguarding the Name

The warning against blaspheming God's Name, for which death by stoning is prescribed by Jewish law (Lev 24:16), refers only to the Four-Lettered Name. The ban does not apply to the other forms appearing as part of theoporic names, such as *Yeho- (Jeho-), Yo- (Jo-), -yah (-iah, -jah), -yahu*. Their pronunciations remain widely known and used.[67]

Writing the Name of God is not prohibited, but erasing or defacing it is forbidden. In Deuteronomy 12:2-4, God told the Israelites through Moses: *"Ye shall utterly destroy all the places, wherein the nations which ye shall possess served their gods, upon the high mountains, and upon the hills, and under every green tree: And ye shall overthrow their altars, and break their pillars, and burn their groves with fire; and ye shall hew down the graven images of their gods, and destroy the names of them out of that place. Ye shall not do so unto the LORD your God."*

According to Jewish tradition, there are "7 Indelible Names of God." (Please see in the Appendix.) Moreover, pious Jews write the words "God" and "Lord" as "G-d" and "L-rd" to avoid sinning by unwittingly destroying or defacing a name of God. The rabbinical opinion, however, is that the caveat applies only to the Hebrew names of God, not to words in English or any other language.

"Hebrew texts containing the name of God are not to be destroyed when they are damaged or worn out but must be buried or placed in an appropriate place, similar to the ancient genizot (singular, *genizah*) established to serve as final resting place for such documents."[68]

For all or just a few?

Will the true Name of the LORD be one day known to all the people in the world? Or to just a few faithful believers chosen by the Father?

Moses intoned in his song, shortly before his death: *"I will publish the name of the LORD: ascribe ye greatness unto our God"* (Deut 32:3). He referred to the LORD as *"our God."* Did he mean to proclaim the sacred Name exclusively to the nation of Israel?

About 1000 B.C., it seems very few knew the Sacred Name. David sang: *"I will declare thy name unto my brethren: in the midst of the congregation will I praise thee"* (Ps 22:22). If his brethren knew, there was no point in David's declaring the Name.

As we have previously read, Christ taught the Name only to the men the Heavenly Father had given Him (John 17:6,26).

After Christ ascended to heaven, it appears the apostles did not teach the Sacred Name to others, either. Peter quoted Joel: *"And it shall come to pass, that whosoever shall call on the name of the Lord shall be saved"* (Acts 2:21). But Joel had originally said *"the LORD"* (Joel 2:32). Peter substituted "Lord" (*Adonai* or *Kyrios*) for "LORD" (*YHWH*) to refer to the Father while speaking in public – before thousands of Jews gathered for the feast of Pentecost in Jerusalem. Did he have in mind what Christ once said? *"Give not that which is holy unto the dogs, neither cast ye your pearls before swine, lest they trample them under their feet, and turn again and rend you"* (Matt 7:6).

End-time prophecies. King Solomon prayed after the Temple was completed: *"Hear thou in heaven thy dwelling place, and do according to all that the stranger calleth to thee for: that all people of the earth may know thy name, to fear thee, as do thy people Israel; and that they may know that this house, which I have builded, is called by thy name"* (1 Kings 8:43).

God moreover said through the prophet Malachi: *"For from the rising of the sun even unto the going down of the same my name shall be great among the Gentiles; and in every place incense shall be offered unto my name, and a pure offering: for my name shall be great among the heathen, saith the LORD of hosts"* (Mal 1:11).

The two passages say *"all people of the earth"* and *"Gentiles"* will know the Name of the LORD. Both verses, however, are prophecies of the end-times and the future kingdom of God.

In Joel's apocalyptic prophecy, *"whosoever shall call on the name of the LORD shall be delivered: for in mount Zion and in Jerusalem shall be deliverance, as the LORD hath said, and in the remnant whom the LORD shall call"* (Joel 2:32b). Since the LORD will call only a remnant, it follows that only those few will know and call on His true Name!

11

Two Substitutes, One Original

nd the LORD shall be king over all the earth: in that day shall there be one LORD, and his name one"

-- Zechariah 14:9.

The true pronunciation of the Tetragrammaton has been "lost" for nearly two thousand years now. During that time, it became a practice for some religious Jews to call the Four-Lettered Name of God *Shem ha-Mephorash, Shem ha-Meforash,* or *Shemhamforasch* (the "explicit," "interpreted," or "distinguished" Name), that is, the ineffable Name of God that should never be pronounced.

The concealment of the true sound of the most sacred Name of God has resulted in a great cloud of uncertainty over its actual pronunciation. It has led theologians to suggest various versions. In 1749, the German Biblical scholar Teller mentioned several pronunciations of God's Name that he had come across in his readings: "Jao" (Diodorus of Sicily, Macrobius, Clement of Alexandria, Saint Jerome and Origen); "Jahe" or "Jave" (Samaritans, Epiphanius, and Theodoretus); "Javoh" (Ludwig Cappel); "Jahve" (Drusius); "Jehva" (Hottinger); "Jehovah" (Mercerus); "Jovah" (Castellio); "Jawoh" or "Javoh" (LeClerc). (Please see the Appendix for a comprehensive list of presumed pronunciations.)

Over the millennia, however, at least two presumed forms have found enough favor and following at one time or another to be used as substitutes for the *Shemhamforasch.*

The first substitute

In the 1ˢᵗ century A.D., Josephus gave his readers an inkling on the pronunciation of the Tetragrammaton in his book *Wars of the Jews*. Writing in *Koine* (common) Greek, the international language of the time, he described the garments of the high priest at the Holy Temple in Jerusalem partly as follows: "A mitre also of fine linen encompassed his head, which was tied with a blue riband, about which there was another golden crown, in which was engraven the sacred name (of God) it consists of four vowels."[1]

Four Greek vowels?

Josephus was a Jew who surely knew the Tetragrammaton consisted of four consonants. "Why Josephus speaks of 'four vowels' is uncertain. The first and third letters are probably 'by nature vowels' (ו, י = i, u), though by usage consonants."[2] According to the editor of the Loeb edition of Josephus's *Jewish Wars*, "He was perhaps thinking of a Greek form."[3] Researcher Voy Wilks agrees: "Josephus spoke of four GREEK vowels in order to accommodate his Greek readers, and did not in any way intend to leave the impression that the four Sacred Letters on the priest's garments were vowels from the Hebrew alphabet. After all, the Hebrew alphabet contained no vowels."[4]

B. Earl Allen notes: "The Greek language does not... have a Y sound, nor an H sound in the middle of a word, nor a W sound."[5] Curiously, all three letters that make up the Tetragrammaton were not part of the Greek writing system!

Rabbi Yeshayahu Heiliczer explains that "when the Greeks borrowed the Phoenician/Paleo-Hebrew alphabet they used leftover consonants that did not occur in their language and used them as symbols for vowels. Robert Whiting adds: 'When the Greeks adapted the Phoenician writing system to their own language they... created signs for vowels... Therefore, the Hebrew *yud* (Y) became the Greek vowel *iota* (I); the Hebrew *hey* (H) became the Greek vowel *epsilon* ("E"); and the Hebrew *vav* (W/V) became the Greek vowel *upsilon* ("U")'."[6]

Hebrew names Hellenized. Josephus, in *Antiquities of the Jews*, admits: "With a view to euphony and my readers' pleasure these names have been Hellenized (made Greek). The form in which they appear is not that used in our country, where their structure and termination remain always the same." He explains further: "It is the Greeks who are responsible for this change of nomenclature; for in after ages they rose to power, they appropriated even the glories of the past, embellishing the nation with names they could understand and imposing on them forms of government, as though they descended from themselves."[7]

Adam Clarke's Commentary adds that "neither Greeks nor Romans could pronounce either the Hebrew or Persian names, and when engaged in the task of transcribing, they did according to their manner of pronunciation."[8] The Jews followed suit. "Once the Jews came under Greek influence, we note a tendency to replace or to translate Jewish names by similar sounding Greek names."[9]

Vowel indicators

The Israelites themselves, though, had developed a rudimentary system for indicating vowels. Choon-Leong Seow writes: "Beginning in the monarchial period (10th to late 7th centuries B.C.E.), certain letters ה [H], ו [W], י [Y]) were added at the end of words to indicate various vowels; these three letters, which grammarians call *matres lectionis* ("mothers of reading"), served to give some general indication of vowel quality until the Masoretes (Jewish scholars of the fifth to eleventh centuries C.E.) introduced vowel points for more precision in pronunciation."[10]

Last Day Ministries of Texas agrees: "It is true that the letters י, ה, ו can function as vowel letters... the *yod* acts as a vowel in the words 'Eli'... 'The ה... at the end of word it is always a mere vowel letter, unless marked by a *Mappiq* as a strong consonant...' The *waw* ו... carries the 'o' sound... Therefore the letters *yod*, *he*, and *waw* can be vowel letters, they can also be consonants, depending on the usage."[11]

The booklet *The Mistaken J* gives us more specific pronunciations.[12] The three letters, called vowel-consonants or semivowels because they can be used either as vowels or consonants (like Y) at the end of words, are pronounced as follows:

י	/	Yod	/ Y	=	*ee* as in "see"
ה	/	Hey	/ H	=	*ah* as in "bah"
ו	/	Waw	/ W	=	*oo* as in "cool"

"IAUA."

If the Greek vowel equivalents (Y=I, H=E, W/V=U) shown by Rabbi Heiliczer were used, the sacred Name *YHWH* would be spelled *IEUE* in Greek. However, if the four consonants are transliterated with the three Hebrew semi-vowel sounds *"ee," "ah," "oo,"* we will get the four Greek vowels I,A,Y,A (capitals) or, in lower case, ι,α,υ,α (*iota, alpha, upsilon, alpha*), forming the English word "IAUA."

B. Earl Allen concludes: "(*YHWH*) would be transliterated correctly into Greek as Ιαυα..."[13] The *Seventh-Day Adventist Dictionary* confirms this from Sumerian inscriptions: "He (namely, the God) (is) spelled *Yaua* in cuneiform records."[14]

The form, though, was not linguistically proper in Greek. Brian Allen says: "For the Greek translators to have preserved the true spelling in Greek (*IAUA*) or (*Iaua*) would have caused a language revolution."[15]

"IAUE."

Last Day Ministries teaches: "The sacred name… was transliterated into the Greek IAUE, the Greeks changed the 'a' to 'e', just as they did with Noah, Judah, Oshea, Korah, etc. The Greeks have it Noe, Jude, Osee, and Core, etc."[16] Other examples are: Nogah/Nagge, Joshah/Jose, Jehoshua/Iesoue, Joshua/Josue, Gomorrah/Gomorrhe, Abishua/Abisue, Jeremiah/Ieremie. What could have been the reason for the change?

Feminine "ah"? Author Jacob O. Meyer rationalized: "The '*h*' (hay) has the vowel sound of an A (aw or ah)… The '*h*' (hay) standing at the end of a masculine name has the vowel sound of short E. The Hebrew long A sound (pronounced aw) is a feminine ending at the end of a name…"[17] Therefore, the "hay, the last letter is pronounced 'eh' (short e) and not 'ah' (short a)…"[18]

Not a rigid rule. The contention, however, is not a rigid Hebrew grammar rule. B. Earl Allen says that, while "ah" is indeed many times a feminine ending in Hebrew, there are also dozens of masculine Hebrew names ending with "ah," such as Beerah, Elishah, Eloah, Ishuah, Judah, Mitzvah, Shammah, Togarmah, Torah, Yah. Add to these the scores of theoporic personal names ending with –*yah, -iah,* and *-jah.* He also cites several undeniably masculine common nouns: *raphah* ("giant"), *asah* ("warrior"), *tsaphah* ("watchman"), *tsebaah* ("soldier"), *muwlah* ("circumcision").[19] Besides, "eh" is not necessarily always masculine, either. There are several feminine Hebrew words that end in "e" or "eh": *dave* (weak, menstruous), *madveh* (sickness, disease), *matveh* (what is spun, yarn), *macveh* (a veil), *miqveh* (hope, collection), *naveh* (beautiful, seemly), *Nineveh* (abode of Ninus), *qaveh* (a line), *shaveh* (plain, level plain).[20]

"IAOUE."

The Greek form "IAUE" was further modified in transliteration. *The Missing J* says, "Early Christian writers such as Clement of Alexandria transliterated it into Greek as IAOUE."[21] Seow reports a number of "Greek transliterations of the name in the early Christian period and in some magical papyri in the early centuries of that era, including *Iaoue, Iaouai, Iabe, Iabai,* and *Iaue.*"[22] The sacred Name ending in Greek became either an "e" or a similar sounding "ai."

Prof. Anson F. Rainey, professor of Semitic Linguistics at Tel Aviv University, cites from his studies: "I mentioned the evidence from Greek papyri found in Egypt. The best of these is *Iaouee* (London Papyri, xlvi, 446-483). Clement of Alexandria said, 'The mystic name which is called the tetragrammaton... is pronounced *Iaoue*, which means, "Who is, and who shall be".'"[23]

"IABE."

Another form of the Name surfaced after about two centuries. "Later on, Theodoret (c. 390-455) and Epiphanius (c. 315-404) transliterated the sacred name as Iabe, but a couple of hundred years had passed since Clement..."[24] *The Jewish Encyclopedia* says "Theodoret ('*Quaest. 15* in *Exodum'*) states the Samaritans pronounced the name 'Iabe'."[25]

However, the Jews and Samaritans have many religious differences. "Professor Eerdman's article showed that it is not safe to follow the Samaritan pronunciation advocated by Theodoret and Epiphanius, because the Samaritans were opposed to the Jewish way. 'They built their own Temple on Gerizim and had their own priesthood. They thwarted the Jews whenever they could. On the account of their attitude we may safely assume that the Samaritans had their own (different) pronunciation of the holy name. For this reason the Samaritan pronunciation should not have been regarded (by modern scholars) as evidence for the Jewish pronunciation.'"[26]

Moreover, Christ told the Samaritan woman that her people did not know the LORD. "*Ye worship ye know not what: we know what we worship: for salvation is of the Jews*" (John 4:22).

"YAHWEH."

Meyer tells his readers, "Now, if we combine these (Greek) letters we have the English word in the letters IAUE. Pronounce them slowly and then rapidly. You will discover you are saying YAHWEH!"[27] *The Missing J* suggests a similar exercise: "When we pronounce the Tetragrammaton IAOUE we get the sound 'ee-ah-ou-eh.' Saying it rapidly we produce 'Yah-way,' which appears as Yahweh in English."[28]

The New Bible Dictionary states: "The pronunciation, Yahweh, is indicated by the transliteration of the name into Greek in early Christian literature... 'by Clement of Alexandria, and by Theodoret'."[29] Thus, this presumed pronunciation became the basis of the present-day pronunciation of the Tetragrammaton.

In view of this, the *Encyclopedia Judaica* concludes: "The true pronunciation of the name YHWH was never lost. Several early Greek writers of the Christian Church testify that the name was pronounced

'Yahweh'."[30] Practically all proponents of the name "Yahweh" quote the preceding statement to support their contention. However, common sense tells us: How can latter-day Greek writers "testify" to the authenticity of the ancient Hebrew Name of God?

Imperfect, causative form? *The New 20ᵗʰ Century Encyclopedia of Religious Knowledge*, says the view "first suggested by Jean Le Clerc early in the 18ᵗʰ century and developed in modern form by Paul Haupt and W. F. Albright... holds that *yahwe* was originally a finite *hiphil* verb derived from a causative stem of the Northwest Semitic root *hwy*, 'to come into being' or 'to exist'."[31] Seow, however, ripostes: "The name YHWH is, in any case, a verb form, commonly believed to be a causative meaning 'he (God) causes to be' – that is, 'he creates,' or 'he brings to pass (promises),' or the like... On the other hand, the causative of the root is not attested anywhere; moreover the etymology of the name given in Exodus 3:14 (*Ehyeh-Asher-Ehyeh*, usually translated 'I am that I am') assumes the simple present ('exist, be present'), not the causative ('cause to exist')."[32]

Meaning of "Yahweh." The advocates of the name "Yahweh" cannot seem to agree on one single meaning. According to *The New 20ᵗʰ Century Encyclopedia of Religious Knowledge*: "The divine name would thus go back to a verbal form meaning 'he causes to come into existence,' or in effect, 'he creates'."[33] The Assemblies of Yahweh slightly rewords the meaning. "And in the imperfect form this means that the Name of the Heavenly Father should be understood as He Who shall cause things to exist or He Who shall cause to be."[34] The Ambassador College in California, though, proposes other definitions: "But Yahweh is a name meaning the Everliving, or the Eternal. There is no one word in the English language that translates it exactly... Actually, Yahweh means the Self-Existent, Everliving, Eternally Living Creating One."[35] We already know the meaning of the Tetragrammaton. The meanings proposed by advocates of the form "Yahweh" are different. The true pronunciation of the Four-Lettered Name of God should carry the original meaning -- "I AM THAT I AM."

Doubts and disagreements.

Wikipedia, the online encyclopedia, states: "The name YHWH is often reconstructed as *Yahweh*, based on a range of circumstantial historical and linguistic evidence. Most scholars do not view it as an 'accurate' reconstruction in an absolute sense, but as the best possible guess."[36] The *Aid to Bible Understanding* also says that "there is by no means unanimity among scholars on the subject (of the form 'Yahweh'), some favoring yet other pronunciations."[37]

Gesenius' Hebrew-Chaldee Lexicon tells us that "this same form (Yahweh) appears on the gems of the Egyptian Gnostics as the name of God... (but these gems are not of the most remote antiquity; they are the work of heretics of the second and third centuries)."[38]

Even those who use the form "Yahweh" maintain a certain amount of reservation. Meyer relates that one of his Hebrew professors once said: "We use Yahweh because it is the best representation of the original letters of the Name, transliterated into English. Scholarship is now quite positive of this form, although our minds are not closed should new evidence be introduced."[39]

Clement of Alexandria (A.D. 150-211/215?), Epiphanius (315-403), and Theodoret (393-458/466?) were among the most prominent leaders of the early Christian Church. We can safely say that Epiphanius and Theodoret had read the writings of their predecessor Clement. If Clement's pronunciation, "Yahweh" (Ιαουέ or Ιαουαι), was beyond the shadow of any doubt, why would Epiphanius and Theodoret propose other pronunciations?

The second substitute

A dark cloud of doubt obviously hangs over the veracity of the pronunciation "Yahweh." If the uncertainty did not persist, Bible scholars and theologians would not have adopted other forms that appeared in the succeeding centuries of the Christian era.

"YaHoWaH."

Sometime from the 8th to the 11th centuries A.D., the Masoretes inserted the vowels of *Adonay* ("a-o-a") in-between the consonants of the Tetragrammaton (Y-H-W-H). On the surface, the process would have resulted in the form "YaHoWaH"; but the intention was to make the vowel points serve as a reminder to the reader not to pronounce the sacred Name, but instead say "Adonay" ("LORD").

According to *Wikipedia*, the early Christian translators of the Torah did not know that pronouncing those consonants and vowel points together was a phonological impossibility in Hebrew. On top of that, rabbinical Judaism does not accept as correct the pronunciation as it is vowel pointed in the Masoretic Text.[40]

"YeHoWaH."

In any case, the "a" in the first syllable was pronounced as an "e." The *Encyclopedia Judaica* details why. "In the early Middle Ages, when the consonantal text of the Bible was supplied with vowel points to facilitate the correct traditional reading, the vowel points for 'Adonai'

(Lord) with one variation – a *sheva* with the first *yod* of YHWH instead of the *hataf-patah* under the *aleph* of *'Adonai* -- were used for YHWH, thus producing the form – YeHoWaH."[41]

Vowels of *Adonai, Eloah, Elohim*. Notes Prof. Rainey: "The fact is that Jewish tradents (who put the vowel points in the Hebrew text) borrowed the vowels from another word, either *adonai* 'my lord(s),' or *elohim* 'God.' They avoided the very short *a* vowel in this borrowing because it might have led the synagogue reader to make a mistake and pronounce the correct first syllable of the Sacred Name, namely – *ya*... The synagogue reader saw *Yehowah* in his text and read it *adonai.*"[42]

Rabbi Heiliczer says, "When the Masorites added vowels to the Hebrew text in the middle ages they substituted the vowels of the word *'Adonai.'* Later the vowels for *Eloah* (singular of *Elohim*) were used for creating *Yehowah.*"[43] We also read in the *Century Bible* that "when the vowel points were added, the vowels of *Adonai* or *Elohim* were written with YHWH, as a direction that these words were to be read instead of the word whose consonants were YHWH. Thus we find the combinations Yehowah and Yehowih."[44] In a few cases where the phrase *Adonai YHWH* appears in the text, the Masoretes inserted the vowels of *Elohim* in the Four-Lettered Name, so the reader would say "Lord GOD," not "Lord LORD." This made the Tetragrammaton look like "YeHoWiH."

"IEHOUA."

According to the *Oxford English Dictionary*, the Tetragrammaton first appeared in Latin form in 1516.[45] Petrus Galatinus (Peter Galatin), confessor to Pople Leo X, spelled the Name of God as "Iehoua" in his popular book *De Arcanis Catholicae Veritatis* ("Concerning Secrets of the Universal Truth").

How did it come about? In Medieval Europe, the sound of the letter *yod* ("Y") of *YHWH* was substituted for by the Latin letter "I." Then, the consonant "W" became a "U." The *World Book* explains: "U... came from a letter which the Semitic peoples of Syria and Palestine called *waw*... About A.D. 900, people began to write u in the middle of a word..."[46] Lastly, the weak sounding "H" at the end of the Four-Lettered Name was dropped, producing "IEHOUA."

"IEHOUAH."

The Sacred Name again took on a new form in the early years of the Reformation: "Iehouah." In a Jehovah's Witnesses booklet entitled *The Name* we read: "The name first appeared in an English Bible in 1530, when William Tydale published a translation of the first five books of the

Bible. In this he included the name of God, usually spelled Iehouah, in several verses."[47]

One of the leading Church reformers in England, Tyndale restored the "H" at the end of the Latin version of the Tetragrammaton in his Bible translations.

"IEHOVAH."

The "U" in IEHOUAH was later replaced with a "V," forming yet another variant of the Sacred Name. The *World Book* tells us: "The Romans, when they adopted the letter (U), dropped its bottom stroke and wrote it as V... During the Renaissance, it became customary among the people to use u as a vowel and v as a consonant."[48]

The *Wikipedia* additionally says: "They took the letters 'IHVH' from the Latin Vulgate, and the vowels 'a-o-a' were inserted into the text rendering IAHOVAH or 'Iehovah' in 16th century English."[49]

Rabbi Heiliczer explains from a Jewish point of view: "Since in modern Hebrew the letter *vuv* is pronounced "V" in place of its ancient pronunciation which is somewhere between a 'W' and a 'V', *Yehowah* became *Yehovah*. This became transliterated in the original King James Version as *Iehovah*..."[50]

"JEHOVAH."

Seow relates: "From this (*IeHoVaH*) the Germanic form *Jehovah* was derived in the early European translations and attested in 17th century English."[51] As we have seen, in the Middle Ages the letter "I" developed a decorative variant with a tail -- "J." The emergence of the dictionary in the 17th century demanded a consistent spelling of words, so the use of "I" as a vowel and "J" as a consonant became established. When the new letter "J" was added to the English alphabet, "Iehovah" became "Jehovah."

The pronunciation, though, also changed. Rabbi Heiliczer protests: "But the 'J' was pronounced as we now pronounce 'Y'... So the 'J' in Jehovah is incorrect, as are the vowels eh-o-ah which actually come from Eloah. In fact only the two 'h's' are correct."[52]

Used in Bibles. In places where the Jewish scribes missed replacing the Tetragrammaton with *Adonay* ("the LORD"), latter Bible translators spelled out YHWH as "Jehovah" -- in such early English Bibles as the Coverdale Bible (1535), Matthew Bible (1537), Bishops' Bible (1568), Geneva Bible (1560). Later translations with that form of the Name are the King James Version (KJV), American Standard Version (ASV), Darby Bible, Green's Literal Translation (LITV), Young's

Literal Translation, Modern King James Version (MKJV), New English Bible, New World Translation.

The verses containing "Jehovah" are Exodus 6:3 and Psalm 83:18. In two places where the Sacred Name is doubled as "YH YHWH," with the Two-Lettered Name and Four-Lettered Name appearing together, the English translation is "LORD JEHOVAH" (Isa 12:2 and 26:4).

Meaning of "JEHOVAH." The Bible reference *Insight on the Scriptures* of the Jehovah's Witnesses gives a meaning for "Jehovah" that is closely similar to those given for the form "Yahweh." "The name Jehovah comes from the Hebrew verb *hawah*, 'become,' and actually means 'He Causes to Become'."[53]

Doubts and disagreements.

There was opposition against this form of the Name from the very first time it was used, Joseph Rotherham, editor of *The Emphasized Bible*, said. "The pronunciation *Jehovah* was unknown until 1520, when it was introduced by Galatinus; but it was contested by Le Mercier, J. Drusius, and L. Capellus, as against grammatical and historical propriety."[54] He categorically stated that the Name of God is "erroneously written and pronounced Jehovah..."[55]

The Jewish Encyclopedia notes: "This name (of God) is commonly represented in modern translations by the form 'Jehovah,' which, however, is a philological impossibility..."[56] Concludes the *Encyclopaedia Britannica*: "The pronunciation 'Jehovah' is an error resulting among Christians from combining the consonants Yhwh (Jhvh) with the vowels of 'adhonay, 'Lord,' which the Jews in reading the Scriptures substituted for the sacred name..."[57]

Either or neither of the two?

The *Encyclopaedia Britannica* further observes: "Although Christian scholars after the Renaissance and Reformation periods used the term Jehovah for YHWH, in the 19th and 20th centuries biblical scholars again began to use the form Yahweh..."[58] The Jehovah's Witnesses explain in print: "While inclining to view the pronunciation 'Yahweh' as the more correct way, we have retained the form 'Jehovah' because of people's familiarity with it since the 14th century."[59] Also, the Roman Catholic translator of the Westminster Version of the Sacred Scriptures confesses: "I should have preferred to write 'Yahwe,' which, although not certain, is admittedly superior to 'Jehovah'."[60] However, *Wikipedia* notes that "neither 'Jehovah' or 'Yahweh' is recognized in Judaism..."[61]

Origins of the Names "Yahweh" and "Jehovah"

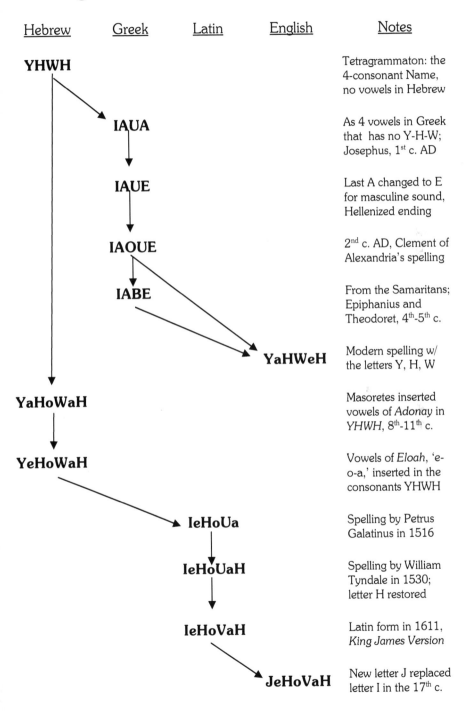

Hebrew	Greek	Latin	English	Notes
YHWH				Tetragrammaton: the 4-consonant Name, no vowels in Hebrew
	IAUA			As 4 vowels in Greek that has no Y-H-W; Josephus, 1st c. AD
	IAUE			Last A changed to E for masculine sound, Hellenized ending
	IAOUE			2nd c. AD, Clement of Alexandria's spelling
	IABE			From the Samaritans; Epiphanius and Theodoret, 4th-5th c.
			YaHWeH	Modern spelling w/ the letters Y, H, W
YaHoWaH				Masoretes inserted vowels of *Adonay* in *YHWH*, 8th-11th c.
YeHoWaH				Vowels of *Eloah*, 'e-o-a,' inserted in the consonants YHWH
		IeHoUa		Spelling by Petrus Galatinus in 1516
		IeHoUaH		Spelling by William Tyndale in 1530; letter H restored
		IeHoVaH		Latin form in 1611, *King James Version*
			JeHoVaH	New letter J replaced letter I in the 17th c.

The original Name

"And God spoke to Moses and said to him: "I am the LORD. I appeared to Abraham, to Isaac, and to Jacob, as God Almighty, but by My name, LORD, I was not known to them" (Ex 6:2-3, NKJV). "God Almighty" is English for *El Shaddai*, which is actually a title.

Sigmund Mowinchel, in a *Hebrew Union College Annual* article in 1961, analyzes the passage: "It is generally recognized that (Exodus) 6:2-3 states that the name (YHWH) was not known till it was revealed to Moses, and that to the patriarchs God had appeared as El Shaddai."[62]

A pre-Mosaic Name?

After Eve gave birth to Cain, she referred to God as "the LORD." *"And Adam knew Eve his wife; and she conceived, and bare Cain, and said, I have gotten a man from the LORD"* (Gen 4:1). As we know, the term "the LORD" has been placed as a substitute in all the verses where the Tetragrammaton had originally been written.

After Adam's grandson Enos by Seth was born, men began to invoke the Name of "the LORD." *"And to Seth, to him also there was born a son; and he called his name Enos: then began men to call upon the name of the LORD"* (Gen 4:25-26).

Abraham, who lived some 500 years before God revealed His Four-Lettered Name to Moses, also called on the Name of "the LORD." *"And the LORD appeared unto Abram, and said, Unto thy seed will I give this land: and there builded he an altar unto the LORD, who appeared unto him. And he removed from thence unto a mountain on the east of Bethel, and pitched his tent, having Bethel on the west, and Hai on the east: and there he builded an altar unto the LORD, and called upon the name of the LORD"* (Gen 12:7-8).

We can see that the first men, long before Moses was born, called on the Name of "the LORD." What was that Name? Did the patriarchs know a primeval sacred Name that was different from *YHWH?*

A deeper meaning?

The *Encyclopedia Judaica* notes the differing opinions: "According to the documentary hypothesis, the literary sources in the Pentateuch known as the Elohist and the Priestly Document never use the name (YHWH) for God until it is revealed to Moses (Ex. 3:13; 6:2-3); but the Yahwist source uses it from Genesis 2:4 on and puts the name in Eve's declaration, 'I along with (YHWH) have made a man,' thus implying that it was known to the first human generation (Gen. 4:1; cf 4:26)."[63]

Mowinchel believes the Name YHWH was known to the first men. "The earliest Israelite historian J uses the name Yahweh in the patriarchal stories without any reservation, and in his opinion it was known already by the third generation of mankind; at the time of Enosh, the son of Seth, (men) – or as the Vulgate says: he – began to call upon the name of Yahweh... the tribes that under the leadership of Moses – became the people of Israel, already knew and worshiped... Yahweh... What Exod. 3:16 tells us is that the deeper meaning of the name was revealed to Moses by Yahweh himself... When the elders of the people hear that he knows even the mysterious meaning of the name, then they must believe that he is telling the truth.

"In J's opinion it was not the name of Yahweh, which was revealed to Moses here – that was known already by Enosh centuries before – but the deeper meaning, which according to Yahwistic tradition and the theology of the 'school' of J, was hidden in the name."[64]

The meaning of His Name that the LORD gave to Moses in Exodus 3:14 is "I AM THAT I AM." On the other hand, Mowinchel fails to say if J (Jahwistic or Yahwistic source) gives the least bit of a hint as to what the deeper, hidden meaning of God's Sacred Name is supposed to be.

Another, earlier Name.

If God revealed the Tetragrammaton for the first time only to Moses, then the Name of God that Adam and Eve, Seth, Enos, Abraham, and others knew and called upon was not *YHWH*. Clearly, it was another, earlier Name. But why does "the LORD," which was used to replace *YHWH* in Scriptures, occur as early as in the book of Genesis?

Could it be that Moses, who wrote the first five books of the Bible, in his great zeal and esteem for the sacred Name revealed to him, began using the Tetragrammaton in the Scriptural text right from the creation of Adam (Gen 2:4)?

Alternative suffixal form

We have seen that in Israelite theoporic names, the suffix *-iah* or *-jah* is actually the abbreviated or Two-Lettered Name of God, *Yah*. The *Encyclopaedia Judaica*, however, informs us that the suffix has yet another form. "This is confirmed, at least for the vowel of the first syllable of the name, by the shorter form Yah, which is sometimes used in poetry (e.g., Ex. 15:2) and the -yahu or -yah that serves as the final syllable in many Hebrew names."[65] The alternative form is *-yahu*.

The *Jewish Encyclopedia* corroborates this, saying that the two short forms of the Name appear as "Yahu or Yah (יהו, יה)" in the second part of such names."[66] Seow gives an example: "In the final position it appears as -*yahu* (-*iah*) or -*yah* (-*iah*) as in the alternate spellings for 'Azariah,' *Azaryahu* and *Azaryah*."[67] In this vein, throughout the Hebrew

Scriptures the name of the prophet Elijah, except on four or five occasions, is spelled Eliyahu, with a *waw* in the end. Is there much difference between the two? They are probably as different as two kingdoms were from one another.

2 kingdoms, 2 suffixes.

After King Solomon died around 975 B.C., the Israelite monarchy broke up into two -- the ten-tribe kingdom of Israel in the north and the two-tribe kingdom of Judah in the south. The separation led to a distinction between the suffix of theoporic names in the north and of that in the south. *Biblical Archaelogy Review* editor Hershel Shanks said in the magazine's May-June 1994 issue: "-*yahu* (was) the common suffix in Judah... (in the northern kingdom of Israel the suffix was *yah*)."[68]

Writer P. Kyle McCarter concurs: "The expected form of the divine name... when it appears as the final part of a Judahite personal name in this period (late 7th to the early 6th centuries B.C.), is *yhw*, pronounced *yahu* (long *a* and *u*)..."[69]

Archeological evidences.

The March-April 1996 issue of *Biblical Archaelogy Review* featured a limestone seal from the 7th century B.C. that reads, "Belonging to Asayahu, servant of the King" (actually a high royal official). The short form "Asaiah" is in 2 Chronicles 34:20 -- "*And the king commanded Hilkiah... and Asaiah a servant of the king's...*"[70]

A 7th c. BC limestone seal with the name *Asayahu*. Suffix YHW seen as 3 leftmost letters in the top line.

The same issue of the magazine had a 7th-6th century B.C *bulla* (seal impression on clay) used by a scribe to seal a document, which reads, "Belonging to Berekyahu, son of Neriyahu, the Scribe." The names have been abbreviated in the Bible: "*Then Jeremiah called Baruch, the son of Neriah...*" (Jer 36:4).[71]

In its May-June 1994 issue, *Biblical Archaelogy Review* showed an inscription

A 7th-6th c. BC *bulla* (seal impression on clay), with the names *Berekyahu* and *Neriyahu*. YHW is in the last 3 letters at the end of lines 1 and 2.

above a rock-tomb in Silwan, Israel, that says: "This is (the sepulchre of ...) *yahu*, who is over the house." The term "over the house" refers to the royal steward, who Bible scholars believe was Shebnayahu (short form, Shebna) in Isaiah 22:15. *"Thus saith the Lord God of hosts, Go, get thee unto this treasurer, even unto Shebna, which is over the house..."*[72]

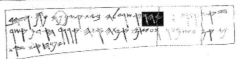

The name suffix -*yahu* seen above the entrance of a rock-tomb in Israel as the 3 Hebrew letters YHW in the top line, with the *yod* partly destroyed to the left of the hole.

Three-Lettered Name

Scholars have found that *Yahu* is more than just a suffix, it actually is another proper Name of God, spelled with only three letters of the Tetragrammaton! This third form became known to "scholars after the discovery of the independent form *YHW* in the Egyptian papyri of the 5th century B.C. from the Elephantine archives..."[73] According to *The New 20th Century Encyclopedia of Religious Knowledge*, in the Old World the form YHW was used by the Jews in the Elephantine Island in Egypt.[74] Last Day Ministries of Texas shares additional information: "There was evidently a Temple built to YHW in Elephantine, Egypt. Many documents from this place show that the sacred name was written YHW..."[75]

Seow suggests that this three-lettered Name is another short form of the Tetragrammaton. "The final *H* in *YHWH* is not a real consonant... the real consonants of the divine name are *YHW*... in several inscriptions from Kuntillet 'Arjud in the Sinai... (a)mong the attestations of the name in the inscriptions from that site is one example of *YHW*... the final vowel not being indicated by the letter *H* in this instance."[76]

Presumed pronunciation.

In the Dead Sea Scrolls from Qumran, Professor Emeritus George Wesley Buchanan of the Wesley Theological Seminary in Washington D.C. found a similar three-lettered Name transliterated in Greek. He speculates: "Clement of Alexandria spelled the Tetragrammaton IAOAI (Ya-oo-ai), IAOE (Ya-oo-eh), and IAO (Ya-oh)... Among the caves of Qumran was a Greek text that included a few Greek word of Leviticus

(4QLXX Lev), one of which was the Tetragrammaton. It was spelled IAΩ (Ya-oh). This is apparently a two-syllable word, but the second syllable is only a vowel. There is no way that it could be rendered 'Yahweh.' This was a transliteration of the Hebrew Ya-ho (יהו). It is the same spelling given in the fifth century B.C. Aramaic papyri. From the Aramaic alone this word could be pronounced either Ya-hoo or Ya-hoh... When the Tetragrammaton was pronounced in one syllable it was 'Yah' or 'Yo.' ...If it was ever abbreviated to two syllables it would have been 'Yahoo'..."[77]

The Century Cyclopedia attests to it. "The early Gnostics, moreover, when they transcribed it in Greek characters, wrote Iao (that is, Yaho)."[78]

Ziony Zevit confirms the "oo" sound at the end of words: "...waw was used to indicate the final vowel 'u'... By employing waw as a m.l. (matres lectionis or vowel indicator) for 'o' in word final positions, some potential ambiguities were eliminated... in this position there was small opportunity for confusion between waw as a m.l. for 'o' and as a m.l. for 'u,' because the first value would occur exclusively with substantives, while the second, most frequently with verbs."[79]

Hence, YHW can be explained as follows: The first two letters YH are the two consonants of the first syllable "YaH," while the third and last letter W is a matres lectionis indicating the vowel "U." Therefore, YHW = YH ("YaH") + W ("U") = "YaHU."

Pronunciation confirmed.

The Century Cyclopedia proves the pronunciation from ancient artifacts: "...we may gather from the contemporary Assyrian monuments that it was pronounced Yahu. Wherever an Israelitish name is met with in the cuneiform inscriptions which, like Jehu or Hezekiah, is compounded with the divine title, the latter appears as Yahu, Jehu being Yahua, and Hezekiah Khazaki-yahu."[80]

Rabbi Heiliczer says it is indeed the pronunciation in the vowel-pointed Hebrew Scriptures. "Moreover the first three letters, yud-hey-vuv (YHW), do appear by themselves in the Tenakh and always with vowels making the pronunciation 'yahu'."[81]

A curious thing, moreover, has been observed. If we try to vocalize YHW as vowels only, using the three consonants used at the end of words to indicate vowel sounds (yod, ee as in "see"; hey, ah as in "bah"; and waw, oo as in "pool"), the resulting sound is: ee-ah-oo = Yahu. It seems that, whether we read the Three-Lettered Name as Hebrew consonants only or pronounce the characters as vowels only, we get the same result -- "Yahu!"

Both a suffix and a prefix

Unlike the Two-Lettered Name "Yah," which is used only as a suffix, the Three-Lettered Name "Yahu" is used as both a suffix and a prefix. The *Jewish Encyclopedia* notes the use of "the forms Jeho or Yeho (יהו), and Jo or Yo (יו, contracted from יהו), which the word assumes in combination in the first part of compound proper names, and Yahu or Yah (יהו, יה) in the second part of such names."[82]

The *Encyclopaedia Britannica* adds that "the usual form is YH or Yhw, occurring in unvocalized texts of the 5ᵗʰ and 4ᵗʰ centuries B.C.E. These forms appear in the Old Testament sporadically as the independent Yah and regularly as Yah or Yahu at the end and Yeho or Yo at the beginning of proper names."[83]

From Yahu to Yeho.

The *Century Cyclopedia* informs us that the Three-Lettered Name YHW, when used as a prefix, "Even according to the Masoretes it must be read Yeho when it forms part of a proper name."[84]

Seow explains the change of *Yahu* to *Yeho* when used as a prefix in theoporic names as a linguistic peculiarity: "...the first vowel was further changed from *a* to *e*, in accordance with rules of Hebrew Grammar."[85] Rabbi Heiliczer thinks it was introduced on purpose. "When a Hebrew name in the Masoretic Tenakh begins with a part of the divine name, the vowels are given as E-O (shortened form of Eh-O-ah from Eloah). Some examples are: Yehoshaphat (Jehoshaphat) YEHO-Shaphat; Yehoshua (Joshua) YEHO-Shua."[86]

From Yeho- to Yo-, Jo-.

Yeho-, though, through syncope or word contraction was further abbreviated to *Y'ho-*, before eventually becoming *Yo-*, then *Jo-*. Author Garrison tells us that the form *Yehoshua*, "in its original Hebrew form it was *Y'hoshua*... frequently abbreviated to *Joshua*."[87] Seow gives another example: "In personal names, what scholars call the 'Yahwistic theoporic element' appears in the initial position as *Yeho-* (*Jeho-*) or *Yo-* (*Jo-*), as in the two forms for 'Jonathan,' *Yehonatan* and *Yonatan*."[88]

Yo- was written as *Io-* in Scriptures before the letter "J" became a consonant. As an Oil Derrick tract explains: "This short form of 'Io' as the sacred name can also be seen in the original 1611 King James Version where it is attached to such Biblical names as Ioshua, Iohn, Ioel, Ionathan, Ioshaphat, Iosedech, Iochebed, Ioram, Ioseph, Ionadab etc. *Strong's Exhaustive Concordance* shows the fuller form of these names as Yehoshua, Yehochanan, Yehonathan, Yehoshaphat, Yehosedech, Yehoseph, Yehoram, Yehonadab."[89]

Names prefixed with YHW.

Emeritus professor Buchanan cites more instances: "The Hebrew for the name 'Jonathan' is Yah-ho-na-than (יהונתן), 'Yaho... has given.' John was spelled 'Yaho-cha-nan' (יהוחנן), 'Yaho... has been gracious.' Elijah's name was Eli-yahoo (אליהו), 'My God is Yahoo...' Ancients often gave their children names that included the name of their deity."[90]

One prominent theoporic name today is the surname of the Israeli prime minister: Netanyahu, which means "given by (netan) Yahu" (Nethaniah -- 2 Chron 17:8, Jer 36:14, etc.). It was adopted by his grandfather in Lithuania in 1920, following the Hebrew language revival that began among the Jews in 17th century Europe. When the sacred suffix is transposed to form the prefix, the name becomes Yahu-netan ("Yahu has given [netan]"), but is spelled Yeho-natan. In the course of time Yehonatan has been contracted to Yonatan. When the new letter "J" became part of the English alphabet, the name became "Jonathan."

Incidentally, Prime Minister Benjamin Netanyahu's elder brother was redundantly named Jonathan (Yonatan) Netanyahu. A major in the Israel Defense Forces, he led IDF commandos in rescuing over 100 hostages held by terrorists in a jetliner at Entebbe Airport in Uganda in 1976. He died a hero's death as the only IDF casualty in the daring raid.

Below is an illustration of how some Biblical names developed.

How "Yahu" Became "Jo" in Theoporic Names

Names w/ Yahu last*	Nethaniah/ Netanyahu	Isaiah/ Yeshayahu	Hananiah/ Chananyahu	Elijah/ Eliyahu	Abijah/ Abiyahu
Meaning	Given (by) Yahu	Salvation (is) Yahu	Gracious (has been) Yahu	My God (is) Yahu	My father (is) Yahu
Same names w/ Yahu first	Yahunatan	Yahushua	Yahuchanan	Yahuel	Yahuab
Meaning	Yahu (has) given	Yahu (is) salvation	Yahu (has been) gracious	Yahu (is) God	Yahu (is) father
First 'a' to 'e,' 'u' to 'o'	Yehonatan	Yehoshua	Yehochanan	Yehoel	Yehoab
'e' lost thru syncope	Y'honatan	Y'hoshua	Y'hochanan	Y'hoel	Y'hoab
'h' dropped over time	Yonatan	Yoshua	Yohanan	Yoel	Yoab
I used for Y, MiddleAges	Ionathan	Iosua	Iohann, Iohn	Ioel	Ioab
New letter J replaced I	Jonathan	Joshua	Johan, John	Joel	Joab

*Modern English Biblical forms over Anglicized traditional Hebrew pronunciations

Old Testament proof

Proof exists in the Old Testament that *Yahu* was truly God's first and original Name that the ancients knew from the time of Adam – the name of Moses's mother. *"And the name of Amram's wife was Jochebed, the daughter of Levi, whom her mother bare to Levi in Egypt: and she bare unto Amram Aaron and Moses, and Miriam their sister* (Num 26:59).

Moses's mother was Jochebed, a granddaughter of Jacob (Israel) by his son Levi. She married her brother Kohath's son Amram, who became Moses's father (Ex 6:16-18,20). Jochebed lived around 3,600 years ago in Egypt during the period of Israelite bondage.

Jochebed means "YHWH is glory"[91] – *chebed* coming from the Hebrew root-word *kabed*, meaning "splendor, glory, honor." The initial letter "J" in her name was anciently a "Y," so *Jochebed* used to be *Yochebed*. Even earlier, it was *Y'hochebed*, from *Yehochebed*. And, long before that, its original form was *Yahuchebed*.

Since Jochebed was born and given her particular theoporic name by her parents <u>before</u> the Creator revealed a new Name to her future son, Moses, that leaves us with but one conclusion: The sacred Name of God that the Israelites knew before the time of Moses was *YAHU*.

"According to Albright (Assyrian Cuneiform scholar) and others the most ancient form of the sacred name (outside of Scripture) is 'Yahu'. YHW or YHU are indicated by the same letter in Hebrew."[92] Researcher James Montgomery, in the *Journal of Biblical Literature* (1944), put the matter to rest: "The earliest form of the Name was doubtless Yahu."[93]

The meaning of *Yahu*. If the Four-Lettered Name *YHWH* means "I AM THAT I AM" and the Two-Lettered Name *YH* stands for "I AM," what does the Three-Lettered Name *YHW* signify?

There are several Biblical names that similarly end in *-hu*, other than those ending in *–yahu*. Let us examine three of them.

1) Abihu, a son of Aaron, Moses's brother (Ex 6:23, etc.). *Abihu* in Hebrew means "My father (*Abi*) is he (*huw*)."[94]

2) Elihu, David's eldest brother, *et al.* (1 Chron 27:18, etc.). *Elihu* signifies "My God (*Eli*) is He (*huw*)."[95]

3) Jehu, a prophet of Israel, *et al.* (1 Kings 16:12, etc.). *Jehu* stands for "The LORD (YHWH) is He (*huw*)."[96] (Note that in all three instances the last letter "w" is lost in personal names. *Huw* is written *hu* in modern Hebrew.)

Based on the foregoing examples, it follows *YAHU* means "I AM (*Yah*) HE (*huw*)." (The original Hebrew wording *Yah huw* is never used in ordinary speech. In common usage, "I am he" is *Ani hu*.)

Obviously, *Yahu* is the abbreviation of *Yah huw*. *Gesenius Hebrew Grammar* explains how it happened: "Assimilation usually takes place when one consonant which closes a syllable passes over into another beginning the next syllable and forms with it a strengthened letter."[97] In other words, if the last consonant of a syllable is the same as the first consonant of the succeeding syllable, the two identical consonants are written as only one letter.

Accordingly, the two words *Yah* and *huw* together form *Yahhuw,* which becomes *Yahuw* in conformity with Hebrew grammar rules, and is further simplified to *Yahu,* as illustrated below:

Yah	+	*huw*	=	*Yahhuw*	=	*Yahuw*	=	*Yahu*
("I AM")	+	("HE")	=					("I AM HE")

Allusion by the LORD.

The LORD alluded to His Three-Lettered Name on many occasions: *"See now that I, even I, am he..."* (Deut 32:39).

"Who hath wrought and done it, calling the generations from the beginning? I the LORD, the first, and with the last; I am he" (Isa 41:4).

"Hearken unto me, O Jacob and Israel, my called; I am he; I am the first, I also am the last" (Isa 48:12; also 43:10,13,25; 46:4; 51:12).

New Testament Proof

YHW appears to have been spoken by Christ Himself, *"Then Judas, having received a detachment of troops, and officers from the chief priests and Pharisees, came there with lanterns, torches, and weapons. Jesus therefore, knowing all things that would come upon Him, went forward and said to them, "Whom are you seeking?" They answered Him, "Jesus of Nazareth." Jesus said to them, "I am He." And Judas, who betrayed Him, also stood with them. Then -- when He said to them, "I am He,"-- they drew back and fell to the ground"* (John 18:3-6, NKJV).

Why did Judas and the band of men fall to the ground? What power did the Three-Lettered Name of God have? We see why in Temple worship practices: "The High Priest spoke the name of God on the Day of Atonement in his recitation of Lev. xvi. 30 during the confessions of sins; and when the priests and the people in the great hall heard him utter the 'Shem ha-Meforash (the Distinguished Name),' they prostrated themselves and glorified God."[98]

Translator H. Danby corroborates this in the *Mishnah,* a collection of Jewish legal traditions. "And when the priests and the people which stood in the Temple Court heard the Expressed Name come forth from the mouth of the High Priest, they used to kneel and bow themselves and fall down on their faces and say, 'Blessed be the name of the glory of his kingdom for ever and ever!' (*Yoma* 6:2)."[99]

Many people get the impression that the men arresting Christ fell backwards. On the contrary, they fell forward on their faces in an act of worship! They were from the Temple, and, as our references relate, they customarily fell to the ground on their faces whenever they heard the Name of God. Apparently, when Christ said "I am He," He used the sacred phrase *Yah huw* – i.e., the Three-Lettered Name YHW (*Yahu*).

Disappearance.

Why is the form *Yahu* not found in the Bible? Allen says, "When the Jews were carried into Babylon in 606 B.C.E. many of the personal names had the element 'yahu'…"[100] Yet, Zevit found that when the Jews returned from Babylonian captivity 70 years later, the suffix had changed from -*yahu* to -*yah*. "An examination of the chronological distribution of the suffix in Judean inscriptions indicates that -yhw is characteristically pre-Exilic, and -yh post-Exilic… Japhet points out that in Ezra-Nehemiah all names with this element are written -yh with one exception…"[101]

After Babylon fell, the Jews began returning to Jerusalem to rebuild the city and the Temple under a decree King Cyrus of Persia issued in 536 B.C. By the time of the Jewish leaders Ezra and Nehemiah, the use of -*yahu* as a suffix in Hebrew theoporic names had ceased.

About 2,000 years later, in Europe, even the rare names which had the suffix -*yahu* in the Hebrew text, such as *Eliyahu*, were transliterated by Bible translators with the more familiar -*iah* and -*jah* suffixes

The 3 Personal Names of God

Below is a summary of the LORD's three Personal Names:

Spelling	Pronunciation	Meaning	Passages	Notes
Y-H (י ה)	**"YaH"**	"I AM"	Ex 3:14; John 8:58	As in *Isaiah* or *Hallelujah*
Y-H-W (י ה ו)	**"YaHU"**	"I AM HE"	Isa 41:4, etc. John 18:5-6	As in *Eliyahu* or *Netanyahu*
Y-H-W-H (י ה ו ה)	God's most sacred Name, known only to a few.*	"I AM THAT I AM"	Ex 3:14; 6:3	The "Ineffable Name," never spoken aloud

*The keys to the sound of the Tetragrammaton are plainly stated in this book. "*They are all plain to him that understandeth, and right to them that find knowledge*" (Prov 8:9).

Called by God's Name

The LORD said Israel is *"my people, which are called by my name..."* (2 Chron 7:14a). God's Name is truly in the names the world calls the Israelite people. Let us review those two Hebrew names.

God renamed Jacob "Israel" after he wrestled all night with an angel (Gen 32:28). Israel is a compound name made up of *sarah* ("to prevail, have power") and *El* ("mighty one, God"), signifying "contender with God," "having power with God," or "ruler with God." The descendants of Jacob's twelve sons became the "Twelve Tribes of Israel." An Israeli today, therefore, has "God" in his designated nationality.

Judah was Jacob's fourth son. His mother said after giving birth to him: *"Now will I praise the LORD: therefore she called his name Judah..."* (Genesis 29:35b). Strong's Greek/Hebrew Definitions says the Hebrew original of "Judah" was *Yehuwdah*. In consequence, Jews as a nation are called *Yehuda*. The traditional term for a Jew is *Yehudi* (plural, *Yehudim*).

Two Biblical names have similar first syllables -- *Jehucal* (Jer 37:3) and its short form *Jucal* (Jer 38:1). The *New Unger's Bible Dictionary* defines *Jehucal* (*Yehuwkal*) as "YHWH is able (*yakol*, "to be able")."[102] It looks like the "Yehu-" in *Yehuda* was originally *Yahu*.

Bottom line: People of Hebrew descent today can be called "Jews" (from *Judah*) or "Israelis" (from *Israel*). Either way, they are truly the "people called by God's Name."

12

A Deadline
for Calling on God?

*eek ye the LORD while he may be found,
call ye upon him while he is near"*

-- Isaiah 55:6.

Can it be true? Is there really a limit to the time that men can call on the Name of the LORD? Unknown to most people, there seems to be a hidden prophecy that says so, couched in symbols in the last book of the Bible, the Revelation, wherein the apostle John recorded his visions of the end-times shown to him by the Lord in the spirit. Let us go over that strange, cryptically worded prophecy.

"And after these things I saw four angels standing on the four corners of the earth, holding the four winds of the earth, that the wind should not blow on the earth, nor on the sea, nor on any tree. And I saw another angel ascending from the east, having the seal of the living God: and he cried with a loud voice to the four angels, to whom it was given to hurt the earth and the sea, Saying, Hurt not the earth, neither the sea, nor the trees, till we have sealed the servants of our God in their foreheads" (Rev 7:1-3).

It is rather unusual that "trees," which represent just one kind of vegetation, should be mentioned as a third entity seemingly on the same class as the "sea" and the "earth." Nevertheless, let us endeavor to discover what these obvious metaphors mean.

Prophetic symbols

John wrote the book of Revelation, also known as the Apocalypse, around 95 A.D. He was then an old man held prisoner in the mining island of Patmos. (The only apostle to die of old age, John is said to have been thrown in boiling oil in Rome earlier, but survived unhurt.)[1]

Many of the prophecies in the book have remained veiled for nearly 2,000 years, because they contain mystifying images. Many, however, have been unlocked in the last two centuries by prophecy watchmen, who realized that most of the keys and clues to Biblical mysteries can be found in the Bible itself. As Paul says, no man can make his own personal interpretation of Bible prophecy. *"Knowing this first, that no prophecy of the scripture is of any private interpretation"* (2 Peter 1:20).

The Bible interprets itself. And when Scripture solves its own riddles and answers its own questions, we can be certain the answers are trustworthy. In the passage we have read, in addition to the "earth," "sea," and "trees," there are two other prophetic symbols: "wind" and "seal." Let us open our Bibles to decipher the hidden meanings of those mysterious metaphors.

"Wind."

Several Biblical verses contain the word "wind." *"I will scatter them as with an east wind before the enemy; I will shew them the back, and not the face, in the day of their calamity"* (Jer 18:17). Nelson's Illustrated Bible Dictionary comments: "In a figurative sense, war is compared to the east wind..."[2]

Another passage presents a similar picture: *"And upon Elam will I bring the four winds from the four quarters of heaven, and will scatter them toward all those winds; and there shall be no nation whither the outcasts of Elam shall not come. For I will cause Elam to be dismayed before their enemies, and before them that seek their life: and I will bring evil upon them even my fierce anger, saith the LORD; and I will send the sword after them, till I have consumed them"* (Jer 49:36-37).

Whirlwind. A concentrated, more violent form of wind seen in other passages is the whirlwind. *"When your fear cometh as desolation, and your destruction cometh as a whirlwind; when distress and anguish cometh upon you"* (Prov 1:27).

"But I will kindle a fire in the wall of Rabbah, and it shall devour the palaces thereof, with shouting in the day of battle, with a tempest in the day of the whirlwind" (Amos 1:14).

"And at the time of the end shall the king of the south push at him: and the king of the north shall come against him like a whirlwind, with chariots, and with horsemen, and with many ships; and he shall enter

into the countries, and shall overflow and pass over" (Dan 11:40). Whirlwinds produce even more devastating scenarios. As we can see, "wind" and "whirlwind" both figuratively mean war, enemy attacks, and invasions, usually as a manifestation of the wrath of the Almighty.

"Sea."

In a vision the prophet Daniel had in Babylon, he saw some of the elements that the apostle John would record in the book of Revelation about 700 years later. *"Daniel spake and said, I saw in my vision by night, and, behold, the four winds of the heaven strove upon the great sea"* (Dan 7:2). Both the "four winds" and the "sea" are mentioned.

"Great Sea" was the term used by the Jews to refer to the Mediterranean Sea vis-à-vis the smaller Sea of Galilee and Dead Sea. The *"four winds"* appear to be the many wars fought throughout the lands of the eastern Mediterranean, the known civilized world in ancient times. As we have learned earlier, the Fertile Crescent was the birthplace of organized warfare.

Four great beasts. In his dream, Daniel saw four strange-looking animals emerge from the "sea." *"And four great beasts came up from the sea, diverse one from another. The first was like a lion, and had eagle's wings: I beheld till the wings thereof were plucked, and it was lifted up from the earth, and made stand upon the feet as a man, and a man's heart was given to it. And behold another beast, a second, like to a bear, and it raised up itself on one side, and it had three ribs in the mouth of it between the teeth of it: and they said thus unto it, Arise, devour much flesh. After this I beheld, and lo another, like a leopard, which had upon the back of it four wings of a fowl; the beast had also four heads; and dominion was given to it. After this I saw in the night visions, and behold a fourth beast, dreadful and terrible, and strong exceedingly; and it had great iron teeth: it devoured and brake in pieces, and stamped the residue with the feet of it: and it was diverse from all the beasts that were before it; and it had ten horns"* (Dan 7:3-7).

An unidentified person standing by in his dream explained to Daniel the meanings of his vision. *"These great beasts, which are four, are four kings, which shall arise out of the earth"* (Dan 7:17). So, "beasts" mean kings. It looks lie they symbolize the four ancient empires that rose one after another in the eastern Mediterranean region: (1) Babylon had winged lions and bulls as royal symbols; (2) Media-Persia, where bears are common, invaded Babylon (the three ribs in its mouth denote its three vassal kingdoms Babylon, Lydia, and Egypt);[3] (3) Greece, represented by the leopard, defeated Media-Persia (its four wings signify the speed of Alexander's conquests; and the four heads, the four divisions of the empire after his death); and (4) Rome, the terrible beast with great iron teeth, used iron extensively in its implements of war as it replaced Greece as the dominant power in the ancient known world.

"Many waters." In the Revelation, John wrote about a monster that emerged from the "sea." *"And I stood upon the sand of the sea, and saw a beast rise up out of the sea, having seven heads and ten horns, and upon his horns ten crowns, and upon his heads the name of blasphemy"* (Rev 13:1). Four chapters later, the monster again comes into view. *"And there came one of the seven angels which had the seven vials, and talked with me, saying unto me, Come hither; I will shew unto thee the judgment of the great whore that sitteth upon many waters... So he carried me away in the spirit into the wilderness: and I saw a woman sit upon a scarlet coloured beast, full of names of blasphemy, having seven heads and ten horns"* (Rev 17:1,3).

The monster with seven heads and ten horns in the "sea" and an identical creature carrying the great whore in "many waters" appear to be the same beast, so the terms "sea" and "many waters" must be synonymous, too. An angel revealed the meaning of "many waters" (the "sea") to John. *"And he saith unto me, The waters which thou sawest, where the whore sitteth, are peoples, and multitudes, and nations, and tongues"* (Rev 17:15).

The "sea," therefore, where the ancient Babylonian, Medo-Persian, Grecian, and Roman empires held sway and where many different peoples and nations live, speaking various languages, represent those parts of Europe, Asia, and Africa around the Mediterranean Sea – known as the "Old World."

"Earth."

Let us next ferret out the prophetic meaning of "earth." We come across a hint to its symbolism in the account of the creation on the third day. When the Creator made heaven and earth, at first there was only water. Then, after He gathered the waters together, dry land appeared. Hence, the surface of the planet consists of only two kinds: the "sea" and the "earth" (Gen 1:9-10). *The New Unger's Bible Dictionary* gives one meaning of "earth" as the "land as opposed to sea."[4] Obviously, the two are opposites.

Extending this principle to prophecy, if the "sea" signifies a region with many different kinds of people in it, "earth" must mean a region with very few or even no people living in it. In that case, if the "sea" is the Old World, then the "earth" stands for the vast, but sparsely populated lands of the Americas that European explorers stumbled onto during the Age of Discovery -- the New World.

Beast from the earth. John saw a beast rise from the "earth." *"And I beheld another beast coming up out of the earth; and he had two horns like a lamb, and he spake as a dragon. And he exerciseth all the power of the first beast before him, and causeth the earth and them which dwell therein to worship the first beast, whose deadly wound was healed. And he doeth great wonders, so that he maketh fire come down from heaven on the earth in the sight of men"* (Rev 13:11-13).

The "beast" or kingdom was like a lamb, meaning it is a young nation and, unlike the Old World kingdoms which rose to power by conquering neighboring countries, its ascent to prominence was relatively peaceful.[5] John said the lamb-like beast spoke like a dragon. How? In Revelation 12:7, the dragon in heaven rebelled against God, so speaking like a dragon likely means speaking against God.

What country in the New World has led others in issuing laws and rulings that contradict or negate the word of God in the name of liberty? Its government has instituted the teaching of biological evolution (thus stultifying Biblical creation), banned prayers in schools, removed the Ten Commandments from public buildings, legalized abortion, upheld gay clergymen, allowed same-sex marriages, in addition to having espoused divorce for a long time.

That the second "beast" would exercise *"all the power of the first beast before him"* indicates it would also become a world power. It would make *"fire"* (figuratively, destruction)[6] *"come down from heaven."* (The word "heaven" in the Greek text is *ouranos*, also the name of the god of the sky in Greek mythology, Uranus. The radioactive element *uranium*, the primary source of nuclear energy, is named after Uranus/*ouranos*.) The nation of the lamb-like beast has truly made "fire" come down from "heaven" (*ouranos*/uranium) -- in the form of the atomic bomb!

"Trees."

What do "trees" symbolize? Speaking to Ezekiel, the LORD likened the Assyrian king and the Egyptian pharaoh to trees. *"Behold, the Assyrian was a cedar in Lebanon with fair branches, and with a shadowing shroud, and of an high stature; and his top was among the thick boughs... To whom art thou thus like in glory and in greatness among the trees of Eden? yet shalt thou be brought down with the trees of Eden unto the nether parts of the earth: thou shalt lie in the midst of the uncircumcised with them that be slain by the sword. This is Pharaoh and all his multitude, saith the Lord GOD"* (Ezek 31:3,18).

In Babylon, Daniel interpreted King Nebuchadnezzar's dream of a great "tree": *"The tree that you saw, which grew and became strong, whose height reached to the heavens and which could be seen by all the earth, whose leaves were lovely and its fruit abundant, in which was food for all, under which the beasts of the field dwelt, and in whose branches the birds of the heaven had their home -- it is you, O king, who have grown and become strong; for your greatness has grown and reaches to the heavens, and your dominion to the end of the earth"* (Dan 4:20-23, NKJV).

The kings of Assyria, Egypt, and Babylon, are likened to great trees. What do they have in common? History tells us these three kingdoms successively oppressed and subjugated the Israelites. The "trees" therefore stand for the enemies and oppressors of Israel, both in ancient times and end-time prophecy. (Egypt, the most populous Arab nation today, has kept the same identity to these modern times, but Assyria and Babylon are no more. Today they form the northern and southern parts of the Arab state of Iraq, respectively.)

A global conflict?

Let us now put together the prophetic symbols whose meanings we have so far discerned. The four angels in the prophecy are *"on the four corners of the earth..."* – denoting the four directions of the compass: north, east, west, and south. So, the scope of their power is worldwide. If "wind" prophetically means war, the *"four winds of the earth"* they are holding back point to a global conflict. The Third World War?

The angels are preventing the global conflict from breaking out prematurely. The other symbols identify the main protagonists and battle zones in the coming warfare: the New World or the Americas (*"the earth"*), the Old World -- Europe, the Middle East, North Africa (*"the sea"*), and the enemies of Israel (*"the trees"*).

See the picture? After the angel from the east shall have finished putting the seal of God *"in the foreheads"* of the *"servants of our God,"* the global conflagration will be allowed to break out. The phrase *"in their foreheads"* (not *on* their foreheads) indicates that the seal will not be a physical mark; it will be an idea or belief implanted in their minds and consciences. Who are *"the servants of our God"*?

The servants of God

John wrote down the number of God's servants who will receive His seal. *"And I heard the number of them which were sealed: and there were sealed an hundred and forty and four thousand of all the tribes of the children of Israel. Of the tribe of Juda were sealed twelve thousand. Of the tribe of Reuben were sealed twelve thousand. Of the tribe of Gad were sealed twelve thousand. Of the tribe of Aser were sealed twelve* thousand. Of the tribe of Nepthalim were sealed twelve thousand. Of the tribe of Manasses were sealed twelve thousand. Of the tribe of Simeon were sealed twelve thousand. Of the tribe of Levi were sealed twelve thousand. Of the tribe of Issachar were sealed twelve thousand. Of the tribe of Zabulon were sealed twelve thousand. Of the tribe of Joseph were sealed twelve thousand. Of the tribe of Benjamin were sealed twelve thousand" (Rev 7:4-8).

Israelites only?

Are the members of the twelve tribes of Israel the only ones who will receive the seal of God in their foreheads? At first blush, that seems to be the case. Yet, a closer examination reveals that it is not so. Let us see further what the Scriptures have to say on the matter.

God has named Israel His "chosen people." *"For thou art an holy people unto the LORD thy God: the LORD thy God hath chosen thee to be a special people unto himself, above all people that are upon the face of the earth"* (Deut 7:6; see also Isa 45:4).

The LORD made a covenant or agreement with them, promising to adopt them as His children if they would serve and worship Him as their God. Paul enumerates God's special favors to *"the people of Israel. Theirs is the adoption as sons; theirs the divine glory, the covenants, the receiving of the law, the temple worship and the promises"* (Rom 9:4, NIV). Thus, the LORD calls them His "sons" and "daughters." *"I will say to the north, Give up; and to the south, Keep not back: bring my sons from far, and my daughters from the ends of the earth; Even every one that is called by my name: for I have created him for my glory, I have formed him; yea, I have made him"* (Isa 43:6-7).

A number of God's chosen people, however, fell out of grace. The Jewish nation, in general, refused to accept God's Only Begotten Son as their long-awaited Messiah. *"Well; because of unbelief they were broken off...* (Rom 11:20). Still, the Almighty Father did not annul His choice of Israel, who remains His chosen people. He simply replaces all the unbelieving Jews with Gentile believers who are taken in as substitutes. *"And if some of the branches be broken off, and thou, being a wild olive tree, wert graffed in among them, and with them partakest of the root and fatness of the olive tree"* (Rom 11:17).

"Spiritual Israel."

Paul explains: *"For he is not a Jew, which is one outwardly; neither is that circumcision, which is outward in the flesh: But he is a Jew, which is one inwardly; and circumcision is that of the heart, in the spirit, and not in the letter; whose praise is not of men, but of God"* (Rom 2:28-29).

The criteria for being considered an Israelite or a Jew are no longer limited to racial descent and compliance with the divinely commanded practice of circumcision. What now counts is not physical, but spiritual circumcision in Christ. *"In him you were also circumcised, in the putting off of the sinful nature, not with a circumcision done by the hands of men but with the circumcision done by Christ"* (Col 2:11, NIV). *"Neither circumcision nor uncircumcision means anything; what counts is a new creation. Peace and mercy to all who follow this rule, even to the Israel of God"* (Gal 6:15-16, NIV). The real Israel no longer consists of the genetic descendants of Jacob, it is now *"Israel of God"* -- spiritual Israel.

"Naturalized Israelites." God's promise of adoption has widened to include all the Gentiles who do His will. They, too, will be His children. *"Wherefore come out from among them, and be ye separate, saith the Lord, and touch not the unclean thing; and I will receive you, And will be a Father unto you, and ye shall be my sons and daughters, saith the Lord Almighty"* (2 Cor 6:17-18). *"For as many as are led by the Spirit of God, they are the sons of God"* (Rom 8:14). Faithful Gentile believers will become citizens of spiritual Israel. *"Now therefore ye are no more strangers and foreigners, but fellowcitizens with the saints, and of the household of God"* (Eph 2:19).

Thus, Gentiles "naturalized" as Israelites will be among the 144,000 members of the twelve tribes of Israel who will receive God's seal in their foreheads.

Two groups. The servants of God will come from two groups, as revealed in two prophetic verses. The first verse: *"And the dragon was wroth with the woman, and went to make war with the remnant of her seed, which keep the commandments of God, and have the testimony of Jesus Christ"* (Rev 12:17).

The *"woman"* has been introduced a few verses earlier. *"And there appeared a great wonder in heaven; a woman clothed with the sun, and the moon under her feet, and upon her head a crown of twelve stars"* (Rev 12:1). *"Clothed with the sun"* means covered with righteousness (holy and upright living) as in the "sun of righteousness" (Mal 4:2; Matt 13:43). The *"moon under her feet"* connotes primacy over false gods. (Ashtaroth, or Ashtoreth, wife of the sun-god Baal, "lord of heaven" [Judg 2:13], was known as the "queen of heaven" [Jer 1:18], whose symbol was the moon. She was called Astarte in Phoenicia, Ishtar in Assyria and Babylonia, Isis in Egypt, Ashtaroth Karnaim in Syria.)[7] The woman's crown of twelve stars, as seen in Joseph's dream (Gen 37:9-10), represents the twelve tribes of Israel.

The *"woman,"* therefore, stands for the original faith that Abraham observed in worshipping God. It became the religion of Israel. So, the "*remnant of her seed*" are observant Jews who obey God's laws, as well as believe Christ is the Son of God.

And the second verse: "*Here is the patience of the saints: here are they that keep the commandments of God, and the faith of Jesus*" (Rev 14:12). Pious Israelites were called "saints" (Ps 16:3, 34:9, etc.). When Christ carried out his earthly ministry, His followers were also called "saints" (1 Cor 1:2; Phil 1:1; etc.). But the foregoing passage appears to combine the two. Hence, "*saints*" today observe two things: the laws of God and the teachings of Christ.

Observant Jews who believe in Christ and faithful Christians who keep God's Old Testament commandments are both called "Messianic."

Undefiled "virgins"

In heaven, John overheard in the spirit what it takes to be part of the 144,000. "*These are they which were not defiled with women; for they are virgins. These are they which follow the Lamb whithersoever he goeth. These were redeemed from among men, being the firstfruits unto God and to the Lamb*" (Rev 14:4). Does the passage close the door to you? Are all married, widowed, divorced people, single parents, and all others who are no longer virgins barred from the ranks of the 144,000? Take heart. There is still hope for you. The word "*virgins*" seems to be symbolic as well.

"Women."

As we now know, "woman" in prophecy personifies a faith, religion, church, or its members. An immoral woman thus represents a corrupt and sinful church. "*And there came one of the seven angels which had the seven vials, and talked with me, saying unto me, Come hither; I will shew unto thee the judgment of the great whore that sitteth upon many waters: With whom the kings of the earth have committed fornication, and the inhabitants of the earth have been made drunk with the wine of her fornication*" (Rev 17:1-2).

On the other hand, a "virgin" is symbolic of the pure and sinless faith. "*What thing shall I take to witness for thee? what thing shall I liken to thee, O daughter of Jerusalem? what shall I equal to thee, that I may comfort thee, O virgin daughter of Zion?...*" (Lam 2:13). "*I have likened the daughter of Zion to a comely and delicate woman*" (Jer 6:2).

"Zion" ("conspicuous object"),[8] which refers to the Temple Mount in Jerusalem, among others, is the dwelling-place of God on earth (Ps 9:11; Isa 8:18). Thus, the terms "virgin daughter of Zion," "daughter of Jerusalem," "virgin of Israel," all point to the pure, righteous faith of the chosen people of God.

In this sense, *"defiled with women"* points to being spiritually tainted by the false teachings and erroneous practices of corrupt churches and religions. A person exposed to such influences is no longer a "virgin."

Virginity regained?

Surprisingly, one can regain lost virginity! Christ actually said something to that effect. *"Jesus answered and said unto him, Verily, verily, I say unto thee, Except a man be born again, he cannot see the kingdom of God"* (John 3:3). A most puzzling statement. Did Christ mean reincarnation? The perplexed disciple could not believe his ears. *"Nicodemus saith unto him, How can a man be born when he is old? can he enter the second time into his mother's womb, and be born? Jesus answered, Verily, verily, I say unto thee, Except a man be born of water and of the Spirit, he cannot enter into the kingdom of God"* (John 3:4-5).

Christ was speaking of baptism (literally, "immersion" in Greek). Paul explains the concept. *"Know ye not, that so many of us as were baptized into Jesus Christ were baptized into his death? Therefore we are buried with him by baptism into death: that like as Christ was raised up from the dead by the glory of the Father, even so we also should walk in newness of life"* (Rom 6:3-4). Immersion in water is symbolic of burial with Christ. Through baptism, a spiritually dead person is buried, but rises again, like Christ, spiritually spotless, to a new life. (Note, however, that spiritual rebirth is twofold: by water and by the Spirit.)

"Therefore if any man be in Christ, he is a new creature: old things are passed away; behold, all things are become new" (2 Cor 5:17). As it were, the baptized person is spiritually born again as an innocent "virgin." Paul uses that term: *"For I am jealous over you with godly jealousy: for I have espoused you to one husband, that I may present you as a chaste virgin to Christ"* (2 Cor 11:2). So, even a person who has married many times can become a virgin again!

Yet, being baptized and spiritually becoming a "virgin" again is no guarantee that one will be counted among the 144,000. Surprised? This is a subtle lesson Christ imparts in another one of His parables.

The ten virgins

Christ related to his disciples: *"Then shall the kingdom of heaven be likened unto ten virgins, which took their lamps, and went forth to meet the bridegroom. And five of them were wise, and five were foolish. They that were foolish took their lamps, and took no oil with them: But the wise took oil in their vessels with their lamps. While the bridegroom tarried, they all slumbered and slept"* (Matt 25:1-5).

The parable is a veiled prophecy of the Second Coming of Christ, represented by the "bridegroom." The "virgins," members of the party of the "bride" (Rev 21:2-10), are believers awaiting His return.

Half left.

"And at midnight there was a cry made, Behold, the bridegroom cometh; go ye out to meet him. Then all those virgins arose, and trimmed their lamps. And the foolish said unto the wise, Give us of your oil; for our lamps are gone out. But the wise answered, saying, Not so; lest there be not enough for us and you: but go ye rather to them that sell, and buy for yourselves. And while they went to buy, the bridegroom came; and they that were ready went in with him to the marriage: and the door was shut" (Matt 25:6-10).

At His Second Coming, Christ will take with Him to the "wedding" (the Rapture or first resurrection) only the five wise "virgins" who are ready. *"Afterward came also the other virgins, saying, Lord, Lord, open to us. But he answered and said, Verily I say unto you, I know you not. Watch therefore, for ye know neither the day nor the hour wherein the Son of man cometh"* (Matt 25:11-13). The ten young women, being "virgins," are all pure and spotless – hence, spiritually saved. Yet, five or half of them will be left out of the "wedding"!

The ten virgins with their oil lamps waiting for the bridegroom.

Other passages in the Gospels confirm the point of the parable: *"I tell you, in that night there shall be two men in one bed; the one shall be taken, and the other shall be left. Two women shall be grinding together; the one shall be taken, and the other left. Two men shall be in the field; the one shall be taken, and the other left"* (Luke 17:34-36; comp. Matt 24:40-41).

Elect of God.

Those who will be taken up in the Rapture, represented by the five wise virgins, are called the "elect." *"And he shall send his angels with a great sound of a trumpet, and they shall gather together his elect from the four winds, from one end of heaven to the other"* (Matt 24:31).

Paul presents a detailed view of the Rapture: *"For the Lord himself shall descend from heaven with a shout, with the voice of the archangel, and with the trump of God: and the dead in Christ shall rise first: Then we which are alive and remain shall be caught up together with them in the clouds, to meet the Lord in the air: and so shall we ever be with the Lord"* (1 Thess 4:16-17). This brings to mind the 144,000. *"These are they which follow the Lamb whithersoever he goeth..."* (Rev 14:4b). Both the elect and the 144,000 will always be in the company of the Son of God. It therefore looks like the 144,000 are the elect.

Let us make an inventory of those who will be taken in the Rapture: (1) The "elect" will be gathered by the angels. (2) The "five wise virgins" went with the "bridegroom" (Christ) to the "wedding" (the Rapture). (3) The "144,000" from (4) the twelve tribes of "spiritual Israel," also called (5) *"the firstfruits unto God and the Lamb"* (Rev 14:4). (In Israel, the firstfruits of the crops and flocks early in the harvest season are brought as offerings to God. *"Firstfruits"* point to a later, bigger harvest.) We can form just one conclusion – all five groups are one and the same, just called by different names.

Two groups have "tickets" to the Rapture. The wise virgins were taken to the wedding because they had oil in their lamps. The 144,000 will be in the company of the Lamb, because they will have the seal of God in their foreheads. Could the "oil" and the seal of God be symbols of the same thing?

The "oil" and the seal

Aside from the "oil" and the "seal," "lamps" appear to be symbolic, too. Surely, the Scriptures must hold their hidden meanings as well.

"Lamps."

Several Bible verses contain the words "lamp" and "lamps." Here are two of the most telling. *"Thy word is a lamp unto my feet, and a light unto my path"* (Ps 119:105). The verse says God's Word, the Holy Scriptures or the Bible, is a "lamp" that lights the way of the believer.

Another verse reads: *"For the commandment is a lamp; and the law is light; and reproofs of instruction are the way of life"* (Prov 6:23). Here we learn that God's commandments are figuratively also a "lamp."

The first five books of the Bible containing God's commandments are collectively called the *Torah* ("instruction, law").[9] It looks like the *Torah* is the "lamp" in the parable.

"Oil."

There are hundreds of verses in the Scriptures with the words "oil" or "oils" in them, but only one stands out in association with "virgins": *"Thine oils have a goodly fragrance; Thy name is (as) oil poured forth;*

Therefore do the virgins love thee" (Song 1:3, ASV). Aromatic oils are likened to the Name of God, which "virgins" cannot resist falling in love with. The "oil" in the parable evidently stands for the Name of God.

"Lamps" and "oil" go together. One needs the other in order to produce light. The same is true with the Torah and the Name of God. As the oil produces light in the lamp, so does the Sacred Name provide the "light" or aura of divine truth to the commandments in the Torah. With God's Name in the Scriptures, we are assured of Who its real Author is, as well as Who is telling us to do His will.

It thus becomes quite clear that the "five wise virgins" with "oil" in their "lamps" allude to believers who know and call on the true Name of God ("the oil") in the Torah ("the lamp").

The seal of God.

John was blessed with a glimpse of the seal of God in the foreheads of His servants. *"And I looked, and, lo, a Lamb stood on the mount Sion, and with him an hundred forty and four thousand, having his Father's name written in their foreheads"* (Rev 14:1).

The seal in the foreheads of God's servants has His Name in it! (The Name of God is not by itself the complete seal, but an all-important part of the seal, which contains other elements.) The Sacred Name being *in* the foreheads of God's servants means they accept, believe in, and call on His true Name.

The "foolish virgins" who have no "oil" with them see and literally read the substitute term "the LORD" as printed in the Bible. On the other hand, the "wise virgins" who have "oil" with them read the Scriptures as though the sacred Name YHWH is spelled out and printed clearly in the Biblical text.

The "deadline" and beyond

To sum up, the number of the 144,000 servants of God who will receive the seal of God in their foreheads will be completed just before the outbreak of the global conflict. So, those who want to be numbered among the elect must know and call upon God's true Name before the war erupts. The beginning of hostilities will be the sign that the angel from the east shall have finished his work. No further sealing will be done. The "deadline" is thus the eve of the Third World War.

No one will know for sure who will have been sealed until after the elect shall have been taken up in the Rapture. However, it will console those who will be left behind to know that the Name of God can still save them, physically, on the Day of Wrath that will immediately follow.

But, first, let us go through the intervening end-time events.

The "Great Tribulation."

The angel Gabriel told Daniel about a coming time of trouble. *"And at that time shall Michael stand up, the great prince which standeth for the children of thy people: and there shall be a time of trouble, such as never was since there was a nation even to that same time"* (Dan 12:1a).

Christ calls that unparalleled time of trouble the "Great Tribulation." *"For then shall be great tribulation, such as was not since the beginning of the world to this time, no, nor ever shall be. And except those days should be shortened, there should no flesh be saved: but for the elect's sake those days shall be shortened"* (Matt 24:21-22).

The Great Tribulation will begin in the middle of the last 7 years. *"And he shall confirm the covenant with many for one week: and in the midst of the week he shall cause the sacrifice and the oblation to cease, and for the overspreading of abominations he shall make it desolate, even until the consummation, and that determined shall be poured upon the desolate"* (Dan 9:27). (The Hebrew word used for "week," *shavua*, can mean a period of 7 days or 7 years. The context indicates it is the latter. The "covenant" is an agreement "confirmed" or ratified by several parties, which will be broken 3½ years later.) The "*he*," in all likelihood, is the end-time Antichrist, a leader who will have the power to stop the offerings (*"the sacrifice and the oblation"*) on Temple Mount and destroy the holy hill (*"make it desolate"*).

The Antichrist. The Antichrist (*"the beast"*), presumed dead after sustaining a mortal wound, will startle the world when he comes back to life. *"And I saw one of his heads as it were wounded to death; and his deadly wound was healed: and all the world wondered after the beast. And they worshipped the dragon which gave power unto the beast: and they worshipped the beast, saying, Who is like unto the beast? who is able to make war with him? And there was given unto him a mouth speaking great things and blasphemies; and power was given unto him to continue forty and two months"* (Rev 13:3-5). His revival will be the work of Satan (*"the dragon"*), who is worshipped as a false god. Under him, the Antichrist will hold power for the next 3½ years.

"Abomination of desolation." The Antichrist will set this up on Temple Mount. *"And arms shall stand on his part, and they shall pollute the sanctuary of strength, and shall take away the daily sacrifice, and they shall place the abomination that maketh desolate"* (Dan 11:31). "Strength" comes from the Hebrew root *azaz* ("to be stout or strong"), so the phrase could mean "sanctuary of God," just like "power" is used to mean God in some verses (Matt 26:64; Mark 14:62).

"When ye therefore shall see the abomination of desolation, spoken of by Daniel the prophet, stand in the holy place, (whoso readeth, let

him understand:) Then let them which be in Judaea flee into the mountains: Let him which is on the housetop not come down to take any thing out of his house: Neither let him which is in the field return back to take his clothes. And woe unto them that are with child, and to them that give suck in those days! But pray ye that your flight be not in the winter, neither on the sabbath day" (Matt 24:15-20).

It seems the "abomination" will bring about instant and far-reaching destruction, because the inhabitants of Judea will have to flee to the mountains without a moment to spare. It will ignite the global war!

The world war. The Antichrist will war against Jews and Christians. *"And it was given unto him to make war with the saints, and to overcome them: and power was given him over all kindreds, and tongues, and nations"* (Rev 13:7). He will prevail and become ruler of the world!

"And when he had opened the fourth seal, I heard the voice of the fourth beast say, Come and see. And I looked, and behold a pale horse: and his name that sat on him was Death, and Hell followed with him. And power was given unto them over the fourth part of the earth, to kill with sword, and with hunger, and with death, and with the beasts of the earth" (Rev 6:7-8). The *"fourth part of the earth"* means some 25% of the world population will become casualties of war (*"sword"*), famine (*"hunger"*), pandemics (*"death"*), wild animals (*"beasts of the earth"*).

"Mark of the beast." The "second beast" will back the Antichrist. *"And he had power to give life unto the image of the beast, that the image of the beast should both speak, and cause that as many as would not worship the image of the beast should be killed"* (Rev 13:15). It sounds like a computer-generated digital image of the Antichrist!

"And he causeth all, both small and great, rich and poor, free and bond, to receive a mark in their right hand, or in their foreheads: And that no man might buy or sell, save he that had the mark, or the name of the beast, or the number of his name. Here is wisdom. Let him that hath understanding count the number of the beast: for it is the number of a man; and his number is Six hundred threescore and six" (Rev 13:16-18). Like the seal of God, the mark of the beast will be an idea or belief.

The Second Coming.

The Great Tribulation will last for 3½ years and end at the Second Coming. *"Immediately after the tribulation of those days shall the sun be darkened, and the moon shall not give her light, and the stars shall fall from heaven, and the powers of the heavens shall be shaken: And then shall appear the sign of the Son of man in heaven: and then shall all the tribes of the earth mourn, and they shall see the Son of man coming in the clouds of heaven with power and great glory"* (Matt 24:29-30).

Rapture! Christ's appearance in the sky will initiate the Rapture or first resurrection. *"And he shall send his angels with a great sound of a trumpet, and they shall gather together his elect from the four winds, from one end of heaven to the other"* (Matt 24:29-31). At this point, the 144,000 – both living and dead – will be caught up to Christ in the sky.

"Behold, I shew you a mystery; We shall not all sleep, but we shall all be changed, In a moment, in the twinkling of an eye, at the last trump: for the trumpet shall sound, and the dead shall be raised incorruptible, and we shall be changed. For this corruptible must put on incorruption, and this mortal must put on immortality" (1 Cor 15:51-53). The 144,000 elect of God shall have attained everlasting life!

The elect in the graves will rise first. *"For this we say to you by the word of the Lord, that we who are alive and remain until the coming of the Lord will by no means precede those who are asleep. For the Lord Himself will descend from heaven with a shout, with the voice of an archangel, and with the trumpet of God. And the dead in Christ will rise first. Then we who are alive and remain shall be caught up together with them in the clouds to meet the Lord in the air"* (1 Thess 4:15-17, NKJV).

Armageddon. The Rapture will take place just before Armageddon, the last great battle on earth -- between Christ and the Antichrist. *"And I saw heaven opened, and behold a white horse; and he that sat upon him was called Faithful and True, and in righteousness he doth judge and make war… And I saw the beast, and the kings of the earth, and their armies, gathered together to make war against him that sat on the horse, and against his army"* (Rev 19:11,19). The battle will be brief.

"For, behold, the LORD will come with fire, and with his chariots like a whirlwind, to render his anger with fury, and his rebuke with flames of fire. For by fire and by his sword will the LORD plead with all flesh: and the slain of the LORD shall be many" (Isa 66:15-16).

The casualties from the world war and Great Tribulation will greatly increase with many more at Armageddon. *"The Lord at thy right hand shall strike through kings in the day of his wrath. He shall judge among the heathen, he shall fill the places with the dead bodies; he shall wound the heads over many countries"* (Ps 110:5-6).

The "Day of Wrath." Armageddon will be fought on the Day of Wrath. *"The great day of the LORD is near, it is near, and hasteth greatly, even the voice of the day of the LORD: the mighty man shall cry there bitterly. That day is a day of wrath, a day of trouble and distress, a day of wasteness and desolation, a day of darkness and gloominess, a day of clouds and thick darkness, A day of the trumpet and alarm against the fenced cities, and against the high towers"* (Zeph 1:14-16).

Terrible, unthinkable things will happen in heaven and earth. *"And I beheld when he had opened the sixth seal, and, lo, there was a great earthquake; and the sun became black as sackcloth of hair, and the moon became as blood; And the stars of heaven fell unto the earth, even as a fig tree casteth her untimely figs, when she is shaken of a mighty wind. And the heaven departed as a scroll when it is rolled together; and every mountain and island were moved out of their places.*

"And the kings of the earth, and the great men, and the rich men, and the chief captains, and the mighty men, and every bondman, and every free man, hid themselves in the dens and in the rocks of the mountains; And said to the mountains and rocks, Fall on us, and hide us from the face of him that sitteth on the throne, and from the wrath of the Lamb: For the great day of his wrath is come; and who shall be able to stand?" (Rev 6:12-17).

Cleansing by fire. Whereas in Noah's time God purified the earth with water, this time around He will cleanse it with fire. Peter wrote: *"Whereby the world that then was, being overflowed with water, perished: But the heavens and the earth, which are now, by the same word are kept in store, reserved unto fire against the day of judgment and perdition of ungodly men"* (2 Peter 3:6-7).

The antediluvians who built the Great Pyramid knew it. The prophet Zephaniah knew it. *"Neither their silver nor their gold shall be able to deliver them in the day of the LORD's wrath; but the whole land shall be devoured by the fire of his jealousy: for he shall make even a speedy riddance of all them that dwell in the land"* (Zeph 1:18).

Peter describes a horrid day. *"But the day of the Lord will come as a thief in the night; in the which the heavens shall pass away with a great noise, and the elements shall melt with fervent heat, the earth also and the works that are therein shall be burned up"* (2 Peter 3:10).

The Name that saves. The LORD will save those left behind who will call on His true Name. *"And it shall come to pass, that in all the land, saith the LORD, two parts therein shall be cut off and die; but the third shall be left therein. And I will bring the third part through the fire, and will refine them as silver is refined, and will try them as gold is tried: they shall call on my name, and I will hear them: I will say, It is my people: and they shall say, The LORD is my God"* (Zech 13:8-9).

"And it shall come to pass, that whosoever shall call on the name of the LORD shall be delivered: for in mount Zion and in Jerusalem shall be deliverance, as the LORD hath said, and in the remnant whom the LORD shall call" (Joel 2:32). Apart from those in Jerusalem, God's "remnant" in other parts of the world will also be saved.

Few men left. A pitifully small number of humans will survive the tempest of fire that will incinerate the earth. *"Therefore hath the curse* *devoured the earth, and they that dwell therein are desolate: therefore the inhabitants of the earth are burned, and few men left"* (Isa 24:6).

After the Day of Wrath, it will be so much easier to find gold than to come across a living human. *"I will make man scarcer than pure gold, more rare than the gold of Ophir"* (Isa 13:12, NIV).

Call on His Name

In this book we have learned two of the LORD's personal Names. Let us make use of them. Let us not pass up this wonderful opportunity to become part of God's elect. We have nothing to lose and everything to gain. We may even attain the glorious privilege of seeing God up close. *"And there shall be no more curse: but the throne of God and of the Lamb shall be in it; and his servants shall serve him: And they shall see his face; and his name shall be in their foreheads"* (Rev 22:3-4).

God's servants will be kings – actual, flesh-and-blood kings -- each ruling over his own kingdom during the Millennium, the thousand years of peace, with Christ as King of Kings. *"And I saw thrones, and they sat upon them, and judgment was given unto them: and I saw the souls of them that were beheaded for the witness of Jesus, and for the word of God, and which had not worshipped the beast, neither his image, neither had received his mark upon their foreheads, or in their hands; and they lived and reigned with Christ a thousand years"* (Rev 20:4). Will you be one of them?

Blessed are your eyes

Is it by mere chance that, of the billions of people now living on earth, you are, at this very moment, holding this book in your hands? The author would like to believe that it is Yahu's will.

Christ had said: *"Because it is given unto you to know the mysteries of the kingdom of heaven, but to them it is not given. For whosoever hath, to him shall be given, and he shall have more abundance: but whosoever hath not, from him shall be taken away even that he hath. Therefore speak I to them in parables: because they seeing see not; and hearing they hear not, neither do they understand... But blessed are your eyes, for they see: and your ears, for they hear. For verily I say unto you, That many prophets and righteous men have desired to see those things which ye see, and have not seen them; and to hear those things which ye hear, and have not heard them"* (Matt 13:11-13,16-17).

May Yahu bless you in the Name of Yahushua, His Only Begotten Son. May your name be found in the Book of Life.

HalleluYah!!! Amen.

Appendix

Old and New Testament Parallelism

	Old Testament	Total			New Testament	Total
I.	**Covenant**			I.	**Covenant**	
	Genesis				Matthew	
	Exodus				Mark	
	Leviticus				Luke	
	Numbers				John	4
	Deuteronomy	5				
II.	**History**			II.	**History**	
	Joshua				Acts	1
	Judges					
	Ruth					
	1 Samuel					
	2 Samuel					
	1 Kings					
	2 Kings					
	1 Chronicles					
	2 Chronicles					
	Ezra					
	Nehemiah					
	Esther	12				
III.	**Teachings**			III.	**Teachings**	
	Job				Romans	
	Psalms				1 Corinthians	
	Proverbs				2 Corinthians	
	Ecclesiastes				Galatians	
	Song of Songs	5			Ephesians	
IV.	**Prophecy**				Philippians	
	Isaiah				Colossians	
	Jeremiah				1 Thessalonians	
	Lamentations				2 Thessalonians	
	Ezekiel				1 Timothy	
	Daniel				2 Timothy	
	Hosea				Titus	
	Joel				Philemon	
	Amos				Hebrews	
	Obadiah				James	
	Jonah				1 Peter	
	Micah				2 Peter	
	Nahum				1 John	
	Habakkuk				2 John	
	Zephaniah				3 John	
	Haggai				Jude	21
	Zechariah			IV.	**Prophecy**	
	Malachi	17			Revelation	1
	Total:	39				27

The Hebrew Alphabet

No.	Name	Char.	Pronunciation	Symbol	Value
1.	Aleph	א	Silent letter	Ox	1
2.	Bet	בּ, ב	B as in Boy, V as in Vine	House	2
3.	Gimmel	ג	G as in Girl	Camel	3
4.	Dalet	ד	D as in Door	Door	4
5.	Hey	ה	H as in Hay	Wind	5
6.	Vav, Vaw, Waw	ו	V as in Vine, W as in Water	Hook, peg, nail, pillar	6
7.	Zayin	ז	Z as in Zebra	Olive tree	7
8.	Chet	ח	CH as in BaCH	Fence	8
9.	Tet	ט	T as in Tall	Serpent	9
10.	Yod	י	Y as in Yes	Hand	10
11.	Kaf	כּ, כ / ך	K as in Kite, CH as in BaCH	Palm of hand	20 / 500
12.	Lamed	ל	L as in Look	Ox goad	30
13.	Mem	מ / ם	M as in Mom	Water	40 / 600
14.	Nun	נ / ן	N as in Now	Fish, seed	50 / 700
15.	Samech	ס	S as in Sun	Post, circle	60
16.	Ayin	ע	Gulping letter	Eye, color	70
17.	Pey	פּ, פ / ף	P as in Pay, F as in Food	Mouth	80 / 800
18.	Tsade	צ / ץ	TS as in NuTS	Fish hook	90 / 900
19.	Qof	ק	Q as in Queen	Back of head	100
20.	Resh	ר	R as in Rain	Head	200
21.	Shin, Sin	שׁ, שׂ	SH as in Shape, S as in Sun	Teeth	300
22.	Tav, Taw	ת	T as in Tall	Sign, cross	400

Instances of Divine Proportion
in Man, Nature, and Man-Made Objects

The human head.

The face of a man.

Body segments of an ant.

Flower structure.

Avian plumage coloration.

The Parthenon in Greece.

Notre Dame Cathedral

Computer monitor screen.

Business cards, playing cards,
credit cards, ATM cards, etc.

Summary of Key Events related to Abraham and Nimrod

B.C.	Event	Notes
2446	Birth of Shem	98 years before the Flood
2348	The FLOOD	
2247	Birth of Peleg	101 years after the Flood (Gen 10:25)
2037	Birth of Nimrod	Son of Cush "in his old age," his favorite son
2126	Birth of Terah	Father of Abram (Gen 11:24)
2017	Leopard coats	Nimrod, 20, began wearing Adam's garments
2008	Tower of Babel; death of Peleg	340 years after the Flood; dispersion after tower builders' tongues confused; Peleg, 239, died
2007	Nineveh built	Nimrod, 30, left Babel, founded Nineveh
1996	Birth of Abram	Nimrod tried to kill Abram, hidden in a cave
1986	Shem's tutelage	Abram, 10, taken to Shem; was taught godliness
1946	Move to Terah	Abram, 50, moved in with father Terah, broke his idols; brought to Nimrod, who killed Haran
1946	Move to Haran	Terah left Ur with Abram, Sarai, and Lot
1921	Death of Terah; move to Canaan	Terah died, 205. Abram, 75, called by God, went to Canaan, the Promised Land
1913	Lot rescued	Abram, 83, rescued Lot from Amraphel/Nimrod
1896	Birth of Isaac	Son of Abram, 100, by Sarah, 90
1857	Isaac's marriage	Isaac, 40, married Rebekah, a niece from Ur
1846	Death of Shem	Shem died at the age of 600
1837	Esau and Jacob	Twin sons of Isaac, 60, by wife Rebekah born
1822	Abraham's and Nimrod's deaths	Abraham, 175, died; Esau, 15, killed Nimrod, 215, ruler of Nineveh for 185 years.

(NOTE: Years in boldface from Archbishop James Ussher's chronology. Dates in regular typeface derived from the Stone *Chumash,* the Book of Jasher, or extrapolated.)

Key Events in the 430-Year Sojourn
and 400-Year Affliction of Abraham's Descendants
in a "Land that is Not Theirs"

B.C.	Event	After	Notes
1921	God's call to Abram	(Start)	Abram, 75, migrated to Canaan; start of 430 years in Ex 12:40-41
1912	First covenant	9 yrs	God made covenant with Abram, 84
1910	Ishmael born	2 yrs	Son of Abram, 86, by the maid Hagar
1897	Names changed; circumcision begun	13 yrs	New names given: Abraham and Sarah; circumcision made sign of the covenant
1896	Isaac born	1 yr.	Son of Abram, 100, by Sarah, 90
1891	Isaac weaned	5 yrs	Ishmael, 19, mocked Isaac, sent away
	Sub-total:	30 yrs	Start of 400 years in Gen 15:13
1857	Isaac had a wife		Isaac, 40, wed Rebekah, a niece from Ur
1837	Esau and Jacob born		Twin sons of Isaac, 60, and Rebekah
1822	Abraham died		Abraham, 175, died in Canaan
1796	Esau married		Esau, 40, took 2 Hittite wives
1753	Jacob, 84, married Leah, then Rachel		Served 7 years for Rachel; tricked into having Leah; given Rachel 1 week later
1745	Joseph born		Jacob's 11th son and Rachel's first child
1728	Joseph sold		Joseph, 17, sold into slavery in Egypt
1716	Joseph appointed as Pharaoh's vicegerent		Joseph interpreted Pharaoh's dream of 7 years of plenty and 7 years of famine
1706	Jacob came to Egypt	185 yrs	Jacob, 130, came with 70 descendants
1689	Jacob passed away		Jacob, 147, died after 17 years in Egypt
1670	Shepherd-kings/ Hyksos rule		Hyksos kings began to rule over Egypt, wielding power for about 100 years
1635	Joseph died		Joseph, 110, after 93 years in Egypt
1571	Moses born		Found in the Nile, adopted by princess
1531	Moses' flight to Midian		Moses, 40, fled after killing an Egyptian
1491	Exodus from Egypt	215 yrs	Moses, 80, led about 2 million Israelites
	Sub-total:	400 yrs	Fulfillment of 400 years in Gen 15:13
	TOTAL:	430 yrs	The 430 years related in Ex 12:40-41

*Years in bold figures from Archbishop James Ussher's Chronology

The "YHWH" Titles

The sacred Name YHWH is combined with many descriptive titles and epithets. Here are some of the most frequently used appellatives.

1. *YHWH Elohim* ("YHWH God" -- Gen 2:4, etc.)
2. *Adonay YHWH* ("The Lord YHWH" -- Gen 15:2, etc.)
3. *YHWH Yireh* ("YHWH will see (to it)" -- Gen 22:8, etc.)
4. *YHWH Ropheka* ("YHWH that healeth thee" -- Ex 15:26)
5. *YHWH-Nissi* ("YHWH my banner" -- Ex 17:15)
6. *YHWH Eloheka* ("YHWH thy God" -- Ex 20:2, etc.)
7. *YHWH Eloheikem* ("YHWH your God" -- Lev 19:3)
8. *YHWH Elohai* ("YHWH my God" -- Ps 13:3, etc.)
9. *YHWH Mekaddishkem* ("YHWH that doth sanctify you" -- Ex 31:13)
10. *YHWH-Shalom* ("YHWH is peace" -- Judg 6:24)
11. *YHWH Tseba'ot* ("YHWH of hosts" -- 1 Sam 1:3, etc.)
12. *YHWH Elyon* ("YHWH most high" -- Ps 7:17, etc.)
13. *YHWH Sal'i* ("YHWH my Rock or Hiding Place" -- Ps 18:2)
14. *YHWH Tsuri weGoali* ("YHWH my Rock and my Redeemer" -- Ps 19:4)
15. *YHWH Roi* ("YHWH my shepherd" -- Ps 23:1)
16. *YHWH Osenu* ("YHWH our Maker" -- Ps 95:6)
17. *YHWH Elohenu* ("YHWH our God" -- Ps 99:5,etc.)
18. *YHWH Elohei Yisrael* ("YHWH God of Israel" -- Isa 17:6)
19. *YHWH Moshi'ek* ("YHWH thy Saviour" -- Isa 60:16)
20. *YHWH Abinu* ("YHWH our Father" -- Isa 64:8)
21. *YHWH Tsidkenu* ("YHWH our Righteousness" -- Jer 23:6, etc.)
22. *YHWH Elohei Dawid* ("YHWH God of David" -- Isa 38:5)
23. *YHWH Shammah* ("YHWH is there" -- Ezek 48:35)

PERMUTATIONS OF THE TETRAGRAMMATON

The Jews anciently believed that the Torah had been written with permutations of the sacred Names of God.[1] Bezaleel, the craftsman who made the Ark of the Covenant and other articles of the Tabernacle, possessed an awesome reputation: "He knew how to combine the letters of the Divine Names with which heaven and earth were created."[2]

In the *Kabbalah,* great importance is placed on the manipulation of letters and numbers, specially those of the Names of God. Jewish mystics believed that hidden in the Torah were guides on how to harness the creative forces of the Hebrew alphabet and the magical powers of the various arrangements of the Tetragrammaton. Israel ben Eliezer, an 18th century rabbi better known as the *Baal Shem Tov* ("Master of the Good Name") was reputed to have miraculously cured many people of their ailments through his esoteric permutations of the Name of God.

The 12 Transpositions

1. YHWH	4. HWHY	7. WHHY	10. HYHW
2. YHHW	5. HWYH	8. WYHH	11. HYWH
3. YWHH	6. HHYW	9. WHYH	12. HHWY

The consonants are considered the "body" of the Name. The vowels, written as dots and dashes over, in, and under the consonants, are the "garments." Permutation may also be made by changing the positions of various vowels in relation to the consonants.[3] Below are some examples:

YaHaWaHa	YeHeWeHe	YaHWaH
YeHaWaHa	YaHeWeHa	YoHeWaH
YiHaWaHa	YoHaWiHa	YHaWoHi
YoHaWaHa	YaHiWeHa	etcetera…

The Vari-Lettered Names of God

Like many Hebrew names, God's Name is said to be the short form of a longer name. It thus has many variations. The *Haggadah* (book of Talmudic stories explaining the law) says the sacred Names of God were used by those who knew their combinations to perform miracles.

One-Lettered Names.

The Name of God may be written with just one Hebrew letter. "In Hebrew literature generally and in Hebrew letter-writing the Name of God is represented by the letter 'he' or 'dalet' with an accent over it"[4]

Hey (ה/H), the simplest, most effortless letter to vocalize, is sounded by mere exhalation. It is found on Western European amulets, either alone or repeated five times. *Dalet* (ד/D) is also the numeral "4," the number of letters in the Tetragrammaton.

ה

(H)

ד

(D)

Two-Lettered Names.

There are two Two-Lettered Names of God, both formed by the letters of the Tetragrammaton. The first, *YH* (*yod-hey*), is the short form of the Four-Lettered Name, sounded "Yah." The second, *YY* (*yod-yod*), which is used in liturgy, is the initial of the Tetragrammaton doubled. It is pronounced with the substituted word *Adonai* ("LORD").

י ה

(YH)

י י

(YY)

The Three-Lettered Name.

The Three-Lettered Name of God is made up of the first three letters of the Tetragrammaton. It is pronounced "Yahu."

י ה ו

(YHW)

Four-Lettered Names.

The Tetragrammaton is the most sacred and most secret Name of God. The High Priest used to utter it once a year -- on *Yom Kippur* ("Day of Atonement") at the Holy Temple in Jerusalem. The Four-Lettered Name, as well as its many permutations, was often used in meditations, amulets, and various types of prayer. Referred to as the "Ineffable Name," the Tetragrammaton is never said aloud.

י ו ה ה

(YHWH)

In prayer, Jews use a four-lettered substitute, usually *Adonay*. Other four-lettered Names are *EHeYeH* ("Existence") and an acronym, *AGLA*.

אדני

(ADoNaY -- "LORD")

אהיה

(EHeYeH -- "Existence")

אגלא

(AGLA: Atoh Gebor LeOlam Adonay –
"Thou art mighty forever, O LORD")

Eight-Lettered Name.

A rare form, the Eight-Lettered Name is said to have been favored by the Jews in Kurdistan and Iraq. Basically, the Name has the vowels of Adonai interspersed with the consonants of the Four-Lettered Name. This form of the Name is numerically equivalent to "Amen."

יאההדונהי

(Y-'-H-d-W-n-H-y)

Twelve-Lettered Name.

The Jewish Encyclopaedia notes its origin: "It appears that the majority of the priests in the last days of the Temple were unworthy to pronounce the Name, and a combination of the letters or of the equivalents of the letters constituting the Name was employed by the priests in the Temple. Thus the Twelve-Lettered Name was substituted, which, a baraita says, was at the first taught to every priest; but with the increase of the number of licentious priests the Name was revealed only to the pious ones, who 'swallowed' its pronunciation while the other priest were chanting."[5]

קתרחכמבי, נה

(QTRChKMBYNH)

Mentioned in the Talmud, this form of the Name, it is said, may also be derived from the first three Sefirot (divine emanations or attributes of God that make up the "Tree of Life") in the Jewish Kabbalah.[6]

Fourteen-Lettered Name.

This little-known form of the Name ("Adonai Elohainu Adonai") is from the Shema ("Hear"), the Jewish confession of faith from Deut 6:4–9; 11:13–21 and Num 15:37–41. It was, for a time, written on the backs of mezuzot (small parchment scrolls inscribed with the Shema inserted in tubes or cases and affixed to the doorposts of Jewish homes). By means of *timurah* (letter transposition), this Name comes out to:

כוזו במוכסז כוזו

(KWZW BMWKSZ KWZW)

Twenty-Two-Lettered Name.

This form of the Name was widely popular. It is found in the *Sefer Raziel* and is attributed to Eleazar of Worms, although it may be much older, since Eleazar drew from Gnostic sources. Among other theories, it is thought to have been transposed from the Priestly Benediction.

The fact that it has 22 letters, corresponding to the 22 letters of the Hebrew alphabet on which the world is said to have been built, gives this Name great significance. No exact pronunciation is known.

אנקתם פסתם פספסים דיונסים

('NQTS PSTS PSPSYS DYWNSYS)

Forty-Two-Lettered Names.

There are two known Names of this kind. One 42-Lettered Name is made up of four combined Names and titles that, when spelled out, total 42 letters.

אהיה יהוה אדוני הויה

('HYH YHWH 'DWNY HWYH)

אהיה	=	'HYH	=	אלף הא יוד הא	=	10 letters
יהוה	=	YHWH	=	יוד הא וו הא	=	9 "
אדוני	=	'DWNY	=	אלף דלת וו נון יוד	=	14 "
הויה	=	HWYH	=	הא וו יוד הא	=	9 "
						42 letters

Of the second, the 12th century Jewish sage Maimonides thought that the 42 letters consisted of several words, each expressing a fundamental attribute of God, together presenting one description of God's divine essence.[7] It has no known pronunciation. The second segment could be interpreted as "break Satan" and was used to protect those who had been attacked by demons. It was frequently inscribed on amulets worn around the neck.

אבגיתץ קדעשטן נגדיכש בטרצתג
חקדטנע יגלפזק שקוצית

('BGYTTs QD'STN NGDYKS BTRTsTG
ChQDTN' YGLPZQ SQWTsYT)

"Forty-Five-Lettered" Names.

Two 45-Lettered Names do not actually contain 45 letters. Rather, 45 is the value of the Hebrew letters in the Names. The first consists of the four letters of the Tetragrammaton spelled out in full in Hebrew. The sum of the values of the letters that form *YHWH* is 45.

יו ד ה ה א ו א ו ה א

(YWD H' W'W H')

(י/*Yod*) י ו ד   (ה/*Hey*) ה א   (ו/*Waw*) ו א ו   (ה/*Hey*) ה א
(10+6+4)   (5+1)   (6+1+6)   (5+1)   = (45)

The second 45-Lettered Name comes from the word "what" (*mah*) in Proverbs 30:4. *"Who hath ascended up into heaven, or descended? who hath gathered the wind in his fists? who hath bound the waters in a garment? who hath established all the ends of the earth? what is his name, and what is his son's name, if thou canst tell?"* In this verse, the word *"what"* (*mah*) is regarded as a Name of God.

Mah ("what") is made up of the two Hebrew letters *mem* (M) and *hey* (H). When the values of *mem* (40) and *hey* (5) are added, they produce the value of 45.

מ ה

(M H)

מ/*Mem*   ה/*Hey*
40   +   5   =   45

Seventy-Two-Lettered Names.

One 72-Lettered Name of God consists of the Hebrew letters in the names of the Twelve Tribes (50 letters), the three Patriarchs Abraham, Isaac, and Jacob (13 letters), and the words *Shivtei Yisrael* ("Tribes of Israel," 9 letters). This Name was inscribed on the *Urim* and *Thummim*[8] (oracular objects used by the High Priest in making decisions).

Names of the 12 Tribes   50   letters
Names of the 3 Patriarchs   13   "
Shivtei Yisrael ("Tribes of Israel")   9   "
                Total: 72   letters

A second 72-Lettered Name does not actually have 72 letters. The number refers to the sum of the values of the letters of the One-Lettered, Two-Lettered, Three-Lettered, and Four-Lettered Names of God when added up, as shown below:

						י/Y/10	=	10
						+		+
				י/Y/10	+	ה/H/5	=	15
				+		+		+
		י/Y/10	+	ה/H/5	+	ו/W/6	=	21
		+		+		+		+
י/Y/10	+	ה/H/5	+	ו/W/6	+	ה/H/5	=	26
10	+	15	+	21	+	26	=	72

The number 72 multiplied by 11 produces 792. It points to the diameter of the earth -- 7920 miles at the equator. In Pythagorean "sacred" geometry (said to have been brought to earth by the fallen angels), 792 times 4 yields 3168, the circumference of the square of the Earth. Bethlehem, Christ's birthplace, is located on the latitude of 31.68 degrees. The values of "Lord Jesus Christ" in Greek, *Kurio Iesous Xristos,* also total 3168.[9]

Seventy-Two "Divided" Names.

These are derived from the words Moses spoke in Exodus 14:19-21, when he parted the waters of the Sea of Reeds, allowing the Israelites to escape the pursuing Egyptians. Each one of the three verses, beginning with *Wayyissa, Wayyabo,* and *Wayyet,* contains exactly 72 letters.

To see the Names, the verses are written in boustrophedon form – the first verse from right to left, the second from left to right (reversed), and the third from right to left again. The resulting 3 lines will have 72 columns of 3 letters each. Read from top to bottom, each letter-triad is regarded as a Name of God or the name of one of 72 angels. Read in reverse, from bottom to top, the letter-triads supposedly reveal the names of 72 demons. Here are the verses and their Hebrew texts (each verse in Hebrew is laid out in 4 lines for lack of space).

Exodus 14:19 -- "And the angel of God, which went before the camp of Israel, removed and went behind them; and the pillar of the cloud went from before their face, and stood behind them."

ו י ס ע מ ל א כ ה כ ה ל א ה י ה מ ה ה ל כ
ל פ נ י נ מ ח ה נ ה י ש ר ע ל ו י ל כ מ
א ח ר י ה מ ו י ס ע ע מ ו ד ה ע נ נ
מ פ נ י ה מ ו י ע מ ד מ א ח ר י ה מ

14:20 -- "And it came between the camp of the Egyptians and the camp of Israel; and it was a cloud and darkness [to them], but it gave light by night [to these]: so that the one came not near the other all the night." (In Hebrew, this verse begins from the leftmost bottom letter.)

ה ל י ל ל ה ל ה כ ה ז ל א ה ז ב ר ק א ל
ו ה ל י ל ה ל ה ת א ר א ' ו כ ש ח ה ו נ
נ ע ה י ה י ' ו ל א ר ש י ה נ ח מ נ י
ב ו מ י ר צ מ ה נ ח מ נ י ב א ב י ו

14:21 -- "And Moses stretched out his hand over the sea; and the LORD caused the sea to go [back] by a strong east wind all that night, and made the sea dry [land], and the waters were divided."

ו י ט מ ש ה א ת י ד ו ע ל ה י מ ו י
ו ל כ י ה ו ה א ת ה י מ ב ר ו ח ק ד
י מ ע ז ה כ ל ה ל י ל ה ו י ש מ ע ת
ה י מ ל ח ר ב ה ו י ב ק ע ו ה מ י מ

In the boustrophedonic English transliteration of the Hebrew letters of Exodus 14:20-21 below, the 72 Names are divided into 4 groups of 18 each, with each group under a letter of the Tetragrammaton.[10]

י (Y)

18	17	16	15	14	13	12	11	10	09	08	07	06	05	04	03	02	01
K	L	H	H	M	Y	H	L	'	H	K	'	L	M	ˋ	S	Y	W
L	'	Q	R	B	Z	H	'	L	Z	H	K	L	H	L	Y	L	H
Y	W	M	Y	H	L	ˋ	W	D	Y	Th	'	H	Sh	M	T	Y	W

ה (H)

36	35	34	33	32	31	30	29	28	27	26	25	24	23	22	21	20	19
M	K	L	Y	W	L	ˋ	R	Sh	Y	H	N	Ch	M	Y	N	P	L
N	W	H	Ch	Sh	K	W	Y	'	R	'	Th	H	L	Y	L	H	W
D	Q	Ch	W	R	B	M	Y	H	Th	'	H	W	H	Y	K	L	W

ו (W)

54	53	52	51	50	49	48	47	46	45	44	43	42	41	40	39	38	37
N	N	ˋ	H	D	W	M	ˋ	ˋ	S	Y	W	M	H	Y	R	Ch	'
Y	N	M	Ch	N	H	Y	Sh	R	'	L	W	Y	H	Y	H	ˋ	N
Th	ˋ	M	Sh	Y	W	H	L	Y	L	H	L	K	H	Z	ˋ	M	Y

ה (H)

72	71	70	69	68	67	66	65	64	63	62	61	60	59	58	57	56	55
M	H	Y	R	Ch	'	M	D	M	O	Y	W	M	H	Y	N	P	M
W	Y	B	'	B	Y	N	M	Ch	N	H	M	Ts	R	R	Y	W	B
M	Y	M	H	W	ˋ	Q	B	Y	W	H	B	R	Ch	L	M	Y	H

The letter-triads of the 72 Divided Names of God, which are also said to be the names of 72 angels, have the following sounds[11]:

Y		**H**		**W**		**H**	
1.	Wehu	19.	Lewo	37.	Ani	55.	Mabeh
2.	Yeli	20.	Pahel	38.	Chaum	56.	Poi
3.	Sit	21.	Nelak	39.	Rehau	57.	Nemem
4.	Aulem	22.	Yiai	40.	Yeiz	58.	Yeil
5.	Mahash	23.	Melah	41.	Hahah	59.	Harach
6.	Lelah	24.	Chaho	42.	Mik	60.	Metzer
7.	Aka	25.	Nethah	43.	Wewal	61.	Wameb
8.	Kahath	26.	Haa	44.	Yelah	62.	Yehah
9.	Hezi	27.	Yereth	45.	Sael	63.	Aunu
10.	Elad	28.	Shaah	46.	Auri	64.	Machi
11.	Law	29.	Riyi	47.	Aushal	65.	Dameb
12.	Hahau	30.	Aum	48.	Miah	66.	Menak
13.	Yezel	31.	Lekab	49.	Waho	67.	Aiau
14.	Mebha	32.	Wesher	50.	Doni	68.	Chebo
15.	Heri	33.	Yecho	51.	Hachash	69.	Raah
16.	Haqem	34.	Lehach	52.	Aumem	70.	Yebem
17.	Lau	35.	Kaweq	53.	Nena	71.	Haiai
18.	Keli	36.	Menad	54.	Neith	72.	Moum

Two Hundred Sixteen-Lettered Name.

This particular Name of God has all the letters of the 72 Divided Names of 3 letters each. All of its 216 letters are pronounced, if at all, as just one glorious and magnificent Name. It is one of the most powerful Names of God that a mystic might use.

In speech and script, the term *Shemhamforash* is used as a substitute for the 72-Lettered Name (as with the Tetragrammaton) for brevity, as well as to avoid desecrating the actual sacred Name.

Tradition has it that anyone uttering this Name of God in a state of impurity or uncleanliness would be struck dead instantly.

Various Presumed Pronunciations of "YHWH"
(Dates refer to either time of usage or publication of reference)

IABAI	Magical papyri, early Christian era
IABE	Epiphanius (d. 404), Theodoret (d. 457)
IAE	Origen (d. 254)
IAHE	Epiphanius, Theodoret
IAHOVAH	16th c. English spelling
IAHUE(H)	Oxford Dictionary, 1871
IAO/JAO	Diodorus (d. 21 BC), Irenaeus (d. 202?), Clement of A. (d. 212), Origen, Macrobius (4th c.), Jerome (d. 420)
IAOAI	Clement of Alexandria,
IAOE	Clement of Alexandria
IAOU/IAOV	Clement of Alexandria
IAOUAI	Clement, magical papyri
IAOUE	Clement of Alexandria
IAOVAI	Clement of Alexandria
IAOVE	Clement of Alexandria
IAPA	Samaritans, Theodoret
IAUA/YAUA	Assyrian, Greek, Syriac, Josephus; LDM (1990s)
IAUE	Ante-Nicene Fathers, magical papyri
IAVA/JAVA	Greek/Syriac forms
IAVE	Epiphanius, Theodoret
IEHOUA	Petrus Galatinus, 1516
IEHOUAH	William Tyndale, 1530
IEHOVA	Petrus Galatinus, 1516
IEHOVAE	Monastery in Germany
IEHOVAH	King James Version, 1611
IEHOVE	Heywood, 1600
IEHUA/IEOUA	Before 1518 (LDM)
IEUO	Philo (d. 45/50)
IHOUAH	P. de Salvaticis, 1303
IOHOUA	Raymundus Martini, 1278
IOHOUAH	Porchetus de Salvaticis
IOUA/IOVA	before 1400s (LDM)
IOUE	Homer, 800-700 BC
IOVE	14th c., Merriam-Webster's
JAHAVEH	Kodesh Name Soc., 1936
JAHOH	D.D. Williams, 1936
JAHOVAH	Faith Magazine, 1938
JAHVAH	Faith Magazine, 1938
JAHVE	J. Drusius, Cath. Encyc.
JAHVEH	J.E. Carpenter, 1869
JAHWE	Cyclopedia of Biblical, Theological & Ecc. Lit.
JAHWEH	J. Grosboll, Steps to Life
JAUOH	Jean Le Clerc, 18th c.

JAVE	Stromata (English trans.)
JAVOH	Ludwig Cappel, Le Clerc
JAWOH	Jean Le Clerc, 18th c.
JEHOVA	Oxford Eng. Dict. 1871
JEHOVAH	17th c., Protestant Bibles
JEHVA/JEVA	Hottinger
JEOVA	Chiesa, Parma, Italy
JEUE/JEVE	Adam Clarke Commentary
JOVA/JOVAE	Origen's Hexapla, 16th c.
JOVAH	Castellio
JOVE	Oxford English Dictionary
YABE	Samaritans, Theodoret
YAHAVAH	Assembly of YHVH, 1939
YAHAVEH	Am. People's Enc., 1952
YAHAWA	Encyclopedia Biblica
YAHAWE	Encyclopedia Biblica
YAHO(H)	Biblical Archeology Review (BAR), 1995
YAHOUAI	Greek writers transliterated
YAHOUE	Greek writers transliterated
YAHOVAH	Faith Magazine, 1938
YAHOVEH	Zola Levitt, 2003-2006
YAHOWAH	BAR, 1995
YAHUAH	Dr. M. Reisel
YAHUVEH	Yeshayahu Heiliczer, 1999
YAHUWA	Jehovah's Witnesses
YAHUWEH	(IAHUEH variant)
YAHVAH	Assembly of Yahvah 1930s
YAHVE	Revised Segond Version
YAHVEH	Moses Montefiore, 1892
YAHUWAH	Last Day Ministries, 1990s
YAHWA	Encyclopedia Biblica
YAHWAH	L.D. Snow, 1943
YAHWE	R.H. Charles, 1899
YAHWEH	19th c., Bible scholars
YAOU	(IAOU/IAOV variant)
YAVE	Spanish variant
YAVEH	Alex. MacWhorter, 1857
YEHOAH	Masoretic texts, 5th-9th c.
YEHOH	Jehovah's Witnesses
YEHOVAH	Codex Leningrad, 1008
YEHOVEH	Voice in the Wilderness
YEHOWAH	Masoretic texts, 5th-9th c.
YEHOWIH	Westminster Version
YEHUAH	Dr. M. Reisel
YEHUVEH	Voice in the Wilderness
YEHUWAH	Voice in the Wilderness
YEHWAH	Codex Leningrad, 1008
YEHWEH	Emphasized Bible
YEHWIH	Codex Leningrad, 1008
YOVA	Turks (B.E. Allen, 2009)

The 7 Indelible "Names" of God

According to Jewish tradition, seven sacred Names and Titles of God may be written, but not erased. The first six are based on two key verses in Exodus:

1) *"And God (**Elohim**) said unto Moses, I AM THAT I AM (**Eheyeh Asher Eheyeh**): and he said, Thus shalt thou say unto the children of Israel, I AM hath sent me unto you"* (Ex 3:14).

2) *"And God spake unto Moses, and said unto him, I am the LORD (**Adonai**): And I appeared unto Abraham, unto Isaac, and unto Jacob, by the name of God (**El**) Almighty (**Shaddai**), but by my name JEHOVAH (**YHWH**) was I not known to them"* (Ex 6:2-3).

The seventh Indelible Name occurs in 291 verses throughout the Old Testament, as in:

3) *"For thy Maker is thine husband; the LORD of hosts (**Sabaoth**) is his name; and thy Redeemer the Holy One of Israel; The God of the whole earth shall he be called"* (Isa 54:5, etc.).

Based on the above verses, the Seven Indelible Names of God are:

1) **El.** "Strong One" or "Mighty One," translated "God" in English.

2) **Elohim.** Hebrew plural for *El*, also translated as singular "God."

3) **Adonai.** Literally, "my Lords," translated "The LORD" as a substitute for the personal Names of God in the Hebrew Scriptures.

4) **YHWH.** The Tetragrammaton or Four-Lettered Name of God, meaning "I AM THAT I AM", spelled only with consonants.

5) **Eheyeh Asher Eheyeh.** Hebrew for "I AM THAT I AM," the etymological meaning of the Tetragrammaton.

6) **Shaddai.** From the Hebrew root *shadad* ("to be powerful"), translated into English as "Almighty."

7) **Sabaoth** (*Tseba'ot*). Plural of the Hebrew *tsaba*, meaning an "army" or "multitude."

The name YHWH and the title Elohim often occur with the word *tsevaot* or *sabaoth* ("hosts" or "armies"), as in *YHWH Elohe Tsevaot* ("YHWH God of Hosts" – 2 Sam 5:10, etc.), *Elohe Tsevaot* ("God of Hosts" – Ps 80:7, etc.), *Adonai YHWH Tsevaot* ("Lord YHWH of Hosts" – Ps 69:6, etc.) or, most frequently, *YHWH Tsevaot* ("YHWH of Hosts" -- 1 Sam 1:3, etc.). In Latin the term was originally transliterated as *Sabaoth* and was printed as such in the 1611 KJV.

Endnotes

1 – Mysteries of Our Maker

1. Deism, *World Book 2005* (Deluxe)
2. Hinduism, *op. cit.*
3. Paul Johnson, *A Quest for God*, 1996, p. 1
4. Ein Sof, *op. cit.*
5. Wernher von Braun, letter to the California State Board of Education, September 14, 1972
6. Ein Sof, *op. cit.*
7. Tzimtzum, *op. cit.*
8. Moses Maimonides, *The Guide for the Perplexed*, 1190
9. Time, *Microsoft Encarta Encyclopedia Deluxe 2004*
10. Big Bang Theory, *op. cit.*
11. Paul Davies, *It's About Time*, 1995, p. 17
12. Study of the Book of Revelation, "Spiritual Time, Space, Mass, Light and Energy," updated 8/20/00, Internet
13. Fred Alan Wolf, *Space-Time and Beyond*, 1987, p. 140
14. Paul Davies, *The Mind of God: The Scientific Basis for a Rational World*, 1992, pp. 199-200
15. "Whence Our 'Reality'?", *Personal Update*, December 2003, p. 3
16. Keith Ward, *God, Chance & Necessity*, 1996, p. 17
17. *The Quotable Einstein*, p. 152; quoted in "The Beginning of the Universe," *Does God Exist?*, 2000, p. 12
18. von Braun, *op. cit.*
19. *Ibid.*
20. Quoted by Fred Heeren, *Show Me God: What the Message from Space Is Telling Us About God*, 1997, frontispiece; cited in "Evidence in Plain Sight," *Does God Exist?*, 2000, p. 5
21. Roger Penrose, *The Emperor's New Mind*, 1991; cited by Gerald Schroeder, *The Science of God*, 1997, p. 22
22. Cosmos, *Encyclopaedia Britannica 2009 Student and Home Edition*
23. M. Mitchell Waldrop, "The Large-Scale Structure of the Universe," *Science*, Vol. 219, 4 March 1983, p. 1050
24. Trefil, p. 93; cited by Walt Brown, Astrophysical Sciences, creationscience.com
25. Universe, *World Book 2005* (Deluxe)
26. Trefil, *loc. cit.*
27. Waldrop, *loc. cit.*
28. Universe, *op. cit.*
29. Aristotle, *World Book 2005* (Deluxe)
30. Quoted by Chuck Missler, *Cosmic Codes*, Revised 2004, p. 337
31. Quoted by Missler, *op. cit.*, p. 338
32. Quoted by Andrew Chaikin, "Are There Other Universes?", *Science Tuesday*, 05 February 2002, Internet
33. Wolf, *op. cit.*, p. 133
34. Paul Davis, *Superforce*, 1948, p. 48; quoted by Missler, *op. cit.*, p. 340
35. Bell's Inequality, *Microsoft Encarta Encyclopedia Deluxe 2004*
36. Wolf, *op. cit.*, pp. 135-136
37. *Op. cit.*, pp. 148-149

38. Paraphrased by Missler, *op. cit.*, p. 337
39. *Op. cit.*, pp. 339-340
40. Miracles, *Fausset's Bible Dictionary*, Electronic Database, 1998
41. *Ibid.*
42. "Computer Takes on the Bible," *St. Louis Post Dispatch*, March 12, 1992; cited by Robert Faid, *A Scientific Approach to More Biblical Mysteries*, 1994, p. 69
43. Moses, *International Standard Bible Encyclopaedia*, 1996
44. Animal Kingdom, *The New Unger's Bible Dictionary*, 1988
45. Animals, *Nelson's Illustrated Bible Dictionary*, 1986
46. Quail, *International Standard Bible Encyclopaedia*, 1996
47. Animal Kingdom, *op. cit.*
48. Weights and Measures, *Fausset's Bible Dictionary*, 1998
49. Herodotus ii. 77; cited in Quail, *op. cit.*
50. Num 11:31-35, *Matthew Henry's Commentary on the Whole Bible*, New Modern Edition, 1991
51. Manna, *World Book 2005* (Deluxe)
52. Manna, *Encyclopaedia Britannica 2009 Student and Home Edition*
53. Manna, *Fausset's Bible Dictionary*, 1998
54. Manna, *Microsoft Encarta Encyclopedia Deluxe 2004*
55. Manna, *Encyclopaedia Britannica op. cit.*
56. David Allen Deal, *The Mystic Symbol*, p. 169; quoted in *Ancient American*; cited in Indian Sabbath Trail tract
57. *The Mind of Mankind*, Chapter 15; cited by Donald L. Hamilton, "The Many Motions of Planet Earth," 1996-2002, Internet
58. Grant Jeffrey, *The Signature of God*, 1996, p. 234
59. Martin Hunter, "Math of the Bible!," National Institute for Inventors, tract, p. 2
60. Chuck Missler, "The Mysterious Mathematical Design of the Bible," *Mysteries of the Bible Now Revealed*, 1999, pp. 188-189
61. J.R. Church, "Jewish Holy Days: The Making of a Baby," Amazing Discoveries, *Prophecy in the News*, June 2006, p. 17

2 – Secrets in Scriptures

1. Michael Drosnin, *The Bible Code*, 1997, p. 21
2. Grant Jeffrey, *The Signature of God*, 1996, p. 205
3. Bible, *International Standard Bible Encyclopaedia*, 1996
4. Ed Spurlin, "God's Preserved Word," tract, 1/3/94
5. William P. Grady, *Final Authority: The Christian's Guide to the King James Bible*, 1993, p. 82
6. Albert Pike, *Morals and Dogma*, p. 547
7. Spurlin, *op. cit.*
8. Grady, *loc. cit.*
9. Pike, *op. cit.*, p. 266
10. Spurlin, *op. cit.*
11. Codex, *Encyclopaedia Britannica 2009 Student and Home Edition*
12. Spurlin, *op. cit.*
13. Chuck Missler, *Cosmic Codes*, 1999, Revised 2004, p. 441
14. Library, *World Book 2005 (Deluxe)*
15. Bible, *op. cit.*
16. Richard Chaimberlin, "The Hebrew Matthew," *Petah Tikvah*, April-June 2011, p. 6
17. Missler, *op. cit.*, p. 109
18. Chaimberlin, *op. cit.*, pp. 3-7

19. *Op. cit.*, p. 6
20. Bible, *op. cit.*
21. *Ibid.*
22. Curious Facts and Interesting Information about the Bible, *The Practical Bible Dictionary and Concordance,* with *The Treasury of Biblical Information*, Renewal 1952, p. 109
23. William E. Nix, "Versions, Ancient and Medieval," *Wycliffe Bible Encyclopedia,* Vol. 2, 1975
24. Versions of the Scriptures, *The New Unger's Bible Dictionary*, 1988
25. Nix, *loc. cit.*
26. Larry Spargimino, "Myths about the Septuagint and Modern Translations," *Prophetic Observer*, September 1999, p. 2
27. Spargimino, *op. cit.*, p. 1
28. Jack Moorman, *Forever Settled: A Survey of the Documents and History of the Bible*, 1999, pp. 17-18
29. Aquila, *Encyclopedia Britannica 2009 Student and Home Edition*
30. Targum, *International Standard Bible Encyclopaedia*, 1996
31. Versions, *The New Unger's Bible Dictionary,* 1988
32. Spurlin, *op. cit.*
33. Vulgate, *Encyclopedia Britannica 2009 Student and Home Edition*
34. Jim Combs, "The Powerful Worldwide Impact of the Bible," *Mysteries of the Bible Now Revealed*, 1999, p. 163
35. Spurlin, *op. cit.*
36. Erasmus, *Microsoft Encarta Encyclopedia Deluxe 2004*
37. Combs, *loc. cit.*
38. Coverdale, *World Book 2005 (Deluxe)*
39. Coverdale, *Encyclopaedia Britannica 2009 Student and Home Edition*
40. Spurlin, *op. cit.*
41. Bible, *World Book 2005 (Deluxe)*
42. Spurlin, *op. cit.*
43. Combs, *loc. cit.*
44. *Ibid.*
45. Spurlin, *op. cit.*
46. Missler, *op. cit.*, p. 442
47. Grady, *op. cit.*, p. 73
48. Floyd Jones, *The Septuagint*, 1995, p. 50
49. Missler, *loc. cit.*
50. Spurlin, *op. cit.*
51. Norman Geisler and William Nix, *A General Introduction to the Bible*, 1974, p. 263
52. Bible Societies, *Microsoft Encarta Encyclopedia Deluxe 2004*
53. Combs, *loc. cit.*
54. "The Tangled Tether," *Personal Update*, April 2005, pp. 14-15
55. Jeffrey Satinover, *Cracking the Bible Code*, 1997, p. 250
56. Wilbur Smith, *The Incomparable Book*, 1961, pp. 9-10
57. J. Barton Payne, *Encyclopedia of Biblical Prophecy*; cited by Missler, *op. cit.*, p. 219
58. Norman Geisler and William Nix, *A General Introduction to the Bible*, 1986, p. 13
59. *Ibid.*
60. Gordon Lindsay, *Signs of the Soon Coming of Christ*, p. 15

61. David Allen Lewis, "The Miraculous Preservation of the Jews, People of the Bible," *Mysteries of the Bible Now Revealed*, 1999, p. 67
62. *Innocents Abroad*, Vol. II, p. 234; quoted by David Allen Lewis, *Prophecy 2000*, 1990, pp. 121-123
63. Howard Fast, *The Jews – Story of a People*, 1968, p. 366
64. J.R. Church, "After Centuries of Exile, They Came Home!," *Prophecy in the News*, October 2008, p. 6ff.
65. out-of-zion.com, Internet
66. *Ibid.*
67. Lindsay, *op. clt.*, p. 14
68. Jeffrey, *op. cit.*, p. 188
69. Lewis, *op. cit.,* p. 68
70. "Israel at 63: An Export Superpower," *Petah Tikvah*, July-Sept. 2011, p. 58
71. Martin Hunter, "The Bible Is the Word of God," Letters to the Editor, December 22, 1995, National Institute for Inventors, tract
72. Missler, *op. cit.*, pp. 47, 476
73. Lindsay, *op. cit.*, pp. 12-13
74. J.R. Church, *Hidden Prophecies in the Psalms,* 1986, pp. 67-69
75. Quoted by Missler, *op. cit.*, p. 133
76. Missler, *op. cit.*, pp. 126-128
77. Michael Drosnin, *The Bible Code*, 1997, p. 19
78. *Ibid.*
79. Quoted by Missler, *op. cit.*, p. 139
80. Drosnin, *op. cit.,* pp. 44-45
81. Missler, *op. cit.*, p. 145
82. Satinover, *op. cit.*, p. 243
83. Drosnin, *loc. cit.*
84. John Weldon, *Decoding the Bible Code*, 1998, p. 100
85. *Op. cit.*, p. 133
86. Drosnin, *op. cit.,* p. 102
87. *Op. cit.*, p. 163
88. *Op. cit.*, p. 165
89. Bob Schlenker, *The Open Scroll*, Vol. 2, No. 1
90. Drosnin, *op. cit.*, pp. 218-219
91. Ed Vallowe, *Biblical Mathematics*, 1998, Foreword
92. Origen, *Against Celsus*, Book I, Chap. XV; cited in *The Ante-Nicene Fathers*, 1952, p. 402; cited by Missler, *op. cit.*, p. 295
93. Vallowe, *loc. cit.*
94. Numbers, *International Standard Bible Encyclopaedia*, 1996
95. Weldon, *op. cit.*, p., 40
96. Gematria, *Encyclopaedia Britannica 2009 Student and Home Edition*

3 – Conundrums of Creation

1. Stephen Hawking, *A Brief History of Time*, 1988, p. 171
2. Hugh Ross, *The Creator and the Cosmos*, 1993, p. 15
3. Fred Heeren, *Show Me God*, 1997, Preface; quoted in "The Beginning of the Universe," *Does God Exist?*, 2000, p. 12
4. Gerald Schroeder, *The Science of God*, 1997, p. 23
5. De Sitter, *World Book 2005 (Deluxe)*
6. Robert Faid, "The Factual Scientific Accuracy of the Bible," *Mysteries of the Bible Now Revealed*, 1999, p. 136

7. Cosmos, *Encyclopaedia Britannica 2009 Student and Home Edition*
8. Robert Jastrow, *Journey to the Stars*, 1989, p. 47
9. Quoted by Grant Jeffrey, *The Signature of God*, 1996, p. 117
10. Cosmos, *op. cit.*
11. Hawking, *op. cit.*, pp. 140-141
12. "Why 'Six Days'?," *Personal Update*, November 2003, p. 11
13. Quoted by Schroeder, *op. cit.*, p. 184
14. Hawking, *op. cit.*, p. 129
15. Paul Davies, *God and the New Physics*, 1983, pp. 31-32
16. Fred Alan Wolf, *Space-Time and Beyond*, 1987, pp. 128-129
17. Quoted in "Whence Our 'Reality'?," *Personal Update*, Dec. 2003, p. 4
18. Quoted by Schroeder, *op. cit.*, Introduction
19. James H. Jeans, *The Mysterious Universe*, revised edition, 1932, p. 181
20. De Broglie, Louis Victor, *World Book 2005 (Deluxe)*
21. Schroeder, *op. cit.*, p. 160
22. Cited by Schroeder, *op. cit.*, p. 58
23. Quoted by Schroeder, *op. cit.*, 1997, p. 184
24. John D. Barrow, *The Origin of the Universe*, 1994, pp. 3-5
25. Cited by Schroeder, *op. cit.*, p. 62
26. Andrew Chaikin, "Are There Other Universes?", *Science* Tuesday, 05 February 2002, Internet
27. Richard Morris, *The Edges of Science*, 1990, p. 25
28. "New Direction in Physics: Back in Time," *The New York Times*, nytimes.com/1990/08/21/science, Internet
29. 1980: Nobel Prizes, *Microsoft Encarta Encyclopedia Deluxe 2004*
30. *Ibid.*
31. Steven Weinberg, "Life in the Universe"; quoted by Schroeder, *op. cit.*, pp. 188-189
32. John Gribbin, "Taking the Lid Off Cosmology," *New Scientist*, August 16, 1979, p. 506
33. Danny Faulkner, "Do Creationists Believe in 'Weird' Physics?", *The New Answers Book 2*, 2008, pp. 328-329
34. Chaikin, *op. cit.*
35. "New Direction in Physics: Back in Time," *op. cit.*
36. Hawking, *loc. cit.*
37. Thales, *World Book 2005 (Deluxe)*
38. Big Bang, *op. cit.*
39. Schroeder, *op. cit.*, p. 190
40. Big Bang Theory, *Microsoft Encarta Encyclopedia Deluxe 2004*
41. Schroeder, *op. cit.*, pp. 189-190
42. Cosmos, *Encyclopaedia Britannica 2009 Student and Home Edition*
43. Hydrogen, *Microsoft Encarta Encyclopedia Deluxe 2004*
44. Helium, *Encyclopaedia Britannica 2009 Student and Home Edition*
45. Quoted by Migene Gonzalez-Wippler, *A Kabbalah for the Modern World*, 1977 edition, p. 37
46. Light, *World Book 2005 (Deluxe)*
47. Cited by Gonzalez-Wippler, *op. cit.*, p. 9
48. *Op. cit.*, p. 11
49. Schroeder, *op. cit.*, p. 171
50. Helen D. Setterfield, "History of the Light-Speed Debate," *Personal Update*, July 2002, p. 10

51. Chris Bennett, *Speed of light slowing down?*, July 31, 2004, WorldNetDaily.com
52. Chuck Missler, *Cosmic Codes*, revised 2004, pp. 343-345
53. Dr. Joao Magueijo of Imperial College in London, Dr. John Barrow of Cambridge, Dr. Andy Albrecht of the University of California at Davis, and Dr. John Moffat of the University of Toronto
54. Jonathan Leake, *London Sunday Times*, June 4, 2000
55. "Astronomers detect new clues on universe's expansion," *The Philippine Star*, March 19, 2006
56. Robert Jastrow, *God and the Astronomers*, 1978, p. 14
57. Schroeder, *op. cit.*, p. 187
58. George Sim Johnston, *Reader's Digest*, May 1991, p. 31
59. "Spiritual Time, Space, Mass, Light and Energy," A Study of the Book of Revelation, updated 8/20/00, Internet
60. Paul Davies, *The Goldilocks Enigma*, 2006, pp. 15-16
61. Quoted by Andrew Chaikin, "Are There Other Universes?", Science Tuesday, 05 February 2002, Internet
62. D. Russell Humphreys, "Seven Years of Starlight and Time," Internet
63. Ralph Woodrow, "Three Days and Three Nights," p. 42; cited in "When Is The Evening, In Scripture?", tract, Last Day Ministries
64. James Ussher, *The Annals of the World*, 1658; translated by Larry and Marion Pierce; book review by Bob Ulrich, *Prophecy in the News*, March 2004, p. 18
65. Lawrence Badash, "The Age-of-the-Earth Debate," *Scientific American*, August 1989; in Dating Methods, *Microsoft Encarta Encyclopedia Deluxe 2004*
66. J.R. Church, "Creation Week," *Prophecy in the News*, Nov. 2005, p. 3
67, Day, *International Standard Bible Encyclopaedia*, 1996
68. Quoted by Schroeder, *op. cit.*, p. 45
69. Creation Science Evangelism, Internet
70. D. Russell Humphreys, "Seven Years of Starlight and Time," Institute for Creation Research, Internet
71. *Ibid.*
72. Terry Mortenson, "Where Did the Idea of 'Millions of Years' Come From?", *The New Answers Book 2*, 2008, pp. 114-117
73. Creationism, *Microsoft Encarta Encyclopedia Deluxe 2004*
74. "Earth's Age: Does Genesis 1 Indicate a Time Interval?", *Creation or Evolution*, 2002, p. 29
75. *Ante-Nicene Fathers*, 1917, p. 342
76. "Earth's Age...", *loc. cit.*
77. *The New Schaff-Herzog Encyclopedia of Religious Knowledge*, 1952, Vol. 3, p. 302; quoted in "Earth's Age...", *loc. cit.*
78. Charles Taylor, "The First 100 Words," undated
79. *The Complete Word Study: Old Testament, KJV*, 1994, p. 3
80. Hugh Ross, *The Fingerprint of God*, 1989, p. 154
81. Arthur Peacocke, "The Challenge of Science to Theology and the Church," *The New Faith-Science Debate*, 1989, p. 16
82. Mortenson, *loc. cit.*
83. Mortenson, *op. cit.*, p. 112
84. Bodie Hodge, "How Old Is the Earth?", *The New Answers Book 2*, 2008, p. 48
85. Cosmology, *Microsoft Encarta Encyclopedia Deluxe 2004*
86. Hubble Constant, *World Book 2005 (Deluxe)*
87. Age of the Universe, *Microsoft Encarta Encyclopedia Deluxe 2004*
88. Big Bang Theory, *op. cit.*

89. Cosmology, *Encyclopaedia Britannica 2009 Student and Home Edition*
90. Big Bang, *World Book 2005 (Deluxe)*
91. Universe, *op. cit.*
92. "Astronomers detect new clues...", *op. cit.*
93. Expanding Universe, *Encyclopaedia Britannica 2009 Student and Home Edition*
94. Schroeder, *op. cit.*, p. 59
95. *Op. cit.*, p. 52
96. *Op. cit.*, p. 59
97. *Ibid.*
98. *Op. cit.*, p. 55
99. *Op. cit.*, p. 65
100. *Op. cit.*, p. 69
101. *Op. cit.*, p. 66
102. *Op. cit.*, p. 65
103. *Op. cit.*, p. 63
104. *Op. cit.*, p. 69
105. *Op. cit.*, p. 66
106. *Ibid.*
107. *Op. cit.*, pp. 63-74
108. *Op. cit.*, p. 70
109. Framework Interpretation, *Wikipedia*, Internet

4 – Primordial Planet Puzzles

1. "The Most Insulting Idol of All," *Personal Update*, January 2004, p. 7
2. Chuck Missler, *Cosmic Codes*, 1999, revised 2004, p. 123
3. Sefer Yetzirah, ix; quoted in Names of God, *The Jewish Encyclopedia*, Vol. 9, pp. 162-163
4. Michael Munk, *The Wisdom in the Hebrew Alphabet*, p. 85
5. Missler, *op. cit.*, p. 109
6. Osios R' Akiva, Internet
7. Munk, *op. cit.*
8. Golem, *Encyclopaedia Britannica 2009 Student and Home Edition*
9. Hugh Ross, *The Creator and the Cosmos*, 1993, p. 15
10. Planets, *World Book 2005 (Deluxe)*
11. Planetary Science, *Microsoft Encarta Encyclopedia Deluxe 2004*
12. "Why 'Six Days'?," *Personal Update*, November 2003, p. 12
13. Walt Brown, Astrophysical Sciences, Internet
14. Erik Asphaug, "The Small Planets," *Scientific American*, Vol. 282, May 2000, p. 54.
15. *Ibid.*
16. Stephen G. Brush, *A History of Modern Planetary Physics*, Vol. 3, 1996, p. 91.
17. Noah's Flood -- Where did all the water come from?, ChristianAnswers.Net, Internet
18. Dennis Petersen, *Unlocking the Mysteries of Creation*, 2002, p. 30
19. ChristianAnswers.Net, *op. cit.*
20. Donald Cyr, "The Crystal Veil," *Stonehenge Viewpoint*, Issue 106, 1995
21. Mitchell Waldrop, "Delving the Hole in Space," *Science*, 27 Nov. 1981
22. Palestine, *Nelson's Illustrated Bible Dictionary*, 1986
23. "Three Days and Three Nights," Las Day Ministries, undated
24. Carl Wieland, "Starlight and time – a further breakthrough," June 26, 2009, Internet

25. D. Russell Humphreys, "The Battle for the Cosmic Center," Internet
26. Ellen G. White, *The Great Controversy*, 1990 Reprint, pp. 677-678
27. Milky Way, *World Book 2005* (Deluxe)
28. Gerald Schroeder, *The Science of God*, 1997, p. 192
29. Atmosphere, *Encyclopaedia Britannica 2009 Student and Home Edition*
30. Earth, *World Book 2005 (Deluxe)*
31. Bacteria, *op. cit.*
32. Cited by Gerald Schroeder, *The Science of God*, 1997, p. 71).
33. ScienceDaily, Mar. 22, 2006, Internet
34. Astronomy, *International Standard Bible Encyclopaedia*, 1996
35. Mazzaroth, *New Exhaustive Strong's Numbers and Concordance with Expanded Greek-Hebrew Dictionary,* 1994
36. Mazzaroth, *Nelson's Illustrated Bible Dictionary*, 1986
37. Missler, *op. cit.,,* p. 200
38. Astronomy, *op. cit.*
39. Zodiac, *World Book 2005 (Deluxe)*
40. "Three Wise Men and a Star," *Strange Stories, Amazing Facts*, 1975, p. 373
41. Zodiac, *Encyclopaedia Britannica 2009 Student and Home Edition*
42. Zodiac, *Microsoft Encarta Encyclopedia Deluxe 2004*
43. F. Chris Patrick, *The Zodiac Conspiracy*, 1993, p. 13
44. Astrology, *World Book 2005 (Deluxe)*
45. Evolution, *Encyclopaedia Britannica 2009 Student and Home Edition*
46. "Reason For Almost Two Billion Year Delay In Animal Evolution On Earth Discovered," ScienceDaily.com, Mar. 27, 2008, Internet.
47. Earth, *World Book 2005 (Deluxe)*
48. Leslie Orgel, "Darwinism at the Very Beginning of Life," *New Scientist*, April 15, 1982, p. 151
49. Cambrian Period, *Microsoft Encarta Encyclopedia Deluxe 2004*
50. Jonathan Sacks, "Genesis and the origin of the Origin of the species," *The Times* (London), August 29, 2008
51. Schroeder, *op.cit.,* p. 117
52. Arthur N. Strahler, *Science and Earth History: The Evolution/Creation Controversy*, 1987, p. 316.
53. Francis Downes Ommanney, *The Fishes*, 1963, p. 60.
54. *Marvels & Mysteries of Our Animal World*, The Readers Digest Association, 1964, p. 25.
55. Gen 1:20, *Barnes' Notes*, 1997
56. Schroeder, *op. cit.,* p. 99
57. Mass Extinctions, *Microsoft Encarta Encyclopedia Deluxe 2004*
58. *Ibid.*
59. Frank M. Carpenter, "Fossil Insects," *Insects*, 1952, p. 18.
60. Mass Extinctions, *loc. cit.*
61. *Ibid.*
62. *Ibid.*
63. Paul Falkowski, "Oxygen Increase Caused Mammals To Triumph, *Science*, Sept. 30, 2005, quoted by ScienceDaily, Oct. 3, 2005
64. Moses Maimonides, *Guide for the Perplexed*, 1:7; cited by Schroeder, *op. cit.,* p. 123
65. Talmud Keliim 8:5; cited by Schroeder, *loc. cit.*
66. Ramapithecus, *Encyclopaedia Britannica 2009 Student and Home Edition*

67. Ramapithecus, *World Book 2005 (Deluxe)*
68. Australopithecus, *Encyclopaedia Britannica 2009 Student and Home Edition*
69. Human Evolution, *Microsoft Encarta Encyclopedia Deluxe 2004*
70. Australopithecus, *loc. cit.*
71. Human Evolution, *loc. cit.*
72. From articles in *Time*, October 12, 2009, and *The Week*, October 16, 2009; cited in "Is 'Ardi' the Missing Link?", *Petah Tikvah*, January-March 2010, p. 22
73. Australopithecines, *Microsoft Encarta Encyclopedia Deluxe 2004*
74. Donald C. Johanson, "Finding Lucy and Other Fossil Treasures," Australopithecines, *loc. cit.*
75. Australopithecus, *World Book 2005 (Deluxe)*
76. Dennis Petersen, *Unlocking the Mysteries of Creation*, 2002, p. 129
77. Bruce Bower, "Evolution's Youth Movement," *Science News*, 2 June 2001, p. 347
78. Matt Cartmill et al., "One Hundred Years of Paleoanthropology," *American Scientist*, July–August 1986, p. 417.
79. Roger Lewin, *Bones of Contention*, pp. 164–165.
80. Solly Zuckerman, *Beyond the Ivory Tower*, 1970, p. 90
81. Richard E. Leakey and Roger Lewin, *Origins*, 1977, p. 86
82. James Shreeve, "New Skeleton Gives Path from Trees to Ground an Odd Turn," *Science*, 3 May 1996, p. 654.
83. Human Evolution, *loc. cit.*
84. Homo habilis, *Microsoft Encarta Encyclopedia Deluxe 2004*
85. Richard Leakey, *National Geographic*, June 1973; quoted by Petersen, *op. cit.*, p. 130
86. Hugh Ross, Reasons To Believe, July 8, 1997, Internet
87. Human Evolution, *loc. cit.*
88. Richard Leakey, "Further Evidence of Lower Pleistocene Hominids from East Rudolf, North Kenya," *Nature*, Vol. 231, 28 May 1971, p. 245
89. Homo erectus, *Microsoft Encarta Encyclopedia Deluxe 2004*
90. Petersen, *op. cit.*, p. 133
91. Eugene Dubois, "On the Fossil Human Skulls Recently Discovered in Java and Pithecanthropus Erectus," *Man*, Vol. 37, January 1937, p. 4
92. Homo erectus, *World Book 2005 (Deluxe)*
93. Homo heidelbegensis, *Encyclopaedia Britannica 2009 Student and Home Edition*
94. Names of God, Kabbalah, *Wikipedia*, Internet
95. *Ibid.*
96. *Ibid.*
97. *The Interpreter's Dictionary of the Bible*, p. 683
98. David Menton, "Did Humans Really Evolve from Apelike Creatures?", *The New Answers Book 2*, 2008, p. 91
99. Mitochondria, "Neandertals Were Not Close Relations, Say DNA Test," *Microsoft Encarta Encyclopedia Deluxe 2004*
100. Human Evolution, *loc. cit.*
101. David Menton, *op. cit.*, p. 92
102. Homo Neanderthalensis, "Neandertals Were Not Close Relations, DNA Testing Finds," *Encyclopaedia Britannica 2009 Student and Home Edition*
103. Prehistoric people, *World Book 2005 (Deluxe)*
104. Human being, *World Book 2005 (Deluxe)*
105. Cro-Magnon, *Encyclopaedia Britannica 2009 Student and Home Edition*

106. Cro-Magnon, *Microsoft Encarta Encyclopedia Deluxe 2004*
107. Neanderthals, *World Book 2005 (Deluxe)*
108. Prehistoric People, *loc. cit.*
109. *Nature,* May 16, 1996
110. "1999: Archaeologists Find Evidence that Neandertals Practiced Cannibalism," *Microsoft Encarta Encyclopedia Deluxe 2004*
111. Human Evolution, *loc. cit.*
112. Prehistoric people, *loc. cit.*
113. Wheel, *Encyclopaedia Britannica 2009 Student and Home Edition*
114. Writing, *Microsoft Encarta Encyclopedia Deluxe 2004*
115. Bronze Age, *Encyclopaedia Britannica 2009 Student and Home Edition*
116. Iron Age, *World Book 2005 (Deluxe)*
117. Ancient Rome, *World Book 2005 (Deluxe)*

5 – Early Earth Enigmas

1. Quoted by Migene Gonzalez-Wippler, *A Kabbalah for the Modern World,* 1974, p. 16
2. Jonathan Sacks, "Genesis and the origin of the Origin of the species," *The Times* (London), August 29, 2008
3. Steven Weinberg, "Life in the Universe," *Scientific American,* October 1994
4. Sir James Jeans, *The Mysterious Universe,* 1930
5. Paul Davies, *The Goldilocks Enigma,* 2007
6. Stuart Clark, "Unknown Earth: Our Planet's Seven Biggest Mysteries," *New Scientist,* Sept. 7, 2008
7. Gerald Schroeder, *The Science of God,* 1997, p. 191
8. Atmosphere, *Microsoft Encarta Encyclopedia Deluxe 2004*
9. ScienceDaily, Mar. 22, 2006, Internet
10. "Rise Of Oxygen Caused Earth's Earliest Ice Age," ScienceDaily, May 7, 2009, Internet
11. "Oxygen Triggered The Evolution Of Complex Life Forms," Exo Life, Jan 29, 2004, Internet
12. Atmosphere, *loc. cit.*
13. *National Geographic,* January 1976; quoted by Dennis Petersen, *Unlocking the Mysteries of Creation,* p. 100
14. Dennis Petersen, *Unlocking the Mysteries of Creation,* 2002, pp. 32-33
15. Petersen, *op. cit.,* p. 35
16. "Oxygen Increase Caused Mammals To Triumph, Researchers Say," *ScienceDaily,* Oct. 3, 2005, Internet
17. Richard Dawkins, *The Selfish Gene,* 1976, p. 16
18. ScienceDaily, Mar. 22, 2006, Internet
19. George Wald, "The Origin of Life," *Scientific American,* August 1954, pp. 49-50
20. Mike Riddle, "Can Natural Processes Explain the Origin of Life?", *The New Answers Book 2,* 2008, p. 66
21. Michael Denton, *Evolution: A Theory in Crisis,* 1985, p. 261
22. Spontaneous Generation, *World Book 2005 (Deluxe)*
23. Spontaneous Generation, *Microsoft Encarta Encyclopedia Deluxe 2004*
24. Michael Behe, *Darwin's Black Box: The Biochemical Challenge to Evolution,* 1996, pp. 23-24
25. Spontaneous Generation, *op. cit.*
26. Gary Parker and Henry Morris, *What Is Creation Science,* 1982, p. 40
27. Fred Hoyle and Chandra Wickramasinghe, *Evolution from Space,* 1981, p. 24

28. C. Folsome, "Life: Origin and Evolution, *Scientific American Special Publication*, 1979; quoted by Schroeder, *op. cit.*, p. 89

29. I. Prigogine, N. Gregoire, and A. Babloyantz, "Thermodynamics of Evolution," *Physics Today*, November 1972, pp. 25:23, and December 1972, pp. 25:38

30. Schroeder, *op. cit.*, p. 89

31. Petersen, *op. cit.*, p. 92

32. Jonathan Wells and William Dembski, *How to Be an Intellectually Fulfilled Atheist (or Not)*, 2008, p. 4

33. L.L. Larison Cudmore, *The Center of Life*, 1977, pp. 13-14

34. Rick Gore, "The Awesome Worlds Within a Cell," *National Geographic*, September 1976, pp. 357-360

35. Peter Gwynne, Sharon Begley and Mary Hager, "The Secrets of the Human Cell," *Newsweek*, August 20, 1979, p. 48

36. Loren C. Eiseley, *Darwin and the Mysterious Mr. X*, 1979, pp. 45–80

37. Wallace, Alfred Russell, *Encyclopaedia Britannica 2009 Student and Home Edition*

38. Ashley Montagu, quoted by Luther D. Sunderland in *Darwin's Enigma*, 1984, p. 119

39. George Gaylord Simpson and William S. Beck, *Life: An Introduction to Biology*, 1965, p. 241

40. Lee Spetner, *Not by Chance*, 1996, p. 138

41. Peo C. Koller, *Chromosomes and Genes*, 1971, p. 127

42. *Encyclopedia Americana*, 1977, Vol. 10, p. 742

43. G. Ledyard Stebbins, *Processes of Organic Evolution*, 1971, pp. 24-25

44. Gordon Rattray Taylor, *The Great Evolution Mystery*, 1983, p. 48

45. P. Moorhead and M. Kaplan, "Mathematical Challenges to the Neo-Darwinian Interpretation of Evolution," *Proceedings of the Symposium*, Wistar Institute of Biology, 1967; cited by Schroeder, *op. cit.* p. 119

46. Pierre-Paul Grasse, *Evolution of Living Organisms*, 1977, pp. 88,103

47. Martin Hunter, "There's a Lot of Holes in Evolutionary Theory," May 12, 1998, tract

48. Francis Hitching, *The Neck of the Giraffe*, 1982, p. 103

49. *On Call*, July 3, 1972, pp. 8,9

50. "Turning Back Nature's Clock," *Strange Stories, Amazing Facts*, 1975, pp. 104-105

51. Enigmas of Evolution," *Newsweek*, March 29, 1982, p. 39

52. David B. Kitts, "Paleontology and Evolutionary Theory," *Evolution*, September 1974, p. 467

53. Norman D. Newell, "The Nature of the Fossil Record," *Adventures in Earth History*, 1970, pp. 644–645

54. "The Evolution of Plants: A Major Problem for Darwinists," *Technical Journal*, 2002, Internet

55. Quoted in "What About Plant Evolution," *The Good News*, November-December 2009, p. 13

56. Frank M. Carpenter, "Fossil Insects," *Insects*, 1952, p. 18

57. David Attenborough, *Life on Earth*, 1979, p. 137

58. Richard Milton, *Shattering the Myths of Darwinism*, 1997, pp. 253-254

59. Ann C. Burke and Alan Feduccia, "Developmental Patterns and the Identification of Homologies in the Avian Hand," *Science*, 24 October 1997, pp. 666–668

60. Richard Hinchliffe, "The Forward March of the Bird-Dinosaurs Halted?" *Science*, 24 October 1997, p. 597

61. John A. Ruben et al., "Lung Structure and Ventilation in Theropod Dinosaurs and Early Birds, *Science*, pp. 1267–1270

62. W. E. Swinton, "The Origin of Birds," *Biology and Comparative Physiology of Birds*, 1960, p. 1

63. Charles Darwin, *On the Origin of Species*, Masterpieces of Science edition, 1958, pp. 136-137

64. David Menton, "The Human Tail and Other Tales of Evolution," *St. Louis MetroVoice*, January 1994

65. J.D. Ratcliff, *Your Body and How It Works*, 1974, p. 137

66. Mario Seiglie, Tom Robinson and Scott Ashley, "Evolution's 'vestigial organ' argument debunked," God, Science and the Bible, *The Good News*, November/December 2006, p. 11

67, Charles Darwin, *On the Origin of Species*, 1859, p. 179

68. Donald G. Mikulic et al., "A Silurian Soft-Bodied Biota," *Science*, 10 May 1985, pp. 715–717

69. Darwin, *op. cit.,* pp. 146,175

70. *Op. cit.,* Sixth Edition, The Modern Library, 1872, p. 66

71. Termite, *World Book 2005 (Deluxe)*

72. Schroeder, *op. cit.* p. 94

73. Madeline Nash, "When Life Exploded," *Time*, Dec. 4, 1995, p. 68

74. Schroeder, *op. cit.* pp. 92-93

75. Paul Chien, "Explosion of Life," 30 June 1997 Interview, origins.org/articles/chien_explosionoflife.html, p. 2

76. *Op. cit.,* p. 3

77. S. Bowring et al., "Calibrating Rates of Early Cambrian Evolution," *Science*, 1993; cited by Schroeder, *op. cit.,* pp. 116-117

78. R. Gore, "The Cambrian Explosion of Life," *National Geographic*, October 1993

79. R. Kerr, "Evolution's Big Bang Gets Even More Explosive," *Science*, 1993

80. Colin Patterson, *Evolution*, 1978, p. 133

81. Alfred S. Romer, "Darwin and the Fossil Record," *Natural History*, October 1959, p. 466

82. Richard Dawkins, *The Selfish Gene*, 1976, p. 14

83. Charles Darwin, *op. cit.,* 1902 edition, Part Two, p. 54

84. David M. Raup, "Conflicts Between Darwin and Paleontology," *Field Museum of Natural History Bulletin*, January 1979, p. 23

85. Steven M. Stanley, *The New Evolutionary Timetable*, 1981, p. xv

86. Stephen J. Gould, "Evolution's Erratic Pace," *Natural History*, May 1977, pp. 13-14

87. George Sim Johnston, "An Evening with Darwin in New York," *Crisis*, April 2006, Internet

88. Adrian Desmond and J. Moore, *Darwin: The Life of a Tormented Evolutionist*, 1991, pp. 475-477

89. C.F. (Frank) Morgan, "Evolution Not Based on Fact," May 4, 1998, "Letters to the Editor," National Institute for Inventors tract

90. I.L. Cohen, *Darwin Was Wrong: A Study in Probabilities*, 1984, p. 209-210

91. Arthur L. Bruce, "Evolution Is a Creation Myth," May 23, 1998, "Letters to the Editor," National Institute for Inventors tract

92. Austin H. Clark, "Animal Evolution," *Quarterly Review of Biology*, December 1928, p. 539

93. Fred Hoyle and N. Chandra Wickramasinghe, *Evolution from Space: A Theory of Cosmic Creationism*, 1981, pp. 96–97

94. John C. Walton, "Organization and the Origin of Life," *Origins*, 1977, pp. 30–31

95. Dawkins, *op. cit.,* Oxford University Press 30th Anniversary Edition, 2006, p. 2

96. Jonathan Sarfati, *DNA: Marvelous Messages or Mostly Mess?*, March 2003, Internet

97. L. Lester and R. Bohlin, *The Natural Limits to Biological Change*, 1989, p. 157

98. Francis Crick, *Life Itself*, p. 88; quoted by Gary Stearman, "Rael, Inc., "Cloning for Life," *Prophecy in the News*, February 2003, p. 12

99. Jan Marcussen, Newsletter, Mid-January Y2K+11, p. 2

100. Michael Behe, *Darwin's Black Box: The Biochemical Challenge to Evolution*, 1996, p. 193

101. Cohen, *loc. cit.*

102. Theistic Evolution, *Microsoft Encarta Encyclopedia Deluxe 2004*

103. "Punctuated Equilibria: An Alternative to Phyletic Gradualism," *Mammals in Paleontology*, 1972, pp. 82-115

104. "Punctuated Equilibrium Comes of Age," *Nature 366*, 1993, pp. 223-227

105. "Punctuated Equilibria: The Tempo and Mode of Evolution Reconsidered," *Paleontology*, 2007, pp. 115-151

106. "Enigmas of Evolution," *loc. cit.*

107. Evolution, *Microsoft Encarta Encyclopedia Deluxe 2004*

108. Fred Hoyle, *The Intelligent Universe*, 1983, p. 242

109. Cited by Gary Stearman, "Rael, Inc., "Cloning for Life," *Prophecy in the News*, February 2003, p. 11

110. Francis Crick, "Life Itself – Its Origin and Nature," *Futura*, 1982; quoted by Mark Eastman and Chuck Missler, *The Creator Beyond Time and Space*, 1996, p. 62

111. J. Horgan, "Profile: Francis H.C. Crick," *Scientific American*, February 1992; quoted by Schroeder, *op. cit.*, p. 90

112. Old Earth Creationism, Wikipedia, Internet

113. Progressive Creationism, Wikipedia, Internet

114. David Menton, "Did Humans Really Evolve from Apelike Creatures?", *The New Answers Book 2*, 2008, p. 85

115. Nicholas Wade, "How Old Is Man?", *The New York Times*, October 4, 1982, p. A18

116. Donald C. Johanson and Maitland A. Edey, *Lucy: The Beginnings of Humankind*, 1981, p. 315

117. Richard E. Leakey and Roger Lewin, *Origins*, 1977, p. 40

118. J. Horgan, "The New Challenges," *Scientific American*, December 1992; and J. Rennie, "Darwin's Current Bulldog: Ernst Mayr," *Scientific American*, August 1994; cited by Schroeder, *op. cit.*, p. 133

119. Menton, *loc. cit.*

120. Johanson and Edey, *op. cit.*, p. 286

121. Hitching, *op. cit.*, p. 224

122. "Anthro Art," *Science Digest*, April 1981, p. 41

123. James C. King, *The Biology of Race*, 1971, pp. 135,151

124. Stephen Jay Gould, *Hen's Teeth and Horse's Toes*, 1983, pp. 201-226

125. The Surprising Animal Kingdom," *Strange Stories, Amazing Facts*, 1975, pp. 91-93

126. "The Divine Proportion," Summum, Internet

127. *Journal of General Orthodontics*, June 1996, Vol. 7 No. 2; Reference: *International Journal of Orthodontics*, Spring 2004, Vo. 15 No. 1

6 – First Family Foibles

1. George Sim Johnston, *Reader's Digest*, May 1991, p. 31; excerpted in "Creation and Evolution: The Biblical Explanation," *Creation or Evolution*, 2000, p. 32
2. *Reader's Digest*, November 1982, cited by Grant Jeffrey, *The Signature of God*, 1996, p. 106
3. Chuck Missler, *Cosmic Codes*, Koinonia House, revised 2004, p. 367
4. Gerald Schroeder, *The Science of God*, 1997, Preface, xii
5. *Op. cit.* p. 143
6. Mainonides, *Guide for the Perplexed*, Part One, Chapter 7; Talmud Eruvim 18A; Jerusalem Talmuc Peah 1:1; annotated by Schroeder, *op. cit.*, p. 147
7. Rick Aharon Chaimberlin, Our Reply, *Petah Tikvah* Mailbox, *Petah Tikvah* (Door of Hope), April-June 2010, p. 45
8. "Genesis and ancient Near Eastern stories of Creation and the Flood: an introduction"; ChristianAnswers.Net
9. *Ibid.*
10. Nahmanides, commentary on Gen 2:7; annotated by Schroeder, *op. cit.*, p. 146
11. Schroeder, *op. cit.*, p. 145
12. Spirit, *The New Unger's Bible Dictionary,* 1988
13. Spirit, *Fausset's Bible Dictionary,* 1998
14. Spirit, *International Standard Bible Encyclopaedia,* 1996
15. Sheldon Z. Kramer, "Jewish Meditation," pp. 226-228
16. Starlight problem, Wikipedia, Internet
17. *Ibid.*
18. Josephus, BJ, II, viii, 11; quoted in Paradise, *International Standard Bible Encyclopaedia*, 1996
19. Dennis Petersen, *Unlocking the Mysteries of Creation*, 2002, p. 31
20. "Noah's Flood -- Where did all the water come from?", ChristianAnswers.Net
21. "More than a Body Can Stand," *Strange Stories, Amazing Facts*, 1975, p. 320
22. Spirit, *The New Unger's Bible Dictionary,* 1988
23. Paradise, *The New Unger's Bible Dictionary,* 1988
24. Paradise, *Nelson's Illustrated Bible Dictionary,*1986
25. Grant Jeffrey, *The Signature of God*, 1996, p. 208
26. Eden, *International Standard Bible Encyclopaedia*, 1996
27. Garden of Eden, Wikipedia, Internet
28. Eden, *op. cit.*
29. *Ibid.*
30. Gary Stearman, "The Trail of the Slithering Serpent," *Prophecy in the News*, January 2001, pp. 10-11
31. Garden of Eden, *op. cit.*
32. Stearman, *op. cit.*
33. Cush, *The New Unger's Bible Dictionary,* 1988.
34. Cush, *Fausset's Bible Dictionary,* 1998
35. Garden of Eden, *op. cit.*
36. Eden, *op. cit.*
37. Garden of Eden, *op. cit.*
38. Eden, *op. cit.*
39. Garden of Eden, *op. cit.*
40. *Ibid.*
41. Babylonia, *Microsoft Encarta Encyclopedia Deluxe 2004*
42. Cyrus H. Gordon and Gary A. Rendsburg, *The Bible and the Ancient Near East*, 1997

43. Tree of the knowledge of good and evil, Wikipedia, Internet
44. *Ibid.*
45. Cecil Adams, "Was the forbidden fruit in the Garden of Eden an Apple?", November 24, 2006, Internet
46. Tree of the knowledge of good and evil, *op. cit.*
47. Fig, *Encyclopaedia Britannica 2009 Student and Home Edition*
48. Alexander Hislop, *The Two Babylons.*; quoted by Stearman, "What You Haven't Heard About the Da Vinci Code," *Prophecy in the News*, July 2006,p.15
49. *Ibid.*
50. Tree of the knowledge of good and evil, *op. cit.*
51. Rashi, commentary on Gen 3:6; paraphrased by Schroeder, *op. cit.*, p. 148
52. Jeremiah 13:22, *The Wycliffe Bible Commentary*, 1962
53. December 4, 2000, *nationalgeographic.com*
54. *SMU News*, March 16, 2000; quoted by Stearman, "The Trail of the Slithering Serpent," *Prophecy in the News*, January 2001, pp. 8-9
55. Snake, *Encyclopaedia Britannica 2009 Student and Home Edition*
56. *Ibid.*
57. "Snake Ancestors Lost Limbs on Land, Study Says," Internet.
58. Snake, *op. cit.*
59. Carl Wieland, "Snakes do eat dust!," Creation Ministries International, Internet
60. Romans 5:12-14, *The Wycliffe Bible Commentary.*
61. *Book of Jasher*, 7:23-26; paraphrased by Gary Stearman, "Nimrod and the Garments of Power," *Prophecy in the News*, September 2001, 15
62. Abel, *International Standard Bible Encyclopaedia*, 1996
63. Prehistoric people, *World Book 2005 (Deluxe)*
64. Testament of Adam; quoted by J.R. Church, "The Millennial-Day Theory," *Prophecy in the News*, June 2008, p. 7
65. Russell Grigg, "Pre-Adamic Man: Were There Human Beings on Earth Before Adam?", Creation, September 2002, Internet
66. *Ibid.*
67. James Ussher, Old Testament Chronology, Treasury of Biblical Information, p. 3; *The Practical Bible Dictionary and Concordance*, 1952
68. Golgotha, *International Standard Bible Encyclopaedia*, 1996
69. *Ibid.*

7 – Wonderful World Wasted

1. Bronze Age, *Encyclopaedia Britannica 2009 Student and Home Edition*
2. Mahalaleel, *Nelson's Illustrated Bible Dictionary*, 1986
3. Mahalaleel, *The New Unger's Bible Dictionary*, 1988.
4. R.H. Charles, editor and translator, *The Book of Enoch*, 1893, p. 63
5. *Ibid.*
6. *Ibid.*
7. Noah, *Fausset's Bible Dictionary*, 1998
8. Chuck Missler, *Cosmic Codes*, revised 2004, p. 201
9. Flavius Josephus, *The Antiquities of the Jews*, Book 1, Chap. 2, Par. 3
10. Korum Megertchian, "Metallurgic Factory," *Bible-Science Newsletter*, Five Minutes section, Feb. 1973, p. 3; cited by Dennis R. Petersen, *Unlocking the Mysteries of Creation*, 2002, p. 189
11. Robert Helfinstine and Jerry Roth, *Texas Tracks and Artifacts*, 1994, p. 91
12. J.R. Church, "Mount Hermon: Gate of the Fallen Angels," *Prophecy in the News*, January 2007, pp.3-4,37-38

13. Josephus, *The Antiquities of the Jews*, Book I, Chap. 3, Par. 1
14. Methuselah, *Fausset's Bible Dictionary*, 1998
15. Larry Pierce and Ken Ham, "Are There Gaps in the Genesis Genealogies?", *The New Answers Book 2*, 2008, p. 61
16. Lamech, *International Standard Bible Encyclopaedia*, 1996
17. Josephus, *op. cit.*, Book I, Chap. 3, p.32
18. Patrick Robinson, A Disciple's Study of the Great Pyramid of Giza in Egypt," 6/5/95, Internet
19. I. Pierce, "In the Days of Peleg," *Creation* 22 no. 1, 1999, p. 106
20. Robinson, *op. cit.*
21. Dennis R. Petersen, *Unlocking the Mysteries of Creation*, 2002, p. 215
22. Robinson, *op. cit.*
23. John Zajac, Who Built the Great Pyramid?, Internet
24. Robinson, *op. cit.*
25. *Ibid.*
26. Peter Lorie, *The Millennium Planner*, 1995, pp. 56-59
27. Peter Lemesurier, *Nostradamus: The Final Reckoning*, 1995, p. 11-12
28. Robinson, *op. cit.*
29. Ancient Egypt. *Encyclopaedia Britannica 2009 Student and Home Edition*
30. Robinson, *op. cit.*
31. Bishop Burnett, *The Sacred Theory of the Earth*, 1816, p. 408; quoted by Grant Jeffrey, *Armageddon Appointment with Destiny*, 1988, p. 179
32. David Jay Jordan, Enoch Designed the Great Pyramid, Internet
33. Alexander MacAlister, Longevity, *International Standard Bible Encyclopaedia*, 1996
34. Josephus, *op. cit.*, Book III, Chap. 9
35. *Op. cit.*, Book I, Chap. 5
36. Petersen, *op. cit.*, p. 35
37. *Ibid.*
38. biblebell.org/creation.html, Internet
39. Paul Falkowski, "Oxygen Increase Caused Mammals To Triumph," *Science*, Sept. 30, 2005; quoted by ScienceDaily, Oct. 3, 2005, Internet
40. Petersen, *op. cit.*, p. 192
41. Noah, *Fausset's Bible Dictionary*, 1998
42. Tim LaHaye and John Morris, *The Ark on Ararat*, 1976, pp. 247-248
43. Mid-Ocean Ridge, *Microsoft Encarta Encyclopedia Deluxe 2004*
44. "Oceans Wild and Wide," *Strange Stories, Amazing Facts*, 1975, pp. 73-74
45. Mid-Ocean Ridge, *op. cit.*
46. Walt Brown, *In the Beginning: Compelling Evidence for Creation and the Flood*, 8th Edition, 2008, Internet
47. Noah's Flood -- Where did all the water come from? ChristianAnswers.Net
48. Ararat, *Encyclopaedia Britannica 2009 Student and Home Edition*
49. Olive, *Fausset's Bible Dictionary*, 1998
50. Amazing Discoveries, *Prophecy in the News*, October 2002, p. 7
51. Ararat, *International Standard Bible Encyclopaedia*, 1996
52. Isaac Preston Cory, *Ancient Fragments*, 1832, p. 54; quoted by Robert Faid, *A Scientific Approach to More Biblical Mysteries*, 1996, p. 15
53. Ararat, *Fausset's Bible Dictionary*, 1998
54. Faid, *op. cit.*, pp. 15-16.
55. Ararat, *Fausset's Bible Dictionary*
56. Nakhichevan, *Encyclopedia Britannica 2009 Student and Home Edition*

57. Ararat, *Fausset's Bible Dictionary*
58. Araxes, Armenia, *Microsoft Encarta Encyclopedia Deluxe 2004*
59. Ararat, *Encyclopaedia Britannica 2009 Student and Home Edition*
60. Bob Cornuke, *The Lost Mountains of Noah*, book review by Bob Ulrich, *Prophecy in the News*, December 2001, p. 7
61. Mario Seiglie, Tom Robinson and Scott Ashley, "Has Noah's ark been found buried under ice on Mt. Ararat?", *The Good News*, July/August 2010, p. 29
62. Flood, *The New Unger's Bible Dictionary*, 1988
63. A. Leo Oppenheim, *Ancient Near Eastern Texts*, 1950, p. 265
64. Flood, *op. cit.*
65. Deluge, *Microsoft Encarta Encyclopedia Deluxe 2004*
66. Noah, *Fausset's Bible Dictionary*, 1998
67. Deluge, *op. cit.*
68. Deluge, *International Standard Bible Encyclopaedia*, 1996
69. Petersen, *op. cit.*, p. 32
70. Terry Mortenson, "Where Did the Idea of 'Millions of Years' Come From?", *The New Answers Book 2*, 2008, p. 114-117
71. Noah, *op. cit.*
72. Hardwick, "Christ and other Masters," 3:16
73. Ken Ham, Jonathan Sarfati, and Carl Wieland, "Where did all the Flood waters go?", *The Revised and Expanded Answers Book*, 2000, ChristianAnswers.Net
74. Sinim, *New Exhaustive Strong's Numbers and Concordance with Expanded Greek-Hebrew Dictionary*, 1994
75. William Whiston, *The Works of Josephus: Complete and Unabridged*, 1987, pp. 36-37
76. Hardwick, *loc. cit.*
77. James Legge, *The Notions of the Chinese Concerning God and Spirits*, 1852, p. 52; in Kang and Nelson's *Discovery of Genesis*; p. 15; quoted by Petersen, *op. cit.*, p. 208
78. Tim Osterholm, "The Table of Nations (Genealogy of Mankind) and the Origin of Races (History of Man), Internet
79. Amazing Discoveries, *Prophecy in the News*, April 2002, p. 7

8 – Full Circle to Square One

1. S.A. Austin, J.R. Baumgardner, D.R. Humphreys, A.A. Snelling, L. Vardiman, K.P. Wise, "Catastrophic Plate Tectonics: A Global Flood Model of Earth History," *Proceedings of the Third International Conference on Creationism*, 1994, p. 609
2. William Overn, "The Tilt of the Earth's Axis, Its Orientation Brings The New Age, Its History Reveals The Flood and Explains the Magnetic Reversals," *Proceedings of the 1992 Twin-Cities Creation Conference*, p. 84
3. Peter Lorie, *The Millennium Planner*, 1995, pp. 60-68
4. Barry Setterfield, "The recent change in the earth's axis," *Science At The Crossroads*, 1983 National Creation Conference, Minneapolis, MN, pp. 82-84
5. Paul D. Ackerman, *It's A Young World After All*, 1986, Web Version
6. Dennis R. Petersen, *Unlocking the Mysteries of Creation*, 2002, p. 32
7. *Ibid.*
8. Dietary supplement, *World Book 2005 (Deluxe)*
9. Ararat, *Encyclopaedia Britannica 2009 Student and Home Edition*
10. Tim Osterholm, "The Table of Nations (Genealogy of Mankind) and the Origin of Races (History of Man)," Internet
11. Arphaxad, *Nelson's Illustrated Bible Dictionary*, 1986

12. Eber, *International Standard Bible Encyclopaedia*, 1996
13. Terah, *The New Unger's Bible Dictionary*, 1988
14. Nimrod, *The New Unger's Bible Dictionary*, 1988
15. *Zohar*, vol. 1, p. 250
16. Nimrod, *Fausset's Bible Dictionary*, 1998
17. Flavius Josephus, *The Antiquities of the Jews*, I, 4
18. Leopard, *Fausset's Bible Dictionary*, 1998
19. Alexander Hislop, *The Two Babylons*, quoted by Gary Stearman, "Night of the Leopard," *Prophecy in the News*, July 2001, p. 13
20. Josephus, *loc. cit.*
21. *Zohar, loc. cit.*
22. Nimrod, *International Standard Bible Encyclopaedia*, 1996
23. Nimrod, *Fausset's Bible Dictionary*, 1998
24. Gary Stearman, "Night of the Leopard," *Prophecy in the News*, July 2001, p. 13
25. *Zohar, loc. cit.*
26. J.R. Church, "Mount Hermon: Gate of the Fallen Angels," *Prophecy in the News*, January 2007, p. 38
27. Hislop, *op. cit.*; excerpted by Church *op. cit.*, pp. 3-4,37-38
28. *Ibid.*
29. Church, *loc. cit.*
30. Josephus, *loc. cit.*
31. Tower of Babel, Wikipedia, Internet
32. Josephus, *loc. cit.*
33. Brian E. Allen, *The Star of Their God*, undated, p. 34
34. Josephus, *loc. cit.*
35. Pam Sheppard, "Tongue-Twisting Tales," *Answers*, April-June 2008, pp. 56-57; cited by Bodie Hodge, "Was the Dispersion at Babel a Real Event?," *The New Answers Book 2*, 2008, p. 311
36. Babel, *International Standard Bible Encyclopaedia*, 1996
37. Nimrod, *Fausset's Bible Dictionary*, 1998
38. *Ibid.*
39. Iscah, *Fausset's Bible Dictionary*, 1998
40. "Abram: The Soul Winner," *Petah Tikvah*, Oct.-Dec. 2007, p. 27
41. Gary Stearman, "Nimrod and the Garments of Power," *Prophecy in the News*, September 2001, 17
42. Nimrod, Wikipedia, Internet
43. *Ibid.*
44. "Abram: The Soul Winner," *loc. cit.*
45. Nimrod, Wikipedia, Internet
46. "Abram: The Soul Winner," *loc. cit.*
47. *Ibid.*
48. Nimrod, Wikipedia, Internet
49. *Ibid.*
50. Flavius Josephus, *The Works of Josephus: New Updated Edition*, book 1, chapter 8; translated by William Whiston, 1987, p. 39
51. Jacob, *International Standard Bible Encyclopaedia*, 1996
52. Jacob, *The New Unger's Bible Dictionary*. 1988
53. Gen 29:9-14, *Matthew Henry's Commentary on the Whole Bible*
54. Joseph, *Nelson's Illustrated Bible Dictionary*,1986
55. Joseph, *The New Unger's Bible Dictionary*, 1988
56. Joseph, *Fausset's Bible Dictionary*, 1998

57. Zoan, *International Standard Bible Encyclopaedia*, 1996
58. Hyksos, *World Book 2005 (Deluxe)*
59. Ancient Egypt, *World Book 2005 (Deluxe)*
60. Hyksos, *Encyclopaedia Britannica 2009 Student and Home Edition*
61. Ancient Egypt, *op. cit.*
62. Chariot, *World Book 2005 (Deluxe)*
63. Hyksos, *Microsoft Encarta Encyclopedia Deluxe 2004*
64. Zoan, *Fausset's Bible Dictionary*, 1998
65. Zoan, *International Standard Bible Encyclopaedia*, 1996
66. Zoan, *Fausset's Bible Dictionary*, 1998
67. Zoan, *International Standard Bible Encyclopaedia*, 1996
68. Zoan, *Fausset's Bible Dictionary*, 1998
69. Dave Ramey, Bible Study, Internet
70. Zoan, *Nelson's Illustrated Bible Dictionary*, 1986
71. Zoan, *International Standard Bible Encyclopaedia*, 1996
72. *Ibid.*
73. Goshen, *Nelson's Illustrated Bible Dictionary*, 1986
74. *Ibid.*
75. Zoan, *International Standard Bible Encyclopaedia*, 1996
76. Exodus, *The New Unger's Bible Dictionary*, 1988
77. Ancient Egypt, *World Book 2005 (Deluxe)*
78. Hyksos, *World Book 2005 (Deluxe)*
79. Joseph, *International Standard Bible Encyclopaedia*, 1996
80. Hyksos, *Encyclopaedia Britannica 2009 Student and Home Edition*
81. Joseph, *The New Unger's Bible Dictionary*, 1988
82. Joseph, *Fausset's Bible Dictionary*, 1998
83. *Ibid.*
84. Jacob, *International Standard Bible Encyclopaedia*, 1996
85. Exodus, *The New Unger's Bible Dictionary*, 1988
86. Josephus, Ant. 2:9, section 2,3; cited in Moses, *Fausset's Bible Dictionary*, 1998
87. Josephus, Ap. 1:9,6; 2:9; cited in Moses, *op. cit.*
88. Moses, *International Standard Bible Encyclopaedia*, 1996
89. Moses, *The New Unger's Bible Dictionary.* 1988
90. Robert Faid, How Many Were There in the Exodus, *A Scientific Approach to More Biblical Mysteries*, 1995, pp. 72-73
91. J. Sanford, *Genetic Entropy and the Mystery of the Genome*, 2005, p. 37
92. Wendy Wippel, "The History of the World in the Molecules of Life," *Prophecy in the News*, December 2006, pp. 36-37
93. 10% of Brain Myth, Wikipedia, Internet
94. Richard M. Restak, *The Brain: The Last Frontier*, 1979, p. 59.

9 – Recurring Riddles Reexamined

1. *Strange Stories, Amazing Facts*, 1975, pp. 421-423
2. *Op. cit.*, pp. 424-427
3. *Op. cit.*, p. 427
4. Duane Gish, *Dinosaurs by Design*, 1992, p. 16
5. Dennis Petersen, *Unlocking the Mysteries of Creation*, 2002, p. 167
6. Roy Mackal, *A Living Dinosaur? In Search of Mokele-Mbembe*, 1987; paraphrased by Petersen, *loc. cit.*
7. Don Patton, interviews with Dr. Javier Cabrera; paraphrased by Petersen, *op. cit.*, p. 165

8. "A Bolivian Saurian," *Scientific American*, 49:3 (1883); quoted by William Corliss, *Incredible Life: A Handbook of Biological Mysteries*, p. 531; quoted by Petersen, *op. cit.,*, p. 168

9. Randall Reinstedt, *Shipwrecks and Sea Monsters of California's Central Coast*, 1975, p. 160

10. Petersen, *op. cit.*, p. 166

11. John Goertzen, "New *Zuiyo Maru* Cryptid Observations: Strong Indications It Was a Marine Tetrapod," *Creation Research Society Quarterly*, June 2001, pp. 19ff.

12. *Strange Stories, Amazing Facts*, p. pp. 436-437

13. *Ibid.*

14. *Ibid.*

15. *Ibid.*

16. Amazing Discoveries, *Prophecy in the News*, May 2004, p. 17

17. Jan Marcussen, "There were giants in the earth in those days," newletter, Mid-August Y2K+5, p. 3

18. Amazing Discoveries, *loc. cit.*

19. Marcussen, *loc. cit.*

20. *Ibid.*

21. *Ibid.*

22. *The World's Last Mysteries*, 1967, p. 94

23. Wendy Wippel, "The History of the World in the Molecules of Life," *Prophecy in the News*, December 2006, p. 37

24. *Ibid.*

25. Noah, *Fausset's Bible Dictionary*, 1998

26. Wippel, *loc. cit.*

27. Semites, *Microsoft Encarta Encyclopedia Deluxe 2004*

28. Japhetites, *Microsoft Encarta Encyclopedia Deluxe 2004*

29. Tim Osterholm, "The Table of Nations (Genealogy of Mankind) and the Origin of Races (History of Man)," Internet

30. Bill Cooper, *After the Flood*, 1995, pp. 49

31. Tim Osterholm, Genesis 10 – the Table of Nations, Updated 09/2009

32. Hamites, *World Book 2005 (Deluxe)*

33. Tim Osterholm, "The Table of Nations (Genealogy of Mankind) and the Origin of Races (History of Man)," Internet

34. Race, *Microsoft Encarta Encyclopedia Deluxe 2004*

35. Osterholm, *op. cit.*

36. *Ibid.*

37. Cathay, *World Book 2005 (Deluxe)*

38. Osterholm, *op. cit.*

39. Noah, *Fausset's Bible Dictionary*, 1998

40. Philip E. Ross, "Hard Words," *Scientific American*, April 1991, p. 144

41. David C. C. Watson, *The Great Brain Robbery*, 1976, pp. 83–89

42. Walt Brown, *In the Beginning: Evidence for the Creation and the Flood*, Internet

43. Writing, *World Book 2005 (Deluxe)*

44. Writing, *Microsoft Encarta Encyclopedia Deluxe 2004*

45. Hebrew Language, *The New Unger's Bible Dictionary*, 1988

46. Writing, *Microsoft Encarta Encyclopedia Deluxe 2004*

47. Writing, *World Book 2005 (Deluxe)*

48. Languages of the Old Testament, *International Standard Bible Encyclopaedia*, 1996

49. The Targums, *The Westminster Bible Dictionary*, p. 625
50. Hebrew language, *World Book 2005 (Deluxe)*
51. Grant Jeffrey, *The Signature of God*, 1996, p. 186
52. Hebrew language, *Microsoft Encarta Encyclopedia Deluxe 2004*
53. David Down, "Ziggurats in the News," *Archaelogical Diggings*, March-April 2007, pp. 3-7; cited by Hodge, *op. cit.*, p. 301
54. Jeffrey, *op. cit.*, p. 39-40
55. *Ibid.*
56. Aubrey de Selincourt, *Herodotus, The Histories*, 1983, p. 181; quoted by Robert Faid, *A Scientific Approach to More Biblical Mysteries*, 1996, p. 51
57. Henry Morris, *The Biblical Basis for Modern Science*, 1984, pp. 414-426
58. Petersen, *op. cit.*, p. 55
59. Population, *Microsoft Encarta Encyclopedia Deluxe 2004*
60. Pyramid, *Microsoft Encarta Encyclopedia Deluxe 2004*
61. *The World's Last Mysteries*, *loc. cit.*
62. Petersen, *op. cit.*, p. 219
63. "Tibetan Sound Levitation Of Large Stones Witnessed By Scientist," 10-3-3; quoted by D. H. Childress, ed., "Anti-gravity and the World Grid"; cited by Bruce Cathie, *Acoustic levitation of stones*, pp. 213-217; Rense.com, Internet
64. Acoustic levitation, Wikipedia, Internet
65. "The Mayan," *National Geographic*, December 1975, p. 783
66. Amazing Discoveries, *Prophecy in the News*, July 2004, p. 17
67. Harry Schwalb, "Electric Batteries of 2,000 Years Ago," *Science Digest* 41, April 1957, 17-19; excerpted by William Corliss, *Ancient Man: A Handbook of Puzzling Artifacts*, 1978, p. 453
68. Amazing Discoveries, *loc. cit.*
69. Petersen, *op. cit.*, pp. 224-225
70. Petersen, *op. cit.*, p. 223
71. Urim and Thummim, *Nelson's Illustrated Bible Dictionary*, 1986
72. North, *The New Unger's Bible Dictionary*, 1988
73. Keil and Delitzsch, Commentary on the Pentateuch, III, 17
74. Astronomy, *International Standard Bible Encyclopaedia*, 1996
75. Ox, *The New Unger's Bible Dictionary*, 1988
76. Astronomy, *op. cit.*
77. Cheiro, *Cheiro's World Predictions*, 1931, reprinted 1986, pp. 170,183
78. Gods, False, *The New Unger's Bible Dictionary*, 1988
79. Astrology, *International Standard Bible Encyclopaedia*, 1996
80. John Salverda, "The Identification of Israel with Saturn," Brit-Am Ephraimite Discussion Group, Internet
81. *Ibid.*
82. Astrology, *op. cit.*
83. J.R. Church, "Two Full Lunar Eclipses in 1996! Both on Jewish Holidays!," *Prophecy in the News*, October 1996, p. 6
84. Salverda, *op. cit.*
85. Alexander Hislop, *The Two Babylons*, p. 269
86. Shield of David, *Microsoft Encarta Encyclopedia Deluxe 2004*
87. Chuck Missler, "The Mysterious Mathematical Design of the Bible," *Mysteries of the Bible Now Revealed*, 1999, p. 206
88. O.J. Graham, *The Six-Pointed Star*, pp. 32,34; cited by Brian E. Allen, *The Star of Their God*, undated, p. 2
89. Shield of David, *op. cit.*

90.   W. Gunther Plaut, *The Magen David*, 1991, pp. 37-39
91.   Asher Eder, *The Star of David*, 1987, p. 15
92.   Shield of David, *op. cit.*
93.   Arcturus, *World Book 2005 (Deluxe)*
94.   F. Chris Patrick, *The Zodiac Conspiracy*, 1993, p. 80
95.   Johann Heinrich von Madler, *Microsoft Encarta Encyclopedia Deluxe 2004*
96.   Pleiades, *Fausset's Bible Dictionary*, 1998
97.   Unidentified Flying Object, *Encyclopaedia Britannica 2009 Student and Home Edition*
98.   *Ibid.*
99.   Unidentified Flying Object, *World Book 2005 (Deluxe)*
100. Unidentified Flying Object, *Encyclopaedia Britannica 2009 Student and Home Edition*
101. Gary Stearman, "Roswell—The Biblical Question," *Prophecy in the News*, October 2001, pp. 8-10
102. Unidentified Flying Object, *World Book 2005 (Deluxe)*
103. Unidentified Flying Object, *Encyclopaedia Britannica 2009 Student and Home Edition*
104. Unidentified Flying Object, *Microsoft Encarta Encyclopedia Deluxe 2004*
105. *Ibid.*
106. *Encyclopaedia Britannica*, Vol. 22, p. 1001
107. Carl Sagan, etc., *Communication with Extraterrestrial Intelligence* (CETI), 1973, p. 66
108. Chuck Missler, *Cosmic Codes*, 1999, Revised 2004, p. 29-31

10 – Personal Names of God

1.   Rabbi Yeshayahu Heiliczer, "The Divine Name," *Messianic Home*, Summer 1999, p. 18
2.   "How the Cocktail Party Effect Works," *Strange Stories, Amazing Facts*, 1975, p. 52
3.   Names of God, Kabbalah, *Wikipedia*, Internet
4.   OT:1961, OT:834, *Biblesoft's New Exhaustive Strong's Numbers and Concordance with Expanded Greek-Hebrew Dictionary.* 1994
5.   B. Earl Allen, *Publish the Name of Yahuwah*, 2009, Revised Edition, pp. 51,52
6.   Names of God, Kabbalah, *op. cit.*
7.   Name of God, *Encyclopaedia Judaica*, Vol. 7, p. 680
8.   *Smith's Bible Dictionary*: quoted by Allen, *op. cit.*, p. 49
9.   Allen, *op. cit.*, p. 51)
10.   Names of God, *The Jewish Encyclopedia*, Vol. 9, p. 162-163
11.   Choon-Leong Seow, "The Ineffable Name of Israel's God," Glossary, *Bible Review*, December 1991, p. 49
12.   Jacob O. Meyer, "Seven Thousand Witnesses," tract, 1972
13.   Allen, *op. cit.*, pp. 51,52,54,55
14.   Name of God, *loc. cit.*
15.   Names of God, *op. cit.*, pp. 160-161
16.   Seow, *op. cit.*, p. 50
17.   J, *Funk and Wagnalls Encyclopaedia,* 1979
18.   "The 1560 Geneva Bible," The Oil Derrick, tract, undated
19.   J, *op. cit.*
20.   J, *World Book 2005 (Deluxe)*
21.   J, *Funk and Wagnalls Encyclopaedia,* 1979

22. *The Mistaken J,* 1996, p. 4
23. J, *World Book 2005 (Deluxe)*
24. Jehovah, *Insight on the Scriptures,* 1988, p. 7
25. OT:3050 Jah, *New Exhaustive Strong's Numbers and Concordance with Expanded Greek-Hebrew Dictionary,* 1994
26. *Encyclopedia Judaica,* Vol. 7, col. 680
27. Names of God, *The Jewish Encyclopedia,* Vol. 9, pp. 162-163
28. God, Names of, *The Jewish Encyclopedia,* Vol. 11, p. 263
29. *Encyclopedia Judaica, loc. cit.*
30. *The Jewish Encyclopaedia,* Vol. 12, p. 119
31. Seow *op. cit.,* p. 49
32. Names of God, *loc. cit.*
33. *Encyclopaedia Britannica,* Vol. 23, p. 867
34. Solomon Zeitlin, *Jewish Quarterly Review,* Vol. 59, No. 4, April 1969
35. *Mackey's Revised Encyclopedia of Freemasonry,* Vol. 1, p. 501
36. *Ibid.*
37. Languages of the Old Testament, *International Standard Bible Encyclopaedia,* 1996
38. *The Jewish Encyclopaedia,* Vol. 12, p. 119
39. Languages of the Old Testament, *op. cit.*
40. Heiliczer, *loc. cit.*
41. Alexander, *Fausset's Bible Dictionary,* 1998
42. Alexander, *International Standard Bible Encyclopaedia,* 1996
43. High Priest, *Fausset's Bible Dictionary,* 1998
44. God, Names of, *op. cit.,* Vol. 1, p. 201-202
45. Simeon the Just, *The Jewish Encyclopedia,* 1901, Vol. 11, pp. 352-353
46. God, Names of, *Encyclopaedia Judaica,* col. 682
47. God, Names of, *The Jewish Encyclopaedia,* Vol. 1, pp. 201-202
48. Quoted by Seow, *op. cit.,* pp. 49-50
49. Seow, *loc. cit.*
50. *The Babylonian Talmud,* Tractate Yoma, p. 39b
51. Names of God, *loc. cit.*
52. Temple, *International Standard Bible Encyclopaedia,* 1996
53. Jesus Christ, *Nelson's Illustrated Bible Dictionary,* 1986
54. Names of God, *loc. cit.*
55. P. Kahle, *The Cairo Geniza,* 1959, p. 222
56. *The Divine Name That Will Endure Forever,* 1984, p. 25
57. Seow, *loc. cit.*
58. Heiliczer, *loc. cit.*
59. *Encyclopedia Americana,* Vol. 23, p. 867
60. Jacob O. Meyer, *The Memorial Name – Yahweh,* 1987, pp. 84-85
61. Names of God, Kabbalah, *op. cit.*
62. *Ibid.*
63. *Ibid.*
64. *Ibid.*
65. *Ibid.*
66. God, Names of, *Encyclopedia Judaica,* col. 680
67. Names of God, Kabbalah, *op. cit.*
68. God, Names of, *The Jewish Encyclopaedia,* p. 290

11 – Two Substitutes, One Original

1. Flavius Josephus, *Wars of the Jews*, Book 5, ch. 5, sec. 7
2. Gesenius, *Hebrew Grammar*, ed. Cowley, pp. 26, 45
3. *Jewish Wars*, Loeb Classical Library, p. 273
4. Voy Wilks, "The Sacred Name YHWH Consists of Four Vowels?", tract, 11\17\91
5. B. Earl Allen, *Publish the Name of Yahuwah*, Revised 2009, p. 62
6. Yeshayahu Heiliczer, "The Divine Name," *Messianic Home*, Summer 1999, p. 19
7. Flavius Josephus, *Antiquities of the Jews*, Book 1, Ch. 6, Sec. 1
8. *Adam Clarke's Commentary*, Vol. 3, pp. 393-394
9. Iesous, *Theological Dictionary of the New Testament*, pp. 284-293
10. Choon-Leong Seow, "The Ineffable Name of Israel's God," Glossary, *Bible Review*, December 1991, p. 49
11. "Four Vowels," Last Day Ministries, tract, undated
12. The Four Vowels, *The Mistaken J*, YNCA, 1996, p. 32
13. Allen, *op. cit.*, p. 89
14. *Seventh-Day Adventist Dictionary*, cited by B. Earl Allen, *op. cit.*
15. Brian Allen, "Open Letter to Tony Sukla," undated
16. Last Day Ministries, tract, undated
17. Jacob O. Meyer, *The Memorial Name – Yahweh*, 1987, p. 83
18. Meyer, *Seven Ancient Witnesses*, 1973, p. 2
19. Allen, *op. cit.*, p. 102
20. Allen, "Open Letter to Tony Sukla"
21. *The Missing J*, Yahweh's Assembly in Messiah, Revised 1996, p. 7
22. Seow, *op. cit.*, p. 50
23. Anson F. Rainey, *Biblical Archaelogy Review*, Sept.-Oct. 1994
24. Allen, *op. cit.*, p. 41
25. The Names of God, *Jewish Encyclopedia*, Vol. 9, p. 161
26. *The Good News*, Nov.-Dec. 1972; quoted by Allen, *op. cit.*, p. 64
27. Meyer, *The Memorial Name – Yahweh*, 1987, p. 83
28. *The Missing J*, *loc. cit.*
29. J.D. Douglas, *The New Bible Dictionary*, 1973, p. 478
30. God, Names of, *Encyclopaedia Judaica*, Vol. 7, col. 679
31. *The New 20th Century Encyclopedia of Religious Knowledge*, 2ND edition, p. 886
32. Seow, *loc. cit.*
33. *The New 20th Century Encyclopedia of Religious Knowledge*, *loc. cit.*
34. Meyer, *op. cit.*, p. 22
35. Faculty Members of Ambassador College, Padadena, California, God Speaks Out on the New Morality; quoted by Meyer, *op. cit.*, p. 8
36. Names of God, Kabbalah, *Wikipedia*, Internet
37. *Aid to Bible Understanding*, Watchtower Tract and Bible Society, p. 885
38. Jehovah, *Gesenius' Hebrew-Chaldee Lexicon*
39. Meyer, *op. cit.*, p. 87
40. Names of God, Kabbalah, *op. cit.*
41. God, Names of, *op. cit.*, cols. 680-682
42. Rainey, *loc. cit.*
43. Heiliczer, *loc. cit.*
44. Adeney and Bennett, *The Century Bible*, Vol. 1, p. 91
45. Jehovah, *Oxford English Dictionary*
46. U, *World Book 2005 (Deluxe)*
47. *The Name*, Jehovah's Witnesses, p. 18

48. U, *op. cit.*
49. Names of God, Kabbalah, *op. cit.*
50. Heiliczer, *loc. cit.*
51. Seow, *loc. cit.*
52. Heiliczer, *loc. cit.*
53. Jehovah, *Insight on the Scriptures*, 1988, Vol. 2, p. 12
54. Joseph Rotherham, editor, *The Emphasized Bible,* Introduction; quoted in *The Mistaken J,* YNCA, 1996, p. 17
55. J.B. Rotherham; quoted in *Is His Name Jehovah or Yahweh?*, YNCA, 1989, p. 3
56. The Names of God, *op. cit.*, p. 160
57. *Encyclopaedia Britannica*, 15th edition, Vo. 12, p. 995
58. *Encyclopaedia Britannica, Micropedia,* Vol. 10
59. Foreword, *The New World Translation of the Christian Greek Scriptures*, p. 25
60. Quoted in *Let Your Name Be Sanctified,* Jehovah's Witnesses, p. 16
61. Names of God, Kabbalah, *op. cit.*
62. Sigmund Mowinchel, "The Name of the Heavenly Father of Moses," *The Hebrew Union College Annual,* 1961, p. 14
63. God, Names of, *op. cit.*, col. 679
64. Mowinchel, *loc. cit.*
65. God, Names of, *op. cit.*, cols.. 679-680
66. YHWH, Names of God, *Jewish Encyclopedia,* Internet
67. Seow, *loc. cit.*
68. Herschel Shanks, "The Tombs of Silwan," *Biblical Archaeology Review,* May-June 1994, p. 48
69. P. Kyle McCarter, "In Private Hands," Queries & Comments, *Biblical Archaeology Review,* May-June 1996, p. 26
70. Shanks, "Fingerprint of Jeremiah's Scribe," *Biblical Archaeology Review,* March-April 1996, p.38
71. Shanks, *op. cit.*, pp. 36-38
72. Shanks, "Isaiah's Ire," *Biblical Archaeology Review,* May-June 1994, pp. 48-49
73. *The New 20th Century Encyclopedia of Religious Knowledge,* 2nd edition, p. 886
74. *Ibid.*
75. "Comments," Last Day Ministries, tract, undated
76. Seow, *op. cit.*, p. 49
77. George Wesley Buchanan, "The Tetragrammaton," Comments & Queries, *Biblical Archaelogy Review,* March-April 1995, pp. 30,31,100
78. *Sayce,* Ancient Monuments, *The Century Cyclopedia* [1900], p. 75; excerpted by Allen in "How Long Halt Ye Between Two Opinions," tract, undated
79. Ziony Zevit, *Matres Lectionis in Ancient Hebrew Epigraphs,* American Schools of Oriental Research, 1980, p. 25
80. *Sayce, loc. cit.*
81. Heiliczer, *op. cit.*, p. 20
82. YHWH, Names of God, *op. cit.*
83. Yahweh, *Encyclopaedia Britannica,* 11th Edition, Vol. 12
84. *Sayce, loc. cit.*
85. Seow, *op. cit.*, p. 50).
86. Heiliczer, *loc. cit.*
87. Garrison, *Strange Facts About The Bible*, p. 81
88. Seow, *op. cit.*, p. 49
89. "Ioua/Iona," The Oil Derrick, tract, undated, p. 1
90. Buchanan, *loc. cit.*

91. Jochebed, *International Standard Bible Encyclopaedia*, 1996
92. "The Mystic Symbol," Indian Sabbath Trail, tract, undated
93. James Montgomery, "The Hebrew Divine Name and the Personal Pronoun *Hu*, Critical Notes, *Journal of Biblical Literature*, Vol. lxiii, 1944, p. 162
94. Abihu, *International Standard Bible Encyclopaedia*, 1996
95. Elihu, *The New Unger's Bible Dictionary*, 1988
96. Jehu, *Nelson's Illustrated Bible Dictionary*,1986
97. *Gesenius Hebrew Grammar*, p. 68
98. God, Names of, *op. cit.*, col. 263
99. *The Mishnah*, translated by H. Danby, 1954, p. xiv
100. Allen, *op. cit.*, p. 7
101. Zevit, *op. cit.*, pp. 12-13
102. Jehucal, *The New Unger's Bible Dictionary*, 1988

12 – A Deadline for Calling on God?

1. John, *Nelson's Illustrated Bible Dictionary*,1986
2. Wind, *op. cit.*
3. Uriah Smith, *Daniel and the Revelation*, Revised 1944, p. 94
4. Earth, *The New Unger's Bible Dictionary*, 1988
5. A. Jan Marcussen, *National Sunday Law*, Ninety-sixth printing, 1990, p. 3
6. Fire, *Fausset's Bible Dictionary*, 1998
7. Moon, *The New Unger's Bible Dictionary*, 1988
8. OT:6725 *tsiyuwn*, *Strong's Greek/Hebrew Definitions*
9. Torah, *The New Unger's Bible Dictionary*, 1988

Appendix

1. *Zohar, Yitro* 87 and *Mishpatim* 124; cited by Chuck Missler, *Cosmic Codes*, revised 2004, p. 123
2. Babylonian *Talmud*, Berachot 55a; cited by Missler, *loc. cit.*
3. Name of God, Temple Emanu-El of San Jose, 2008, Internet
4. Names of God, *The Jewish Encyclopedia*, Vol. 9, pp. 162-163
5. *op. cit.*, p. 163
6. Sir E. A. Wallis Budge, *Amulets and Talismans* , 1961, p. 377
7. Adolphe Franck, *The Kabbalah: The Religious Philosophy of the Hebrews*, 1967, p.19; cited in A Study of the Book of Revelation, Internet
8. Names of God, *loc. cit.*
9. A Study of the Book of Revelation, Temple Emanu-El, Internet
10. Migene Gonzalez-Wippler, *A Kabbalah for the Modern World*, 1977, p.30
11. *Ibid.*

38449741R00244

Made in the USA
San Bernardino, CA
07 September 2016